Robert Browning's Literary Life

From First Work to Masterpiece

Robert Browning's Literary Life

From First Work to Masterpiece

Gertrude Reese Hudson

EAKIN PRESS ★ Austin, Texas

Contents

List of Illustrations   vii

Acknowledgments   ix

Preview   xiii

I   A Boyish Work   1
Pauline, 1833

II   Evidences of a New Genius for Dramatic Poetry   24
Paracelsus, 1835

III   First Attempt at Playwriting   45
Strafford, 1837

IV   Frustration   75
Sordello, 1840

V   Appeal to a Pit-Audience   99
Pippa Passes, 1841

VI   Two Plays Rejected and Poems for Popularity's Sake   112
King Victor and King Charles, 1842; *Dramatic Lyrics*, 1842; *The Return of the Druses*, 1843

VII   A Play Accepted   133
A Blot in the 'Scutcheon, 1843:
Rehearsal, Performance, Reception

VIII   A Play Restaged and Recalled to Mind   147
A Blot in the 'Scutcheon, 1843:
Later Opinion and Defense

IX   Farewell to the Stage   168
Colombe's Birthday, 1844

X   Working in a New Light   187
Dramatic Romances and Lyrics, 1845:
Completion and Publication

XI   A Step Forward   198
Dramatic Romances and Lyrics, 1845: Reception

XII   Plays for Reading   217
Luria and *A Soul's Tragedy*, 1846

XIII   Further Encouraging Signs   239
                    Poems, 1849

XIV   Retrospection   259
                    1833–49

XV   A Religious Poem   270
                    Christmas-Eve and Easter-Day, 1850

XVI   Prose and Finances   288
                    Essay on Shelley, 1852

XVII   Newer Manner Than Matter   299
                    Men and Women, 1855: Form and Technique

XVIII   Limited Recognition   322
                    Men and Women, 1855: Values and Substance

XIX   Nonprofessional Opinion in the Fifties   347

XX   Attracting Readers   375
                    Selections from the Poetical Works of
                    Robert Browning, 1863

XXI   A Broad View   396
                    The Poetical Works of Robert Browning, 1863

XXII   Timely Topics and Wider Acceptance   410
                    Dramatis Personae, 1864

XXIII   Critics Against Critics   434
                    Dramatis Personae, 1864

XXIV   Republications and Inclusive Reviews   444
                    The Poetical Works of Robert Browning, 1865;
                    A Selection from the Works of Robert Browning, 1865;
                    The Poetical Works of Robert Browning, 1868

XXV   The Masterpiece: Inception to Publication   463
                    The Ring and the Book, 1868–9

XXVI   The Masterpiece: Assessments   475
                    The Ring and the Book, 1868–9

XXVII   The Masterpiece: Comprehensive Appraisal   501
                    The Ring and the Book, 1868–9

XXVIII   Nonprofessional Opinion in the Sixties   521

Overview   548

Reviews of Browning's Works in British Periodicals, 1833–70   563

Abbreviations Used in Notes   582

Notes   585

Index   629

Illustrations

John Forster, 1868, age fifty-six. Baylor University,   51
    Armstrong Browning Library.
William Charles Macready. Victoria and Albert Museum.   53
Playbill, *Strafford,* May 1, 1837. Theatre Museum, London.   55
Account of *Sordello* with Moxon. Colorado College, Colorado Springs.   91
Playbill, *A Blot in the 'Scutcheon,* February 11, 1843.   138
    Theatre Museum, London.
Playbill, *A Blot in the 'Scutcheon,* November 27, 28, 29, 1848.   159
    Theatre Museum, London.
Samuel Phelps. Victoria and Albert Museum.   160
Alma Murray as Mildred in *A Blot in the 'Scutcheon,* March 15, 1888.   162
    Miss Elsa Forman.
Playbill, *Colombe's Birthday,* April 25, 1853.   180
    Theatre Museum, London.
Helen Faucit, role unidentified. Victoria and Albert Museum.   181
Scene from *Colombe's Birthday. Illustrated London News,* April 30, 1853.   182
Alma Murray as Colombe in *Colombe's Birthday,* November 19, 1885.   185
    Miss Elsa Forman.
Robert Browning, by William Fisher, 1854. Wellesley College   302
    Library, Special Collections.
Robert Browning reading *The Ring and the Book,*   468
    by William W. Story, September 1869.
    Pierpont-Morgan Library, 1954.5.

Acknowledgments

For permission to quote from manuscripts and autograph letters and to use photographs I am indebted to the Armstrong Browning Library, Baylor University; Beinecke Rare Book and Manuscript Library, Yale University; Henry W. and Albert A. Berg Collection and Gilbert H. and Amy Angell Collier Montague Collection, Rare Books and Manuscripts Division, New York Public Library; British Library; Harry Ransom Humanities Research Center, University of Texas at Austin; Houghton Library, Harvard University; Pierpont Morgan Library; Victoria and Albert Museum, Board of Trustees; Wellesley College Library, Special Collections. For assistance in obtaining this permission I wish to thank Roger L. Brooks, Baylor; Vincent Giroud, Yale; Wayne Furman, New York Public Library; Shirley Nicholson, British Library; Thomas F. Staley, University of Texas; Rodney G. Dennis and Elizabeth A. Falsey, Harvard; Charles E. Pierce, Jr., Pierpont Morgan Library; Susanna Robson, Victoria and Albert Museum; Ruth R. Rogers, Wellesley.

Of the many librarians that I am grateful to, my particular thanks go to Hannah French, Anne Anninger, Wilma R. Slaight, and Jean Berry of Wellesley College Library for giving generously of their time and knowledge; to Veva Wood and Betty Coley of the Armstrong Browning Library and Elizabeth Airth of the University of Texas Library for extended assistance; to G. W. Murray of Marlborough College, Wiltshire, for identification of the authorship of a review. During many periods of work in the British Library, I received much helpful attention from the staff in Great Russell Street. In searching for reviews, I have profited extensively by the resources provided by the Newspaper Collection of the British Library at Colindale, the Library of Congress, the New York Public Library, the University of London, and the University of Texas Library at Austin. For other published materials I have relied chiefly on the British Library, the New York Public Library, and the University of Texas Library.

For various kinds of information and assistance, I thank others, including G. St. J. Barclay of the Alexander Turnbull Library, Wellington, New Zealand; W. R. Cunningham, the University, Glasgow; James A. Davies, University College of Swansea; Aurelia Brooks Harlan, Corpus Christi, Texas; Jack Herring, Armstrong Browning Library; E. A. Horsman, University of Otago, New Zealand; Claire Hudson, Theatre Museum, London; J. Hutton Hynd, South Place Ethical Society, London; Sylvère Monod, Paris, France; Barbara Neilon, Charles Leaming Tutt Library, Colorado Springs; Millicent M. Oldham, University College, London; E. V. Quinn, Balliol College, Oxford.

Miss Doris M. Domett of Richmond, Surrey, most generously sent Joseph Arnould's Letterbook to me for examination, and she and her sister, Jasmine B. N. Domett, gave me permission to quote from it. Miss Elsa Forman, who recalled Browning from the days of her childhood, talked to me of the association of Browning and her mother, the actress Alma Murray (Mrs. Alfred Forman). Miss Forman had copied for my use portraits of her mother in the roles of characters in Browning's plays. Through the kindness of Sibylla Jane Flower I gained useful information and obtained permission from Lt. Col. Henry Flower to publish the letter from Eliza Flower to R. H. Horne. Dorothy Hewlett's generosity and friendship were invaluable during my periods of study in England. She led me to useful correspondence, including the Browning-Story letters in the Keats-Shelley Memorial House in Rome, and to people who had particular knowledge of Browning; and she shared with me her own knowledge of Elizabeth and Robert Browning.

To A. J. Armstrong of Baylor University I acknowledge with appreciation my first encouragement in the study of Browning; and to Philip Graham and J. B. Wharey my indebtedness for turning me to an extended study of Browning and Victorian literature. To the University of Texas and to Southwest Texas State University I am grateful for research assistance and to the American Association of University Women for the Margaret M. Justin Fellowship, which enabled me to work in England for a year.

I wish to express my gratitude to Mr. Ed Eakin for the production of this book. I appreciate the work of his staff, especially that of Mr.

Tom Hayes and Mrs. Geraldine Pickens. I also thank Mr. Barkley Edwards for his part in the final stages of production.

I am grateful to Mr. John Murray for allowing me to read Browning's letters to George Smith and for permission to quote from them and from other letters of Browning protected by his copyright.

I am most indebted to my husband, who read the manuscript, offered many helpful suggestions, and encouraged me to complete this study.

Preview

This study concentrates on the literary career of Robert Browning from the publication of his first work, *Pauline* (1833), through the appearance of *The Ring and the Book* (1868–9), which established him as one of the two foremost English poets of the day. With relation to parallel intellectual and religious movements of the mid-century, it maps the course of criticism in its slow advance to the recognition of Browning's achievement, and it takes into account his efforts to employ his genius effectively and at the same time attract readers, and also his response to the reception of his works. An examination of specific comments that Browning made relative to his exertions in conceiving, composing, and revising his poetry provides a realistic perspective of the poet at work. This accords with recent critical studies that show him as a deliberate literary craftsman.

Browning's career illustrates the difficulties that confront a great original poet and also those who assess his work. That the critics in their blindness retarded Browning's attainment of fame by their unfavorable criticisms is an oversimplified notion. Early critics in general did not exert sufficient effort to go beyond the inherited and prevailing standard to evaluate his contribution. Impatience and irritability clouded their judgment. They faltered not only because of their natural inclination to resist poetry that was original in both content and style but also because of the necessity of coping with Browning's individuality in the various forms which he tried as he moved toward the one best suited to his genius. The result of all this was that after more than a quarter of a century Browning had not yet succeeded in gaining wide recognition. But the critics were not altogether blind. From the time of his earliest works they saw Browning as a poet with unusual ability and they repeatedly noticed praiseworthy qualities. Nor were they altogether resistant to change. In confused or contradictory statements there were often signs of reaching toward understanding.

Browning's writing up to the time of the establishment of his reputation falls into three periods. The first extended from the publication of his earliest work (1833) through his collected edition of 1849, the period of search and experimentation. The second covered the fifties, the period in which his art reached maturity. The third, the decade of the sixties, was the period in which his works secured his place as a great poet.

By the time of Browning's first collected edition changes in the criticism that led to a better understanding had begun to take place. In the fifties the acceptance of techniques and subject matter individual to Browning advanced, though laboriously. Besides the negative reaction to both *Christmas-Eve and Easter-Day* and *Men and Women,* there was also receptivity that foreshadowed future approval. The sixties brought success to the critics as well as to Browning. With the repeated exposure to his individuality and a climate favorable to acceptance of *Dramatis Personae* and *The Ring and the Book,* the critics reacted favorably to the timeliness of one and the greatness of the other. *The Ring and the Book* would not have had the recognition it deserved without the preceding slow and steady acclimatization to the original qualities of Browning's poetry and the arrival at a revised notion of the function of poetry. There had been no sharp turning point in the growing acceptance and appreciation of the intellectual, spiritual, and dramatic in Browning's character portrayal.

An analysis of the reviews during these periods reveals specific lines of criticism that at first tended to appear separately and later combined to lead toward the establishment of Browning's reputation. Decided progress came with the changes that took place in the standards for evaluating poetry and in the character of periodicals and of reviewing as well as in the contemporary frame of thought. There were effective shifts, too, in Browning's successive productions and in his mode of presenting his poetry to the public. An attempt is made to explain all of these changes and show how they were related to the development of his reputation. In addition an attempt is made to indicate how far the criticism in periodicals was in agreement with nonprofessional criticism by drawing conclusions from a broad sampling of contemporary opinion.

Statements about the attitude of the critics can be oversimplified, and comments on Browning in relationship to his career can be based on insufficient observation of his struggle to fulfill his potentialities as an original poet and to gain recognition. A fair picture can be drawn from extensive and unprejudiced observation of Browning at work: he wrote and revised, then took advantage of all available possibilities of gaining and holding readers, and he gave serious consideration to both professional and nonprofessional criticism.

Browning was receptive to criticism and in some respects profited by it, and he made concessions to contemporary taste. At the same time he persevered in the exercise of his highly innovative and original genius, never seeking to gain public approval at the price of his artistic integrity. He was steadfast in moving toward the mature expression of his individuality and as he progressed he revealed something of the character of his poetic thinking and intentions. These revelations came sometimes when he was defending his works, and his defense underscores the strong feeling he had about his contribution to literature.

Browning was confident of his own powers, but individual and press criticism taught him early in his career how difficult it was for an original poet to gain approval. With determination to succeed, he could rebound from failures, particularly early in his career, but he was sensitive to whatever impeded the acceptance of his poetry. He anxiously awaited reviews, and since he felt that they were a powerful factor in the recognition of his works he often spoke out freely and harshly about the writers of derogatory ones. He was at times volatile, but he was appreciative of a sympathetic approach to his poetry and often expressed gratitude for the help he had received.

There are pitfalls for one who appraises Browning in the frame of his literary career. His temperament was not monochromatic and his remarks cannot always be readily evaluated. He was patient and impatient, courageously confident and discouraged almost to the point of despair, assertively self-reliant and dependent upon others, aggressive and restrained. From comments Browning made and contemporaries made about him, it is easy to take a statement here and there and arrive at quick decisions and unwarranted generalities. Sometimes Browning's statements belied the real situation because of his carelessness of details, peculiar manner of expression, or self-deception. These miscues and the cover-up of his true feelings have resulted in a surprising number of facile observations made by both his and our contemporaries. Contradictions and half-truths lie in the large body of comments by and on Browning that we have at our disposal. Weighing the comments in the context of the whole and testing them by his behavior are the proper means of arriving at valid conclusions..

In Browning's early life lay clues to his later attitudes and behavior. Only the broadest view of his literary life will yield a trustworthy picture. In spite of Browning's extensive destruction of sources of information, there remains enough evidence, both firsthand and secondary, to make possible a fruitful examination of his concerns and activities in advancing his reputation. His comments and the related comments of others indicate his efforts to find the best medium of expression for his genius and his determination to protect its central force, his means of attracting and holding readers, and his reaction to his critics and their criticism. An examination of his behavior in the light of the slow movement toward recognition of his works results in a better understanding of Browning the man and the poet. His ambitions, impulses, and sensibilities — altogether human qualities — supported by the urge of his genius can be orchestrated so as to bring out the function that they played in the total composition of his literary career.

Studies that have dealt with the reception of Browning's works have appeared at intervals throughout this century. Thomas R. Lounsbury, in *The Early Literary Career of Robert Browning,* covered the years from 1833 through 1846. Besides dealing with the critical reception he included pertinent facts of Browning's life and commentaries of his own on Browning's works. Since his chapters were originally written for a series of lectures, Lounsbury passed over details that would have been tedious to an audience. D. C. Somervell, in "The Reputation of Robert Browning," made valid generalizations but said little that contributed specifically to the development of his subject. In the first part of *Browning: Background and Conflict* F. R. G. Duckworth considered the reception of Browning's works in the eighteen-fifties, the eighteen-nineties, and nineteen-twenties. The brief discussion of the eighteen-fifties chiefly concerned the negative judgment of Browning.

More detailed studies were made of the reception of Browning's works within limited areas. Reviews of the sixties were studied by C. C. Watkins in "Browning's 'Fame within These Four Years' "; by H. P. Pettigrew in "The Early Vogue of 'The Ring and the Book' "; by B. R. McElderry, Jr., in "Browning and the Victorian Public in 1868–69" and "Victorian Evaluation of *The Ring and the Book.*" E. A. Khattab examined both contemporary and modern reviews in "The Critical Reception of Browning's 'The Ring and the Book,' 1868–1889 and 1951–1968." The titles of Maurice B. Cramer's articles on the attitude toward Browning's work outside the press indicate the direction of his investigation: "Browning's Friendships and Fame before Marriage, 1833–1846"; "What Browning's Literary Reputation Owed to the Pre-Raphaelites, 1847–1856"; and "Browning's Literary Reputation at Oxford, 1855–1859."

In various ways others have covered the whole of Browning's works. DeVane, in his *Handbook,* contributed something to the subject of Browning's reputation in the section titled "After-History" for each work, but he did not undertake to give much specific information on contemporary reviews and on opinions of Browning outside the press. In his earlier chapters he sometimes referred his readers to Lounsbury. James P. McCormick, in his dissertation "Robert Browning's Reputation in the Nineteenth Century in England and America," brought together a large body of material and made acute observations. Boyd Litzinger and Donald Smalley, editors of *Browning: The Critical Heritage,* reprinted a generous number of contemporary reviews or parts of reviews of Browning and other commentaries of the time on his work, a number of them not otherwise easily available to students. They sometimes provided pertinent headnotes and included in their introduction comments on Browning, the reception of his works, and his attitude toward his critics.

All of these scholars have contributed to the subject of Browning's reputation. In two of the more recent studies dealing with Browning, reviews by his contemporaries are cited. Philip Drew in *The Poetry of Browning: A Critical Introduction* and Isobel Armstrong in *Victorian Scrutinies* made perceptive observations on selected reviews — Drew in his chapter "Browning and His Critics before 1914" and Armstrong in her discussion of changes in the character of the criticism in the sixties (she reproduced the text of two reviews of *The Ring and the Book*).

The criticisms or excerpts that Smalley and Litzinger chose are helpful in giving the reader material to form a definite notion of certain aspects of the reception of Browning's poetry, but some of the omitted sections (not always indicated) show important lines, or strands, of criticism that have been generally neglected. What is needed in the study of the development of Browning's reputation is an analysis of the reviews that will place emphasis on the continuity of various lines of criticism and their progressive modification and give adequate attention to the positive as well as the negative attitude in the three periods under consideration. Moreover, present-day studies have passed over reviews that appeared in the late forties and the fifties. This oversight in the scholarship has left a discontinuity between what preceded and what followed these years. My account attempts to repair the discontinuity and provide a more complete explanation of Browning's eventual rise to fame. A charting of the development of Browning's reputation from *Pauline* to *The Ring and the Book* has involved a study of some two hundred and eighty reviews.

Most of the studies thus far cited dealt primarily with contemporary opinion. A few scholars have considered Browning's professional activities by way of his response to criticism and help for his readers. In "Browning and His Critics" K. L. Knickerbocker called attention to Browning's negative reaction to the reviews of *Men and Women;* the article was helpful in that it quoted for the first time from Browning's letters to Edward Chapman, publisher of the collection. Lounsbury deserves credit for correcting some notions of the reception of his poetry that Browning had imagined and that had consequently been accepted by others. But Lounsbury was wide of the mark when he accused Browning of being indifferent to the needs of his readers. In their introductory commentary Litzinger and Smalley pointed to what is often deemphasized or ignored: Browning's gratefulness for helpful reviews. In "Commented It Must Be" Ian Jack has examined an important aspect of Browning's career: his efforts to provide guidance for his readers.

To some extent Browning's activities as they relate to his career have been discussed in full-length biographies and shorter biographical studies. Partly because of the difficulty and the extent of the task of examining sources for the numerous details of Browning's professional life, biographers have sometimes made use of what had already been generally accepted, occasionally including false notions and incorrect facts. Since my study focuses on the professional side of Browning's life, it involves a fuller examination of certain activities of his that are related to the shaping of his career. The result is the bringing together of details that reveal his sensitivity, his work habits, and his reaction to critics and criticism. These details and the analysis of many reviews have made it possible to bring out new aspects of old topics, enlarge upon old ones, and correct misstatements of fact. Some of the revised notions become obvious as chapters advance.

Largely because of the number of published misrepresentations, some minor, I have made silent corrections, but I have tried to provide the necessary support for revised opinions or facts. When for some reason I have called attention to a particular questionable or incorrect impression in a much-used and generally reliable and valuable study or biography, I have as a rule specifically named the work in an effort to prevent the repetition of inexactness or error. I have found a number of errors or incomplete references in the various listings of reviews of Browning's works from the first through *The Ring and the Book*. It would be awkward to call attention to each of these. The manner for handling the problem is explained in the headnote to the bibliography of reviews.

Something should be said about the organization of this study. The overall order is chronological. Most of the chapters include something on the inception and the time of composition of the work under consideration and Browning's activity in placing it before the public; an analysis of the reviews with the pointing up of lines of criticism and at times observation of nonprofessional reaction to the work; and then Browning's response to the reception, though his comments sometimes immediately follow the discussion of the review that attracted his attention. Chapters XIX and XXVIII deal more fully with the reception of Browning's works outside the press.

The presentation of the content of reviews varies. In the early chapters individual reviews are taken up in the order of publication so that the character of reviews in runs of the same periodical and in periodicals appearing at different intervals (weekly, monthly, quarterly) can be evaluated. This examination of individual criticisms makes it possible to emphasize significant aspects of a review as a whole, to correct misleading notions concerning certain reviews, and to facilitate later references to reviews already discussed. After the chapter on the last number of *Bells and Pomegranates* the analysis of reviews does not always follow the same pattern. As the book advances there is an increasing need for emphasis on the aspects of the reviewing that influenced the shaping of Browning's reputation. The reason for the method chosen for presentation of the content of the reviews is clear from the text of each chapter.

Besides occasional references to the remaining decades of Browning's life beyond the period covered in the book, the time past the sixties is drawn upon to bring out misconceptions and to show his extreme and persistent sensitivity. His later description of unfair treatment of *Pauline, Paracelsus,* and *A Blot,* presented along with a discussion of the situation as it existed at the time of the first publication, shows his defensive attitude toward early works. Reference to a time past that of immediate publication of *A Blot* and *Colombe's Birth-*

day is made to show continued critical opinion that these plays were not stageworthy.

Quotations play an important part in the study. Often only Browning's own words can reveal the intensity of his feeling, the substance of his professional thinking, or a potentiality for misinterpretation. Direct quotations from contemporary opinion serve to indicate the tone of criticisms, help establish important lines of thought, and controvert misleading notions resulting from incomplete or partial representations of certain statements in reviews. When others by quoting only part of a sentence or passage from a review have given an impression that is not valid in the light of the complete passage, I have quoted as much as will correct the impression.

I have not dealt with Browning's allusions to critics and criticism in his poetry. Though their negative quality in itself is not a negligible factor in a study of his attitude toward the critics, their complexity and extent make it impossible to include them here. I have not dealt with Browning's revisions except as they relate to readability. For statements about them I have turned to those who have made a study of the texts, and have given them credit in appropriate places. I have tried to take account of personal influences on Browning but I have said little of sources he used for various works. For my discussion of his relations with his publishers I have depended chiefly on letters Browning wrote to them or remarks he made about them, which provide considerable illumination. I have not gone outside the correspondence for information concerning the business and technical aspects of Browning's publishing history.

Two other procedures need explanation. Quotations from Browning's works are taken from the first editions. In later periods sometimes two reviews of a work appeared in the same periodical. In that case the review being discussed is identified by its date in parenthesis following the name of the periodical.

There follows a chronological list of books and articles referred to in the Preview.

Lounsbury, Thomas R., *The Early Literary Career of Robert Browning*. New York: Charles Scribner's Sons, 1911.
Somervell, D. C., "The Reputation of Robert Browning," *Essays and Studies by Members of the English Association*, XV, 1929, 122–38.
Duckworth, F. R. G., *Browning: Background and Conflict*. New York: E. P. Dutton & Co., 1932.

Knickerbocker, K. L., "Browning and His Critics," *Sewanee Review*, XLIII, July 1935, 283–91.

Pettigrew, Helen P., "The Early Vogue of *The Ring and the Book*," *Archiv für das Studium der neuern Sprachen*, n.s. LXIX, 1936, 36–47.

McCormick, James P., "Robert Browning's Reputation in the Nineteenth Century in England and America," Ph.D. dissertation, Northwestern University, 1937.

McElderry, B. R., Jr., "Browning and the Victorian Public in 1868–69," *Research Studies of the State College of Washington*, V, Dec. 1937, 193–203.

McElderry, B. R., Jr., "Victorian Evaluation of *The Ring and the Book*," *Research Studies of the State College of Washington*, VII, June 1939, 75–89.

Cramer, Maurice Browning, "Browning's Friendships and Fame before Marriage, 1833–1846," PMLA, LV, Mar. 1940, 207–30.

Cramer, Maurice Browning, "What Browning's Literary Reputation Owed to the Pre-Raphaelites, 1847–1856," *A Journal of English Literary History*, VIII, Dec. 1941, 305–21.

Cramer, Maurice Browning, "Browning's Literary Reputation at Oxford, 1855–1859," PMLA, LVII, Mar. 1942, 232–40.

DeVane, William C., *A Browning Handbook*, 2d ed. (1st ed., 1935.) New York: Appleton-Century-Crofts, 1955.

Watkins, Charlotte Crawford, "Browning's 'Fame within These Four Years,' " *Modern Language Review*, LIII, 1958, 492–500.

Drew, Philip, *The Poetry of Browning: A Critical Introduction*. London: Methuen & Co., 1970, 363–7, 382–5.

Litzinger, Boyd; Smalley, Donald, eds., *Browning: The Critical Heritage*. New York: Barnes & Noble, 1970.

Armstrong, Isobel, *Victorian Scrutinies: Reviews of Poetry, 1830–1870*. London: Athlone Press, 1972, pp. 56–9, 245–87.

Khattab, Ezzat Abdulmajeed, *The Critical Reception of Browning's* The Ring and the Book, *1868–1889 and 1951–1968. Salzburg Studies in English Literature*, vol. LXVI, 1977.

Jack, Ian, "Commented It Must Be," *Browning Institute Studies*, IX, 1981, 59–77.

CHAPTER I

A Boyish Work

Pauline, 1833

Robert Browning once said that he could not remember when he was not writing rhymes. Before the age of five he composed something in imitation of Ossian, which he "thought exceedingly well of, and laid up for posterity under the cushion of a great armchair."[1] At thirteen or thereabouts he wrote verses modelled on Byron, which in his youthful modesty he called *Incondita* (confused, disordered). Escaping the fate of the earlier poems, these came into the hands of family and friends who were favorably impressed by them.

Among the friends who admired the juvenilia were Eliza and Sarah Flower. Sarah, known as the author of *Nearer, My God, to Thee,* was a poet, and she had a talent for acting. Eliza was a musical composer of merit — "of real genius," Browning said — and her singing brought praise from many who heard her. The young Robert, who was attracted to music, drama, and poetry, looked upon these young women — Eliza nine and Sarah seven years his senior — with admiration; and they became interested in the precocious youth.

On behalf of the young Browning, the sisters appealed to William Johnson Fox, a Unitarian minister, who was their father's friend and after his death their guardian. His active interest in literature and drama as well as in social and political reform extended his influence far beyond the pulpit. For his opinions he found a channel of expression in various journals that he contributed to regularly.[2]

Sarah sent Fox a sample of Browning's verses, along with her own enthusiastic impression of them. Eliza, too, had her share in promoting the boy poet, as we know from Browning's own words when he was trying later to destroy all traces of his juvenilia: ". . . perhaps at twelve or thirteen, I wrote a book of verses which Eliza read and wrote to me about, — I wrote back, — then came the acquaintance with Fox, if meeting him one evening be worth that name, — but she gave me his opinions at second hand, and more letters came of it. . . ."[3] Fox was a gentle and kindhearted critic of the boy's verses, "which verses he praised not a little; which praise," said Browning, "comforted me not a little."[4] It was perhaps later that Fox admitted to Browning the "too great splendour of language and too little wealth of thought" of *Incondita*.[5] In time the boy-author "saw the proper way" and put his "blessed" poems into the fire.[6]

Then came a period of trying to channel his creative ability, of soul-searching and mind-searching, which *Pauline*, his first published poem, testified to. Browning wrote, "I don't know whether I had not made up my mind to *act*, as well as to make verses, music, and God knows what. . . ." On October 22, 1832, during his time of indecision, he saw Edmund Kean play in *Richard III*: according to Browning, on this evening he conceived the plan of *Pauline*.[7]

Browning must have completed his poem by January 1833, the date of the prefatory note. His aunt, Mrs. Christiana Silverthorne, gave him £30 for the publication, which covered the cost of printing and advertising. In March the poem was published anonymously by Saunders and Otley with the title *Pauline; A Fragment of a Confession;* not even the publisher knew the author's name.[8]

Browning wanted publicity for his poem. He thought of Fox, who he believed was associated with the *Westminster Review*. Browning wrote him. This was his first of many moves throughout a long stretch of years to advance his poetry. The letter to Fox shows a combination of artifice and humility and a seriousness underlying a carefree manner — characteristic qualities of many of his early letters designed to smooth the way for the furtherance of his reputation.

Dear Sir, — Perhaps by the aid of the subjoined initials and a little reflection, you may recollect an oddish sort of boy, who had the honour of being introduced to you at Hackney some years back — at that time a sayer of verse and a doer of it, and whose doings you had a little previously commended after a fashion — (whether in earnest or not God knows): that individual it is who takes the liberty of addressing one whose slight commendation then, was more thought of than all the gun drum and trumpet of praise would be now, and to submit to you a free and easy sort of thing which he wrote some months ago "on one leg" and which comes out this week — having either heard or dreamed that you contribute to the "Westminster."

Should it be found too insignificant for cutting up, I shall no less remain,

Dear sir,
Your most obedient serv^t.
R. B.

I have forgotten the main thing, — wch is to beg you not to spoil a loophole I have kept for backing out of the thing if necessary, "sympathy of dear friends," &c. &., none of whom know anything about it.

Monday Morning; Rev. — Fox[9]

Fox was no longer connected with the *Westminster.* In 1831 he had bought the *Monthly Repository,* which he had freed from the restrictions of a religious magazine and directed toward a broader and more diversified audience. One of the results of his editorship was a marked attention to literary criticism; he was not afraid to promote the works of older writers generally ignored or to assist fledglings. In answering Browning, he made an offer of help; and the young poet lost no time in taking advantage of the kindness. He even prepared the way for a further meeting with Fox, who could, and did, open useful doors.

Dear Sir, — In consequence of your kind permission I send, or will send, a dozen copies of "Pauline" and (to mitigate the infliction) Shelley's Poem — on account of what you mentioned this morning. It will perhaps be as well that you let me know their safe arrival by a line to R. B. junior, Hanover Cottage, Southampton Street, Camberwell. You must not think me too encroaching, if I make the getting back "Rosalind and Helen" an excuse for calling on you some evening — the said "R. and H." has, I observe, been well thumbed and sedulously marked by an acquaintance of mine, but I have not time to rub out his labour of love.

I am, dear sir,
Yours very really,
R. Browning.

Camberwell: 2 o'clock[10]

The prospect of a review prompted another letter, in which Browning wrote, "I can only offer you my simple thanks — but they are the sort that one can give only once or twice in a life: all things considered, I think you are almost repaid, if you imagine what I must feel. . . ."[11] It is not difficult to imagine something of his feelings at the outset of his career. Throughout the years he continued to be grateful for sympathetic criticism, and he did not hesitate to express his gratitude to supportive reviewers when the occasion offered itself.

Fox did write a review but his was not the first notice of *Pauline*. On March 23 the *Literary Gazette* gave judgment on the poem in a single sentence: "Somewhat mystical, somewhat poetical, somewhat sensual, and not a little unintelligible, — this is a dreamy volume, without an object, and unfit for publication." Brief as it was, this first public notice of Browning made the complaint against his works that for many years was to be as sustained as organ point — that of unintelligibility.

The opinion that *Pauline* was unfit for publication was not shared by the authors of three reviews that appeared in April. The *Athenaeum* published a review on April 6. In it the objections were softened by a genial spirit of praise:

> There is not a little true poetry in this very little book; here and there we have a touch of the mysterious, which we cannot admire; and now and then a want of true melody, which we can forgive; with perhaps more abruptness than what is necessary: all that, however, is as a grain of sand in a cup of pure water, compared to the nature, and passion, and fancy of the poem. We open the book at random; but fine things abound: there is no difficulty in finding passages to vindicate our praise. . . .

The critic hoped the poet's next strains would be as original as these and more cheerful. In his final sentence he sought to palliate the probable fate in store for the author. ". . . the day is past, we fear, for either fee or fame in the service of the muse; but to one who sings so naturally, poetry must be as easy as music is to a bird, and no doubt it has a solace all its own."

The *Atlas* reviewed *Pauline* on April 14. The critic said that in the poem, which was intended to be "metaphysical," the poet did not always effect the confessional to his mistress with proper dignity. Many of the lines had a prosaic character, the metrical construction was occasionally faulty, and the plain language was often unsuited to the mystical image. Although the *Atlas* was harsher than the *Athenaeum* in its derogatory remarks, this review like the earlier one commented on the good qualities of the poem and the author's promise for the future. "But there are many passages in the piece of considerable beauty, and a few of such positive excellence that we augur very favourably of the genius that produced them." The critic then quoted the now well-known passage from *Pauline* on Shelley, the "Sun-treader," and ended his review on a hopeful note: "The poem has created in us just so much interest as will induce us to look with some curiosity to the author's next essay."

The review in the *Monthly Repository* also appeared in April. In it Fox gave ten pages to a summary, long quotations, and comments. One comment, it is interesting to note, calls attention to qualities that critics were to emphasize as Browning's career unfolded.

> The scenery is in the chambers of thought; the agencies are powers and passions; the events are transitions from one state of spiritual existence to another. And yet the composition is not dreamy; there is in it a deep stamp of reality. Still less is it characterised by coldness. It has visions that we love to look upon, and tones that touch the inmost heart till it responds.

Fox recognized indications of poetical genius. "We felt certain of Tennyson, before we saw the book, by the few verses which had straggled into a newspaper; we are not less certain of the author of Pauline." He dealt gently with the immaturity of the poem: though hastily and imperfectly written, *Pauline* had truth and life in it. His criticism of its inferior melody he qualified with the adjective "perhaps"; and after calling attention to a few passages that were somewhat obscure, he added, "but that's not much." Fox felt that the absence of light lyrics would prevent the poem from becoming popular, but he showed in the quotations from it that there was no lack of "picturesque faculty," "grace," and "sentiment," and he ended his review on an encouraging note.

The obviously Shelleyan *Pauline* received further publicity in the *Monthly Repository*. A few months later, in June, Fox wrote a paragraph under the title "Local Logic," in which he used an extended metaphor associating the poem with Eliza (Lizzie) Flower:

> Shelley and Tennyson are the best books for this place. . . . They . . . if planted . . . would grow. . . . Last Autumn L——— dropped a poem of Shelley's down there in the wood, amongst the thick, damp, rotting leaves, and this spring some one found a delicate, exotic-looking plant, growing wild on the very spot, with

"Pauline" hanging from its slender stalk. Unripe fruit it may be, but of pleasant flavour and promise, and a mellower produce, it may be hoped, will follow.

By the end of April the outlook for *Pauline* seemed auspicious. Although there had been only a few reviews, the adverse criticisms, barring the sentence in the *Literary Gazette,* had been temperate and not unfair, the favorable comments generous, and the tone agreeable. Furthermore, that his first work had been noticed by two influential weeklies, especially the *Athenaeum,* and also reviewed by the *Monthly Repository* was enough to gratify Browning. At this point launching his career probably looked like smooth sailing to the twenty-one year old poet. But two notices of *Pauline* to come after a few months proved otherwise.

In August *Tait's Edinburgh Magazine* succinctly dismissed the poem: "*Paulina {sic}, a Fragment of a Confession;* a piece of pure bewilderment." The last of the contemporary reviews appeared in the December issue of *Fraser's.* The third of a series of articles entitled "The Poets of the Day" was published with the subtitle "Batch the Third." In it Browning's poem was subjected to the impish savagery of the magazine's reviewers. The poet was accused of being as mad as Cassandra, without her power of prophecy or even the ability to construct a connected sentence. He was labeled the Mad Poet of the Batch, "as being mad not in one direction only, but in all." The critic had weighty reasons, so he maintained, for attributing the production to one or all of the Whig ministers; here was the "same folly, incoherence, and reckless assertion" that characterized their pamphlet on the Reform Ministry and Parliament. The critic selected passages of the poem and related them to Whiggery; thus he identified *Pauline* with the Whigs, who were subjects of repeated *Fraserian* attacks. Such antics of the pen speak for themselves. In reading these two notices Browning saw his poetry dealt with in the hostile tone that characterized much of the reviewing of the time and that became prominent in reviews of his poetry.

John Stuart Mill wrote a criticism of *Pauline* but it was never published. By the time Browning's first poem was completed Mill had begun to take an interest in poetry, and he was encouraged by Harriet Taylor (a member of Fox's circle), who was later to become his wife. Mill published two articles on poetry in the *Monthly Repository* in 1833 — "What Is Poetry?" in January and "The Two Kinds of Poetry" in October. When Fox received the twelve promised copies of *Pauline* from Browning he thought of Mill, then contributing to the *Examiner*. Hoping that he would review Browning's poem for that periodical, Fox sent him a copy. On May 18, 1833, Mill reported: "I have written nothing lately but a short article on that 'Pauline', which will not, I believe, be too long for the Examiner, and if so, will probably appear there. *That* I have written chiefly because you wished it." [12]

In June Mill explained to Fox that the notice of *Pauline* "could not be inserted" in the *Examiner* and that he would alter and enlarge it for *Tait's*. [13] In the following month he gave additional information about the proposed article to Carlyle. (He had already written Carlyle on December 27, 1832, that his limited knowledge of poetry and art had kept "What Is Poetry?" from being satisfactory. [14]) He wrote in his letter of July 5, 1833:

> I think I mentioned to you that I have carried the investigation (rightly or wrongly as it may be) one step farther in a paper (being a review of a new poem) which I wrote for the Examiner: it proved too long for Fonblanque [the editor], and it is to appear in Tait, after such additions and alterations as I see it absolutely requires, and which I have not yet found time to give it. [15]

Before Mill could find time to rewrite his article, *Tait's* ran its contemptuous dismissal of *Pauline*. At this point he could see no reason why he should complete it and send it in. On August 6 he wrote William Tait:

> You must have been a good deal surprised at hearing nothing from me respecting the literary article which was to be transferred from the Examiner to your Magazine. The fact is that for some weeks past the pressure of other occupations had left me no time to take the article in hand and fit it for your use: and now at length when I had begun to rewrite it for you, I find that the work it is a review of (a poem named Pauline) has been disposed of in your last number by a passing notice, in terms of contempt which though I think the poem was overpraised in the Monthly Repository, I cannot consider it to deserve. So I hope you will receive this as my apology for not fulfilling my engagement. [16]

Browning explained nearly fifty years afterwards that Mill "had been forestalled by a flippant line" in *Tait's*. [17] It is true, as Browning said and commentators on Browning have repeated, that Mill had been forestalled. Browning thought that if Mill's article had appeared in *Tait's* it would have greatly hastened his recognition as a poet of consequence. But, as we shall see, it would hardly have been as favorable and influential as Browning supposed it would have been.

In a letter to Fox on October 10 Mill made his last statement concerning his efforts to deal with *Pauline:* "I send 'Pauline,' having done all I could — which was to annotate copiously in the margin, and *sum up* on the flyleaf — on the whole the observations are not flattering to the author — perhaps too strong in the *expression* to be shown him." [18]

Fox, who had been considerate of the poet's feelings in his own criticism, sent Browning the copy of *Pauline* with Mill's comments, which Mill himself felt were "perhaps too strong in the expression" for the author to see. The copy, which was later given to John Forster and is now in the Forster and Dyce Collection in the Victoria and Albert Museum, has attracted the attention of various scholars. [19] Mill's commentaries and Browning's reaction to them are important in this study, in which they will be placed in a larger frame of reference than that of previous discussions. Browning's attitude toward the reception of *Pauline* and toward Mill's projected article and its fate becomes increasingly significant as the account of his career advances.

When Browning received the annotated copy from Fox, he found Mill's remark "too much pretension in this motto" above the Latin passage taken from Heinrich Cornelius Agrippa, and he found favorable and unfavorable notes in the margins of the text. [20] A considerable number of the unfavorable ones were complaints of obscurity. By the time Mill reached page eighteen he decided upon a shortcut for designating obscure passages: "The passages where the meaning is so imperfectly expressed as not to be easily understood, will be marked X." He saw other faulty composition, including a passage "not even *poetically* grammatical," an image not "appropriate," and "a bad simile"; and he noted criticism such as "self-flattery" and "a curious idealization of self-worship" followed by "very fine, though." Then there were favorable marginal comments, including "beautiful," "*most* beautiful," "striking," "finely painted," "deeply true," "good descriptive writing."

When Browning came to Mill's summing-up on two blank leaves at the end of the book, he found criticism severer than that in the margins, though it was not devoid of commendation. In the first sentence Mill recognized Browning's ability and then he made a sharp thrust: "With considerable poetic powers, this writer seems to me possessed with a more intense and morbid self-consciousness than I ever knew in any sane human being. . . ." This was followed by a discussion of the place of Pauline in the speaker's existence. "I should think it a *sincere confession* though of a most unloveable state, if the 'Pauline' were not evidently a mere phantom." Mill thought that if she did exist the poet's behavior was subject to criticism, because of his inconsistent attitude toward her and his ungenerous and unfeeling treatment. As in the first part of the commentary, Mill prefaced the last part with a favorable remark: "A cento of most beautiful passages might be made from this poem — & the psychological history of himself is powerful and truthful, *truth-like* certainly all but the last stage." Mill thought that the poet described well the self-seeking and self-worshipping state, though beyond that he was limited by his emotional condition. He did not write as if the "badness of his state" were "purged out of him." He felt not remorse, only disappointment. "Meanwhile he should not attempt to shew how a person may be *recovered* from this morbid state — for *he* is hardly convalescent. . . ."

Browning went through the annotated copy and marked it. ("R Browning / *October 30th 1833*" was written on one of the end flyleaves — not in Browning's hand, probably in Sarianna's.) It is easy to imagine the ambitious young poet turning the pages and examining the notes: relishing the favorable comments; reading Mill's objection to his ambiguous and obscure use of *so* in the sense of *therefore* or *accordingly* and with satisfaction writing a defense of his choice of the word, with examples to show that his use was "perfectly authorized"; and further on blithely answering a question on an obscure point with, "Why, 'that's tellings,' as schoolboys say." Browning took the annotations in good spirit, if we can judge by the rejoinders he made to them in the margin. Nor is there any indication that Mill's summary comment caused him displeasure as he examined the annotated copy. While Browning was going through the poem he had ideas of his own for improvement in wording and punctuation and made changes, some of which he never used in subsequent editions, partly because he did not have this copy in hand.

In all likelihood it was at a later time that Browning made a further comment on page four:

> The following Poem was written in pursuance of a foolish plan which occupied me mightily for a time, and which had for its object the enabling me to assume & realize I know not how many different characters; — meanwhile the world was never to guess that "Brown, Smith, Jones, & Robinson" (as the Spelling-books have it) the respective authors of this poem, the other novel, such an opera, such a speech &c &c were noother {for "no other"} than one and the same

individual. The present abortion was the first work of the *Poet* of the
batch, who would have been more legitimately *myself* than most of
the others; but I surrounded him with all manner of (to my then notion) poetical accessories, and had planned quite a delightful life for
him.

Only this crab remains of the shapely Tree of Life in this Fools
Paradise of mine.

<u>RB</u>

In tone this note is unlike Browning's marginal comments. They
are lively and spontaneous, as if made in the first excitement of reading
Mill's criticisms of his poem. The note on page four is different. It is
sober, not lighthearted. It is apologetic; there is no spirit of apology in
any of Browning's marginal notes, whether by way of explanation, defense, or pert rejoinder. Browning may well have written the foolish-
plan note after enough time had elapsed for him to recover from the
first pleasurable excitement of seeing various criticisms of his work and
to take seriously the adverse criticism here and also in published reviews.

The opinion once generally accepted, and still not entirely dissi-
pated, was that Mill's criticism caused Browning to look upon *Pauline*
with aversion and turned him to quite another kind of writing; that is,
he would henceforth write so as not to reveal himself. It is important
for us to understand that neither the history of his next three works nor
his attitude toward Mill indicates such an influence.

When we look from various standpoints at the early poetry following *Pauline,* we can see nothing that indicates Mill's particular influence on Browning's choice of subject or manner of presentation.
Paracelsus, Strafford, and *Sordello* were published in this order. Browning started *Sordello* first, but he did not complete it until after *Paracelsus* and *Strafford* were published. *Strafford* was written as the result of
William Charles Macready's suggestion that Browning write a play for
him, and as a historical play it offered no occasion for the author to reveal or conceal himself. Paracelsus was suggested to Browning as a subject by a friend, and he read about Sordello while studying Italian.
Both were historical figures who in themselves were interesting to him
— it is not likely that he saw them as characters which he could treat
without the risk of becoming confessional or otherwise self-revelatory.

It might be supposed that Mill's influence would be shown in the
next poem Browning worked on after *Pauline.* According to DeVane,
Browning began *Sordello* soon after the publication of *Pauline* in March

1833. At this time he did not have Mill's notes and comments in hand; he did not see them until after October 10. At the beginning of *Sordello*, unless this part was rewritten later, Browning admitted the attraction of staying out of view before seeing Mill's criticism. After going through the marked copy of *Pauline*, he was not influenced to conceal himself. In fact, Browning is the narrator in his own person. In the opening of Book I he says he would have preferred to have Sordello tell his own story, "myself kept out of view," but then he says he will use the narrative method because a writer who deals with unusual and new subJects must make everything clear for his readers and critics. In *Sordello*, in which Browning was exploring the possibilities of the narrative method, he did at times speak directly to his readers.

There is no evidence that Mill's review influenced Browning to choose his mode of presentation for *Paracelsus*. In it, as in *Sordello*, he followed no conventional pattern. At the beginning of his Preface he made clear that he was trying something "novel." At the end of the Preface he stated that the poem was an "experiment" which he would be "in no case likely to repeat." It was natural that with a genius that proved to be as innovative as his Browning would do something different with the dramatic, which had figured prominently in his informal education; he made clear that he was writing a "poem, not a drama" and that he was trying something unconventional by emphasizing the mood rather than external events. Statements in the Preface and the poem itself point to a continuation of experimenting that he started before he saw Mill's comments and that further attracted him when he realized from the criticisms as a whole the extent of the confessional element in *Pauline*.

From the beginning he was interested in experimentation. According to his own admission on page four of the Forster-Mill copy of *Pauline*, he had thought of trying poetry, novel, opera; and at the end of the same copy he admitted the attractions of acting, writing poetry, and composing music. Once he had settled on poetry, he continued to show versatility and originality, as his career clearly demonstrates. *The Ring and the Book* of 1868 and 1869 and the *Parleyings* of 1887 were two later original achievements of a poet who had begun to try something unusual in his second published work.

The early works themselves show that the influence Mill was supposed to have exerted on the direction of Browning's writing can be easily discounted. And his attitude toward Mill further discounts such an influence. In the first stages of his career Browning was eager for criticism. With the exception of the curt dismissal in *Tait's,* seemingly he was not hurt by any particular review of *Pauline,* nor is there any indication that Mill's comments stung him. In fact, Browning hoped that through Fox's influence "a certain writer who meditated a notice (it matters not laudatory or otherwise) on 'Pauline' in the 'Examiner' " would not be an idle spectator when *Paracelsus* was published.[21] In mentioning Mill's criticism of *Pauline* to Elizabeth Barrett in 1845, Browning did not show any upsetting effects;[22] and by the last part of his career he was crediting Mill with a remarkable degree of appreciation of *Pauline.*

Browning was ambitious and intelligent, and, as we shall see in later chapters, he often took to heart comments in reviews of his work. The criticisms of *Pauline* as a whole, not just Mill's comments, helped to open his eyes to the character of his first poem. The April reviews, in which *Pauline* received praise, contained some objections similar to Mill's. One critic hoped for more cheerfulness in the next work and did not admire "a touch of the mysterious" *(Athenaeum).* Another wrote, "The author is in the confessional, and acknowledges to his mistress the strange thoughts and fancies with which his past life has been crowded." This critic objected to the manner in which the poet expressed these thoughts: "He does not always speak of his agonies in language worthy of one who evidently understood them so well; he sometimes runs slip-shod through his afflictions" *(Atlas).* Fox said, "We have never read any thing more purely confessional" *(Monthly Repository),* though in the discussion of this quality as well as of others, he tempered his criticism.

Like many another writer who in time became embarrassed by his first publication, Browning hoped that *Pauline* would be forgotten, and he did what he could toward that end. He obtained the printed but unbound copies of the poem from the publisher. In 1846 he wrote Elizabeth that he had "a whole bale of sheets at the house-top."[23] This precaution could not conceal *Pauline* from Browning's future readers. Surprisingly he later gave John Forster the copy annotated by Mill, but in time he must have regretted having done so, for he tried to get it back, though without success.[24]

In spite of his reticence about his first work, others learned of it. In January of 1846 Browning did not want Elizabeth Barrett to see a recent issue of the *New Quarterly Review* because it made mention of *Pauline.* (This *Review* was to mention the poem again in January 1847.) After he did send her his copy of the periodical, she vainly teased him to let her read the poem. She wrote on January 10: "Then, I *shall have* *'Pauline' in a day or two* — yes, I shall & must . . & *will.*" Browning replied the next day: "Must you see 'Pauline'? At least then let me wait a few days, — to correct the misprints which affect the sense, and to write you the history of it; what is necessary you should know before you see it." On the 13th Browning went to see Elizabeth — without a copy of *Pauline.* She continued to urge him to bring her the poem, and Browning was still reluctant:

> Will you, and must you have "Pauline"? If I could pray you to revoke that decision! For it is altogether foolish and *not* boylike — and I shall, I confess, hate the notion of running over it — yet commented it must be; more than mere correction! I was unluckily *precocious* — but I had rather you *saw* real infantine efforts . . (verses at six years old, and drawings still earlier) than this ambiguous, feverish — Why not wait?

When Elizabeth agreed to wait if Browning would promise to show her *Pauline* later, Browning answered: ". . . you shall see it when I can muster resolution to transcribe the explanation [his] which I know is on the fly-leaf of a copy here." Elizabeth gave in to Browning for the time being, consoling herself with the promise of seeing *Pauline* later: "I seem to understand that you would really rather wish me not to see it now. . . ."[25]

Alfred Domett and Joseph Arnould, both of Camberwell, who became intimate friends of Browning's after the poem was published, learned about it. Arnould read it, and on September 19, 1847, a year after Browning's marriage, he wrote to Domett: "By-the-bye, did you ever happen upon Browning's 'Pauline'? a strange, wild (in parts singularly magnificent) poet-biography: his own early life as it presented itself to his own soul viewed poetically: in fact, psychologically speaking, his 'Sartor Resartus': it was written and published three years before 'Paracelsus,' when Shelley was his God."[26]

If Browning did not want Elizabeth Barrett, Domett, or Arnould — with all of whom he otherwise discussed his poetry — to read his first work, he must have taken care to guard his secret. But he was not completely successful. Near the time when Domett learned about *Pauline,* Dante Gabriel Rossetti inferred from internal evidence that Browning was the author and wrote him for confirmation.[27] Some learned that it was an unacknowledged work of Browning's from a book by Thomas Powell, first published in America in 1849 and republished, with changes, in England in 1851.[28] Others could have seen the mention of it in the two criticisms in the *New Quarterly Review,* the one of January 1846 (probably partly written by Powell) and the one of January 1847. The poem did not entirely escape notice when *Men and Women* was published in 1855; the *Christian Remembrancer* (1857) made a reference to it in a footnote. On September 17, 1863, Browning wrote to Moncure Daniel Conway, who was going to review the 1863 collected edition: "No poem has been omitted, and none added to the present edition, — always excepting one very early thing, never known as mine, nor likely to be remembered by anybody."[29]

When Browning said *Pauline* was never known as his, he was making free with the facts. He knew that at least a few had been aware of his authorship. He sent Elizabeth the *New Quarterly Review* article that mentioned *Pauline,* and Rossetti had written him concerning it. In a letter to Thomas J. Wise in 1886, he indicated that more than a few had known about *Pauline;* ". . . the book was undoubtedly 'still-born,' . . . despite the kindly offices of many friends, who did their best to bring about a successful birth."[30]

If Browning thought *Pauline* was not likely to be resurrected in the sixties, when his works were more attentively examined, he was wrong. The *Eclectic Review* (May 1863) carried a criticism of the 1863 *Selections* in which *Pauline* was mentioned: "His [Browning's] first effort as a poet — 'Pauline' — we suppose has passed from everybody's recollection. Its author does not seem desirous that it should be retained." Then Conway in his article in the *Victoria Magazine* for February 1864 gave four sentences to *Pauline;* he referred to it as a "very impressive and vigorous work" and regretted its omission from the 1863 collected edition.

Three years after Conway's article was published, Richard Herne Shepherd, a bibliographer who had a penchant for publicizing juvenilia of famous people, asked Browning for permission to quote excerpts from *Pauline* in a projected work to be called "Unknown Works of Well-Known Authors." Browning's answer was first published by William Lyon Phelps. On February 1, 1867, Browning reluctantly gave permission:

> I hardly know what to say in reply to your request: I cannot but have repugnance to any exhibition of a boyish attempt, which never bore my name, and, as yourself remark, from my keeping it out of all collections of my poems these thirty years and more, must have enjoyed my best wishes for its abolition: but nobody cares about an

author's feelings in such a matter, and I can hardly do more than make a grimace and submit to whatever mine may have to undergo.

His permission carried certain restrictions:

> I do not wonder that you refused to edit the whole poem for America, though I am obliged greatly by your sense of justice and gentlemanliness as shown by such a refusal; and in consequence I will bring myself to say that — in reliance upon those two qualities — if you will strictly confine yourself to "a few extracts" — and will preface these with mention of the fact that the poem was purely dramatic and intended to head a series of "Men & Women" such as I have afterwards introduced to the world under somewhat better auspices, — mentioning this on your own authority, and not in any way alluding to this of mine — and, further, if you will subject the whole of the extracts to my approval — (*not* a single remark upon them, — only the passages themselves) — in this case, and not otherwise, I give the leave you desire. I may add that I am glad you do not refer to any early works of my wife: I should be compelled to prevent any extract from them.[31]

Phelps stated that Shepherd possibly did not reply, but in fact he answered on the following day:

> Accept my best thanks for your kind letter, and the provisional permission you have accorded me.
> By the same post I take the liberty of forwarding you a transcript of *Pauline,* in which, for facility of reference, I have numbered the lines in pencil. I propose to quote the opening passage to line 75; lines 280–329; lines 385–389; lines 466–475; lines 564–578; lines 735–809; and the conclusion 11. 1005–1050: altogether two hundred and seventy-five lines out of 1050. If I am asking too much, you will veto any particular passage or passages enumerated to which you object. I would also inquire if I am correct in the rectification of line 567, which seems to be disfigured by a printer's error.[32]

The excessive number of lines to be quoted might have given Browning concern. He might also have heard something of Shepherd, who at times thought more of his own interests than of the wishes or rights of others. Browning, who had already had experience with literary knavery, became cautious. The fear of a mutilated publication by Shepherd or an unauthorized publication by someone else was enough to make him realize that he must reprint *Pauline* to protect himself. Phelps deduced from Browning's answer to Shepherd that Browning republished

Pauline in 1868 because of Shepherd's proposal. His deduction can be substantiated by information given by Browning and recorded by William Rossetti:

> *Pauline* is included in the edition, in consequence of his having received a letter from somebody who professes a great enthusiasm for the unacknowledged works of distinguished authors, and who contemplated publishing some considerable part of P[auline] in some form — so B[rowning] found the best thing to do would be to take the affair into his own hands, and republish the whole poem with proper press-corrections — not any re-writing, which he objects to.[33]

By December 25, 1867, Browning had made his decision to reprint *Pauline* in its entirety; this was the date of the introductory note for the second edition of the poem.

Browning's suspicion was well founded. Shepherd prepared *Pauline* for inclusion in his proposed book, but, as he later explained, this collection, "from a combination of causes, was never destined to see the light."[34] Phelps said that Shepherd "never did print the 'extracts' he had in mind when he wrote Browning," and DeVane and recent biographers have accepted Phelps's statement.[35] In fact, as is indicated in the *Browning Society's Papers* (I, 97), Shepherd's excerpts with his interpolations were published in *St. James's Magazine* in August 1871 (n.s. VII, 485–96). Shepherd said in his preface what Browning had wanted him to and he quoted only the 275 lines which he had indicated, but did not refrain from making remarks of his own. In his letter of February 1867 Browning had given Shepherd permission to use a "few extracts" with "not a single remark upon them." The quoted passages were interspersed with full summary links, and there were concluding comments besides the prefatory ones, so that the whole performance covered eleven pages. The result was a pointing up of the confessional nature of *Pauline*, which Browning thought had already received too much emphasis. Not only in the matter of *Pauline* did Shepherd disregard Browning's wishes. Some years later, in 1878, he did a more damnable thing in Browning's eyes: he published Elizabeth's early poems in spite of Browning's emphatic prohibition.[36]

When the 1868 collected edition appeared, *Pauline*, which had been left out of the 1849 and 1863 collections, was for the first time presented to the public with the author's name. A prefatory note (untitled), like the foolish-plan note, was apologetic:

The poems that follow are printed in the order of their publication. The first piece in the series, I acknowledge and retain with extreme repugnance, indeed purely of necessity; for not long ago I inspected one, and am certified of the existence of other transcripts, intended sooner or later to be published abroad: by forestalling these, I can at least correct some misprints (no syllable is changed) and introduce a boyish work by an exculpatory word.

Looking back, Browning saw in *Pauline* the beginning of his experiments in dramatic writing.

The thing was my earliest attempt at "poetry always dramatic in principle, and so many utterances of so many imaginary persons, not mine," which I have since written according to a scheme less extravagant and scale less impracticable than were ventured upon in this crude preliminary sketch — a sketch that, on reviewal, appears not altogether wide of some hint of the characteristic features of that particular *dramatis persona* it would fain have reproduced: good draughtsmanship, however, and right handling were far beyond the artist at that time.

Just as his authorship of *Pauline* became publicized, Browning was reaching the summit of his fame. Quite naturally his readers became interested in his first poem, and copies of the octavo volume of seventy pages, bound in drab paper-covered boards, which, Browning said, no one bought at the time of its first publication,[37] became more and more a coveted book. But copies were scarce. Of those that had been given away not many survived. Near the end of her life Sarianna Browning said that while they were living in Hatcham she helped her brother destroy all the copies (sheets, Browning said) he had got from the publisher except one.[38] After the poem was republished in 1868 Browning had three copies in hand. The one he had corrected for the collected edition he gave to Frederick Locker-Lampson in 1869.[39] One of the other copies he gave to James Dykes Campbell; the remaining one he kept for his son.

With the scarcity of copies not many people were as fortunate as Frederick Locker-Lampson and James Dykes Campbell. The next best thing was a facsimile reprint, which was made for the members of the Browning Society in 1886. Browning expressed no objection to the reprint, but when he was asked to write an introduction for it, he succinctly refused: "I really have said my little say about the little book elsewhere, and should only increase words without knowledge."[40] The attention belatedly given to his first poem afforded Browning some satisfaction, but it was best for him not to take the risk of involving his emotions. Just as he had found it difficult in 1846 even to transcribe an explanatory note on the flyleaf of a copy for Elizabeth Barrett, he now drew back from the ordeal of getting close to the poem by writing an introduction. He was unwilling to stir up his deeper feelings.

Wise, who had unsuccessfully tried to get one of the last two copies that Browning had, later obtained a copy for £22.10 and asked Browning to inscribe it. Browning answered on January 31, 1888: "Of course I will cheerfully do what you please to require so kindly with the copy of *Pauline,* which you have purchased, as far as I can remember, at about two thirds of the price paid for printing the whole edition fifty-five years ago." His inscription also referred to the change in value: "I see with much interest this little book, the original publication of which can hardly have cost more than has been expended on a single copy by its munificent Proprietor and my friend — Mr. Wise."[41]

Browning's old humiliation and new pride were at odds with each other. At the time when Wise obtained his copy of *Pauline,* Browning was working on his last collected edition. He had not planned to include *Pauline,* but after receiving the proofs of the first volume he changed his mind. On February 27, 1888, he wrote to his publisher.

> When I received the Proofs of the 1st. vol. on Friday evening, I made sure of returning them next day — so accurately are they printed. But on looking at that unlucky *Pauline,* which I have not touched for half a century, a sudden impulse came over me to take the opportunity of just correcting the most obvious faults of expression, versification and construction, — letting the *thoughts* — such as they are — remain exactly as at first: I have only treated the imperfect expression of these just as I have now and then done for an amateur friend, if he asked me and I liked him enough to do so. Not a line is displaced, none added, none taken away. I have just sent it to the printer's with an explanatory word: and told him that he would have less trouble with all the rest of the volumes put together than with this little portion.[42]

Contrary to his statement that he had not touched *Pauline* for half a century, he had made changes in the 1868 version of the poem. And in this final form the alterations were considerable.[43] He reprinted the prefatory note of 1868 and made an addition, including the following:

Twenty years' endurance of an eyesore seems more than sufficient: my faults remain duly recorded against me, and I claim permission to somewhat diminish these, so far as style is concerned, in the present and final edition where "Pauline" must needs, first of my performances, confront the reader. I have simply removed solecisms, mended the metre a little, and endeavoured to strengthen the phraseology — experience helping, in some degree, the helplessness of juvenile haste and heat in their untried adventure long ago.

Here is the same distaste and apology for the poem that Browning had expressed in the note he wrote in the Forster-Mill copy at some time after it was returned to him and that he had again expressed in the 1868 introductory note. But now there was a difference. In 1868 he republished *Pauline* under something of a compulsion. In 1888 he wished to include it in his final collected edition. Behind the public apology, which was not as strong as his earlier statements, was his personal satisfaction in the attention now given to his early works, including the poem that he said had been stillborn.

In Wise's copy he had referred to the contrast between the early financial history of the poem and the current value placed upon it. He spoke of this contrast again when he replied in June of 1888 to an invitation to become a member of the Roxburghe Club:

I must (as a bibliophile) remain contentedly amused at the fact that a little affair of my own, published more than half a century ago at my own expense, — and absolute loss of every penny, — then selling (were there buyers) at some three shillings and six pence, now is hardly procurable for £25, and has already been reprinted in *facsimile* as a curiosity![44]

Browning would have been more than amused had he known how the sale price of copies of the first edition of *Pauline* would increase with time. In the 1890's, copies sold for $260, $210, and £145; in the early 1920's they brought $2560 and $2400; in 1929 the price reached $16,000.[45]

In the days of his fame Browning felt some pride in the resurrection of his first poem; coupled with this pride was a sensitiveness that had developed as professional disappointments accumulated. In time he came to feel the need to explain the tardy recognition of his works. To satisfy this need, Browning was led into unintentional misrepresentation of his early literary career. He made the statements about *Pauline* that have already been cited — the one to Conway in 1863 that

Pauline had never been known as his and the one to his publisher in 1888 that he had not touched *Pauline* for half a century. These were not misrepresentations of consequence. More misleading were the ones related to Mill's criticism and the notice in *Tait's*.

Browning included Mill's criticism in the reviews which he told Frederick James Furnivall were "good natured."[46] He gave Edmund Gosse information about his life and later expressed approval of what Gosse had written, which included the statement that *Pauline* "delighted" Mill "in the highest degree."[47] Other accounts that he gave to his contemporaries after he became famous contained misrepresentations concerning Mill's criticism as well as mistaken notions concerning the beneficial effect on his reputation that would have followed a review by Mill in *Tait's*. Although only in the letter to Furnivall do we have Browning's own words, it seems safe to accept statements that are in agreement with each other in three reports of Browning's conversation, especially since in part they are in accordance with the comment in his letter to Furnivall and the comments in the Browning-approved account by Gosse.

The first was given by F. W. Farrar in his *Men I Have Known:*

> He [Browning] said that when one of his earlier volumes came out —I think, *Bells and Pomegranates* — a copy fell into the hands of Mr. John Stuart Mill, who was then at the zenith of his fame, and whose literary opinion was accepted as oracular. Mr. J. S. Mill expressed his admiration of the poems, and of the originality of the lessons they contained; and he wrote to the editor of *Tait's Magazine,* then one of the leading literary journals, asking if he might review them in the forthcoming number. The editor wrote back to say that he should always esteem it an honor and an advantage to receive a review from the pen of Mr. J. S. Mill, but unfortunately he could not insert a review of *Bells and Pomegranates,* as it had been reviewed in the last number. Mr. Browning had the curiosity to look at the last number of the magazine, and there read the so-called review. It was as follows: *"Bells and Pomegranates,* by Robert Browning: *Balderdash."*[48]

A footnote explained that "Balderdash" may not have been the exact word, that possibly the reminiscence was a little blurred. Farrar heard more on the subject:

> "It depended, you see," said Mr. Browning, "on what looked like the merest accident, whether the work of a new or as yet almost un-

known writer should receive an appreciative review from the pen of the first literary and philosophic critic of his day" — a review which would have rendered him most powerful help, exactly at the time when it was most needed, — or whether he should only receive one insolent epithet from some nameless nobody. "I consider," he added, "that this so-called 'review' retarded any recognition of me by twenty years' delay."

The second account was given by Oscar Browning (no relation to Robert) in *Memories of Sixty Years:*

He used sometimes to complain to me, as he did in his poems, of the early neglect of his poetry, and of the lateness with which recognition had come to him, compared, for instance, with Tennyson. It was well known that John Stuart Mill was one of the first to make known to the world the genius of Tennyson, and that he did so in an article published in the *London Repository,* then edited by Fox, a well-known patron of Letters. Mill showed similar acuteness in discovering Browning's first poem "Pauline," surreptitiously printed by him at Richmond, and he desired to review it favourably in Fox's magazine, but he received an answer that it had been already noticed in a previous number. Upon a close examination he found, at the end of a half column, the two words "Pauline — balderdash." The explanation was that a single line was required to complete the page, and the editor, taking up the first book on which he could lay his hand, and thinking it insignificant and pretentious, described it as I have stated above. Browning declared that by this accident his public recognition had been delayed for twenty years.[49]

Frances Horner gave the third account in *Time Remembered:*

Browning said to me that he had very early learned not to be affected by praise or blame, or by the critics. When his early book of poems, called *Bells and Pomegranates,* came out, John Stuart Mill offered to review it for him in an important magazine. Browning was very much pleased but learned to his surprise that this could not be, as the book had already been reviewed in their pages. He searched all the back numbers diligently, and finally discovered in a part called, I think, "The Editor's Table," the following mention of his poems:
Bells and Pomegranates
           by   Balderdash.
     R. Browning.
     This prevented his having an appreciative review from a well-known literary man — and he said it taught him fortitude under criticism.[50]

The wrong identification of magazine and editor, the confusion of *Bells and Pomegranates* with *Pauline,* the use of "Balderdash" instead of the phrase in *Tait's* can all be dismissed as trivial mistakes easy to make in reporting long-past details. Other misrepresentations that either two or three of these accounts have in common are more serious. They concern Mill and *Tait's* and seemingly reflect Browning's attitude. In the first place, Browning gave the impression that Mill's main feeling for the poem had been one of admiration and that he wished to review it. Mill's own words show that he undertook the review not because he wished to but because Fox wanted him to. That Mill's chief impetus in writing the review grew out of Fox's request Browning might well have not known, but neither could he have known that Mill wished to review *Pauline.* Even though Mill made favorable comments, how could Browning think that his principal feeling had been one of admiration? His rejoinders to Mill's remarks in the margins of the Forster-Mill copy suggest the enthusiasm that the youthful poet felt when he first read the criticisms, but his foolish-plan note, probably written some time after his first reading of Mill's comments, was subdued. It indicated that the remarks Mill considered perhaps too severe to show the poet quite possibly came home to him as he thought of similar objections in the reviews of *Pauline.* Yet at no time did Browning express a negative reaction to Mill and his criticism.

In the second place, according to the accounts of Farrar, Oscar Browning, and Horner, Browning gave the impression that a review by one of Mill's prominence would have been of inestimable value. If his influence in 1833 was as great as Browning represented it, the public would probably have been more aware of the weakness of *Pauline* from Mill's projected article than from the few words in *Tait's.* But Browning exaggerated the weight that Mill's review would have carried in 1833. Mill was not yet established in the intellectual areas in which he later became famous, and certainly he did not exert influence as a literary critic.[51] His words to Carlyle, quoted earlier in the chapter, show his feeling of inadequacy in writing about poetry and art.

Browning, then, presented John Stuart Mill to his believing contemporaries as his aggressive supporter and the failure of the review to appear as a great loss. He went so far as to say, according to two accounts, that the notice published in place of Mill's criticism retarded his reputation twenty years. *Tait's* was the villain. Browning did not know that it was by Mill's default that the notice in *Tait's* appeared; furthermore, Browning ignored the fact that he had concealed his authorship of *Pauline* for many years. It is difficult to conceive that the appearance in *Tait's* of a full-fledged review based on the annotations in the Forster-Mill copy of *Pauline* might have made such an appreciable difference in Browning's reputation as he indicated — a review written about an anonymous poem by a man trying his wings in literary criticism and published in a magazine that had no claim to literary influence at the time. Browning was deceiving himself. As we shall see, this was not the only instance of his self-deception in matters concerning his literary career. Before judging him severely for his faulty reconstruction of the Mill-*Tait's* affair, we should follow his long and hard struggle for recognition and consider the effect of that struggle on a highly sensitive poet.

CHAPTER II

Evidences of a New Genius
For Dramatic Poetry

Paracelsus, 1835

In *Pauline* the confessional element gave evidence that Browning, like the speaker in the poem, was mind-searching and soul-searching. He continued his search in *Sordello*, which he began soon after the publication of *Pauline* in March 1833, or perhaps even between its completion and its appearance in print. *Sordello* was destined to have a long history of composition with several interruptions before becoming his fourth publication. When in March of 1834 he had the opportunity to go to Russia with Chevalier George de Benkhausen, the Russian consul-general, he put *Sordello* aside.

In three months he was back in England. In all likelihood he had resumed work on *Sordello* when he made a new friendship which led to another interruption. Through an uncle he met, in late summer of 1834, Comte Amédée de Ripert-Monclar, a French Royalist about his own age. Similar interests attracted the two young men to each other, and during their association Monclar suggested that Browning write a poem on the subject of Paracelsus. It was to this friend that he dedicated his second published poem.[1] Although Monclar later changed his mind about the suitability of the subject for a young man, Browning had his own ideas for the poem; and in order to write it he put *Sordello* aside for the second time.

In his Preface to *Paracelsus*, dated March 15, 1835, Browning explained that the poem "had not been imagined six months ago," which would have been September 15, 1834. During this interval he was ex-

24

amining his sources and writing his poem, as his letters to Monclar show. On December 5, 1834, he informed his friend that he had written 3000 lines in three months and would publish the poem after polishing a few scenes. Browning at times gave the impression that once he started composing he moved at a good pace. He indicated to Monclar that it was not writing the poem but examining his sources that had been time-consuming. On March 2, 1835, he wrote that an illness had kept him from working for a month or more. *Paracelsus* was now completed and ready to be published.[2]

After completing *Paracelsus* in March, Browning was faced with the problem of publication. Neither the warning given by the *Athenaeum* reviewer of *Pauline* that the day had passed for "fee or fame in the service of the muse" nor the difficulty of finding a publisher for poetry daunted Browning. The youthful poet — "full of ambition, eager for success, eager for fame, and what's more, determined to conquer fame and to achieve success"[3] — made the most of his then limited acquaintance with people who might help him. Fox, who had read *Incondita* and bestirred himself in Browning's behalf when *Pauline* was published, was again to be called upon for assistance. Next door to Fox lived Vincent Novello and his family, including Mary Novello and her husband Charles Cowden Clarke, who had been a publisher and therefore knew others in the business. Clarke could furnish a letter of introduction to the publisher Edward Moxon. On April 2, 1835, Browning wrote to Fox, "You will oblige me indeed by forwarding the introduction to Moxon. I merely suggested him in particular, on account of his good name and fame among author-folk, besides he has himself written — as the Americans say — 'more poetry 'an you can shake a stick at.' So I hope we shall come to terms."[4]

The introduction was forwarded, and though Browning was hopeful and moved with dispatch, the first attempt came to nothing, as he reported to Fox in a letter written on April 16:

> Your communication gladdened the cockles of my heart. I lost no time in presenting myself to Moxon, but no sooner was Mr. Clarke's letter perused than the Moxonian visage loured exceedingly thereat — the Moxonian accent grew dolorous thereupon: — "Artevelde" [a poem by Henry Taylor] has not paid expenses by about thirty odd pounds. Tennyson's poetry is *"popular at Cambridge,"* and yet of 800 copies which were printed of his last, some 300 only have gone off: Mr. M. hardly knows whether he shall ever venture again, &c. &c. and in short begs to decline even inspecting, &c. &c.[5]

Without hesitation Browning made another attempt; this time he approached Saunders and Otley, the publishers of his first poem. He was hopeful by temperament, but by now he had learned something of the realities of getting poetry into print. He continued his account to Fox, "I called on Saunders and Otley at once, and, marvel of marvels, do really think there is some chance of our coming to decent terms — I shall know at the beginning of next week, but am not over-sanguine." He was turned down by Saunders and Otley. There was also communication, probably near this time, between Browning and Sarah Flower, now Mrs. Adams, about Murray. Browning reported that as he had anticipated there was no chance with Murray; he, like Moxon, expressed a disinclination to run a risk with poetry: ". . . Lord Byron is 'no mo' & Poetry 'no go.' "[6] In the end, with Browning's father paying the expenses, Effingham Wilson published the poem, more "on the ground of radical sympathies in Mr. Fox and the author than on that of its intrinsic worth."[7]

While Browning was searching for a publisher, he was trying to get Fox's opinion of the poem. He had confidence but it by no means precluded a desire for criticism that might be profitable. He made his appeal:

> . . . though I am rather scared at the thought of a *fresh eye* going over its 4,000 lines — discovering blemishes of all sorts which my one wit cannot avail to detect, fools treated as sages, obscure passages, slipshod verses, and much that worse is, — yet on the whole I am not much afraid of the issue, and I would give something to be allowed to read it some morning to you — for every rap o' the knuckles I should get a clap o' the back, I know.[8]

Even with his generosity and desire to help, Fox in his busy life did not at once provide the occasion for the reading. Browning kept the topic alive, for Fox's opinion was of great importance to him; and in the end Fox did hear Browning read *Paracelsus*.[9]

Just after Browning had examined the review of *Pauline* in the *Monthly Repository* he wrote Fox, "I am . . . not altogether hopeless of justifying, by effort at least, your most generous 'coming forward.' " Before reading *Paracelsus* to Fox, Browning expressed the same sentiment, "I also hope my poem will not turn out utterly unworthy your kind interest, and more deserving your favour than anything of mine you have as yet seen; indeed I all along proposed to myself such an endeavour, for it will never do for one so distinguished by past praise to prove nobody after all. . . ." This was not mere courtesy. The remarks can be taken seriously, as can his assurance to Fox that "not a particle" of the criticism of *Pauline* had "been rejected or neglected" and his expression of hope that *Paracelsus* would bear the "marks of the influence under which it was undertaken." [10]

Browning's eagerness for success was backed by earnest attempts to profit by Fox's criticisms. His concern for "obscure passages, slipshod verses" indicates that he had in mind Fox's comments on "inferior melody" and "rather obscure" passages in his review of *Pauline*. Fox had explained in his first review that the absence of light lyrics would prevent *Pauline's* popularity. Browning also heeded this; he included lyrics in *Paracelsus*. Fox was not unmindful of these efforts, as his review of *Paracelsus* would show.

Browning later said that Fox was his literary father and still later called him his Chiron. [11] Fox's help was of the kind that gave encouragement to an aspiring and unrecognized poet. Short poems of Browning's were appearing from time to time in Fox's *Monthly Repository*. [12] Browning turned to the older man for advice and help; with faith in his generosity he wrote the letter in which he reported with some banter the results of searching for a publisher, assured Fox that he had heeded his criticism, and solicited the opportunity to read *Paracelsus* to him. In his request to read the poem he spoke incidentally of the part of *Sordello* that was already written as "not so decisive and explicit on a point or two" and then came to the topic of immediate concern — *Paracelsus:*

> — so I decide on trying the question with this: — I really shall *need* your notice, on this account; I shall affix my name and stick my arms akimbo; there are a few precious bold bits here and there, and the drift and scope are awfully radical — I am "off" for ever with the other side, but must by all means be "on" with yours — a position once gained, worthier works shall follow. . . . [13]

There followed what has already been referred to in the preceding chapter — Browning's courting a review from Mill through Fox. One can hardly imagine a poet more determined to get his works before the public or more confident that they would be worth the attention of readers and critics. Mill was not to be numbered among the reviewers, but Fox was.

On Saturday, August 15, 1835, *Paracelsus* was published. The first reviews were unfavorable, but the critics recognized Browning's poetic ability. A glance at the poem gave the impression that *Paracelsus* was a drama — it was divided into five scenes; it had dialogue; speakers and setting were indicated at the beginning of each scene. In his prefatory remarks, however, Browning stated that he did not wish *Paracelsus* to be mistaken for a play and judged by inapplicable principles. He had "endeavoured to write a poem, not a drama." The novelty of his work he explained thus:

> I am anxious that the reader should not, at the very outset — mistaking my performance for one of a class with which it has nothing in common — judge it by principles on which it was never moulded, and subject it to a standard to which it was never meant to conform. I therefore anticipate his discovery, that it is an attempt, probably more novel than happy, to reverse the method usually adopted by writers whose aim it is to set forth any phenomenon of the mind or the passions, by the operation of persons and events; and that, instead of having recourse to an external machinery of incidents to create and evolve the crisis I desire to produce, I have ventured to display somewhat minutely the mood itself in its rise and progress, and have suffered the agency by which it is influenced and determined, to be generally discernible in its effects alone, and subordinate throughout, if not altogether excluded. . . .

Dramatists, Browning says, usually reveal mental and emotional states "by the operation of persons and events," by which he means that the internal condition of a particular character is brought to light as it is influenced by other characters and the events of the play. Unlike the typical dramatist, Browning had not used "an external machinery of incidents." He had dealt in detail with the origin and course of a "mood" and had left the outside influences working upon it to be inferred from their effects. This was Browning's technique in *Paracelsus.* He realized, as he stated later in his Preface, that he was placing a burden upon his readers, who would have to supply omissions and connections for themselves. In parenthesis he referred to *Paracelsus* as "an experiment I am in no case likely to repeat."

On the weekend when the poem was published it was reviewed in three weekly publications — the *Spectator,* the *Atlas,* and the *Weekly Dispatch* — and on the following Saturday, August 22, a two-sentence notice appeared in the *Athenaeum.* Not one of the critics for these early weeklies wrote a favorable review, though the three who first reviewed the poem found in it indications of poetic ability.

The three indicated an awareness of the novelty of the design but did not approve of it. The critics for the *Spectator* and *Atlas* did make some effort to explain why they objected. The one for the *Spectator* said the defect in the structure was that it had "neither action nor incident; scarcely even a story to excite the attention of the reader." Of this, he commented, Browning seemed "to be in some sort conscious," and then he quoted from the Preface. He further explained his objections to the plan.

> But admitting all this to have been designed, the design may still be very injudicious: for the form of dialogue precludes those descriptions and digressions by which the author in a narrative poem can vary his subjects and "interchange delights;" whilst the fundamental plan renders the whole piece a virtual soliloquy, each person of the drama *speaking up* to Paracelsus, in order to elicit his feelings, thoughts, or opinions. For these reasons, we conceive that such a poem contains in its structure the elements of tediousness, which no execution could obviate; and, unfortunately, the execution of *Paracelsus* is not of a nature to overcome difficulties.

The critic found "no nice conception and development of character, nothing peculiar or striking in the thoughts." It was a "sceptico-philosophical poem," and the philosophical thought should have been shown by examples.

The reviewer for the *Atlas* stated at the outset that the story of Paracelsus was "ill-judged for the uses of poetry"; it was suited to the historical novel, which allowed for expansion and variety, qualities that the *Spectator* also desired and which, according to the *Atlas,* Browning's poem did not have. Whatever the poet intended, the execution of his design was unsatisfactory. "The form . . . can scarcely be called dramatic, although it is in dialogue, for the whole use of the three persons who are introduced is to give *Paracelsus* an excuse for talking, and to draw out his character through his own confessions."

In the quotations given here from the *Spectator* and the *Atlas* the critics called attention to Browning's introduction of characters solely for the purpose of providing Paracelsus "an excuse for talking" and revealing himself. Here lay the germ of Browning's dramatic monologue; the critics were remarking upon a technique to be developed in a form that would make Browning famous, but they had no way of anticipating this. Repeatedly in the future other critics would point out certain techniques of Browning's poetry without being aware of the significance of their statements.

The *Weekly Dispatch,* in a one-paragraph discussion, also disapproved of the plan and execution of the poem. After recognizing that

Browning wished to "institute something like a new school of poetry," the critic commented that the history of Paracelsus was a "meagre theme for poetic imagination," and the poet had handled it "with corresponding weakness."

The reviewers for these weeklies objected not only to the subject and the plan of *Paracelsus;* they also complained of its obscurity and criticized its versification and language. The *Athenaeum* gave two sentences to the poem, chiefly to chide the author for imitating Shelley's faults: *Paracelsus* was "dreamy and obscure." Likewise, the *Spectator* said that the language in which the thoughts were clothed gave them "an air of mystical or dreamy vagueness," the *Atlas* asserted that the thought often labored through a "haze of ambiguous words," and the *Weekly Dispatch* could not name a single work that had been so puzzling. There was disapproval also of the poetic line: the frequent false quantity *(Weekly Dispatch)* and the often discordant and even more often prosaic meter *(Atlas)*. If there were objections to style there was also recognition of Browning's ability. The *Spectator* found "evidences of mental power, perhaps of poetical talent." The *Atlas* acknowledged "powers far above the ordinary level" and "an eloquence of no common order." The *Athenaeum* also found talent in the poem.

An enthusiastic review of *Paracelsus* appeared three weeks after its publication, on September 6, in the *Examiner*. It was written by John Forster, who was soon to become a friend of Browning's. Forster, already moving toward a position of influence as journalist and biographer, liked to control situations and people, often in an irritating manner. Though he was given such names as "tuft-hunter," "vulgar swell," and "Bumbeadle of Creation," many Victorians, including some who were exasperated by his behavior, recognized in him a capable and helpful friend. He became such to Browning after the appearance of his review of *Paracelsus,* the first of his many reviews of Browning's works.

Not since the publication of Henry Taylor's *Philip van Artevelde* had Forster found such evidences of "poetical genius" and "general intellectual power" as in *Paracelsus,* a poem giving "a philosophical view of the mind of Paracelsus, its workings and misworkings, its tendencies and efforts and results." Browning's plan was explained and the reader was told to be prepared for the severe effect of the "mode of treatment." He would find enough beauty to make up for the tedious passages, even if they were ten times as obscure and tedious. "A rich vein of internal sentiment, a deep knowledge of humanity, an intellect subtle and inquisitive" would soon "fix his interest, and call forth his warmest admiration." A long summary with copious quotations followed. The review continued with praise to the end. It had been some time since Forster had read a work of "more unequivocal power." He concluded that its author was a young man, since he recollected no other publication by him. If he continued true to the "promise of his genius," he would have a brilliant career.

By October discussions began to appear in monthlies. The first was in the *Metropolitan Magazine,* a miscellany that carried book notices at the end of each issue. In a one-paragraph notice in October the critic thought the contents crude and supposed that the poet "did not wish his work to be very comprehensible." Yet there were "many touches of beauty, almost Shakespearian" in this "ambitiously unpopular poem." *Tait's,* the monthly whose unfavorable notice of *Pauline* had lodged in Browning's mind, carried a short paragraph on *Paracelsus* in the November issue. The critic referred to one passage with approval and said that in spite of Browning's presentation of the work as nondramatic the finest passages were in fact dramatic.

Other and more effective reviews of *Paracelsus* appeared in monthlies that were influential in varying degrees — the *Monthly Repository, Fraser's,* and the *New Monthly Magazine.* Fox continued his efforts in Browning's behalf; he reviewed the poem in the *Monthly Repository* in November. He explained Browning's design according to the Preface, bringing out that although in form a dialogue the poem was "often in spirit a monologue, the other speakers being introduced as subservient to the delineation, by Paracelsus himself, of the several states of his mental being." Fox recognized in the protagonist an "individualization of humanity," in whom the poet exhibited its "alternate conditions of aspiration and attainment." He stressed the intellectual quality of the poem and saw in it great purpose, which was necessary for poetry to live. To read *Paracelsus* with understanding required work, but it was the kind of work that was compatible with poetic enjoyment.

Fox, who had commented on the lack of light lyrics in *Pauline,* did not fail to notice Browning's use of them in *Paracelsus;* they were distinguished by a "luscious sweetness of imagery and versification." Furthermore Fox, who had earlier pointed out the intellectual aspect of *Pauline,* found that the "strong powers of thought" were combined with an "intense poetical sense" and that often the metaphorical illustration was exquisitely adapted to sentiment and character. Along with the good qualities, Fox found a need for condensation in some parts; he thought the poem would be improved, even in clearness, by avoidance of amplification and repetition.

Fox censured earlier reviewers of the poem, especially those for the weeklies. Unaccustomed to reviewing poems that required thought, they were faced with *Paracelsus* and gave their verdict: it was a "work of genius, or else a worthless abortion; the world may find out which: and when the world has found it out, the critics discover the reasons, and set them forth in learned dissertations."

The other two favorable reviews in monthlies did not appear until March of 1836. In the meantime there was encouraging criticism in a weekly. Leigh Hunt was in all likelihood the reviewer of *Paracelsus* in *Leigh Hunt's London Journal and the Printing Machine* on November 21. Hunt did not fall into the class of critics that Fox had considered incapable of knowing their own minds. His criticism was of a high quality. He did say that he would have been better pleased "with the absence both of the statement in the preface, that the poem had not been imagined six months before its publication, and of any ground for making such a statement." With more time Browning could have produced a "still finer" poem. Whether accounted commendable or the reverse in the abstract, the peculiarities of Browning's poetry were indispensable to the perfection of the style, for they were a "reflection of mental habits" which helped to make the poetry what it was. Hunt continued:

> We do not therefore object generally to his long and often somewhat intricately involved sentences, or to forms of phraseology and construction, of occasional occurrence, which are apt for a moment to perplex or startle on the first reading, or to any other deviations of a similar kind from ordinary usage or the beaten highway prescribed by our books of authority in grammar, rhetoric, and prosody, in so far as such unusual forms are the natural and unaffected product of the writer's genius, working its purposes in its own way.

Long before it was generally recognized that Browning's poetry should not be reviewed as if it observed current concepts of poetic composition, Hunt realized the need to judge it on its own merits. Foreshadowing others, he acknowledged the demands it made but pointed to the reader's satisfaction after he became accustomed to its originality. That much in the diction and versification had a "harsh, awkward, and disappointing effect at first" arose from the poem's "not being cast in a common mould, or formed so much as most new poems are upon the ordinary models." *Paracelsus* was not a mere variation of an old air, and therefore could not be read so easily as most poetical productions of the day. Once the distinctive characteristics became familiar, they acquired a power of enhancing the pleasure of reading Browning's poetry. But like every writer who aimed at being original the poet should be warned against the dangers of slovenliness or affectation. "We think there is in the present poem a slight degree occasionally of both the one and the other; and to many readers it will probably appear that there is a great deal of both." Though some questions might be raised about the execution of *Paracelsus,* Hunt thought that there could be no doubt of its poetic power.

After the critical remarks and a discussion of Browning's plan of the poem, Hunt gave the remainder of his long article to summary and quotation. It is regrettable that this potentially helpful review appeared in a periodical directed to readers ill-qualified to take advantage of it. In his *Autobiography* Hunt wrote that this one of his literary periodicals, selling for twopence, had a short life because it was of "too aesthetical a nature for cheap readers in those days."[14]

In March of 1836 *Fraser's Magazine* and the *New Monthly Magazine* contained reviews of *Paracelsus,* both laudatory. In spite of its flippancy, the discussion in *Fraser's* should be taken seriously. It gave the poem more attention — mainly in the form of summary with generous quotations — than any of the other works included in the same review. Following one of the quotations was a statement that though the versification was imperfect something in its roughness kept the sense above the sound and made the reader attend whether he wished to or not. Then the critic divided poetry into four large classes according to the dominance of sound, words, thought, and ideas. He found in *Paracelsus* little of the first two but very much of the third and more than glimpses of the fourth.

The critic emphasized the superiority of Paracelsus to the then popular *Philip van Artevelde.* He thought that *Artevelde* was a "mechanic" work, derived from the Lake School of poetry and German systems of transcendentalism; it was almost faultless because it was made up "to shew not life in itself, but skill in its maker." On the other hand, *Paracelsus* was organic, with the "thoughts growing up, and acquiring body and stature." There were defects, but they were acceptable because the poem was a "moving, breathing thing." The critic wished that the six years Taylor had spent on *Artevelde* had been six months and that the six months Browning had worked on *Paracelsus* had been six years. Though Browning's poem had not gestated long enough, the critic preferred *Paracelsus* with its "life, passion, motion, growth" to Taylor's poem with its imitation and cleverness.

The most enthusiastic discussion of Browning that appeared in the three favorable reviews in monthlies was the one in the *New Monthly Magazine*. This magazine had started as a Whig periodical in 1814, but the political emphasis weakened as it became an important literary periodical in the twenties. Its continued wide influence during the nineteenth century was advantageous to any writer favorably reviewed in its pages. The treatment of *Paracelsus* in March 1836 was the second criticism of that poem written by John Forster.

Forster began with the statement that *Paracelsus* opened a "deeper vein of thought, of feeling, and of passion, than any poet has attempted for years" and without the "slightest hesitation" named Browning at once with Shelley, Coleridge, and Wordsworth. In this review Forster began to emphasize Browning's dramatic genius. After explaining the content of the Preface, he commented on Browning's notion of leaving the outside influences on the mood to be inferred from their effects. Forster held that the reader was most vividly sensible of the presence of the very agents by which the results had been determined. He made it clear that he was interested in the dramatic quality of Browning's work; the title ("Evidences of a New Genius for Dramatic Poetry. — No. I"), he said, suggested the intended direction of the review. But since he considered Browning a philosophical as well as a dramatic poet, he felt that he could not restrict himself to the dramatic element alone.

Forster, therefore, promised the reader "a wholly new ground of philosophical inquiry into character," or at least a suggestion of valuable and interesting trains of thought. Throughout twenty pages he discussed the real Paracelsus and Browning's imaginative treatment of him. After this "glance at the philosophical claims of Paracelsus," Forster reverted to the dramatic quality of Browning's poetry, which he planned to discuss in another article.

> In a future paper we shall restrict ourselves to *The poem, Paracelsus,* and prove from that, and from other works we have had the pleasure of receiving lately, that dramatic genius, — perfectly new, born of our own age, the offspring of original thinking and original expression, grafted upon those noble points of universal character which only are enduring, — is now actually amongst us, and waits only the proper opportunity of exercise, to redeem the drama, and to elevate the literary repute, of England.

He never wrote the promised paper; but as a steady reviewer of Browning's work, he was to comment later on the originality and the high purpose that prompted Browning's writing and was to hope for some years that Browning would exercise his dramatic genius in writing successful stage plays.

In the early part of the review in the *New Monthly Magazine* Forster referred to *Paracelsus* as a "scantily-noticed volume" and in the conclusion he alluded to the book that had been "buzzed at" by the critics and about which Christopher North (John Wilson of *Blackwood's*) had been silent. Forster, already assuming his role as Browning's staunch supporter, was heightening the notion of his own influence and the neglectfulness of other critics.

On April 9 a short-lived conservative weekly, the *Metropolitan Journal,* announced that it would review *Paracelsus.* The review appeared in two parts, on April 16 and April 23. The critic wrote, "It is long since we have been so much gratified with any modern poetry." In thought and imagination few writers of their time could equal Mr. Browning, whose mind had the "happy mean betwixt the philosopher and the poet." Browning's choice of subject was bad: Paracelsus was unworthy of the poet, but he had wrought a very good poem out of a very bad subject. If there was a fault, it came from the imperfection of the plot; if the language was bald and insufficient, the character Paracelsus must be blamed. One serious blemish that Browning should eliminate in the second edition was his repeated and indecent use of God's name. The reviewer felt that Browning was spiritually akin to Paracelsus, the impassioned being who longed for distinction and a passport to fame. And he assured the poet he would win them both.

The reviews of *Paracelsus* show that on the whole it had what must be called a moderately good reception, especially since it was the poet's first acknowledged work and it was constructed on an experimental design. Half of the reviews discussed in this chapter warmly endorsed the poem. The outstanding weeklies that wrote with disfavor of it — the *Atlas,* the *Spectator,* and the *Athenaeum* — were more than offset by the important periodicals that endorsed it — the *Examiner,* the *New Monthly Magazine,* and the *Monthly Repository.* Browning was launched as a thoughtful poet (*Examiner, Monthly Repository, New Monthly Magazine, Metropolitan Journal*); his dramatic bent was recognized (*Tait's, New Monthly Magazine*); and his particular employment of subservient characters to help reveal the main character — the experiment which would bear fruit in later monologues —

was pointed out *(Spectator, Atlas, Monthly Repository)*. *Paracelsus* was associated with the then popular *Philip van Artevelde;* Browning was included among the acknowledged poets of the time; and a future of great promise was predicted for him.

It is significant that the majority of the reviews of *Paracelsus* appeared in weeklies. When Browning began to publish, five weeklies that were to have long life and considerable influence were in existence. The *Examiner,* the *Atlas,* and the *Spectator* were concerned with politics and literature; the *Examiner,* initiated in 1808, was without a rival in its field until the appearance of the *Atlas* in 1826 and the *Spectator* in 1828. There were two prominent weeklies of a purely literary nature; the *Literary Gazette* was started in 1817 and held first place in its sphere until the appearance of the *Athenaeum* in 1828. These weeklies played an important role in the history of Browning's reputation through the time of the collected edition of 1849. The number of reviews that they carried during this span of time was almost as many as the total number of reviews in the dailies, monthlies, and quarterlies combined. Over twenty reviews of Browning's works appeared in other weeklies as well.

The reviews in the weeklies were usually the first to appear. This might have had some effect on the critics' comprehension of and attitude toward the piece in hand. When facing a pressing deadline, the critics for the weeklies did not always have sufficient time to consider the work carefully and frame judicious remarks. They could deal adequately with run-of-the-mill poetry, but they were at a disadvantage when something in a new vein claimed their attention. *Paracelsus* had a novel plan that was difficult to grasp. The unreceptive attitude toward the plan was indicative of the difficulties which critics writing under the pressure of time would continue to face.

Whatever the objections of the reviewers, whether writing for weeklies or for other periodicals, they were not blind to Browning's poetic ability. This simultaneous disapproval of the work reviewed and recognition of Browning's genius was to be a marked characteristic of future criticism. Other aspects of the criticism of *Paracelsus,* some of which had been present in the reviews of *Pauline,* were to attain prominence in the future: objections to metrical irregularity and obscurity; observation of Browning's interest in human nature and of the dramatic and reflective as well as the philosophical quality of his poetry.

The year of the publication of *Paracelsus* and the year following were momentous ones for Browning. Besides being fairly launched by the reviewers, *Paracelsus* was admired by people prominent in literary and dramatic circles. Browning met some of them and established friendships both pleasurable and profitable. On the evening of November 27, 1835 — by this time at least nine reviews of *Paracelsus* had appeared — Browning went to Fox's home after dinner. There he met Richard Henry Horne — poet, critic, and dramatist — and William Charles Macready, the eminent tragedian, through whom Browning would soon be professionally and emotionally involved in the world of drama.

As noted in his *Diaries*, on September 6 Macready had read extracts from *Paracelsus* in the *Examiner's* review and praised them highly, and on the night before he went to Fox's he again read extracts from the poem — "beautiful and touching" — perhaps this time in Fox's review in the *Monthly Repository*. He was pleased to meet the poet, and thought his face full of intelligence. "I took Mr. Browning on, and requested to be allowed to improve my acquaintance with him." [15] It is evident from Macready's comment that Browning was equal to the occasion: "He expressed himself warmly, as gratified by the proposal; wished to send me his book; we exchanged cards and parted." The actor read *Paracelsus* during the next week and recorded on December 7: ". . . a work of great daring, starred with poetry of thought, feeling and diction, but occasionally obscure; the writer can scarcely fail to be a leading spirit of his time." On the next day Macready finished the poem and again praised it and again commented on its obscurity. Soon after meeting Browning, Macready created an opportunity to improve the acquaintance; he invited Browning with other guests for New Year's. One guest, we learn from Macready's *Diaries*, was Forster, who had already written the review for the *Examiner*.

Because of their interest in *Paracelsus*, Forster through the press and Macready by word of mouth influenced others to read it. Macready put the poem into Harriet Martineau's hand when she was staying at his house. She read a canto before she went to bed and confessed that for the first time in her life she "passed a whole night without sleeping a wink." [16] He also gave a copy to Fanny Haworth, who lived near his home at Elstree. [17] Browning and Miss Haworth met at Macready's, and in this woman, eleven years his senior, Browning found a friend sympathetic with his literary interests. Juliet Pollock, who first came to know Macready after his association with Browning, gave an instance of the actor's continued promotion of *Paracelsus*.

He was disturbed by the discovery that I had not read "Paracelsus," and that I knew nothing of Browning beyond his name. He lifted his eyebrows; he muttered expressions of wonder; he once or twice said, "Oh, good God!" he took a turn or two up and down the room, and then said, "I really am quite at a loss; I cannot understand it."

I pleaded the claims of the babies; they left me little time, etc.

To which he replied, "Hand over the babies to the nurse, and read 'Paracelsus.' "[18]

Other women besides Miss Haworth who played a part in Browning's life told of their admiration for the poem. Anna Jameson, a writer on art who would be a helpful friend during Elizabeth and Robert's journey to Italy after their marriage, knew nothing that would compare with *Paracelsus* since Goethe and Wordsworth.[19] Helen Faucit, who was to perform the leading role in *Stafford, A Blot in the 'Scutcheon,* and *Colombe's Birthday,* regarded the poem as a favorite.[20] By late summer of 1836 — ten years before marrying Browning — Elizabeth Barrett had read *Paracelsus* and was giving her opinion of it to Mary Russell Mitford:

> But have you seen Paracelsus? I am a little discontented even *there,* and would wish for more harmony and rather more clearness and compression — *concentration* — besides: But I do think and feel that the pulse of poetry is full and warm and strong in it, and that — without being likely perhaps to be a popular poem — it "bears a charmed life". There is a palpable power — a height and depth of thought — and sudden repressed gushings of tenderness which suggest to us a depth beyond, in the affections. I wish you would read it, and agree with me that the author is a poet in the holy sense. And I wish besides that some passages in the poem referring to the divine Being had been softened or removed. They sound to me daringly — and *that* is not the appropriate daring of genius.[21]

John Kenyon had taken Elizabeth Barrett a copy of *Paracelsus.* He was Elizabeth's cousin, a wealthy man whose generosity, social graces, and fine sense of values benefitted the lives of many. Kenyon made himself known to Browning one evening when they were having dinner at a friend's house. He questioned the young man about his father, who, it turned out, had been a schoolmate of his. At a later time Kenyon asked Browning to dine with him. Browning sent the following reply, dated May 26, 1837: "I shall be most happy to dine with you on the day you have appointed: we can then, I hope, make some arrangement to procure my Father a pleasure for which he has been very anxious this . . . I regret to say . . long while, for such it has been since I had the gratification of meeting you."[22] Browning was successful in bringing about the renewal of Kenyon's earlier contact with Browning Senior. Kenyon was to be no idle bystander in the converging lives of Robert Browning and Elizabeth Barrett.

Browning's horizon was extending in other ways. At Covent Garden on May 26, 1836, Macready staged with remarkable success *Ion,* a play by Thomas Noon Talfourd. One critic wrote of the performance:

> It was . . . the vital, pathetic excellence of the drama, and the rich poetry of the diction, which, on the night of the production of the play at Covent Garden, filled that great theatre with an audience the like of which, in point of distinction, I have never seen in any English theatre. There were the flower of our poets, the best of our lawyers, artists of every world and every quality.[23]

It was Talfourd's birthday, and after the play more than sixty guests, many of them distinguished, had supper at his home. Wordsworth was there and also Landor and near them the youthful Browning, who by now was sufficiently known for his *Paracelsus* to be included in the toast given to "The Poets of England" and who responded with "grace and modesty."

Three guests at this dinner — Forster, Fanny Haworth, and Landor — called attention to *Paracelsus* in 1836 in publications other than reviews. In Forster's *Sir John Eliot* lines apposite to a description of Eliot were quoted from a poet "whose genius has just risen amongst us." In a footnote the poet was identified by name as the author of *Paracelsus* and complimented: "There would be little danger in predicting that this writer will soon be acknowledged as a first-rate poet. He has already proved himself one."[24] In September two sonnets addressed "To the author of 'Paracelsus' " were published in the *New Monthly Magazine* (XLVIII, 48). They were both written by Miss Haworth. She, like others, referred to Browning's "mind's rich store" and his originality. At the end of the second sonnet she wrote of the time to come: "Unconsciously, / Perchance, his musing spirit is the guest / Of future ages, who shall prize him best."

Paracelsus made a brief appearance in Landor's *A Satire on Satirists, and Admonition to Detractors,* published in December of 1836, which

was chiefly an attack on *Blackwood's* and Wordsworth. The comment in
it on the reception of *Paracelsus* resembles Fox's pronouncement on the
hesitancy of critics to accept Browning's poem.

> To such the trembling verse-boy brings his task,
> Of such the one-spurr'd critick begs to ask,
> Hath Sheffield's glorious son the genuine vein?
> Did *Paracelsus* spring from poet's brain?
> When all expect it, *yes* will never do,
> The cautious and the business-like say *no*.
> Criticks and maidens should not smile too fast;
> A *yes*, though drawl'd out faintly, comes at last.[25]

On August 10, 1836, Landor had written Forster: "When you told us
that the author of Paracelsus would be a great poet, you came rather
too late in the exercise of prophecy — he was one already, and will be
among the greatest. I hope he does not relax in that scirocco of faint
praise which brother poets are fond of giving. Such as yours will brace
him against it."[26]

In the forties Joseph Arnould wrote to Alfred Domett, "I still believe as devoutly as ever in 'Paracelsus,' and find more wealth of
thought and poetry in it than [in] any book except Shakespeare. The
more one reads the more miraculous does that book seem as the work
of a man of five-and-twenty."[27]

In fact, there were not many contemporaries of Browning who
left on record an unfavorable opinion of the poem. In later years Mary
Russell Mitford, James Anthony Froude, and Carlyle said that they did
not like the poem. Miss Mitford, in writing a friend the news of Miss
Barrett's marriage, spoke of *Paracelsus* and other works of Browning's
as "so many riddles."[28] In 1862 Froude wrote, "I tried *Paracelsus*
twenty years ago unsuccessfully, and this, I suppose, has prevented me
from exciting myself about him as I ought."[29] Carlyle's remark was
recorded by Conway: "When he published 'Paracelsus' I did not make
much out of it: it seemed to me to have something 'sensational' as they
say about it. . . ."[30] Coventry Patmore said he admired the poem
"with a reservation."[31] Such opinions as these were in the minority. In
general, comments indicated that *Paracelsus* was considered the work of
a new poet of ability. Faults were indicated — obscurity in particular
— but they were considered of less importance than the qualities that
gave promise of a poet of genius.

Before its publication Browning wrote Monclar that *Paracelsus* was novel in both conception and execution and as such was not likely to be popular; after its publication he told him it had been much more successful than he had expected.[32] He was never ashamed of it as he was of *Pauline*. Until the time of his marriage every work except *Sordello* carried on its title page "By Robert Browning, author of 'Paracelsus.' " In proportion to the pride he took in the poem was the sensitiveness he began to show towards the early reviews of it ten years after its publication. This sensitiveness is apparent in a letter written on December 9, 1845, to Elizabeth Barrett, in which he compared the reception of Talfourd's *Ion,* performed in 1836, with that of *Paracelsus,* published in 1835. Browning and Elizabeth's brother George had just been at Talfourd's house, where they saw a "portentous book, lettered II, and thick as a law-book, of congratulatory letters on the appearance of 'Ion.' "[33] Among the letters in the book bound in green morocco were one that Talfourd had received from Browning and another from Elizabeth Barrett. Talfourd's display of vanity and the chagrin that Browning and Elizabeth felt in knowing that their own letters were on exhibit led them to a free interchange of opinion.

In the letter of December 9 to Elizabeth, Browning turned the clock back ten years.

> . . . to say the truth, I might have remembered the most justifying circumstance in my case . . which was, that my own "Paracelsus," printed a few months before, had been as dead a failure as "Ion" a brilliant success — for, until just before . . Ah, really I forget! — but I know that until Forster's notice in the "Examiner" appeared, *every* journal that thought worth while to allude to the poem at all, treated it with entire contempt . . beginning, I think, with the "Athenaeum" which *then* made haste to say, a few days after its publication, "that it was not without talent but spoiled by obscurity and only an imitation of — Shelley!" — something to this effect, in a criticism of about three lines among their "Library Table" notices. . . .[34]

The statements that Browning made in the letter were not altogether true. No one who reads the reviews could fairly say that *Paracelsus* was a dead failure. Nor was it true that before Forster's criticism in the *Examiner* every journal that discussed *Paracelsus* treated it with "entire contempt." Of the four generally unfavorable reviews antedating the *Examiner's* criticism, all except the *Weekly Dispatch* found poetic ability in the poem and even it acknowledged "some happy thoughts and well-turned periods." It is true that the brief comments in the *Athenaeum* and in the *Weekly Dispatch* gave no adequate notion of the content. But even though they found fault with *Paracelsus,* the critics for the *Spectator* and *Atlas* included a summary, discussed the design of the poem, and explained their objections. They both commented on the function of the supporting characters — to draw out the nature of Paracelsus. They observed the course of the poem, though instead of appreciating the novelty of the treatment they wished that Browning had chosen the conventional narrative form for his subject. Neither critic dismissed *Paracelsus* succinctly or gave the impression that it was not worth consideration; in fact, the critic for the *Atlas* devoted almost as much space to *Paracelsus* as to four other poems treated together in his section on poetry; and he included long quotations, which he praised. Whatever the disapproval and shortsightedness of these reviews, there was no contempt, as Browning stated in his letter to Elizabeth. And almost without exception the objections made in the first four reviews were also made in one or more of the favorable reviews that came later.

Browning continued his letter.

. . . and that first taste was a most flattering sample of what the "craft" had in store for me — since my publisher and I had fairly to laugh at *his* 'Book' — (quite of another kind than the Serjeant's —) in which he was used to paste extracts from newspapers & the like — seeing that, out of a long string of notices, one vied with its predecessor in disgust at my "rubbish," as their word went: but Forster's notice altered a good deal — which I have to recollect for his good. Still, the contrast between myself and Talfourd was so *utter* — you remember the world's-wonder "Ion" made, — that I was determined not to pass for the envious piece of neglected merit I really *was not* — and so! —

Clearly the *Athenaeum's* review, which Browning erroneously remembered as the first one, was not what he said it was — a sample of what the "craft" had in store for him. There was recognition of his poetic ability, and two of the earliest reviewers were not thoroughly blind or ungenerous in their assessment. And it should be added that in none of the four early reviews was the word "rubbish" — or any similar word — used.

Forster's notice altered a good deal — this was Browning's opinion. But will it stand scrutiny? After the *Examiner's* review in September, the criticism in the *Metropolitan Magazine* came out in October and the one in *Tait's* in November; both were hardly more helpful than the earlier *Athenaeum* comment, which so much offended Browning. The writers of the other reviews that followed the *Examiner* were more than likely not affected by what Forster had said. Neither the veteran journalist Leigh Hunt nor the reviewer for the incisive *Fraser's* was apt to lean on Forster's opinion: and clearly enough Fox was prepared to praise Browning before Forster appeared on the scene.

Thomas R. Lounsbury, in his *Early Literary Career of Robert Browning,* pointed out the folly of supposing that the early reviews did much damage. "Further, if Forster's review established a barrier sufficient to withstand the raving, roaring tide of detraction which had set in against the poem, the inundation of disparagement could hardly have assumed an overwhelming character by the time he had erected it."[35] The early reviews were published on August 15, 16, and 22; Forster's review in the *Examiner* appeared on September 6 — hardly enough of an interval to harm the reputation of a new poet.

Lounsbury also showed that Browning was not justified in the contrast of *Ion* as a success and *Paracelsus* as a failure. Talfourd was well known to the public: he was an author before Browning was born, had contributed frequently to periodicals, and had a legal reputation. Furthermore the acting of Macready in *Ion* gave it publicity. Something can be added to Lounsbury's pertinent remarks by looking at the situation in another way. Was Browning thinking only of the contrast between the success of Talfourd's *Ion* and the "dead" failure of his *Paracelsus,* which was certainly not unsuccessful as a first acknowledged poem and which was not a play? Or did he have more definitely in mind the contrast between the successful play *Ion* and his own unsuccessful period of writing for the stage, which had ended in the year before he wrote this letter to Elizabeth? Gosse's account of the early plays (which he had from Browning) includes the following statement: "There was every expectation that the tragedy [*Strafford*] would have no less favorable a 'run' than *Ion* had enjoyed. . . ."[36] It was inevitable that Browning should associate his disappointment with his first attempt, as well as succeeding ones, to write for the stage with the acclaim that was accorded *Ion.* As one play after another had failed, Browning had gone through much turmoil and frustration, from which he never fully recovered. The agitation caused by the *Blot* experience apparently had been quiescent, but Browning saw the comments on *Ion* in Talfourd's portentous book during a time when he often demonstrated his extreme sensitivity — the waiting period after the publication of a new work (this time *Dramatic Romances and Lyrics*) but before enough reviews had appeared to determine its reception. Already on edge, he could not read the praises of *Ion* without awakening the emotions so deeply entangled with his poetic ambition and self-confidence.

Even with good reviews in the *Examiner* and the *New Monthly Magazine,* Forster did not have the influence on the reception of *Paracelsus* that Browning claimed for him. In his fantasy he placed him on a pinnacle, just as in his mind he accorded Mill a potential significance not justified by his notes and comments on *Pauline.* Browning gave the manuscript of *Paracelsus,* now in the Forster and Dyce Collection, to Forster. The inscription reads: "To *John Forster Esq* (my early Understander) with true thanks for his generous & seasonable public Confession of Faith in me. RB. *Hatcham, Surrey, 1842.*"

The passage in Browning's letter to Elizabeth of December 9, 1845, could be set aside as a temporary lapse if Browning had not repeated to others his mistaken version of the early history of *Paracelsus's* reception, with a similarity in wording in one instance. In a letter to George Grove, dated February 4, 1876, he said this of *Paracelsus:* ". . . that poem was treated with the utmost contempt by every weekly and daily journal without a single exception till Forster, wholly a stranger to me, wrote a generous article in the *Examiner* — forty years ago."[37] Browning's reconstruction of what the "craft" of reviewers had done to *Paracelsus* had not changed in thirty years. He harbored an exaggerated idea of the poor treatment of his second poem and of Forster's part in its early reception. When others adhered to the more accurate version of its early history, Browning did his best to controvert that opinion, sincerely believing his own to be right.[38] A distorted notion had formed in his mind and it remained there for the rest of his life.

CHAPTER III

First Attempt at Playwriting

Strafford, 1837

Browning's interest in plays, playacting, and playwriting was awakened early in life. In his poem *Development* he told how his father had acted out with him, a boy of five, the siege of Troy, with household personae and props. Sarianna, his sister, said that he had his schoolmates act plays, some of which he had written himself.[1] As time passed, his extensive reading in classical as well as English literature led him to familiarity with dramatic works, and the stage made a strong appeal. Seeing Edmund Kean act in the early thirties was for the young poet a stirring experience. With health and money gone in his last years, Kean in 1831 leased the theater on Richmond Green, which had been built in 1765. There in the Theatre Royal his performances included *Richard III, Othello,* and *Hamlet* in 1832.[2] Several times Browning walked the ten miles from Camberwell to see him act.[3] One of these nights fell on October 22, when he saw *Richard III* and conceived the plan of *Pauline.* In later years Justin McCarthy indicated how vividly Browning had retained the memory of Kean's acting:

> I shall never forget an account which he gave me once of his early
> recollections of Edmund Kean's acting. Browning, of course, was
> very young when he saw Edmund Kean, but he had carried away in
> his mind a perfect picture of the great tragedian's style and manner;
> and I must say that with all I had read of Kean, nothing ever impressed me with such a comprehension of his genius and of his style
> as did that rapid description by Browning, given, not to the company in general, but to me at a London dinner table.[4]

Browning transferred something of the fire of his own imagination into Kean's acting, for the vestiges of the tragedian's greatness scarcely remained in the lamentable performances at the end of his career. Kean died in May of 1833. Among the stream of people who went to Richmond for the funeral were three men, strangers to each other at the time. Two of them — Macready and Forster — met just before the service. Browning was the third. In a few years the three would be for a time closely associated in the theater world in which Kean — with his brandy bottle, his charm, and his brilliant acting — had played a vital part and had been a formidable rival of Macready's.

It was on New Year's Eve of 1835 that Browning paid his first visit to Macready's home and became acquainted with Forster. The good impression he made was noted in Macready's *Diaries:* "Mr. Browning was very popular with the whole party; his simple and enthusiastic manner engaged attention and won opinions from all present; he looks and speaks more like a youthful poet than any man I ever saw."[5] Macready regretted that he had no opportunity to detain him when the guests were departing the next day. Entries in the *Diaries* for February show how the poet continued to win favor: he had already become Forster's *"all-in-all"* by February 1; on the 27th Macready rejoiced when visitors left him — "excepting Browning, whose gentle manners always make his presence acceptable."

Browning talked plays, went to plays, and gathered with a select few in Macready's dressing room after performances. The lure of the theater was irresistible. *Paracelsus* had given the promise of a great dramatic poet, according to Forster's review of the poem in the *New Monthly Magazine;* the stage would provide an outlet for Browning's talents. Not surprisingly he soon began to turn his attention in that direction. Macready recorded on February 16:

> Forster and Browning called, and talked over the plot of a tragedy which Browning had begun to think of: the subject, Narses [Roman official and general, c. 478 — c. 573]. . . . It would indeed be some recompense for the miseries, the humiliations, the heart-sickening disgusts which I have endured in my profession if, by its exercise, I had awakened a spirit of poetry whose influence would elevate, ennoble, and adorn our degraded drama.

But the play had to wait. *Sordello* was still incomplete; by this time work on it had already been interrupted twice. Furthermore, early in the year Browning gave some assistance to Forster, who had become ill while completing a biography of Strafford.[6] With *Sordello* still in hand he went to the supper following the performance of Talfourd's *Ion* on May 26, 1836. Macready, discouraged by the low quality of stage performances and always hoping to discover promising dramatists, had eagerly welcomed Edward Bulwer Lytton, who, already established as a novelist, wished to succeed as a dramatist. At the time of the success of Talfourd's *Ion,* the first of Bulwer Lytton's plays in which Macready acted was being revised for the stage. Talfourd, Bulwer Lytton — why not the author of *Paracelsus* too? At the end of the celebration where conviviality reigned and talk flowed freely the actor said, "Write a play, Browning, and keep me from going to America."

The evening with celebrities, including Wordsworth and Landor; public recognition as a poet (in a toast); and at the end the invitation from Macready to write a play — these were strong stimulants. Browning was moving closer and closer to the writing of plays, as his response to Macready's remark indicated; it was written on the 28th, only two days following the tempting invitation. After an effusive preamble Browning came to the heart of his message:

> I am now engaged in a work which is nearly done: I allow myself a month to complete it: from the first of July I shall be free: if, before then, any subject shall suggest itself to you — I will give you my whole heart and soul to the writing a Tragedy on it to be ready by the first of November next: should I be unequal to the task, the excitement and extreme effort will have been their own reward: — should I succeed, my way of life will be very certain, and my name pronounced along with yours.[7]

This response prompted the actor to record with comparable effusion on May 30: "What can I say upon it? It was a tribute which remunerated me from the annoyance and cares of years: it was one of the very highest, may I not say the highest, honour I have through life received."

Macready was struggling for the maintenance of his reputation and for better theater standards at a time when legitimate drama had strong competition with attractions designed purely for money-making through an appeal to large and uncritical audiences. Melodrama and opera or anything else possible was adapted to spectacle. A trained dog as chief attraction in *The Caraven;* lions from Paris in *Hyder Ali, or the Lions of Mysore;* a stagecoach and six horses in *Paul Clifford;* Burmese bulls and ostriches from the Surrey Zoological Gardens in *Thalaba the Destroyer;* blue-fire melodrama in *Joan of Arc* — such attractions brought box office returns. Macready saw in Browning a hope for good drama with audience appeal.

Browning said he would have *Sordello* completed by July. Towards the end of that month Macready invited him to his home in Elstree, and Browning accepted on Saturday, July 23, for the following weekend. His pleasure was unmistakable in the acceptance note, which he wrote with his characteristic youthful flair:

> My dear Macready,
>   I am very sensible of your goodness in thus breaking in upon your brief breathing-time for the purpose of being hospitable to one "who could find it in his heart to bestow all his tediousness on your worship," in season and out of season: — I confess myself unable to compete with so signal generosity, and instead of vying with you in self-denial and refusing to come, shall look forward to next Sat^y with indecent impatience. Would I had a previous engagement! that, setting it aside, I might — but there would be no virtue in that, unless it were as attractive as yours: — until I shall be favoured with such an one I must remain,
> Dear Macready,
>   Yours ever truly and obliged
>   Robt Browning[8]

On Monday, August 1, Macready (reading a play by Bulwer Lytton) and his guests, including Forster, William Harrison Ainsworth, and Browning, went back to London by Billings's coach. After the stimulation of the weekend the still incompleted *Sordello* was destined to rest again in Browning's portfolio. He could no longer resist the magnetism of the stage. On August 3 Macready learned from Forster that Browning had decided to write a play on Strafford, a subject that pleased the actor. The decision was a natural one since Browning had worked with Strafford's life while assisting Forster earlier in the year.

The impression given from time to time — by Browning or by others when it may well have emanated from him — that he wrote his works with great speed could have an unfortunate effect. Macready, to his dismay, heard on October 4 that *Strafford* had been completed in ten days. On the 10th he was rejoiced to find that such was not the case. On October 31 Browning told Macready the play was finished; but when he brought it to him on November 19 the fourth act was incomplete. At Macready's request Browning "wrote out the story of the omitted parts." On the next day Macready noted in his *Diaries* that he was "greatly pleased" with Browning's manuscript. Browning called on November 21 "in some anxiety" to have the actor's opinion. He was gratified by Macready's comments, accepted his objections, and promised "to do everything needful to the play's amendment." With the play again in hand on November 23 Macready began *"very attentively"* to read it again. He saw its weakness: ". . . I find more grounds for exception than I had anticipated. I had been too much carried away by the truth of character to observe the meanness of plot, and occasional obscurity."

In his *Handbook* DeVane has traced the events leading up to the performance of *Strafford* in 1837. For the present study certain aspects of the situation and of Browning's behavior are pointed up for their importance in the sequence of Browning's attempts to write plays and the results: Macready's recognition of the weakness of the play, his fears for its success, and his as well as Forster's exertions in its behalf; on one hand Browning's wish to make changes appropriate to stage presentation and on the other a mixture of inability and reluctance to revise. In his first play Browning felt the expediency of following suggestions for changes, but he was frustrated in his efforts. Once he had conceived and written the work, basic revision, which the play obviously needed for stage production, seemed virtually impossible for him.

In his *Diaries* Macready, the experienced actor, recorded his awareness of the shortcomings of *Strafford* as a play for the stage. Browning had admirably portrayed "the policy of the man, and its consequence upon him, not the heart, temper, feelings, that work on this policy"; the play was too historical for the stage (Mar. 19, 1837). The management of the story would not arouse interest (Mar. 21). There was a "want of connection in the scenes" (Apr. 5). The play lacked action and lightness (Apr. 8); it was feeble and heavy (Apr. 11). Macready continued to bemoan its shortcomings, and on the Friday (Apr. 28) before the opening performance on Monday he made a comparison. He considered the strength of Shakespeare's historical drama in having only "such events as act on the individuals concerned." How different was *Strafford!* "But in Browning's play we have a long scene of passion — upon what? A plan destroyed, by whom or for what we know not, and a parliament dissolved, which merely seems to inconvenience *Strafford* [underscored] in his arrangements. There is a sad want of judgment and tact in the whole composition." Macready, like many who passed judgment later, saw that *Strafford* was not stage-worthy.

Though full of doubt, Macready earnestly desired that the play should succeed for his sake and for Browning's. He was unable to give much time to it until the spring of 1837. Over a period of six weeks — from March 19 down into the day of its first performance on the evening of May 1 — his benefit night — Macready did all that he could to prepare it for stage presentation, constantly working against odds. Habitually he took counsel with others on the fitness and revision of plays, and Forster was among those whom he depended on. Forster eagerly assisted in the efforts to revise *Strafford*. One day during the first week of the revision period Macready and Browning read and discussed the play before dinner and continued their discussion after dinner. At this time the *Diaries* indicate no desire on Browning's part to heed suggestions for changes; it is possible that he even defended his work as it was, for Macready, "seeing no other course," resolved to read *Strafford* again. He was by no means "sanguine . . . on its success." On Tuesday of the second week, March 28, he went to Forster's and talked about the play, and after his performance of *Othello* that night he, Forster, and Browning discussed the plot until two o'clock. Browning brought the play with revisions on Wednesday; "he looked very unwell, jaded and thought-sick." His spirits rose on the following day when he learned that the manager of the theater after hearing Macready read *Strafford* "caught at it with avidity" and agreed to pay £12 for each of the first twenty-five nights and beyond that period £10 for each of ten nights. Macready had made memoranda of emendations in the manuscript and Browning promised to work hard.

The gravity of the situation lay in Browning's failure to revise effectively or revise at all, and during the third and fourth weeks of preparation, from April 3 to 14, it was up to Macready and Forster to try to get the play into shape for acting. Browning took notes, he brought alterations — and at times very quickly. But they were "feebly written" or "mere feeble rant — neither power, nor nature, nor healthful fancy." On one occasion he had complete writing paralysis. Early in the day on April 14 he brought "some scraps of paper with hints and unconnected lines — the full amount of his labour upon the alterations agreed on." He and Macready went "all over the play *again* (!) very carefully," and he resolved to bring the amendments by eleven that evening. Browning returned in the evening — but without the amended play. "He had done nothing to it; had been oppressed and in-

John Forster

capable of carrying his intentions into action." During this period it devolved upon his friends to do his work. They "entirely surrendered" one day to *Strafford;* Macready sent for Forster and explained the "dangerous state of the play," and they "altered, omitted, and made up one new scene." At another time Macready cut the manuscript and gave it to Forster, who approved of the omissions.

So there were goings to and comings from various points: Browning's home in Camberwell, Covent Garden, Macready's chambers, and Forster's place at 58 Lincoln's Inn Fields. Nerves jangled. In the delicate situation twice there were altercations between Forster and Browning. Macready wrote of mutual complaints and of blame that rested on one and then the other. Browning knew that it was not expedient to quarrel with Macready about alterations, which he complained about to others, but he did let himself go to Forster. His futile attempts at revision and his having to stand by while Forster helped with the alterations were enough to grate on Browning's artistic ego. And Forster, as many Victorians testified, could be overassertive.

Fatigue, frustrations, and fears were not ingredients for harmony. But the days passed without the violent explosion that would precede the performance of *A Blot*. Even if Forster's temper now and then got out of control, he behaved, as Macready observed, in "the most earnest spirit of devotion." Where the play was concerned, he was at Macready's beck and call; and he persuaded Longmans to publish it. Macready kept his head. Although he hoped that something would happen to necessitate cancellation of the performance — that the objection of the actors would perhaps be effective — he behaved with circumspection. When Browning himself, after his experience of writer's paralysis, wished to recall *Strafford,* Macready cautioned him against any "precipitate steps and insisted on a conference with Forster. In spite of his strong desire to withdraw the play, Macready wanted no responsibility in such a move, and, as a man of uneven disposition he could well write, "I thank God I felt quite satisfied with my conduct throughout this delicate affair of Browning."

The weeks went by, and the situation did not improve. As the time for the production drew near, Macready's fears increased. He wrote on April 23: "The more I consider the play the lower my hopes smile upon it; I expect it will be damned — grievously hissed at the end — from the unintelligibility of the motives, the want of action, and consequently of interest." On the other hand, with the revision period behind him Browning became more confident. On the 22nd he

William Charles Macready

was "very pale, and apparently suffering from over-excitement." After the 23rd there is no indication in the *Diaries* of further efforts on Browning's part to revise, and by the 27th he was confident that his play would succeed. The still troubled Macready wrote: "Browning amused me much by his confidence in the success of the play; he looked at the acting and movement of a subject in which he had a deep interest — ensure that same *interest* in the audience, and I will ensure its success — but the question is: will the audience be kindled to such an interest?"

The question was soon to be answered. Macready playing in a new drama on his benefit night was a big attraction, and the critics were prepared to welcome the author, whose preceding work showed promise of a dramatic talent; but Macready was aware of the risk. He wrote on the 28th: "There is no chance in my opinion for the play but in the acting, which by possibility might carry it to the end without disapprobation; but that the curtain can fall without considerable opposition, I cannot venture to anticipate under the most advantageous circumstances."

On the evening of May 1 the curtain at Covent Garden Theatre raised to a full house. Browning was there with his father. The audience's anticipation and Macready's superior acting carried the play through this first night. At the end Browning's friends loudly called for the author, among them Frederick Young, who later recalled being one of the claquers.[9] And William Bell Scott, an artist and an admirer of *Paracelsus,* was there to applaud.[10] After the play Browning took his father to Macready's dressing room to shake hands with the great actor. Others were in Macready's room, including Talfourd, Forster, Edward Bulwer Lytton, and his brother Henry Bulwer. It was a night of exhilaration for the twenty-five-year-old poet.

But if Macready's feeling of the possible good effect of his acting on the first night was justified so was his fear of the unfavorable opinion of the play. It was withdrawn after four performances — May 1, 3, 5, 9 — and then given again on May 30. The short run, the reviews with their reservations and adverse criticism, the comments of others — all these show clearly the outcome of Browning's first attempt to write a play for the stage.

Strafford, dedicated "in all affectionate admiration" to Macready "by his most grateful and devoted friend," was published on May 1, the day of the first performance. It was the only work before Browning's marriage not to be published at the expense of the family. The

Playbill, Strafford, May 1, 1837

first part of the Preface indicated that, no matter what Macready considered the demands of the stage, Browning was still influenced by the technique of *Paracelsus*.

> I had for some time been engaged in a Poem of a very different nature [*Sordello*], when induced to make the present attempt; and am not without apprehension that my eagerness to freshen a jaded mind by diverting it to the healthy natures of a grand epoch, may have operated unfavourably on the represented play, which is one of Action in Character rather than Character in Action. To remedy this, in some degree, considerable curtailment will be necessary, and, in a few instances, the supplying details not required, I suppose, by the mere reader.

According to the Preface, when Browning was persuaded to undertake *Strafford* he was occupied with *Sordello*, a poem of "a very different nature" — that is, a poem (like *Paracelsus*) stressing internal states. The consequence of this was that he put much into *Strafford* that was not appropriate to a stage play and omitted details that were necessary. In part, these faults could be remedied on the stage (changes could be made even after performances began) by shortening some passages and supplying details required by playgoers but not by readers. Browning's classification of *Strafford* as a play of "Action in Character rather than Character in Action" seems to be a neat but cryptic formulation reflecting his conviction that internal states or struggles are of paramount importance. Whatever his meaning, this statement was puzzling to his critics, especially since *Strafford* offered considerable movement on the stage.

The Preface reflects Browning's interest in character and Macready's insistence on the action required for stage production. Character must have been emphasized in the original version of the play since Macready was at first impressed by the "truth of character" and on second reading by the "meanness of plot." Browning was frustrated during the period of preparation because in part he thought the revisions were detrimental to his intention to emphasize character. He was relieved when he saw the last rehearsal on May 1, according to the entry that Macready made in his diary on that day: his portrayal of Strafford was "full recompense," so Browning told Macready, "for having written the play, inasmuch as he [Browning] had seen his utmost hopes of character perfectly embodied." As we shall see, Browning's later behavior concerning *Strafford* also indicated his primary concern with character.

On the day of its publication and first performance Browning sent a copy of *Strafford* to W. J. Fox, who had generously helped to place the poet's first two works before the public. It was accompanied by the following note:

> Dear Sir, — All my endeavours to procure a copy before this morning have been fruitless. I send the first book of the first bundle. *Pray* look over it — the alterations tonight will be considerable. The complexion of the piece is, I grieve to say, "perfect gallows" just now — our *king*, Mr. Dale, being . . . but you'll see him, and, I fear, not much applaud.
> Your unworthy son, in things literary,
Robert Browning.
> P.S. A most unnecessary desire, but urged on me by Messrs. Longman: no notice on Str. in to-night's True Sun, lest the other papers be jealous!!! [11]

Fox again obliged Browning, and what he and other reviewers said leaves no doubt of the unfavorable reception of *Strafford*. He reviewed the play in the *True Sun* on May 2, starting with a report of the crammed theater and the fine acting of Macready. The play he had not read; he realized that its "extraordinary characteristics deserve something more than the hasty notice of almost extempore criticism." Its author was already known by the dramatic poem *Paracelsus*. The charm of that poem was in "its bold metaphysics and its luxuriant poetry." *Strafford* was different, with its "power of a most business-like reality of character and action, and a diction of severe truthfulness to the persons and circumstances." There was no digression from history, "no impertinence of got-up sentiment or description." All was historical, including Strafford's conflicts.

Fox said what he could in support of *Strafford*, but he could not ignore its weakness as a stage play. He could not "but feel the want of a stronger leading sympathy." The interest in the character and conduct of Strafford made it "rather the development of a philosophical question than an action upon the emotions of the audience." The result was "too cold and curious an interest for the theatre." The play implied more knowledge of history than a theatrical audience would likely have. In fact a "studious perusal" was needed to appreciate Browning's progress as a poet.

Other reviews of the first performance appeared in the dailies — in the *Constitutional*, the *Morning Post*, the *Morning Chronicle*, and the *Times* on the 2nd; and the *Morning Herald* had a review of the second performance on the 4th. The praise accorded *Strafford* in these reviews, like that in the *True Sun,* had a dubious quality about it. The critic for the *Constitutional* hedged. He said a little about Browning's close adherence to history in portraying the characters and wrote mostly of the performance, since he had seen, not read, the play. In compliment to Macready and to the "noble tragedy" the house was thronged. Not having examined the work himself, the critic could only "testify" to its "signal and deserved success" on the stage and therefore could not speak "so confidently" as others.

The short discussion in the *Times* ended with the following: "This is Mr. Browning's first dramatic effort, and it is one of no little promise." The critic thought the drama so historical that one who did not know the minutiae of the period would find it almost unintelligible, and he almost feared it would not become as popular as its intrinsic merits deserved. Browning had the secret of "concise and pointed" language; no character said more than he had to. But in some instances this "closeness" was carried too far; it was up to Macready to make the obscurities clear. The Earl of Strafford was admirably drawn, but Pym was not more than an "outline portrait" and the character of the Countess of Carlisle wanted fullness.

A report of the second performance was given by the reviewer for the *Morning Herald,* who began with an allusion to the promise of *Paracelsus.* He wrote favorably of the display of passion, the language, and the pure "general style" and said he did not hesitate to pronounce *Strafford* the best tragedy that had been produced for many a year in any of the theaters. After giving nothing but high praise for act after act and concluding that all was "put together with great judgment," he expressed the regret that Browning had not reserved the subject for his maturer years.

The reviews thus far discussed leave the impression that the critics wished to review the play favorably. They recognized in the author of *Paracelsus* a candidate for high poetic honors, and they wrote enthusiastically of Macready's fine performance and of the full house and good reception on Macready's benefit night. But they failed to produce a convincing endorsement of *Strafford.* To say on one hand that because of its extraordinary characteristics it deserved to be read in order to be reviewed more advantageously and on the other that it had no theatrical appeal; to have no confident opinion because of not having studied the play; to talk of the play's promise and then specify characteristics that did not foretell better plays to come from the same author; to feel that *Strafford* was the best tragedy produced in many years, yet regret that Browning had not reserved the subject until his art was mature — all of this indicated that the reviewers had not assured themselves that Browning had fulfilled in *Strafford* the promise given in *Paracelsus*.

The two remaining reviews were different from each other and from the four reviews just discussed. There was no praise, dubious or otherwise, of *Strafford* in the *Morning Post*. The success of the perform-ance was attributed to Macready's acting, not to the play. The critic for the *Morning Chronicle* said he had not had such a high regard for *Para-celsus* as others and therefore came with no preconceived idea of what Browning's play would be like. He had read the play and had been un-favorably impressed; but the performance convinced him he had done the author an injustice. Browning had written a play that did him great credit, though in the part of Strafford the credit belonged to Macready, not Browning. It is impossible for us to tell whether the critic would have changed his mind for the better if Macready had not injected his histrionic talent into a performance which inspired the en-thusiasm of both Macready's and Browning's friends.

A concentration of reviews appeared in the weeklies on the 6th and 7th, the weekend after the first three performances. As usual the reviewers commented on the quality of the acting. Macready received the greatest praise, and Helen Faucit received high praise also; Van-denhoff drew favorable and unfavorable comments in about the same degree; and the others, if they were mentioned at all, came in for mostly unfavorable criticism. The slight passage of time had permitted a clearer view of the play itself. A falling off in audience following Macready's benefit had a sobering effect and critics could evaluate the play from reading it as well as from seeing it on the stage. Its weak-nesses were more consistently pointed out, but there were still efforts to sustain it. Some critics, like earlier ones, indicated that *Strafford* had not disappointed expectations, but their specific criticisms were to the contrary. Others thought of *Strafford* not in terms of fulfilled expecta-tions, but of promise for the future success of its author.

Two weeklies — the *Parthenon* and *Bell's Life in London* — wrote primarily of the reception and the performance, giving most praise to Macready's acting. The *Court Journal, Weekly Dispatch,* and *John Bull* were impressed by the play's promise but not by its intrinsic merits. They criticized the style, considered the handling of history not con-ducive to audience appeal, and two of them objected to the characteri-zation. When they made a favorable comment, they usually contra-dicted it before ending the discussion.

The severest reviews appeared in the major weeklies. Only the critics of the *Literary Gazette* and the *Examiner* tempered their disapproval. The *Atlas* was representative of the out-and-out unfavorable review; the *Literary Gazette* exemplified the review that spoke in contradictions; and the *Examiner* illustrated the way in which some gave support to the play even as they saw its faults. Both the *Atlas* and the *Literary Gazette* spoke of the prior expectations for the author of *Paracelsus*. The critic for the *Atlas* could not discover any traces of the same hand. He found the whole performance so obscure, the action so spasmodic, the dialogue so full of sudden exclamations, jerks of words, and broken sentences, and explanations and motives so vague that even the most experienced playgoer would be at a loss unless he knew the history of the period. The effect of this style was ludicrous. Strafford was historically incorrect; the best exertions of Macready did not "infuse a spirit or meaning into the curious character he was called upon to impersonate." Although a few — "a very few" — perfect sentences were a help to the audience, they could not sustain the interest and they made the surrounding obscurity more obvious. There was further condemnation of the style with emphasis on obscurity.

According to the *Literary Gazette, Strafford* had fulfilled expectations raised by the author of *Paracelsus,* but after briefly calling attention to much vigor and genuine poetry in the play, the reviewer cited no further evidence of fulfilled hopes. The "abrupt and interrupted" dialogue with its "broken and declamatory" sentences often affected the sense of the drama, even more on the stage than in the closet. As a stage play, the critic felt that interest failed after the third act. Emphasis on characterization was centered almost entirely on Strafford to the sacrifice of others in the play. "Where Strafford is not, there is nothing to care for; and where he is, is turmoil. . . ."

Forster, in the *Examiner,* explained away the faults of *Strafford* that others had found. He had announced in the review of *Paracelsus* for the *New Monthly Magazine* that the dramatic genius of Browning waited only for the proper opportunity to redeem the drama of England. Knowing that Browning's efforts, even with Macready's guidance, had not made the play a success on the stage, he could not say that the time of redemption had come, but he still had great expectations of Browning's future as a dramatist. The "highest objects and triumphs of dramatic literature" that the author of *Strafford* was capable of were not achieved in this play, but they were there "in the rough." *Strafford* seemed to promise the "most brilliant career of dramatic authorship" of the time; Forster was not sure that the career would be realized, but he had reasons for strong hope.

After these general remarks came the specific criticisms. Forster considered the characters of the independent party to be drawn in a masterly way, but could not say as much for Strafford and the King. The blemishes of the play were due to Browning's faulty conception of these characters. Where other critics condemned elliptical expressions and sudden transitions, Forster explained them as an outgrowth of the characterization of Strafford, who was presented "rather as the victim of an extreme and somewhat effeminate sensibility, than as a fearless and heroic champion of arbitrary power." He called attention to specific scenes in which the inequality of language was due to Browning's conception of Strafford's character. Yet even in some of these scenes the style of writing was dramatic. In the first scene, though "probably pitched too high," he felt "distinct and tangible collision" and "local truth and freshness" to such an extent as he had never encountered in any scene in any other drama.

The *Athenaeum* and the *Spectator* followed in the steps of other major weeklies. None exhibited such inclusive and unrelieved severity in condemning the play as the *Spectator*. As for the *Athenaeum's* review, the objections were there also and with them was suggested the best method of understanding the speeches: "to take care not to follow the speaker too closely, but to hear the opening of a sentence, and supply the remainder by imagination."

On May 13 the *Casket of Literature, Science, and Entertainment* began a long summary of *Strafford* with an extensive quotation and occasional references to historians who had dealt with Strafford. It was continued on May 20 and concluded on May 27. In the May 13 issue there was a separate discussion of the play under another head. In it were expressed approval and hope that the author would continue his efforts, for he had the "right passport into the company of the illustrious shadows of the past, intense sympathy with their struggles — an ennobling apprehension of their greatness." Most of the review consisted of an introduction to the principal characters; an account of the sources, which Browning had mentioned in his Preface; and a long quotation from the first scene of Act IV, a sample of the "beautiful style" to support the high praise which the critic felt "impelled to award" the play.

These were good words but they did not save the play. On May 14, after four performances, the *Examiner* announced its fate.

Strafford was winning its way into even greater success than we had
ventured to hope for it, but Mr Vandenhoff's secession from the theatre has caused its temporary withdrawal. It will be only temporary,
we trust; no less in justice to the great genius of the author, than to
the fervid applause with which its last performance was received by
an admirably filled house.

It is not easy to reconcile the "greater success," "fervid applause," and
"admirably filled house" with the discontinuance of the play, for, as
Lounsbury pointed out, the departure of a single minor actor, who
could be replaced, would hardly be reason enough for withdrawing a
play that was still in demand.[12] Forster, Browning's strong supporter
who had reviewed *Strafford* for the *Examiner,* in all likelihood wrote
this notice hoping that the performances, with Macready still in the
leading role, would be resumed.

Although there was an announcement on a playbill of May 15
that *Strafford,* which had been "attended . . . with most complete success," would be repeated early in the following week, two weeks went
by without another performance. On May 27 the *Court Journal* informed its readers that *Strafford* would be given on the 30th with Elton
as Pym in the place of Vandenhoff. It was performed on the benefit
night of Edward Fitzball, who thought the play had been "uncom-
monly well received" on Macready's benefit night, and for the first
time Browning's name was on the playbill.[13]

In June, after the last performance, two monthlies noticed *Strafford.* The *Metropolitan Magazine,* in an account of Macready's benefit
night, expressed an attitude which in several ways was unusual. The
critic predicted that *Strafford* would occupy a prominent place on the
stage, but would not be a favorite closet drama. In spite of its lack of
imagination, rough and halting blank verse, commonplace sentiments, and obscurely developed plot to those unread in history, *Strafford* was eminently successful "chiefly owing to the admirable conception, and . . . faithful delineation of the characters, and the stirring
action of the incidents." Most of the review was given to a favorable
discussion of Browning's treatment of the historical characters and the
performance of the actors.

The short discussion in the *New Monthly Magazine* (June) of the
performances of *Strafford* must surely have been written by Forster. He
had announced his discovery of Browning's dramatic genius in the earlier review of *Paracelsus* in the same monthly (Mar. 1836), to which he
alluded here. *Strafford,* he now said, bore out the impression made by

Paracelsus that the author might become a liberal and illustrious contributor to the treasures of dramatic poetry. Forster was pleased that within the preceding month the production of *Strafford* was one of the two events that had occurred "to throw a grace" upon the last of the theater season. Macready's "admirable delineation" of Strafford "perfectly filled up, with as much delicacy as force, the bold, varied, and original design of the author." Contrary to the notice of May 14, this one suggested public apathy. To achieve triumph as an acting drama, *Strafford* "must be played only to audiences of more than average intelligence."

Two reviews from Edinburgh bring to an end the discussion of Browning's first play by early professional critics. Both departed from the straightforward approach that had been previously used in discussions of *Strafford* and the performances of it; each gave an unsatisfactory representation of the play. In July the *Edinburgh Review,* in a nineteen-page article, characteristically approached the work through a discussion of a more general subject, the degraded condition of drama. The reviewer said Browning's defects were "fostered by a corrupt taste in theatrical matters." That Browning was capable of writing well was demonstrated when he ignored current fashions and chose to write sustained dialogue and declamation. The "considerable share of success" on the London stage — the "favourable run" — was proof that his work afforded "striking situations and dramatic interest."

The *Dramatic Spectator* of Edinburgh included a review on September 30th in the tenth and last issue of the weekly's life. The critic objected to the language and obscurity of *Strafford,* as others had objected to them, but his impertinent levity and sarcasm left the impression of an attempt to display cleverness rather than a desire to evaluate the play.

The comments made by twentieth-century scholars on the reception of *Strafford* have not been in agreement and they have not been convincing. Boyd Litzinger and Donald Smalley in their introduction to *Browning: The Critical Heritage* made the following comment. It came after a statement concerning Macready's fears for the play. "Browning's hopes were not much higher, for he could sense that Macready's heart was not in the play. It came, therefore, as something of a surprise when the reviews proved to be generally favourable and of such a nature that Browning could blame the failure of the play upon Macready rather than upon himself."[14] These writers did not discuss at length the reception of *Strafford,* for they were writing a commentary on all of Browning's publications in the compass of an introductory chapter. In the body of the book their readers have the excerpts from nine reviews of *Strafford*. Close examination of the excerpts raises questions about the editors' generalization on the reception of the play.

DeVane, in his *Handbook,* was also limited in the extent of his discussion. He referred to Lounsbury for the best account of the reception given *Strafford* and made the statement that the "dramatic critics varied widely in their comments." Actually what stands out more than the variety is the agreement in the criticism. Lounsbury was correct in saying that contemporary accounts were almost unanimous in considering the play a failure.[15] For support of his conclusion that *Strafford* "would not take permanent hold upon the stage," Lounsbury cited two pieces of evidence: the article in the *Edinburgh Review* and Forster's concession that it would not. (In his not entirely favorable review in the *Examiner,* Forster did make this concession, but he put the play's chances for success in a slightly different light when he stated later in the *New Monthly Magazine* that to be successful it would require an audience of above average intelligence.)

The discussion of the reviews has indicated, and a few concluding remarks will emphasize, what the critics actually thought of *Strafford.* An examination of each review as a whole has shown that with few exceptions whatever praise was given was counteracted by contradictions or weakened by qualifications. After the first few reviews there was general agreement that objectionable verse and obscurity were detrimental to the success of the play. Some critics might make excuses for these faults or say that in spite of them the play showed promise. Yet they acknowledged the presence of faults, and this was damaging to the play's reputation.

The pronouncements on the historical accuracy of the play were in disagreement, but there was considerable agreement that Browning's handling of historical facts and characters did not constitute a good dramatic presentation. The complaint was made repeatedly that the play did not hold the interest of the audience, a complaint overlapping that of obscurity. Understanding the play required more knowledge of history than most of the audience possessed, Browning adhered to history with too much strictness, the details were dry, the personal politics were too minute — such reasons were given for *Strafford's* failure to maintain the audience's attention, a prime requisite for a successful stage play.

Nor, according to the critics, did Browning understand the dramatic management of historical personages for the stage. In his Preface he said that the play was "one of Action in Character rather than Character in Action." Perhaps the play was what Browning asserted it to be, said the *Court Journal;* we are puzzled, said the *Literary Gazette;* in his next play let him have character in action, wrote *John Bull.* Others — the *Casket* and the *New Monthly Magazine* — commented on Browning's statement as a faulty principle on which to write a stage play. To some it might explain the weakness of *Strafford,* which with very few exceptions was looked upon as a play to be performed. Without a doubt Browning intended *Strafford* as a play for the stage. As such it was criticized and as such, according to the consensus of opinion, it failed in character portrayal. Strafford, being the title character, received the largest share of disapproval, King Charles next, and Pym third. Some critics objected to the emphasis on Strafford's attachment to the king, which gave him an effeminate quality rather than the magnitude needed for a leading dramatic role.

It would be easy to say that the frequent references to the audience's support were evidences of favorable reception. Except for the remarks in the *Examiner* of May 14 and the *Edinburgh Review,* comments on the successful reception of the play, even when made after later performances, had reference to Macready's benefit night. The attraction of the first performance for the majority of the audience was seeing Macready in a new play on his benefit night; for Browning's supporters it was welcoming a play of his with Macready in the leading role. And Macready's acting made the weaknesses of the play less obvious at first. There were, however, some dissenting voices among the critics, even concerning the reception of the first performance. The *Morning Post* reported that "something unseemly" in the closing scene "produced a laugh from a few of the audience." The *Spectator* noticed a "few hisses at the conclusion." More unfavorable audience reaction on Macready's benefit night was reported by William Bell Scott. As an admirer of *Paracelsus,* he had determined to go and applaud.

> From the first scene it became plain that applause was not the order. The speakers had every one of them orations to deliver, and no action of any kind to perform. The scene changed, another door opened, and another half-dozen gentlemen entered as long-winded as the last. Still I kept applauding, with some few others, till the howling was too overpowering, and the disturbance so considerable that for a few minutes I lost my hat. The truth was that the talk was too much

the same, and too much in quantity; it was no use continuing to
hope something would turn up to surprise the house.[16]

According to the repeated accounts of the success of the first night, it
seems unlikely that there was overpowering howling and considerable
disturbance. The "few hisses" and a "laugh from a few" are probably a
more accurate representation of the audience's behavior. Macready had
feared hisses, and he was right when he told Browning after the first
performance that the play had had a grand escape.

The real test came after the first performance. The success of the
benefit was tenuous since it owed much to Macready's eminence and
his acting, and apparently the success was not repeated. The critic for
the *Morning Herald* reviewed the second performance, when, he said,
the play was not received with as much applause as it deserved. The
Weekly Dispatch might have been writing of more than one performance
when it said the play had been "coldly received." We have just seen
that there were two reports of good reception by the audience after the
first night. The comment made by Forster in the *Examiner* of May 14
that *Strafford* was winning its way into even greater success than was
hoped for was, as has been pointed out, probably aimed not so much at
accuracy as at keeping interest in the play alive. When he wrote of the
play in the *New Monthly Magazine* after the fifth and last performance,
Forster no longer referred to its success. The *Athenaeum's* prediction
of a "temporary existence" had come true. In the long run the good
acting of Macready and Helen Faucit could not keep the play alive
any more than the poor acting of the other characters could cause its
collapse.

Strafford was not the play to establish Browning as a dramatist.
Not even Forster could claim as much in his review in the *Examiner;*
and his support of Browning throughout the troubles of preparing for
the performance and his earlier introduction of Browning as a great
dramatic genius gave him every reason to pronounce the play successful
if it were possible to do so.

Although the reviews show without doubt that the play was a
failure and that it did not have a favorable reception (despite the applause on the first night), they did, to be sure, carry Browning's name
over a large area and to an assortment of readers — the conservative
High Church reader of *John Bull,* the sportsman of *Bell's Life,* the family fireside reader of the *Spectator,* the literatus of the *Athenaeum,* and
the liberal of the *Weekly Dispatch.* Although some of the periodicals
that reviewed *Strafford* did not exert much influence, there were

enough that were influential to advance Browning's name had *Strafford* been a good play. In spite of its shortcomings, however, the ground-work of hope prepared by *Paracelsus* was still firm enough for the building of Browning's reputation. The criticism, as clear as it was about the failure of the play, contained repeated expressions of faith in what Browning would write in the future. The critics were looking forward to his next work.

Outside the press *Strafford* was dismissed with a few remarks that did not disagree with the general verdict of the reviewers. On May 25, 1837, Richard Monckton Milnes wrote to Aubrey de Vere: "*Strafford* is like a drawing of Michael Angelo. It is odd to have to complain nowadays of a style being too broad, but this is the case here. He [Browning] says himself very truly of the play that it is rather action in character than character in action; and thus there is a stiffness as of cramp about the very vigour of the piece." [17] Thomas Lovell Beddoes, who read excerpts that Forster chose and praised in the *Examiner,* thought them "not exactly dramatic." [18] In a general comment on recent British achievement in drama, Edward Bulwer Lytton avoided specific comment on the stageworthiness of *Strafford* when he mentioned it along with other plays which, "varying in their degree of success on the stage, have all at least been of an order calculated to refine and heighten the public taste in theatrical exhibitions." [19]

The passage of time did not bring forth a good word for Strafford. R. H. Horne wrote a sympathetic review of Browning's poetry for the *Church of England Quarterly* of October 1842, in which he had something favorable to say for all of the poet's acknowledged works except *Strafford,* which he considered "a maimed thing, all over patches and dashes." Even those more personally concerned with Browning's welfare saw the play as a failure. In 1861 Elizabeth Barrett Browning referred to it as Browning's "poorest work of all." [20] In 1891, Helen Faucit, then Lady Martin, was asked about the productions of Browning's plays upon the stage. She wrote this of *Strafford,* in which she had played the part of Lady Carlisle:

> . . . although many doubtful forecasts were made in the green-room as to the ultimate attraction of a play so entirely turning on politics, yet all were determined to do their very best to insure its success. . . .
> I can remember . . . that I went home very sad; for, although the play was considered a success, yet, somehow, even my small experience seemed to tell me, it would not have a very long life. . . . [21]

In his letter of commitment to Macready following the *Ion* dinner Browning wrote that should he be unequal to the task of writing a play the excitement and effort would be their own reward. And he said in his Preface to *Strafford:* "While a trifling success would much gratify, failure will not wholly discourage me from another effort: experience is to come, and earnest endeavour may yet remove many disadvantages." Although the statement in the Preface expressed his long-term attitude, what he said of discouragement did not hold true immediately after the performance of the play. He was dissatisfied and he vowed that he would write no more plays.

For a high-strung artistic nature, the accelerated tempo of experience was unsettling. Even the bright side of the experience contributed to the disturbance. To have his first play performed by Macready at Covent Garden under any circumstances would have been a heady experience. The wonder of the situation was that Browning, the author of only one acknowledged poem, was invited by Macready to write a play and that Macready accepted Browning's effort without making him wait for a decision. Eliza Flower was thinking of Browning's achievement in having Macready produce his play, not its actual reception, when she gave news of *Strafford* to someone who knew the poet, ". . . it is a great deal to have accomplished a successful tragedy. . . ."[22] And Horne, a playwright himself, in his 1842 review of Browning wrote of the play, "which, 'marvelous to relate,' he got acted immediately — an event quite unprecedented on the modern stage, except with those two or three dramatic authors who have previously passed through the customary delays preceding representation."

The anticipation of having his play performed was accompanied by the excitement and trials of preparing it for presentation. Besides the alterations there were problems of staging that seemed intolerable. The costumes were not suitable and they were the subject of press ridicule. All was not well otherwise — "perfect gallows," said Browning, who reported the necessity of writing out the meaning of the word *impeachment* for some of the actors who thought it meant *poaching*.[23] He, Macready, and the reviewers complained of the performances of some of the minor actors, especially of Dale, the actor with defective hearing, who played the part of King Charles. Browning was "incensed at Mr. Dale's unhappy attempts" on Saturday and then "quite in raptures" over Macready's performance at the last rehearsal on Monday, May 1. These extremes belonged to the fever pitch of excitement Browning was experiencing. On May 2, the day after the first performance of *Strafford,* he heard from Macready that the play was "a grand escape" and that he ought to regard it only as such, a statement hardly conducive to a satisfactory state of mind. That night he wrote a note of appreciation to Fox for the review in the *True Sun;* in it he said he was "much annoyed and unwell." [24]

The annoyance was not over for Browning or for Macready even after *Strafford* began its run. With other problems that he faced and with the trouble and fears which the play had already caused him, Macready would have been relieved to dismiss it from his mind as soon as possible. But Browning kept the atmosphere troubled; and Macready's emotions, admirably controlled before the play was first performed, were now released. On May 9, the day of the fourth performance, he was irritated by Browning's attitude toward Forster's review in the *Examiner:*

> Called on Forster, who informed me how much he had been hurt by Browning's expressions of discontent at his criticism, which I myself think only too indulgent for such a play as *Strafford.* After all that has been done for Browning with the painful apprehension of failure before us, it is not pleasing to read in his note, "Let [me not] write any future tragedies"! Now, really, this is too bad — without *great assistance* his tragedy could never have been put in a condition to be proposed for representation — without great assistance it never could have been put upon the stage — nor without great assistance could it ever have been carried through its "perilous" experiment. It is very unreasonable and indeed *ungrateful* in him to write thus.

There was other provocation. More than once Browning troubled Macready about the fate of his play, as the entry in the *Diaries* on the 18th showed: "Browning . . . again evinced an irritable impatience about the reproduction of *Strafford.* . . ." Then, to make matters still worse, in the following week Macready was asked to give more time and energy to the revision of a play that had failed; he was not accustomed to such behavior on the part of playwrights, even experienced ones. His reaction, recorded on May 22, is not surprising:

> Called on Forster, who gave me a letter from Browning, at which I was surprised and annoyed; as if I had done nothing for him — having worn down my spirits and strength as I have done — he now asks me to study a speech at the end of the second act, and an entire scene which I am to restore in the fourth act. Such a selfish, absurd, and useless imposition to lay on me could scarcely have en-

tered into any one's imagination. I was at first disgusted by the sickly and fretful over-estimate of his work and was angry; but reflected that he did not know what he required me to do, and had forgotten what I have done; "so let him pass, a blessing on his head!" I shall not do it.

Browning's behavior was all that Macready said it was — and more. It was not true, as Browning thought it would be, that in the event of the play's failure he would consider the effort and excitement their own reward. Ego, resistance to defeat, desire to attract an audience, the process of evolving his principle of "Action in Character" — these were strong and troublesome forces. A close look at Macready's *Diaries* shows that Browning's own notion of the character of Strafford governed to some extent his behavior toward Macready and Forster.

According to Macready's understanding, Browning had asserted that "no change had been made in the conduct of the play since its first draught." This was recorded on April 7. Macready and Forster, who had already spent considerable time on the revision, would naturally disagree with him. Browning's statement suggests that the word "conduct" meant something particular to him that it did not mean to them. If we assume that Browning equated conduct and his intended characterization, such an interpretation would agree with his expression of delight at seeing in the last rehearsal "his utmost hopes of character perfectly embodied" in Macready's acting. His strong feeling for his characterization also furnishes a gloss on his "expressions of discontent" at the criticism made by Forster, in whose review the faults of the play were attributed to Browning's conception of Strafford and the King. Relieved of the agony of revising and carried away by the last rehearsal, Browning had praised Macready's portrayal of Strafford. His later expressions of discontent to Forster and Macready came in the interval between the performances at the beginning of May and the last performance on the 30th. With the revision period behind him, Browning was again thinking of the play as he had originally conceived and written it. His request of May 22 that Macready study a speech at the end of the second act and restore an entire scene in the fourth act before the last performance was to Macready an indication of Browning's "sickly and fretful over-estimate of his work." Browning saw the request as a reasonable one.

We learn more of the whole situation from Anneliese Meidl's helpful and revealing study of the manuscript version of *Strafford* that was submitted by the manager of Covent Garden to the Lord Chamberlain for licensing — that is, the acting copy — as set over against Browning's published version of 1837.[25] This study has shown how Macready's struggles for revision of the play, as we have seen them reflected in his *Diaries,* led to a version that aimed at stage representation and clarity. "Browning's drama deals with a subject that cannot be easily dramatized. Hence the experienced actor attempted to draw the audience's attention to the essential conflicts. He eliminated epic elements, most of the elaborate historical framework, reflections and description, as well as poetic ornaments."

Macready's revisions of the passages in Act II and in Act IV and Browning's reaction to them are of particular interest. Macready cancelled passages and, according to the acting copy, presented a more stageworthy hero. Then why did Browning want them restored? We can go to the first edition for the answer. They emphasized the psychological aspect of Strafford's support of a king who was unworthy of his support. This internal action was more important to Browning than action of a strong and decisive leader, which Macready realized was more effective on the stage. As indicated in the Preface, Browning preferred Action in Character, though he surely recognized the necessity of Character in Action in the play intended for the stage.

Browning was not capable of handling historical action on the stage. Nor had he yet learned to profit by criticism of his faulty attempt and still present his own idea of character. The drastic changes in his own work — revisions, cuts, replacements — left him unsettled. Since he could not think of the acting copy as his own, he published his version on the day of the first performance. If it was imperfect as a stage play, it at least placed emphasis where Browning wanted it, on the inward aspect of character. The information from Macready and from Meidl's article shows that Browning was often unable or reluctant to make changes and that he and Macready were far apart in their notions of characterization.

There was other work to do and the time came for Browning to put *Strafford* out of mind as far as possible, to leave behind the frustrations of the revising period and of the performances and reviews. The reviews he could destroy and probably he tried to, for one that he possessed still exists and has written on it in his sister's hand, "Saved from the scizzors, Aug. 2, 1839."[26] He did not include the play in his 1849 collection, though it appeared in all successive collections. The mention or discussion of it in later reviews and the stage history confirm the early failure. Since the five performances in 1837 it has been acted only a few times and never with real success. Browning showed his feelings about one of the later performances in a letter to Furnivall, dated December 13, 1886.

Alma Murray was asked to play in a production of *Strafford* that the Browning Society was to sponsor on December 21, 1886. She had already played in *In a Balcony* (1884) and in *Colombe's Birthday* (1885), and had pleased Browning with her performance in Shelley's *Cenci*. She consented, but complications arose and she withdrew.[27] In his letter to Furnivall, cofounder of the Browning Society and otherwise a Browning promoter, Browning asked, "Do not you think this is a very proper occasion for postponing the representation?" He then referred to a notice in the *Daily News* (Dec. 13, 1886) of the projected performance, in which excerpts were given from the reviews of the 1837 run. These recalled the failure of the play, which Browning faced in his letter:

> The only conclusion to draw is that a play which did not obtain the enthusiastic praise of the critics *then,* cannot deserve a better fate *now,* under quite other conditions. I would strongly advise that you run no such risk, but let a thing which has so long lain dormant, sleep a little longer. Of course I do not know what the engagements are, and whether it is not too late to recede, but surely with the loss of Alma Murray goes the last chance of a gratifying result.[28]

It was Furnivall's wishes and not Browning's that were to rule; the performance was given. William Rossetti attended, and on the next day, December 22, he wrote Furnivall a four-page enthusiastic letter on *Strafford*. "If the theatre-goers of our present day had a heart for the great drama of the world, & not merely for the passions mirrored in a pretty face, I feel a clear conviction that Strafford w^d be a fine established stagepiece. . . ."[29] But it never attained this status. The explanation for Rossetti's satisfaction in the tragedy as opposed to the unfavorable reception it had on its first run and the lukewarm reviews that appeared in 1886[30] probably lies in his familiarity with it. A humorous proposal was made by a reviewer of the Oxford University Dramatic Society's production of *Strafford* in 1890: "The only way to gain a genuine success for this finely written tragedy would be to hold an examination in Browning, which every member of the audience must pass; for nothing but the closest acquaintance with the text and the methods of thought of all the characters could make their words and deeds quite comprehensible."[31] In his letter William Rossetti said that he had been familiar with the play "from early youth." He had shared his brother Dante Gabriel's knowledge of and efforts to promote Browning's poetry.

In later years Browning did not go to great ends to defend *Strafford*, as he did to explain why *A Blot* failed; but whenever the subject of the tragedy came up, his comments followed the pattern of defense which had taken shape in his mind through the years. Late in life Browning spoke or wrote about the fate of *Strafford* to three people — Gosse, Furnivall, and William Archer, an actor. We can examine Gosse's report (1881) of Browning's version of what happened; it agrees with statements that Browning made in the letter to Furnivall (1886) on the projected performance of *Strafford* and in notes enclosed in a letter to Archer (June 29, 1888).[32] In preparing for a life of Macready, Archer had asked Browning to comment on entries in Macready's *Diaries* concerning *Strafford* and *A Blot in the 'Scutcheon.*

Gosse referred to the financial situation, inadequate staging, and poor acting.

> *Strafford* was produced when the finances of Covent Garden Theatre were at their lowest ebb, and nothing was done to give dignity or splendor to the performance. "Not a rag for the new tragedy," said Mr. Osbaldiston. The king was taken by Mr. Dale, who was stone-deaf, and who acted so badly that, as one of the critics said, it was a pity that the pit did not rise as one man and push him off the stage.[33]

A passage in Browning's letter to Furnivall echoes the points and wording of Gosse, who must have been closely following the account given him by Browning. The reference to "the judicious remarks of the Critic" is ironic — the critic does not make clear, according to Browning's notion, the causes adversely affecting *Strafford's* chances of success.

> You see the judicious remarks of the Critic in this morning's *Daily News:* not a doubt as to whether the bankrupt management of that day did what was requisite for the success of the piece, whether the wretched acting of the inferior people might not have done harm (a stone-deaf Charles, a silly, simpering Carlisle, &c.), and whether the management "that dressed the Scots Commissioners in kilts" might not refuse, as it did, "one rag for the new piece."

There is no reason to question the accuracy of Browning's comments on the poor performance of some characters and on the poor staging. These reports accord with the established facts, as we know them from Macready, the reviewers, and others.

Other points in Browning's accounts were not dependable. According to Gosse, ". . . the three plays which he [Browning] has brought out have all succeeded, and have owed it to fortuitous circumstances that their tenure on the board has been comparatively short." The three plays included *Strafford,* which, Gosse reported, was enjoying an "undiminished popularity" when the performances ended. This must have been an accurate report of Browning's statement since it agrees with the one he made in the notes he sent Archer: the play "met with no 'opposition' at all." He did not wish to recall the reception of the second night, which according to all evidence was less enthusiastic than that of Macready's benefit night. He was present on the second night, "muffled up in a cloak,"[34] and must have seen for himself how the audience was responding. Fifty years later the memory of the first night had blocked out the memory of the second.

Nor did Browning recognize that alterations were made in an attempt to remedy the deficiencies. Gosse's comment "All sorts of alterations were made in the text" represents the situation accurately; but Browning's own words to Archer made the incompetent minor actors serve as his whipping boys. After referring to those who acted well, he wrote of "the rest, — for the sake of whose incompetence the play had to be reduced by at least one third of its dialogue, — *non ragionam di loro!*"

The "simpering Carlisle" in the letter to Furnivall was an unimportant error of the kind that sometimes accompanied Browning's more consequential misrepresentations or misleading emphasis as he reviewed earlier periods of his career. Lady Carlisle, who was played by Helen Faucit, would not have been simpering. Browning must have been thinking of another character.

What stands out in Browning's retrospective comments on Strafford is that, as with *Pauline, Paracelsus,* and *A Blot,* he was reacting defensively to the painful memory of what he considered neglect and mistreatment of an early work. His sensitiveness about his literary offspring and the retarded recognition of his achievement could lead him into inaccurate reconstructions.

CHAPTER IV

Frustration

Sordello, 1840

In 1840, three years after the publication of *Strafford, Sordello* was published. Its history is a remarkable one — the long drawn-out composition with interruptions for other writing and for travel, the ironical notion held by some of Browning's friends before it was published that it would do for the poet's reputation what *Strafford* had failed to do, the quips it evoked, Browning's early faith in the acceptance of the poem and his continued defense of it, a long period of notoriety along with recognition by a few of poetic wealth in it, and a reevaluation of it in reviews of the sixties.

Browning wrote *Paracelsus* in six months or less; the composition of *Sordello* stretched over seven years, with interruptions. This was a longer span of time than that extending from the beginning to the completion of any other work — even *The Ring and the Book.* In the later poem Browning adopted a plan and moved straightforward toward his goal. The composition of *Sordello* was doomed to suffer setbacks as the poet was compelled to shift his approach several times. DeVane has distinguished four periods of activity in his article "*Sordello's* Story Retold."[1] It will be helpful to review these four periods here.

Browning began *Sordello* at about the time of the publication of *Pauline* in March 1833. He went to Russia in March of 1834 and was writing *Paracelsus* from the autumn of 1834 to March of 1835. Then he realized he had duplicated much of his notion for *Sordello* in *Paracelsus,* and he started the second period, which lasted for two years or more;

he was considering a different Sordello. During this period he helped with Forster's life of Strafford and wrote his own *Strafford* for the stage. He wrote Macready on May 28, 1836, that Sordello was "nearly done,"[2] and an advertisement affixed to *Strafford,* published May 1, 1837, announced it as "Nearly ready." Similar comments made in the other periods of composition afford a glimpse of his effort to complete the poem.

On July 15, 1837, another setback came when Mrs. W. Busk published her *Plays and Poems,* which included a long poem entitled *Sordello;* its romantic treatment of the subject caused Browning to look at his poem in another light. A third period followed in which Browning revised his poem, and again there was news that it would soon be done — given to Miss Martineau on December 23, 1837.[3] But he was having trouble, and the third period ended when he left for Italy on April 13, 1838, with the hope of completing *Sordello* there. He did not complete it in Italy, but he reached conclusions that enabled him to begin his last period of composition after his return in July. He wrote Miss Haworth at the end of that month, "You will see Sordello in a trice, if the fagging-fit holds."[4]

On May 26, 1839, Browning reported to Macready that *Sordello* was completed. In his experimental stage of writing, Browning, faced with interruptions and circumstances that threatened to divert him from his original conception, produced a poem with a confusion of direction and details. DeVane wrote at the end of his article, "Psychology, love, romance, humanitarianism, philosophy and history encounter each other feverishly throughout the poem."

While Browning was occupied with *Sordello* hopes ran high for the poem in his circle of friends. Those that he talked to must have been affected by his enthusiasm and confidence as well as by the promise they had found in *Paracelsus.* In his early years Browning talked freely of his works; he did not have the reticence toward them that people often attributed to him in later years. He talked of them to Eliza and Sarah Flower, Fox, Fanny Haworth, Harriet Martineau, Forster, Macready, Domett, Arnould, Elizabeth Barrett, and to a good many others no doubt — probably to anyone who was interested and willing to listen. He talked of projected works, difficulties, disappointments, ambitions; requested criticism; and expressed confidence in his progress. He talked of *Paracelsus, Strafford, Sordello,* and of all the *Bells.*

He spoke of *Sordello* with confidence: it would reach the pubic. In his Preface to *Paracelsus,* dated March 15, 1835, he referred to productions which "may follow in a more popular, and perhaps less difficult form." In writing to Fox of *Paracelsus* on April 16, 1835, he said he had "another affair on hand, rather of a more popular nature."[5] When he made these comments, he had *Sordello* in mind; he was in the early stage of its composition, before the accumulation of attempts at different approaches to his subject. By the time it was completed he might have felt that he had heeded the critics' wish for narrative in *Paracelsus* and their objection to mysticism and vagueness as well as Fox's desire for condensation.

Others besides Browning were confident that the poem would succeed. Macready looked forward to it with assurance of its success. On April 28, 1837, when he felt that *Strafford* would fail, he wrote in his *Diaries.* "Browning will efface its memory by the production of *Sordello.* . . ." Miss Martineau was looking forward to the new poem; her delight in *Paracelsus* had given her "unbounded expectation."[6]

Forster believed in the poem. He was reading passages from it to Macready as early as February 15, 1836. He was a man of enthusiasms, and wherever his enthusiasm lay he was likely to set himself up as prime mover of events. During the summer of that year, when Browning was working in the second period of composition and thought he was nearing the end of his efforts, Forster took it upon himself to find a publisher. One of his friends was the novelist William Harrison Ainsworth, whose *Rookwood,* published in 1834, had brought him popularity. Forster set about converting Ainsworth to Browning and *Sordello,* and Ainsworth was in turn to persuade his publisher, the young and ambitious John Macrone, to produce the poem. Convinced that *Sordello* would bring credit to its publisher, Ainsworth wrote Macrone on June 14, 1836:

> Forster, whom I saw yesterday, tells me that Colburn is anxious to publish Browning's new poem *Sordello.* I hope you will not let this work, which will, at all events, do you credit as a publisher, slip through your hands without due consideration. It is impossible to foretell in such a case as the present whether the work will *pay* or not. My own opinion, from all I hear and know of Mr. Browning, is that it will do so. But at all events, it will do what I am so desirous you should do for yourself — contribute to *fan* your character as a publisher of taste and discrimination; and viewed only in this light is a very desirable undertaking for you. You should see Forster as soon as you can, and come to some positive understanding on this point. . . .[7]

On July 29 Ainsworth again praised Browning to Macrone:

> I had yesterday, as I anticipated, the pleasure of making your
> new Poet's acquaintance, and from what I saw of him — and from
> what I heard and saw — I am induced to form a very high opinion of
> him. He is full of genius. . . . *Sordello* complete, he is to write a
> Tragedy for Macready — and I feel quite sure that he has great dra-
> matic genius. As, moreover, his Tragedy is to be written for and
> produced next season, you will have no reason to regret your imme-
> diate undertaking.[8]

The letter leaves the impression that Macrone had already decided to
publish *Sordello:* Ainsworth was no longer trying to persuade him to do
so but instead he was writing of Browning as "your new" poet and of
"your immediate undertaking." Whatever the decision, Macrone died
soon after these letters were written. His death defeated Forster's plan
for *Sordello* and left the road clear for someone else to fan his "character
as a publisher of taste and discrimination." Someone else turned out to
be Moxon, who because of the great risk of publishing poetry had declined even to read *Paracelsus*. Perhaps the fair success of that poem encouraged him to take a chance with *Sordello*.

Before *Sordello* was published, others besides Forster were eager to
help in some way. Miss Martineau discussed with Browning the use of
preface and notes; she felt he must choose between being historian or
poet and advised him "to let the poem tell its own tale."[9] And, according to Orr, she introduced him to John Robertson, who was assisting
J. S. Mill in editing the *London and Westminster Review;* Robertson, an
admirer of *Paracelsus,* promised a review of *Sordello*. Always alert to the
possibility of a review, Browning did not want the promise to be forgotten. Before leaving for Italy on April 13, 1838, he unsuccessfully
tried to see Robertson and then wrote him a note, no doubt intended
as a reminder. According to the account of the association of Browning
and Robertson, first commented on by Orr and later by others, the
poet lost his review because he refused to send an advanced copy,
thinking that doing so would be unfair to other critics.[10]

A further look raises a question about the reason given for the loss
of the review. In a letter that Mill sent to Robertson from Paris on December 28, 1838, eight months after Browning wrote Robertson his
note, there is no evidence that Browning said he would not provide an
advanced copy. Mill advised, "Use Browning's means of conveyance as
much as you can, but if he sends Sordello we must not let him suppose

that we can promise a review of it in the February number."[11] At least, there must have still been talk of a review of the poem. And even if Browning later refused to send an advanced copy to Mill or Robertson, it was surely not at the time of publication because by then Mill was terminating his control of the *Review*.

Mill, who was to review *Sordello,* had thought he would get a copy early enough to write the review before he left England. In Paris, he felt that he would not have time to do it. Perhaps that was best, he said, for he could not "honestly give much praise" to either *Strafford* or *Paracelsus.* Yet he did not know whom he and Robertson could get to do the review. We can muse upon the possible contents of a review of *Sordello* by Mill. In his marginal notes on *Pauline* he said that he had read that poem four times. Would he have endured reading *Sordello* a sufficient number of times to write a review of it? And if he had, what effect would his review have had on Browning's later accounts of Mill's part in the early history of his career?

In the *Literary Gazette* of February 29, 1840 — three years lacking two months after the performance of the unfortunate *Strafford* — Moxon announced the publication of *Sordello.* It was published on March 7, the date inscribed in his mother's copy and the date of a note accompanying a copy sent to Domett. On the following weekend, March 14 and 15, two weeklies introduced the poem to the public. In all, there were nine reviews, four of them very short, spread over the eleven weeks from March 14 to May 30.

On March 14 there appeared in the *Spectator* a few remarks showing the impatience that would characterize more than half of the criticisms of *Sordello.*

> What this poem may be in its extent we are unable to say, for we *cannot* read it. Whatever may be the poetical spirit of Mr. Browning, it is so overlaid in *Sordello* by digression, affectation, obscurity, and all the faults that spring, it would seem, from crudity of plan and a self-opinion which will neither cull thoughts nor revise composition, that the reader — at least a reader of our stamp — turns away.

Oddly enough the only press notice of *Sordello* that did not make the charge of obscurity was *Bell's Life in London and Sporting Chronicle,* and, further, it was one of the only two publications that gave an indication, slight though it was, of the nature of the poem. In the March 15, 1840, issue in addition to the sections on chess, pigeon-shooting, and other diversions there was a section on literature, which contained two reviews, one of a book on hunting and another, three times as long, of *Sordello*. Thus it was that the followers of the diversions of life (the weekly boasted a sale of over 23,000 copies) had their attention called to *Sordello*, a poem of a "higher and more ambitious tendency" in a more mature form than *Paracelsus*. It was the "psychological biography of Sordello. . . , an exposition of the sensations, aspirations, and progress of the poetic mind and character." In the space allotted to literature no attempt could be made to give an analysis "adequate to its merits and importance." The poem required and would richly repay, the critic thought, a "careful and patient study," though he had not yet "been able to afford it." A quotation served as a sample of the "many and rare beauties throughout the book" which showed the "impress and true cunning of a master-hand."

Quite a different impression was given in the *Atlas* two weeks later, on March 28. *Sordello*, even more than *Strafford*, disappointed the critic, who had seen the promise of *Paracelsus*. In *Paracelsus* the merits made amends for the faults; in *Sordello* "all the faults recur in exaggerated shapes, without being relieved or compensated for by an equal amount of excellence in any single point of view." Browning did not make amends even by occasional fragments of the beautiful which his genius was able to produce. "The whole structure is faulty, not only in its entire outline, but in its minutest details." A quotation of nearly fifty lines from *Sordello* demonstrated the peculiarities of Browning's poetry, obvious in *Paracelsus* and more pronounced in *Strafford* — "the same pitching, hysterical, and broken sobs of sentences — the same excisions of words — the same *indications* of power — imperfect grouping of thoughts and images — and hurried, exclamatory, and obscure utterance of things." Instead of improvement in his latest poem Browning had demonstrated not only that experience had been of no benefit to him but that the sins of his verse were "premeditated, wilful, and incurable."

A short comment in the *Metropolitan Magazine* in April showed that this reviewer, like the one for the *Atlas,* was irritated by *Sordello,* in particular by its obscurity. "If it were possible to understand the meaning of the writer of this poem, we should be delighted to impart the information to our readers." A passage quoted from Book III included the lines "And sonnets on the *earliest ass* that spoke" and "Mark ye the dim first oozings?" which induced the taunt in the final sentence of the comment: "We had rather write sonnets on the *latest,* as well as the earliest *speaking ass,* than be doomed to read such unintelligible oozings of nonsense." In the same month, the *New Monthly Belle As-sembléе,* in three sentences, condemned Browning's poem because of its obscurity and nonsense. "He calls it poetry, we term it trash of the very worst description."

In May there were four reviews of *Sordello.* The critic for the *Dublin Review,* a quarterly, spelled out its failure. He included several definitions of the poem, all sarcastic; an account of the hopeful expectations that *Paracelsus* had generated and that were unfulfilled in *Strafford* and remained so in *Sordello;* and a criticism of the peculiar syntax, versification, language, and narration. Browning's faults were "exaggerated and profusely displayed, to the destruction of all interest, comprehension of the narrative, sympathy with the author, or approbation of his intellectual pretensions." Although the reviewer expressed fear of what the future held for Browning as the result of his defects, he had not lost hope for him. "He has given indication of powers, that if faithfully, diligently, and loftily cultivated, might place him in an honourable and benificent [*sic*] position. . . ."

Two monthlies and one weekly noticed the poem in May. The objections in all three were strong, but the reviews in the two monthlies showed a composure lacking in the forthcoming *Athenaeum.* George Henry Lewis, the critic for the *Monthly Chronicle,* had opened *Sordello* with the "most pleasurable anticipations, and closed it with the most painful disappointment." In it he found the faults and missed the good of the "deep-thinking and delightful" *Paracelsus.* In *Sordello* there were the "short abrupt sentences" of *Strafford* and also dullness and wordy metaphysics. "The story is badly and tediously unfolded — the reflections for the most part are commonplace and prosaical — the versification every where rugged, imperfect, and inharmonious — and the imagery seldom novel or striking." Browning has forgotten that art must be beautiful; ". . . when this want of a sweet flowing beauty both in thought and versification . . . is coupled with a positive want of dramatic or speculative interest in the story, and a by no means new or newly put moral, we may be pardoned if we say we regard 'Sordello' as a failure *in toto.*" Lewes expressed regret for finding so much fault with the work of an author who had given "such indications of genius as are to be found in 'Paracelsus.' "

According to the *Monthly Review,* in a single paragraph given to *Sordello,* "affectations of language and invertions [*sic*] of thought" and other causes of obscurity detracted from the pleasure of reading the poem. Yet, like the writer for the *Dublin Review,* this critic had not lost hope for Browning. He seemed even confident of his future.

But after all, we are much mistaken if Mr. Browning does not yet prove himself a poet of a right stamp, — original, vigorous, and finely inspired. He appears to us to possess a true sense of the dignity and sacredness of the poet's kingdom; and his imagination wings its way with a boldness, freedom, and scope, as if he felt himself at home in that sphere, and was resolved to put his allegiance to the test.

On May 30, nearly three months after the publication of *Sordello*, the *Athenaeum* reviewed it. T. K. Hervey, the critic, was more fretful than the reviewers for the monthlies, but it must be pointed out that they had made no attempt to give an indication of the content of the poem as a whole. Hervey undertook to do this — not an easy task. His effort was somewhat weakened by the persistency of his objection to the poem's obscurity. The review began, "If it were Mr. Browning's desire to withdraw himself from the inquest of criticism, he could scarcely have effected that purpose better than by the impenetrable veil, both of manner and language, in which he has contrived to wrap up whatever truths or beauties this volume may contain." Accepted grammatical forms and euphony were to be respected. Mastering the "novelties of mere construction" necessary for grappling with the "peculiarities of expression" handicapped the reader. Getting at the meaning was a problem. The "occasional outbreaks of light, giving assurance of a spiritual presence," took the reader onward, and the "air of philosophic pretension" about the work left the impression that it must contain something worthwhile. After a difficult and discouraging search, the critic stated what he thought Browning's object was, though he was not sure.

> If we understand Mr. Browning's philosophic purpose, it is to paint the contest between the spiritual aspirations of an ardent nature and the worldly influences by which it is opposed; the disappointment which an enthusiastic heart, nursed, amid natural influences, into dreams of perfectibility, experiences in its attempts to impress its own character upon surrounding objects, and confer, by the act of its own will, those boons upon its fellow men, which are the slow and gradual gift of ages.

Besides the principal meaning there were "minor philosophical ventures," which turned out to be "commonplace truths."

It should be noted that the review was not entirely disparaging. At the end long passages were quoted: either to show "the author's profundities, and his peculiar manner of enunciating them," when he chose to be "most intelligible"; or to show that from time to time "pregnant thought, and quaint poetry, and significant illustration" lured the reader on over rough ground; or to show that "the quaintness of the style has not overlaid the poetry, nor originality become mere extravagance." These examples might satisfy the reader of the advisability of Browning's taking trouble "to use the language of ordinary men, and to condescend to be intelligible, which need not prevent his being profound."

Near the first of the review the *Athenaeum* had a warning that the "author who chooses deliberately to put 'his light under a bushel' of affectations, must not be surprised if men refuse the labour of searching it out, and leave him to the peaceable enjoyment of that obscurity which he has courted." Whether or not the reviewers of *Sordello* labored to search for the light, only two made any attempt to state Browning's aim in writing the poem — *Bell's Life* briefly and the *Athenaeum* somewhat more completely. The other critics scarcely got beyond commenting adversely on the obscurity of meaning, the rough or irregular lines, and the peculiar language — repeating criticisms that had been made of *Strafford*. Several called attention to the disappointing *Strafford* and *Sordello* after the promise shown in *Paracelsus*. Although hope for Browning's future could still be expressed (*Dublin Review, Monthly Review*) and his genius was still recognized (*Atlas, Monthly Chronicle*), the harm done to his reputation even more by *Sordello* than by *Strafford* would be difficult to repair.

Tendencies that were to become prominent in future criticism began to appear. The critics for the *Monthly Chronicle* and the *Athenaeum* made it clear that they expected the conventional in poetry; both specified euphony and the *Athenaeum* also specified acceptable grammatical forms. Whatever justification their statements might have had on these points when Browning was in his initiatory struggle for individual expression, the critics were to be shortsighted in harping on his failure to follow tradition after his style matured. A critical motif of impatience and irritability was introduced, one that for some time would hamper critics in seeing what was worthwhile in Browning. The *Atlas* called his sins "wilful" and the *Dublin Review* feared that the defects were the result of some obstinate system already too long at work to permit future good to emerge. Either the word "wilful" or a synonym was to appear with dismal frequency.

Browning watched for reviews. Little suspecting the severity of the criticisms in store for him, he read what *Bell's Life* had to say of *Sordello* and wrote Domett an imaginary and playful account of the contents of the issue.[12] The appearance of a review in *Bell's* raises questions. In the first place, why was *Sordello*, as well as *Strafford*, reviewed in a weekly devoted to sports? And how could a writer for such a periodical, who admittedly had not given the poem "careful and patient study," see that *Sordello* was a psychological biography? Even reviewers experienced in reading literary works had not grasped this. Is it possible that Browning, as usual eager to get his works introduced to the pubic, had an opportunity to talk of his poem to a writer for *Bell's?* At any rate, he had the pleasure of seeing in print at least one account that contained no unfavorable comments on *Sordello.*

It might be expected that Browning's friend Forster would have come to his support soon after the publication of *Sordello,* but Forster made no public comment until he reviewed *Pippa Passes* a year and a half later. In the *Examiner* of October 2, 1841, Browning could read a statement that was unusual for the time. Forster began his review with a reference to *Paracelsus* and continued thus:

> Mr Browning has published since then: in our opinion, not so well. But yet not so, as to falsify any anticipation formed of the character of his genius. To write a bad poem is one thing: to write a poem on a bad system is another, and very different. When a greater curiosity about the writer shall hereafter disentomb *Sordello,* it will not be admired for its faults, but, in spite of them, its power and its beauty will be perceived. It had a magnificent aim, and a great many passages in which justice was done to that, and to the genius of the designer. The temptations which too easily beset a man's pride in his own originality; the enticing and most dangerous depths of metaphysics, which are, to the young and genuine thinker, as the large black eyes of Charlotte were to Werter, *a sea, a precipice;* into these the poet fell.

Forster's qualified praise was surely intended to give Browning encouragement after the adverse criticism of *Sordello.*

Outside the reviews there was no dearth of comments on *Sordello* as there had been on *Strafford.* The poem was a prominent subject of conversation and anecdote; some of the reputed comments may never have been made or may have been improved as they were repeated. Miss Martineau wrote in her *Autobiography* that her unbounded expectations were sadly disappointed; she was so unable to understand *Sor-*

dello that she thought she was ill. [13] Although Macready had supposed before its publication that the poem would save Browning's reputation, he did not fare any better than Miss Martineau. He recorded in his *Diaries* on June 17, 1840: "After dinner tried — another attempt — utterly desperate — on *Sordello;* it is *not* readable." Douglas Jerrold, dramatist and journalist, could make nothing of the poem and finally exclaimed, "O, God, I *am* an idiot!" [14]

Tennyson said that he understood only two lines and that they were both untrue — the first line, "Who will, may hear Sordello's story told," and the last line, "Who would has heard Sordello's story told." [15] Charles Gavan Duffy lent the poem to a friend, who returned it with the inquiry "whether by any chance it might be the sacred book of the Irvingite Church, written in their unknown tongue." [16] Mrs. Carlyle said that she could not tell whether Sordello was a "book, a city, or a man." [17] Doubtless those who read the poem could not forget the struggle easily. Hervey, who, unlike other immediate reviewers, made a real effort to understand it, later maintained that it was "absolute nonsense." [18] Seemingly Browning's father was one of those who had trouble. According to a comment in a letter to W. H. Griffin, Browning Senior gave a copy to a friend and fellow-worker in the Bank of England. "The tradition goes that when he brought it he said, 'Mr. Earles, my son sends you his last poem — perhaps *you* can make head or tail of it but I confess *I* can't.' " [19]

Quips on *Sordello* have been bandied about a good many years, often by people with but limited knowledge of Browning's poetry in general and none of the poem itself. Two opinions have escaped broadcast flippancy, one attributed to Fox, interesting for Browning's comment on it, and the other expressed by Eliza Flower to Horne, one of Browning's earnest supporters. Fox, who had reviewed the poet's first three works, apparently took no public notice of *Sordello,* though he continued to write reviews of literary works for various periodicals. In a letter accompanying a gift copy of *Sordello* to Macready, Browning told what Fox thought of the poem: "Our friend Fox, I am given to understand, pronounces it abundantly 'unintelligible' — but Fox is lecturing now on the Devil, and can hardly fail to be full of his subject. . . ." [20] Remarks on Browning's works made during these early years by Eliza Flower and other members of the Fox family circle have found their way into print. To these remarks should be added Eliza's as yet unpublished opinion of *Sordello.*

Ah Sordello! It is *madness* I think. One never minds, one likes, ob-scurity, & misty shrouding: haze is often excess of light: and the out-line may be as faint as possible through the veil, & so much the more stimulative & suggestive. Infinity has no boundary line: and sensa-tion we know can distance thought. But Sordello has none of this charm: it is intertwisted & involved to distortion: confusion worse confounded: it is like walking over the rough & spiky shingles that give way on the shelving beach, while you make no way, and get your shoes full of stones: meanwhile the consciousness of a lovely & melodious ocean felt at intervals. I am as sure as I am of my own ex-istence, sure that Robert Browning is a natural born Poet, & of a very superb quality: he dives deep, & his pearls are of the largest & the loveliest order: and that he should be satisfied with that mon-strous failure is I am clear, delirium, or infatuation as to approach to it. The close of the fifth book is the most extraordinary part: is it not like the incoherent snatches & raving of a mad man?[21]

Two other friends read *Sordello* and were concerned because of its obscurity — Alfred Domett and Joseph Arnould, who both, like Browning, lived in Camberwell. All three were members of a set, the Colloquials — "Poets, in Embryo, Philosophers, Scientific — *literary* all — & so light & lively!"[22] — who held debates and had their own magazine. Arnould, whose father was a doctor in Camberwell Grove, won the Newdigate Prize in Oxford, took his degree, became a fellow of Wadham College, was entered at the Middle Temple, and was called to the bar in 1841. Though after privately printing some poems he gave up any idea of the serious writing of poetry, he did not give up writing. When he was making little money from his profession, he de-pended on journalism to supplement his income and wrote a book on the law of marine insurance, which was to be recognized as an author-ity. In 1859 he became Judge of the Supreme Court at Bombay and re-ceived the title of knighthood.

Domett, whom Browning had in mind when he wrote *Waring, Time's Revenges,* and *The Guardian Angel,* came of a family of seafaring and shipping interests. He entered St. John's College, Cambridge, but never took a degree. In his youth twice he indulged his desire to travel in other lands and twice he published a volume of poetry — *Poems* (1833) and *Venice* (1839) — and also some poems in *Blackwood's.* Like Arnould, he was entered at the Middle Temple and called to the bar in 1841. On April 30, 1842, he left England again and this time it was to settle in New Zealand for many years and achieve distinction there.

With the candor and intimacy of their early association, Arnould and Browning wrote Domett about their professional lives and the activities of the literary and political world. Their letters and Arnould's letters to Browning[23] follow the course of Browning's publications and provide insight into his poetic concerns during the years of writing preparatory to his greatest works. Only one other published correspondence — that of Browning and Elizabeth Barrett — is more valuable for understanding the poet in his early career.

The first two of Browning's published communications to Domett were written not long before Domett left for New Zealand. Both concerned *Sordello;* one was the note accompanying a copy of the poem and the other a letter in reply to Domett's criticism — "blame as well as praise."[24] What the praise was Browning's letter did not reveal; clearly it revealed that the blame was for his unintelligibility. Domett had objected that he was "difficult on system." Browning's response is included in a later discussion in this chapter that shows his serious consideration of criticism made by his friends, including Domett.

In a verse epistle that Arnould was to write to Browning when *Dramatic Lyrics* was published in 1842, he looked back to the problem that *Sordello* had presented to the poet. He saw Browning's need to discipline the wealth of his mind so that he could be understood by his readers:

> His struggling thought, to struggling language glows,
> [O]ne truth half-phrased, another is behind
> The swift succession tasks his labouring mind
> Light makes him dark, & too clear vision, blind.
> So it will ever be; the full rich soul
> O'erteemed with truths, too restless for controul
> Chasing the fire-flies of thought that glance
> Before, around him, in delirious dance
> Clutching with too quick grasp each glittering prize
> Impairs its beauty for the general eyes —
> Such was Sordello's fault. . . .[25]

Among those to whom Browning regularly sent copies of his works during these years was Carlyle. Doubtless Browning eagerly awaited the older writer's opinion, for he set high value on it. In June 1841 Carlyle wrote Browning concerning *Pippa Passes,* a copy of which he had just received, and also *Sordello,* received "many months" before. In the opening paragraph of the letter he confessed, with gentleness and guarded honesty, that the two poems gave rise to many reflections, "not without friendly hopes and anxieties in due measure." He explained, "Unless I very greatly mistake, judging from these two works, you seem to possess a rare spiritual gift, poetical, pictorial, intellectual, by whatever name we may prefer calling it; to unfold which into articulate clearness is naturally the problem of all problems for you. This noble endowment, it seems to me farther, you are *not* at present on the best way for unfolding. . . ." [26]

Browning, who had been gratified by Landor's praise in *A Satire on Satirists,* addressed some lines in *Sordello* (III, 950–66) to him and sent a copy of the poem with an accompanying request for his opinion. In his reply Landor gave an excuse for postponement of criticism, whether pretended or real, and spoke of *Paracelsus,* which Browning's well-wishers were looking back to. "Three days have nearly slipped by since I received your poem, and a family which came to Bath about the same time, claiming all the rights of old acquaintance, has prevented me from enjoying it. You much overrate my judgment: but, whatever it is, you shall have it, before I have read it so often as I read *Paracelsus.*" [27] Landor was usually generous in his encouragement of young writers, and, lacking a follow-up letter to Browning, we can only wonder what he said about *Sordello.* A statement he made to Forster in all likelihood refers to the poem. "You were right as to Browning. He has sent me some admirable things. I only wish he would atticise a little. Few of the Athenians had such a quarry on their property, but they constructed better roads for the conveyance of the material." [28]

Horne also saw wealth in *Sordello.* After reading through Book I he set down his impression for his friend Fox:

> I . . . firmly believe that I understand almost everything in it, except the story; the connection of the sentences; the perking interrogations; the grammatical structure of most of the longer sentences; the showery aptitude of the historical pepper-box. One poem seems chiefly addressed to gulp-Gorton-swill-Guthrie readers. But what pure diamonds of the first water are to be found in this confused setting! His genius is equal to his perversity — the pity of it is that the shades run so continually into each other. We cannot skip. The poem wants a second volume of unreadable notes, to make it quite perfect. What a waste of genius! — so far as I can judge from Book I, and about fifty dips in the devious whole. [29]

Horne was to shape this opinion into a comment for a discussion of Browning in the *Church of England Quarterly* (Oct. 1842), later to be used for his discussion of *Sordello* in his *New Spirit of the Age*. He wrote in the *New Spirit:* "The poem of 'Sordello' is a beautiful globe, which, rolling on its way to its fit place among the sister spheres, met with some accident which gave it such a jar that a multitude of things half slipt into each other's places."

Like Arnould, Carlyle, and Landor, Horne saw wasted riches in *Sordello.* "Never was extraordinary wealth squandered in so extraordinary a manner by any prodigal son of Apollo." Others persisted and had something good to say of the poem. Miss Haworth, to whom Browning addressed some lines in *Sordello,* asked for explanation of them and praised the poem. He answered, "You say roses and lillies and lilac-bunches and lemon-flowers about it while everybody else pelts cabbage stump after potato-paring. . . ."[30]

Elizabeth Barrett, whose critics sometimes accused her of subjecting her own readers to obscurities, found the poem difficult. After she and Browning had started corresponding with each other but before they had met, Elizabeth, in writing to Thomas Westwood, classified *Sordello* as belonging to "Sphinxine literature," yet worth the study necessary for understanding it.

> I am delighted that you should appreciate Mr. Browning's high power — very high, according to my view — very high, and various. Yes, 'Paracelsus' you *should* have. 'Sordello' has many fine things in it, but, having been thrown down by many hands as unintelligible, and retained in mine as certainly of the Sphinxine literature, with all its power, I hesitate to be imperious to you in my recommendations of it. Still, the book *is* worth being *studied* — a study is necessary to it, as, indeed, though in a less degree, to all the works of this poet; study is peculiarly necessary to it. He is a true poet, and a poet, I believe, of a large *'future in -rus, about to be.'* He is only growing to the height he will attain.

In the next letter to Westwood she admitted the charge of her own "sin of Sphinxine literature" and asked that he tell her honestly if he saw in her works "anything like the Sphinxeness of Browning." She thought his fault was great but, for her and Westwood, the depth and power of the significance, when it was apprehended, glorified the puzzle. In the following month — after Browning's first call on Elizabeth — she was encouraging the same correspondent to persevere with *Sordello,* from which they, as poets, could learn much, for Browning spoke "true oracles."[31] She defended the poem to others besides Westwood, as Fox indicated in a statement made soon after her marriage: "I wonder whether she is still angry with anybody that does not understand *Sordello*. She almost quarrelled with H. Martineau for her want of perception."[32]

"If a favorable word can be found for the work in any quarter, even the obscurest, it seems to have escaped so far the hardest search," Lounsbury stated. We may ask about his later quotation from the more favorable part of Forster's comment on *Sordello* in his review of *Pippa Passes*. It is understandable that Lounsbury missed the discussion in *Bell's Life*, but it is not understandable why he did not take into account Forster's opinion. Furthermore, when he discussed the *Athenaeum's* review and Elizabeth's letters to Westwood, he ignored the designation of good qualities in quoted passages and he misrepresented Elizabeth's letters to Westwood, disregarding some relevant passages and making misleading statements about others. The editors of *Browning: The Critical Heritage,* in omitting (without indicating the omission) the last of the *Athenaeum's* review, ignored what has already been brought out — a statement of the philosophical purpose of the poem and some favorable comments with illustrative quotations. Thus it is that whatever good was said of the poem in Browning's early career has been generally passed over.[33]

Forster's brief comment and others already cited in this chapter help to show that a few saw beyond *Sordello's* faults of expression and presentation. We can add a postscript to the tiresomely repeated comment made by Jerrold, who, according to Horne, returned to *Sordello* after his first reading and fared better. "When Jerrold took up the poem a second time he found there was a world of sense and new light in it."[34] A few persevered and found thought and beauty in spite of all obstructions.

Elizabeth Barrett saw the consequence of the close and attentive reading required for Browning's poetry: he was not read except in a "peculiar circle very strait and narrow."[35] In 1855 the poet had from the publisher Edward Moxon an account of the sale of *Sordello* from the time of its publication on March 7, 1840, until July 20, 1855. Of the edition of 500 copies, 157 had been sold and 86 had been given away, and 257 were still on hand. Beside an entry for May 1840, the sale of 41 copies was recorded.[36]

The most damaging effect of *Sordello* was its initiation of the feeling that Browning had ability but did not make the effort necessary to reach his readers. In spite of all that has been said to the contrary, he did make the effort to be intelligible. If his words and his actions are

Robert Browning, Esq. in account with *Edward Moxon*

1855				1855
1848 to	Printing 37 copies of Sordello at 4⅔		12 4	July 20th 1855
1855	Advertising	3 3		By 42 net copies at 4/6 9 4 6
"	Commission 10 per cent on £9.4.6		18 5	
	Sundries			Sold May 1840 ——— 41
				Oct. 31 1842 ——— 6
				—— 1843 ——— 6
				—— 1846 ——— 46
				—— 1847 ——— 16
				July 20 1855 ——— 42
				Author's Account &c ——— 86
				On hand ——— 257 / 600
July 20	Private Account	1 14		
"	Cash	2 16 9		
		£9 4 6		£9 4 6

Account of Sordello with Moxon

examined, the seriousness of his efforts and the accompanying desire to carry his readers along with him cannot be doubted. He had trouble in seeing his writing as others saw it, a fault not by any means restricted to Browning. He tried to see and tried to improve his poetry. According to John Westland Marston, Browning sent *Sordello* to him to read before its publication, "saying that this time the public should not accuse him at any rate of being unintelligible."[37] The statement may be apocryphal, but Browning's early unawareness of the difficulties presented in *Sordello* came out in a comment that can be relied upon. At the time of its publication Miss Haworth asked him to make clear some lines addressed to her in Book III; he sent an answer that no one but Browning could think was clear and then asked, ". . . what is involved here?" He added, "Only one does not like serving oneself as a certain 'Watson' served Horace in a translation I have. . . ."[38] Watson had injected needless explanations in his translation. There was no arrogance in Browning's comment but rather a simple question and a statement resulting from his failure to see the need for clarification. Near the end of his letter to her he wrote, "Don't fear . . . any more unintelligible writing."

Browning reacted in the same way to Domett's criticism of *Sordello*. After thanking his friend for both praise and blame, he wrote a confusing passage which indicated his failure to anticipate that a reader might have problems with the poem. He added, "I wish I had thought of this before. . . ." Intent on doing his best, Browning welcomed criticism and determined to consider the needs of his readers:

> . . . meantime I am busy on some plays . . . that shall be plain enough if my pains are not thrown away — and, in lieu of Sir Philip and his like, Stokes may assure himself that I see him (first row of the pit, under the second oboe, hat between legs, play-bill on a spike, and a "comforter" round his throat "because of the draught from the stage"), and unless he leaves off sucking his orange at the pathetic morsels of my play, I hold them nought.[39]

In September of 1845, five years after the appearance of *Sordello*, Miss Barrett was writing Browning of the poem, which was "like a noble picture with its face to the wall." She felt that it wanted "drawing together & fortifying in the connections & associations" rather than added verses, which he had talked of on the preceding day. It might be brought out into the light by his hand. The next month she was inquiring about the "new avatar of 'Sordello,' " which he had taught her to look for. Two months later he told her that one day when they were together he meant "to set about that reconsidering 'Sordello.' "[40]

The year preceding his marriage was not a propitious time for revising the poem. When friends urged him to clarify it, Browning realized how difficult the task would be. He told Miss Barrett that his thoughts could not be so readily expressed.[41] He did not include *Sordello* in the 1849 collection, but had plans for its improvement. When G. W. Curtis, an American, visited the Brownings soon after they went to Florence in 1847, the poet was thinking of a revision. Upon learning that Curtis had not read *Sordello,* Browning said to him, "So much the better. . . . Don't read it, except in the revised form, which is coming."[42] In the summer of 1855 the Brownings left Casa Guidi for a visit to England; they had with them the manuscript of *Men and Women,* which was to be published in November. In October, after the proofs were read, they went to Paris, where they spent the winter.

At last Browning was to direct his attention to *Sordello.* On September 6 he had written from London the first of six letters to the American publisher J. T. Fields, with whom he was making arrangements for the publication of *Men and Women.* They are revealing in their references to *Sordello.* In the first one Browning said that he was going to "revise thoroughly and do justice" to *Sordello.* He hoped to interest Fields in the publication of it and *Strafford.* He returned to the subject of the two poems in a letter written on October 3. On October 9, in writing again of the poems, he said of *Sordello:* ". . . it is my best performance hitherto: I am not without evidence that the good of it is to be got at even now by the pains-taking, — and I hope & believe that, by myself taking proper pains in turn, — I shall make the good obtainable at a much easier rate." He planned to "augment" *Sordello* "considerably"; as we have seen, he had expressed a like intention to Elizabeth in 1845. Without having both sides of the correspondence, we can assume from Browning's letter of February 4, 1856, that Fields had heard of the difficulty of understanding *Sordello.* Browning wrote from Paris: "As for 'Sordello' — I shall make it as easy as its nature admits, I believe — changing nothing and simply *writing in* the unwritten *every-other-line* which I stupidly left as an amusement for the reader to do — who, after all, is no writer, nor needs be."[43] In the same month Elizabeth wrote Mrs. Jameson, "Robert . . . is much occupied with 'Sordello,' and neither of us receive anybody till past four o'clock."[44] Seven years were to pass before a revised *Sordello* appeared, first in England (1863) and then in America (1864). The revisions were not so ambitious as those projected in Browning's letters to Fields.

At no period of his life did Browning want a public more than in the decade in which he tried to revise *Sordello*. In the second half of this decade he was disheartened because of the poor reception of his poetry. Nothing would have pleased him more than to produce a revised *Sordello* that would satisfy him and meet with the approval of his readers, and he worked hard to make it more easily understandable. But it was a virtual impossibility to convert a poem that had suffered from distractions, shifts in plan and emphasis, confusing historical details, and difficulties of style into a direct, readable poem. Although Browning wrote to Fields of more revision than he actually made, he did make numerous changes in order to help his readers: for clarification he made changes in the phrasing and the punctuation and broke up long sentences, and to guide readers he added page-headings. Domett had written questions and remarks in the margin of his copy of *Sordello*. Browning borrowed the copy and must have noted the indicated difficulties before he returned it, for when he revised the poem he made some changes in accordance with Domett's observations.[45]

Browning published the revised *Sordello* in his 1863 collected edition with a dedication to Joseph Milsand. In his dedication he bared much of his poetic self to the public — his confidence in his writing and his desire for approval; his disappointment and sense of futility when he was not understood.

> Let the next poem be introduced by your name, and so repay all trouble it ever cost me. I wrote it twenty-five years ago for only a few, counting even in these on somewhat more care about its subject than they really had. My own faults of expression were many; but with care for a man or book such would be surmounted, and without it what avails the faultlessness of either? I blame nobody, least of all myself, who did my best then and since; for I lately gave time and pains to turn my work into what the many might, — instead of what the few must, — like: but after all, I imagined another thing at first, and therefore leave as I find it. The historical decoration was purposely of no more importance than a background requires; and my stress lay on the incidents in the development of a soul: little else is worth study. I, at least, always thought so — you, with many known and unknown to me, think so — others may one day think so. . . .

Lounsbury's comment on the dedication shows how Browning's statements could lead to misunderstanding of his wish and efforts to make his work acceptable.

> In dedicating "Sordello" later to his friend Melsand [*sic*], of Dijon, the poet told him that he blamed nobody for its failure, least of all himself. This last phrase is significant. It reflects his invariable mental attitude. His faults of expression, he acknowledged, were many; but people might have surmounted the difficulties caused by them, had they cared to take the pains; if they did not care enough for the book or its writer to do this, what would avail its faultlessness? Never was there a more unblushing declaration on the part of an author of his willingness to shift upon the reader the burden of clearing a path through the jungle of his expression which he himself was too indolent or too indifferent to open up.[46]

Since Browning had trouble in recognizing the difficulty of following his expression, he could well have felt that some of the fault lay with his readers, who he thought should have some responsibility. But his statement was not a declaration of unwillingness to help them; it was more a declaration of his disappointment that they could not overcome the difficulties. To say that he was indolent or indifferent at any time is not to recognize how much he worked to gain a public. He was perfectly willing to shoulder the burden of clearing the path through the jungle of *Sordello* and did shoulder it. There is every reason to believe that, as he said, he gave time and pains to turn *Sordello* into what readers might like; he worked at the revision in the middle fifties, a period when he was conscious of his mature powers and wished with his whole being to achieve recognition. It was impossible for him to make the poem into something that the many would like. He could write with feeling and with justification that he did not blame himself for the failure of *Sordello*. No one could know better than he did the effort and trials of writing it, the problems of modifying his first conception, and the frustrations of attempting later to revise the poem. Lounsbury's conclusion regarding this work is typical of the underestimation of Browning's desire and hard work to reach his readers.

Although Browning revised *Sordello* considerably before he included it in the *Poetical Works* of 1863, he made it clear that he never thought of the revisions as being equivalent to a rewriting. In September he wrote to M. D. Conway, who was to review the collected edition of 1863: "*Sordello* is corrected *throughout;* not altered at all, but really elucidated, I hope, by a host of little attentions to the reader: the 'headlines,' or running commentary at the top of the page, is added for the first time.[47] In 1886, in a letter to Furnivall, he again stated firmly that he had not made a basic change in the poem:

> I don't understand what Mrs Dall can mean by saying that "Sordello" has been "re-written": I did certainly at one time intend to rewrite much of it, — but changed my mind, — and the edition which I reprinted was the same in all respects as its predecessor — only with an elucidatory heading to each page, and some few alterations, presumably for the better, in the text — such as occur in most of my works: I cannot remember a single instance of any importance that is "rewritten" — and I only suppose that Mrs Dall has taken project for performance, and set down as "done" what was for a while intended to be done.[48]

Browning's insistence that the poem had not been rewritten is reminiscent of the statement that during the process of shaping *Strafford* for the stage no change had been made to alter or obscure the hero's "conduct," by which he seemed to mean that his concept of Strafford's inner being had remained the same. Seemingly once Browning put into words his conception, it was difficult for him to alter his basic idea. The statement in his Dedication of *Sordello* to Milsand, "I . . . leave [it] as I find it" did not mean that he had made no revisions of any kind but that he had made no major changes. He had written Fields that in his revising he was changing nothing, simply adding lines for the sake of clarity. In 1868, William Rossetti recorded a comment of Browning's on *Pauline* that shows his attitude toward revision: ". . . B[rowning] found the best thing to do would be to . . . republish the whole poem with proper press-corrections — not any re-writing, which he objects to."[49]

Browning responded to the unfavorable criticism of *Sordello* by acknowledging its faults and trying, unsuccessfully, to amend them, but he never lost faith in his poem. This contrasts with his reaction to the reception of *Pauline,* which for a long while he did not claim as his own. In writing *Sordello* Browning had given expression to ideas of concern to him about problems that man faced, about the possibilities for his growth, and particularly about the nature and function of the poet and of poetry. These were all matters of great importance to him. The adverse criticism of his poem did not cause him to consider disavowing it; in the light of the unfavorable estimate of *Sordello,* Browning's faith in the poem is significant.

For a time he believed that others would come to like *Sordello*. He had no notion that the difficulty of the poem would be a barrier to its acceptance. On March 9, 1840 — soon after its publication — he lightly answered Eliza Flower's objection to its obscurity. "Of course, I understand your objections — how else? But they are somewhat lightened already . . . will go on, or rather go off, lightening, and will be — oh, where *will* they be half a dozen years hence?"[50] Even after the reviewers had criticized the poem severely, he retained his confidence, as Macready noted in August 27, 1840: "Browning came . . . and really *wearied* me with his obstinate faith in his poem of *Sordello*, and of his eventual celebrity. . . ." Eventually he had to recognize that *Sordello* did not produce the desired effect on readers, but he never reached the point of depreciating it, no matter how many complaints or quips about its unintelligibility might have reached him. As we have seen, he wrote to Fields in 1855 that it had been his best performance up to that time. When Edward Dowden asked him questions about it in 1866 he answered:

> I . . . will try and answer off-hand, premising that I have a fa-cility at forgetting my own things once *done* and that, in this case, I have put this particular poem away and behind me long ago — not at all meaning to undervalue it thereby, but because it is good hus-bandry of energy in an artist to forget what is behind and press on-ward to what is before.[51]

Browning was pleased when he learned that William Rossetti was considering an exposition of the poem. He wrote him on December 31, 1858: ". . . the 'Exposition' of *Sordello* you had a thought of mak-ing — how can I be other than honoured and gratified in every way by such a thought, and benefitted by such an act if it arrives so far?" Browning emphasized to him as he did to others the nature of his re-working of the poem; it consisted purely of "additions, accretions, in-nestations, merely explanatory." He added, "I change *nothing,* but in-terpolate. . . ."[52] *Change* had a particular meaning for him. William Rossetti said he never wrote the exposition, but he sent an explanation of the poem — about twenty pages — to William Bell Scott, who thought the explanatory essay as obscure as the poem itself. Rossetti defended Browning's treatment:

> As to Sordello, I must give you up, hoping that the pains of heresy don't await you round the corner somewhere or other. The particulars of his life given — *not given,* you would say — by Brown-

ing are nearer the truth than most people suppose, or at least nearer some versions and hints of the truth, for his life is involved in great obscurity. . . .[53]

Casual readers have been easily deceived by Browning's later remarks on *Sordello*. As he listened to the old quips, he joined in the amusement that they afforded. But to do so was not a real indication of his feeling. What should a poet and a man of the world do when people persisted in the ridicule of one of his valued poems?

Sordello was not always to be the object of derision, as later chapters will show. A sonnet by one of the most enthusiastic of its partisans closes the present discussion. It was written in D. G. Rossetti's hand at the end of a copy of the first edition of the poem.[54]

SONNET ON A FIRST READING OF "SORDELLO"

"Sordello's story," (the Sphinx yawned and said.)
"Who would has heard." Is this enough? Who could,
('Twere not amiss to add.) has understood, —
Who understood, perhaps has profited.
For my part, I might tell a tale, instead.
Of one who, dreaming of no likelihood
Even that the book was going to stop for good,
Turned the last leaf — and lo! The book was read.
Now shame on thee, weak soul of mine! With hand
Guarding thy gathered brows, thou peerest at
A perfect Image built into the Sun,
And say'st " 'Tis small and dim." Nay, 'tis too grand
With height and sunshine: and because of that,
Fools scoff. But will thou too be such an one?

D. G. R.

In future years there were to be readers who instead of scoffing would recognize the significance of the poem.

CHAPTER V

Appeal to a Pit-Audience

Pippa Passes, 1841

*S*ordello was published during the first week of March 1840. At the end of the volume, three works were announced as nearly ready — *Pippa Passes, King Victor and King Charles,* and *Mansoor the Hierophant* (later called *The Return of the Druses*). These were to be No. I, No. II, and No. IV of eight pamphlets that came out from 1841 to 1846 under the title of *Bells and Pomegranates.* Besides the three works announced at the end of *Sordello,* the series eventually included two collections of short poems — *Dramatic Lyrics* (III) and *Dramatic Romances and Lyrics* (VII); and four plays — *A Blot in the 'Scutcheon* (V), *Colombe's Birthday* (VI), and *Luria* and *A Soul's Tragedy* (VIII).

In the late spring or early summer of 1839, after Browning had done an indeterminate amount of work on *King Victor* and the *Druses* and had completed but not published Sordello, he probably wrote *Pippa Passes.* In March of 1840 he referred to it in a letter to Eliza Flower: "By the way, you speak of *Pippa.* . . . The Lyrics *want* your music — five or six in all — how say you?" [1] *Pippa* was not to be published for a year. During the rest of 1840 Browning was giving his attention to plays intended for the stage. As we shall see in the following chapter, he was disappointed in his plans for their production. For the time being they remained unpublished and he decided to bring out *Pippa Passes.* He approached Moxon, who might well have demurred at the idea of accepting the poem, for after rejecting *Paracelsus* he had published the unfortunate *Sordello* in 1840.

99

Browning tried to see Moxon early in 1841, at first unsuccessfully: ". . . I called for the purpose of begging your advice about a work of mine I want to publish. . . ."[2] As he continued his letter he adroitly used his family's recent move to New Cross as an excuse to set a time for seeing him:

> . . . I have removed, you must know, deeper into Uninhabitableness than Camberwell even, and may call on and miss you, therefore, next week as this: do I draw too largely on your kindness if I say I shall be in Town on Wednesday — and at Dover St by 1. o*clock*? Of course you wouldnot [for "would not"] dream of setting aside the least important engagement you may happen to have for that hour. — but if this mention of my purpose should merely postpone a ride or walk for a few minutes, it will greatly oblige
>
> Yours very truly,
> Robert Browning.

When publisher and poet met, whether or not shortly after Browning's letter, Moxon was mindful of the cost of *Paracelsus* and *Sordello* to Browning's father. He told the young poet, who was determined to keep trying to attract readers, about an inexpensive edition of Elizabethan dramatists that he was publishing.[3] Browning at once grasped the possibility of bringing out his own works in the form of cheap pamphlets, and an agreement was made. His father was to assume the cost, which turned out to be approximately £16 for each number of *Bells and Pomegranates;* this low cost was made possible by fine print, double columns, and paper wrappers. *Pippa Passes* sold for sixpence. The confusing title *Bells and Pomegranates* for the series of eight works was suggested by the bells and pomegranates in Exodus 28: 33–4, which, as Browning later explained to Elizabeth, were symbolical of "Pleasure and Profit, the Gay & the Grave, the Poetry & the Prose, Singing and Sermonizing."[4]

Pippa Passes was published in April 1841; it was dedicated to Talfourd.[5] Eight reviews appeared in a stretch of eight months, the first in the *Spectator* on April 17 and three in May. In slow succession other reviews followed until the end of the year, the last one in the *Athenaeum* on December 11.

When the critics turned to the title page, they found the following: Bells and Pomegranates. / No. I. — *Pippa Passes.* / By Robert Browning, / Author of "Paracelsus." / London: / Edward Moxon, Dover Street. / MDCCCXLI. Then they turned to the Advertisement on page 2 and read:

Two or three years ago I wrote a Play, about which the chief matter I much care to recollect at present is, that a Pit-full of goodnatured people applauded it: — ever since, I have been desirous of doing something in the same way that should better reward their attention. What follows I mean for the first of a series of Dramatical Pieces, to come out at intervals, and I amuse myself by fancying that the cheap mode in which they appear will for once help me to a sort of Pit-audience again. Of course such a work must go on no longer than it is liked. . . .

The "No. I" on the title page in conjunction with "doing something in the same way" as *Strafford* and "the first of a series of Dramatical Pieces" in the Advertisement got the early critics off on the wrong foot.

The difficulty shows up in the one-paragraph notice in the *Spectator*. *Pippa Passes* was considered as only part of a work. "Allowance is to be made for every first number; especially when it exhibits only part of a play, and that part of necessity the least stirring in its action and the least interesting from its passion." The critic did not think Browning's scheme likely to succeed unless the mode of execution was changed. What he saw was "not a drama, but scenes in dialogue, without coherence or action; not devoid of good thoughts poetically expressed, but perfectly ineffective from being in a wrong place." The irony of the review was that while the critic charged Browning with lack of coherence in *Pippa Passes,* he saw how Pippa provides the connection between the four episodes. The title, he said, "apparently means that Pippa, the heroine, only *passes* over the stage, talking to herself, and stimulating the conduct of others by her appearance." The review ended with disapproval of the moral tone of the Ottima-Sebald scene, of the scene of the courtesans, and of the scene in the last of the poem with the planned prostitution. Such a tone, said the critic (who was writing for a paper that was often read aloud in the family circle), was not likely to be accepted on or off the stage.

Two of the three reviews that appeared in May were in monthlies — a paragraph in the *Metropolitan Magazine* and a longer criticism in the *Monthly Review*. The reviewer for the *Metropolitan* was puzzled. Was the poem a fragment or was it complete? Was it an "exhibition of great power, merely to show that the power is possessed, the curvettings and prancings of a stately war-horse, which advance him nothing?" The critic would have to wait for the second part to see how the work was allied to its title. All was mystery, but he found the poem "full of snatches of the most beautiful poetry, mystical and impassioned. . . ."

Even the sympathetic critic for the *Monthly Review* was confused. He opened his discussion by wishing that the experiment of the cheap form to get readers would be successful; the poet, "who, with high poetic endowments, and a fervent desire to influence through his art the thoughts, feelings and characters of his fellow men," wrote in gloomy days for poetry, when few stopped to read it. This critic gave his readers a better notion of *Pippa Passes* than did the one for the *Spectator*. He introduced Pippa, who worked in the silk-mills, as she was anticipating her one holiday of the year and designated the four scenes of the poem and the characters in each who were influenced by Pippa's song. He saw that the scenes were connected "by the agency of the silk-girl," whose songs produced "the climax of each scene." Her passings were the "moving causes of effects incalculable." But he, too, did not think that the poem was complete in itself; he said it would readily be seen from his analysis that it was fragmentary. Perhaps the consciousness of this, he said, reacted on the author's mind and caused obscurity that was offensive in some parts of the poem, particularly in the scene of Jules and Phene. To show that the kinds of poetical imperfections that he designated were the result of lack of care, not inability, he quoted passages of merit. These included the lines from the Ottima-Sebald scene that were often to be quoted and praised, beginning, "Buried in woods we lay. . . ." The review ended with thanks to Browning for what he had already done and with anticipation of better work.

The *Atlas* carried the third review in May, and, like the others, it showed the confusion of the early critics. The reviewer went so far as to recognize *Pippa Passes* as a work "dramatic in form, and poetical in treatment," which he saw as sequential to *Paracelsus* and *Strafford;* Browning was making an effort to sustain the reputation he had acquired by each. The critic thought of *Pippa Passes* as the first part of a work with an incomprehensible title, and it was likely to produce a pit-audience that would get sulky and hiss: ". . . the whole affair, from beginning to end, as far as this first part proceeds, is a chaos of speeches, dialogues, and figures, in which we can discover neither coherency nor positive meaning." The reviewer commented on Pippa's passings and on Ottima and Sebald as they talked of the murder, yet so deficient did he find the poem in "unity, action, and human character" that he did not think it difficult to foresee the issue of the experiment unless unexpected interest was developed in the ensuing parts. Though he was incapable of comprehending the originality of the poem and wished some passages to be more intelligible, he praised others. The tone of impatience at the first of the review, where the critic emphasized his incomprehension of both plan and title, disappeared when he turned to long individual passages, which he showed no difficulty in understanding. He quoted one-third of the Ottima-Sebald scene and Pippa's song beginning, "A king lived long ago . . ." and ended on a note of praise.

A short discussion appeared in *Tait's Edinburgh Magazine* in June. The critic stated that *Pippa Passes* was the first part of a dramatic poem with an obscure title, which seems to mean that the heroine passes before the readers, many of whom might imagine that it refers to "some new-fangled flourishes in the noble art of self-defence." After flippantly underscoring "the danger of an affected or equivocal title," the critic concluded with a vague generalization. "The opening of the poem promises well, and contains some beautiful poetry, imbued with the philosophy conspicuous in *Paracelsus*.

Thus far the critics had not been of much help to Browning. Only the critic for the *Monthly Review* had shown any comprehension of the content of *Pippa Passes*, and he thought the poem fragmentary. Not until three months after publication was there encouragement in the reviews. The author of the criticism that appeared in the *Morning Herald* on July 10 was not disturbed by the title page. The poem under its "piquant and poetic designation" promised to be one of the "most remarkable of the day." Pippa, seemingly, was intended "to bring into something of unity four different actions with different *dramatis personae*, which, in this libretto, are thrown into juxtaposition." Her songs came "home with a touching significance to their feelings." The *Morning Herald* went beyond the *Monthly Review*. For one thing, it was the first to comment at all on Browning's treatment of character in *Pippa Passes*. The *Monthly Review* had done little more than name the characters; the *Morning Herald* gave some indication, slight though it was, of Browning's artistry in character representation: "highly dramatic, glowing with strong and original conception, and combining the darker and more gentle passions in vigorous contrast." It also saw *Pippa Passes* as a completed work, a "masterly and singular dramatic composition" instead of only a fragment. The scenes had a certain "waywardness of tone," which occasionally tended to obscurity, but they also had "abundant compensating contributions of genuine poetry."

The *Examiner,* which had not reviewed *Sordello,* had nothing about *Pippa Passes* until October 2. After briefly discussing *Sordello,* Forster carried his discussion of *Pippa Passes* through more than three of the long columns of the *Examiner.* Favorable remarks were accompanied by generous quoting. *Pippa Passes,* a "piece of right inspiration," was worthy of the author of *Paracelsus.* Forster thought that the transitions between the four parts were fine and that the poem's highest beauty was lyrical. He gave praise that foreshadowed his later attention to Browning's skill in adapting his verse to the particular occasion. The "rich variety of verse, embodying the nicest shades of poetical and musical rhythm, flows in a full tide of harmony with each lightest change of sentiment." After indicating the contents, he stated his interpretation of the poem's message.

> It is to inculcate the faith in higher than mere actual things: it is to encourage the hope that all who do rightly and cheerfully what duty they are called to, however humble, may aspire to their share of influence on the whole great scheme of the world: it is to express the truth that, at once encircling the meanest and the greatest, there is a fulness of divine life which acts upon our own existence, to be made suddenly visible or sensible by the lightest thing; and that all, even when the greatest contraries appear to be at work, is yet, to the mind of thoughtful insight, interdependent and harmonious.

It seemed to Forster that the conception had "extraordinary beauty"; the defect in the execution of the work lay in the scene of the young sculptor and his bride, a scene that the *Monthly Review* had objected to. He noted the "clear and manly prose" in the student scene and the intensity of the Ottima-Sebald scene.

The review of *Pippa Passes* in the Athenaeum showed clearly the unfortunate effect of *Sordello.* It was written by T. K. Hervey, who had reviewed *Sordello* and given more evidence than any of the other critics of making an effort to understand the poem. His review of *Pippa Passes* had a long introductory paragraph of irritable denouncement. He said that he had "taken more than common pains" to understand Browning — perhaps more trouble than the poet would prove to be worth — because of his "air of originality" and "apparent disposition to *think.*" His faith in Browning remained, said Hervey, but his patience was lost: even though more familiar with Browning's manner, he found his writing to be almost as obscure as ever, yet admitted getting "a glimpse, every now and then, at meanings which it might have been well worth his while to put into English." Hervey's earlier warning against obscurity, given in the review of *Sordello,* was repeated: "We have already warned Mr. Browning that no amount of genius can fling any lights from under the bushel of his affectations."

The title page of the new poem was an irritant. Hervey gave up on the general title "Bells and Pomegranates"; he considered the title "Pippa Passes" a "very pretty exercise of the reader's ingenuity," which he ventured to say he had succeeded in solving. Unlike most of the other critics, he saw *Pippa Passes* as the first entire work in a series of dramatical pieces. Like the critic for the *Atlas,* he was scornful of Browning's fancy that the cheap form would attract a pit-audience, for it was not at all likely that such an audience would be willing to hunt for deliberately concealed treasures. Because of Browning's statement in the Advertisement that "such a work [as this] must go on no longer than it is liked," Hervey spoke with the "reverence and forbearance which one is accustomed to exercise towards the dead."

While Hervey was severe in his discussion of Browning's obscure manner of writing, he was liberal in his praise of the thought expressed in *Pippa Passes.* The last sentence of the irritable introductory paragraph turned attention away from his objections to the poem and to what he considered its beauty and immortal spirit. The "idea," he said, was remarkably beautiful and well worth being worked out in language suitable to its simple and healthy moral. He gave a partial summary of the poem, commented on its plan, explained that it was dramatic because it was in dialogue form, singled out the Ottima-Sebald scene for praise, and placed most stress on the element of thought. With no unity of action, the poem was held together by the "single unity of its moral." Pippa influenced the characters guilty of corruption, of intrigue and passion, "carrying everywhere her moral that 'God's in his heaven,' and the world beneath his eye — scattering sophisms and startling crime." As Hervey continued to emphasize the value of the thought, he noted the originality of its presentation. "Not only have we the trite, but valuable, moral that happiness is more evenly distributed than it seems, enforced in a new form, — but also that other and less popularly understood one . . . that the meanest . . . has his appointed value in God's scheme. . . ." But even in his appreciation he could not resist jabs at Browning's making mummies of his living thoughts and forcing his readers to unwrap them. When he admitted that he found beauties in the poem he talked of the obscurities that soon appeared, and when he quoted he said he was choosing examples most unencumbered by faults. It was difficult for the critic to give unqualified praise. His objections might have been valid for *Sordello,* but not for *Pippa Passes.*

Merely to indicate the obtuseness of those who did not understand and appreciate *Pippa Passes,* as has been done, is not sufficient for a full and fair comprehension of the critical situation. That comes primarily from seeing the whole picture of the poem and its presentation and examining the reception in its broader significance. The reviews reflected tendencies pointed out in the discussion of *Paracelsus.* As with that poem, the unfavorable criticism came principally in the earliest reviews of *Pippa* (here they were not all in weeklies as they were following the publication of *Paracelsus*); the critics of both works were handicapped in being the first to review a work of originality, and Browning's introductory paraphernalia hindered rather than helped their grasp of the poem. The later reviewers were more perceptive; they showed the benefit of a lapse of time between the publication and the reviewing. In the reviews of *Paracelsus* some critics were calling attention to techniques without realizing their significance; two critics of *Pippa Passes* commented on the passings of Pippa, yet saw no unity or coherence in the work.

Another common feature of the reception of *Paracelsus* and *Pippa Passes* was praise for Browning as a poet by those who did not understand or appreciate the work before them. Along with the unfavorable as well as the favorable commentaries came recognition of Browning's poetical ability in *Pippa Passes:* "not devoid of good thoughts poetically expressed" *(Spectator);* "full of snatches of the most beautiful poetry" *(Metropolitan Magazine);* "high poetic endowments" *(Monthly Review);* "some highly poetical passages," some "replete with that wild and fanciful beauty which Mr. Browning pours out so richly into his productions," "ripe spirit of poetry" *(Atlas);* "limbs and lineaments of beauty" and "traces of an immortal spirit" *(Athenaeum).*

The bad effect of miscomprehension on the mood of the reviewers was a foreboding of the future when originality would again merit sympathetic consideration but be received with confusion and irritation. Often, as with the reviewer for the *Atlas,* the less a critic understood what was new to him, the more positive and quarrelsome was his expression of disapproval. The last part of this review — where the critic was not writing about an unfamiliar dramatic form — was entirely different in tone. The critic for the *Athenaeum,* positive in his denunciation of obscurity, was typical of many reviewers who transferred this accusation from one poem to another without an unbiased examination of the new work; Hervey saw in *Pippa* the same difficulties that confronted the readers of *Sordello*.

It is easy to point out the blindness and querulousness of the critics. It is fairer to look further. The disadvantageous effect of the title and the Advertisement has been pointed out. We should also recognize the difficulty of evaluating original genius at work. For example, let us take the Jules-Phene scene, which troubled two critics. Park Honan, in *Browning's Characters* has shown how this scene indicated progress in the development of Browning's dramatic monologue. The employment of diction, syntax, and imagery appropriate to Jules and Phene are evidence of an improved portrayal of character.[6] In writing of this part of the poem, the *Examiner* and the *Monthly Review* objected to the language and apparently to the sentences also. The language was, said Forster, with some exception "fitful and obscure, the thoughts themselves . . . wild and whirling." Unable to see in this part what he recognized in the rest of the poem, he continued, ". . . the very reverse of this, is the general style of the poem: suited to what it has to express. . . ." The critic for the *Monthly Review* also found fault with the language; in objecting to the style of this scene he was more specific than any other critic. "The very language seems in places fragmentary and enigmatical, not merely from the abstruseness of the thoughts it embodies, but from its own mechanical imperfection. In the lyric parts the ear is often pained by the involved and difficult construction of the words, the awkward breaks, and misplaced pauses." We should not judge the early critics of *Pippa Passes* too severely for not seeing what a first-rate critic of today has pointed out.

In another area, credit is due the critics. They considered the scene between Ottima and Sebald praiseworthy. Lounsbury's statement that it "awakened an occasional protest" and "profoundly outraged" the moral feelings of some of the critics[7] is too sweeping. Of the periodicals with reviews discussed by Lounsbury, as well as the additional ones considered here, only the *Spectator* found this part of the poem offensive morally; the *Athenaeum* thought the public would find it so; the critic himself found it "written with such power of passion and of painting . . . as marks a master-hand." Three praised it, including the *Atlas* (Lounsbury ignored this praise in demonstrating the obtuseness of the reviewer), which quoted almost a hundred lines and said there was "power" and "vivid dramatic truth" in it in spite of the obscurity of its diction. The critic for the *Monthly Review* was impressed by the scene and quoted a "vigorous passage." Forster said the intensity and sensual extravagance issued rightly from the "drunken deed of passion and of blood."

If the reaction of the critics of *Pippa Passes* was generally one of bewilderment sometimes relieved by recognition of Browning's poetic ability, how did the nonprofessional readers fare? At least two of them valued the poem sufficiently to record their impatience with the blindness of the critics. Domett wrote a poetic attack, which was later published in his *Flotsam and Jetsam* under the title *Lines Sent to Robert Browning, 1841, on a Certain Critique on 'Pippa Passes.'* It included the following:

> A black squat Beetle, potent for his size,
> Pushing tail-first by every road that's wrong,
> The dirt-ball of his musty rules along —
> His tiny sphere of grovelling sympathies, —
> Has knocked himself full-butt with blundering trouble
> Against a Mountain he can neither double
> Nor ever hope to scale. So, like a free,
> Pert, self-complacent Scarabæus, he
> Takes it into his horny head to swear —
> There's no such thing as any mountain there![8]

In a letter to Mary Russell Mitford, Miss Barrett chided the *Athenaeum* for its criticism of *Pippa Passes:*

> Mr. Browning deserved better than that light, half jocose, pitifully jocose, downward accent of critical rallying — 'Forsooth they are almost tired of him! and yet he has some good stuff — but they have almost lost their sublime critical patience!!' Why what if he did mouth in his speaking, — was there nothing worth reverence in his speech? — worth a critic's reverence — or a world's! I would not speak so of Mr. Browning in a whisper — I would not dare — even to myself.[9]

It should be noted that the poetic outburst was produced by a friend of Browning's and that Elizabeth's comment to Miss Mitford, written in January of 1842, did not represent her initial reaction. Her first comment on *Pippa Passes* to Miss Mitford was written in July of the preceding year.

> But really 'Pippa passes', I must say, Mr. Browning's ordinary measure of mystery. Now laugh at me. Laugh, as you please. I like, I do like the 'heart of a mystery' when it beats moderate time. I like a

twilight of mysticism — when the sun and moon both shine together. Yes — and I like 'Pippa' too. There are fine things in it —
and the presence of genius, never to be denied! At the same time it is
hard . . *to understand* — isn't it? Too hard? I think so! And the fault
of Paracelsus, — the defect in harmony, is here too. After all,
Browning is a true poet — and there are not many such poets — and
if any critics *have,* as your critical friend wrote to you, 'flattered him
into a wilderness and left him' they left him alone with his *genius,* —
and where those two are, despair cannot be. The wilderness will
blossom soon, with a brighter rose than 'Pippa'. In the meanwhile
what do you think of *her?* Was there any need for so much coarseness? Surely not. But the genius — the genius — it is undeniable —
isn't it? [10]

The immediate effect of the poem upon Miss Barrett was pretty much
like its effect upon the critics: she had difficulty in understanding it.
She recognized fine things in it and the presence of genius and persisted in her efforts to understand the poem. The next day she was
writing Miss Mitford again about *Pippa,* this time with a difference:

> But I must tell you . . . I read it three times — in correspondance
> [*sic*] with Mr. Chorley's four — and in testimony both to the genius
> and the obscurity. Nobody should complain of being forced to read
> it three or four or ten times. Only they would do it more gratefully
> if they were not forced. I who am used to mysteries, caught the light
> at my second reading — but the full glory, not until the third. The
> conception of the whole is fine, very fine — and there are noble,
> beautiful things everywhere to be broken up and looked at. That
> great tragic scene, which you call 'exquisite' — and which pants
> again with its own power! [11]

It took a second reading for Elizabeth to catch the light and a
third to see the "full glory" of *Pippa Passes.* The professional critics
hardly had the time or inclination to persevere with a poem by the author of *Strafford* and *Sordello,* even if they recalled their expectations for
Browning after reading *Paracelsus.*

Elizabeth was well read in the literary works of her contemporaries, and she was a great admirer of Browning and Tennyson. It is not
surprising that after a study of *Pippa Passes* she became and remained
one of its most ardent supporters. She rose to Browning's defense in
two letters to Miss Mitford in October of 1842. In one she set Browning beside another writer of the time:

Ah — you speak more severely of Mr. Browning, than I can say 'Amen' to. Amen would stick in my throat — even suppose it to rise so high. There is a unity and nobleness of conception in 'Pippa passes' which seems to me to outweigh all the riddles in riddledom — and verily a great many 'lie hid' in that same 'Pippa'. Give me my choice, — only give me my choice, between Mr. Milnes's genius and Mr. Browning's, and you will see if I dont take the last and say 'thank you'. . . . Pippa, dark as she is, is worth all those rhymes you speak of — in my eyes, not blinded by friendship. [12]

Elizabeth wrote to Miss Mitford about *Pippa* several years before she started her correspondence with Browning. In the first letters she and Browning exchanged, they wrote much about their works, and it was not long before she told him that she could find it in her heart to covet the authorship of *Pippa Passes,* and in a later letter to him she classified the poem as one of the masterpieces of the world. [13] She also praised it to Thomas Westwood: ". . . 'Pippa Passes' I lean to, or kneel to, with the deepest reverence." [14]

The alertness of Domett and Miss Barrett to Browning's poetic accomplishment was shared only to a very limited extent by Miss Mitford and Eliza Flower and apparently not at all by Carlyle. If we judge from Miss Barrett's defense, Miss Mitford must have criticized *Pippa* rather severely, though she did call the Ottima-Sebald scene "exquisite." Eliza, who along with her sister had praised Browning's boyish verse and who had persuaded Fox to read his *Incondita,* had become less enthusiastic by the time of the first *Bell.* With *Pippa* in mind she wrote to a friend:

I send you *Bells and Pomegranates,* not because you will like the thing any more than I do, but because you won't like it less than I do. It is just like *his way.* This time he has got an exquisite subject, most exquisite, and it seemed so easy for a poet to handle. Yet here comes one of those fatal ifs, the egoism of the man, and the pity of it. He cannot metempsychose with his creatures, they are so many Robert Brownings. Still there are superb parts, the very last is quite lovely. But *puppets,* what a false word to use, as if God worked by puppets as well as Robert Browning! [15]

As the preceding chapter indicated, Carlyle lumped *Pippa* with *Sordello,* seeing them both as evidence of poetical endowment not yet unfolded into "articulate clearness" and gave Browning advice that he so often gave to poets, "If your own choice happened to point that way,

I for one should hail it as a good omen that your next work were written in prose!" He added, "Not that I deny you poetic faculty; far, very far from that."[16] Some other earlier supporters of Browning had given up. Others were for the present standing by — silent. But *Pippa Passes* would find its way and not too slowly.

In writing *Pippa* Browning no longer felt the urgency to write poems that provided him with a medium for considering the direction of his own life. Nor was he inclined to consider the demands of the stage, for which he had already written two plays *(Strafford* and *King Victor)* and started another (the *Druses).* He chose a simple plan that unified four dramatic scenes. In each Pippa's song served as the motivating force at a crucial moment in the lives of the characters. He had walked out of his father's library into Dulwich Wood and there the idea for *Pippa Passes* came to him. Instead of drawing on an earlier historical period, as he had done in *Paracelsus, Strafford,* and *Sordello,* he depended on firsthand observation of contemporary life and the setting of Asolo. He included lyrics, doubtless still remembering Fox's comment in his review of *Pauline* on their desirability, and he achieved clarity of expression, surely keeping in mind criticisms of his obscurity.

In the Advertisement he said that he wanted a pit-audience again and desired to provide a better reward for the "pitfull of goodnatured people" who had applauded *Strafford.* He had already written to Domett, in answer to his friend's complaint of the obscurity of *Sordello,* that he was busy on the plays he had advertised in *Sordello* and that he had his eye on the first row of the pit. The immediate reviews could not have convinced Browning that he had gained the audience he referred to in his Advertisement and in his letter to Domett. After the first criticisms, however, the poem started to gain supporters, and by the end of the forties it had attained a place of favor that it would never lose. When Elizabeth at the beginning of their correspondence expressed her great admiration of the poem, Browning admitted his own preference for it; he liked it better than anything else he had written, he said. Yet a little later, in summing up his feelings toward the whole of his work after his last *Bell* was published, he made no specific mention of it or any other work. As we shall see, he considered all that he had done as experimental; *Pippa Passes* and his other works served merely as preparation for better things to come.

CHAPTER VI

Two Plays Rejected and Poems for Popularity's Sake

King Victor and King Charles, 1842;
Dramatic Lyrics, 1842; *The Return of the Druses,* 1843

Within two years after *Pippa Passes* was published four more numbers of *Bells and Pomegranates* appeared: *King Victor and King Charles* (No. II) in March and *Dramatic Lyrics* (No. III) in November of 1842, followed by *The Return of the Druses* (No. IV) in January and *A Blot in the 'Scutcheon* (No. V, introduced here and fully discussed in the next two chapters) in February of 1843. In an account of the development of Browning's reputation the order in which his works were published is of basic importance, but the order in which they were written is also important because it brings out the complexity of his literary life. The short poems in *Dramatic Lyrics* were composed between 1834 or 1836 and 1842, and the three plays just named were completed before the publication of *Pippa Passes* in 1841.[1] Browning wrote the plays with the hope that they would be performed by Macready, and the history of his writing them and of his efforts to get them accepted and performed shows how much he was obsessed with playwriting, how desperately he wanted and tried to reach the public, and how his youthful confidence moved him to persist in his attempts in spite of repeated failures. His works, along with his comments, demonstrate his natural leaning toward a kind of character revelation that was unsuitable to the stage but greatly important in the development of his genius.

This chapter starts with a reversion to the time of *Strafford* in order to show the continuance of Browning's efforts at playwriting, which were interspersed with the composition and publication of his

112

poems. Whether or not he turned back to the neglected *Sordello* immediately after the performances of *Strafford* in the first part of May 1837, from his discussions with Macready and Forster we have seen that he still had his mind on the play during most of that month. By June he must have been seriously at work on *Sordello* again, but entries in Macready's *Diaries* for this month show that Browning did not lose touch with Forster and Macready. Then after the frustrating setback in his work on *Sordello* because of the publication in July of Mrs. Busk's poem on the same figure, he again turned his thoughts toward the stage in spite of his earlier vow that he would not write another play. A letter sent to Fanny Haworth about August 1 shows that two plays were taking shape in his mind, *King Victor and King Charles* and *The Return of the Druses*, which he first called *Mansoor the Hierophant*.

> I am going to begin the finishing Sordello — and to begin thinking about a Tragedy (an Historical one, so I shall want heaps of criticisms on "Strafford") — and I want to have *another* Tragedy in prospect, I write best so provided; I had chosen a splendid subject for it, when I learned that a magazine for next, *this* month, will have a *scene* founded on my story: vulgarizing or doing no good to it: and I accordingly throw it up. I want a subject of the most wild and passionate love, to contrast with the one I mean to have ready in a short time: I have many half-conceptions, floating fancies: give me your notion of a thorough self-devotement, self-forgetting; should it be a woman who loves thus, or a man? What circumstances will best draw out, set forth this feeling?[2]

Browning's historical tragedy was *King Victor and King Charles*. He wrote to Miss Haworth of getting it ready "in a short time." Here again, as in the prefatory note to *Paracelsus,* Browning left the impression of being a rapid composer. His expectation of having *King Victor* ready in a short time is reminiscent of the reported completion of *Strafford* within ten days. If Browning did get *King Victor* into final or nearly final form soon after his letter to Miss Haworth, for two years — from 1837 to 1839 — he made no move to submit it to Macready, though he continued to be one of the intimates who visited the actor's dressing room after performances, dined by invitation with him, and was one of six invited in December 1838 to his home to hear the reading of Edward Bulwer Lytton's *Richelieu* and write an opinion of it. During this time he went to Italy, completed *Sordello,* and possibly in the spring or early summer of 1839 wrote *Pippa Passes.*

On August 21, 1839, he tried to find out from Macready what his chances were for the production of another play. Macready recorded the meeting:

> Found Browning at my lodgings on my return, and was kept by him long; but he left me where he found me. His object, if he exactly knew it, was to learn from me whether, if he wrote a really good play, it would have a secure chance of acceptance. I told him certainly, and after much vague conversation, he left me to read and rest as I could.

After this, Browning moved with considerable alacrity in placing his second play in Macready's hands. In two weeks' time Macready had read *King Victor,* which he considered a *"great mistake."* No vagueness clouded his verdict, given on September 5: "I called Browning into my room and most explicitly told him so, and gave him my reasons for coming to such a conclusion." The reasons must not have convinced Browning; on September 20, Forster told Macready "of Browning's intemperance about his play which he read to Fox, Forster, etc." Whatever intemperance Browning had shown, according to Macready he was in control of his feelings when he visited him at the end of September and said "all that sympathy and friendly feeling could suggest."

The verdict on *King Victor* did not discourage Browning from submitting other plays to Macready. On March 7, 1840, *Sordello* was published, and not much time elapsed between its publication and Browning's resumed attempts to get a play produced. He intended to send Macready a copy of *Sordello,* probably on March 7, and with it a letter to herald his next play, *Mansoor the Hierophant,* later called *The Return of the Druses.* It was the play with the subject of a "most wild and passionate love" that he had told Miss Haworth he was looking for. There was not only love in it but action, colorful language, and surprises as well. He indicated to Macready in the letter of March 7 that he had written it with the demands of the stage in mind.

> I have advertised three plays, or attempts at plays, one of which, I think, might succeed on the stage — now the poor but genuine compliment to yourself implied by such a course, was this — all things considered, I had rather publish, that is print — this play, sell a dozen copies, and see the rest quietly shelved — than take the chance of a stage success that would in the highest degree gratify and benefit me, at the *risk* of "mettre du gêne" in a friendship which I trust I know how to appreciate, by compelling you once more to say "No," where you would willingly say "Yes."[3]

But he decided to retain the copy of *Sordello* and the letter announcing the *Druses*. Macready left London on March 8 for an engagement in Bristol, and Browning, with his way of holding on to some of his works for revision, probably decided to give more attention to the play. On March 23 he wrote Domett that he was busy with plays advertised in *Sordello*.[4] They were *Pippa Passes, King Victor,* and *Mansoor the Hierophant* (the *Druses*). On the 29th Macready recorded that Browning brought him a copy of *Sordello;* probably the letter preparing the way for the *Druses* was still with it. Browning, according to Macready, came on May 5 "to speak about his play." Sometime during this month the poet told Miss Haworth he was "in treaty with Macready" and was going to send the play to him. He said he thought it clever but Macready, he added prophetically, would think it stupid.[5]

The *Druses* had a longer probation period than *King Victor*. Macready read it and suggested revisions. Browning wrote him in June that he had "considerably altered" and, he hoped, improved the play; he had followed the advice to make the three acts five.[6] He said he would send the play as soon as possible, but he was unable to bring his revisions to an end as readily as he thought he could. Not until July 31 did he take it to Macready. The actor's first impression was that it *"does not look well."* On August 3 he recorded his general opinion of Browning's writing: "Read Browning's play, and with the deepest concern I yield to the belief that he will *never write again* — to any purpose. I fear his intellect is not quite clear. I do not know how to write to Browning." Browning called on the 12th. When he talked of the *Druses* and of *Sordello,* Macready "most honestly" told him his opinion of both, expressing himself "most anxious" that Browning "should justify the expectations formed of him, but that he could not do so by placing himself in opposition to the world." Macready continued his report of the conversation: "He wished me to have his play done for nothing. I explained to him that Mr. Webster [the manager] *would not* do it. . . ." Macready promised to read the play again, probably to take the edge off his criticism.

By the 23rd Browning learned that the actor had not changed his opinion of the *Druses*. A man with less tenacity of confidence in his work and more restraint of his impulses would have resigned himself to failure. Not so, Browning, who now defended his play in a letter to Macready. This letter leaves no doubt that Browning had worked hard to fashion a character to suit Macready and thereby suit the public.

> . . . to confess a truth, I have worked from the beginning somewhat
> in the spirit of the cucumber-dresser in the old story (the doctor, you
> remember, bids such an one "slice a platefull — salt it, pepper it,
> add oil, vinegar etc etc and then . . throw all behind the fire") —
> spite of this, I *did* rather fancy that you would have "sympathized"
> with Djabert [for Djabal] in the main scenes of my play: and your
> failing to do so is the more decisive against it, that I really had you
> *here,* in this little room of mine, while I wrote bravely away — *here*
> were you, propping the weak, pushing the strong parts (such I
> thought there might be!) — now majestically motionless, and now
> "laying about as busily, as the Amazonian dame Penthesilé" — and
> *here,* please the fates, shall you again and again give breath and blood
> to some thin creation of mine yet unevoked — but *elsewhere — en-*
> *foncé!*[7]

Macready obviously had objected that the audience would not be familiar with the Druses. But Browning did not feel that the play exacted too much effort on the part of the audience any more than he
later felt that the dramatic monologue demanded too much of the
reader, as the critics thought it did. We see Browning's mind at work
in his defense:

> Your other objections I think less material — that the auditory, for
> instance, know nothing of the Druzes and their doings *until I tell*
> *them* (which is the very office I take on myself) that they are men and
> women oppressed and outraged in such and such ways and desirous
> of being rid of their oppressor and outrager: if the auditory thus far
> instructed (and I considered that point sufficiently made out) call for
> a previous acquaintance with the Druzes before they will go along
> with such a desire . . are they not worthy compatriots of the Hyde-
> park gentleman who "could not think of pulling a man out of the
> Serpentine to whom he had not been previously introduced"?

On the 27th, a few days after writing this letter, Browning, as on
the 12th, again spoke to Macready of *Sordello* as well as of the *Druses.*
He "really *wearied*" him "with his obstinate faith in his poem of *Sordello,* and of his eventual celebrity, and also with his self-opinionated
persuasions upon his *Return of the Druses.*" Browning had the confidence of a man following the urge of his genius while the actor feared
he was "for ever gone." His persistency made the situation trying and
awkward for Macready; in the end Browning was "consenting" (Macready's ironic word) to leave the manuscript for another perusal. Macready did read it once more about two weeks later — that is, read what

he could bring himself to read of the "mystical, strange and heavy play of the *Return of the Druses*" — and still could not find it good. He wrote Browning his "reconsidered opinion" (still the same) and Browning came two days later, on September 17, for the manuscript.

Although during one year's time, from September 1839 to September 1840, Macready had rejected two plays (*King Victor* and the *Druses*), Browning was not yet ready to give up the stage. In December 1840 he wrote Macready: ". . . monstrously ambitious thoughts begin to rise like clouds within me!"[8] Macready faced the ordeal of examining the third play since *Strafford* — *A Blot in the 'Scutcheon.* Browning soon sent another letter showing that he had taken Macready's criticisms to heart in an effort to display more action on the stage.

> "The luck of the third adventure" is proverbial. I have written a spick and span new Tragedy (a sort of compromise between my own notion and yours — as I understand it, at least) and will send it to you if you care to be bothered so far. There is *action* in it, drabbing, stabbing, et autres gentillesses, — who knows but the Gods may make me good even yet? Only, make no scruple of saying flatly that you cannot spare the time, if engagements of which I know nothing, but fancy a great deal, should claim every couple of hours in the course of this week.[9]

When *Pippa Passes* was published in April 1841, Macready had *A Blot* in hand. If he accepted it, the play could be published as the second *Bell.* But the months went by and Macready made no move. Browning and Forster, in whose association dissonances arose from time to time, had recently had one of their clashes, but the difficulty had been resolved and Forster was in a helpful mood. Macready recorded on September 26th: "Forster importuned me after dinner to read Browning's tragedy, which I did. He had taken *enough* wine, and was rather exaggerating in his sensibility and praise. I was not prepared, and could not do justice to it in reading."

As Macready did nothing, Browning grew restless. No matter how often he talked of his works to Macready or how strongly he expressed faith in *Sordello* and the *Druses,* he knew it was recognition by others, not his own opinion, that his reputation depended on. *Pippa* had not yet won many readers, and *A Blot* remained unproduced. Browning felt he was losing his tenuous hold on the public. In December 1841 he wrote Miss Haworth that he would print *King Victor* by February.[10] In March 1842 this play that Macready had summarily rejected was published as the second *Bell* — four and a half years after Browning said he would soon have it ready.

The critics were faced with a work that Browning himself considered "a very indifferent substitute" for *A Blot*. They read the Advertisement, in which Browning again introduced a new work to his readers. Not having received general critical approval of his interest in character as stated in the Prefaces to *Paracelsus* and *Strafford*, Browning in his Advertisement to *Pippa Passes* had made an appeal to a "sort of Pit-audience" without bringing in character explicitly. In his Advertisement to *King Victor* he avoided a direct statement concerning his emphasis on character but indicated it subtly. Whereas in the Preface to *Strafford* he had in the first sentence associated the "grand epoch" with his intention to stress character, here he placed the "terrible event" and its historical background in the initial spotlight.

So far as I know, this Tragedy is the first artistical consequence of what Voltaire termed "a terrible event without consequences;" and although it professes to be historical, I have taken more pains to arrive at the history than most readers would thank me for particularizing. . . .

In other words, the play was based on an actual event and professed to be historical; Browning took pains to establish the history involved, but spared his readers the particulars. After indicating a few sources, the details of which he supposed they did not care to learn, he summarized what he considered essential for them to know — the characteristics of each of the major participants in the tragedy. Thus the train of thought in the Advertisement moved from "a terrible event" — that is, an action — to character, Browning's principal interest.

Before taking up the reviews of *King Victor*, we should note that Browning also moved from plot to character, or soul states, in his remarks on the *Druses* in his letter to Fanny Haworth of August 1837, quoted above. He first said to Miss Haworth that he wanted "a subject of the most wild and passionate love," and then asked her, "What circumstances will best draw out, set forth this feeling?" Park Honan has said of this passage, "It is clear that Browning once again is interested not primarily in the representation of an action but in the depiction of a state of being."[11] The "circumstances" of the letter and the "terrible event" of the Advertisement would both function as a means of revealing character. In Browning's statements they led up to character, his main concern.

The critics of *King Victor* saw that character assumed more importance than events. Within four and a half months five reviews of *King Victor and King Charles* appeared, about a month apart — four in weeklies and the other in a monthly. The first was the one in the *Spectator* on March 5. After giving a summary, the reviewer discussed the characters as they existed in history and as they were presented in the play. Examination of the play left an unfavorable impression: "To the character of a drama *King Victor and King Charles* has no pretension, scarcely to that of a modern dramatic poem." It was "a Dialogue of the Dead in blank verse" with the defect "that, presenting results without the reasons on which they are founded, and very often in an allusive and mystical way, it will not convince those who are acquainted with the period and will be unintelligible to all others." If considered as a poem, the critic thought, it had "some passages of a quaint and peculiar beauty or power." The whole, however, caused him to regret that Browning persisted in misusing his ability; he appeared to be a man who cultivated his weeds rather than his flowers.

Forster, who had welcomed the dramatic genius of a new poet when *Paracelsus* was published and had, like others, tried to place *Strafford* in a good light, was now faced with reviewing *King Victor and King Charles*. He knew Macready's opinion of Browning's plays and the impasse that the actor and the dramatist had reached. On the other hand he considered himself Browning's champion, in spite of ups and downs in their personal relationship. In his review in the *Examiner* of April 2 he still expressed confidence in Browning's ability to write a successful play, but, like the critic for the *Spectator,* Forster felt impatience with him for the "wayward perverseness of a man of true genius." His view of the historical events and characters as set over against the use made of them in the play took up much of the space in the review. What Forster did not like about the characterization resulted from "the love of a too decisive contrast" — an error common among the best of young poets, he said. He saw two general faults in the play: its defects of versification as a poem and the "substitution of the metaphysics of character and passion for their broad and practical results" in a dramatic work. Forster was to comment on versification and character analysis as he reviewed future works. Turning from the faults that he found in the play, he said that the reward came in the "many beautiful, powerful, and pathetic passages." He quoted several to illustrate the character of King Victor, whom Browning had best depicted, and one extract to show Browning's dramatic faculty. The review ended on a hopeful note: "Sooner or later — unless he defers it till too late! — Mr. Browning will write an entirely worthy, manly, and well matured dramatic work. It is *in* him, and ought to be *out*."

Though the review of *Pippa Passes* (Dec. 11, 1841) and the one of *King Victor* (Apr. 30, 1842) in the *Athenaeum* probably were not written by the same critic, they both began with a prefatory sermon delivered from a position of critical authority commonly assumed in the nineteenth century. After a derogatory reference to the "whimsical title of 'Bells and Pomegranates,' " the reviewer said that his prediction of a limited audience for Browning was fulfilled since the price of admission had been doubled. "If such be the case, even in the teeth of our infallibility, we regret it, for we have faith in Mr. Browning, and trust to see him realize a higher destiny than that of the thousand and one claimants to the laurel crown."

At this point the reviewer dropped his tone of condescension. The "highly dramatic" plot was worked out with skill, and the characters were drawn with "breadth and great distinctness of colouring." The critic then introduced the characters, who, he thought, were "pictured with unity and vigour." But Browning allowed "his manner to interpose between his own fine conceptions and the public." His poems indicated an author possessing thought, learning, and fancy; they also showed him as "cumbered, rather than strengthened by the number of his possessions." Going again from protest to praise, the critic quoted long self-revelatory speeches by the principal characters; these passages, he said, did credit to Browning. According to the conclusion of the review, the play might give the author a "little popularity among the many," but it would "confirm the few in their anxiety to see him take 'the one step more' out of the labyrinth in which he lingers too fondly."

The *Metropolitan Magazine*, in its June issue, had nothing but praise for *King Victor*. Browning had portrayed the characters with "considerable truth and accuracy"; the sketch of them in the review was in keeping with Browning's brief descriptions in his Advertisement preceding the play. The character of Polyxena, "singularly beautiful," received most praise; she was "one of the most admirable creations of the feminine character that could well have been imagined." The plot was "simple, and yet powerful" and the dialogue "highly characteristic, tender, poignant, sarcastic" as occasion required, "always energetic, and expressive of the passion or purpose of the speaker."

The *Atlas* carried a review on July 16. The critic confessed that he had made little headway with the play. Except for "two very strongly-contrasted personages moving through the tessellated dialogue" all was "palpable obscurity." The critic had expressed his objection to the title of the series in his review of *Pippa Passes*. He repeated it here with more irritation. "The title, to say the least of it, is utterly unintelligible. Bells and pomegranates! Pips and grasshoppers! Mr. BROWNING has high poetical powers; — why does he waste them in these silly vanities?"

The critic for the *Atlas* had apparently made little or no effort to read *King Victor and King Charles*, but the other four critics had read it and Browning's Advertisement as well. Unlike the reviewers of *Strafford*, these expressed little objection to Browning's conception of the historical personages. They did object, however, to the lack of action. They saw Browning's primary interest in character but the external working out that would bring the stage figures to life was lacking. Good passages were there; but these alone would not make good drama. Only the *Metropolitan Magazine* did not complain about what Forster called the "metaphysics of character" without theatrical action. Most critics agreed that Browning had shown ability; that he did not fulfill his potentialities led to one conclusion — he was perverse. The play has never been considered any more praiseworthy than it was at the time of publication; in fact, few critics have taken the trouble to give it serious attention.

John Kenyon's report to Elizabeth Barrett at the end of March 1842 that Browning was "a little discouraged by his reception with the public"[12] was surely an understatement. The appearance of only one review of *King Victor* in March, the month in which it was published, intensified Browning's feeling of frustration as the result of Macready's rejections and the recent paucity of favorable reviews. The future held no immediate relief from his professional disappointments. While the unpromising reviews of *King Victor* were appearing from March to July of 1842, Macready still made no move concerning *A Blot*, which he had kept by him a year or more. In April 1842 Browning wrote him in an effort to get some definite action. He began his letter in his customarily tactful manner by referring to Macready's professional situation and saying that he wished to cause him no trouble and would acquiesce in whatever decision he recommended. Browning then presented his own situation:

> But, here is my case — that quiet, generally-intelligible, and (for me!) popular sort of thing, was to have been my *Second Number* of

Plays — on your being gracious to it, I delayed issuing any farther
attempts for nearly a year — and now have published a very indifferent substitute, whose success will be problematical enough. I have
nothing by me at all fit to be substituted for the work in your hands.
Will you have the kindness to say if I am mistaken in my conjecture
as to your intentions? — And if you will at all object to my withdrawing it, in that case, and printing it at once — the booksellers'
season being no[w] in the prime?[13]

Several things are clear from the letter: Browning had been sob-
ered by his frustrations though his manner was still artful; in writing
the play, he had made an effort to be clear and he had considered popular taste; he appeared to think that Macready had given him some sort
of encouragement about the production of *A Blot;* his excuse for getting his play back — to have something fit to publish — was a pretext
for forcing Macready's hand (Browning had the still-unpublished
Druses), and, if that was impossible, to recover the manuscript.

In a letter of May 22 to Domett, Browning referred to Macready's
answer, which he had received about May 1: ". . . a couple of days
after you left, I got a note from Macready — the disastrous issue of the
play you saw of Darley's brother, had frightened him into shutting the
house earlier than he had meant. Nothing new this season, therefore,
but next, &c., &c., &c. So runs this idle life away, while you are working!" With Macready's commitment still suspended and two plays already rejected (one of them published and poorly received), Browning's
hardiness suffered: "At present, I don't know if I stand on head or
heels: what men require, I don't know — and of what they are in possession know nearly as little."[14] So ardently at this time did he want
acceptance of his plays that it seemed he would find the highest degree
of satisfaction in Macready's performance of them.

In October 1842 a streak of light appeared in the gray clouds that
had been gathering. The *Church of England Quarterly Review* published
the first over-all review of Browning's works. This comprehensive discussion gave a clearer notion of the character of Browning's contribution than could the reviews of single publications, and the admonition
that Browning's work was worth the effort it required was timely. In
eighteen pages of summary, comments, and quotations, the author,
R. H. Horne, discussed all of the works published up to this time except the anonymous *Pauline,* a discussion that he would in part use in
his book *A New Spirit of the Age.* Although Horne agreed with other
critics in thinking well of *Paracelsus* and poorly of *Strafford,* he thought

more highly of *King Victor* than other critics did. Like the majority of reviewers of *Pippa Passes* he appreciated the Ottima-Sebald scene, and he belonged with those who understood Browning's plan and aim in the poem. His real departure from the criticism of the time came in his discussion of *Sordello,* which covered nearly ten of the eighteen pages. Feeling that it had not been fairly estimated, Horne pointed out the difficulties that kept readers from seeing the wealth buried in the poem. With explanation and quotations he showed that it held promise for the future.

Presenting Browning's works as if they were worth being examined rather than nagging him for his wilfulness was encouraging at this low point in his career. Browning told Domett about the article in September, and in his next letter in December he spoke of the generosity of the reviewer who wrote so "of an unappreciated man." [15] In September he dwelt on the editorial changes made inconsiderately in Horne's review, which Browning said he had seen in manuscript. But the review was not spoiled for him; his gratification came through in the light tone of his letter:

> And there is an estimate of me and mine — by, I can't guess whom — which some wiseacre of a sub-editor has been allowed to travel over and spoil in as many points as he has touched; for you must know, the MS. was forwarded to me, by a friend of the unnamed penman, to *assay* my good nature — which is virgin gold when these matters are concerned — and I, not being "offended" (the friend's word!) at the sharp bits, or what are meant for such, here and there — have furnished some third party with a pretext for softening of the soft bits the wrong way — so that instead of flaring heaven-high, as Carlyle would say — I only range with the gas-lamps in ordinary. Read and laugh, for thereto I send it! [16]

Browning added that in a week or two he would send some lyrics which he thought of printing. These he had mentioned to Domett in May, outlining his immediate plans: "I shall go to the end of this year, as I now go on — shall print the Eastern play you may remember hearing about — finish a wise metaphysical play (about a great mind and soul turning to ill), and print a few songs and small poems which Moxon advised me to do for popularity's sake!" (The plays were the *Druses* and *A Soul's Tragedy.*) Browning little dreamed of the significance to his career of a few songs and small poems written for popularity's sake, nor was he fully aware of the importance of the sentence which followed: "These things done (and my play out), I shall have tried an experiment to the end, and be pretty well contented either way."[17] It was not to be the end of the experiment, and Browning was not to be contented with the outcome of the play. The poems were published in November 1842 under the title of *Dramatic Lyrics*. In the short dramatic pieces, not in the plays, Browning had found the form of expression suited to his genius and conducive to his ultimate fame.

Since the poems were to be published for "popularity's sake," Browning wanted to do what he could so that they would be understood and appreciated by the public. To show that they were dramatic, he gave them the title *Dramatic Lyrics* and in the Advertisement provided an explanation:

> Such Poems as the following come properly enough, I suppose, under the head of "Dramatic Pieces"; being, though for the most part Lyric in expression, always Dramatic in principle, and so many utterances of so many imaginary persons, not mine.

Without the explanation readers might fall into the error of Leigh Hunt, who failed to see that feature of Tennyson's poems. Browning later wrote to Domett, "Hunt's criticism is neither kind nor just, I take it — he don't understand that most of Tennyson's poems are *dramatic* — utterances coloured by an imaginary speaker's moods." (Browning was thinking of his own poems.) "Thus 'the mermaid' [in the poem so titled] is not purely sea-woman enough for him — too coquettish and conscious, and like a girl of our own[,] *fancying* 'the only blessed life, the watery': whereas: it *is* just that, a *girl*, looking characteristically at what might be viewed after many another fashion — Ariel's, for instance."[18]

Besides helping his reader by explaining the nature of the poems, Browning considered the time of publication. For the choice of season he depended on his publisher's knowledge and for the more specific time on the possibility of Forster's best presentation. In a letter to Moxon he suggested scheduling a publication date so that Forster could give the poems a good introduction: ". . . he [Forster] wants to get the start of such Squintowls as the *Spectator*, etc., and yet thinks his notice had better be delayed till the Saturday after next, — as he is forced to cumber *this* number with Annual poetry and the praise of it."[19]

This letter was written on Thursday, in all likelihood on November 17. Forster thought that the poems should not be published before the beginning of the following week — the one beginning November 21. On the Saturday of that week, November 26, Forster introduced

Dramatic Lyrics to readers of the *Examiner*. To some extent he anticipated the evaluation of a later day. Of the critics he alone saw any reason for terming the lyrics dramatic: they were "full of the quick turns
of feeling, the local truth, and the picturesque force of expression,
which the stage so much delights in." Furthermore, he saw purpose
and idea in whatever Browning wrote: "Often there is thought of the
profoundest kind. . . ." As for his language, which to many others had
seemed difficult or unpoetic, Forster pointed out that the "best passages are full of the best Saxon words." In the art of versification,
Browning "must be called a master." Forster stood out from the early
critics in the attention he gave to Browning's skill in versification, especially to its suitability in individual poems:

> It is his surpassing facility in this particular, that now and then plays
> bewildering pranks with his reader's ear — distracting, dazing and
> confusing it, in mazes of complicated harmony. On more happy oc-
> casions, the flow with which his lines gush forth into the kind of
> music most appropriate to the thoughts that prompt them, is to us
> extremely charming; and for the neatness of his rhymes in his lighter
> efforts, we think that Butler would have hugged him.

The review gave some notion of the content of the collection and
quoted all of two short poems and much of *The Pied Piper*.

On this as on other occasions Forster was not slow to give himself
credit for the recognition of Browning's poetry. His perspicacity may
have ordinarily come as much from conversations with the poet as from
his own critical ability, but we must remember that he first praised
Browning before he ever met him and was now publicly supporting a
poet whose reputation was in a precarious state. We must also give him
credit for having an open mind. He was responsible for pointing out
Browning's change for the better. This was needed to encourage new as
well as earlier readers who had been disappointed by *Sordello* and the
plays.

> The collection before us is welcome for its own sake, and more wel-
> come for its indication of the poet's continued advance in a right di-
> rection. Some of this we saw and thanked him for in his *Victor and
> Charles*, much more in his delightful *Pippa Passes*, and in the simple
> and manly strain of some of these *Dramatic Lyrics*, we find proof of
> the firmer march and steadier control.

To Forster the poems indicated that Browning was ridding himself of
the fault that had hindered his progress: ". . . on the whole they con-

firm what we have said of Mr. Browning's genius, and prove that he is fast reclaiming it from the 'vague and formless infinite' of mere metaphysical abstraction."

Since Forster had a deeper insight into Browning's poetry than most contemporary critics, his review was particularly valuable during this low period in Browning's career. One *Bell* after another was having a poor reception. In May Browning had written with discouragement to Domett. It might be inferred from the following statement in the *Examiner* that Forster had been with Browning during one of those moments when despondency overshadowed confidence. "In a word, Mr. Browning is a genuine poet, and only needs to have less misgiving on the subject himself, to win his readers to as perfect a trust, and an admiration with as little alloy in it, as any of his living brethren of the laurel are able to lay claim to."

Other reviews of *Dramatic Lyrics* followed at intervals: in the *Spectator,* December 10, 1842; the *Morning Herald,* December 20, 1842; the *Metropolitan Magazine,* February 1843, after the appearance of the *Druses;* and the *Athenaeum,* April 22, 1843, after the appearance of the *Druses* and *A Blot.* Only the paragraph in the *Morning Herald* was entirely receptive. In it a number of poems were singled out for praise; all of them, the critic said, were "marked by a strongly original tone and a vivid vein of imaginativeness." The other reviews showed confusion and irritation.

The critic for the *Spectator* started out by saying that *Dramatic Lyrics* struck him as being "the best, or at least the most readable and intelligible of his works; because the form and structure of the lyric, scarcely permits the affectation and obscurity which may take place in a longer poem." Even in the worst poems of the collection Browning was less discursive and obscure than usual. The critic grouped the poems according to the order in which he thought they deserved recognition, starting with the best: "In the few direct lyrics written to be sung, or at least taking the form of song, he has displayed a vigour and spirit which show him capable of better things than he has yet published, if he would but resolutely root up his mannerisms and affectations." *Marching Along,* one of the *Cavalier Tunes,* which he considered perhaps the best poem in the collection, he quoted to exemplify this group.

The effectiveness of the second group, consisting of epigrams or stories, was "only dashed by peculiarities of composition." In this group fell *The Pied Piper* and *Camp* (later called *Incident of the French*

Camp). Then came the comment on the next group: "In others — such as 'Italy' [*My Last Duchess*], and in a lesser degree 'France' [*Count Gismond*] — the mode of telling the story, the quaintness of the sentiments, or the choice of the metre and the character of the pauses, obtrude the writer so constantly on the reader, that every thing in art or nature is subordinate to Mr. Browning and his *manner.*" Even worse were the poems "where a vicious nature, fostered by self-indulgence, has contrived to defeat Necessity herself, and compress into a page the species of faults that have hitherto been spread through a poem." Although not named, *The Spanish Cloister, Johannes Agricola,* and *Porphyria's Lover* may well have been assigned to this group. Stanzas from *In a Gondola* were quoted to show "how common thoughts and natural images can be rendered constrained and unnatural by the position of a rhyme and an occasional expression." The trouble with Browning was that he was "wise in his own conceit." He seemed to think that his own conceptions were sufficient, "intrinsically better than anything to be found in nature, and requiring no rules of art to exhibit them to advantage — 'he is a man, too great to scan.' "

Like the *Spectator,* the *Metropolitan Magazine* objected to the technique of the *Dramatic Lyrics,* a "poetical caracoling." The critic's irritation is predominant, in spite of a slight concession.

> Never, surely, did the steed of bard so prance, and prove so restive
> — now floundering in the mud of obscurity, until, finding we are
> like to receive nothing but splashes, we are tempted to abandon him
> altogether, and then breaking into fire and energy, and carrying us
> into some scene where we suddenly catch sight of showers of the
> gleams of shattered diamonds. . . . It is of no use for Mr. Browning
> to put in his plea that he has taken out a license for poetical frenzy;
> we hold that sanity is essential to sense, and we look for coherence,
> at least, in poetry.

Hervey, the reviewer for the *Athenaeum,* did not grasp the intention of *Dramatic Lyrics,* though he had had some success in understanding *Pippa Passes.* He was as captious as ever about Browning's unintelligibility. The tone was set in the first sentence: "That it is Mr. Browning's pleasure to be enigmatical, may now, we suppose, be considered as an accepted condition of his literary dealings with the public. . . ." The critic felt that it would be a waste of his time to try "to obtain better terms." Accordingly, he would abandon the subject of Browning's mannerisms with one final hint. The hint expanded into another diatribe against the unintelligibility of the poetry. Hervey was further irritated by the mysterious title of the series, *Bells and Pomegranates*, which he supposed would be eventually unriddled, and by the classification "Dramatic Pieces." Mr. Browning, who had a "regal way of disposing of all such trifling difficulties," explained that the poems were for the most part lyric in expression and dramatic in principle. Hervey admittedly had not been able to discover any dramatic quality whatever in more than half of the poems; to him they were not even poems: "In any case, however, they are mere fragments, varying in length from half a dozen lines upwards — apparently thoughts jotted down for after use — or rejected from their places in longer pieces, and denoting foregone conclusions — but scarcely important enough to have formed the materials of an independent publication."

Thus the critic dismissed the publication before he quoted for the last of his review all of *Camp* [*Incident of the French Camp*], *Cloister* [*Soliloquy of the Spanish Cloister*] and *Marching Along*. He did say of the *Cloister* that it "may deserve the title of dramatic . . . being a quaint, amusing, and graphic expression of that concentrated spite which is both fed and fettered by the pressure of conventional arrangements." The diatribe against Browning's obscurity that Hervey had started in his review of *Sordello* and continued in his review of *Pippa Passes* was mitigated to some extent by statements that resulted from his attempt to understand those works. In this review of *Dramatic Lyrics*, his third of Browning, Hervey let his impatience get the upper hand; apparently he exerted little or no effort to understand the poems.

Dramatic Lyrics, published "for popularity's sake," attracted few reviewers at the time of publication, and of these only the *Examiner* and the *Morning Herald* showed appreciation. The trouble came in judging by traditional norms. It seemed that Browning had no rules of composition, did not scan, was incoherent, used pauses without consideration of art — in short, that he had taken out a license for poetical frenzy. His statement in the Advertisement that the poems were often lyric in expression and always dramatic in principle was not a sufficiently serviceable guideline for the reviewers. Forster explained wherein they were dramatic. The reviewer for the *Athenaeum*, who was confused by Browning's statement, could not find much of the dramatic except perhaps in the *Cloister*. To critics who thought a poem should have a beginning, middle, and end some of these poems were unacceptable. The *Athenaeum's* statement that here were fragments or rejections from other poems was a sample of the inability of reviewers to cope with original poems — ones written to attract readers.

The deficiencies — so labeled — meant obscurity to the critics, who felt that Browning refused to help himself or others by making his poetry intelligible. They never doubted that their irritation was justified, that he had talent and misused it. The *Metropolitan Magazine* expressed a common attitude toward him during these years: "In truth, we admire Mr. Browning so much, that we wish he would allow us to admire him more."

How many of Browning's nonprofessional supporters might have shared this sentiment, we have no way of knowing. There is only a meager record of private opinion. We have two letters from Elizabeth to Miss Mitford and one letter from Joseph Arnould to Domett and another from him to Browning. Elizabeth's first impression of *Dramatic Lyrics* was not favorable. She wrote Miss Mitford: "There are fine things — yes, and *clearly* fine things. But there is much in the little (for the publication consists of only a few pages) which I, who admire him, wish away — impotent attempts at humour, — a vain jangling with rhymes . . I mean of *mere* rhymes . . and a fragmentary rough-edgedness about the *mounting* of some high thoughts."[20] In another month the poems had a stronger appeal for Elizabeth. She resolved to persuade Miss Mitford to set more value on Browning. She sent her a copy of *Dramatic Lyrics* and again expressed her opinion: "Certain of the poems should not, I think, have been published, — but several of them are very fine and individual — 'original', my dearest friend, according to my impression and conviction. They are at least *new to me.*"[21]

There was no qualification in Arnould's praise of *Dramatic Lyrics*. He wrote Domett of their "extraordinary beauty and power" and of the "delight and enthusiasm" which they gave him.[22] And in a letter to Browning he showed how far ahead he was of others in appreciation. Before commenting on individual poems he wrote:

> Finding it utterly impossible to express in prose the tumult of delight which your most noble Dramatic Lyrics have given me I have ventured as you will see to express, however imperfectly a tithe of what I felt in the following most crude & hasty lines, dashed off at haphazard in the intoxication of the moment. I wish you could have seen the delight with which my wife & myself devoured your "Pomegranate" & the singing of "Bells" we set up afterwards.[23]

The verse epistle that accompanied Arnould's letter traced Browning's progress. Although the poet had "taught / Language to be the *minister* of Thought," in *Sordello* "Too steeply soaring in his Godlike flight / He half forgot the multitude he meant / To carry with him in his grand intent." Then "Three giant strides each firmer, than the last" had set him free — "erect & godlike." The strides were taken in *Pippa Passes, King Victor,* and *Dramatic Lyrics.*[24] The verse epistle of over one hundred and fifty lines was one of the very few refreshing drops of encouragement in an arid stretch for Browning. In the letter accompanying the copy of *Dramatic Lyrics* sent to Domett, Browning referred to Arnould's "cleverest, gratefullest *verse*-thanks." Concerned mostly with news of their friends and the literary world, Browning said little about the poems. Probably thinking of *Dramatic Lyrics* as merely another move in his series of experiments, he asked Domett for criticism and expressed the hope that his future poems would be better.[25]

Some weeks after Browning heard from Arnould and before the last of the reviews of *Dramatic Lyrics* had appeared, he published *The Return of the Druses,* earlier rejected by Macready. It came out in January of 1843 and the limited attention it received confirmed Macready's opinion. On February 4 the *Spectator* had a short paragraph. The story was considered improbable and uninteresting. It was not told intelligibly; the actors were "mere phantasmagoria, *talking Browning.*" The critic saw in the play Browning's usual faults and little of his power. In July, after publishing its derogatory reviews of *A Blot* and of *Dramatic Lyrics,* the *Athenaeum* carried a criticism of the *Druses.* It was not characterized by the carping tone of earlier reviews in that periodical. The critic, like others, thought that Browning's intentions were not always clear, but he was not querulous in stating his objections. Furthermore he gave considerable space to quotation of "a good specimen of the poetry" and a summary of the play, in which he saw powerful dramatic elements that in many respects were employed with great skill.

In January 1844, one year after the *Druses* was published and nearly a year after the performance of *A Blot,* an interesting review of the *Druses* appeared in the *Foreign and Colonial Quarterly* (later titled *New Quarterly Review, or Home, Foreign, and Colonial Journal*). It has the mark of having been written by someone who knew at first or second hand about Macready's professional habits and about the relationship between him and Browning. The reviewer — who, as it will appear later, was Horne — made a few statements about *A Blot* and then discussed certain aspects of the *Druses.*

Horne praised the characters in the *Druses,* especially the main one, on which Browning had unsuccessfully labored in order to please Macready. "The character of Djabal is a masterpiece, and of the highest order of dramatic portraiture." The support given for this statement looks toward the later recognition of Browning's use of character in the dramatic monologue.

> It is at once complicated and clear; the motives intervolved and con-
> flicting, yet "palpable to feeling as to sight;" and all his actions,
> their results, and his own end, are perfectly in harmony with these
> premises. Anything in him that puzzles us, is only in the progress of
> the drama; for eventually he stands out in the finest relief, as though
> upon "the mountain" to which his dying steps lead on his emanci-
> pated people.

Horne pointed out Djabal's acuteness in self-analysis and quoted one of his speeches by way of demonstration. "This is to write drama," he added, "and psychological history at the same time." In the discussion of the protagonist as well as other characters "scarcely less admirably drawn . . . though not so elaborately finished" and of their effective-ness on the stage, Horne remarked that Macready could not play Dja-bal. "He would never feel that he rightly understood the character." This pointed directly to Macready's lack of sympathy with the part Browning had designed for him.

One of Macready's objections was that Browning postponed the explanation required immediately for understanding a play. Horne agreed with Macready. He gave examples, one being the first speech in the play. "Puzzling the head does not excite and suspend an interest, but delays or prevents our feeling an interest." Horne called Brown-ing's method "reversing the dramatic principle," and it was this re-versing principle that Browning had defended in his letter to Macready and later developed in the dramatic monologues that did the most to establish his reputation.

Two other deficiencies were indicated. Sometimes Browning did not depict precisely and clearly the feelings of the characters, a criti-cism also made by the *Athenaeum.* The other deficiency consisted of a lack of "perspicuous distribution of the action." This deficiency, Horne seemed to think, might have been remedied easily by Macready "with far less trouble than is always taken with the works of Mr. Knowles, or Sir E. L. Bulwer, or with any of the 'great discoveries' and failures of Mr. Macready." Horne thought that the *Druses* possessed "in the highest degree" the main requisites for a successful acting tragedy

— character and passionate action. He gave it an elevated place. "We take our leave of this production of Mr. Browning, by observing, that we consider it, 'as a whole,' to be one of the finest of modern dramatic works, and that with no more than the usual adaptation, it would be a good acting drama." To him it was strange that it had not had an adequate review, not even a notice in the press (in this last statement he was wrong).

In spite of this review, the reception of the *Druses* by the reading public was dismal. Even Arnould was disappointed in the play: ". . . it was too full of the old faults of style, and the object not plain enough."[26] The later history of *King Victor* and the *Druses* has not proved them to be good acting plays. They were not staged even by the Browning Society. In 1888 there was talk of a production of the *Druses* with Alma Murray,[27] but nothing came of it. Neither play has been generally accepted by critics of our time as stageworthy.[28]

Both works can be called failures as plays for the stage, but the *Druses* cannot be dismissed so easily as *King Victor*. Browning gave no indication at any time that he had a high regard for *King Victor*. Even though an audience would have difficulty in following the ambiguities in the *Druses*, Browning worked hard on it. He made concessions to Macready, and he had confidence in his continuing experiments with character revelation. According to his defense of the play to Macready and to the explanation that he might well have given his friend Horne, he saw the play as evidencing advancement in his writing. When in the last decade of his life his plays were again much on his mind, he resurrected his early feeling about the *Druses*, as is indicated in a letter written by Edmund Gosse to Arthur Pinero.

> It was in the Spring of 1881, and some little play of Tennyson's in blank verse (perhaps *The Cup?*) was running at the Lyceum. I dropped in on Browning, as I often did on my way down in the morning; and he said, "What do you think? Irving wrote me a letter yesterday in which he asked me to write him a play in verse, like Tennyson's." I replied, "Well, and I hope you will agree to do it. What have you said to him?" "I have just answered his letter, and I have said that it is very kind of him, very civil and all that, but that if he wants to act a play of mine there is *The Return of the Druses* ready waiting for him!"[29]

To someone who does not know as much as we do about the history of the play, it would be startling that in the eighties Browning still thought of the *Druses* as being fit for the stage.

CHAPTER VII

A Play Accepted

A Blot in the 'Scutcheon, 1843:
Rehearsal, Performance, Reception

W hen Macready performed in *Strafford*, he was acting under the managership of someone else. When he received *A Blot* during a season at the Haymarket, he was probably already considering the managership of Drury Lane Theatre and would soon be involved in plans that led to its opening late in 1841 under his direction. Being both actor and manager was trying, especially with Macready's high aims for improvement of the drama. He gave much of his energy to searching for good new plays and restoring the original text of Shakespeare. He carried out his resolution to relieve the deadening effect of long runs by providing variety; his sacrifice of successful productions in order to avoid routine performances helped to drain his treasury. He gambled and lost on new plays. Debts piled up, his health suffered, and his spirits sank. Near the end of his first season he produced a new play by C. F. Darley called *Plighted Troth*. In spite of the confidence that he and his advisers had in its success, it was a complete failure. The outcome was a blow to Macready, not only because of the pecuniary loss but also because of his misjudgment.

It was less than a week after this failure, on April 26, 1842, that Browning made his attempt to get some sort of commitment from him concerning *A Blot* and was told that there would be no more new plays during the remainder of the season.[1] Macready might well hesitate before trying another new play at this time, especially since it was by Browning, whose dramatic ability he no longer believed in. Arnould,

Browning's staunch supporter, could see that after *Strafford* Macready might possibly "have looked doubtfully at Browning's chance of writing a play that would take."[2]

When Macready closed his first season at Drury Lane in May 1842, he had had *A Blot* for well over a year. His second season began in October. On November 25, Dickens, having been asked to read the play, wrote what he thought of it:

> Browning's play has thrown me into a perfect passion of sorrow. To say that there is anything in its subject save what is lovely, true, deeply affecting, full of the best emotion, the most earnest feeling, and the most true and tender source of interest, is to say that there is no light in the sun, and no heat in blood. It is full of genius, natural and great thoughts, profound and yet simple and beautiful in its vigour. I know nothing that is so affecting, nothing in any book I have ever read, as Mildred's recurrence to that "I was so young — I had no mother." I know no love like it, no passion like it, no moulding of a splendid thing after its conception, like it. And I swear it is a tragedy that MUST be played; and must be played, moreover, by Macready. . . . And if you tell Browning that I have seen it, tell him that I believe from my soul there is no man living (and not many dead) who could produce such a work.[3]

It might have been this praise that provided sufficient impetus for Macready to take definite steps for the production of *A Blot*. Browning wrote Domett on December 13: "Macready is getting on poorly enough; he pledges himself to keep his Theatre open till he has played my Tragedy — I don't know what will be the end of it."[4] Although Macready no longer thought that Browning could write a really good play, it seems that he did not immediately feel so strongly opposed to *A Blot* as he had to *King Victor* and the *Druses;* instead of rejecting it, he held it without recording the disapproval that he had expressed of the earlier plays. He wrote Bulwer Lytton on July 17, 1842, that he had several tragedies on hand, "one, and really a very touching one, and with scenes of great passion by Browning. . . ."[5] In later years John Westland Marston thought it was *A Blot* that he had heard Macready speak of in 1842 with "emphatic admiration."[6]

Whatever he had found good in the play and whatever Dickens had said of it, Macready's interest in Browning and his writing had diminished during the time when Browning was presenting *King Victor* and the *Druses* for his opinion. By October 1842 Macready had apparently gone far enough to exclude the once welcome poet from his room after a performance.[7] In spite of this coolness and his recent disappointment in new plays by other writers, he agreed to produce a second play by Browning. On January 25, 26, and 28 of 1843 he was reading *A Blot*, preparatory to the rehearsals. The entry in his *Diaries* for January 27 indicated one of his depressive moods caused by the burdensome work of the theater: "Low in spirits and worn down in body. I do not know how I am to wear through this effort, but I cannot help feeling that it is very hard with such endeavours, such objects and such means I am not more successful!"

This was scarcely a mood to fortify Macready against the days ahead. After one actor declined his request to read *A Blot* in the greenroom, he made the mistake of turning the task over to the prompter Willmott, an aging man with a wooden leg. The incongruity of this unimposing figure reading all parts, feminine as well as masculine, raised laughter, so that Macready thought the play had not been taken seriously. Browning was displeased to learn that instead of reading *A Blot* himself Macready had left to someone else the introduction of his play to the actors. Added to this grievance was Macready's advice on the 29th to alter the second act of the play; Browning was weary of following his suggestions for alterations — to no avail. More and more the situation was becoming ripe for the impending debacle that was to mark the end of Browning's efforts to reach the public with Macready's assistance. Whatever restraint there had been in the delicately balanced association was giving way. Macready recorded Browning's behavior on the 31st:

> Went to Drury Lane theatre. Found Browning waiting for me in a state of great excitement. He abused the doorkeeper and was in a very great passion. I calmly apologized for having detained him, observing that I had made a great effort to meet him at all. He had not given his *name* to the doorkeeper, who had told him he might walk into the green-room; but his dignity was mortally wounded. I fear he is a very conceited man. Went over his play with him, then looked over part of it. Read it in the room with great difficulty, being *very unwell.*

On the following day, with the memory of the difficulties during the *Strafford* production and of Browning's more recent behavior, Macready continued to work on the revision of *A Blot* but felt unequal to the situation in his role as actor and manager. He complained of his inability to meet commitments. According to one report he said that he could not perform in Browning's play unless the whole work of the theater stopped, that it would be best to let the part of Tresham be taken by Samuel Phelps. According to another report he said he could not play the part unless the play was postponed until after Easter. Browning, impatient for the play's performance and probably suspicious of Macready's intentions, unhesitatingly accepted Phelps as the substitute for the star of the company. Rehearsals began; Phelps became ill; Macready understudied his part. Phelps, who was playing under Macready's management for the second time, thought that he was generally mistreated because good parts were denied him, and now he was losing this chance to take the leading role. He appeared on February 10, the day before the first performance, somewhat recovered, and wished to regain his part. By that time Macready was well into the play. Browning positively stated his preference for Phelps.[8]

The clash on February 10 was highly emotional. According to Macready, at a quarter past one word came that Phelps would do the part of Tresham if he "died for it." Macready then offered to give Browning and Phelps suggestions which he considered helpful. "Browning, however, in the worst taste, manner, and spirit, declined any further alterations, expressing himself perfectly satisfied with the manner in which Mr. Phelps executed Lord Tresham. I had no more to say. I could only think Mr. Browning a very disagreeable and offensively mannered person." In May Arnould gave a similar version in a letter to Domett:

> . . . our Robert does not fall prone at his feet and worship him for his condescending goodness — not that at all does our Robert do, but quite other than that — with laconic brevity he positively declines taking the part from Phelps, dispenses with Macready's aid, &c., and all this in face of a whole greenroom. You imagine the fury and whirlwind of our managerial wrath — silent fury, a compressed whirlwind, volcano fires burning white in our pent heart.

Browning's uncontrolled arrogance toward Macready in his own theater and in the presence of others was the lowest point in their professional association. Something can be said for each major participant in this off-stage tragedy. Macready was beset by financial worries and troubled by defeated efforts during his management of Drury Lane, and he had lost faith in Browning's ability to write a play that the public would like. Browning was the unproved playwright, Macready the famous actor and the manager of the theater; Browning the suitor, Macready the sued. Moreover, Macready had tried to help Browning and had exercised a good deal of patience throughout his unsuccessful but persistent attempts at writing plays for the stage and had had to bear with what he considered Browning's unjustified confidence in his ability.

On the other hand, no matter how hard Browning tried, it was impossible to please Macready. His confidence, verbalized earlier to the point of making Macready fear for the poet's sanity, became less steady, though probably the change went unnoticed by the actor. Browning had introduced the last two plays submitted to Macready by advanced letters that had an undertone of wariness. It was hard for him to understand why Macready was not more receptive. He was blind to the merit of the part of Djabal in the *Druses,* written expressly to suit him. Besides, he had kept *A Blot* for two years, neither rejecting nor producing it at a time when Browning needed the favorable publicity he thought it would give him. The delay put him on tenterhooks; Arnould wrote how even his friends contributed to his unhappy frame of mind: "Meanwhile judicious friends, as judicious friends will, had a habit of asking Browning when the play was coming out — you can fancy how sensitively Browning would chafe at this." After seriously considering the production of *A Blot,* Macready still showed signs of indifference; then he tampered with the play that Browning had shaped so that it would have Macready's approval and also public appeal — "a sort of compromise between my own notion and yours," he had written Macready.

The wonder is that the relationship lasted as long as it did between two highly sensitive and explosive men, each pulled in a different direction by his dramatic talent and each increasingly disappointed in the expectations he had of the other. The final eruption of feelings produced a professional situation beyond repair. Because Browning resented the damage he considered Macready was doing *A Blot* by revisions and cuts, Moxon rushed the play through publication just as Browning had written and revised it, so that it appeared as *Bell* No. V on the day of its first performance. The poet whose gentle manners had made his presence acceptable to Macready in the first months of their acquaintance became one of the "wretched insects" about him and "the puppy" when Browning refused to speak on one occasion a few years after the first run of the play.

A Blot was performed only three times in 1843 — on February 11, 15, and 17. Two dailies reviewed it on February 13, bringing out

NEVER ACTED.

Theatre Royal, Drury Lane.

To-morrow. SATURDAY, February 11th. 1843,
Her Majesty's Servants will perform

A NEW TRAGIC-PLAY,
IN THREE ACTS, called

A BLOT IN THE 'SCUTCHEON.

Thorold, Lord Tresham,	Mr. PHELPS,
Henry, Earl Mertoun,	Mr. ANDERSON.
Austin Tresham,	Mr. HUDSON.
Gerard,	Mr. G. BENNETT,
Andrew.	Mr. MELLON.
Arthur.	Mr. SELBY,
Ralph, (retainers of Lord Tresham)	Mr. YARNOLD,
Joseph,	Mr. C. J. SMITH,
Martin,	Mr. HOWELL,
Walter.	Mr. BENDER,
Mildred Tresham,	Miss HELEN FAUCIT.
Gwendolen Tresham.	Mrs. STIRLING.

Playbill, A Blot in the 'Scutcheon, February 11, 1843

both its good and bad points. Then followed on the weekend of February 18 and 19 the major weeklies, which with the exception of the favorable *Examiner* showed a strong aversion to the play, and two weeklies with temperate criticism. Three brief comments ended the reviews at this time. One was in a monthly in March and two in quarterlies — in May and in January 1844.

The *Morning Post* and the *Times* were the first ones to review the play, the *Post* with nearly two of its long columns and the *Times* with almost the whole of one. The *Post* thought that Browning had tried to improve his style but was still a mannerist. The critic was willing to endure the oddities for the sake of the feeling. He knew that "the prude and the unhealthy moralist" would object to the incident upon which the plot was founded, but he defended Browning's choice. He gave highest praise to the element of passion; there Browning's dramatic strength lay; and in it and in thought he was a true poet. But even so the critic could not be blind to his lack of skill in the construction of a play, which in this instance led to improbabilities in the characters' behavior. Though scenes of strong feeling smoothed over such difficulties, they had a bad effect on the audience.

The *Times* praised the vigor and the striking effects Browning had achieved, but these were overbalanced by the faulty construction and the "strange idiosyncrasies" the author gave to his characters "on purpose to force them into difficulties." Even though recognizing a writer with poetical qualifications of no common order, the reviewer disapproved of the improbabilities arising from poor plot construction and of the prominence of the breach of chastity acknowledged by Mildred and Mertoun. These were characteristics that most of the critics complained of.

The severity of the criticisms in the *Spectator*, the *Atlas*, the *Literary Gazette*, and the *Athenaeum* — all published on February 18 — must have contributed much to the unfortunate aftereffects of the *Blot's* early history on Browning's mind. They concentrated mainly on complaints concerning plot construction and subject matter. Admittedly *A Blot* would have suited the critic of the *Spectator* better had it been reduced to one act and best had it been left unwritten. It was "brief, yet tedious: shocking, but unimpressive; and melodramatic, without being effective." The subject itself was unfit for tragedy. And Browning tried to excite strong emotions by making what was disagreeable horrible, but instead he created a predominating feeling of aversion; the unchasteness of Mildred and the attendant events were fatal to dramatic sympathy. Furthermore, in constructing the drama Browning had so unskillfully managed stage business that at the end of a scene the audience was forced to listen to a narration of what had already passed before them. The motives, situation, and purpose of the characters were unaccountable, with no light thrown on them by soliloquy or dialogue; the ideas were so farfetched and the phraseology so quaint that the drift of the speeches was scarcely to be followed.

Even though the *Atlas* considered the first production of *A Blot* somewhat successful, its measure of success was attributed to the actors, "who managed to invest an unpleasant and unsatisfactory theme with the charms of powerful elocution and action." Admiration of vigorous passages in the printed version was overborne by realization that the tragedy was "faulty in material points of construction, rough and eccentric in its language, wiredrawn in its unfoldings of thought, and abrupt in the conduct of its action." Browning's rough versification, his innate love of subtle argument and ill-timed disquisition, and his failure to adapt his style of writing to the stage were also censured. But it was the moral action that most offended the critic: ". . . it behoves the poet to discard incidents which are more offensive to the feelings than beneficial to the morals." Although both lovers suffered the critic's displeasure, Mildred came in for a larger share. The concluding verdict was that Browning, a poet of acknowledged power, must be consigned to the ranks of poets "without *essential* dramatic genius."

The review in the *Literary Gazette* was in keeping with the typical professional estimation at the time of its first performance. The critic thought that the success of the first night was a doubtful one, "though the audience in general certainly went along with the author." Even if some of the scenes and much of the dialogue were too long, the variety and constant moving of the action kept the audience from noticing the faulty plot. It would require a moment of reflection to become aware that "human nature, physics, and metaphysics, must be outraged, or there would be no play at all." The critic recognized the "fine marks of genius in the working-out of his [Browning's] conception, and not a few beautiful touches of genuine pathos and poetry — half lines worth a world of declamation," but even though in poetical composition the play was far above the mediocre efforts of ordinary writers, the disagreeable subject and the defiance of probability in handling the plot would prove fatal. The critic was no more complimentary to the other *Bells,* which, since the *Literary Gazette* had not reviewed them, he now referred to in a footnote.

The *Athenaeum,* designated by Browning forty years later as Macready's upholder, carried one paragraph, in which the critic showed his disgust. "If to pain and perplex were the end and aim of tragedy," Browning's drama would have been worthy of admiration, for it was a very "puzzling and unpleasant piece of business." The plot was clear enough but the behavior of the characters was "inscrutable and abhorrent" and their language "as strange as their proceedings." The critic saw no future for such a drama, even if it had been artfully constructed.

Forster foresaw the severe criticism that appeared in the weeklies on the same day (Feb. 18) as his review in the *Examiner.* "People are already finding out . . . that there is a great deal that is equivocal in its sentiment, a vast quantity of mere artifice in its situations, and in its general composition not much to 'touch humanity.' " Forster, echoing Dickens, defended the play: ". . . we would give little for the feelings of the man who could read this tragedy without a deep emotion." The play was sad, perhaps needlessly so, but "unutterably tender, passionate, and true." He defended the handling of the plot by answering specific objections that were being made. Furthermore, he found no "equivocal morality in it, no false sympathies to set the judgment halting between right and wrong; no good that deters, no bad that encourages." He went beyond answering the objections by praising the play's originality. Browning did not imitate other authors; his play, with its "animated pathos" and "freshness and unexaggerated strength," was his own creation. Though it might have only a short existence on the stage at first, Forster prophesied that it would not die.

Four more critics had something to say about its moral aspect. Three had definite complaints concerning moral conduct — the *New Monthly Belle Assemblée* (Mar. 1843) in a brief and negligible comment and *John Bull* (Feb. 18, repeated 20) and the *Era* (Feb. 19) — both weeklies — in discussions of both the good and the bad in the play. *John Bull* recognized the behavior of the lovers as the "radical defect of the piece" and then noted the occasional power in the language and the "quick situation and novel construction of the piece, taking you like a bold, unfinished sketch," which had secured for the play a temporary success. After a reference to the objectionable subject of illicit love, the *Era* dwelt on the good qualities: fine dramatic feeling with a natural construction and characters standing out from the canvas. The "fine gush of feeling" was untainted by farfetched epithets and old-fashioned words. "We discover no borrowings or adaptations from the elder dramatists, the sentiments are not arrayed in tricksy phraseology, and were the inversions (the author's besetting sin) less frequent, his blank verse would be unexceptionable." The critic, who at the end of the discussion mentioned the series of *Bells and Pomegranates* and referred favorably to *Paracelsus* and *Strafford,* thought that Browning was a poet of undoubted genius, that if he were "less of a mannerist" he would be one of the leading poets of the day.

The comments on the moral aspect of the play that particularly attract our attention appeared in the last notice of *A Blot* at this time. It was written by Browning's friend Horne and included in a review of several poets in the *Foreign and Colonial Quarterly Review* (Jan. 1844). The section on Browning indicates Horne's firsthand knowledge of the Macready-Browning relationship. The greater part of it concerned the *Druses* and has already been discussed. The beginning paragraph dealt with *A Blot.* At the end of this paragraph Horne, in all likelihood with Browning's complaints of Macready's treatment of his play in mind, alluded to the indifferent staging. Most of the brief commentary concerned the moral conduct of the lovers. Like Forster and the critic for the *Morning Post,* Horne did not censure them, though in fact he thought the morality of the play was not altogether clear. He probably was thinking of the effect of Macready's changes. "The play was intended to be nobly and boldly unconventional, and as it was therefore proportionately dangerous, it contained several strong conventional speeches carried to absurdity, with a view to 'carry *off*' the danger." The result was that "at last we did not know which was meant for the true morality."

The remaining criticism of *A Blot* appeared in the *Westminster Review* (May 1843), in which George Henry Lewes presented four dramas as failures. In his discussion of their faults, he gave only *A Blot* specific attention. The whole dramatic nature of the play was false — "an instance of very clever superstructure on very rotten basis" and a display of preposterous brother's love.

Half of the critics indicated little or no sympathetic interest in *A Blot.* The other half had praise for it, but with the exception of Forster and Horne all of them pointed out weaknesses. This reception is particularly interesting because *A Blot* indicated that Browning, with the previous objections of Macready and of the reviewers in mind, had made concessions. Dramatically Browning had not handled historical facts and characters well in *Strafford,* he had not brought the historical characters to life in *King Victor,* and he had not made himself clear in presenting details, historical or otherwise, in the *Druses.* And he had considered character more important than action in *King Victor* and the *Druses*. In *A Blot* Browning did not depend on history for his plot and he chose a domestic situation involving characters in a great house, which he thought would appeal to the actor-manager, the critics, and the audience; he emphasized action and he made an attempt to avoid distractions that would impede the movement of the plot. There had been a general complaint of obscurity and so he worked for clarity of expression.

The reviewers, who to a considerable extent would sympathize with Victorian tastes and Macready's notion of stage requirements, passed judgment upon the results of Browning's effort to write a successful play. They were not severe in the matter of obscurity, but otherwise they were not pleased. Providing pathos in a domestic tragedy accorded with Victorian preferences; but Browning took as his subject a moral situation that the reviewers, reflecting the attitude of the public, found distasteful and that the Lord Chamberlain might have questioned.[9] There was action; but the critics pointed out that the plot was designed without due consideration of probability, that Browning placed his main characters in positions producing incredible behavior. After the performance and publication of *Strafford*, the critics still had had hopes for Browning as a stage dramatist. After *A Blot* there were no longer false expectations. Its immediate reception as a stage play was unfavorable. Even as the critics recognized the failure of *A Blot*, they saw in it marks of a true poet *(Morning Post)*, of a poet of no common order *(Times)*, of one having acknowledged power *(Atlas)*, and of one possessing real genius *(Literary Gazette, Era)*.

Those who had a personal knowledge of Browning and his career could think of *A Blot* in more liberal terms than could the critics. Although Arnould did not consider it a good stage play, he saw it as a contribution to Browning's reputation.

> With some of the grandest situations and finest passages you [i.e., Domett] can conceive, it does undoubtedly want a sustained interest to the end of the third act; in fact the whole of that act on the stage is a falling off from the second act; which I need not tell you is for all purposes of performance the most unpardonable fault. Still, it will no doubt — nay, it must — have done this, viz. produced a higher opinion than ever of Browning's genius and the great things he is yet to do, in the minds not only of a clique, but of the general world of readers.

Browning reminded Arnould of Webster; "in vigour, grandeur, and fire," they seemed to him much alike. "Of course in intellect Browning has the superiority, just as Webster certainly beats him in plot and stage effect, and also . . . in dramatic style, though in this respect I think the 'Blot in the 'Scutcheon' was a great improvement on anything since 'Paracelsus.' " [10]

John Kenyon went to one of the performances — perhaps the first — and reported to his cousin Elizabeth Barrett, who in turn wrote Miss Mitford, "Mr. Kenyon saw it acted at Drury Lane and witnessed the sensation in the house, the tears upon stedfast faces, the silence and applause not offered but compelled." Elizabeth, of course, read the play herself. She wrote her opinion to Miss Mitford.

> It is a fine production, I think, — this 'Blot on the 'Scutcheon'. . . .
> As a composition, I seem to be aware of a little weakness towards the
> close — but I always believed that Mr. Browning was a master in
> clenched passion, . . concentrated passion . . burning through the
> metallic fissures of language — and this last trial of his, and the last
> but one 'The return of the Druses' do not cause me to waver. [11]

Although, according to the critics, *A Blot* was not suitable for performance, it was the best liked of the plays that Browning wrote for the stage, particularly by those who read instead of seeing it. "Bravo, Browning," William Allingham recorded upon first reading the play in 1848, and he was still praising it in 1868. [12] Later in life Charles Gavan Duffy said that from the time of reading it in an "ill-printed pamphlet" he had regarded Browning as the "first poet of his age and country." [13] Such comments are scattered throughout Victorian letters and memoirs. Although usually the praise came as the result of reading, not seeing the play, one exception was the American critic W. L. Phelps. He saw *A Blot* in New York (1905) and judged it to be a successful stage play by the way it affected him; he could not keep from crying. [14] That the play so stirred his emotions helps to account for the fact that it has been performed more times than any other play of Browning's in spite of the critical opinion that it was not a good stage play.

Browning felt that *A Blot* had not had the chance for success that it deserved and he never recovered from the wounds received in his last professional experience with Macready. Although after the early performances he seemingly made an attempt to avoid discussion of the clash with Macready, his discontent came to the surface from time to time throughout forty years. In the last decade of his life he was quite explicit in his efforts to vindicate himself. When in May of 1843 he wrote to Domett, his intimate and sympathetic admirer in New Zealand, he did not let himself refer to the recent disturbing experiences except in a parenthetical remark that Macready had used him vilely. In the same paragraph, however, he struck out against critics who he felt stood in the way of his success:

> They take to criticising me a little more, in the Reviews — and God send I be not too proud of their abuse! For there is no hiding the fact that it is of the proper old drivelling virulence with which God's Elect have in all ages been regaled. One poor bedevilling idiot, whose performance reached me last night only, told a friend of mine, the night before that, "how *in reality* he admired beyond measure this and the other book of Mr. B.'s, but that *in the review*, he thought it best to," &c., &c. This Abhorson boasted that he got £400 a year by his practices![15]

In the autumn of 1843 Browning helped Horne choose mottoes for some of the chapters (Elizabeth chose others) in his book on contemporaries called *A New Spirit of the Age.* One of the chapters that needed a motto was that on Macready and the dramatist Sheridan Knowles. In a letter to Horne, Browning offered one (which was used) and wrote that he knew of something else fitting from *Faust* which he could not locate at the moment.[16] Later he did find what he had in mind and copied out a passage in German for Horne,[17] who used it in translation for his second motto. The lines are from the Prelude to *Faust* and are of interest because Browning felt they could have come right out of his experience with Macready. In them the director says there must be action, plenty of it, in order to attract and hold the audience, and the poet-playwright protests against such hackwork as the director wants, which does not befit a real poet.

In this letter to Horne with the lines from *Faust*, Browning included a "Quarlesian bit," quoted from *Divine Fancies*, Book 2, which he had already mentioned. It was for Horne's "own admonition to detractors." The irritation in the following lines (only a part of the quotation), showing through a pose of indifference, resembles the mood and language later present in *Pacchiarotto:*

> Hath men's censorious baseness gone about
> With her rude blast to puff my taper out?
> It hath: and let their full mouthed bellows puff!
> It is their breath that stinks, and not my snuff.

I let them snarl & burst that I may smile.
Do, let them jerk, and I will laugh the while.
They cannot strike beyond my patience: no —
I'll bear, and take it for an honor too.[18]

Though Browning's feelings of resentment were in danger of
being aroused, there is evidence that he did control them to the extent
of leaving a general impression of forbearance. Before the end of 1843
Arnould wrote Domett of Browning and the trouble with Macready: "I
think Browning seems thoroughly to have left behind him any soreness
or annoyance which for the time no doubt must have been caused by
such extraordinary malignity."[19]

The play was revived by Samuel Phelps in 1848, and Browning
apparently could think with resignation of the past affair. Married and
settled in Italy, he was far removed from reminders of the theatrical environment that had so bestirred his emotions. He wrote to Horne, "As
nothing worse can well come than *did* come, I care very little about the
event, — always wishing Phelps well, of course, and the play, too, for
one or two friends' sake moreover, yours preeminently, staunch supporter of mine that you always were."[20] Mrs. Orr said that in 1881
Browning, in writing on the subject to Lady Martin (the former Helen
Faucit, who had played the part of Mildred in *A Blot*), spoke "very
temperately of Macready's treatment of his play, while deprecating the
injustice towards his own friendship which its want of frankness involved. . . ."[21] The next chapter will deal fully with the affair of *A
Blot* as Browning saw it in retrospect.

CHAPTER VIII

A Play Restaged and Recalled to Mind

A Blot in the 'Scutcheon, 1843:
Later Opinion and Defense

Browning, determined to succeed in the world of letters, made an effort to profit by criticism. Though he was a very sensitive person, he withstood adverse criticism remarkably well up to a certain point. Try as he might to put his disappointments behind him, they would submerge and then on occasion surface in strange guises. We have seen how he distorted facts in referring to what he considered the mistreatment of *Pauline, Paracelsus,* and *Strafford.* A reminder of his past defeats could arouse dormant emotions, so that in defending his early works he imagined situations that never existed.

In spite of outward signs of recovery from the unpleasant experiences associated with *A Blot,* the wound did not heal. Browning's restrained emotional turmoil was released in a barrage of explanation when the play and its early history were brought into the spotlight in the eighties. His life had become a topic for wide commentary; the existence of the Browning Society and the late production of some of his plays attested to the increasing interest taken in him. He was gratified by the recognition, but with it came a search into his past by the scrupulous and also the unscrupulous. The arrival of an account of his life in the mail on a morning in February 1881 was one of many occasions of annoyance; it prompted him at once to consent, after earlier refusals, to give Edmund Gosse information about himself for publication, which included a discussion of the early history of *A Blot.*[1]

The play came to the fore of his mind again in 1884. In the summer of that year Lawrence Barrett, an American actor, called on Browning in London and gained permission from him to give a series of performances of *A Blot* in the United States, with whatever changes seemed advisable. The first performance in Washington, D.C., on December 19, 1884, was followed by others in various cities.[2] A paragraph that referred to the Barrett productions and to the early failure of the play was to appear in the (London) *Daily News,* and Frank Hill, the editor, sent the projected discussion to Browning. The critic had quoted from the unfavorable *Athenaeum* review of 1843. Since Browning felt, with justification, that the *Athenaeum* had been unfair to the play and that the critic for the *Daily News* had misrepresented the situation, the paragraph was upsetting. On December 15 he wrote to Hill a spirited seven-page explanation, which Hill or someone else made use of in writing a paragraph to supersede the original one.[3]

Browning did not stop with one letter. He sent five letters to Hill and then two to Mrs. Hill over a period of approximately four months, expressing his strong feeling concerning the early history of the play.[4] In the second letter he wrote, "I only took the occasion your considerate letter gave me to tell the simple truth which my forty years silence is a sign I would only tell on compulsion." He explained that the account given by Macready and his intimates was no longer confined to their limited number. "But of late years I have got to *read,* not merely *hear,* of the play's failure 'which all the efforts of my friend the great actor could not avert:' and the nonsense of this untruth gets hard to bear." Browning was aroused to correct the nonsense.

Soon after the play was revived by Lawrence Barrett, Furnivall, the persistent Browningite, made a plea to Charles Fry, professional stage manager of the Irving Dramatic Club, to produce one of Browning's plays. The result was that Fry directed two performances of *A Blot* (Apr. 30 and May 2, 1885) under the auspices of the Browning Society and the New Shakspere Society.[5] His old feelings revived, Browning told of the early abuse of the play to Hill and Gosse and also to Barrett, Fry, and Alma Murray, who was the last outstanding performer to act in *A Blot* in Browning's lifetime. He also gave his version of the *Blot* story to William Archer for his life of Macready, published in 1890.[6] Unlike Arnould, Domett, Horne, and Helen Faucit (now Lady Martin), these people were new on the scene; they had no first-hand knowledge of the injuries that Browning thought his play had suffered. He spoke freely to them of its "mistreatment," giving some details to Fry and Archer and more to Gosse and Hill.

A reading of his comments to these people shows how much Browning's urge to defend the play influenced his version — so much so that he was blinded to realities. His statements are filled with inconsistencies, half-truths, and outright misrepresentations. Macready and Forster were the offenders, and the one-paragraph review of *A Blot* in the *Athenaeum* assumed a place in Browning's mind besides *Tait's* failure to publish Mill's review of *Pauline* — the paragraph in the *Athenaeum* damaged the reputation of *A Blot* and the passing notice of *Pauline* in *Tait's* retarded his reputation. Macready bore the brunt of the accusations.

Lounsbury (pp. 115–26) discussed errors in the first two of the letters from Browning to Hill and in Browning's account as reported by Gosse, who stated that it "was inspired and partly dictated, was revised and was approved of, by himself [Browning]."[7] Archer, Fry, Macready (in the fuller edition of his *Diaries*, 1912), and Browning's five additional letters to Hill or Mrs. Hill (as well as other sources) furnish a larger canvas than Lounsbury had — all of these enable us to see the extent to which Browning's imagination played him false. His errors of wrong dating of events and his confusion of plays came from a forgetting or easy disregard of details after a span of many years. More serious were other misrepresentations. Browning professed ignorance of Macready's financial situation and of certain theatrical practices, and he placed the blame on Macready for circumstances destructive of the success that he felt *A Blot* should have had.

Browning lamented that he did not have knowledge that would have affected the situation in his favor. Knowing about Macready's financial difficulties, he fancied in later years, would have prompted him to withdraw his play; then it would have escaped its ill fortune. Macready did him a disservice, he said to Hill, in not telling him of these difficulties in the name of friendship — "a friendship which had a right to be simply and plainly told that the play, I had contributed as a proof of it, would, through a change of circumstances, no longer be to my friend's advantage, — all I could possibly care for." This comment, made on December 15, 1884, is similar to one made in the preceding month to Lady Pollock. In writing of her recently published book on Macready, Browning referred to Macready's seeming unjustness to their friendship "simply for want of the word of explanation which would have prevented a moment's estrangement between us."[8] After describing to Archer the situation involving the staging of *A Blot,* Browning said, ". . . how easy to have spoken, and what regret it would have spared us both!" Two questions need to be answered. Did Browning know about Macready's financial situation? And with such knowledge would he have withdrawn his play?

In his first letter to Hill, dated December 15, 1884, Browning explained that only a little time before writing to him had he learned "the extent of his [Macready's] pecuniary embarassments [sic]" in the forties. He might not have known the "extent" of the financial difficulties but he certainly knew they existed. On April 20, 1842, C. F. Darley's *Plighted Troth* was performed. On May 22 Browning wrote Domett of the "disastrous issue" of the play for the actor-manager; it "had frightened him into shutting the house earlier than he had meant." This knowledge had not kept Browning from writing Macready a very short time after the failure, probably on April 26, to exert pressure for acceptance of his play.[9] His state of mind was indicated in the letter that Arnould wrote to Domett about May of 1843, after the performance of *A Blot:* "At length the paramount object with him became to have the play played, no matter how, so that it was at once." Forty-two years after Browning wrote Domett of the difficulties confronting Macready, he explained to Hill that Macready had told him not once but twice of his financial difficulties: first, when J. W. Marston's *The Patrician's Daughter* and Darley's *Plighted Troth* failed; second, when he said that harrassment by "business and various trouble" would not permit him to prepare for the part of Tresham in January of 1843. This was in the same letter in which Browning informed Hill that he had learned only recently of the extent of Macready's financial difficulties. Browning was confused when he disclaimed knowledge of the seriousness of Macready's pecuniary situation and when he thought that a knowledge of Macready's financial affairs would have prompted him to withdraw his play.

In this letter to Hill Browning said that he lacked still other information that would have made a difference in the outcome of his play. Browning wrote, ". . . and again I failed to understand, — what Forster subsequently assured me was plain as the sun at noon-day, — that to allow at Macready's Theatre any other than Macready to play the principal part in a new piece was suicidal. . . ." And he told Archer that he was unaware of the folly of having under Macready's management "any other protagonist" than the actor himself until the more learned subsequently enlightened him, and then he was "angry and disinclined to take advice." Knowledge of the importance of the actor-manager to a play was plain as the sun at noon-day to friends and acquaintances of Browning's who had submitted their plays to Macready. Innocence of this aspect of play-producing was strange for a man who knew as much about what was going on in the theater as Browning did in the days when he was writing plays, associating with other playwrights, and frequenting the theater. Arnould, who did not move in the theatrical environment as Browning did, wrote to Domett: "Now, there can be no doubt whatever that the absence of Macready's name from the list of performers of the new play was the means of keeping away numbers from the house." How could Browning have been oblivious to the importance of having Macready in *A Blot* when he had designed the part of Tresham with him in mind?

Browning surely knew of the value of having Macready in his play and of his financial difficulties, but this knowledge did not govern his movements. What was most important to him, as Arnould said, was to have the play on the stage without further delay. The description of the situation by Arnould shows that this was his primary concern:

> With these feelings he forced Macready to name an early day for playing it. The day was named, Macready was to take the part of Austin Tresham, which was made for him, and everything was going on swimmingly, when lo! a week or so before the day of representation, Macready declines altogether his part unless the play can be postponed till after Easter. Browning, naturally in "a sulky chafe" at this, declines postponement with haughty coolness; indicates that if Mr. Phelps will take the part he shall be perfectly satisfied. . . .

Browning had no notion of postponement — certainly not of withdrawal of the play. The passage was written by Arnould soon after the events took place and the information could have easily been given to him by Browning. Arnould's reporting was probably reliable; though he was Browning's supporter he said he was "making all allowance for both sides." He was capable of doing so, for he was a levelheaded person who knew how to make objective observations.

Some of the statements in this passage from Arnould's letter to Domett serve as commentary on Browning's later reports. The statement that Macready would play the part after Easter belies the impression Browning gave to Hill in his second and third letters that Macready wished to keep himself out of the play for the purpose of damaging its chances. "Macready's plan was frustrated," he wrote; Phelps' performance was not the failure "it was intended to be." The statement that Browning declined the postponement and professed satisfaction if Phelps would take the part of Tresham (which bears out the facts of the early preparations) places some of the responsibility on Browning for the choice of Phelps before the beginning of rehearsals; it conflicts with Browning's "corrections" in his letter of December 25 to Hill of what someone wrote in the eighties about the play's history: "My corrections are — that the substitution of Phelps for Macready was altogether proposed by Macready, and not myself, & that, instead of 'pressing for the play to be acted' I was simple enough to fancy that the pressure to have it acted, even under unfavourable circumstances, was altogether from Macready." The first of this sentence does not make allowance for Browning's complete satisfaction with the choice of Phelps and the last of it does not take into consideration Browning's insistence after Macready's long holding of the play that it be staged.

Any reader who might try to disentangle fact from fancy in Browning's remarks would realize the extent to which he went to convince others — and himself — that his play had treatment detrimental to its chances of success. Fry heard from Browning, "Macready took no interest in the production." [10] It is easy to believe that Macready was reluctant to face the ordeal of staging A Blot, especially since his letters show that at the time when he was doing nothing to bring out Browning's play he was hoping for a new one by the more pliable and promising Bulwer Lytton. [11] But he certainly bestirred himself to make all productions in his theater succeed; with that end in mind he made customary alterations and understudied Phelps' part. How plausible is it that Macready would accept a play and then sabotage it to spite the author? A failure would surely cause him to suffer a loss in revenue and also in prestige.

In his second letter Browning told Hill that Macready deprived A Blot "of every advantage, in the way of scenery, dresses and rehearsing." The poor state of scenery and dresses need not be questioned, but a comment is in order. After the recent setbacks, the outlay of money on A Blot was a gamble Macready would not wish to take. On December 12, 1842, after a dubious success with Marston's The Patrician's Daughter, he wrote, ". . . I begin to doubt the success of any play now," and on January 1, 1843, he wrote, "I will not advance one farthing more than I see absolute occasion for." Perhaps Macready withheld money for scenery and dresses, but he did not deprive the play of advantage in the way of rehearsing. The number of rehearsals was in keeping with that for other new plays while he was manager as well as star. Whatever injury might have occurred as the result of an inadequate number of rehearsals, Browning himself caused more injury by insisting on the day before the performance that the ailing Phelps take the part of Tresham from Macready, who had been understudying it and who as a member of the cast would have added to the drawing power of the play. Browning, who so often attempted to make a way to the public for his works, by his own actions diminished his chance of attracting attention to *A Blot*.

Browning also felt deeply that Macready's alterations and cuts were harmful to the play and he resented them. Fantastic as the notion was, he said that Macready's intent in making the changes was to damage *A Blot*. He could hardly have escaped knowing how much cutting and altering were a part of the procedure of the theater, with the sole aim of producing a good play that the audience would like. Bulwer Lytton, an established novelist and a successful playwright of the period, deferred to Macready's knowledge and experience in planning, cutting, and revising his plays. *Richelieu,* the play that Browning with others heard read and passed judgment on, went through a period of considerable alteration. Bulwer Lytton, as well as many others, expected and even welcomed the suggested changes of the actor-manager and sometimes also of advisers that he depended on.

Browning was not so amenable. His hostile attitude toward Macready's alteration of his play, especially the considerable reduction of it, he clearly exhibited at the time of its production and also later. In May of 1846 he sent Elizabeth Barrett the copy used by Macready. He said that the appearance of the play in print, hastened by his urging, had its intended effect, to prevent further excisions. He continued with a show of strong feeling, ". . . it would have been too ludicrous to leave out the whole of the first scene, for instance (as was in contemplation), and then to tell the public 'my play' had been acted." [12]

Browning again had the acting copy in hand when he wrote his first letter to Hill, who also learned of Browning's objection to Macready's cutting as well as to other alterations:

Macready at once wished to reduce the importance of the "play," — as he styled it in the bills; tried to leave out so much of the text, that I baffled him by getting it printed in four-and-twenty hours, by Moxon's assistance. He wanted me to call it, "The Sister"! — and I have before me, while I write, the stage-acting copy, with two lines of his own insertion to avoid the tragical ending — Tresham was to announce his intention of going into a monastery! all this, to keep up the belief that Macready, and Macready alone, could produce a veritable "tragedy," unproduced before.

Three months later, on March 11, 1885, Browning recurred to the acting copy and to Macready's notes for shortening the play. Domett, having returned to England, was commenting to Browning on the "slight controversy that had been going on in the *Daily News* about Macready and the first production of the *Blot,*" for Domett remembered that many years before in New Zealand he had received Arnould's report of the 1843 embroilment. Browning told Domett that Macready had cut out "about one third" of the play for the stage production, and in recalling the long-passed experience he concluded, "Ah, a sad business."[13]

This manuscript copy that rankled in Browning's mind was the subject of a very serviceable study by Joseph W. Reed, Jr., of the Macready-Browning relationship, particularly in the *Blot* affair.[14] From this study we learn that on the stage-acting copy Macready made suggestions for cuts and revisions in pencil and Browning went over in ink the suggestions that he accepted. "Thus it is possible to discern some of Macready's aims and principles in revision and to see to what extent Browning was willing to compromise his creation in order to get it produced." Reed stated that the proposed cuts amounted to about one-fourth of the play. He explained how in the context of Macready's position and of the nineteenth century theater "almost all" of Macready's changes were "understandable or justifiable," but still "Macready's cuts did violence" to good passages in the play.

In the character Guendolin, Browning had achieved a more real figure than in the major participants in the tragedy. Macready objected to certain of her lines and cut them. Browning disapproved of the suggested deletions "understandably," said Reed. "As he saw it they [the cuts] undermined the characterization of Guendolen and they had an even more serious indirect effect on his supposedly tragic hero." Browning resisted whatever might change his characterization once it was completed. It was shown in Chapter III that he was displeased with alterations of his first play and wished to restore one scene not long before the last performance and that his behavior showed confidence in his original characterization. Then there was Djabal in the *Druses,* whom Browning defended to Macready.

The marked copy of *A Blot* shows what the whole history of the Macready and Browning relationship has demonstrated as it has been narrated in this account of Browning's literary career: the goals of the two men were too far apart for either one to understand or accept the other's dramatic principles. Macready's notions had already been shaped by his training and experience; Browning's dramatic technique, still not fully developed, was being directed away from the stage by the originality of his genius. There could be no common meeting ground for the two men. Browning had tried to make adaptions, and Macready had acted in good faith when he suggested alterations that he thought would make the play more acceptable. If Browning could not mold his ideas to Macready's as easily as Bulwer Lytton and others could, it was because his creative impulse was too strong to be turned aside.

The conflict over the ending, which Browning spoke of in a letter to Hill already quoted, showed how difficult it was for the two to reach an agreement. Macready, who recommended that tragic endings be softened in the plays of other dramatists, recorded on February 10 that his suggestion to have Tresham take refuge in a convent instead of dying was a *"particularly valuable one."* Macready's alteration, rejected by Browning, consisted of two lines. Beneath these lines in the acting copy Browning wrote a note in 1884 in which he indicated his opinion of the suggested change. "The above, in Macready's handwriting, was the substitution for [what] he found written: this to avoid giving the piece the dignity of a Tragedy, and Mr. Phelps the distinction of playing in one!" [15]

In resurrecting injuries he had never fully recovered from, Browning recalled the defense that others had made for Macready. In his second letter he told Hill about the account of the early production "which Macready and his intimates gave currency to at the time" without considering what had been said and done in his behalf. Arnould wrote Domett about the activities of Macready's partisans, as they were probably related to him by Browning. "We say nothing, of course, but we do our spiteful uttermost; we give no orders — we provide paltry machinery — we issue mandates to all our dependent pen-wielders — to all tribes of men who rejoice in suppers and distinguished society. Under penalty of our managerial frown they are to be up and doing in their dirty work." Arnould later referred to "the miserable pettinesses and villainies of Macready." [16]

Browning also had his defenders. The trouble at Drury Lane was noised abroad. Miss Mitford must have heard and written of it to Elizabeth Barrett. Remarkably well informed in her sick room of events in the literary world, Elizabeth echoed the opinion of Browning's supporters in her answer: "Yes! Mr. Macready, from all that I can understand, behaved execrably to Mr. Browning: would and would not act his play — and at last acted it *for damnation.* This is friendship — but

notwithstanding every possible disadvantage, the poetry triumphed —
and *that* was victory!"[17] Horne's partisanship was publicized in his reviews of January 1844 and April 1845. The *Athenaeum,* which Browning accused of being Macready's "upholder" in 1843, in its review of
the first performance in the 1848 run looked back at the earlier situation from another position: "The circumstances attending the original
production under Mr. Macready's management at Drury Lane were
thought, at the time, to be peculiarly illustrative of the relative positions of poet and manager — little to the credit of the latter and not to
the profit of the first."

Browning blamed Macready for the mistreatment of his play and
Macready's supporters for circulation of their account of the *Blot* affair.
Furthermore, he blamed Forster for withholding Dickens' praise from
the public for thirty years, on the assumption that a public knowledge
of it would have made a difference in the reputation of *A Blot.*[18] Mrs.
Orr said in her biography of Browning:

> He also felt it a just cause of bitterness that the letter from Charles
> Dickens, which conveyed his almost passionate admiration of *A Blot
> in the 'Scutcheon,* and was clearly written to Mr. Forster in order that
> it might be seen, was withheld for thirty years from his knowledge,
> and that of the public whose judgement it might so largely have in-
> fluenced.[19]

Literary Anecdotes of the Nineteenth Century had a similar comment:

> . . . he [Forster] kept its contents to himself — and some thirty
> years were to elapse ere the poet knew how deeply his work had
> touched the great novelist. The letter was made public for the first
> time in Forster's *Life of Dickens* . . . and Mr. Browning made no se-
> cret of his regret that the nature of its contents had been so long
> withheld: naturally feeling that such an expression of opinion from
> one so prominently before the public would have been invaluable to
> himself and his work at that period of his career.[20]

Dickens' high opinion had not been withheld, for it was made public
as early as November 1848 in *Sharpe's London Magazine:* ". . . Charles
Dickens . . . is known to consider and declare this poet's 'Blot on the
Scutcheon' [*sic*] the most poetic, pathetic, and generally beautiful of
domestic tragedies." In a book by Thomas Powell, published in 1849
in America and in 1851 in England,[21] and in a review of the first
American edition of Browning's poems in the December 1849 issue of

Graham's Magazine, there were also references to Dickens' praise of the play. Although Browning might not have known of these or of other possible publicizings of the novelist's opinion, he seems not to have thought that such reports might have been made without his knowledge when he was living in Italy.

Certainly it would have meant much to Browning to learn in 1842 of Dickens' opinion from Forster, and we can wonder why Forster withheld it — he who was closely associated with Browning and who in the face of the unfavorable reviews of *A Blot* spoke out in its defense. When Browning did learn of Dickens' opinion after Forster's *Life of Charles Dickens* was published in the early seventies, he assumed that others had not known either. Browning could have added a grievance against Forster to his resentment of Macready's conduct in connection with *A Blot.* Whatever Browning might have said elsewhere about Forster's silence on Dickens' praise of *A Blot,* there is only a passing allusion to it in his comments to Hill on the early history of the play. Forster's strange behavior never kept Browning from giving him credit for his professional support even though there was a temporary rupture in their friendly relationship in the year following Browning's return to England in 1861.[22]

Browning felt that in spite of all that was done to keep the play from succeeding, it had a good reception on the first and second runs. He said that Macready's intention to damage the play was frustrated by the good acting of some of the cast. As evidence of the success of the play he pointed to Macready's declaration that it was successful, the applause, and the first run of "three nights in the same week" followed by a second longer run in 1848.[23] For Macready's declaration we have only Browning's word, and his general confusion about the play's history precludes dependence on his word alone.

The reviews of 1843 did not testify to the play's success, nor did the applause, as Arnould, Browning's friend, made clear in his account to Domett of the performances. Browning's friends rallied to his support. The first night was a "triumph"; there was "no mistake at all about the honest enthusiasm of the audience." On the second night Arnould was one of "about sixty or seventy in the pit," and they seemed crowded "when compared to the desolate emptiness of the boxes"; but the gallery was still full. Arnould went again on the third night and a glance at the "miserable, great, chilly house, with its apathy and emptiness" indicated that this would be the last performance. Forty years later Browning was remembering only the fanfare of the first night.

The play had a longer run in 1848 and 1849. Samuel Phelps, whom Browning had supported for the lead in *A Blot* in 1843, became co-manager, then manager of Sadler's Wells Theatre. During his successful management from 1844 to 1862 he revived Browning's play. It was given on November 27, 28, and 29 and December 7, 8, and 9 in 1848 and on February 2 and 3 in 1849. The run was longer, but as a stage play its reception was no more favorable than that in 1843.

There were reviews in the *Athenaeum, Literary Gazette,* and *Theatrical Times* on December 2; in the *Era* and *Weekly Dispatch* on December 3; and in the *Examiner* on December 9. Like the earlier critics, the reviewers saw that *A Blot* was not a successful stage play; they applied such phrases as "but a sketch," a "poet's play" *(Theatrical Times);* "more a poem than a play" *(Weekly Dispatch);* "the poet's, and not the playwright's art" *(Era).* Not surprisingly, therefore, several reviewers considered it a theatrical risk. Although the critic for the *Athenaeum,* after referring to the earlier trouble and approving of the new trial, said the "experiment perfectly succeeded," he thought the play's "interest to be of too painful a sort to permit its having a long run." Clearly the critics felt that whatever success the play had was due to good acting and mounting. The performance received most of their attention; the play itself was scarcely discussed beyond a reference to it as a poetical rather than a dramatic work. The *Athenaeum* gave a summary, but only the *Era* made an attempt to appraise *A Blot.*

Among the friends who expressed pleasure in seeing the play at the time of its revival in 1848 were Arnould, Henry F. Chorley, and Forster. Arnould wrote Browning of his going to the first performance with Chorley and "many other" of Browning's friends and of the "delight & gratification" that they "in common with a crowded audience" felt at the revival. He called it a "grand triumph."[24] On the night when Chorley saw the play he sent the Brownings a welcome report: "never . . . was a more complete and legitimate success."[25] Forster wrote Phelps on the 29th: "I am going to avail myself of your kindness [of a box] to-night, and shall again see the play myself. There are very few other things going I should care to see twice — or even once."[26] The support of his friends, however, did not provide convincing evidence that *A Blot* had good stage qualities. The review of the performance in the *Examiner* (in all likelihood by Forster) had only a paragraph on the good acting, nothing about the quality of the play itself. The critic for the *Athenaeum* (who could have been Chorley — he wrote some reviews of Browning for this weekly) saw the play as a successful "attempt to give a poetic interest to a melo-dramatic subject."

THEATRE ROYAL,
Sadler's Wells.
Lessees, Messrs, GREENWOOD and PHELPS.

UNDER THE MANAGEMENT OF
Mr. PHELPS.

MONDAY, Nov. 27th, TUESDAY, 28th, & WEDNESDAY, 29th

Will be produced a Tragedy, in Three Acts, by ROBERT BROWNING, Esq entitled

A BLOT IN
THE
'SCUTCHEON.

With New Scenery, Dresses, and Decorations.

The Scenery by Mr F. FENTON, and Mr. BRUNNING.

The Decorations & Properties by Mr HARVEY.   *The Costumes by Mr COOMBES & Miss BAILEY.*

Thorold, Lord Tresham,	—	Mr. PHELPS
Austin Tresham,	—	Mr HOSKINS
Henry, Earl Mertoun,	—	Mr G. K. DICKINSON
Gerard,	—	Mr. GRAHAM

Ralph,	·		·	Mr HARRINGTON
Frank,	·	Retainers	·	Mr C. FENTON
Richard,	·	of	·	Mr KNIGHT
Walter,	·	Lord Tresham	·	Mr STILT
Phillip	·		·	Mr FRANKS
Peter,	·		·	Mr WILKINS

Mildred Tresham,	—	Miss COOPER
Guendolin Tresham.	—	Miss HUDDART

Playbill, A Blot in the 'Scutcheon, *November 27, 28, 29, 1848*

Samuel Phelps

Nor in the eighties and nineties, when *A Blot* was presented as the play of a famous man and acted by amateurs and professionals, was it considered a successful stage drama. Much of the acting was good, and the critics appreciated it. But they still saw the weakness of *A Blot* as a stage play. After one of Lawrence Barrett's productions in America, the reviewer for the Washington *National Republican* of December 20, 1884, expressed admiration for the acting, but saw what was so often observed: that as it stood *A Blot* could "hardly be called a good acting play."[27] The *Athenaeum* (May 9, 1885) reported of the Fry production: "The work . . . will always be more of a favourite in the closet than on the boards." Fry himself wrote, ". . . lengthy criticisms appeared in all the leading papers, though I must honestly confess they were by no means altogether favourable, except as regards the enthusiasm and ambition which led to the production."[28]

Alma Murray played the role of Mildred in a performance given at the Olympic Theatre on March 15, 1888, under the auspices of the Browning Society, and she received great applause; but according to the *Athenaeum* (Mar. 24, 1888), as an acting drama *A Blot* made "strong demands upon the power of faith in an audience." On June 15, 1893, a performance was given at the London Opera Comique Theatre. The review in the *Times* of June 16, 1893, brought in the following verdict: "Browning's tragedy has already been tried on the stage, and has been found wanting." These were representative criticisms. If Phelps, Barrett, or Alma Murray could not convince the public that *A Blot* was a good acting play, Macready, with all his ability and his power as a manager, could not have made it into what it was not. Yet Browning never weakened in his defense of it as a stage play.

Whatever the critics had said of *A Blot* in 1843 and in 1848 and 1849, Browning wished to think that his play had been successful. There is pathos in the words of a writer of great poems longing for recognition of an early play; he felt that the "success" of the eighties vindicated his belief in it. In the face of the production of *A Blot* in America he sometimes played variations on his theme that the early performances had succeeded in spite of Macready's desire to damage it. *A Blot* had run "only" a few nights, he said to Fry; with adequate treatment by Macready it would have had the usual success of plays, he wrote Mrs. Hill (Mar. 7, 1885). He indicated his anxiety about the Barrett performances in his statement (Dec. 29, 1884) that a play "proper enough for representation forty-one years ago" would not have any success in the eighties when played to an audience with different

Alma Murray

demands. He was happy, and probably relieved, when he could say
(Mar. 7, 1885) that Barrett had reported the American performance to
have been a decided success. Near the end of the letter he wrote, ". . .
I should much prefer to be let alone in this matter henceforward and
forever — the American revival having fully answered my purpose — if
I ever had one!" The purpose, we can hardly doubt, was to have public
proof of the stageworthiness of *A Blot.*

In giving the welcome news of the success to Mrs. Hill, Browning showed that he was pleased to think that this success would bring
enlightenment to critics.

> . . . the expressions in the letter [from Mr. Barrett] seem to register
> "a hit" — that being the word: and if so, I might ask the critics who
> supposed, this long while, that, the most having been already done
> for the play, its chance — on any possible revival — was out of the
> question, — whether, in the face of what happens through the enter-
> prise of a stranger, the likelihood is not rather that, had my friend
> Macready dealt fairly by it, the play would have enjoyed the luck
> usual to such works in that day of moderate successes.

Four days later he again was thinking of the play's having been denied
the treatment that he felt would have at once proved its worth. In referring to Barrett's production in America, he said to Domett: "If that
can be done in the green, what should be done in the day! A man one
never heard of [Barrett] can succeed in the character [Tresham]
there!"[29] Furthermore, Browning received a check from Barrett — "all
in strange contrast with my English experience so many years ago."[30]

Though Barrett had permission to make changes, in November of
1884 he wrote Browning that he would give *A Blot* as it had been written.[31] To present it in its original form would further justify the value
Browning placed on the play. Supposing that Barrett had made no
changes, he wrote Hill on January 15, 1885, "The main thing observ-
able [in the reported success of one of Barrett's performances] is that,
with the exception of the song, the whole piece was played as written
— in contrast with Macready's treatment, which cut out a full
quarter." But *A Blot* was not played as written; when the time came to
prepare it for the stage, Barrett did make cuts and changes.[32] In numerous reports that Browning received from America he must have
learned of these alterations. On April 10, 1885, he wrote Mrs. Hill, "I
could not but allow Mr Barrett to adopt them [the changes], sure as I
was of his zeal in the cause, — but the satisfactory thing would have

been that the play was given just as the playwright intended." One of
Barrett's changes was the omission of the opening scene; Browning had
complained to Elizabeth Barrett of Macready's having cut this scene.

So buoyed up was Browning by the welcome news of the American performances that he was persuaded a short time later to go incog-
nito to Fry's production. On April 25, 1885, he asked a friend if he
would like to accompany his sister Sarianna to the performance on May
2. "For myself, I shall be dining with the R.A.s that evening, — not
that I should go at any time to see my own work."[33] But Browning did
go to the performance on April 30. He sat in a box "covered in with
muslin curtains" (this is reminiscent of his going to the second performance of *Strafford* "muffled up in a cloak"), and after the performance he went on the stage to thank the actors and Fry, "expressing his
great pleasure at the representation." He went home and at once wrote
to Furnivall:

> Before I go to bed I must tell you how more than pleased I was
> with the play this evening: all was done capitally — all that was req-
> uisite for getting a fair judgment of the thing: and when I contrast
> the pains which must have been bestowed on rehearsals, &c., by
> those kind and sympathetic amateurs with the carelessness and worse
> of Macready — the purist [restorer of Shakespeare's text] and pre-em-
> inently capable actor, — I feel very grateful indeed. I am glad I was
> persuaded by Mr. Fry to go: he kept my incognito faithfully. . . .[34]

His pleasure in "getting a fair judgment" of his play from the
Barrett and Fry productions revived in him the old urge to write plays.
He confided to Barrett: "When I look back to the circumstances under
which the piece was brought out in London — forty-two years ago — I
may well wonder whether, — if my inclination for dramatic writing
had met with half so much encouragement and assistance as you have
really gratuitously bestowed on it, — I might not have gone on, for
better or worse, play-writing to the end of my days. . . ."[35] After he
saw Alma Murray (Mrs. Forman) perform in *A Blot* he wrote, "Such
treatment as yours to a play much maltreated so many years ago, goes
near to reviving in its author something of the old impulse once strong
in him to try afresh in that direction," an impulse to become alive
again near the end of his life.[36]

Taking her cue from this statement, Miss Murray continued the
topic of a fresh attempt. Browning's real feeling emerged from the
graceful compliment in his reply:

It would be superfluous indeed to assure you that I shall always take a deep interest in such an undertaking as you announce to be possible. As for my own interposition — were it on the account of any person or of any thing in the whole world it should be in the case of my own especial Heroine. But I dare not say more than that *if* an idea strikes me as being altogether available for representation on the stage — the stage being yours, and the chief representative yourself, — I will not disobey what Socrates calls the "Daemon" — but he observes that it invariably was efficacious in dissuading him from an enterprise, — not in urging him to become enterprizing: and so with me.[37]

Browning expressed himself similarly to Hill, ". . . I write no more plays" (Dec. 21, 1884). Old longings were brought to life for brief moments as he enjoyed the satisfaction of feeling that the old story was discountenanced — that *A Blot* "proved a failure in spite of Macready's best endeavours" (Apr. 10, 1885). But at this time he seemed to have no real desire to make any further attempts in the medium that had cost him so much misery even though from time to time there were suggestions from others besides Alma Murray that he write another play.

His satisfaction was not undiluted. The letters to Hill marked the depth of his bitterness. He wrote in his first letter, "I hardly wish to revive a very painful matter." Once revived after his forty-year silence, it was like a root bearing gall and wormwood; and he was not able to curb his emotions as one letter followed another though more than once he gave the promise of the "last word" to Hill. Finally the promised word came in a letter to Mrs. Hill: "I should never have troubled you with all this detailed explanation, had I not wished to justify the suppression of that friendly old piece of criticism (from the 'Athenaeum') which your critic — I am sure in all good faith — would have given as a fair report of how the failure came to be — and now an end to the matter. . . ." Even though Browning in general succeeded in putting aside the upsetting experience of *A Blot's* failure until its revival in the eighties, one effect of his early experience was that thereafter he attended the theater only upon rare occasions. This he lamented in a letter to the actor Squire Bancroft: "As it happened, an early disillusion gave me a distaste which I have not been wise enough to get the better of — and hence comes that rarity of my attendance at the Play, which I remorsefully acknowledge now that I know how much I have irrevocably lost by it."[38]

But to some extent he did get the upperhand of his bitterness. Macready of the *Blot* affair came to be disassociated from the old friend. Browning did not speak to Macready in the days following the early run, but as time passed their personal relationship was resumed. After the death of a daughter of Macready's in 1850, Browning sent him a message of sympathy through Forster. When Macready's first wife died in 1852 Browning wrote a letter of condolence, in which he said, ". . . and if some few of the idler hopes of that time came to nothing, at least all the best and dearest memories of a friendship I prized so much remain fresh in my heart as ever. . . ." In April of 1853 Browning expressed to Forster sincere concern for Macready, who had recently lost a son. "How does dear Macready bear up — I have no heart to send a word to him — God bless and comfort him, I can say to you at least."[39]

That Browning did value the friendship was clear from his reference to a meeting that took place in 1855 in London. He wrote of it to Kenyon.

> Yes — it was a gratifying thing to reknit affection with Macready: he did not come that evening from a sudden, severe attack of illness. Forster dined with us and I afterward went to Macready who was in the Doctor's hands: next day we all dined together *lovingly* at Forster's — next day, he called here and sat with Ba for two hours and more — we parted old friends and something more.[40]

Browning spent an evening with Macready and Dickens, and Macready called on the Brownings when they were all in Paris in 1856. Elizabeth wrote her sister: "Macready called on us, found us at dinner, and comes again. You must know he rather likes me — Robert of course."[41] In answer to an invitation from Macready when the three were in London later in the year, Browning took pains to explain why he and Elizabeth might not be able to see him before leaving England for Italy; he also made clear that the invitation in itself was gratifying, "I can't hope to say how strangely it touches & thrills me, — how happy I am to be where I feel myself in your regard — & you must know how truly & peculiarly I valued *that* ever."[42]

After reading Lady Pollock's book on Macready, Browning told her how he felt when he put aside the interval of misunderstanding: ". . . I can associate myself with you in esteeming Macready as altogether noble and love-worthy as well as — on the whole — the most admirable actor I ever saw."[43] At the end of his biography of Macready, William Archer gave Browning's "estimate" of the actor:

I found Macready . . . and happily, after a long interval, resumed him, so to speak — one of the most admirable and indeed fascinating characters I have ever known: somewhat too sensitive for his own happiness, and much too impulsive for invariable consistency with his nobler moods.[44]

Archer added, "Macready in a nutshell!"

There was something, too, of Browning in this description. Where his work and reputation, as well as his wife and son, were concerned, sensitive spots were sometimes touched in such a way as to disturb him severely. And his impulsive behavior toward Macready in the forties was inconsistent with his usual gratitude for support of his interests. The frustrated efforts in playwriting over a period of seven years and the lack of general acceptance of his poetry over a longer stretch left their mark. After Browning became famous he overexplained to himself and to others why his early works were not recognized. In his mind he distinguished the perpetrators of damage to three of his early works from those who saw their value and were willing to give them recognition.

If we ask why a poet after he was widely acclaimed felt so bitter about the years of public indifference, we can find at least part of the answer in a letter written to a friend in the last decade of Browning's life, in which he referred to the favorable reception of *A Blot* in Washington: "I should have liked to tell this to my father and mother in the old days — now, it seems to matter so little to anybody and less still to me."[45] It must have been painful to him that those near to him who believed in his ability never knew of the recognition of his poetry. So intensely had he felt the disappointments of his early career that not even fame could keep them submerged in his memory without occasional reappearance.

CHAPTER IX

Farewell to the Stage

Colombe's Birthday, 1844

Browning was able to put his completed works behind him and turn readily to new ones, often thinking of different types of poetry. His brain was teeming with ideas. After the publication of *Sordello,* he wrote Eliza Flower, "Do me all the good you can, you and Mr. Fox . . . for I have a head-full of projects — mean to song-write, play-write forthwith." He added in a postscript that he hoped to " 'build' a huge Ode."[1] In facing defeat after his efforts to please Macready with the *Druses,* he wrote to the actor, ". . . tomorrow will I betimes break new ground with So and So — an epic in so many books . . . let it but do me half the good 'Sordello' has done — be praised by the units, cursed by the tens, and unmeddled with by the hundreds!"[2]

Browning took earnestly to the craft, never in these years allowing discouragement to hamper his efforts. When Arnould wrote Domett of the failure of *A Blot,* he said of Browning, "But I am sure in whatever way he regards it, whether as a failure or a partial success, the effect on him will be the same, viz. to make him still to work, work, work."[3] The unsuccessful *Blot* was performed in February 1843. It was not long until rumors of Browning's professional activities were being circulated. On May 4 Elizabeth Barrett wrote Miss Mitford, "But I must tell you first that Mr. Browning is said to have finished two plays, one for Charles Kean and the public, the other for himself and Bells and Pomegranates."[4] The one for Kean was *Colombe's Birthday,* and the rumor that he had completed it was not altogether accurate.

168

On May 15, a short while after Elizabeth's comment to Miss Mitford, Browning wrote to Domett, "I have a desk full of scrawls at which I look, and work a little. I want to publish a few more numbers of my 'Bells' — and must also make up my mind to finish a play I wrote lately for Charles Kean, if he will have it."[5] He obviously intended to work further on the play.

Nearly a year was to pass before *Colombe's Birthday* was published — a breathing spell after the quick succession of the publication of the preceding three works within three months. Whether at the time Browning wrote Domett he was working little or much on his "scrawls," he was making plans for the future after the unfortunate result of his attempt to shape *A Blot* to suit Macready. By autumn of 1843 he said he was "chin-deep in work (having four new works in forwardness)."[6] The new works must have been *Colombe's Birthday, A Soul's Tragedy,* and *Dramatic Romances and Lyrics* (which he originally planned to publish as two *Bells*).

His writing did not consume all of his waking hours. Though there is little information about his activities in the months after his break with Macready, it is certain that he had no dearth of companionship outside the actor's circle. One of his many friends whose professional interests were related to his was Horne. In the autumn of 1843 Browning was helping him choose mottoes for chapters in his *New Spirit of the Age.*[7]

One chapter was given to Browning and John Westland Marston. For the discussion of Browning, Horne made use of the eighteen-page article he had published in the *Church of England Quarterly* in October 1842. He deleted several passages and a number of quotes, most of them long. Among the additions was a paragraph on *The Return of the Druses,* a duplication of a passage in the article on that play in the January 1844 issue of the *Foreign and Colonial Quarterly* (later called the *New Quarterly Review*). It must therefore have been the author of *A New Spirit* who had previously spoken out in defense of Browning's *Druses.* Horne was just the one to lend a sympathetic ear to Browning's account of the fate of his plays because he himself had not been able to come to terms with Macready when he had submitted plays to him in 1835 and 1839.[8]

Browning fared better than a number of those chosen to represent the new spirit of the age. The task of putting the book together was beyond the capabilities of the author, and many were quick to express their objections when the criticism did not please them.[9] Elizabeth

Barrett, who gave considerable assistance to Horne in preparing the essays on their contemporaries,[10] wrote Browning later, ". . . it was not merely putting one's foot into a hornet's nest, but taking off a shoe and stocking to do it."[11] Even though the reception of Horne's book was hostile more often than not, the distaste for it did not cancel the good effect of the discussion of Browning. In a work that reached a second edition in six months, Browning shared the spotlight with such authors as Tennyson, Carlyle, Wordsworth, and Dickens as well as others whose names were not to be so well remembered after their time.

Browning was grateful to Horne for his help. After learning of the authorship of the article in the *Church of England Quarterly,* published in October 1842, he had thanked him for it,[12] the first of continued and varied expressions of gratitude to Horne. He read *A New Spirit* with interest as soon as it appeared and again thanked Horne, this time for the "very kind, handsome, generous, good-purposed and good-producing" notice of him. He thought Horne's discussion of *Sordello* better than anything else in the book.[13] An illuminating paragraph in a letter that Browning was to write to Elizabeth in 1845 also showed his appreciation of Horne's efforts as well as the lurking venom that was apt to imperil his peace of mind, even if momentarily, during the months of his courtship.

> I feel grateful to him, I know, for his generous criticism, and glad & proud of in any way approaching such a man's standard of poetical height. And he might be a disappointed man, too — for the players trifled with and teazed out his very earnest nature, which has a strange aspiration for the horrible tin-&-lacquer 'crown' they give one from their clouds (of smooth shaven deal done over blue) — and he don't give up the bad business yet, but thinks a "small" theatre would somehow not be a theatre, and an actor not quite an actor . .
> I forget in what way, but the upshot is, he bates not a jot in that rouged, wigged, padded, empty headed, heartless tribe of grimacers that came and canted me; not I, them, — a thing he cannot understand — *so,* I am not the one he would have picked out to praise, had he not been *loyal.*[14]

Browning was still exerting his energies for what he called the "tin-&-lacquer" crown when he was writing *Colombe's Birthday.* By the time *A New Spirit of the Age* was published on March 5, 1844, he was at the end of work on his play. He had been writing, he said, for nine or ten hours nearly every day for five weeks.[15] As he sat down to write, there was not just the tug of his highly original genius but also that of a decade of criticism. His problem was how to reconcile the two. He was fully conscious of both and had been for some time. The introductory words to his second work, *Paracelsus*, had signalized the departure from tradition by stressing the mood in a work that gave the appearance of being a drama; the Preface to *Strafford* had expressed his intention to avoid the usual emphasis on external action; the Advertisement to *King Victor* had called attention particularly to the individual characters. It was clear that Browning was primarily interested in presenting character dramatically and that his ideas for doing so were unconventional. *Pippa Passes* had shown the extent and success of his originality. In the letter to Macready of 1840 in which he defended the *Druses*, Browning had indicated his strong attraction to untrodden paths.

> Kean wants to be Macbeth three times a week . . people go to see if he can manage it; *you are* and have been this — how many years? — Macbeth — as everybody knows: why not be something else? Were I *you* (save the mark!) — it should be my first condition with a playwright that his piece should be new, essentially new for better or for worse: if it failed . . who that has seen you perform in some forty or fifty parts I could name, would impute the failure to you who were Iago on Thursday and Virginius on Saturday? If it did not fail . . were it even some poor *Return of the Druzes*, it would be something yet unseen, in however poor a degree — something, therefore, to go and see.[16]

He added, leaning upon Lear: "Laugh at all this — I write, indeed, that you may . . for is it not the characteristic of those who withdraw from 'the scene' to 'take on us the mystery of things, as if [we] were God's spies'? — 'And we'll wear out, in a walled prison' (my room here) 'sects and packs of great ones that ebb and flow by the moon'!"

Browning did "wear out" some writers considered great in his day, and to a certain extent he did withdraw from "the scene." He held fast to his own developing ideas of character revelation. That he prized originality and a poet's adherence to it came out again in a passage on Tennyson's *Poems* of 1842. When he sent the two volumes to Domett, he lamented that Tennyson had omitted " 'everything that is his,' as distinguished from what is everybody's!"[17]

The other tug — that of criticism — was strong though Browning was frequently accused of indifference and wilfulness. He knew it was important to his success to consider what others said of his work, and he welcomed criticism when he felt it was given for his benefit.

While working on *Colombe's Birthday* he gratefully acknowledged advice Domett had sent him and indicated the serious and continued attention he gave to his poetic line.

> I . . . thank you heartily for your criticism, which is sound as old wine. The fact is, in my youth (i.e. childhood) I wrote *only* musically — and after stopped all that so effectually that I even now catch myself grudging my men and women their half-lines, like a parish overseer the bread-dole of his charge. But you will find a difference, I think, in what has reached you already, even, and *more* in what *shall* reach you, D. V. I really feel it awkward to beg you to say your mind, and at length, on what I send — SO INESTIMABLE a favour is it, which those quiet words require![18]

How much Browning wanted criticism and appreciated Domett's comments was shown in a letter from Arnould to Domett:

> Your advice to him as to his language, rhythm, &c., was admirable, and he seemed *really* grateful for it: — "now this," he said, "is what one wants; how few men there are who will give you this." He read it out to us himself; I can assure you there was not in his manner the slightest semblance of anything approaching to offence; on the contrary, he seemed to feel what he said, "How friendly this is."[19]

Again, as in writing *A Blot,* he kept professional criticism in mind. The play *Colombe's Birthday* itself gave evidence of changes that were appearing in areas in which he had been criticized. Horne and Macready had objected to Browning's not helping his readers understand the situation early in his plays, Macready had objected to the first scene of *A Blot,* which cluttered the stage to little effect, and reviewers of *Strafford* had objected to his not gaining or holding the interest of the audience. Critics had complained that Browning's handling of historical details clogged the understanding. *A Blot* had offended the critics' sense of morality and many thought its pathos was marred by improbability of behavior. We know that Browning read reviews of his works. *Colombe's Birthday* suggests that he turned some of the criticisms to good account. He revealed the situation early in the play. Politics and history were unobtrusive. He used an acceptable love plot that was probable within the bounds of romance. He let the love story ride easily on the crest of state events.

But Browning did not heed one criticism that had been made by Macready and by the critics of *King Victor* — that of too little action.

Though he had made concessions, he had indicated time after time that his interest lay in internal rather than external action. Since he did not have to consider Macready's wishes in *Colombe's Birthday,* he felt free to explore in his own way the drama of the mind and heart of his characters, and in this exercise he advanced toward his dramatic monologue.

With his belief in the technique of character analysis that he was using for the stage, Browning felt that Macready had failed to appreciate what he was doing. Charles Kean was just the one to show that Macready had been wrong and Browning had been right in evaluating the plays. During his early professional years Macready had Edmund Kean as his competitor; by the forties he had Kean's son Charles, of lesser talent, to reckon with. In his strong feeling against his rival, Macready was backed by his followers. Among them were Forster, who actively assisted him, and Browning, who had asserted his support until the trouble with *A Blot* ended their professional ties.

After the bitter experience with Macready, Browning wrote *Colombe's Birthday* with Charles Kean in mind. If he had written most of the play when he told Domett of it in May 1843 — and he gave that impression — he had some ten months before completion in which he could work on it at will, certainly by his own words "writing for nine or ten hours every day" during the last five weeks he had it in hand. Finally he again faced the ordeal of subjecting a play of his to the verdict of an actor. On March 9, 1844, he took his play to Kean and read it to him and his wife. On the next day he sent news of the outcome to his friend Christopher Dowson,[20] one of the Colloquials who was much interested in the theater. After the reading, Kean "approved of" the play but found reasons for not using it at any time soon; he wanted to keep it until Easter of the next year — "unpublished all the time." Taken "by surprise," Browning on the spur of the moment promised him a copy and "a fortnight's grace, to come to terms in," before publishing it or accepting another offer. But once away from Kean he changed his mind, no doubt thinking of the bitter experience of waiting for *A Blot* to be performed, and on the same day he sent the manuscript to press. He "merely put the right of *the acting*" at the disposal of Kean, who never chose to stage the play. It remained unacted until 1853.

Browning explained to Dowson his reasons for changing his mind: ". . . I . . . *will* do no such thing as let this new work lie stifled for a year and odd, — and work double-tides to bring out something as likely to be popular this present season — for something I *must* print, or risk the hold, such as it is, I have at present on *my* public." He thought that two or three hundred pounds from Kean would pay him "but indifferently for hasarding the good fortune" which seemed "slowly but not mistakeably setting in" upon him. He had written Domett in the preceding October, "People read my works a little more, they say. . . ."[21]

How can Browning's optimistic reports to Domett and Dowson of his increased following be reconciled with the unfavorable reviews of *A Blot* published in February of 1843? He was not necessarily thinking of these reviews. Encouragement was coming in other ways, as we shall see in the following paragraphs. At the end of the discouraging reception of *A Blot* four reviews were devoted to various publications by Browning. The *Athenaeum* had reviewed all of his works in order through *King Victor,* but it did not keep pace with the quick succession of the next three works — *Dramatic Lyrics* in November 1842, the *Druses* in January 1843, and *A Blot* in February 1843. In accordance with the usual practice it dealt with *A Blot* soon after the stage production. Thus the *Athenaeum's* negative review of the play (Feb. 18, 1843) took precedence over the irritable one of *Dramatic Lyrics* (Apr. 22, 1843) and the better disciplined one of the *Druses* (July 1, 1843). These reviews in the *Athenaeum* and the delayed favorable criticism of the *Druses* (with the introductory paragraph on *A Blot*) in the *Foreign and Colonial Quarterly Review* of January 1844 have already been discussed along with related criticism; they are mentioned here because of their place in the chronology.

Another criticism — not yet discussed — between the reviews of *A Blot* and the publication of *Colombe's Birthday* was a short one in the *Gentleman's Magazine* (Aug. 1843) of *Bells* Nos. I through IV. At this time it was unusual to include several of Browning's works in one critical estimate. Because of its brevity and sketchiness it was not helpful, as the over-all review in the *Church of England Quarterly* of October 1842 had been. But examining Browning's works together in one place was important in that it would soon lead to critics' relating them in order to explain the underlying qualities. Though Browning surely was not pleased by the unfavorable review of *Dramatic Lyrics* in the *Athenaeum,* he probably welcomed the more sympathetic tone of the longer and more effective one of the *Druses* and might have recognized the singularity of the one in the *Gentleman's Magazine.* He certainly must have felt encouraged by Horne's review of the *Druses* and also his general discussion in The New Spirit of the Age, which fell into the time span between the last of the reviews of A Blot in 1843 and the publication of Colombe's Birthday in 1844.

Browning might well have known of projected reviews. His movements, personal and professional, extended to profitable sources of influence. In May 1843 he wrote Domett that he had access to several editors.[22] One of them was in all likelihood the editor of the Foreign and Colonial Quarterly Review, retitled in 1844 the New Quarterly Review, or Home, Foreign, and Colonial Journal,[23] which would publish two articles on Browning within a year after the appearance of Colombe's Birthday, one in October 1844 and one in April 1845. Browning knew the value of keeping his fences mended. Some of the well-deserved favorable reviews of his works had been written by members of the circles in which he moved, reviews that contributed partly to his "good fortune." And the few criticisms of Colombe's Birthday were written by friends.

Some friends who were not critics were Browning's partisans. One of these was Bryan Waller Procter, who had already started a verse epistle to Browning, to be published later under Procter's pseudonym, Barry Cornwall. Outside his practice of law Procter's literary interests extended to the writing of plays and poetry and to companionship with many literary people. Browning wished to dedicate Colombe's Birthday to him and asked for his permission. In his answer of March 21, 1844, Procter indicated how high he placed Browning among his contemporaries.

> And now to thank you for your kindness — or rather — if you will let me use the word — your friendship. I am a bad thanker — but I mean all that I say, when I say that it will give me a great pleasure to have my name associated with you in any way — and I am not very sure that I could say as much — as far as poetry goes — to anyone else, except Tennyson. I accept therefore your kindness in the same spirit as it is offered, and am very proud of the alliance.[24]

Procter, whose own play Mirandola had gained him recognition, like others looked upon Browning as a dramatist. He continued:

> I am glad to hear your account of your play and I have no doubt about it. I am quite sure — and have always (and to everybody) said that — if you would give yourself fair play you would be sure to do great things — and you will do better than you now have done (whatever it may be). Avant! onward is the word. But you must shun brain

fever and loneliness (the word is loneliness not loveliness) — and
with health and the resolution to do — and to look at the thing
fairly, I will back you against any of the Dramatists of the day. . . .

Colombe's Birthday, with the dedication to Browning's staunch
friend, was published in April of 1844. After his disappointing experience with Kean, the quick decision to send his manuscript to the
press, and the publication of his play, he again awaited the reception of
a work written for the stage. The reviews were slow to start, and there
were few of them. Forster reviewed the play in the *Examiner* on June
22, two months after it was published. He thought it gave proof of
Browning's genius; there was a "want in it: but not of passion, nor of
thought." It was a "building of strength and stateliness, notwithstanding its intricate passages, and galleries of too quaint device: raised by a
man of rich imagination, and many fine and noble sympathies." Nerve
and vigor of writing, noble images, great force and beauty in the situations and in the struggles of Colombe, a simple story in contrast to its
subtlety of treatment — all of these Forster noted as he summarized
and illustrated with quotations.

But with this praise there was ill-tempered fault-finding at the
beginning and end of the review. Since Forster was one of Macready's
clique, Browning's negotiations with Kean perhaps had something to
do with the abusive tone. No doubt, said Forster, Browning could give
good reasons for the effort he exacted for the pleasure of his poetry; it
was Browning's responsibility to write so as to make his good qualities
apparent. Forster's attitude of the moment was clear. "As far as he has
gone, we abominate his tastes as much as we respect his genius."

Four months later two favorable reviews appeared. Chorley reviewed *Colombe's Birthday* in the *Athenaeum* on October 19. The beginning paragraph is noteworthy. "Fertility of invention is a merit which
Mr. Browning may claim, and must have allowed. Paracelsus, Pippa
Passes, the Druses, the Dramatic Lyrics, a Blot in the 'Scutcheon,
whatever may be their relative merits or demerits, have all essential
differences; and the dramatic tale before us has its own distinctive character." This recognition of fertility of invention Browning needed particularly now because in a low point of his career it would help prevent
the sharp criticism of individual works from overshadowing his total
contribution. Similar recognition came later and played an important
part in the establishment of his reputation. In another way Chorley anticipated later opinion in his evaluation of the play — "beautiful in the
lofty and chivalrous spirit it illustrates, in the noble lesson it teaches."

He also indicated the skill of Browning's characterization of Colombe and the "rich and poetical eloquence" of language.

The tone of condescension and contempt, the attack upon mannerisms, the repeated reference to the puzzling title "Bells and Pomegranates" — earlier complaints of the *Athenaeum* — were noticeably absent in this review written by a critic who was Browning's friend. Instead, general praise and a few pertinent remarks along with a summary and quotations directed the reader to Browning, who had advanced "many steps nearer to simplicity, without his fancy, or feeling, or stores of imagery showing a trace of impoverishment."

The other review published in October appeared in the *New Quarterly Review or Home, Foreign, and Colonial Journal*. The critic was delighted with the play as a whole and proceeded to enumerate its merits briefly. It was "a masterpiece of dramatic unity, both in conception and execution, and a poetical embodiment of a simple tale which realises our most happy visions of the 'Pure Ideal.' " The development of the character of Berthold could not be praised too highly and Colombe was one of the series of women that Browning had so remarkably portrayed. The only adverse criticism came at the end in the mild reproof for the needless obscurity caused by Browning's punctuation and his omission of stage directions.

A remarkable article on Browning's plays appeared six months later, in April 1845, in the same periodical, entitled "Living English Dramatists." The opinions expressed and the phrasing indicate that the reviewer who wrote this article had also written the article on *Colombe's Birthday* for the *New Quarterly Review* of October 1844 as well as the one on the *Druses* for the *Foreign and Colonial Quarterly Review* of January 1844 (which became the *New Quarterly Review*). Since we know that the review of the *Druses* was written by Horne and incorporated in his *New Spirit of the Age*, we conclude that it was this friend of Browning's who reviewed *Colombe's Birthday* and then discussed his plays in the article on dramatists. Beyond this point it will be assumed that it was Horne who wrote the review of *Colombe* (Oct. 1844) and that of the plays in general (Apr. 1845), both in the *New Quarterly Review*.

It was pointed out in the discussion of the review of the *Druses* that the critic — that is, Horne — in all likelihood knew of the Browning-Macready association. That the writer of the review of April 1845 — Horne — had heard Browning's side of the affair is also apparent. We are told that *Strafford* "succeeded perfectly in its representation at Drury Lane." We are also told that *A Blot* had been mistreated and that it had been at first successful. "It was, however, (why we know not,) speedily removed from the bills; and it had been brought out, as we are informed, with little or no care, so altered through the manager's suggestions, as to have lost that dramatic unity in a great degree, which, in its present form, so peculiarly distinguishes it." There was also a statement of the "disadvantage to which his plays are exposed, from being infamously stopped; so badly, indeed, as frequently to destroy the sense of very beautiful passages; and further, from being often deprived of the needful stage directions." (By "stopped" the reviewer meant "cut.")

Horne, who repeated Browning's complaints against Macready, was ahead of other critics at this time in comprehending Browning's technique. He wrote discerningly of Browning's use of the language of his day and the natural speech of the characters. Since Browning did not have his characters explain the motives for their conduct and speech but left the reader to infer from their "casual expressions" their feelings and the "workings of their souls," there was an apparent obscurity. This was explanation and defense of the technique in the plays that matured into the dramatic monologue.

Horne reverted to a criticism he had made in the review of the *Druses* — that Browning did not allow his readers to see from the beginning what became clear only later in the play. This again was a technique to be developed in the dramatic monologue, the one Browning had defended in his letter to Macready on the *Druses*. Though Horne objected to this plunging into the middle of things, he saw that the objection was most applicable to *King Victor* and the *Druses*. These were the plays, we know, that were written before Browning made a marked attempt to accommodate his ideas of playwriting to Macready's.

Horne pointed out that, besides satisfying the soul, the plays gave pleasure to the mind. His other remarks on the plays as a whole were summed up in the following sentence: "Thus we have dramatic power, intense feeling, and above all, reality, combined in the plays of this author." They had all the requirements for "unparalleled dramatic success," with faults "comparatively slight and incidental." Horne commented on each play in turn. *A Blot*, he said, was the best known of Browning's works. We have seen that only he and two other reviewers had not criticized the morality of the play after its performance and publication in 1843. In the review of 1845 Horne asserted that the play contained a Christian lesson. "The moral, in as far as it teaches that evil must ever spring from evil, and that man is never justified in revenge, is truly Christian."

Browning, who had struggled for acceptance of his plays, must surely have been pleased with this article. In sixteen pages it covered all of them, praised all except *Strafford,* treated them as plays suited to the stage, and devoted twelve pages to *Colombe's Birthday* "for a more special illustration of Browning's great merits." It explained techniques peculiar to Browning. And it left the impression that the poet himself had sought to leave — that *Strafford* was successful and that *A Blot* was mistreated. Browning later complained that Macready's side of their association had been aired in print, implying that his side had been passed over; but here as in Horne's discussion of *A Blot* and the *Druses* in January of 1844 is an instance of public support of which Browning must have had knowledge.

Only Horne in the *New Quarterly Review,* in all likelihood writing with Browning's defense of his play in mind, considered that *Colombe's Birthday,* along with his other plays, had the qualities requisite for dramatic success. *Colombe's Birthday* was not acted at the time of its publication. It was performed, however, in 1853, and the critics at that time could take its measurement as an acted play.

Helen Faucit, who had played in *Strafford* and *A Blot,* was now Mrs. Theodore Martin. When she knew early in 1853 that she was to make a return appearance on the stage, she requested of Browning a renewal of the permission he had given her earlier to play in *Colombe's Birthday.* [25] He gladly reaffirmed his consent, even including the liberty to reduce the play to the three acts that the manager at first desired. Browning asked only that the corrections in the revised 1849 edition, which were "important to the sense," be observed, [26] a request that shows his concern for improving his works.

Elizabeth — by this time she and Robert were living in Italy — admitted being "anxious" about the reception of the play. She was relieved when she heard that it had "taken rank . . . as a true poet's work," [27] just as she had been "anxious" and then relieved at the report of the "complete and legitimate success" of the first of the 1848 performances of *A Blot.* [28] Did her anxiety grow out of a fear that the deep-seated hurt of Browning's earlier disappointments might be reawakened? Was he as composed about the reception of *Colombe's Birthday* as his and Elizabeth's comments indicated? [29] Elizabeth said she was more concerned about the play than he, and in the fifties it is possible that he felt no return of his agitation, removed as he was from his experi-

NEVER ACTED!

THEATRE ROYAL,

HAY-MARKET.

Under the Management of - - Mr. BUCKSTONE.

FIRST NIGHT OF A PLAY, IN FIVE ACTS, entitled

COLOMBE's BIRTH-DAY

IN WHICH

Miss HELEN FAUCIT

Who is engaged for TEN NIGHTS, will make her First Appearance under the present Management.

TWENTY-FIFTH NIGHT of Mr BUCKSTONE'S

ASCENT OF MOUNT PARNASSUS

Which will be performed EVERY EVENING.

This Evening, MONDAY, April 25th, 1853,

Will be presented (NEVER ACTED) a Play, in Five Acts, entitled

COLOMBE's BIRTH-DAY

By ROBERT BROWNING, Esq. Author of "Paracelsus," &c.

The New Scenery by Mr GEORGE MORRIS and Mr O'CONNOR.   The Properties by Mr FOSTER

The Dresses by Mr BARNETT and Miss CHERRY.

Prince Berthold, *(Claimant of the Duchy)*   Mr HOWE
    Melchior, *(his Confidant)*   Mr ROGERS
Valence,   -   *(Advocate of Cleves)* -   Mr BARRY SULLIVAN
   Guibert,   Mr WILLIAM FARREN
   Gaucelme,   } *Courtiers* {   Mr H. CORRI
   Maufroy,   Mr BRAID
   Clugny,   Mr TILBURY
  Adolf, *(a Page)*   Mr VINCENT—*His First Appearance in London.*
Colombe of Ravestein, Duchess of Juliers & Cleves, Miss HELEN FAUCIT
    Sabyne, *(her Attendant)*   Miss A VINING

Playbill, Colombe's Birthday, *April 25, 1853*

Helen Faucit

Illustrated London News, *April 30, 1853*

ences with the London stage. Apparently he looked primarily upon the performances of his play as an advertisement of the collection (1849) in which it was printed.[30]

According to the playbills, *Colombe's Birthday* was performed in its original five acts at the Haymarket in 1853 — on April 25, 27, 28, 29 and on May 2, 6, 11; and Miss Faucit included it in performances she gave in Manchester in June. The consensus of critical opinion of the London performances was that the feeling, thought, and beauty of *Colombe's Birthday* qualified it for the closet but that it did not fulfill the requirements for the stage. The typical response is represented by the following phrases: a "dainty dramatic poem," "utterly unfitted for the purposes of stage-representation," "essentially made for private study" *(Spectator);* "deficient in the most essential elements of stage effect, plot, and incident," "best appreciated in the closet" *(John Bull);* "much thought, and occasionally much passion," "better fitted for private perusal than for theatrical representation" *(Daily News);* "scarcely a poem less fitted for stage representation" *(Times);* "charming poem, rather than drama" *(Athenaeum).* The few who did feel that *Colombe's Birthday* had possibilities as a stage play said, with almost no exception, that others had not recognized or would not recognize it as such.

Most of the critics thought that the first-night reception was good, but it was apparent to them that the play would not have a permanent stage success; they felt that much of its initial success was due to Helen Faucit's acting. There was enthusiastic praise for her and for the fine staging of the play. Although both Browning, who received reports from England, and Miss Faucit's biographer lamented the inadequate effect of the performance of the other actors,[31] it is doubtful that the participation of Phelps as leading man or producer (he has been erroneously said to have been one or the other[32]) or even of Macready, now retired, would have made a difference in the reception of *Colombe's Birthday* as an acting play. The two critics (for the *Morning Post* and *Atlas*) who considered *Colombe's Birthday* one of the best of modern plays realized that its merits might not ensure its success on the stage.

The reviewers of 1844 and of 1853, like future critics, found *Colombe's Birthday* praiseworthy, but, with the exception of Horne, they did not commend it as a play for the stage. They were impressed by the portrayal of various characters, especially Colombe, but realized that reading, not seeing, the play brought out the refinement of Browning's characterization. In the remarks of two people who saw the play in 1853 there was no variation of opinion from that of the critics. Anna Swanwick commented on its "charm of beauty, grace, and truth" and Westland Marston saw what "poetic acting" contributed to "poetic thought."[33] Letters of the Brownings to others who had written them of the performances did not reveal specifically what these well-wishers thought of *Colombe's Birthday*.[34]

When there was a surge of interest in Browning's plays in the last decade of his life, Alma Murray, under the auspices of the Browning Society, played in *Colombe's Birthday* at St. George's Hall on November 19, 1885. Though the performance gave much satisfaction to the Society, professional critics — such as those for the *Athenaeum* (Nov. 28) and *St. James's Gazette* (Nov. 20) — continued to consider *Colombe's Birthday* unacceptable as a stage play. A review by Sidney Lee in the *Academy* on November 28, 1885, best summed up the situation involving the performance of *Colombe's Birthday* and also of other plays of Browning's that were performed in the eighties.

> There is no need to conceal the fact that none of these experiments will convince the everyday theatre-going public that Mr. Browning is worthy of their patronage. But the members of the Browning Society will doubtless rest content if these representations prove their poet's plays to possess more dramatic stuff than the student of modern literature ordinarily gives them credit for.

Like the critics of 1853, the reviewer acknowledged that *Colombe's Birthday* was not for the stage; he was more specific than most critics in discussing the play's compensatory qualities. He said, "It may be admitted at once that all who were merely acquainted with 'Colombe's Birthday' as a poem learned from last week's rendering of it that it had some sterling dramatic qualities which they had not previously recognized." He had to go a step further. "Mr. Browning has nothing of the purely theatrical instinct, which is a pitiful substitute for the dramatic feeling of the poet, but is none the less its indispensable accessory."

Sidney Lee explained why Browning's plays were not suitable for performance and wherein they possessed qualities that compensated for their shortcomings. He then paid a tribute to the actors who had to make up for Browning's deficiencies as a writer of plays intended for stage production.

> We can conceive of no higher testimony to an actor's or an actress's capacity than to be able to state that he or she has interpreted one of Mr. Browning's characters so as to excite the interest of a large au-

Alma Murray

dience. Thirty-two years ago Miss Helen Faucit accomplished so much for the part of Colombe at the Haymarket; Miss Alma Murray did little less at St. George's Hall last week.

At various times Browning indicated his gratitude to Helen Faucit and Alma Murray. But at the end of his defeated attempts in the forties to win recognition as a writer of plays for the stage he let it be known that actors and managers in general were anathema to him. In writing to Elizabeth Barrett of Horne as a playwright and a helpful critic of his work, he stated his low opinion of stage people. He wrote to Horne of the "puddling the clear spirit" of poets by stage managers.[35] And in referring to his conference with Kean, who said he needed two months to study *Colombe's Birthday*, Browning informed Dowson of the comparative merits of men of letters and actors: "The poorest Man of letters (if *really* of letters) I ever knew is of far higher talent than the best actor I ever expect to know: nor is there one spangle too many, one rouge-smutch too much, on their outside-man — for the *inward* . . can't study a speech in a month! God help them . . . ."[36] Browning had had enough of actors, managers, and the theater in general.

CHAPTER X

Working in a New Light

Dramatic Romances and Lyrics, 1845:
Completion and Publication

After *Colombe's Birthday* was published in April 1844, Browning made no further attempt to use the stage as a medium of expression. With his elasticity of spirit he was ready to turn in another direction. At the end of July he wrote Domett: ". . . I feel myself so much stronger, if flattery not deceive, that I shall stop some things that were meant to follow, and begin again. I really seem to have something fresh to say. In all probability, however, I shall go to Italy first . . . for my head is dizzy and wants change."[1]

He went to Italy in August. In the same month a collection of Elizabeth Barrett's appeared under the title *Poems.* Her cousin John Kenyon gave the two volumes in dark green cloth boards to Sarianna, Browning's sister. After his return to England in December, Browning read the poems; he came upon a reference to himself in *Lady Geraldine's Courtship.* It was a happy-ending ballad of a poor and low-born poet and a great lady. The poet read aloud to Lady Geraldine

> at times a modern volume, — Wordsworth's solemn-
> thoughted idyl,
> Howitt's ballad-dew {so in 1st ed.}, or Tennyson's
> enchanted reverie, —
> Or from Browning some "Pomegranate," which, if cut
> deep down the middle,
> Shows a heart within blood-tinctured, of a veined
> humanity! —

Browning's name had appeared earlier in a work by Miss Barrett. Shortly after Wordsworth's *Poems, Chiefly of Early and Late Years* was published in 1842, she reviewed it in the *Athenaeum*. In the review she named Browning and Tennyson as two of the "high-gifted spirits" who would work and wait for results.[2]

Browning and Elizabeth Barrett, who was recognized as a learned woman and outstanding poet, had never met. During a prolonged period of invalidism Miss Barrett had maintained her social and professional contacts chiefly through correspondence. Though with her usual reluctance to receive strangers she rejected Kenyon's attempt early in the forties to introduce Browning to her "sofa-side," she was interested in reports of him and in his poems, which she often defended in letters to her correspondents. She also valued his opinion of her own works. When she heard of his comment on her *Greek Christian Poets,* articles published in the *Athenaeum* in 1842, she indicated her pleasure in a letter to her brother and in another to a friend; and she asked her cousin to let her keep a letter written to him by Browning in praise of one of her poems which Kenyon had shown him in manuscript.[3] With no less interest on his part Browning heard from Kenyon and also from others of the poetess at 50 Wimpole Street. He was ready to be introduced to her when Kenyon's effort to bring them together was ineffective. Browning later explained to Elizabeth that instead of writing with Kenyon's backing in an attempt to become one "of the foolish crowd of rushers-in upon genius" he chose to let his admiration for her poetry go "its natural way in silence."[4]

So it was that reticence and magnetism were already threaded in the pattern of their lives when Browning read the Pomegranate passage in Elizabeth's ballad.[5] A day or two later he saw Kenyon. They talked of Miss Barrett's poems and Browning ventured a suggestion that he might write her about them. At this time Kenyon encouraged him to do so and later sent a note to reassure Browning that his cousin would be pleased to hear from him.[6] On January 10, 1845, Browning sent the first of many letters to her. He began, "I love your verses with all my heart" and later in the letter repeated and added to the praise, "I do, as I say, love these books with all my heart — and I love you too. . . ."[7]

Elizabeth did not consent to a visit for over four months, but the correspondence flourished and Browning at once sensed that a new life lay before him. He and Elizabeth were on common ground intellectually and poetically. From the beginning there were exchanges of confidence on subjects they were interested in as poets — their reading and writing; critics, criticism, and reputations — and on their literary contemporaries.

Browning wrote of his ambitions for the future and of his hard work in the past. He drew on the deeper reserves of his nature as he discussed his art. One comment must have surprised the woman to whom reading was a joy and writing the mainstay of existence and who lamented the handicap of her isolation: that he no longer cared for reading but he read "to get words and forms for 'the public' "; that he "hated" the society he had put up with lest "some unknown good" escape him. And he added: "I have no pleasure in writing myself — none, in the mere act — tho' all pleasure in the sense of fulfilling a duty. . . . After all, there is a great delight in the heart of the thing; and use and forethought have made me ready at all times to set to work — but — I don't know why — my heart sinks whenever I open this desk, and rises when I shut it."[8]

At the time of these revelations Browning had already made progress on the collection of poems that were to make up his seventh *Bell.* It as well as the last *Bell* was to be published before the correspondence ended in September 1846, when the poets were married and went to Italy. Through the letters we observe Browning as he completed the works to be included in the last two numbers of the series, made revisions, and saw them through the press; and we learn of comments that others outside the press made about the works, of his response to some of the comments, and also of his reaction to the remarks of the professional critics or their silent neglect.

On February 26, before many letters were exchanged, Elizabeth heard from Browning something about *Luria* and *A Soul's Tragedy;* but before going on to them he said he would first "have some Romances and Lyrics, all dramatic, to dispatch."[9] For two months he made little reference to specific works of his. On May 1 Elizabeth asked to hear more of *The Flight of the Duchess,* which had already been published in part. He answered her question and added a word on *Saul,* which, he confessed, he would like to show her — "an ominous liking," for nobody, he said, saw what he wrote until it was printed. "But as you *do* know the printed little part of me, I should not be sorry if, in justice, you knew all I have *really* done. . . ."[10] Ten days later he gave her notice that in the next letter he would say how she must help him with his "new Romances and Lyrics, and Lays & Plays, and read them and heed them and end them and mend them!"[11]

On May 20, 1845, Browning paid his first visit to Elizabeth; it was followed by a precipitous proposal of marriage, her thrusting him back into reality, and his awkward retreat from his position and attempt to save the situation after being "soundly frightened" at having endangered their growing friendship. Poetry, which had brought them together, was to smooth the path for a more gradual shift from friendship to Elizabeth's submission to the overpowering force of love. He read and commented on her new translation of *Prometheus Bound* and in letter after letter she gently urged him to let her see his poems; she would be grateful if he would let her see any work he had. It was easier for him to turn to her *Prometheus* than to his own work. He had become weary of writing in the face of successive failures, and the emotional was crowding the poetic in his life. Repeatedly he confessed to her that he was writing about one thing and thinking of another. On June 14 he wrote, "But have you not discovered by this time that I go on talking with my thoughts away?" [12]

He realized that he could not continue to ignore his obligation to complete his *Bells,* nor could he further put aside Elizabeth's plea to see works already mentioned in his letters — *The Flight of the Duchess, Saul, Luria, A Soul's Tragedy.* The intention he had expressed in February that he was going to dispatch "some Romances and Lyrics" was repeated now in June, during the recovery period after the proposal. "I must make an end, print this Autumn my last four 'Bells,' Lyrics, Romances, The Tragedy, & Luria." [13] This time he acted upon his resolution. But instead of being published as four *Bells,* these works appeared as two: No. VII — *Dramatic Romances and Lyrics* and No. VIII — *Luria* and *A Soul's Tragedy.*

To give assistance, along with others, to Thomas Hood in his last illness, Browning had published five poems in *Hood's Magazine* between June 1844 and April 1845 — *The Laboratory, Claret and Tokay, Garden Fancies, The Boy and the Angel, The Tomb at St. Praxed's* (later called *The Bishop Orders His Tomb at St. Praxed's Church*), and part of *The Flight of the Duchess.* [14] These and other poems were to be included in the collection published as the seventh *Bell.* Browning completed and then Elizabeth read *The Flight of the Duchess* in July with his request for criticism in mind. Before the end of the month she had in hand the other poems printed in *Hood's.* In August, September, and October the work continued. [15] Elizabeth, who saw some poems before they went to the printer and some not until they were in proof, did help "mend" and "end" the *Dramatic Romances and Lyrics.*

During the process of working with the *Bells,* Browning revealed something of his habits of writing and revising and of his problems and aims. When he received her comments on *The Flight of the Duchess,* he wrote, "I shall let it lie, (my poem) till just before I print it; and then go over it, alter at the places, and do something for the places where I (really) wrote anyhow, almost, to get done." [16] Later he referred to other poems that he had taken her: "I shall correct the verses you have seen, and make them do for the present — " [17] According to these passages Browning let his verses rest between periods of working on them — not an extraordinary procedure for a writer but one to be set against accusations made by critics of Browning's negligence in revising and of wilfulness in not helping his readers.

A few days before he went to see Moxon about printing the poems, he turned to the revisions. A week later, on Wednesday, October 15, he wrote, "My poems went duly to press on Monday night — there is not much *correctable* in them, — you make, or you spoil, one of these things, — that is, *I* do. I have adopted all your emendations, and thrown in lines and words, just a morning's business. . . ." [18] The passage is the kind that might be isolated by readers tempted to show Browning's indifference to or carelessness in the improvement of his poems. It should not be considered in isolation. Other statements in the letters to Elizabeth show clearly enough that Browning spent serious thought and time on his poems, both before and after he wrote them. In acknowledging his tendency to forget his poems after first writing them, he indicated his habit of revising:

> I must have mentioned to you that I forget my own verses so surely after they are once on paper, that I ought, without affectation, to mend them infinitely better, able as I am to bring fresh eyes to bear on them — (when I say "once on paper" that is just what I mean and no more, for after the sad revising begins they do leave their mark, distinctly or less so according to circumstances). . . . [19]

It is difficult to imagine that the "sad revising" was done with the abandonment suggested by the comment made on October 15. Quite the contrary. Both writing and revising were done seriously, not entirely free from frustration and often accompanied by much weariness and frequent headaches, which Elizabeth was becoming well aware of.

Early in their correspondence Browning wrote Elizabeth of the effort that went into his work: his "scenes and song-scraps" were escapes of his inner power that came out after weary intervals — likened to the

light in the Mediterranean phares (lighthouse) that revolves in a dark
gallery and leaps out for a moment;

> and, no doubt, *then,* precisely, does the poor drudge that carries the
> cresset set himself most busily to trim the wick — for don't think I
> want to say I have not worked hard — (this head of mine knows bet-
> ter) — but the work has been *inside,* and not when at stated times I
> held up my light to you — and, that there is no self-delusion here, I
> would prove to you, (and nobody else) even by opening this desk I
> write on, and showing what stuff, in the way of wood, I *could* make
> a great bonfire with, if I might only knock the whole clumsy top off
> my tower![20]

During an exchange of opinion on George Sand, Browning wrote
more specifically of his work, this time of the difficulty of his task as a
dramatic poet:

> And what easy work these novelists have of it! a Dramatic poet has
> to *make* you love or admire his men and women, — they must *do* and
> *say* all that you are to see and hear — really do it in your face, say it
> in your ears, and it is wholly for *you,* in *your* power, to *name,* charac-
> terize and so praise or blame, *what* is so said and done . . if you don't
> perceive of yourself, there is no standing by, for the Author, and
> telling you: but with these novelists, a scrape of the pen — out
> blurting of a phrase, and the miracle is achieved — [21]

This passage was written on August 10, 1845, a few days after a visit
to Carlyle, which the Sage of Chelsea reported to his wife, adding, "He
. . . is about publishing new Pomegranates, no, new Something-elses,
on an improved principle; had I been in clearer mood, he would have
been welcome to me."[22] Indefinite as the report is, the "new . . . on
an improved principle" brings to mind Browning's intention to begin
again — with something fresh to say — that Domett had learned of in
July of 1844.

Browning indicated to Elizabeth, as he had to Macready and
Domett,[23] the high estimate he set on originality. In an exchange of remarks on the value of different influences on their writing, Elizabeth
lamented the loss caused by her isolation from experience in the outer
world. Browning answered:

> And one thing I want to persuade you of, which is, that all you
> gain by travel is the discovery that you have gained nothing, and
> have done rightly in trusting to your innate ideas — or not rightly in

distrusting them, as the case may be; you get, too, a little . . perhaps a considerable, good, in finding the world's accepted *moulds*
every where, into which you may run & fix your own fused metal, —
but not a grain Troy-weight do you get of new gold, silver or brass.
After this, you go boldly on your own resources, and are justified to
yourself, that's all.[24]

Later Browning recurred to the subject. In a letter to Elizabeth he
praised a recently published collection of Horne's poems more highly
than she did in a letter that crossed his. In his second comment on
them he wrote, "You are entirely right about those poems of Horne's
— I spoke only of the effect of the first glance, and it is a principle with
me to begin by welcoming any strangeness, intention of originality in
men — the other way of safe copying precedents being *so* safe!"[25]

While Browning was thinking of something fresh to say, of beginning again, of the problems that faced a dramatic poet, and of the
value of originality, he was getting further away from the conventional
requirements for stage plays, from character revelation through external action, and nearer his individualized dramatic poem, with characterization by means of internal action.

Browning's talk about trusting his own ideas, working hard, and
revising was not mere talk; it was backed up by active effort to produce
results. He added lines to *The Englishman in Italy* (first called *England
in Italy*) and discarded sixty lines of *Saul*. This information comes from
the love letters,[26] but much more knowledge of his poetic activity exists outside the letters. All along Browning had welcomed from friends
criticisms that he felt were made in his interest. Of far greater value to
him was Elizabeth's opinion. He respected her ability, and her works
had been well received. Furthermore, the attraction for each other that
extended beyond the poetical made her opinion all the more acceptable. First she wanted to know about his works in progress, and then
she wished to see them. In answer to one of her requests to see his
poems, he wrote, "You do not understand what a new feeling it is for
me to have someone who is to like my verses or I shall not ever like
them after!"[27]

He wanted her help and she gave it generously. In addition to her
comments on the poems in her published letters to Browning, she
wrote fifty-six separate octavo pages of suggestions for thirteen of the
twenty-one poems in *Dramatic Romances and Lyrics* and for the last two
plays in his *Bells;* eleven and a half pages were on *The Flight of the Duchess* alone.[28] She praised as well as criticized, and he let her know how

much he appreciated her notes and benefitted by them. Of her written comments on *The Flight of the Duchess* he said, ". . . all the suggestions are to be adopted, the improvements accepted. . . ."[29] After Elizabeth went over one batch of proofs and returned it with her remarks, he wrote, ". . . I have corrected all the points you noted, — to their evident improvement."[30] At the end of his work on the poems he explained, "See your corrections . . and understand that in one or two instances in which they would seem not to be adopted, they *are* so, by some modification of the previous, or following line . . as in one of the Sorrento lines . . about a 'turret' — see!"[31]

To what extent did Browning "adopt" the suggestions that Elizabeth made in addition to the comments included in her letters? Let us give our attention to twelve of the thirteen poems involved and then turn to an estimate of Elizabeth's influence on *The Flight of the Duchess* already made by Edward Snyder and Frederic Palmer, Jr.[32] Of the changes that Elizabeth suggested for the twelve poems, Browning accepted almost half verbatim and made some use of almost a third. Sometimes she merely raised a question and he made a revision, and after examining her notes he occasionally left lines as he had written them. Her most frequent objections had to do with lines which she considered defective in rhythm and next in frequency were her criticisms of obscurity. Her comments on lack of clarity prompted him to make alterations which in a number of places did improve understanding, and more than likely they made him even more conscious of the difficulties that readers had with his poetry.

How much he profited from her criticisms of rhythm is a moot question. As much as Elizabeth appreciated his genius, she, as well as others who were sympathetic with his poetry, could not altogether grasp his prosody. Browning liked compactness and when he followed Elizabeth's suggestions for longer lines and for the addition of specific short words — such as relative pronouns, articles, and conjunctions — too often the lines lost the compressed strength and energy that characterize his poetry. He was learning how to achieve a variety of effects that could not come from the regularity and smoothness of the kind of lines that Elizabeth favored.[33]

Snyder and Palmer, in examining Elizabeth's notes on *The Flight of the Duchess,* have found that "Browning actually accepted verbatim at least twenty-six of her emendations, adopted at least thirty-four more with independent changes of his own in the wording, and rejected, or missed the point of, four." In nine cases they could not determine how

Browning's manuscript read originally. As in the shorter poems, Elizabeth objected to more lines for rhythm in *The Flight of the Duchess* than for anything else and second in number were her criticisms of obscurity. Snyder and Palmer concluded that Browning, whom they called a "brilliant but careless young poet," was given "lessons in prosody by the greatest poetess England has ever produced." Her notes, they said, reminded Browning of certain facts important to him; one was the necessity of "perfection of rhythm."[34] Undeniably Elizabeth enriched not only Browning's life but also his poetry, but she cannot be given credit for improving the nature of his rhythm, as they have asserted.

Why did Browning, with his aggressive sense of prosody, sometimes take Elizabeth's advice when it negated the effectiveness of his line? There may be an explanation. He was influenced by her poetry. In his first letter to her he wrote, "I love your verses with all my heart . . . ." He read her recently published poems over and over and, probably unconsciously, he was swayed by her versification as well as by her criticism, so that he now and then allowed his rhythm to be emasculated.[35] Roma King has discussed Elizabeth's influence on Browning's *Saul,* including that on the rhythmic movement. "Although Elizabeth Barrett contributed in many ways to Browning's general development," he concluded, "it would seem that her influence in this poem was not entirely wholesome."[36]

As a rule Browning was not inclined to take criticism to heart without being convinced that he would benefit by it. He wrote Elizabeth that he failed to understand why Keats and Tennyson could " 'go softly all their days' for a gruff word or two" from the critics; Tennyson read the *Quarterly* and did as its reviewers bade him, "with the most solemn face in the world — out goes this, in goes that, all is changed and ranged. . . ."[37] He relayed to Domett what he had learned from Moxon (publisher of both Tennyson and Browning) about Tennyson: ". . . that he is miserably thin-skinned, sensitive to criticism (foolish criticism). . . ."[38] In his study of Tennyson and his reviewers, E. F. Shannon has shown that both Robert and Elizabeth were off the track in judging Tennyson's reaction to his critics.[39] Here we are interested in Browning's statements not so much for their accuracy or inaccuracy in a judgment of Tennyson as for their reflection of Browning's reluctance to sacrifice his integrity as an artist.

Browning, with confidence that he was working out something new in poetry, took pains to achieve his desired effects. We can take seriously his statement to Elizabeth of his trimming the wick in the

weary intervals between the leaping out of the light. Earnest premedi-
tation of his works was characteristic of his poetic activity. There is evidence also that he gave careful consideration to his lines after as well as
before they were written.

With his great longing to have his poetry accepted — but accepted as the original work it was — he was attentive to its quality. He
was no less attentive to its presentation. He and Elizabeth both had notions about helpful accessories to the revisions. Shortly before Browning went to see Moxon about printing his poems Elizabeth suggested
the insertion of titles for some of them.

> And now when you come to print these fragments, would it not be
> well if you were to stoop to the vulgarism of prefixing some word of
> introduction, as other people do, you know, . . a title . . a name?
> You perplex your readers often by casting yourself on their intelli-
> gence in these things — and although it is true that readers in gen-
> eral are stupid & cant understand, it is still more true that they are
> lazy & wont understand . . & they dont catch your point of sight at
> first unless you think it worth while to push them by the shoulders
> & force them into the right place.

She explained by the use of an example:

> Now these fragments . . you mean to print them with a line between
> . . & not one word at the top of it . . now don't you! — And then
> people will read
>   "Oh, to be in England"
> and say to themselves . . "Why who is this? . . who's out of Eng-
> land?" Which is an extreme case of course; but you will see what I
> mean . . & often I have observed how some of the very most beauti-
> ful of your lyrics have suffered just from your disdain of the usual
> tactics of writers in this one respect.[40]

Browning answered, "Thank you, thank you — I will devise titles — I
quite see what you say, now you do say it."[41] Here, as in an earlier letter to Domett, Browning quickly recognized a stumbling block for his
readers after it was pointed out to him, and resolved to do what he
could to clear the path.[42]

Elizabeth also suggested that he explain the title *Bells and Pomegranates* in *Dramatic Romances and Lyrics*.[43] As a result of criticisms in
the reviews, Browning had probably already decided to provide an explanation in the last number. He was tactful in his answer: "I will
make a note as you suggest — or, perhaps, keep it for the closing num-

ber, (the next) when it will come fitly in with two or three parting words I shall have to say."[44]

Browning, as well as Elizabeth, was thinking of ways to attract and hold readers. Some "easy" verses that he wrote out for Elizabeth were, as he explained, ones "out of a paper-full meant to go between poem & poem . . . and break the shock of collision."[45] Furthermore, just as he had depended on Forster in determining the best time for publication of *Dramatic Lyrics,* he now heeded the advice of another friend associated with the press — Henry F. Chorley. On August 3, he wrote Elizabeth that Chorley had said there was no use in printing "before November at earliest."[46] On October 12, which fell on a Sunday, Browning gave her more definite information about the publication of No. VII. "On Thursday I saw Moxon — he spoke rather encouragingly of my own prospects. I send him a sheetful to-morrow, I believe, and we are 'out' on the 1st. of next month."[47] Elizabeth answered: "How fast you print your book, for it is to be out on the first of November! Why it comes out suddenly like the sun."[48] The poems went to press on October 13.

There were still proofs for Browning to take care of with Elizabeth's help. Finally the work came to an end. With the last proofs in hand on October 28, he wrote, ". . . I don't know how I have got tired of this."[49] The poems, which were inscribed to John Kenyon,[50] were published on November 6, 1845.

CHAPTER XI

A Step Forward

Dramatic Romances and Lyrics, 1845: Reception

The significance of the press criticism of *Dramatic Romances and Lyrics* has not been adequately recognized. Lounsbury wrote of the reception of these short poems: "There was even more than lack of appreciation; there was sometimes positive condemnation. Along with the censure of some professional reviewers, indeed, praise was bestowed upon them by others; but it was always praise accompanied with qualifications."[1] He did not mention any reviews to support this comment, and it has gone unchallenged. DeVane, writing of *Dramatic Romances and Lyrics* in the section "After-History" in his *Handbook,* said that the reception was "indifferent" and limited himself to two sentences on the *Athenaeum* and the *Examiner.* In the introduction to *Browning: The Critical Heritage,* Litzinger and Smalley made several general statements about the reception of *Bells and Pomegranates* and in their text included excerpts from five reviews of *Dramatic Romances and Lyrics.* These enable the reader to get a fairly representative notion of the reviews, though some of the omitted sections (on pp. 104, 105, 106, 110 — not always indicated) are helpful in showing how the critics had advanced in evaluating certain distinctive qualities of Browning's short poems. It is important to analyze a number of criticisms of *Dramatic Romances and Lyrics* and determine their place at this point in the development of Browning's reputation.

After the publication on November 6, 1845, there was certainly no great rush to consider the poems. In that month only one review ap-

198

peared. Most of the criticisms were published in the two following months, three in December and four in January. Then the pace slowed down; two reviews came out in April and one in June — the last. Contrary to the earlier situation, the number of monthlies and quarterlies together more than doubled the number of the weeklies that reviewed the preceding two *Bells*. The *Atlas, Literary Gazette,* and *Spectator,* which had been almost uniformly negative in their early reviews of Browning, did not consider it worthwhile to discuss the last three *Bells*. Possibly their failure to continue to the end and the more leisurely appearance of other criticisms, mostly in monthlies and quarterlies, had something to do with the increasingly receptive attitude and better understanding noticeable in the reviews.

Lounsbury left the impression that there was more unfavorable than favorable criticism and that the unfavorable sometimes went to the extreme. In fact, only *Fraser's* was thoroughly condemnatory. If the scales tipped at all, they did so on the side of the favorable. Even two religious periodicals that were concerned with the unwholesome in Browning made favorable comments on some of the poems. Besides the condemnation in *Fraser's* and the complaint of unwholesomeness, other strictures were not unduly prominent.

Furthermore, Lounsbury's comment did not take into consideration what is most important of all. The critics were casting light where it was needed: on Browning's interest in character; on the variety of his works and the fertility of his genius; on his individual use of diction and the relationship between his choice of versification and his conception of a poem; on the good employment of his dramatic bent. Furthermore, something was said of the beneficial effect these poems would have on his reputation.

Forster, who had shown resentment when Browning submitted *Colombe's Birthday* to Charles Kean, Macready's rival, was the first to review *Dramatic Romances and Lyrics*. In September Browning received a letter from his "old foe," with tickets for a private theatrical.[2] A month later Forster called on Browning and was "very profuse of graciosities"; they would, Browning told Elizabeth, "go on again with the friendship, as the snail repairs his battered shell."[3] When the collection of poems was published, Elizabeth remembered "in inglorious complacency" that Forster was "no longer anything like an enemy."[4]

The review was published in the *Examiner* on November 15. Forster reminded his readers that he had ranked Browning's muse high and had grieved when "she lost her way in transcendental or other fogs."

He was repeating an earlier complaint. His objection, which Elizabeth disapproved of,[5] was that metaphysics had been "too abundant for his poetry"; the analytic and imaginative powers never worked well together. Browning was freeing himself from this fault, the only one that "retarded his advance."

For the most part Forster dwelt on the merits of the short dramatic pieces, in which he found "a busy life, a stir of human interest." He pointed out the same outstanding characteristics that he had called attention to in the earlier collection of short poems — dramatic quality, ideas, appropriate versification — and also the "stamp and freshness of originality" that he had praised in A Blot. Though later critics were to give better and fuller analysis of these qualities, Forster was the first to call attention to them repeatedly. He realized that the verse must be judged by the use Browning made of it for the particular poem. "There are some twenty pieces in the collection; each marked out from its fellow by an idea of its own, to which it moves with corresponding music; from the breathless gallop of 'How they brought the good news from Ghent to Aix' to the calm simplicity of the 'Boy and the Angel.' " Browning was master of verse in "all its most poetical and most musical varieties."

Forster gave his readers succinct comments on half of the poems and quoted liberally. He praised Browning's poetic use of "the most natural and unaffected terms of ordinary every-day language" in The Flight of the Duchess and in the minute picture of Italian life and scenery in England in Italy (The Englishman in Italy). He called attention to the earnestness present in the collection: the noble and universal truth in The Boy and the Angel, the noble ideal of The Lost Leader, and the concerns of life and death in The Tomb at St. Praxed's (The Bishop Orders His Tomb). The poems were "already packed up and on their way to posterity."

The next seven reviews came out within six weeks, and all showed some appreciation, if not always understanding, of Browning's poems. Douglas Jerrold's Shilling Magazine, "mainly devoted to a consideration of the social wants and rightful claims of the People," as the preface to the first issue announced, ran for three years (1845–8). It carried short reviews of both of the poet's works that were published during its existence. The one dealing with Dramatic Romances and Lyrics appeared in December. The poems in the collection were written by one of the few "real poets" of the age; however, he was not popular even with the multitude of literary men, doubtless because of his "disdain of popular arts." His poetry appeared abrupt, fragmentary, and, to those slow in responding to suggestion, obscure because with his soul of fire, he cast away every detail and thought that did not "ministrate to the pourtrayal of the passion with which every line of his productions is fraught." As in true poetry, there was no straining after effect; the language was "simple and plain" and the effort was devoted to the "just conception of the image or idea."

The qualities that some considered as blemishes, Jerrold, if he was the reviewer, took as proof of the poet's genuine inspiration and originality; they displayed the "terrible energy of his conceptions, — the truth and earnestness of his visions." To avoid wordiness and hackneyed phraseology Browning sometimes missed the finest expression of his thought. His versification might seem rugged to those who were accustomed to common versification. "To the reader impregnated with the passion of the matter, it starts however into a harmony new, congenial, and invigorating." Like Forster, Jerrold saw that the verse would not be properly appreciated unless it was seen in relation to the artistic intention of each poem. "The rhythm that the true poet utters is a part of his mental conception, and cannot be separated from it without producing dissonance." Browning could not be judged in the ordinary way. "To those . . . who come in simple honesty to hear the poet uncontaminated by the cant of academical criticism, and with but a moderate share of impulse and imagining power, there can be no doubt the god will reveal himself in his 'might, majesty, and dominion,' and Browning will be acknowledged a poet."

On the appearance of *Dramatic Romances and Lyrics* several critics took occasion to review in addition most of Browning's previous works. One such discussion in the High Church *English Review* in December dealt with three poets, two of them being Robert Browning and Elizabeth Barrett. According to Browning, the review was written by Eliot Warburton,[6] an acquaintance of his. He at once gave recognition to Browning as a poet: "Mr. Browning unites within himself more of the elements of a true poet than perhaps any other of those whom we call 'modern' amongst us: yet there are few writers so little read, so partially understood." The review consisted of a running account of Browning's works from *Paracelsus* through No. VII of *Bells and Pomegranates,* with the exception of *Strafford.* The critic commented on *Paracelsus* favorably and on *Sordello's* bad influence on Browning's reputation. But the neglect would be only temporary.

As if in defiance, Browning gave his truthful and genuine poems
that followed *Sordello* the fantastic name of *Bells and Pomegranates* and
the first of the series the incomprehensible title of *Pippa Passes*. Browning's fine judgment of character and his varied genius were best proved
by his *Bells*. They had every kind of composition "from the most
stately tragic, to the airiest lyric." *Pippa Passes* showed to the best advantage Browning's versatility. The plays, with "thought, poetry, and
feeling," were for reading only. The critic commented briefly but specifically on the *Druses*, *A Blot*, and *Colombe's Birthday*. In the next to
last paragraph the shorter poems, those in *Dramatic Lyrics* and *Dramatic
Romances and Lyrics*, were discussed. On the one hand, they were "vigorous, versatile, original." On the other, the knowledge of nature and
truthfulness they displayed were expressed in strange words, ingenuity
of rimes was carried to an extreme, and Browning often omitted information that he supposed his reader had. Nevertheless the two collections of short poems would alone vindicate Browning's fame.

Elizabeth objected to the heading given to Browning's poetry,
Paracelsus, and Other Poems:

> . . . I quite understand that it is doing no manner of good to go
> back so to Paracelsus, heading the article 'Paracelsus & other poems,'
> as if the other poems could not front the reader broadly by a divine
> right of their own. Paracelsus is a great work & will *live,* but the way
> to do you good with the stiffnecked public . . . w^d have been to hold
> fast & conspicuously the gilded horn of the last living crowned crea-
> ture led by you to the altar, saying 'Look HERE.' What had he to do
> else, as a critic? Was he writing for the Retrospective Review?[7]

She was right in thinking of the drawback of overstressing *Paracelsus*
and understressing the short poems, but Browning was in part to
blame for the critics' harking back to his earlier work. He presented
himself on the title page of *Strafford* and all his *Bells* as the "Author of
'*Paracelsus.'* "

A third review appeared in December; it was in the *Critic*. The reviewer had just become acquainted with Browning's poetry, and in
spite of the faults he thought that the "few leaves" of *Dramatic Romances and Lyrics* merited more attention than many a splendid quarto
submitted for examination. He started his discussion with praise:

> Robert Browning is a true poet; in every page is the presence of ge-
> nius; the spirit of song glows within him. Moreover he is an earnest,
> sincere man; he speaks because he has something to say, and not

from any vanity to collect a crowd about him, and make himself the
idol of the hour; he has a mind of his own; writes what he thinks in
such manner as accords with his mood, and cares very little for the
formulas of critics, or the freaks of fashion. He throws himself heart
and soul into his subject, and seldom fails to bring out something
new. He is one of those whom the more you read, the better you
love.

Yet with these merits Browning was not a popular poet. The critic
specified the reasons for this: carelessness; deficiency in the "musical
ear for metre and rhyme"; "loose" lines; lack of attention to the selection of words and a needless plainness of speech; a too obvious aim at
originality. These faults should not "have militated against his great
and many merits" to the extent that they had. His works should be
more widely known. The critic was surprised to find how much "real
poetry" was in *Dramatic Romances and Lyrics.* He thought that the best
of the poems was *The Flight of the Duchess,* from which he quoted generously; he quoted another poem in part and two shorter ones in their
entirety. Although the review has some contradictions and it does not
indicate any particular astuteness, it gives the impression that the
writer found in Browning's poetry the faults that others had attributed
to it, but that at the same time he was agreeably surprised to recognize
for himself that it had merits and wanted to tell his readers of them.
Like others, he could not see the relation of what he praised and what
he found fault with.

    In January 1846 there appeared in a ladies' magazine, the *New
Monthly Belle Assemblée,* a short review of *Dramatic Romances and Lyrics*
by Camilla Toulmin, later Mrs. Newton Crosland. It commended
Browning for his sympathy "with all that is great and good and beautiful." From reading these poems Miss Toulmin felt that no writer was
more original than Browning. The result was "fresh thoughts" in
"fresh coinage"; this was startling to readers until they "let in the light
of his new method," which then illuminated the poem before them.
She praised his descriptive powers and his highly dramatic genius,
which was not to be confused with the "lesser talent of theatrical adaptation." Even in her brief discussion, now and then she named or
quoted a poem for illustration.

    In the same month the *Oxford and Cambridge Review, and Univer-
sity Magazine* carried a short commentary on *Dramatic Romances and
Lyrics* and quoted from one poem, with best wishes for the success of a
publication "so cheap, and yet so good." The critic said that if he were

disposed to be severe he might mention with "proper censure" the many faults, but the beauties were exceedingly more numerous and he was better pleased to enlarge upon them. The short poems in the collection happily possessed "many of the characteristics of real poetry, and more especially its simplicity."

Also in January, the *New Quarterly Review* included a discussion of *Dramatic Romances and Lyrics* in an article called "Poetical Contrasts," possibly written in collaboration by James A. Heraud and Thomas Powell. In it the reviewers emphasized the qualities of power, intellect, and originality in Browning's poetry as a whole and then commented on individual works. They began, "It is always refreshing to meet with the poetry of Robert Browning: we may be quite sure that we shall meet with no soundings, commonplaces, or simple drivellings; all is firm, vigorous, original, and daring." To show the contrast with the work of Charles Mackay, a journalist and lesser poet who was also discussed in the review, the critics stressed the power of Browning's poetry:

> . . . rough, Herculean thoughts, developed in a style as startling and Titanian as are those which jostle you in every page of the "Bells and Pomegranates" . . . burning madnesses tearing the brain, which you, by a fatal fascination, read over and over again; sometimes to reduce to an intelligible shape, at another time to feel its full galvanic shock thrill through your poetic frame. . . .

The intention was to explain Browning's limited appeal and at the same time praise the distinctive qualities of his poetry; but because of the critics' manner of statement, their commendation was subject to misunderstanding. They wrote:

> Alas! that we do not meet with the "sensuous." The poetry of the "Bells and Pomegranates" wants "flesh and blood;" wants that coming home to men's bosoms which makes the poet for the million. No! Browning is the poet of the mind; the brain is the organ to which he appeals, and certainly with great success. He is possibly the most intellectual poet of the day. . . .

Taken in context, the observation that Browning was not sensuous and lacked flesh and blood led to an explanation of his limited reputation and his intellectuality. His poetry did not have the sensuous, that which would make him popular; its appeal was made through the intellect. The critics found another deficiency in Browning, "the total absence of all sympathy with the efforts, wishes, and struggles of his fellow-man," a great defect. If Browning's works were dug up and examined without clues there would be nothing in them to identify his period, no reflection of the struggles of his contemporaries. In other words, Browning did not write about his own time, and this limited his appeal. This, as well as his intellectual bent, worked against his popularity, but popularity was "no test of original genius." Browning's genius was of the intellect and would be recognized by future generations.

Browning thought that the article in the *New Quarterly* was "outrageously eulogistical" and "stupidly extravagant," as he wrote Elizabeth. In her reply she took exception to its assertion that he was lacking in two respects: ". . . it is the dreariest impotency to complain of the want of flesh & blood & of human sympathy in general."[8] But, she conceded, the review was right about Browning's intellectuality.

The critics suggested still another obstacle to the growth of Browning's reputation: readers might object to his strange subjects, but they thought Browning was defensible on this score. Even though the themes that Browning chose might be distasteful, he was no commonplace poet. The matter and manner of his poetry were of his own begetting. Even the discussion of Browning's obscurity was relieved of the usual sting. "The Italians have lately created a professorship to expound Dante; a like doubtful compliment might well be paid, from his obscurity, to the illustrious author of 'Sordello.' " This served as introduction to a paragraph on the "finish" of Browning's style: from the first he had been perfect in this respect.

Besides dealing favorably with four poems from *Dramatic Romances and Lyrics* and quoting liberally from two, the critics brought in Browning's early long poems, including the anonymously published *Pauline*. Here, seemingly for the first time, Browning was publicly identified as the author, a revelation that, as we have seen, prompted Elizabeth's desire to see the poem — to Browning's chagrin. The mention of Browning's first work here and again in the same periodical later in the year (*New Quarterly*, Oct. 1846) seemed to arouse no curiosity among reviewers. The reference to *Pauline* argues for Browning's attributing the authorship of the article in part to Thomas Powell, who a short time before this review appeared had been in close touch with him and had learned something of his professional activities.[9]

The best review of Browning's works in the *Athenaeum* (Jan. 17, 1846) before the establishment of his fame was that of *Dramatic Ro-*

mances and Lyrics. It, like the favorable one of *Colombe's Birthday,* was
written by his friend Chorley. He began by mixing praise of Browning's fertility of invention and complaint of his obscurity. "Though his
manner changes less than might be wished — since the mist, if it rises
and reveals a clear prospect for half a page, as certainly falls again, —
there are few of his contemporaries who embrace so wide a field of subjects; be they of thought, or description, or passion, or character." Unlike others, Chorley did not consider Browning a careless poet. "Sometimes *baroque,* Mr. Browning is never ignoble: pushing versification to
the extremity of all rational allowances, and sometimes beyond it, with
a hardihood of rhythm and cadence little short of Hudibrastic, — he is
rarely careless."

Other critics merely mentioned the character-drawing in these
poems, but Chorley emphasized it. The collection was made up of a
"gallery full of human creatures — not abstractions." He commented
specifically on the dying Bishop, "a study of a human being"; the
Spanish girl in *The Confessional;* and four of the figures in *The Flight of
the Duchess.* Seemingly he was the first to call attention to one of the
distinguishing marks of Browning's short poems, portrayal of the
spirit of a period and a country: ". . . the French lady in 'The Laboratory,' with her profligacy and her passion, her frivolity and her feroc-
ity, gives us a story, a country, and an epoch, in twelve short stanzas
of what at first seems merely inconsequent talk. . . ." Chorley praised
and illustrated at length with quotations the poet's descriptive powers
and character-drawing. He regretted leaving untouched *Saul, The
Glove,* and the love poems, but he felt he had given enough evidence
to prove that the works in this collection would enhance the poet's
reputation. The inclusion of long extracts pleased both Browning
and Elizabeth.[10]

Two religious quarterlies carried reviews in April. The Nonconformist *Eclectic Review* had a sketchy discussion of all the *Bells* up
through *Dramatic Romances and Lyrics.* The critic thought that the
works in this series, chiefly dramatic in form, possessed all the beauties
and blemishes of the writer. He was concerned about Browning's lack
of clarity and of higher purpose. "There is a sensual taint about his
writings which will bring him one day a bitterness that no amount of
reputation will be found an antidote for." If Browning would free himself from affectations and aim at "advocacy of great principles, and inculcation of great sentiments," he could be a poet of high order. With
powers capable of fulfilling such aims, he made "himself merely a puz-

zle to those that see here and there really brilliant passages in him, and to the general reader — caviare." For a long time the critic had been inclined to think Browning insane, because it was hard to believe that a man with his power would voluntarily assume a "form of confused and crazy eccentricity, merely for the poor pleasure of making people wonder." But then came *A Blot*, as "clear and rational in language as any plain understanding can desire," demonstrating that Browning could write intelligibly if he would.

If Browning understood his own abilities, he should have known that the "lasting reputation of a poet cannot spring out of the buffoonery of a barbarous style, but out of great truths, truthfully and clearly enunciated." Hopeful signs that such knowledge was dawning upon him were evident in the increasing clarity of *Bells and Pomegranates*. The critic named the titles of the seven *Bells* and indicated Browning's continuing progress from the first to the seventh; in the last there was clearness and also higher purpose. He quoted a passage from *Pippa Passes* to show what he considered the early cloudiness and another passage from *Italy in England* to show the improved clarity of style. Who could, he asked, believe that the confusing passages of *Pippa Passes* were written by the author of *The Flight of the Duchess*, *The Lost Leader*, *Italy in England* (later, *The Italian in England*), and *England in Italy* (later, *The Englishman in Italy*), which were rich with "descriptive power and brilliant thought"? More than two-thirds of *Italy in England* was quoted to show the mode of writing that Browning should pursue. The "sense of what is noble in these lines," if followed, would lead him to fame. Perhaps nothing in these works, however, had more evidence of great poetical power than *Pictor Ignotus*.

In an article entitled "Recent Poetry" the High Church *Christian Remembrancer* gave a scant treatment of the *Bells* through *Dramatic Romances and Lyrics*. The critic said that Browning's merits should be noticed though his offences were many and unpardonable. He quoted from *The Flight of the Duchess* to show how much power Browning had to excite "real, living, human interest." Browning was a poet of cosmopolitan sympathies. "But as, on the one hand, he has no Bible Society mission to excuse his ravings about 'their Saints, their Priests, their Pope,' and the like, — so, on the other, he has none of the aversion to foreign vices to which that character must in some degree have pledged him." No page of *Dramatic Romances and Lyrics* could "be read freely and without reserve." It would have been better had Browning replaced the objectionable poems by ones like *The Flight of the Duchess* and *The Pied Piper.* The critic found it strange that the poet who had so much dramatic power wrote dramas that fell short of his other works. The historical plays threw little light upon his characters and the times they represented. *A Blot,* he said incorrectly, had been acted with success, but it had "false" sentiment and "questionable" morality.

Seven months after the publication of *Dramatic Romances and Lyrics, Fraser's* commented briefly on Browning in the second part of an article entitled "Past and Present Condition of British Poetry," which began in May and concluded in June 1846. The critic opened with a general condemnation. He thought that contemporary poetry was in a sorry plight if it had to depend on Tennyson and Browning for the hereditary honors of its existence, in spite of what the *Examiner* and *Athenaeum* had said. "A page out of every ten in Herrick's 'Hesperides' is more certain of an hereafter than any one dramatic romance or lyric in all the 'Bells and Pomegranates' of Mr. Browning." He was "unquestionably" a poet. But sentiments did not spring naturally from his subject; his poetry at times was overlaid with affectation, "the common conceit of men who affect to tell common things in an uncommon manner"; the verses were clogged with too many consonants and too many monosyllables; and he carried the "sense too frequently in a very ungraceful manner from one line to the other." At the end of the discussion specific condemnation was given. *England in Italy,* quoted in part, was considered "torture to read," and *Home-Thoughts from Abroad,* quoted in full, was introduced as "mere twaddle of a Cockney at Calais or Cologne."

A few concluding remarks on professional criticism will emphasize the aspects that indicated a forward movement in the understanding of Browning's poetry. Obscurity, which had for so long been a target, was not a serious charge in the evaluation of *Dramatic Romance and Lyrics.* More than half of the critics made no complaint of it; others placed but slight emphasis on this point. It was not dwelt upon as it had been in the past, in particular since the publication of *Sordello.* The critic for the *English Review* had something to say about obscurity and also faulty diction and rhymes, but his objections were not belabored; on the positive side he praised the qualities which in the short poems would "vindicate" Browning's fame. Chorley's reference to "mist" was far outweighed by his laudatory remarks. The critic for the *Eclectic* observed the increasing degree of clarity in each of the successive *Bells.* The *New Quarterly Review* said that the poet "appears" to speak in riddles. More positive help came in the brief general explanation in *Douglas Jerrold's Shilling Magazine* of why Browning seemed to be obscure.

With the exception of the reviewer for *Fraser's* and perhaps the one for the *Christian Remembrancer,* the few critics who discussed other faults considered that the merits more than compensated for them. Two periodicals directed attention to the poetic line — *Douglas Jerrold's Shilling Magazine* and the *Examiner.* They gave some praise to the diction and approved of the rhythm as inherent in the artistic conception. This criticism looked to future criticism as did that which indicated Browning's interest in man, his poetic range, and his dramatic quality. The reviewers recognized Browning's interest in the study of man — "paintings of characters" in a "gallery full of human creatures — not abstractions" *(Athenaeum),* the power of "exciting real, living, human interest" *(Christian Remembrancer),* "fine judgment of character" *(English Review),* "a stir of human interest" *(Examiner).* And with this went the recognition of Browning's breadth and observation *(English Review* and *Athenaeum)* and the awareness that he had made good use of his dramatic turn in the short pieces *(Christian Remembrancer, New Monthly Belle Assemblée,* and *Examiner).* Most of the critics approved of his originality.

One set of contradictions in the reviews is significant. There had been earlier objection to the unwholesome quality of *A Blot.* Complaint about this quality in Browning's work came now chiefly from the religious press, which was beginning to give attention to the poet's work and was to play an important part later in the shaping of his reputation. Of the three religious periodicals that reviewed *Dramatic Romances and Lyrics,* the *Eclectic Review* and the *Christian Remembrancer* represented the attitude expressed in the religious periodicals of the forties that Browning's poetry did not always conform to Christian ideals. The *English Review,* in seeing the wholesome in *Paracelsus* and *Pippa Passes,* foreshadowed the favorable attitude that the religious press was to adopt by the late fifties. And it agreed with critics of *Dramatic Romances and Lyrics* who saw in Browning's poetry noble and universal truth *(Examiner),* aims of truth and freedom *(Athenaeum),* "truth and earnestness" *(Shilling Magazine),* "sympathy with all that is great and good and beautiful" *(New Monthly Belle Assemblée).*

In artistic insight the criticism of *Dramatic Romances and Lyrics* was clearly far ahead of the criticism of Dramatic Lyrics, its predecessor. *Dramatic Romances and Lyrics* had twice as many reviews; its reception was more favorable than unfavorable, whereas only the *Examiner* and the *Morning Herald* had spoken out wholeheartedly for the earlier collection. Though the critics in 1845–6 were still prone to single out for praise poems following conventional patterns, they were beginning to be attracted to what was more characteristic of Browning's poetry than of traditional poetry. Not one critic had made a favorable comment on *My Last Duchess* when reviewing the 1842 collection; three appreciated *The Bishop Orders His Tomb (Examiner, New Quarterly, Athenaeum)*, published in the 1845 collection. It might seem that at this time the strong anti-Catholic feeling in England would be likely to attract interest in a poem placing a bishop in a bad light, but such was not the case. The comments on the *Bishop* indicated that the critics were interested in the poem, not as an unflattering study of a Catholic churchman, but as a penetrating study of the human heart — a hopeful sign for the understanding of the dramatic monologue. The carping tone that had been prominent in the early reviews was far less noticeable in 1845, and more substantial quoting was effective. Apparently *Dramatic Lyrics* had prepared the way for the better reception of *Dramatic Romances and Lyrics*. Three reviewers saw the short poems as being sure to advance Browning's reputation.

After copies of *Dramatic Romances and Lyrics* came to him on November 6 Browning set about his "dreadful dispatching-business" at once — "friend A. & B. & C. must get their copy, and word of regard, all by next post!" [11] It is likely that he did not forget people like Camilla Toulmin, whom he had met at a social gathering in the early forties. At that time, she said, she had not read a line of Browning's. He did not speak very much, but she was struck by his "quiet dignity" and "commanding intelligence." Soon afterwards he sent her several numbers of the *Bells*. In the January 1846 issue of the *New Monthly Belle Assemblée*, which she was editing, she reviewed *Dramatic Romances and Lyrics* with praise, as we have seen above. Browning immediately (Jan. 5, 1846) wrote her a letter of thanks. [12] Thus did a chance social acquaintanceship, with some encouragement from Browning, result in a favorable public notice capable of adding its bit to the furtherance of his reputation.

Indirectly we learn something of the opinions of those who received the copies of *Dramatic Romances and Lyrics*. Elizabeth wanted to know what his correspondents said about the new work and he took her letters he had received. She was not altogether pleased with them. There was one from Chorley, written two months before his review appeared. "Mr. Chorley speaks some things very well — but what does he mean about 'execution,' *en revanche?* but I liked his letter & his candour in the last page of it." She found fault with a letter from Sir John Hanmer, a friend of Browning's and a minor poet. "Sir John Hanmer's, I was half angry with! — Now *is* he not cold? — and is it not

easy to see *why* he is forced to write his own scenes five times over &
over? He might have mentioned the 'Duchess' I think, — & he a
poet!"[13] Browning defended Hanmer ("this coldness . . . is part of
him") as he was later to defend Chorley when his review of *Dramatic
Romances and Lyrics* appeared in the *Athenaeum* and Elizabeth thought it
too fell short in its evaluation.[14]

Kenyon also wrote Browning. We learn not from a reference to his
letter but from Elizabeth's relay of his verbal comments to her on how
he praised the "works of a highly original writer & of such various faculty!" including *How They Brought the Good News* and *The Flight of the
Duchess. Saul* greatly impressed him. Elizabeth reported, "He reads it
every night . . . when he comes home & just before he goes to sleep,
to put his dreams into order, & observed . . . that it reminded him of
Homer's shield of Achilles, thrown into lyrical whirl & life."[15] Elizabeth's comment after she learned what W. J. Fox thought of the poems
indicated that Browning's old friend might have qualified his praise:
"And how glad I am that Mr. Fox should say what he did of it . .
though it wasn't true, you know . . not exactly." She continued with
her own praise:

> Still, I do hold that as far as construction goes, you never put to-
> gether so much unquestionable, smooth glory before, . . not a single
> entanglement for the understanding . . unless 'the snowdrops'
> [stanza 4 of *The Lost Mistress*] make an exception — while for the un-
> deniableness of genius it never stood out before your readers more
> plainly than in that same number! — Also you have extended your
> sweep of power — the sea-weed is thrown farther (if not higher), —
> than it was found before. . . .[16]

The summit of the praise of *Dramatic Romances and Lyrics* came
from Landor. His letter, dated November 12, had welcome words:
"Before I have half read thro your Dramatic Romances I must acknowledge the delight I am receiving. . . . What a profusion of imagery,
covering what a depth of thought! You may stand quite alone, if you
will — and I think you will."[17] There was more from Landor — a poem
of fourteen lines in blank verse, often repeated by lovers of Browning's
poetry.

> There is delight in singing, though none hear
> Beside the singer; and there is delight
> In praising, though the praiser sit alone
> And see the prais'd far off him, far above.
> Shakespeare is not *our* poet, but the world's.

Therefore on him no speech; and short for thee,
Browning! Since Chaucer was alive and hale,
No man hath walk'd along our roads with step
So active, so inquiring eye, or tongue
So varied in discourse. But warmer climes
Give brighter plumage, stronger wing; the breeze
Of Alpine heights thou playest with, borne on
Beyond Sorrento and Amalfi, where
The Siren waits thee, singing song for song.

Elizabeth and Robert were delighted with Landor's praise. Browning set it quite apart from other laudatory remarks:

> Of course, Landor's praise is altogether a different gift, — a gold vase from King Hiram; beside he has plenty of conscious rejoicing in his own riches, and is not left painfully poor by what he sends away: *that* is the unpleasant point with some others — they spread you a board and want to gird up their loins and wait on you there: Landor says 'come up higher and let us sit and eat together.'[18]

In letters to Moxon and Domett, Browning commented on Landor's "happy epithet 'hale' as applied to Chaucer."[19]

From Landor's letter Elizabeth thought that he understood and gave a true description of Browning's poetry; he put his finger on the characteristics that she, before she knew Browning, studied and despaired of being able to approach, "taking them to be so essentially & intensely masculine that like effects were unattainable, even in a lower degree, by any female hand."[20] Landor's verses, she said, must be printed. She and Browning both hoped they would be published in the *Examiner* by Forster, to whom Landor had sent a copy. They were not, but they did appear in the *Morning Chronicle* on November 22 through the efforts of Moxon, to whom Browning had sent a copy. And Browning's father had copies of the poem printed for distribution.[21]

With the exception of Landor's praise, Browning showed little interest in the comments of his correspondents. Once he half apologized for sending Elizabeth "all those good-natured letters, desperate praise and all." He confessed of the most laudatory of all, "I *skimmed* once over with my flesh CREEPING — it seemed such a death-struggle, that of good nature over — well, it is fresh ingratitude of me, so here it shall end — "[22] It was not ingratitude. Browning appreciated the good motive behind the words of praise, but what he needed and almost desperately wanted was criticism that would reach many readers.

He was concerned about the reception of his seventh *Bell* by the press, which he recognized as a strong factor in the making of a reputation. With his high degree of sensitiveness to the reception of his poetry, Browning reacted to professional criticism in various ways. Much depended on the situation and on his own state of mind at the moment. On February 11, 1845, he made a generous statement about critics to Elizabeth. "I do sincerely esteem it a perfectly providential and miraculous thing that they are so well-behaved in ordinary, these critics. . . ."[23] But this statement was only part of a long discussion of critics; as his astute correspondent read the whole passage she saw indications of a not altogether placid acceptance of misunderstanding of his works. Elizabeth was to learn more about Browning's variegated moods. In his letters to her and to others he sometimes praised writers of the reviews, grateful for their help and aware of problems that Chorley and other reviewers faced. At times he was provoked to lash out. Now and then he wrote only of the disappointment at the futility of his efforts, ". . . how heartbreaking a matter must it be to be pronounced a poor creature by Critic This and acquaintance the other."[24] Fortunately Elizabeth was a wise and understanding woman. Once she wrote to a friend: "You must learn Robert — he is made of moods — chequered like a chess-board; and the colour goes for too much — till you learn to treat it as a game."[25] We have to recognize that his struggle to establish himself was a very serious and sometimes painful game.

In his correspondence Browning often showed uneasiness in anticipation of the reception of his works, having experienced both sharp attacks and disquieting silence. After the publication of *Dramatic Romances and Lyrics* in November, he anxiously watched for the reviews, ready to show disapproval or appreciation. A few days after the first review appeared, that in the *Examiner,* Browning wrote Moxon of his gratefulness for Landor's verses and added, "Forster's notice . . is that not most generous, too?" Resentment was in the same letter. Browning complained that people were always "snubbing" him, "like friend Harness." Of Reverend William James Harness, who wrote for the *Quarterly Review,* Browning had more to say, "If he goes and does the 'quizzing article' he hints at, I'll be hanged if I don't rhyme him to death like an Irish Rat!"[26] In *Pacchiarotto* Browning later proved how capable he was of carrying out such a threat; fortunately the review by Harness did not appear.

Browning learned that there was to be an article on him and Elizabeth in the *English Review,* but December passed and they did not see it. During this month there is in their letters reference to only a one-sentence announcement of *Dramatic Romances and Lyrics,* which Elizabeth had copied from the *New Monthly Magazine.*[27] Browning visited Elizabeth on December 29. On the following day she wrote to him: "What a *misomonsism* you fell into yesterday, you who have so much great work to do which no one else can do except just yourself! — & you, too, who have courage & knowledge, & must know that every work, with the principle of life in it, *will* live, let it be trampled ever so under the heel of a faithless & unbelieving generation. . . ."[28]

The *Athenaeum* had not given its customary attention to the poet's new publication. Browning was doubtless watching the review section and hoping to find an article by his friend Chorley. He had his mind on the *Athenaeum* and Chorley when he wrote Elizabeth on January 11:

> How you know Chorley! That is precisely the man, that willow blowing now here now there — precisely! I wish he minded the Athenaeum, its silence or eloquence, no more nor less than I — but he goes on painfully plying me with invitation after invitation, only to show me, I feel confident, that *he* has no part nor lot in the matter . . . . For myself — if I have vanity which such Journals can raise; would the praise of them praise it, they who praised Mr. Mackay's own, own Dead Pan, quite his own, the other day?[29]

The letter shows how the absence of critical attention could set Browning on edge and how his imagination led him into error. Elvan Kintner, editor of the courtship letters, has pointed out that Browning in his objection to the *Athenaeum's* recognition of Charles Mackay's poem was mistaken in supposing that Elizabeth's *Dead Pan* was published before Mackay's *Death of Pan.*[30] Furthermore, Browning professed that a review of his own poems in the weekly would have no great effect on his feelings. Yet in the following passage in the same letter he showed that the *Athenaeum* carried weight with him:

> You shall see they will not notice . . unless a fresh publication alters the circumstances — until some seven or eight months — as before; and then they *will* notice, and *praise,* and tell anybody who cares to enquire, "*So* we noticed the work." So do not you go expecting justice or injustice till I tell you: it amuses me to be found writing so, so anxious to prove I understand the laws of the game, when that game is only "Thimble-rig" and for prizes of gingerbread-nuts —

But even with no review in the *Athenaeum* the scene was already beginning to shift by the first of January of 1846. On the 4th Brown-

ing was looking forward to receiving the *English Review* with the promised article; at about the same time he read the review by Camilla Toulmin in the *New Monthly Belle Assemblée* and in his prompt
acknowledgment he paid Miss Toulmin a compliment with a flourish
reminiscent of his remarks in early letters to Fox and Macready.[31] On
January 6 he received his copy of the *English Review* with its article on
him, Elizabeth Barrett, and Coventry Patmore, which Browning read
in haste and sent at once to Elizabeth. His accompanying note was
hardly more than an expression of disappointment that the section on
her poetry did not do her justice. On the same day he received a copy
of the *New Quarterly Review* with its criticism, which he had been led to
believe was unfavorable. In the exchange of comments on the article
between Robert and Elizabeth, cited above, he revealed that he was
surprised when he read it. In his letter to her he said he was mentioned
in three other articles discovered by his sister in the same periodical.

> Last night, I received a copy of the New Quarterly — now here is
> popular praise, a sprig of it! Instead of the attack I supposed it to be,
> from my foolish friend's account, the notice is outrageously eulogist-
> ical, a stupidly extravagant laudation from first to last — and in *three
> other* articles, as my sister finds by diligent fishing, they introduce
> my name with the same felicitous praise (except one instance,
> though, in a good article by Chorley I am certain). . . .[32]

Kintner located the three articles that Sarianna had found by diligent
fishing.[33] In the article attributed to Chorley Browning is called a Min-
nesinger, in another he is named along with other "scribblers," and in
a third he is given credit for "magnificent productions." The attention
given him obviously helped to improve his frame of mind.

On January 17 the *Athenaeum* finally published its review of *Dramatic Romances and Lyrics,* which Browning supposed to be by Chorley
and which Elizabeth labeled "cold & cautious" and found at fault for
"what is said of 'mist.' "[34] On the day of its appearance Browning
wrote with relief and appreciation as he made excuses for the complaints of obscurity.

> Do you see the Athenaeum? By Chorley surely — and kind and sat-
> isfactory. I did not expect any notice for a long time — all that about
> the "mist," "unchanged manner" and the like is politic concession to
> the Powers that Be . . because he might tell me that and much more
> with his own lips or unprofessional pen, and be thanked into the bar-
> gain — yet he does not — But I fancy he saves me from ,a rougher
> hand — the long extracts answer every purpose — [35]

To Browning the faults that Elizabeth found with the *Athenaeum*, the *New Quarterly Review*, and the *English Review* were insignificant in the total. if limited, favorable criticism that had appeared. A letter to Domett reflected Browning's good spirits when the anxious days after the publication and reception of *Dramatic Romances and Lyrics* were over. In November 1845 he had sent his friend a copy of this latest work; in March 1846 he again wrote him, expressing his gratification at Landor's poem and enclosing a copy of it. He also expressed, though with ironical undertones, his satisfaction with his share of press criticism: "I never was much disturbed in my natural post of 'most unintelligible of writers,' nor, consequently, got a tithe of the notice bookmakers get as a matter of course — yet my gettings, what all the unintelligibility and unpopularity in the world could not preserve me from getting — quite enough [it] has been, indeed!"[36]

At the moment the outlook was encouraging. In addition to the sympathetic understanding that his poems had received, the information in December 1845 from Moxon that his poems were "going off 'rather heavily'" was superseded by the report in the following February of Moxon's anticipation of a possible second edition, then the news on March 3 of his books that were "selling and likely to sell," and a further favorable report on March 23.[37] The "new green leaves" which Elizabeth discerned with pride in Browning's "bay"[38] were a sign that his artistic achievement was receiving fuller recognition. At least, gain in understanding and appreciating Browning's qualities was apparent in the reviews and in the sale of his poems. Browning's trust in his own ideas and his "improved principle" (Carlyle's phrase) was vindicated by his advancement from *Dramatic Lyrics* to *Dramatic Romances and Lyrics*. The second collection was in the line of development that would lead to *Men and Women*, which signalized the maturity of Browning's genius.

CHAPTER XII

Plays for Reading

Luria and *A Soul's Tragedy*, 1846

Two plays made up the eighth and last number of *Bells and Pomegranates*. On February 11, 1845, Browning wrote to Elizabeth of one of them, "this darling 'Luria' — so safe in my head, & a tiny slip of paper I cover with my thumb!"[1] On February 26 he told her more of it and introduced *A Soul's Tragedy*. He sketched his plan for "golden-hearted" Luria and named characters, including the Moor Luria's adversaries with their "worldly-wisdom and Tuscan shrewd ways." And he added a statement that revealed the poetic process taking place in his mind, ". . . for me, the misfortune is, I sympathise just as much with these as with him. . . ."[2] The effectiveness of this attitude — Browning's "misfortune" — was demonstrated in later outstanding monologues.[3]

Luria had to wait. At the beginning of May, Browning wrote, "I have had a constant pain in the head for these two months, which only very rough exercise gets rid of, and which stops my 'Luria' and much besides."[4] With his short dramatic poems to complete and his mind on 50 Wimpole Street, he did nothing on his play for some months. On October 6, before his *Dramatic Romances and Lyrics* went to press, he wrote, ". . . the plays can follow gently."[5] When in the next week he spoke of "just a morning's business" of the last revisions, he added, ". . . but one does not write plays so."[6] It was not without qualms that he thought of playwriting, though when he saw the proofs of the poems and wearily looked at their faults he said *Luria* would be better than they were.

Nearly two weeks passed and Elizabeth, who had censured the stage for its vulgarizing effect,[7] learned something of his play that must have pleased her. On October 27 he wrote, "Yesterday I took out 'Luria' & read it thro' — the skeleton — I shall hope to finish it soon now. It is for a purely imaginary Stage, — very simple and straightforward." He went further, "Would you . . no, Act by Act, as I was about to propose that you should read it, — that process would affect the oneness I most wish to preserve."[8] Elizabeth did read it act by act, the first one on November 13 and the last one on or near February 9, 1846, the day Browning took it to her. She read the acts more than once, and the exchange of comments in their letters shows Browning's wavering attitude toward the play. Since it was not for the stage, he had the satisfaction of working from the dictates of his genius, but he was unable to achieve the desired results.

The writing moved slowly. As Elizabeth read and commented on the first three acts, with some reservations she praised them. On January 11, 1846, after Browning had finished Act IV but before he took it to her, he said he did not "on the whole, feel dissatisfied . . . with the effect" of it. Then he wrote Elizabeth concerning the nature of his writing. "It is all in long speeches — the *action, proper,* is in them — they are no descriptions, or amplifications — but here . . in a drama of this kind, all the *events,* (and interest), take place in the *minds* of the actors . . somewhat like Paracelsus in that respect. . . ."[9] When Browning took Act IV to Elizabeth a week or so later, she read it and remembered his comment on the long speeches as coinciding with her own impression of them. "And, do you know, I agree with yourself a little when you say . . (did you *not* say? . .) that some of the speeches . . Domizia's for instance . . are too lengthy. I think I should like them to coil up their strength, here & there, in a few passages."

There was another objection. Upon learning that Luria took poison at the end of Act IV, Elizabeth could scarcely resign herself to his suicide "as a necessity . . . the act of suicide being so unheroical." She reconsidered. "But you are a dramatic poet & right perhaps, where, as a didactic poet, you would have been wrong. . . ." It was, Elizabeth decided, Luria's natural reaction to the circumstances. "Also, it is satisfactory that Domizia, having put her woman's part off to the last, should be too late with it. . . ."[10] Browning was relieved. She had just the feeling he wanted her to have about Domizia and the suicide of Luria, which he proceeded to justify. He then concluded his remarks. "But I know there is very much to improve and heighten in this fourth act, as in the others — but the right aspect of things seems obtained and the rest of the work is plain and easy — " [11]

The rest of the work did not prove to be easy. When Browning brought Elizabeth Act V on February 9 he made a comment that she referred to in her letter written the next day, ". . . I agree with you, that a little quickening & drawing in closer here & there . . . would make the effect stronger. . . ." Again when Browning gave her an opening she indicated her objection to the length of the speeches. She lightened her criticism by praise expressed in general terms: "moral grandeur" and "noble exposition of the ingratitude of men against their 'heroes.' " One troublesome spot especially disturbed her. "Domizia disappoints me rather. You might throw a flash more of light on her face — might you not? But what am I talking? I think it a magnificent work. . . ." After more praise Elizabeth could not resist a parting sigh for stronger characterization. "Ah — Domizia! would it hurt her to make her more a woman . . a little? . . I wonder!" [12]

In his letter of February 11 Browning said he realized that Domizia was "all wrong . . . her special colour had faded. . . ." He would follow his procedure of letting the work rest; after a week or two he would see what he had forgotten.

> One of my half dozen words on my scrap of paper . . . was, under the "Act V," *"she loves"* — to which I could not bring it, you see! . . . I will try and remember what my whole character *did* mean — it was, in two words, understood at the time by "panther's-beauty" — on which hint I ought to have spoken! But the work grew cold, and you came between, and the sun put out the fire on the hearth. . . . [13]

On March 22 Browning was depressed as he considered *Luria;* he had thought it a failure at first, he said, and now found it "infinitely worse." [14] Elizabeth had made critical notes on the play, and he had been going through them. A week later he liked it better in proof. When Elizabeth saw the play in proof, she continued her praise of it and her criticism of Domizia.

> The proof . . the printed Luria . . I mean . . has more than pleased me. It is noble & admirable; & grows greater, the closer seen. The most exceptionable part, it seems to me, is Domizia's retraction at the last, for which one looks round for the sufficient motive. But the impression of the whole work goes straight to the soul — it is heroic in the best sense. [15]

Whereupon Browning confessed his own dissatisfaction:

> . . . I *could not* bring her to my purpose. I left the neck stiff that was
> to have bowed of its own accord — for nothing graceful could be ac-
> complished by pressing with both hands on the head above! I meant
> to make her leave off her own projects thro' love of Luria: as it is,
> they in a manner fulfil themselves, so far as she has any power over
> them, and then, she being left unemployed, sees Luria, begins to
> see him, — having hitherto seen only her own ends which he was
> to further.

Then he added, "Oh, enough of it!" [16]

Browning had worked with difficulty for three months and more
on *Luria* and had held it longer. He was weary of writing and was
thinking of preparing for his last *Bell* a play probably composed several
years earlier.

Browning had started *A Soul's Tragedy* as early as May 22, 1842,
the date on which he wrote Domett that he was going to "finish a wise
metaphysical play (about a great mind and soul turning to ill)," and he
might have written it in 1843,[17] on the rebound from disappointing
attempts to write for the stage.[18] Elizabeth learned about it on February 26, 1845, when Browning indicated the content of *Luria* and told
her that *A Soul's Tragedy* was finished but not right for the last work of
his *Bells*. A year later, after *Dramatic Romances and Lyrics* had been published and he was at the end of *Luria,* she asked him about *A Soul's
Tragedy.* He answered on February 11, 1846, "For the Soul's Tragedy
— *that* will surprise you, I think — There is no trace of you there, —
you have not put out the black face of *it* — it is all sneering and *disillusion*
— and shall not be printed but burned if you say the word. . . ."[19]

That night he read the play again and was afraid it would have a
bad effect on his reputation. Although a few points still impressed him
as "successful in design & execution," the play was not a good ending
for the series. He gave his reasons:

> . . . subject-matter & style are alike unpopular even for the literary
> *grex* that stands aloof from the purer *plebs,* and uses that privilege to
> display & parade an ignorance which the other is altogether uncon-
> scious of — so that, if Luria is *clearish,* the Tragedy would be an un-
> necessary troubling the waters; whereas, if I printed it first in order,
> my readers, according to custom, would make the (comparatively)
> little they did not see into, a full excuse for shutting their eyes at the
> rest . . . but, at bottom, I believe the proper objection is to the im-

mediate, *first* effect of the whole — its moral effect, — which is dependent on the contrary supposition of its being really understood, in the main drift of it. . . .[20]

Browning was not expressing a low opinion of the play but a fear that it would not be received well. He had been encouraged by the reception of *Dramatic Romances and Lyrics* and hoped his work on *Luria* would facilitate the reader's understanding; he wanted to run no risk of ending his series with a play that would present problems. He was inclined to put *A Soul's Tragedy* aside for the present. ". . . I wrote it with the intention of producing the best of all effects — perhaps the truth is, that I am tired, rather, and desirous of getting done. . . . I have lost, of late, interest in dramatic writing, as you know — and perhaps, occasion."[21] He was weary of writing but also he knew only too well the hazard of publishing a work as innovative as *A Soul's Tragedy*.

The play was not easily dismissed. Elizabeth could not resist showing her desire to read it. And Browning at this point, as well as at other times, expressed the need to disburden himself of works already conceived, and in this instance already written. On February 24, 1846, he looked over the play again and changed his mind. "I . . . think it will do after all . . . ." He added, ". . . there are some things in the 'Tragedy' I should like to preserve and print now, leaving the future to spring as it likes, in any direction, — and these half-dead, half-alive works fetter it, if left behind."[22] On March 9 he took Part I to Elizabeth. After his previous remarks on the play, she was surprised when she read it. She wrote:

> Dearest, I read your 'Soul's Tragedy' last night & was quite possessed with it, & fell finally into a mute wonder how you could for a moment doubt about publishing it. It is very vivid, I think, & vital, & impressed me more than the first act of 'Luria' did . . though I do not mean to compare such dissimilar things, . . & for pure nobleness 'Luria' is unapproachable . . will prove so, it seems to me . . But this "Tragedy" shows more heat from the first . . & then, the words beat down more closely . . well! I am struck by it all as you see.[23]

In less than ten days later Browning had done with *A Soul's Tragedy*. When he was with Elizabeth on March 28 he must have shown further uncertainty of it. Having read the whole play, she continued to praise it: "I am not to admire it . . am I? And you really think that anyone who can think . . feel . . could help such an admiration, or ought to try to help it. Now just see — It is a new work with your

mark on it." Again there was Elizabeth's comparison of *A Soul's Trag-*
edy with *Luria:* "I am not at all sure that if I knew you now first & only
by these two productions, . . Luria and the Tragedy, . . I should not
involuntarily attribute more power and a higher faculty to the writer of
the last — I *should*, I think — yet Luria is the completer work . . I
know it very well." There were no reservations in her praise of *A Soul's*
Tragedy, as there had been in her remarks on *Luria:*

> Such thoughts, you have, in this second part of the Tragedy! — a
> 'Soul's Tragedy' indeed! No one *thinks* like you — other poets talk
> like the merest women in comparison. Why it is full of hope for both
> of us, to look forward & consider what you may achieve with that
> combination of authority over the reasons & the passions, & that
> wonderful variety of plastic power![24]

Elizabeth was right in preferring *A Soul's Tragedy* and Browning
was right in his anticipation of its effect upon those who were soon to
read the play. In his uncertainty about the impression that the play
would leave, he wrote Elizabeth: "How you surprize me . . . by liking
that Tragedy! It seems as if, having got out of the present trouble, I
shall never fall into its fellow — I will strike, for the future, on the
glowing, malleable metal; afterward, *filing* is quite another process
from hammering, and a more difficult one. . . ."[25]

As difficult as it was, filing as well as hammering was part of the
process of being a poet, and Browning saw his task through. We can
stand on the sideline and observe something of the process as he was
finishing and then revising the plays, just as we did when he was working on *Dramatic Romances and Lyrics*. Excerpts already given from the
love letters have shown Browning writing the plays and expressing his
opinion of them. The letters also show him revising them. As the result of Elizabeth's objections to the length of some of the speeches in
Luria, he cut down the play, and before he took Part II of *A Soul's*
Tragedy to her he removed a long speech, "a huge kind of sermon";
later he added a few phrases in order to throw light on one of the characters in *A Soul's Tragedy*.[26] At the last moment he was still anxiously
scrutinizing both plays in proof for possible improvements.[27]

Elizabeth's criticism of *Dramatic Romances and Lyrics* and Browning's reaction have been discussed. And what was his reaction to the
separate pages of comments she made on the plays? Her notations on
Luria came to approximately fifty. A little over a third of the questions
or suggestions for revision applied to inversions and a third to lack of

clarity. Criticisms for lack of clarity included questions concerning diction and the omission of connectives or pronouns. The frequent inversions caused Elizabeth at times to come out with such comments as ". . . where nothing is gained by an inversion, the simpler form seems better," "Why object to natural sequency of words?" and "O you inverter." There were so many undesirable inversions that at times she made the change to the natural order of words without labeling it.[28]

After receiving her suggestions Browning wrote Elizabeth, "I adopt every one. . . ."[29] Although almost without exception he heeded them, he did not always adopt them verbatim. It is interesting that in several instances a change he made for the *Luria* of 1846 in accordance with her suggestion was cancelled in editions published after Elizabeth's death and the original was restored; where his first writing seemed better than her suggested change, he might have reverted to it without remembering her criticism. Bernice Fox has shown that in some instances Browning also reverted in his 1863 *Poetical Works* to the original reading in *Paracelsus* after making changes in that work for the 1849 collected edition.[30] When she wrote her article a comment of Browning's on the changes had not yet been published. He wrote to M. D. Conway, who reviewed the 1863 collection *(Victoria Magazine,* Feb. 1864), ". . . in the instance of *Paracelsus* the few changes are simply a return to the original reading, which I had polished a little, in the second edition [1849], and done no good to."[31]

It might be asked whether Elizabeth influenced Browning to polish the original for the 1849 edition. Miss Fox commented on the result of the changes. "The revised *Paracelsus* is certainly a more graceful composition than the original, although the refinement of style necessarily results in a loss of rugged strength." As can also be seen by an examination of the variorium readings of *Paracelsus,* some lines that were compact and forceful in the original edition were changed in the 1849 edition to smoother expanded ones (of the sort that Elizabeth suggested in her notes on *Dramatic Romances and Lyrics* and *Luria*) and changed back in subsequent editions to Browning's original lines.

At this point we can make two observations about Elizabeth's influence on Browning's style. The first is that whatever gain or harm she might have been responsible for in *Dramatic Romances and Lyrics, Luria,* and the collected edition of 1849, on the whole *Luria* seemingly profited in 1846 by her criticisms; the number of them accounted for Browning's finding "this sad *Luria*" infinitely worse than he had thought it was. The other observation is that, although, as Thomas J.

Collins has pointed out, Elizabeth's "stylistic influence [on Browning] has been thoroughly documented,"[32] very little has been said about Browning's occasional inclination to follow or revert to his own course instead of accepting her suggestions.

If Browning had as much trouble with the "filing" of *A Soul's Tragedy* as he did with *Luria*, we have no evidence of it. Since the harness of stage tradition fit even more loosely upon *A Soul's Tragedy* than upon *Luria*, Browning might have written more naturally and easily in the last play of the *Bells*. Elizabeth noted only four objections to *A Soul's Tragedy*. If she had had the play in hand as long as she had *Luria*, she might have found more, but the love letters show that she undoubtedly favored *A Soul's Tragedy*. She recognized its originality. Furthermore she pronounced the play "as light as day."[33]

That remark surely pleased Browning. In writing and revising he kept in mind the often-repeated criticism of obscurity. While he was writing the last act of *Luria*, a reminder of such criticism launched him into a discussion, in a letter to Elizabeth, that showed how facile and indeterminate he thought the attacks could be. Furthermore, he indicated his own position on clarity of expression. "Of course an artist's whole problem must be, as Carlyle wrote to me, 'the expressing with articulate clearness the thought in him' — I am almost inclined to say that *clear expression* should be his only work and care — for he is born, ordained, such as he is — and not born learned in putting what was born in him into words. . . ."[34]

Near the end of the work on the plays, Elizabeth again brought up the matter of the title of the series:

> Dearest, I persist in thinking that you ought not to be too disdainful to explain your meaning in the Pomegranates. . . . Consider that Mr. Kenyon & I may fairly represent the average intelligence of your readers, — & that *he* was altogether in the clouds as to your meaning . . had not the most distant notion of it, — while I, taking hold of the priest's garment, missed the Rabbins & the distinctive significance, as completely as he did. . . . Now why should you be too proud to teach such persons as only desire to be taught? I persist — I shall teaze you.[35]

Luria and *A Soul's Tragedy* were published on April 13, 1846. This last *Bell* was dedicated to Landor,[36] whose congratulatory poem written after the publication of *Dramatic Romances and Lyrics* had given much gratification to Browning. When Elizabeth received her copy of the pamphlet of thirty-two pages, she turned over the leaves "ever so proudly." She confessed that one of her first searches was for the explanation of the title. She "looked, and looked, & looked, at the end, at the beginning, at the end again." Finally she turned to *A Soul's Tragedy* and found it on the verso of the half title. "Having submitted to explain, quite at the point of the bayonet, you determined at least to do it where nobody could see it done."[37]

Browning gave Elizabeth his reasons for placing the explanation as a foreword to *A Soul's Tragedy:*

> The explanatory note fills up an unseemly blank page — and does not come at the end of the "Soul's Tragedy" — prose after prose — still it does look awkwardly — but then I don't consider that it excludes this last from the "Bells" — rather it says this *is* the last, (*no, nine* if you like, — as the title says eight *and* last' — from whence will be this advantage — that, in the case of another edition, all the lyrics &c may go together under one common head of Lyrics & Romances — and the "Soul's Tragedy," — profiting by the general move-up of the rest of the numbers, after the fashion of hackney coaches on a stand when one is called off, — step into the place and take the style of No. 8 — and the public not find themselves defrauded of the proper quantity!)[38]

Browning optimistically had his mind on a second edition.

The explanation of the title read:

> Here ends my first Series of "Bells and Pomegranates:" and I take the opportunity of explaining, in reply to inquiries, that I only meant by that title to indicate an endeavour towards something like an alternation, or mixture, of music with discoursing, sound with sense, poetry with thought; which looks too ambitious, thus expressed, so the symbol was preferred.

There was more to Browning's explanation but we need not follow it here.

Forster, who managed to obtain the first copy of the last *Bell,* published a review in the *Examiner* on April 25. He gave most of his attention to *Luria.* He did not recollect better writing in any of Browning's works than that in this play. He summarized it and quoted generously. Although his remarks were on the whole favorable, he again complained of Browning's metaphysics and again lamented the poet's failure to succeed as a stage dramatist. Had Browning's *"tone* of treatment" been "simpler, less remote, less abstrusely metaphysical, the stage would in him have found its noblest supporter in these latter days." Forster felt that when Browning got away from what clogged and obstructed him and into the "region of uncontrollable emotion," he displayed an extraordinary power. Few writers equalled him in the "intensity and individuality of his thoughts and emotions" as few failed to surpass him in "ease and simplicity." In concluding his remarks on *Luria,* Forster recognized that "genius is to be thanked, not quarrelled with"; if Browning's writing had fewer faults it might not be so strong and original. *A Soul's Tragedy* was briefly introduced near the end of the review.

The *New Monthly Magazine* of May carried a paragraph with namby-pamby support of Browning and his last *Bell.*

In June both plays were reviewed in the *New Monthly Belle Assemblée,* which recognized lofty purpose in each one. Camilla Toulmin was in all likelihood the writer of the review, which bears similarities to her criticism of *Dramatic Romances and Lyrics. Luria,* which the critic did not suppose to be intended for the stage, was praised for its "unity of plot and purpose" and "power of a fresh coinage, stamping some truth which we instantly recognize in the glowing words which make it Poetry." Although Miss Toulmin quoted generously for the reader's benefit, she felt that the passages were weakened by their isolation from the play. *A Soul's Tragedy,* "a very different production from 'Luria,' " the reviewer did not readily understand. "On a first perusal we were inclined to deem it inferior, and we still think it obscure; but a light dawns as again and again we refer to its pages, fascinating enough from the philosophic truths and quaint similies in which they abound." The concluding sentences are of interest for their suggestion of Browning's growing reputation.

> Robert Browning's genius is so much in advance of all that is vulgar and trite and common-place, that . . . his appreciators must be a gradually enlarging circle. That it is already so large as it is, we look upon as a hopeful sign of mental advancement in the popular mind; which shows that this is becoming of a different quality from that which had to be taught to recognize so many of its now acknowledged masters.

Another review of the last *Bell* appeared in June, in *Douglas Jerrold's Shilling Magazine.* Here Browning was recognized as a poet of very high rank. "He has great perceptions and conceptions, and his delight is in his own might, not in the vain plaudits of those who mistake skill for genius, and smartness for originality." The reviewer stressed Browning's ability to understand and portray character. The secret of his strength and hardness lay in his lack of sentimentality. Conducive to the portrayal of character in all the "nakedness and hideousness of true passion" was his choice of time and country. Deeply imbued with and informed by the spirit of the Middle Ages, Browning demonstrated his dramatic strength as he nobly realized in *Luria* a great idea — "the conflict of mind and matter, of will and intellect." The reviewer, probably Jerrold, felt that *A Soul's Tragedy*, with its masterly revelation of the villain, was one of the "most intensely dramatic" works ever written, and in it Browning fulfilled the mission of the poet and the dramatist in new and valuable illustrations of the weak and degraded in contrast with the good and noble sides of human nature. Although the critic did not think it likely that these dramas would be performed, certainly not until there was a change in taste for acted plays, he was sure of Browning's dramatic ability.

Along with the praise there sounded a discordant note.

> He [Browning] may perchance have a touch too much, with the proud Roman, of resting on his own powers, and if not despising, disregarding his reader. He understands character and human emotion profoundly, and delineates it powerfully. He never aids the reader by narrative or obtrusion of himself. There are character, passion, and poetry, flung down on the paper, and it is certainly the reader's fault or misfortune if he does not perceive them.

As in some other favorable reviews, the injected suggestion that Browning was guilty of self-indulgence was more in accord with the general opinion of his poetry than with the critic's favorable measurement of it, which came out clearly in the rest of the review.

An extremely unfavorable criticism appeared in *Hood's Magazine* in August 1846. (By contributing poems to this magazine, Browning had helped Hood at the last of his life.) The heading indicated a review of the last *Bell*, but only *Luria* was discussed. After a harangue on Browning's obscurity, the critic gave an example of his "better-class writing" and then repeated lines from the example to show how bad they were. There was also objection to "loose, hastily-constructed, unpolished, and unmusical lines which grate, past endurance, on a correct ear." The reading public was warned not to be misled by the praises of friendly worshippers of an elliptical, abrupt, and often puzzling style, not to mistake it for "the perfection of recondite beauty" and "the model of future fine writing." This review of *Luria* was used as the occasion for a persistent and heavy-handed attack against all of Browning's writing.

Although the heading of an article on poetry of the day in the *New Quarterly Review* for October 1846 promised a review of *Luria* and *A Soul's Tragedy*, more space was given to comments on other works of Browning's than to the two plays in the last *Bell*. In the introductory remarks of the review, *Pauline* as well as *Paracelsus* was mentioned. At the beginning of the section on Browning, the critic at once identified him as one of the psychological poets of the day. He dwelt on his obscurity generally and then showed more specifically that he had found *Paracelsus*, *Strafford*, and *Sordello* increasingly obscure; Browning redeemed himself with *Pippa Passes*, "a beautiful poem." It was followed by four plays unsuited to the stage. The critic said he was happy to report that *Luria* and *A Soul's Tragedy* were "generally intelligible," and he indicated briefly the content of each play. Though the unfavorable criticism of Browning was more prominent than the praise, it was not colored by irritation, as had often been the case in reviews of the forties. The reviewer thought that the persistent reader would be repaid for his effort. In the conclusion he noted some familiar objections but at least he did not place the whole blame for Browning's lack of popularity on the poet alone. ". . . Mr. Browning, notwithstanding his perversity and obscurity, is in the first class of poets. He soars out of sight, indeed; but it is the spectator's weakness that he cannot follow him. Would the poet, mighty as he is, condescend to public appreciation, no man would be more successful."

Browning had made a step forward in his reputation with the publication of his second volume of short dramatic pieces as *Bell* No. VII, but his return to the form of a play for *Luria* and *A Soul's Tragedy* in his last *Bell* threw his readers off course. One review was written by a friend (John Forster) and two reviews were apparently written by people whose paths Browning had crossed (Camilla Toulmin and Douglas Jerrold). The plays would have had a dismal reception without these criticisms. Each contained favorable remarks and the reviewers did not consider the plays as intended for the stage. But they could hardly be expected to take the next step: seeing that *Luria* and *A Soul's Tragedy* approached what was later to be called the dramatic monologue inasmuch as interest is directed toward one figure and the others are subordinated. Several reviewers, it should be recalled, had been aware of this aspect of *Paracelsus* when it was first published. The critic for *Douglas Jerrold's Shilling Magazine* had a keener sense of Browning's dramatic strength in portraying human nature than the other critics of the last *Bell*. With the exception of the complaint of unintelligibility in *Hood's*, the discussions of the two plays provide relief from the accusation of obscurity and the quarrelsomeness that had been present in many reviews since the publication of *Sordello*.

Of the two plays *Luria* received the more ready approbation. When Browning was planning it, he doubtless had in the back of his mind the objection that Macready as well as critics had made to his postponement of explanation needed at the beginning. In *Luria* the early unfolding of the situation facilitated the reader's understanding. Browning wrote Elizabeth that it was "very simple and straightforward," as indeed it was in its act-by-act direct movement toward the end. He might have added that the play's resemblance to *Othello* was also a staff for the reader to lean upon.

A Soul's Tragedy was not so well adapted to immediate appreciation, as Browning was aware. In it, as in *Pippa Passes,* he gave himself free rein to follow his individual dramatic inclination. *A Soul's Tragedy* was unlike works the readers were familiar with. They had no clear signals at the beginning as to what was to follow and no straightforward movement as in *Luria.* They had a play in two parts, each with a remarkably independent character portrayal, as Park Honan has pointed out,[39] and they had to read both parts attentively in order to appreciate the sophisticated penetration of mind.

Elizabeth, who had been immersed in Browning's developing techniques in character presentation and who happily accepted a work far removed from the stage, could appreciate *A Soul's Tragedy.* Others were not so fortunate. *Hood's* ignored it; Forster did little more than refer to it; the critic for the *New Monthly Belle Assemblée* confessedly had to read it repeatedly to understand it; the *New Quarterly Review* labeled it "intelligible" and indicated its content. Only *Douglas Jerrold's Shilling Magazine* praised it highly and did so without hesitation.

As far as we can tell from the love letters, the nonprofessionals who went beyond a general statement about the last *Bell* showed a preference for *Luria.* Mrs. Paine, Elizabeth's enthusiastic visitor from Farnham, read *Luria* and wrote Elizabeth, ". . . I feel inclined to call Browning the greatest dramatic genius we have had for hundreds of years." George Barrett thought *Luria* "very fine." After Elizabeth read a letter from Chorley to Browning, she wrote, "If Mr. Chorley did not

read Luria at once, he speaks of you in the right words. . . ." Nothing
was said of his opinion of A Soul's Tragedy.⁴⁰

Elizabeth's report of Kenyon's opinion suggested his preference
for Luria. "A very noble creation, he thought it, & heroically pathetic
. . & much struck he seemed to be with the power you had thrown out
on the secondary characters, lifting them all to the height of humanity,
justifying them by their own lights. Oh — he saw the goodness, & the
greatness, the art, & the moral glory. . . ." She confessed that he tried
"to find out a few darknesses," but she proved "that they were clear
noonday blazes instead, & that his eyes were just dazzled." His opinion
of A Soul's Tragedy, however favorable, was less definite, ". . . the
'Soul's Tragedy' made the right impression — a wonderful work it is
for suggestions, & the conception of it as good a test of the writer's genius, as any we can refer to."⁴¹ From the love letters come echoes of
praise that Browning received from others — Arnould, Horne, Mrs.
Jameson, W. C. Bennett of Blackheath, and Browning's "old sailor-
friend" James Pritchard.⁴²

Browning had skimmed over the most laudatory of the letters on
Dramatic Romances and Lyrics with his flesh creeping, and now, he confessed, he could not read Bennett's comment on the last Bell. The
opinions of two of the greater lights in the literary world — Carlyle
and Landor — fell into a different category. After walking to Carlyle's,
Browning reported, "He told me he had read my last number [Bell
VIII]; and that he had 'been read to' — some good reader had repeated
'The Duchess' [The Flight of the Duchess in Bell VII] to him — altogether he said wonderfully kind things and was pleased to prophesy in
the same spirit, — God bless him!"⁴³

Scarcely more definite than the report of Carlyle's comment was
Landor's opinion of the plays expressed in his letter acknowledging the
work dedicated to him. Browning read the first paragraph: "My dear
Browning, — Let us agree to drop Sirs for ever. And now accept my
thanks for the richest of Easter offerings made to anyone for many
years. I staid at home last evening on purpose to read Luria, and if I
lost any good music (as I certainly did) I was well compensated in
mind." At this point Browning faced two longer paragraphs that contained no definite remarks on the plays. The first started with an
expression of appreciation for the dedication, which, with its reference
to Shakespeare, allowed Landor to discuss in both paragraphs Shakespeare's rather than Browning's plays. In the fourth and last paragraph
Landor referred to works as yet unwritten: "Go on and pass us poor

devils! If you do not go far ahead of me, I will crack my whip at you and make you spring forward."[44]

Landor was more definite in a letter to Forster:

> I have written to Browning; a great poet, a very great poet indeed, as the world will have to agree with us in thinking. I am now deep in the *Soul's Tragedy*. The sudden close of *Luria* is very grand; but preceding it, I fear there is rather too much of argumentation and reflection. It is continued too long after the Moor has taken the poison. I may be wrong; but if it is so, you will see it and tell him. God grant he may live to be much greater than he is, high as he stands above most of the living: *latis humeris et toto vertice*. But now to the *Soul's Tragedy*, and so adieu till we meet at this very table.[45]

Landor had read *Luria* without the benefit of Browning's explanation that the action proper takes place in the minds of the characters and is revealed in their speeches. We can see that the "argumentation and reflection" in Luria's long speeches were a movement leading to the perfection of the dramatic monologue.

Elizabeth showed a livelier interest than Browning in all of these personal comments on his plays. It was professional criticism of his *Bells* that he was concerned about and watching for as he discussed with Elizabeth published reviews of works by other writers. He expected attention from the *Examiner* and the *Athenaeum*. When Forster's criticism of *Luria* and *A Soul's Tragedy* did appear (nearly two weeks after publication), he was relieved of some of his anxiety and at once wrote Elizabeth of his appreciation of Forster's efforts in his behalf.

> Well Ba, do you see the "Examiner"? That is very kind, very generous of Forster: there are real difficulties in the way of this prompt, efficient, serviceable notice — for he has a tribe of friends, dramatists, actors "conflicting interests" &c &c to keep the peace among, — and he quite understands his trade, — how compensation is to be made, and an equilibrium kept in the praises so as to offend nobody, — yet see how he writes, and with a heap of other business on his shoulders! I thank him very sincerely, I am sure.[46]

Elizabeth answered, "Very good Examiner! — I am pleased with it & with Mr. Forster for the nonce, though he talks a little nonsense here & there, in order to be a true critic, & though he doesn't talk at all, scarcely, of the *Soul's Tragedy* . . . how is one to bear it?"[47]

From the beginning of his career Browning had set great store on the effect that criticism in the press had on his reputation. In one ref-

erence to the review in the *Examiner* Browning wrote: "Well, now —
see the way a newspaper criticism affects one, nearly the only way! —
If this had been an attack — how it would affect you and me matters
nothing — it might affect others disagreeably — and thro' them, us.
So I feel very much obliged to Forster in this instance."[48]

Browning doubtless expected the *Athenaeum* to review his last
Bell, but the weeks passed by and no review appeared. Elizabeth grew
impatient with the silence. Nettled by the disregard of his work, one
evening in August Browning released his feelings to Chorley, his
friend and a reviewer for the *Athenaeum.* They argued about two other
men who had been of service to Browning in writing reviews of his
works — Horne and Forster. Browning defended Horne as a poet and
Forster as a critic. According to Browning's report to Elizabeth, the
subject of Forster and the *Examiner* brought uncontrolled words from
Chorley. We read Browning's account of proving his points and are left
to imagine the extent of his own control.

> I proved another thing too — that Forster was not a whit behind his
> brethren of the faculty, in literary morals — that the Examiner,
> named, was quite as just and good as another paper, unnamed.
> Whereat Chorley grew warm and lost his guard, and at last, — de-
> claring I forced him into corners and that speak he *must; instanced the
> Examiner's treatment of myself as not generous* . . Luria having been no-
> ticed as you remember a week after the publication, and *yet,* or
> never, to be reviewed in the Unnamed! — *Ces Misères!*[49]

There can be no doubt about Browning's feelings toward the *Athenaeum's* disregard of his last plays, though at the end of his work on
them he himself called them "manque, failures" to Elizabeth. Since
the time of *Paracelsus* he had been working out his own methods of dramatic presentation, and these two plays as well as statements of his
about them showed how far he had developed an original technique of
character revelation. But plays, even for an imaginary stage, were no
longer suitable to his needs. After he had written Domett in 1842 of
his works in progress — *A Blot,* "a few songs and small poems" *(Dramatic Lyrics),* an "Eastern play" *(Druses),* and a "wise metaphysical
play" *(Soul's Tragedy)* — he said that he would be contented with the
outcome of his experiment.[50]

He had not been content with the results then and was not content in 1846. At the end of his *Bells* he felt that it was time to complete the works he had been impelled to write, take poetic inventory,

and proceed to better effect. As he had written Elizabeth, he wished to relieve his mind of his "half-dead, half-alive works." He wrote to Domett on July 13, 1846, after his last *Bell* was published, ". . . I felt so instinctively from the beginning that unless I tumbled out the dozen more or less of conceptions, I should bear them about forever, and year by year get straiter and stiffer in those horrible cross-bones with a long name, and at last parturition would be the curse indeed."[51]

In what Browning called "the Author's flourish" later in this let-ter to Domett, one passage is significant for Browning's consideration of his past writing. He presented two possibilities for a man who meets disappointment at the end of a stretch of work.

> It seems disinspiriting for a man to hack away at trees in a wood, and at the end of his clearing come to rocks or the sea or whatever disap-points him as leading to nothing; but still, turn a man's face, point him to new trees and the true direction, and who will compare his power arising from experience with that of another who has been confirming himself all the time in the belief that chopping wood is incredible labour, and that the first blow he strikes will be sure to jar his arm to the shoulder without shaking a leaf on the lowest bough?

Since from the beginning Browning had placed great value on experi-ence, his choice is not surprising.

> I stand at present and wait like such a fellow as the first of these; if the real work should present itself to be done, I shall begin at once and in earnest . . . not having to learn first of all how to keep the axe-head from flying back into my face; and if I stop in the middle, let the bad business of other years show that I was not idle nor alto-gether incompetent.

A few months before he wrote Domett of the value of past expe-rience to future works, he had taken stock of his situation in a letter to Elizabeth.

> I have told you, and tell you and will tell you, my Ba, because it is simple truth, — that you have been "helping" me to cover a defeat, not gain a triumph. If I had not known you *so far* THESE works might have been the *better*, — as assuredly, the greater works, I trust will follow, — they would have suffered in proportion! If you take a man from prison and set him free . . do you not probably cause a sig-nal interruption to his previously all-ingrossing occupation, and sole labour of love, of carving bone-boxes, making chains of cherry-

stones, and other such time beguiling operations — does he ever take
up that business with the old alacrity? — No! But he begins plough-
ing, building — (castles he makes, no bone-boxes now). I may
plough & build — but these, — leave them as they are![52]

Even before Browning met Elizabeth his desire to begin a new
chapter in his poetic endeavors was so strong that he was scheming
"how to get done" and go to his "heart in Italy."[53] After he met her he
felt even more that he could gain from an end to the early poetic experiences. She had shown him the way to greater possibilities; in the life
lying ahead there would be a fresh start.

He repeatedly expressed belief that he would produce better
works in the future. When he was dispirited early in 1842, he wrote
Domett, "The true best of me is to come, and you shall have it. . . ."
Late in the same year, in referring to *Dramatic Lyrics,* he wrote, "I shall
have more ready ere long, I hope — and better."[54] In spite of his occasional times of discouragement he was generally optimistic during his
experimental period of writing. One of the themes running throughout his letters to Elizabeth was that he would do "quite other and better things."

Browning's confidence in his future can be set beside the observation that Fanny Haworth had made in her sonnet on him, published
in 1836: he was "assured in genius too intense / For doubt of its own
power." He knew what he had done, compared with "the dim thrill of
what shall be / When glorious visions find reality." Browning had the
confidence that an original artist must have, especially in the face of
failures, and he had a strong belief in his destiny as a poet. He said to
Elizabeth, thinking of himself, that you must write "if you fear God."
And later he wrote her, "I desire in this life . . . to live and just write
out certain things which are in me, and so save my soul."[55] The charge
laid upon Paracelsus was one he felt to be his own.

> How know I else such glorious fate my own,
> But in the restless irresistible force
> That works within me? . . . . . .
>   Be sure that God
> Ne'er dooms to waste the strength he deigns impart.
>
> . . . .
>
> Be sure they sleep not whom God needs; nor fear
> Their holding light his charge, when every hour
> That finds that charge delayed is a new death.

During the years in which Browning "tried an experiment to the end," he developed the art of social intercourse, which he came to consider important to his career. He was not always inclined to the gregariousness later attributed to him, as is shown by Procter's advice in 1844 to shun loneliness.[56] In the thirties, so Carlyle reported, Browning "seemed to have set his heart on the gift of silence."[57] Arnould reported to Domett that Browning, whom they remembered as hardly able to do justice to himself in a social gathering, had improved as a result of acquiring "the habit of good and extensive society." Again later, in 1845, Arnould wrote of him, "Glorious Robert Browning is as ever, but more genial, more brilliant, and more anecdotical than when we knew him four years ago. . . ."[58]

Once he had adjusted himself to the serious business of knowing men and their ways and of becoming known, Browning learned to turn his intellectual assets to good account. In professional-social circles he was then recognized as a man of grace and poise with a wide and varied knowledge. Elizabeth heard echoes of his charm in her secluded existence. But his active life could and did pall at times. In strong language he once revealed to Elizabeth that he had moments of distaste for his efforts to please and for those he was trying to please: "I . . . who have been at such pains to acquire the reputation I enjoy in the world . . . dine, and wine, and dance and enhance the company's pleasure till they make me ill and I keep house. . . ."[59] He came to realize that the socializing which he had initially found difficult kept him and his work in the eyes of others and provided him with a fund of knowledge and observation upon which he could draw for whatever might benefit his poetry.

Whether alone or in a group, Browning was always thinking of himself as a poet and striving to improve his art, and he hoped to win the approval of those whose opinion he valued and whose friendship might prove advantageous in some way. In the beginning, the Fox household offered him a social and also a professional atmosphere, where he had his first sweet taste of the possibility of having his works known and where he met men who were to be vital to his poetic concerns. He became one of the Colloquials, who, according to a later report by Arnould, had "such thorough sifting into the very heart of things as used to delight" their "more boisterous, but more joyous colloquies of old."[60] Their magazine and debates furnished an outlet for the expression of their views on literature, politics, and the theater; Browning found in the group lovers of poetry and in Domett a brother poet as well. In time Browning also moved in circles made up of men already recognized in fields of poetry, drama, and criticism — including Landor, Procter, Macready, and Forster.

Among Browning's friends and acquaintances he had loyal supporters, and there was considerable talk back and forth of his poetry and of his personal and professional welfare. Overwork and too intense pursuit of his goal were concerns of some friends. Procter advised him not only to shun loneliness but also to be wary of brain fever. Domett wrote from New Zealand in 1846: "I am greatly afraid you overwork that brain of yours . . . . You *brood* too much over your conceptions . . . ." He advised him to let his brain "lie fallow" for a season.[61]

Another concern of those close to Browning was the difficulty of his poetry. As we have seen, Macready as well as other friends warned him of the danger to his reputation. Domett sent him an impassioned plea:

> Do for heaven's sake, *try to write commonplace* [underlined twice]. Strain as much for it as weaker poets do against it. And always write for *fools;* think of them as your audience instead of the Sidneys & Marvels & Landors or others you talk to in Sordello. Make your language and thoughts such as a tripe man in St Giles's or a milliner in Cranbourne Alley may take into their slender or fat wits at one glance.[62]

Domett continued along his line of advice, though he feared Browning would not take it. Yet he knew that herein lay his "truest course."

Browning had his turn. He expressed his appreciation for Domett's "cautions and warnings" concerning his "well-being, mental and physical," and assured him that he had done his best in his most recent works to get rid of defects of obscurity and imperfect expressions. But Browning would not countenance any suggestion by his friend Domett that he thought might stifle or thwart his genius — or by Arnould, Macready, or anyone else. In answering Domett he defended his poetic stance: ". . . from the beginning, I have been used to take a high ground, and say, all endeavour elsewhere is thrown away. Endeavour *to think* (the real *thought*), to *imagine,* to *create,* or whatever they call it . . . ."[63] Browning believed that though the effort to think, imagine, and create might fail, it should be undertaken nevertheless. Later in the letter he strongly affirmed his feeling that *real* work is not done in vain, no matter what the outcome.

The difference between the creative and the mechanical in writing he discussed in a letter to Elizabeth. The mechanical part of his art

should be studied, he said; but the "more one sits and thinks over the
creative process, the more it confirms itself as 'inspiration,' nothing
more or less." He continued:

> Or, at worst, you write down old inspirations, what you remember
> of them — but with *that* it begins: "Reflection" is exactly what it
> names itself — a *re*-presentation, in scattered rays from every angle of
> incidence, of what first of all became present in a great light, a whole
> one. So tell me how these lights are born, if you can![64]

And so it was that when the proper occasion presented itself,
Browning, absorbed as he was in his art, was ready to talk about poetry
and explain or defend his manner of writing it. As we have seen, he
discussed *Sordello* with Miss Martineau; he had the ear of Fox and Forster, and they both wrote sympathetic reviews; he presented to Macready, and at times defended, his notions of writing plays. He was full
of his scheme of dramatic portrayal, and Horne apparently listened to
him explain it. He acquainted Carlyle with his "improved principle"
of writing and repeatedly made clear the high value he set on originality. He wrote Elizabeth of the difficulties of a dramatic artist, of his
sympathy with Luria's adversaries, and of his practice of having events
take place in the mind of his characters.

But Carlyle was too busy annotating Cromwell's letters and
speeches and too set against the use of poetry for the best expression of
ideas to take in Browning's improved principle, and conventional
stagecraft was too deeply ingrained in Macready's thinking for him to
open his mind to Browning's method of character portrayal, on or off
the stage. Browning fared somewhat better with Fox, Forster, and
Horne. As poet, scholar-critic, and beloved confidante, Elizabeth was
better able than anyone else to understand and appreciate his poetry,
though even she did not always grasp his innovations in rhythm.

It is no wonder that Browning explained to Domett that his problem was "stopping the ears against the noise outside." He continued,
". . . but all is next to useless — for there is a creeping, magnetic, as-
similating influence nothing can block out. When I block it out, I
shall do something."[65] The noise outside must not silence the voice
within.

But, as he well knew, the noise outside could be of some value if
it did not drown out the inner voice. Browning wrote short poems "for
popularity's sake" and he was grateful for and heeded sincere criticism
as long as it did not threaten what he considered his own poetical pow-

ers. Critics and even friends often cried out against what they considered the misuse of his genius. To a considerable extent Browning exercised restraint in his response; but a seething force within a very intense poet, lurking just below the surface, sometimes became activated by neglect of his work or a needling criticism.

Browning himself gave an insight into his disposition in a letter to Elizabeth: "I myself am born supremely passionate — so I was born with light yellow hair — all changes; that is the passion changes its direction and, taking a channel large enough, looks calmer, perhaps, than it should — and all my sympathies go with quiet strength, of course — but I know what the other kind is."[66]

Various facets of Browning in his early career — his dedication and hard work in the face of defeat, his inclination to talk of his writing, his consideration of the advice as well as the limitations of his readers, his sensitiveness, his variegated moods of satisfaction and chagrin, and his participation in a social-professional life in the service of his poetry — all should be viewed in connection with his later behavior. And in his early as in his later life none of these aspects should be considered in isolation. To see them as they fit together to make a whole pattern should result in a better understanding of the poet as he moved toward the wide acceptance and appreciation that he desired.

CHAPTER XIII

Further Encouraging Signs

Poems, 1849

In 1846 Robert and Elizabeth married and left England. Between this time and 1850, when Browning's first new work after his marriage was published, *A Blot* had its second run on the stage (1848–9) and a collected edition of his works appeared (1849). Reviewers of the late forties, some writing before and some after the publication of this collection, looked back over Browning's work and took stock of his special achievement. Several reviewers had tended in this direction when dealing with *Dramatic Romances and Lyrics*. Encouraging signs that had become evident at that time continued to be present: recognition of variety and fertility; awareness of Browning's interest in the portrayal of character; and the beginning of a clearer notion of his particular dramatic quality. Encouraging also were a decline in irritability, which helped to clear the mind for a sympathetic approach, and along with it a more pronounced inclination to accept Browning's highly individual style and make an attempt to explain rather than condemn it.

While the last of the reviews of the eighth *Bell* were appearing and before the publication of the collected edition, special attention was given in two periodicals to earlier individual works. The reviews are noteworthy because they were written to attract readers to Browning, not only by summaries of particular poems, but also by explanation of the difficulties of reading his poetry and assurance of the rewards of becoming familiar with it. As guides for the reader, the reviews were precursors of others to follow.

239

Chorley, Browning's friend and a reviewer for the *Athenaeum*, wrote two of the articles (this is a better term because they are not reviews in the ordinary sense) before Browning's marriage and departure for Italy. They were published in the *People's Journal*, a weekly designed to entertain and instruct the poor, both intellectually and morally. The first, which appeared on July 18, 1846, was a summary of part of *Pippa Passes* with introductory and concluding remarks and the second, published on August 22, was a summary of *Colombe's Birthday*.

At the beginning of the first article Chorley stated that when a poet by issuing his works in cheap form invites the great public to read them and at the same time uses such a title as *Bells and Pomegranates*, one of two results is to be expected. He will be disregarded as one who speaks in parables "not worth the unriddling" or an interpreter will explain the beautiful and great that is veiled to the common gaze. Instead of dismissing Browning because of a "few strange individualities," Chorley would display one of the "noblest contemporary geniuses in all its strength of variety and passion."

Admittedly Browning was not clear; his obscurities did not come from affectations "but from the over-richness of a mind embossed and encrusted, so to say, with the learning and imagery of all schools, of all countries, of all periods." He worked more "by the accumulation than by the digestion of his materials." He was original and reflective, with no intention to puzzle his readers or " 'come over' the vulgar multitude with the Charlatan's robe." How was it best to deal with a writer "at once so difficult, so full of meaning, and so sincere"? The answer was by "*translation* rather than criticism; by dilution as well as analysis." But such a procedure would be impossible for all of the *Bells and Pomegranates;* the works, each as "full as an egg," covered a great territory of subject matter. Therefore the critic would discuss only one or two.

Chorley chose *Pippa Passes* as the subject of his first article. He took his reader through the "Proem," "Morning," and "Noon" and ended his summary with a warning. Anyone who cared only for "easy-going verse, with the sense on the surface," "rhythm making a music to step or dance to," and "imagery reviving old associations" should not read Browning's poetry. In it there were suggestive phrases, broken versification, and many remote and recondite allusions. Those who were willing to put forth labor for pleasure would be made nobler and better by the "lesson" they would find in *Bells and Pomegranates*.

Browning read Chorley's discussion of *Pippa* as soon as it appeared and called it "very kind and gratifying" in a letter to Elizabeth — "this is true, *live* lovingness of him — I will tell him so."[1] A month later Chorley's second article in the *People's Journal* appeared. Explaining that a discussion of the rest of *Pippa Passes* might prove too gloomy for a fair representation of the poet's works, Chorley this time introduced *Colombe's Birthday,* a "beautiful drama," to his readers in an article of two and a half pages, most of it summary. He regretted that there no longer existed a dramatic company that could appreciate the "lights and shades" of the characters in the play. If *"finely* acted," *Colombe's Birthday,* he thought, would be successful on the stage. Again Browning read Chorley's article as soon as it was published. He wrote Elizabeth, "By the way, Chorley has written another very kind paper, in that little Journal of today, on Colombe's Birthday — I have only glanced at it however. See his goodwill!"[2] Elizabeth replied, "There is not much in the article by Mr. Chorley, but it is right & kind as far as it goes."[3] Even though the first part of her statement could not be denied, Chorley's article was designed for the *People's Journal,* and Browning appreciated his friend's effort to place his works within reach of a wider public.

The third article, intended like Chorley's two in the *People's Journal* to help the reader approach Browning and secure favorable attention for *Pippa Passes,* was published in *Sharpe's London Magazine* in 1848. It began in the November issue and concluded in December. Though the "best and worthiest" appreciated Browning, the critic realized that the poet was not "generally popular"; and he, like Chorley, wanted to convince readers unacquainted with him that his work warranted careful study.

In the first installment various writers of poetry and of drama were briefly mentioned, and Browning was ranked high among them. He was asserted to be "pre-eminently, if not exclusively, a dramatist." The critic disapproved of *Sordello;* saw *Paracelsus* as being vague and shadowy, though it was a fine dramatic poem; and merely alluded to the "dramatic utterances in the shape of lyrics." He was impressed by the plays and called particular attention to *Strafford* as a "very remarkable tragedy." Browning's dramas had particular qualities. "It is not . . . in technical adaptability for performance, but intensity of passion and truthfulness of characterisation, combined with high dramatic interest, that Robert Browning's plays surpass the productions of the English school." His plays were not generally appreciated because "not a speech, not a line, scarcely a word is introduced, which does not tend to exhibit some phase of character, which has not a direct bearing on the development of the plot, which does not contribute to the unity of the whole creation."

The critic discussed the first work in *Bells and Pomegranates* — *Pippa Passes,* "which is couched in a peculiar form and vein, but which, nevertheless, must command the sympathies of all who have once learned to understand it." He gave an extended summary accompanied by highly favorable comments, pointing out the individuality, psychological truthfulness, and dramatic force of the characters. Both before and after the summary he offered explanations of Browning's peculiarities as a poet. His works required close reading; the critic was impelled to confess the existence of a needless obscurity characteristic of Browning. Certain defects made the first reading of the poetry a study rather than an ordinary reading: the omission of all relative pronouns and other small words and stage directions as well, for brevity's sake; concentration of thought and passion within the narrowest possible space; assumption of the reader's understanding of recondite allusions. The obscurity to some extent accounted for the slow progress of Browning's reputation. But the professional critic who should have overcome the difficulties could not be excused for the lack of study necessary to appreciate the poetry.

The writer of the article admitted his own difficulty on first reading one of the plays — he thought it was the *Druses.* Like Horne, he disapproved of delaying the explanation needed for immediate understanding. In compensation familiarity revealed beauties and a "sacred melody." Though the critic objected to Browning's sanction of regicide in *Pippa Passes,* he observed that a patrician and Christian "delicacy of sentiment" was the prevailing characteristic of his works, "combined with a force and truthfulness which are sometimes surprising." The gain was worth the effort required. "And, finally, where we at first drew back with a feeling of dismay, we weep, perchance, from the overflowing of our hearts in love, and recognise the presence of the Divine." This discussion, which shows considerable perception, was designed, like Chorley's, to widen Browning's audience. It looked toward the future recognition of Browning's moral and spiritual seriousness and of his emphasis on character; approval of the individual quality of his plays; acceptance of the hard work necessary for understanding his poetry; and explanation of the peculiarities of his writing.

Unlike the articles in the *People's Journal* and *Sharpe's London Magazine* was the nineteen-page review that appeared between them in the

British Quarterly Review in November 1847. It was written by George Henry Lewes, who, though admitting that Browning was recognized as an outstanding poet, showed little ability to understand his individuality. The critics for the *People's Journal* and *Sharpe's* called attention to Browning's style with very little complaint as they prepared readers for difficulties. Lewes condemned his manner of writing: he did not take pains to write clearly and musically; his obscurity was tiresome, not suggestive. The writers of the articles perceived his dramatic genius and his skill in characterization; of these Lewes said nothing. They appreciated *Pippa Passes* and presented it with the purpose of attracting readers; Lewes was as confused about it as its first reviewers. Although he was not irritable in stating his objections, he showed little perception and lacked sureness. He praised Browning's intellect, then said he was "rather a thinker than a singer" and yet not "accepted as a remarkable thinker." He praised his "power of seeing for himself and writing in his own language," and later, in discussing his style, Lewes wrote of his "aping originality and attracting attention." In his fumbling criticism Lewes made it apparent that he did not like Browning's poetry. With the exception of *The Lost Leader,* which he praised, and *How They Brought the Good News,* he found fault with all of the works he discussed.

When the review in the *British Quarterly* appeared in November 1847 Browning had revised his poems for the collected edition, and when the discussion in *Sharpe's London Magazine* appeared at the end of 1848 the edition was in the press. He had begun his revisions while he and Elizabeth were in Pisa, where they sojourned for six months after they left England. Elizabeth wrote Miss Mitford on December 19, 1846, "Robert is busy preparing a new edition of his collected poems which are to be so clear that everyone who has understood them hitherto will lose all distinction."[4]

Browning approached Moxon, but his erstwhile publisher, despite his earlier encouraging reports of the sale of *Dramatic Romances and Lyrics,* was not ready to rush into the venture. Elizabeth wrote to her sister Arabel on February 8, 1847: ". . . we have both had excellent reports from Moxon as to poetry — the *proceeds* this year being seventy pounds! There's riches for you! — all expenses paid!" She continued, "Moxon desires however, as some copies remain of some of Robert's works, that the issue of the new edition sh'd be delayed till our return to England, in order to secure, as he says, 'an immediate success.' "[5]

Browning was not in favor of a delay, and he continued to present his own position in the matter when he wrote Moxon late in February:

> But the point which decided me to wish to get printed over again was the real good I thought I could do to *Paracelsus, Pippa,* and some others; good, not obtained by cutting them up and reconstructing them, but by affording just the proper revision they ought to have had before they were printed at all. This, and no more, I fancy, is due to them. . . . When you speak of postponing this till my return to England you may be thinking of a speedier return than is probable.[6]

Browning attempted to persuade Moxon that it was in the interest of both publisher and poet to bring out a collected edition in the near future. He wrote, ". . . you know infinitely best what our policy is; 'ours,' for if we keep together, there is not such a thing as your losing while I gain."[7]

Some of Browning's friends had evidently warned him against publication in cramped typographical form like that of the *Bells.* Browning himself liked the compactness, but he so desired to do whatever might attract and keep readers that he passed along their advice to Moxon. "They will have it that the form, the cheap way of publication, the double columns, &c., do me harm, keep reviewers from noticing what I write — retard the sale — and so on. For myself, I always liked the packed-up completeness and succinctness, and am not much disposed to care for the criticism that is refused because my books are not thick as well as heavy."[8]

With copies of Browning's works still on hand, Moxon must have thought that consideration of a collected edition was unrealistic. He certainly was not eager for immediate publication. In later years, Browning wrote Locker-Lampson of his relationship with Moxon:

> He printed on five [for *nine*] occasions, nine poems of mine, wholly at my expense — that is he printed them, & subtracting the very moderate returns, sent me in duly the bill of the remainder of the expense. When I married, I proposed that he should publish a New Edition at his own risk which he declined. . . . Moxon was kind & civil, made no profit by me, I am sure & never tried to help me to any, he would have assured you.[9]

Elizabeth wrote of the financial situation with Moxon to her sister Arabel, who wanted specific information about their publisher's payment to them: ". . . you ask about the proceeds from Moxon. The seventy five pounds this year represent both Robert's & my poems — and then you are to remember that he published last summer *three* 'Bells & Pomegranates' which made a certain expense, all safely covered & having an overplus." Her comments to Arabel on Browning's earnings had an air of vagueness. She reported that 180 copies of her poems remained, as well as copies of his. The immediate past was good, the future promised to be even better: "For several years now the expenses of publication have been so surely covered in his poems, that Moxon has sent him in no bill even. . . . His poems (having survived all the flat years of poems) are getting on now . . it will be all clear gain now, says Moxon . . & there will be a regular income. . . ."[10]

This statement of Elizabeth's seems to bear out what Browning had written to her before marriage about his confident expectations.

As to my copyrights, I never meant to sell them — it would be foolish: because, since some little time, and in consequence of the establishment of the fact that my poems, — even in their present disadvantageous form, without advertisements, and unnoticed by the influential journals — do somehow manage to pay their expenses, I have had one direct offer to print a new edition, — and there are reasons for thinking, two or three booksellers, that I know, would come to terms.[11]

Browning had painted his picture with bright colors in 1846, but now that he was in Italy the two or three booksellers in England did not come to terms so easily. He had told Elizabeth before their marriage, "Smith & Elder . . . wrote to offer to print any poem about Italy, in any form, with any amount of advertisements, on condition of sharing profits . . taking all risks off my hands . . concluding with more than a hint that if that proposition was not favorable enough, they would try and agree to any reasonable demand."[12] After the discouraging exchange of letters with Moxon on the collected edition, Browning turned to George Smith. Smith, with whom Browning had earlier become acquainted and to whom he had presented his books, knew that as the result of a severe financial setback in his firm in the later forties he had to turn down any book considered a financial risk. Therefore when Chorley approached him for Browning about the publication of his works, Smith in his strained position had to move carefully.[13] He depended on his literary adviser, who thought that the poems ought to be republished, but that "he could not advise it as a pecuniary speculation."[14] Again Browning had to look elsewhere for a publisher.

Forster, who had been reviewing Browning's works since 1835 and had assisted him in other ways during this time, was able to use his influence with Chapman and Hall, for whom he was literary adviser.[15] Chapman agreed to publish the two volumes, even at the firm's expense; this was the first time with the exception of *Strafford* that a publisher had taken a chance on Browning's work. Friends in England were helpful. Elizabeth thanked Kenyon for his and Chorley's and Forster's "kind dealings with Robert's poems."[16]

On November 19, 1848, Elizabeth wrote her sister Henrietta that the new edition was coming out soon, and in the same letter she said that Phelps had obtained permission to stage a revival of *A Blot*.[17] As has already been shown, the play was performed three times in November and three in December 1848 and twice in February 1849, and the reviewers saw it more as poetry than as drama. The play was having this second run when Chapman and Hall announced in the *Athenaeum* on December 2, 1848, that *The Poetical Works of Robert Browning*, in two volumes, would be published in December, and on December 16 and 23 announced publication. The title page bore the date 1849 (though the volumes were published in 1848) and the title *Poems by Robert Browning*, with the label *A New Edition*. Evidently Browning chose this label because the works included had been previously published. (The announcements that appeared in the *Athenaeum* indicated a new edition, with numerous alterations and additions.) More accurately, this was his first collected edition, since it included all of his published works except *Pauline, Strafford, Sordello*, and a few short poems. In this chapter it has already been, and will continue to be, referred to as "the collected edition."

Browning's introductory remarks included this statement: "The various Poems and Dramas have received the author's most careful revision." Browning commented on the revisions to several people; he considered them important. As stated in Chapter IX, he requested that the corrections in *Colombe's Birthday* made in the collected edition be observed when Helen Faucit asked permission to perform the part of Colombe in 1853.

Five reviews of the collected edition appeared in 1849 over a period of eight months — in the *Atlas, Literary Gazette, English Review, Eclectic Review*, and *Examiner*. Three more appeared in 1851 — in *Fraser's*, the *Guardian*, and *Christian Remembrancer;* two of these also included discussions of *Christmas-Eve and Easter-Day*. These later discussions of the collected edition are to be considered here along with the first ones. By examining prominent topics in these reviews we can get a better overall picture of the reception of Browning's literary output as represented by the collected edition, which is important in itself, in its relation to the earlier attitude of the critics, and in foreshadowing the later evaluation of Browning's work.

The reviews varied in the extent and adequacy of their examination. The one in the *Atlas* came out in January of 1849, soon after publication. The critic did not write an unfavorable review such as had appeared again and again in the *Atlas*. He was surprised to see how much Browning had written; perhaps the quantity kept him from attempting to evaluate individual works or point out the distinguishing characteristics of Browning's poetry, though he expressed his gratitude for the collection "of one whose claims the world will yet recognise more ungrudgingly than it has hitherto consented to do." His attention was mainly directed to a discussion of Browning's revisions, most of which he did not like. Two months later the *Literary Gazette*, also departing from its previous negative attitude, in two sentences referred to its earlier praise (which in fact had been overshadowed by blame) and said the *Poems of Robert Browning* had "far more to admire than to criticize."

The other reviewers covered more ground and were more specific in both praise and blame. The *English Review* (June 1849) and the *Eclectic Review* (Aug. 1849) were most helpful in emphasizing aspects of Browning's poetry that showed the progress of his genius toward maturity; the *Examiner* (Sept. 8, 1849) and the *Guardian* (Mar. 12, 1851) came next in measuring his accomplishments; and *Fraser's* (Feb. 1851) and the *Christian Remembrancer* (Apr. 1851) did more to misdirect than direct their readers to an understanding of the works. The critics dealt with these topics: his dramatic genius, intellectual quality, moral and ethical sense, and style.

Now that they had a bird's-eye view of Browning's works, they were impressed by the dramatic quality that underlay all of them. To the *English Review* his genius was "pre-eminently dramatic, — so much so, indeed, that whatever he writes, takes consciously or unconsciously a dramatic form." Browning did not write *about* people; he "shows you the people themselves, thinking, feeling, acting." The *Guardian* also saw Browning's genius as being "essentially dramatic"; it was "displayed not only in the occasional felicitous touches which are to be found in all his works, but in the conception and delineation of his characters generally." Even *Paracelsus*, though not properly called a drama, remained still perhaps "the most splendid proof of his dramatical no less than of his poetical powers." Forster said in the *Examiner* that at this time Browning claimed attention mainly as a dramatic poet. "He has the true tact of the dramatist; and seems, almost unconsciously, to cast all he writes in the mould of dramatic presentation." The critic for the *Eclectic Review* saw the poet's genius as "essentially dramatic, but not in the sense which the word vulgarly bears." This critic, like the one for the *English Review*, associated Browning's dramatic genius with his particular technique of character portrayal. All of his works were "mostly the drama of character, not of incident, or scenic effect," with "too absolute a development of interior, mental action" for them to be considered "representable drama."

As for Browning's intellectual quality, the *Eclectic* (Cyrus R. Edmonds was probably the reviewer) did not raise the old objection to mental action on the grounds that it kept his plays from being stageworthy. Although in earlier reviews of other works Forster had at times praised the intellectual content, more often he had seen the analytical element as a fault, especially since it kept Browning from developing into a great dramatist for the stage. In reviewing the collected edition, he related what he considered the weakness of Browning's poetry to a characteristic of the age.

> The most remarkable feature of Mr Browning's genius is the equi-potency of the imaginative and the reasoning powers in his composition. He is a subtle analyst of the human mind, and is endowed at the same time with a rarely equalled power of imaginative creation. It is an error characteristic of the age, and therefore one which he could hardly be expected to escape, that poets should now be too apt to substitute the elaborations of metaphysical analysis for the visions which imagination bodies forth out of many impressions from without. . . . Poetry is perverted into metaphysics. It is the sense of a lingering taint of this kind about Mr Browning's poetry, and a belief that he has yet the power altogether to work himself clear of it, that induced us to anticipate at the outset of these remarks the possibility of still greater works by him in [the] future.

The *Guardian* saw the intellectual aspect of Browning's poetry from another angle. Browning was so engaged upon the thoughts he was to deliver that he was not attentive to the manner in which he was to deliver them. The result was that for readers unwilling to make the effort to comprehend — and many were unwilling — the ideas would not be clear. The critic was not objecting to the intellectual as such. He was typical of most of the earlier reviewers, who accepted and usually praised this quality in passing. To those who reviewed the collected edition it presented different kinds of problems and consequently their remarks varied considerably. *Fraser's* felt that Browning's learning set him above other writers but that his thought and imagery were "welded artificially together." The critic for the *Christian Remembrancer*, who stressed the immorality in the works, said Browning had "more faculties than soul," more intellect than worthy aims. The *Eclectic* foreshadowed the later expanded and more specific consideration of Browning's intellectual quality. The critic saw that the bent of his genius was "eminently and exclusively recondite," displayed in subject matter and manner, and that it was inseparable from his originality and power. Browning could see "innumerable bearings and aspects of the matter in hand, *not* seen by others." This was exemplified in *The Glove*, with its "recondite treatment" and "refinement of sympathy with humanity," which was also characteristic of Browning.

The combination of the intellectual, the dramatic, and the humanly sympathetic in Browning's genius resulted in his presentation of a wide range of characters, bad as well as good, which was acceptable, or even pleasing, to some and repugnant to others. The duality of opinion concerning the moral and ethical sense that had been noticeable in 1845 after the publication of *Dramatic Romances and Lyrics* was present in the reviews of the collected edition. Browning was interested in characters of various kinds, and some critics were able to appreciate his enlarged canvas for depicting human nature. In discussing *A Soul's Tragedy, Douglas Jerrold's Shilling Magazine* (June 1846) had observed the valuable illustration of both the weak and the noble in humanity. In his discussion of the collected edition the critic for the *Eclectic Review* did not object to the comprehensive view. "The phenomena of humanity, in the largest application of the word, form the province and distinctive prerogative of poetry, of the development of poetic truth." In Browning's works, he emphasized, thought was bound up with the large human world.

But when Browning probed the mind and heart of characters that he chose to reveal dramatically, he sometimes found and displayed what the Victorians did not want represented on the printed page or the stage, just as when he brought to his writing his knowledge of the remote in time and place he also aroused criticism. In his review the critic for the High Church *Guardian*, a newcomer among the reviewers of Browning, made a passing statement that none of the dramas "would probably command the attention of a mixed audience." *Fraser's* complained of the poems with their coarse, vulgar, and irreverent expressions, with the flesh and not the spirit of the past, and with Italian rather than English subjects. If these two periodicals pointed out objectionable subject matter, what was the attitude of the three religious periodicals that had already reviewed Browning?

The High Church *Christian Remembrancer* had objected to the subject matter in a review of *Dramatic Romances and Lyrics,* and there was no change of opinion in the criticism of the collected edition. What Browning had to say was "heathenish or coarse"; his poetry asserted "the supremacy of our lower instincts and passions" or gloated over "our nature's savage propensities"; often it was profane. Poem after poem was discussed in the light of this pronouncement.

The earlier criticism of Browning in the High Church *English Review* (Dec. 1845), written by Eliot Warburton, with whom he was acquainted, had contained no complaint on the score of morals. The critic who reviewed the collected edition for the same periodical did have some objections but they were offset by praise. He felt that the sympathy Browning created for the lovers in *A Blot,* about whose morality some questions might be raised, could be dangerous in effect; there was "so much of moral, and even religious beauty" in the play that he knew not how to condemn it. He criticized Browning's support of regicide and his exaltation of suicide, he felt the poet's lack of sufficient regard for certain external decencies, and he regretted the use of themes "which had better been left untouched." But he considered that the moral and religious beauties counterbalancing these errors to be "so great, as to call for the genial appreciation of all true lovers of poetry or of truth." Browning was "always reverential, and sometimes directly Christian." The two volumes made a strong impression on the critic: ". . . the works contained in this edition . . . may be said to be *all* great works, and worthy of serious consideration: they are characterized by deep earnestness, sweet pathos, high purpose, and intense dramatic truthfulness." He called attention to the noble, the religious, and the moral in individual works. The Dissenting *Eclectic,* which earlier (Apr. 1846) had complained of a sensual taint and muddiness of matter, now took no notice of such defects. The critic referred instead to the aspiration and the elevation of human action that he found in reading Browning. The review contained mainly defense, explanation, and praise.

In addition to directing attention to the high plane of thought that characterized Browning's works, the critics for the *English Review* and the *Eclectic* bestirred themselves to put their readers in the right frame of mind for coping with his special style. Effort was necessary for reading Browning, warned the *English Review*. This poet rushed into the subject without explanation and clues, and he presupposed knowledge that the reader probably did not have. Another handicap was the number and concentration of recondite facts. Browning could consider "the expediency of prefixing either arguments or prologues to his principal works, which should not themselves be dramatic, but simply preparatory, explanatory, demonstrative." Many of the difficulties could be eliminated by a second reading, and those who studied the poetry would pass their knowledge on to others. No author was in more need of interpreters, and the critics of the time could not be counted upon to provide this assistance.

In a perceptive review of eleven pages, the *Eclectic Review* stressed Browning's individuality and the need for study which this imposed. Beginning with a discussion of the limited recognition of genuine new poetry, the reviewer said that Browning, a "great and original poet," one among the greatest since the beginning of the century, understandably lacked fame. The expression of his genius must rank as an original manifestation of poetic art. New works must be governed by their own laws, not by the laws of an old code. Those who failed to give time and study could not understand Browning's poetry. He presupposed an intelligent and thoughtful reader; herein lay the primary source of difficulty. He left unexplained not only much that a "less bold or abstract poet *would* explain; but also much in the conception of character, to be comprehensively imagined out; or seen at once — taken for granted, as the ground-work for the after-realization of the poet's creative working." Although Browning's strength lay in his depiction of mental life, there was obscurity in his neglect of incident and external material.. A first reading was also made difficult by Browning's associative imagination, which caused him to follow out the remotest suggestion that might cross his path. Obstacles for the reader arose not from niggardliness but from profusion of poetic wealth, "not from insufficient sight of those ideas within his possession" but from the "number and reconditeness of the ideas themselves." He faced the difficulty of having much given to him in a small space.

But Browning should not change. "Popular or not, he must be a poet after his own fashion; if at all." The critic for the *Eclectic*, as well as the one for the *English Review* and, as has already been said, the one for the *Atlas*, lamented revisions that Browning had made in his poems. Where he had amended his expression, as in *A Blot*, the result was sacrifice, not enrichment, according to the *Eclectic Review*. The reader must not think that all of Browning's poetry was difficult; he would find passages and whole poems in which meaning and beauty would be recognizable at once. The reviewer praised his "mastery over language," and instead of complaining of the roughness of his lines, he grasped the appropriateness of the metrics to the subject matter. Like many others, he thought that Browning's poetry was not as finished as Tennyson's, but he was one of the few during the first part of Browning's career to see his versification as an "efficient instrument, a noble servant." He wrote:

> It is always, — in whatever measure, strictly individual and characteristic, and of exceeding power and facility — the facility of energy, not of smoothness. It is marked by such licence and freedom dangerous only to the poetaster, from merely arbitrary rules, as is proper to the right poet, who is his own lawgiver — following the law of use intelligently, not blindly, only so far as is consistent with the end of this law, — in the first instance proceeding from such as himself.

With their intention to guide the reader to Browning's poetry by explanation of its individuality and to encourage him to see that in spite of the difficulties the effort was worthwhile, the *Eclectic* and the *English Review* followed the pattern of the earlier *People's Journal* (July 18 and Aug. 22, 1846) and *Sharpe's London Magazine* (Nov. and Dec. 1848) and foreshadowed the persuasive instruction that was to come. The other reviews gave relatively little attention to Browning's style. The *Guardian* and the *Examiner* had complaints of Browning's manner of writing but their objections did not blind them to the high quality of the poetry. The *Guardian*, admitting the "cleverness, spirit, and graceful conception" of many of the shorter pieces, thought the harshness or inelegance of execution often marred them. Forster, instead of displaying the perceptive approval of earlier years, complained of the verse, but his objections, like those in the review in the *Guardian*, did not cancel the good effect of the praise.

Fraser's on one hand complained of "the crabbed and confused sentences, the absence of graceful grammatic flow, the exceeding harshness and cacophony of metre, and false and often ludicrous rhymes" and on the other hand approved of "raciness of expression." The *Christian Remembrancer* briefly commented that the verse was unmusical, and hence not pleasurable, though once or twice there were passages of melody showing what Browning could have done had he cultivated rather than vitiated his taste. The difference between the comments in these reviews and those in the reviews discussed in the preceding paragraph was that along with the objection to the manner of writing came a marked disapproval of the low grade of subject matter. With the exception of the *Christian Remembrancer* and *Fraser's* the pervading tone of the reviews continued to show the improvement that had been apparent in the criticisms of *Dramatic Romances and Lyrics*.

There were also encouraging signs in comments on individual works. Throughout the years critics had remembered *Paracelsus* as a remarkable poem, though the praise sometimes came with qualifications. Browning's friend Archer T. Gurney, writer and clergyman, had reviewed it favorably in the *Theologian* in June 1845, ten years after its publication.[18] The essence of Christianity, he said, pervades the poem, and he again pointed out in the October issue the religious spirit of this and of other works of Browning's. With one exception *(Christian Remembrancer)* reviewers of the collected edition wholeheartedly recommended *Paracelsus*. *Pippa Passes* had begun to have support not long after its early negative reception and in the later forties had been the subject of two full-length articles that more than offset two short dissenting discussions *(Eclectic Review,* Apr. 1846; *British Quarterly Review,* Nov. 1847) during the same time. Reviewers of the collected edition indicated the favor that *Pippa* had won. The questioning of the morals, when it occurred, was accompanied by praise. In *Fraser's,* Charles Kingsley (probably the critic) said that he himself did not entirely agree with others who gave the poem a high place.

The most surprising aspect of the reviews was the interest in *Sordello*. Although Browning had not included it in his collected edition. four of the six reviewers (this excludes those for the *Atlas* and the *Literary Gazette*) who discussed the two volumes considered it of sufficient importance among Browning's works to say something about it. Exceptions to the earlier and generally devastating criticism had occurred in Forster's comment in his review of *Pippa Passes* in 1841 and in Horne's much longer discussion in the *Church of England Quarterly* in 1842; both critics recognized *Sordello* as a work not to be scorned. The majority of critics had gone out of their way to heap ridicule on *Sor-*

dello; these later critics went out of their way to say something in its favor, if no more than a bare comment. The *Guardian* called it a "powerful but not very pleasing story."

Other critics had something to say. Even *Fraser's,* more inclined to complain than praise, said that *Sordello,* marred as it was by defects, was poetry "that such as not three men in England now can write"; the critic thought that it and *Paracelsus* distinguished Browning from the herd of scribblers, quoted a long passage, and said that for such passages and for itself as a whole *Sordello* must be praised. *The English Review* objected to it because it was unintelligible, its style was abrupt, and its tendency was morbid; but the critic concluded that it was a work that only a great man could have created. The critic for the *Eclectic Review,* who indicated in his heading that he would discuss *Sordello* as well as the collected edition, thought that it was superior to *Paracelsus.* Besides making several favorable scattered references to it, he gave nearly a page to the poem — three sentences to the obstacles Browning set in the way of understanding it and the rest to high praise for it as Browning's "longest, most characteristic, every way most important poem — his highest, fullest, poetic flight." The collected edition without *Sordello,* he said, was like *Hamlet* without the part of Hamlet. He thought that the omission could be seen as the temporary withdrawal of a poem which because of its inherent difficulties might endanger the favorable hearing sought by the author.

The space taken up by the plays in the collection prompted more attention to them than to the shorter pieces. It seemed to the critic for the *Christian Remembrancer* that Browning thought of himself primarily as a dramatist in the usual sense — a view that critics had once had but had generally abandoned by this time.

> Besides Paracelsus, and Pippa Passes, both in the dramatic form, these two volumes contain six regular plays, five of which are tragedies, and these embrace more than half Mr. Browning's poetical works. It is clear, therefore, that he feels his genius to lie especially in the drama; that he believes it to be the best and aptest means for the expression of his powers. If, pursuing this persuasion to its probable conclusion, he goes on to think that he writes good dramas, that he has the gifts needed by a dramatic poet, we do not think he could have made a greater mistake.

After a long discussion of what a play should and should not be, the critic gave specific reasons for denouncing *Luria* as stage drama.

There are good passages and some just observations, but as a dramatic effort it is simply monstrous. . . . All the characters of the piece, however else opposed, man or woman, soldier or civilian, crafty Italian or half-savage Moor, agreeing in talking metaphysics in the precise moment for action; analysing to one another, in the most critical junctures, and in situations of the most direct hostility, their own motives and their views of life; and this with a prolixity and zeal for philosophical inquiry not to be equalled by any class of human debaters ever met together for the sole purpose of discussion.

The reviewer could not see as others had come to see that *Luria* was not written to be performed and that Browning's dramatic genius for revelation of character, but not through external action, was the guiding force for both poems and plays. By contrast, his attitude throws into relief the progress that had been made in general. Aside from the long discussion in the *Remembrancer* and a brief one in *Fraser's,* there was a noticeable absence of the persistent early complaints that Browning's plays were not successful stage dramas. Since the publication of *Colombe's Birthday,* the critics had more and more approached the plays on the assumption that they were not for the stage.

The reviewers of the collected edition discussed the plays as intelligible or unintelligible, historical or unhistorical, moral or immoral; sometimes they wrote only of the content; sometimes they attempted classifications. Three critics set *Pippa Passes* and *A Soul's Tragedy* apart from Browning's other plays. The *Eclectic* called them "indeterminate drama"; Kingsley, in *Fraser's,* said that Browning's characteristic personality showed itself more clearly in them than in the others; the *Examiner* said that they, along with *Paracelsus,* might be thought of as "embodiments of the author's abstract conceptions of men and society, in creatures more or less of his own imagination." Some reviewers made specific reference to one or more as reading plays. The *Guardian* thought of *A Blot* as a beautiful play for the closet. The *English Review* said that *Colombe's Birthday* was likely to be a favorite with "lady-readers." The *Eclectic* explained, as has already been observed, that none of the plays was "representable drama." General acceptance of the plays for reading is a happy sequel to the few favorable remarks on them in 1845 and 1846 as closet drama. It is a credit to the critics that they dispassionately examined them in this light.

If the critics had advanced far enough by the later forties to accept the plays and not condemn them because of their unworthiness for the stage and if they had seen the dramatic force of all of Browning's work, we might expect them to appreciate the individuality of the short dramatic poems, especially since there had been increased comprehension of them when they appeared in *Dramatic Romances and Lyrics,* Browning's second collection of short pieces. But with so much of the space in the collected edition given to the long works, the spotlight was not yet sufficiently on the short ones to encourage an understanding of the specific direction that Browning's genius was taking. Two critics pointed out that Browning had written poems with a distinctive quality; others saw them from a limited viewpoint. The critic for the *Christian Remembrancer* said that Browning's power lay in his shorter poems, but he found most of them degrading in content. According to the reviewer for the *Guardian* some of the short pieces "in their way" were "first rate; rough, vigorous, lyrical sketches, dashed off with apparent haste and ease, and very little finished; but instinct throughout with life and power."

We turn to the *Examiner,* remembering that Forster had called attention to the appropriate versification in *Dramatic Romances and Lyrics* and praised the poems for their human interest, originality, and dramatic quality. In his review of the collected edition he said that even the short pieces were essentially dramatic in spirit. Then he wrote of Browning's technique.

> Whether he gives vent to the musings of a solitary mind, or to reflections struck out by the collision of assembled minds, he expresses them in address or soliloquy. He pictures to himself a scene occupied by a person "to himself talking;" or by persons interchanging thoughts and sentiments. But with a felicitous and delicate instinct, he gives just so much as his persons would really say; conscious and confident that the words will suggest the accompanying actions, the relative positions of the speakers, and the surrounding scenery.

As a consequence of this observation we might think that when Forster pointed to specific poems they would be those that were dramatic in Browning's manner, but he did not direct his reader's attention to any of these particularly characteristic pieces. Near the end of the review he gave the shorter poems only two sentences, naming *The Pied Piper, Good News,* and *Cavalier Tunes* as "masterpieces of bold, vigorous, easy ballad melody" that along with the *Incident of the French Camp* could be compared with Schiller's best poems in the same class.

The two critics who at this time wrote most perceptively of Browning's works in general commented on the individual quality of his short poems, though the space given to them was restricted. Twenty-eight pages on Browning's other works crowded the shorter pieces into four pages at the end of the discussion in the *English Review*. The critic managed to refer to over half of the total number; his treatment was necessarily brief but it was suggestive. Though he thought some of the poems "abrupt," he praised them in general, saying that they seemed to him unlike anything else he had ever read. "That passion, that intensity, that power, which is the marked characteristic of Mr. Browning, is conspicuous throughout them." He saw the poems as "so many monodramas, that is, directly dramatic utterances under special circumstances of so many imaginary speakers, in lyric forms." (*Monodrama*, which was used by Lamb in 1823 and by Carlyle in 1831,[19] would be an appropriate term, but the later *dramatic monologue* is more clearly self-defining.) The critic recognized that some poems were exceptions to the individuality of Browning's monodrama; one of these, he said, was *Cavalier Tunes*. *My Last Duchess* received more attention than any other one of the short pieces; the reviewer quoted one passage that showed the Duke's jealousy and another that had "the colloquial style of the majority of Mr. Browning's lyrics." He praised most of the considerable number of poems that he commented on briefly, but when he got to *The Bishop Orders His Tomb* his critical insight deserted him — all he could say was that it and *The Confessional* had merit but were sometimes painful.

The critic for the *Eclectic Review* was not concerned that acted drama was no longer a living form in England. The dramatic impulse could take another direction. "Let our drama, then, develop itself in other, fresh, and genuine forms; as realized by a Chaucer in the fourteenth century, by a Tennyson — by the author of 'St. Simeon Stylites,' 'Ulysses,' 'Ænone' — in the nineteenth; and by Mr. Browning himself, in so large a proportion of his creative working." He went on to say that the "highest success of poetic and creative power" was achieved in Browning's "*un*formal" drama; "in nearly all his lyrics, so living and deeply suggestive; and in 'Pippa Passes.' " He referred to the "rich suggestive gallery of minor dramatic sketches, including pieces so wondrously rife in deep thought and creative speech." Despite such recognition, with one exception the critic did no more than name a few of the short pieces (here called monodramas, as in the *English Review*).

Of the short poems, the critics liked best *The Lost Leader, How They Brought the Good News, The Pied Piper, The Flight of the Duchess,*

and *Pictor Ignotus*. Some of Browning's experimental poems, such as
The Confessional and *The Laboratory*, they all but ignored. It is interesting to see how *My Last Duchess* and *The Bishop Orders His Tomb* fared.
Only the *Eclectic* and the *English Review* noticed *My Last Duchess*. They
both praised it but only the *English Review* singled it out from the short
poems for special attention. More reviewers noticed *The Bishop*, but
only the *Eclectic* gave it unqualified praise and that came for it as one of
a group. The *English Review* and *Fraser's* each had a favorable comment,
but they as well as the *Christian Remembrancer* found it painful or degrading. Past obstacles were cleared from the approach to the shorter
dramatic pieces, but the critics did not observe their significance
though two of them had progressed nearer an appreciation of Browning's innovative artistry.

There were not many reviews of the collected edition, but these
along with the articles published between the appearance of the last of
the *Bells* and the edition of 1849 are significant. In spite of the limited
appreciation of the short pieces and other indications of the failure to
overcome the traditional evaluation of poetry, clearly the reviews
showed progress and contained points of criticism that were faint har-
bingers of the future. Complaints of lack of action in the plays had almost entirely disappeared. It began to be obvious that Browning's
command of a great variety of knowledge and his interest in a broad
range of humanity would lead the critics either to commend him for
seeing the whole of life — both good and bad — or to complain because he included the undesirable. There were signs that the more attention some critics paid to moral and spiritual content, the less inclined they were to find fault with Browning for failing to observe
conventional literary canons. More perceptive and conscientious critics
coped with the unconventional by explaining why his poetry was difficult and by assuring readers at the same time that it was worth the
effort required to understand it.

CHAPTER XIV

Retrospection

1833-49

The account that has been given in the preceding chapters of Browning and the steady publication of his works during the thirties and forties and their reception is not complete without further consideration of the relative worth of reviews, the difficulties confronting the critics, and nonprofessional opinion of Browning's poetry.

It is necessary to recognize the misleading direction of some reviews that were apparently favorable, the limited value of others that were sympathetic to Browning's works, and the deterrent force of an unfavorable reception or no notice at all by influential journals. There were reviews seeming to be favorable in content that were not entirely conducive to the recognition of Browning's genius, though a number of them were written by his friends and acquaintances. Forster and Horne wished to promote Browning's reputation, but each assumed a critical position that misdirected readers. The frequent reviews in the *Examiner* were helpful in keeping Browning's works before the public, particularly in repeatedly indicating the suitability of his verse, but Forster's persistence in seeing Browning as a potential writer of plays for the stage, with only the "metaphysics" of character standing in his way, placed his dramatic talent in the wrong light. Just as damaging was the attitude of Horne toward Browning's dramatic talent in otherwise beneficial reviews. He presented Browning's plays as stageworthy, evidently a reflection of Browning's opinion, when it would have been better for him to evaluate them as closet dramas.

There were other drawbacks. The favorable reviews were frequently of limited influence. Sometimes they appeared in periodicals that were read by a restricted audience (the *Monthly Repository*, for example), or were short-lived *(Leigh Hunt's London Journal)*, or were published for readers who were not likely to be attracted by poetry on a high level (the *People's Journal*). Unfortunately the influential periodicals were of little service to Browning's reputation. There was some truth in his statement that he had gone unnoticed by them. The *Edinburgh Review*, still a prominent quarterly, did carry a criticism of *Strafford* but its effect was probably negligible. For the most part the widely influential quarterlies and monthlies ignored or abused Browning. *Blackwood's*, a monthly, had been silent. *Fraser's*, another monthly, reviewed him, but with the exception of its discussion of *Paracelsus*, it offered little illumination. A favorable review of *Dramatic Romances and Lyrics* in *Fraser's* would have been of much assistance; its abuse was particularly damaging. The tone was improved in its discussion of the collected edition, but limited perception handicapped the critic. Browning's friend Chorley helped by his reviews in the *Athenaeum*, but the considerable inflexibility of other critics for that influential weekly did much harm in the totally or partly blind attitude to the better early works. It was important for Browning's works to be reviewed immediately upon publication, but hurried critics were usually unprepared to deal with the difficulty and originality of his poetry.

These were discouraging facts that must be recognized, but they did not negate the good signs that appeared. Favorable recognition of Browning's poetic qualities and perceptive commentaries that appeared from time to time formed the base for better understanding. In the later forties lines of criticism began to stand out, and they were to develop and eventually do much to turn the tide in Browning's favor. Until it was firmly established, his reputation was distinguished by its gradual degree of development. From our vantage point we realize that although some of the beneficial criticisms did not at once reach a broad audience they would be influential in the future. As was pointed out, now and then during Browning's life readers who were receptive to his poetry often had the desire to win others over to it. And thus the number of those who read and supported Browning would eventually be multiplied.

We might well question the value to Browning's reputation of the favorable reviews that appeared in periodicals of limited influence. We do not need to doubt that unfavorable reviews in influential periodicals had a retarding effect. Even though disapproving critics recognized his genius very early and made some progress in evaluating it, in many cases their blindness and bad temper obstructed their critical perceptions or their contentious attitude tended to obscure the occasional discerning observation. It is unfair, however, to condemn them summarily, as has often been done, without consideration of the situation that they faced in reviewing Browning's works. At appropriate places in the preceding chapters we have referred to their difficulties, but for the sake of a clearer account of the critics' role in Browning's early literary life we should do well to give concentrated attention to their problems. Browning set stumbling blocks — certainly unintentionally — in their way. *Paracelsus* gave his reputation a good start; after its publication he was hailed as a promising dramatic poet. Two years later *Strafford* was performed; it was a failure. Next the puzzling *Sordello* appeared. Then after *Pippa Passes* play after play kept Browning before the public as a dramatist (or a would-be dramatist), and he was at first looked upon as such, though as time passed he produced nothing that met the requirements for an acceptable Victorian stage production.

Drama was a time-honored form; but emphasis on internal action, which was the guiding principle in Browning's artistic development, was unsuited to the stage. Contemporary critics could not see what Park Honan has explained in *Browning's Characters:* how Browning was working toward the maturity of his particular genius for character portrayal. They made their judgments by the formulas for the stage that they were familiar with and found Browning's plays wanting; their general evaluation of the individual plays was more often than not the opinion that continued to be expressed after Browning's name was established.

One of the greatest difficulties for all critics is exposure to writing that does not conform to the existing patterns. Consider, then, the situation of having a confusing mixture of the original and the familiar. The critics were faced with plays traditional in appearance but original in Browning's experimenting with character portrayal. The publication of play after play overshadowed the more distinctive short poems and *Pippa Passes.* The critics' attention was further deflected from these works by Browning's publicizing his authorship of *Paracelsus* on the title page of all his early works except *Sordello,* as if he wished it to be remembered as his principal contribution.

Browning's good intentions often had repercussions. Sometimes he chose titles that gave trouble. Literal as it was, the title of *Pippa Passes* misled critics, and so did the "No. I" on the title page, which Browning intended to signify the first *Bell* but which some thought indicated the first part of *Pippa*. *Bells and Pomegranates,* with its symbolical significance, was positively disturbing. The *British Quarterly Review* of November 1847 reported that "in no scanty number of families may one hear energetic protests against the 'affectation' of the title . . . ." Several prefaces were confusing and one left the impression that Browning wrote with speed, not a good recommendation for a poet considered to be careless.

Browning's choice of pamphlet form for the *Bells and Pomegranates* series was not entirely fortunate. After the more extensive *Paracelsus* (boards, 6 shillings), *Strafford* (paper, 4 shillings), and *Sordello* (boards, 6 shillings sixpence), he turned to the cheaper format for his *Bells*. Set in fine type, printed in double columns, and bound in paper wrappers, No. I was sold for sixpence, Nos. II–VI for 1 shilling each, No. VII for 2 shillings, and No. VIII for 2 shillings sixpence. The trouble was that the small print and double columns were not compatible with Browning's style of writing, which demanded concentrated attention. In later years a number of Browning's early admirers commented on the poor readability of the *Bells*. At the time of the change from the poor to the better format of the collected edition, Arnould wrote Browning about the difference in effect, "I like much your external shape & from what I can hear & learn think it not unlikely that you may be much more widely circulated in cloth at 16 s than in the former little well-beloved tracts at 2 s 6 d." After he had time to examine the volumes he continued the subject, ". . . I could not have supposed the mere difference of type & form could have made so advantageous a difference in the ease & pleasure of the reading."[1]

Browning's critics, like others, faced the problem of payment for their work. Horne, in telling Leigh Hunt what terms to expect from the *Foreign and Colonial Quarterly* for reviews, complained of the inadequate payment and the unreliability of the management. "I never have really known *what* I was writing for — nor *when* it would be paid; though I thought I did each time."[2] Browning wrote Elizabeth that his publisher spoke with enlightenment on the situation of the critics.

I can tell you nothing better, I think, than this I heard from Moxon the other day . . it really ought to be remembered: Moxon was speaking of critics, the badness of their pay, how many pounds

a column the "Times" allowed, and shillings the Athenaeum, — and
of the inevitable effects on the performances of the poor fellows.
"How should they be at the trouble of reading any *difficult* book so
as to review it, — Landor, for instance?" — and indeed a friend of
my own has promised to write a notice in the "Times" — but he
complains bitterly, — he shall have to *read* the book, — he can do no
less, — "and all for five or ten pounds"! All which Moxon quite
seemed to understand — "it will really take him some three or four
mornings to read *enough* of Landor to be able to do anything effec-
tually. . . ."[3]

If Landor was difficult to read, what about Browning? Reasonable
payment for critics might have helped. Certainly time, perseverance,
and an open and capable mind were necessary, even after Browning's
poetry reached the stage of maturity. According to the critic for the *Eclectic Review* (Aug. 1849), "The higher the poetry, the fuller, deeper,
its spirit, the more consummate and individual its expression, the
fewer those competent to receive and welcome it, and the greater the
obstacles to its reception. . . ." It has been made clear that even the
less discerning reviewers often noted the outstanding qualities of
Browning's work and had an inkling of his genius. Their greatest disadvantage was that they had no precedents by which to judge the original works. Their greatest transgression was that they allowed their irritation to color their views; occasionally they were guilty of nagging
at the beginning and the end of an otherwise perceptive discussion.

The published response outside the periodical press not yet introduced here, as well as that already discussed, parallels significant tendencies in the professional reception of Browning's works. In the thirties
Forster had introduced him in *Sir John Eliot* and Landor in *A Satire on
Satirists,* and Fanny Haworth had written and published two sonnets to
him. Similarly, in the forties friends paid tribute by dedicating books
to him, as did Thomas Powell[4] and John Kenyon,[5] or referring to him
in prefaces to published works. Talfourd's reference in the Preface to
his *Tragedies* to Browning as a playwright was an echo of the general
label that had been given to him.

> If the Stage, in spite of its emancipation, shall fall to decay, I
> shall deplore it — if it be only for what we shall lose in him [Horne],
> and in the younger genius of Robert Browning — a genius only yet
> dimly perceived, but deeply felt, and which requires and deserves
> the noble discipline of dramatic conditions.[6]

In the Preface of his *Love's Legends* Gurney, who wrote of Browning's poetry in two issues of the *Theologian* of 1845, pointed to a quality of his writing that would be increasingly emphasized in the future: "I make no pretension in these poems to the reflective wisdom of a Wordsworth, or to the deep psychological utterances of a Browning."[7]

In addition to these tributes there were impressions of Browning not dressed up in print. These had a considerable range from admiring, even worshipful, acceptance to distasteful rejection. Besides recalling some opinions already referred to, let us look at some as yet unmentioned, in order to get an idea of how Browning had affected his non-reviewing contemporaries down to the end of the forties. Although Procter had admired works by Browning, usually those of the generation preceding Browning's were more likely to limit themselves to what they were accustomed to and found easy to read. Either, like Carlyle and Landor, they saw Browning as a gifted poet but had reservations about his poems or, like Wordsworth, Samuel Rogers, and Henry Crabb Robinson, did not care for him as a poet.

According to Mrs. Andrew Crosse, "Miss Mitford . . . shares Wordsworth's views with respect to the author of 'Paracelsus' ";[8] and Miss Mitford, we know, made it clear that she did not like Browning's poetry. Chorley reported that he had heard Rogers being "absolutely venomous and violent . . . in dissection, or in wholesale abuse, of the verses of Tennyson, Browning, Milnes. . . ."[9] Robinson branded Browning as "author of unreadable books" and "the crazy poet." In time he learned to like the man, but the poetry never won him over; he confessedly dreaded new poems by anybody.[10]

The peers of Browning were less apt to be fixed in their tastes. Just as Chorley and Forster were attracted to his works, certain young people not associated with the press greatly admired Browning's early poetry. Domett and Arnould were supporters. In New Zealand Domett met a fellow Cantabrigian who said that Browning was the only poet worth reading, an opinion that Domett relayed with pleasure to Browning.[11] Then there was the youthful Robert Lytton (son of Edward Bulwer Lytton), who wished to make a career of writing and continued to compose and publish poetry throughout his life but whose real achievement lay in the field of diplomacy. He first became acquainted with Browning's works through Forster in the later forties and read them "with enthusiasm, feeling at once for their author the almost worshipful admiration of a youthful disciple for a great master."[12]

Late in life well-known Victorians spoke to others or wrote of their youthful attitude toward Browning. Oscar Browning, who became master at Eton and afterwards lecturer at Cambridge (no relation to Robert), recorded that he was familiar with Browning's poetry from his "earliest years." He considered himself more fortunate than others because he became acquainted with it through his older brother, who was a "passionate admirer of his namesake."[13] The cheaply printed *Bells* were not a deterrent to him, nor were they to the Irish patriot and writer Charles Gavan Duffy, who in his youth asked Carlyle about Browning:

> I begged him to tell me something of the author of a serial I had come across lately, called "Bells and Pomegranates," printed in painfully small type, on inferior paper, but in which I took great delight. There were ballads to make the heart beat fast, and one little tragedy, "The Blot in the 'Scutcheon," which . . . I could not read without tears.[14]

George Boyle, who became Dean of Salisbury, had also felt the attraction of Browning's poetry when he was young. In his later years he said, ". . . he has been one of my chiefest interests since I was a schoolboy. . . ."[15] In the eighties George Meredith wrote Arthur Symons of his book on Browning, "I . . . have gone through it with advantage — with some of my old thrills of love for him, when as a boy I chafed over the reviews of *Bells and Pomegranates*. You have done knightly service to a brave leader."[16]

Interest in Browning's poetry was being shown by other young contemporaries. The most enthusiastic of them was Dante Gabriel Rossetti, richly endowed with imagination, independence of spirit, and intellectual curiosity. One day in 1847 Rossetti, only nineteen but already an acute and inquiring reader of poetry, chanced upon a copy of *Pauline* in the British Museum (now the British Library) and thought that Browning had written it. Finding something that excited his attention often prompted him to write the author. On October 17, 1847, he sent a letter to Browning, with an account of his experience.

> It is now two or three months ago that I met, at the British Museum, with a Poem published in 1833, entitled "Pauline, a Fragment of a Confession," which elicited my warm admiration, and which, having failed in an attempt to procure a copy at the publisher's, I have since transcribed. It seems to me, in reading this beautiful composition, that it presents a noticeable analogy in style and feeling to your first acknowledged work, "Paracelsus"; so much so

indeed as to induce a suspicion that it might actually be written by yourself.[17]

It is notable that Rossetti knew Browning's poetry well enough to identify him as the author of *Pauline*, which he liked so much that he copied the whole of it. With his contagious enthusiasm he led his close friends to become Browning partisans.

During the early period in his study of painting, Rossetti met two art students who later became famous — John Everett Millais and William Holman Hunt. Though different in temperament and in background, the three young men had one desire in common: they wanted to break away from the stagnant art of the time and direct it into fresh channels. As they talked, the idea of uniting themselves in pursuit of this goal led to the formation of the Pre-Raphaelite Brotherhood. To these three principal members were added others, and they all set to work with the ardor of reformers. Poetry was important to the members of the Brotherhood and their associates. They took subjects for their paintings from poetry, they included poets in their list of immortals (Browning was among them), and Gabriel Rossetti wrote and published poetry.

Since Browning was high on his list of favorites, Gabriel "by readings, recitations, and preachments" imposed him "as a sort of dogmatic standard, upon the P.R.B."[18] He could quote twenty pages at a time from *Paracelsus* and *Sordello* and "in turn came the shorter inventions of Browning, which were more within the compass of attention suddenly appealed to."[19] Thomas Woolner, sculptor, and Frederic G. Stephens, artist and later art critic, became converts; and William, Gabriel's brother, paid "unbounded homage" to Browning as the author of *Bells and Pomegranates* and "above all of *Sordello*."[20] As Maurice Cramer has shown in his article on Browning and the Pre-Raphaelites, the proselytizing continued.[21] Friends of the members of the Brotherhood were exposed to Browning, with varying results.[22]

Only a short while after the formation of the P.R.B. in 1848, *A Blot* was revived by Phelps. Rossetti heard that it was to be acted and wanted Woolner to accompany him and his brother, and perhaps William Holman Hunt, to the first performance on November 27, 1848. He had this to say about *A Blot:* "I think you do not know this play. It is a most wonderful production, and possessed moreover of that real, intrinsic, and unconventional purity which never fails to excite the moral execration of the enlightened Briton."[23]

Although William Allingham, a young Irish poet, did not come to know Rossetti and share his admiration of Browning until later, he was acquainted with the poet's works by 1847. Allingham considered *Sordello* "nothing but a piece of rich confusion," but he was attracted to *Pippa Passes* and *A Blot*.[24] Eager for news of literary men, when he made his first trip to London in 1847 he sought out Leigh Hunt, who answered freely his questions about contemporary writers. In his Diary, a liberal source of information on writers of his day, Allingham recorded more conversation with Hunt on Browning than on any other contemporary writer. There is a passage quoting what Hunt, who had criticized *Paracelsus* with discernment, replied to Allingham's inquiry. "Browning — lives at Peckham, because no one else does! a born poet, but loves contradictions. Shakespeare and Milton write plainly, the Sun and Moon write plainly, and why can't Browning? . . . He's a pleasant fellow, has few readers, and will be glad to find you admire him."[25]

Seen in retrospect, the picture of Browning's standing among nonprofessionals had its bright and dark sides. Browning's name and poetry were known and admired by a number of people in the professional circles in which he moved, and some of them in their own works called attention to him as a man of letters; younger people who did not know him personally read and discussed his poetry with enthusiasm; and an eminent man of letters, Landor, stood up for *Paracelsus* in his *Satire on Satirists* and later praised Browning in a poem that was published in a daily of large circulation. That was the bright side. There was a darker one also. To be set over against the published praise under Landor's name was the almost complete absence of public testimony of other creative writers of eminence. Carlyle, for example, even with his objections to individual works thought well of Browning's genius and a word in season would have carried weight, but he made no public statement. With few exceptions the young people who read and liked Browning's poetry had little or no influence with the public in the forties. Even the opinion of the Pre-Raphaelites was of little importance beyond their own circle. Like much professional criticism, the praise often had little weight and for the most part failed to come from those who could have done the most good for Browning's reputation in this decade. But with the nonprofessional as with the professional criticism the time would come for bearing the fruits of earlier recognition.

After examining the state of Browning's reputation at this turning point in his literary life, we should like to know what Browning himself was saying about his writing and his professional situation. There is little on record. We do know, as was brought out in the preceding chapter, that in February of 1847 he made his plea to Moxon for publication of his works. A few months later, he revealed to Fanny Haworth something of the arduousness of his writing, even with Elizabeth's encouragement. In his letter to Miss Haworth he first remarked on her failure to apply herself diligently to her work and then asserted his resolution to continue in an endeavor which was not pleasing to him, as he had admitted in the beginning of his correspondence with Elizabeth.

> I should not altogether wonder if I do something notable one of these days, all through a desperate virtue which determines out of gratitude — (not to man and the reading public, by any means!) — to do what I *do not* please: I could, with an unutterably easy heart, never write another line while I have my being — which would surely be very wrong considering how the lines fall to poets in the places of this world generally. So I mean to do my best whatever comes of it. . . .[26]

During a lull in his literary activities following the revisions for the collected edition, Browning wrote to Horne. In his letter he referred with indifference to the outcome of the second run of *A Blot* and briefly to the collected edition of his poems, "My new edition . . but you will see — I have done my best at correcting enough and not too much."[27] This was written on December 3, 1848. By now he and Elizabeth were living in Florence. Many changes had taken place in his day-to-day existence. Along with the pleasurable activities of their new life, Browning concerned himself always about Elizabeth's health, went through the anxiety of her miscarriages, searched for suitable apartments in Florence, made several moves before they settled in Casa Guidi (their home base for the rest of their lives in Italy), and managed their finances. Making adjustments in his new way of life crowded into a corner worry about the goodness or badness of reviews and how many there were at this time.

Their son, Robert Wiedeman Barrett (better known as Pen), was born on March 9, 1849, and Browning's mother died soon after. "While he was full of joy for the child," wrote Elizabeth, "his mother was dying at a distance, and the very thought of accepting that new affection for the old became a thing to recoil from. . . ."[28] She said she had never seen a man "so bowed down in an extremity of sorrow — never"[29] Elizabeth's letters indicate that for more than six months

Browning could not bring himself to "do his best," as he had told Miss Haworth he always intended to do.

No new work had appeared since 1846, and after a while writing had to be faced, at least for the sake of income. Browning, who had said with confidence that he could earn £50 from his writing the year following his marriage,[30] hoped for good returns from his collected edition, but he was disappointed. Although Arnould was told at Chapman and Hall's that the "sale was going on very steadily" soon after its publication,[31] copies of the edition remained on the shelf for a long time. In 1854, six years after publication, Browning made a statement to Forster on his financial situation. He was more definite than Elizabeth had been earlier about his standing with his publisher: "Chapman's account has come in, — I daresay you know the result, — this half year we have sold 70 copies of the *Poems,* and I have at last a balance in his hands — or better say, on his little finger tip — of seven pence!"[32]

The content of reviews, the influence of periodicals in which criticisms appeared, the sale of his works, and the weight of opinions outside the press are important factors influencing a writer's reputation. By these measurements Browning's overall achievements had not been remarkable, in spite of the support which he had received in some quarters. There had, however, been signs in the later forties of improved critical insight that boded well. Browning, instead of being indifferent or resistive to criticism, had for fourteen years been receptive to, even solicitous of, criticism that he thought might be helpful and he had at times heeded criticism. He had worked with determination to direct his poetical energy and gain public acceptance but had not attained the success that he desired. He had yet to see what would be the reaction to the better poetry to come, which he had often spoken of to Elizabeth before their marriage.

CHAPTER XV

A Religious Poem

Christmas-Eve and Easter-Day, 1850

From the last *Bell* in April of 1846 until *Christmas-Eve and Easter-Day* in April of 1850 no new work by Browning appeared. Some five months after their marriage Robert and Elizabeth were considering a joint publication. ". . . by Xmas, Providence helping," Browning informed Moxon in February 1847, "my wife and I want to print a book as well as our betters, after what we think a new and good plan. . . ."[1] In the following month Elizabeth wrote Arabel, ". . . before the year closes we hope to bring out a collection of poems on Italy, with our separate signatures."[2] Perhaps they were thinking of Smith and Elder, who had earlier offered to publish any poem of Browning's about Italy. The book of poems that they talked of was never published, but a wealth of poetry growing out of their Italian years lay in the future.

The dissipation of their plan to collaborate in writing poems on Italy was probably due to various circumstances in their lives. As we have seen, George Smith was unable to risk the publication of the collected edition of 1849; he was out of the picture, at least for the time being. After Browning worked on the revision of his poems for this collection and went through the trials of publication, he turned away from writing for the first time in many years. On October 1, 1849, during his period of poetic inactivity following the death of his mother, Elizabeth confessed to Mrs. Jameson, "What am I to say about Robert's idleness and mine? I scold him about it in a most anti-

270

conjugal manner, but, you know, his spirits and nerves have been shaken of late; we must have patience."[3]

When Browning did resume work, either late in 1849 or early in 1850, he began to compose *Christmas-Eve and Easter-Day*, which was to be shaped by a combination of influences. Elizabeth's strong religious beliefs, Browning's religious introspection following the proximity of his child's birth and his mother's death in 1849, the religious beliefs of his early home life, his exposure to higher criticism of the Bible — these influences modern critics have sufficiently discussed.[4] What needs to be stressed here is that several years before beginning *Christmas-Eve and Easter-Day* Browning had resolved to depart from the earlier forms that he had experimented with. He made this resolution before Elizabeth suggested that he turn from dramatic writing and speak directly to his readers.

When at the first of their correspondence Elizabeth indicated her wish that Browning should not write for the stage, he had already forsworn the writing of plays for performance. Charles Kean's reaction to *Colombe's Birthday* had given the coup de grace to his attempts in that direction. When it was published in 1844, one of the two remaining plays to appear in the *Bells* series was being written or perhaps was already completed — *A Soul's Tragedy*. Browning wrote the other play — *Luria* — for the "imaginary" rather than the real stage, as he said, but he was not yielding to Elizabeth's influence, for he already had it "safe" in his head and on a "tiny slip of paper" when he started writing her.

Not only should we note that Browning turned away from the stage before being exposed to Elizabeth's influence; we need also to observe that it was he, not Elizabeth, who broached the subject of revealing himself to the reader. In his second letter to her he wrote:

> . . . for you *do* what I always wanted, hoped to do, and only seem now likely to do for the first time. You speak out, *you*, — I only make men & women speak — give you truth broken into prismatic hues, and fear the pure white light, even if it is in me: but I am going to try . . so it will be no small comfort to have your company just now . . . it seems bleak melancholy work, this talking to the wind (for I have begun) — yet I don't think I shall let *you* hear, after all, the savage things about Popes and imaginative religions that I. must say.[5]

Back and forth they bounced the ball. "After all, you know nothing, next to nothing of me . . . ," he said.[6] Elizabeth, who believed that the production of an artist partakes of his real nature, answered, ". . . it is not true that I know little of you . . . ."[7] Browning countered, ". . . what I have printed gives *no* knowledge of me — it evidences abilities of various kinds, if you will — and a dramatic sympathy with certain modifications of passion . . *that* I think: but I never have begun, even, what I hope I was born to begin and end, — 'R. B. a poem.' "[8]

It is clear from these passages, as F. R. G. Duckworth has pointed out, that Browning expressed his resolution to make a departure from his earlier objective presentation before Elizabeth took up the subject of writing directly to the reader.[9] Once the idea was in motion, Elizabeth said that she had had in mind a monologue of Aeschylus just before his death. "But my chief *intention* just now is the writing of a sort of novel-poem . . . running into the midst of our conventions, & rushing into drawing-rooms . . . & so, meeting face to face & without mask the Humanity of the age, & speaking the truth as I conceive of it, out plainly."[10] Browning's expression of approval revealed that from the first he had had a somewhat similar intention, which he hoped to realize in the future.

> The poem you propose to make, for the times, — the fearless fresh living work you describe, — is the *only* Poem to be undertaken now by you or anyone that *is* a Poet at all, — the only reality, only effective piece of service to be rendered God and man — it is what I have been all my life intending to do, and now shall be much, much nearer doing, since you will be along with me.[11]

In her next letter she wrote: "I am inclined to think that we want new *forms* . . as well as thoughts. The old gods are dethroned. Why should we go back to the antique molds. . . . Let us all aspire rather to *Life* — & let the dead bury their dead. . . . For there is poetry *everywhere* . . the 'treasure' . . . lies all over the field. And then Christianity is a worthy *myth*, & poetically acceptable."[12]

Christmas-Eve and Easter-Day, as could be seen after its publication, did in fact reflect contemporary life and was concerned with Christianity. Certainly the germ of a religious poem lay in Browning's mind when he wrote Elizabeth at the beginning of their correspondence of the "savage things about Popes and imaginative religions" that he must say. In all likelihood Browning had already written *The Bishop Orders His Tomb;* and when, soon after his letter to Elizabeth, he sent it for publication in *Hood's Magazine*, he wrote the editor, ". . . I pick it

out as being a pet of mine, and just the thing for the time — what with
that Oxford business, and Camden society and other embroilments."[13]
It was Browning's habit to think about possible subjects well in advance of beginning to write. While he was finishing one work he was
looking for another subject. "I write best so provided," he said.[14] His
superactive mind easily leapt into the future and often turned in a new
direction.

Browning's planned departure from his past work at the time he
started his correspondence with Elizabeth fits into the pattern of his repeated experiments in writing. He was a confirmed innovator, as we
have seen from his prefaces, from his remarks to Carlyle, Domett, and
Elizabeth, and from the character of the works themselves. Even without Elizabeth's influence the publications following *Bells and Pomegranates* would in all likelihood have been different in some way.

Outside influences combined with his own genius as he made and
carried out his plans for the writing of *Christmas-Eve and Easter-Day*.
Did he still feel as he had four years earlier when he discussed with
Elizabeth the fearless work he intended to write? ". . . I always shiver
involuntarily when I look . . no, glance . . at this First Poem of mine
to be. '*Now*,' I call it, what, upon my soul, — for a solemn matter it
is, — what is to be done *now*, believed *now*, so far as it has been revealed to me — solemn words, truly. . . ."[15] Whatever Browning's intentions had been when he wrote of his "First Poem" and of "R. B. a
poem" which he had hoped he was born to begin and end, in this new
work he was not speaking directly to his reader. Nor was he following
any of the experimental forms of his earlier dramatic writing. *Christmas-Eve and Easter-Day* does not have the external appearance of a play
and does not read like a dramatic monologue, though it has speakers,
scenes, and sequences. There are similarities between certain elements
in Browning's poem and such medieval patterns as the quest, the
dream vision, and the debate.

The religious spirit had informed some of Browning's earlier poetry; in *Christmas-Eve and Easter-Day* religion stood full-face as the
main subject of consideration. The title names the initial and concluding points of Christ's mission to the world to save mankind. On
Christmas Eve and Easter the speaker in each part (the hard believer in
Easter-Day) has a visionary encounter with Christ in which he learns
all-important spiritual truths.

Christmas-Eve and Easter-Day consists of two divisions or parts
dealing with closely related religious problems, worship in the first

part and faith or belief in the second. In the first part there is a search on Christmas Eve for the one best mode of worship, on the assumption that there is such a mode. The searcher visits a Dissenting chapel, has a vision of Christ and by grasping the hem of his garment is transported to St. Peter's in Rome and then to a rationalistic lecture hall in Germany. He returns to the chapel, which he chooses because Divine love predominates there.

In the second part a hard believer maintains in an argument with an easy believer that it is difficult to be a Christian. The hard believer then recounts a vision or dream of Judgment which he had on Easter Day three years earlier. In it Christ tells him that at the moment he is lost because he has chosen the world instead of the spirit. The hard believer says he will now choose love as it exists between human beings. With a show of wrath, Christ responds that he has not understood or accepted God's love, the basis of his plan for the whole. Let him not doubt that God manifested his love by taking on flesh and undergoing death to save mankind. Thus in the second as in the first part of the poem Browning gives primary importance to Divine love. At the conclusion the speaker still finds it hard to be a Christian, but he hopes that God's infinite mercy will not allow him to be shut out of heaven forever.

Browning sent his completed manuscript to London, and Forster, who continued to be helpful, probably took care of the proofs. He read *Christmas-Eve* from the proof sheets to the members of the Fox household.[16]

The book was published on April 1, 1850, for six shillings. The title page read: *Christmas-Eve and Easter-Day* with the label "A Poem" underneath. The title, unaltered, was used as the running title throughout. There were two divisions, the first headed *Christmas-Eve* and the second *Easter-Day*. All of this, if nothing else, should have indicated that here was a poem in two parts or two companion poems to be considered together as making up a whole. The reviewers did not pay attention to the typographical clues. Most of them treated *Christmas-Eve and Easter-Day* as separate poems without inquiring into the relationship between them.

Though at present *Christmas-Eve and Easter-Day* is not generally given a high rank among Browning's poems, contemporary critics came to look favorably upon it, and their attitude toward Browning's place as a poet was influenced by it. At first it was the old story of confusion among the critics. They had gained something in the forties by repeated exposure to Browning's poetry, but now they were confronted with a poem quite unlike his preceding works.

Any critic would have been struck immediately by the doggeralized poetic style; he would have supposed that he had in hand a non-serious poem. Most of the critics who wrote for the weeklies, in which the earliest reviews of *Christmas-Eve and Easter-Day* appeared, decided at once that the poetic style was unsuited to religious subject matter — again Browning had been perversely misusing his talent. In *Christmas-Eve* — perhaps they read no further — they found that the meaning was not clear, the tone was flippant, and the mixture of the bizarre and the elevated manner bewildering. Some of them discovered a resemblance to Butler's satirical *Hudibras*. Though most of the early critics could not accept the incongruous or grotesque in *Christmas-Eve*, later reviewers noted its strangeness but felt its power and fascination. Still later ones tended not to comment on Browning's manner at all.

Browning foresaw the danger. He had learned that readers could easily mistake his poetic intention. At the end of *Christmas-Eve* he had a warning.

> I have done! — And if any blames me,
> Thinking that merely to touch in brevity
> The topics I dwell on, were unlawful, —
> Or, worse, that I trench, with undue levity,
> On the bounds of the Holy and the awful,
> I praise the heart, and pity the head of him,
> And refer myself to THEE, instead of him;
> Who head and heart alike discernest,
> Looking below light speech we utter,
> When the frothy spume and frequent sputter
> Prove that the soul's depths boil in earnest!
> May the truth shine out, stand ever before us!

Ultimately seven weeklies criticized the work. On the Saturday following publication on Monday (Apr. 1), three of these carried reviews — the *Spectator*, the *Athenaeum*, and the *Examiner*. The *Spectator* was representative of the majority of the weeklies in its negative approach and limited interpretation. The critic indicated the contents of both parts and by quotation called attention to the vision of Christ. He stated that, in so far as he could "form a conclusion from what is too purely Browninglike to be very intelligible," *Christmas-Eve* pointed the moral that love is the "main characteristic of Christianity, and that the mercy of God is infinite." He thought that Browning had not ad-

vanced himself by the new work. "His every-day subjects are commonplace in their images; though an affected quaintness may give them an
air of novelty. His loftier themes are rather shrouded than presented;
they pass for anything to the eye of faith, they are nothing in the eye of
reason." He concluded: "Passages of merit, though perhaps scarcely
equal to the theme, may be pointed out; but the whole is strange as poetry, and mystical as Christianity."

In the degree of receptiveness the *Athenaeum* lay in between four
derogatory reviews and two favorable ones in the weeklies. Early in his
review the critic, J. Westland Marston, disapproved of Browning's
chosen vehicle of expression. "The form of doggrel — carried to excess
by strange and offensive oddities of versification — is not that in which
the mysteries of faith, doubt, and eternity can be consistently treated."
Marston thought that those who read the first section would be greatly
offended by the "flippant" tone used for such a weighty theme.
Browning would have only himself to blame for a limited recognition
of *Christmas-Eve and Easter-Day.* "If, in spite of many unquestioned excellencies, we turn from what Mr. Browning *has* done to speculate on
what he *might have* done, it is his own genius that provokes the comparison and enhances the regret."

Objections to the "coarse and grotesque" and "verbal trickery"
did not hinder Marston from appreciating the descriptions of the rainbow and the Last Judgment. Nor did his objections prevent a sympathetic attempt to examine the meaning of *Christmas-Eve and Easter-
Day.* The two poems, he said, "though distinguished by separate titles, are virtually one." He continued, "The former division points out
the essential truth which underlies various beliefs — insisting, nevertheless, that only one belief can be perfect. It is, in fact, an argument
for the divinity of Christ, — conducted, however, in a large catholic
spirit towards the writer's opponents."

Most reviewers devoted less attention to *Easter-Day* than to
Christmas-Eve or said nothing of it. Marston did give his interpretation
of it, though he did not wish to state his opinion of Browning's theology, an exposition of which he ended thus: "Men fail to read the proofs
of an immortal future because they are wedded in their hearts to the
mortal present." Praise followed: "Subtle, analytic, and often brilliant,
Mr. Browning almost exhausts the various phases by which Christian
belief is modified, — and his argument is full of suggestiveness and
mystical beauty." The poet's genius was most evident in the concluding pages, which aimed at "showing that the very mystery which

wraps the future is necessary to spiritual growth and aspiration, and that good if limited by the bounds of sensible demonstration would leave no room for faith or progress."

Elizabeth wrote of the review to a friend: "You will be sure to think I am vexed at the article on my husband's new poem. Why, certainly I am vexed! Who would *not* be vexed with such misunderstanding and mistaking." The accusation of flippancy and wilfulness alone would have annoyed her. After denouncing the *Athenaeum* she praised the *Examiner:* "On the same day came out a burning panegyric of six columns in the 'Examiner,' a curious cross-fire." [17]

The laudatory review in the *Examiner* was in all likelihood written by Forster. He did not suppose that a thoughtful or earnest reader would need Browning's warning at the end of *Christmas-Eve* against hasty judgment of what might seem an occasional levity of tone: ". . . the book before us can hardly be received but as an expression of the writer's spiritual experiences in their utmost force and intensity." He stated the "joint teaching" of both portions of the poem: "to express belief in Christianity, not without doubts, but against doubts." He said Browning's stand was "to declare with all humility his acceptance of the truth, that only from uncertainty can genuine faith be born, that only from modesty and self-distrust can spring true resolution and self-reliance." The poet, Forster explained, follows the external evidences of faith through the first poem, then goes to the internal conflicts of faith in the second. After this introduction to *Christmas-Eve and Easter-Day* more details of the argument followed.

Here, as in his earlier reviews, Forster related the argument to the mechanics of Browning's poetry. To clear up possible misunderstanding of the "machinery" of *Christmas-Eve and Easter-Day,* he supported, by explanation and by quotation, Browning's expression, which purposefully passed from the real (the chapel and the lecture hall) to the ideal (St. Peter's during high mass and the supernatural vision). "It is an effluence of irrepressible thought, in harmony with each varying shade of the sentiment conveyed by it, and flushed and quickened throughout as in a man's actual utterance of what has agitated or raised him." Forster knew no modern poet who could "give to the most natural and unaffected terms of the commonest every-day language, an ideally perfect expression," and "without the use of a superfluous word" could put into "easy verse the elaborate niceties of a metaphysical argument." The purist, he said, might object to the proximity of the serious and the light, but the verse was in keeping with the intention of the writer. Among the quotations — liberally given in a running commentary on *Christmas-Eve* — were lines from the account of the chapel, which Forster thought to be in the "highest feeling of Crabbe and Wordsworth"; lines from the description of the Rationalist professor, which he considered a masterpiece of "minute accuracy of detail"; and, in contrast to these, lines from the descriptions of the rainbow, the vision, and St. Peter's, which was "majestically described."

In Forster's review there was no running commentary on *Easter-Day* and no quoting from it. This poem, Forster thought, had more of the poet's old obscurity, though a "more sustained dignity and seriousness" than *Christmas-Eve*. Quite clearly with *Christmas-Eve and Easter-Day* in hand, Forster was no longer looking at Browning as a potential dramatist: he had been reclaiming his genius from his earlier "vague and formless infinite" and this work was "full of the richest future promise." The last of the review praised qualities of Browning's poetry that had been pointed out by the critics from the beginning of his career. He would yet be recognized for what he truly was, one of the most original poets of the day. "He is equally a master of thought and emotion, and joins to a rare power of imaginative creation that which is still more rarely found in union with it — the subtlest power of mental reasoning and analysis." Furthermore, Forster would challenge for such a writer the attention of even those who disagreed with the views — he himself was not in entire agreement with them — because the feeling of the work would "waken very many to the 'better part' suggested by its theme," and would "stir and quicken thought in all."

Four more weeklies were to carry reviews of *Christmas-Eve and Easter-Day*. The critics for three of them — the *Literary Gazette*, the *Critic*, and the *Atlas* — were so repelled by the style that they were not receptive to the subject matter. The other review, in the *Leader*, was of a different sort.

The reviews in the *Literary Gazette* and the *Critic* appeared within the second week after publication. The *Literary Gazette*, which ignored *Easter-Day*, carried its review on April 13. Starting with a diatribe against writers of obscure poetry and against the critics who supported them, the reviewer turned to Browning's new work. He condemned *Christmas-Eve and Easter-Day* in general for the incomprehensibility of "the main design and the conduct of the argument," though he could make out portions of the whole. That the querulous critic made almost no headway in the correct reading of *Christmas-Eve* comes out in his only comment on the argument: "The Romish religion is ridiculed like that of the dissenting chapel." He objected specifically to the "vicious, fantastic, and unallowable" versification and the "*simplicities,* prosaic triteness," quoting from the description of the Dissenting chapel to enforce his point. To show that Browning attempted the beautiful, he quoted the entire description of the lunar rainbow and then asked if there was ever "such rapture, such foolishness!" He admitted his annoyance and since he had hopes of Browning lamented his waste of talent. "The enthusiasm displayed in the whole performance is painful to contemplate. We cannot shut out the dread of that condition of mind on which it evidently so closely borders." Thus ended this review marred by snappishness and misrepresentation.

According to the *Critic* of April 15, Browning had ability but he misused it. He was read, for in spite of whimsical expression there was always thought in what he wrote. Though a great deal of poetry worth reading was scattered throughout *Christmas-Eve and Easter-Day,* the work had more "conceits" than earlier works; admittedly the critic did not understand the "idea" of *Christmas-Eve* and suspected Browning could not tell what it was either. He saw "a series of disquisitions on religious and philosophical topics, more or less mystically expressed, and leading to no intelligible conclusion." He did not like the sermonizing and thought that the sentiments were sometimes questionable. This reviewer, like others, was perplexed by conflicting effects of the verse: "It is neither serious nor comic, but a sort of mixture of both, that gives it the appearance of burlesque, and, probably, it was intended as a sort of Hudibrastic satire." There were lengthy quotations, given to show the style of *Christmas-Eve,* "whose excellences and faults are so mingled, that the critic is bound to dispense an almost equal measure of praise and censure." Although this reviewer was milder in tone than the one for the *Literary Gazette,* he was more liberal with censure than with praise.

Nearly two weeks later, on April 27, one of the two favorable reviews of *Christmas-Eve and Easter-Day* in weeklies appeared in the *Leader,* a recently launched periodical of positivistic liberalism. It was written by George Henry Lewes. He paid high tribute to the originality of Browning's poetry in the opening paragraph and then objected to its lack of music, both of which qualities he had noted in the indecisive review of Browning's early works that he had written for the *British Quarterly Review* in 1847. (He had objected to the inharmonious and rugged versification of *Sordello* in the *Monthly Chronicle* in 1840.) After his introductory remarks in the *Leader* on the characteristics of Browning's poetry, he turned to the new work.

Lewes was most interested in the first part, which he had read three times — "and with increasing admiration." Everything that Browning had written was worthy of attention and nothing was more worthy of it than *Christmas-Eve*. "It is a great theme powerfully conceived, picturesquely, sometimes grotesquely handled. In distinctness of purpose, pregnancy of meaning, and power of illustration it shows the masterhand." In his comments on the chapel the critic warned his readers not to be disconcerted by the rough realism in the poem and not to complain that the tone was unsuitable to the gravity of the subject. He said that Browning with his keen eye for truth never idealized and that this was the source of his strength and also of his weakness.

Lewes' running commentary on *Christmas-Eve* was interspersed with quotations, selected from the "admirable" description of the chapel, the account of the vision, and the description of the "hawk-nosed high-cheek-boned professor." According to the review, the substance of what the speaker in *Christmas-Eve* had learned is expressed in *Easter-Day* — "Christianity is Love." Lewes applauded the sincere and earnest spirit which breathed through the poem, realizing that to many the sincerity would look like levity; he had heard of some who thought the tone was not elevated enough. He recognized the value of Browning's original style. "His style is swayed by the subject. It is a garment, not a mould; it takes the varying shapes of varied movement, and does not force its one monotony on all."

Like others, Lewes, without objecting, saw a resemblance to Butler's satirical *Hudibras* and like others he was capable of appreciating the realism of the passages involving the chapel and the lecture hall, yet he could not give up the conventional idea of beauty as a requisite of poetry.

> What it [*Christmas-Eve*] wants to make it an enduring work of art is that which the author cannot give it, has not to give — the magic and mystery of Beauty. But of its kind it is really great. . . . Since Butler no English poet has exhibited the same daring propensity and facility in rhyming. If the verse is sometimes rugged it is but the better exponent of the thought. Realism in Art has Truth as an aim, Ugliness as a pitfall.

Lewes faced the situation that some critics were to experience in reviewing *Men and Women*. He deplored the absence of what was ordinarily considered beauty in poetry, yet appreciated the very qualities that were not conducive to that particular kind of beauty which in 1847 he had characterized as having grace and melody. If he did not go quite as far as Forster, who had evaluated the individuality of Browning's verse without invoking traditional models, we must remember that he had not had the opportunity of hearing Browning discuss his poetry. He had advanced from his position of 1847. Along with the review in the *Examiner*, this one in the *Leader* stood out from the others that appeared in the weeklies.

Before the reviews in the weeklies came to an end, Browning received support from two articles in the May issue of the Pre-Raphaelite *Germ* (now titled *Art and Poetry*), published monthly. Since the writers belonged to a group of ardent readers of Browning's poetry, it is not surprising that both discussions were directed toward those who objected to his manner of writing. In an article called "Modern Giants," written by Frederic Stephens, Browning, the "greatest, perhaps, of modern poets," was singled out as one who had "looked into the heart of man, and shown you its pulsations, fears, self-doubts, hates, goodness, devotedness, and noble world-love." Browning did not write in the weak or worthless manner of some contemporary writers but "with the firm knowing hand of the anatomist, demonstrating and making clear to others, that the knowledge may be applied to purpose." But the public, Stephens said, did not profit. "All this difficult task is achieved so that you may read till your own soul is before you, and you know it; but the enervated public complains that the work is obscure forsooth. . . ."

To the same issue of the *Germ* William Rossetti contributed an extended discussion that included references to Browning's intellectual subtlety, "diversified conception" of character, dramatic quality, and knowledge of "outward nature," but was concerned particularly with the test of style — appropriateness of treatment to subject, adaptation of style to artistic intention. In Browning's works a "deliberate unity of purpose" was "strikingly apparent." Aware of some readers who assumed that he spoiled "fine thoughts by a vicious, extravagant and involved style," Rossetti asked questions to elicit answers which would affirm that the poet's mode of expression was appropriate. His detailed discussion was undertaken "to explain and justify the state of feeling" necessary for consideration of a new poem of Browning's, this of course being *Christmas-Eve and Easter-Day*. Though Rossetti did not name the work in his discussion, the title stood at the head of the review. As

Rossetti later explained,[18] the review was to be continued in another issue; but the *Germ,* a periodical of short life and limited influence, soon ceased to be published and Browning's new work lost what could well have been an energetic defense of its style.

The last of the unfavorable reviews of *Christmas-Eve and Easter-Day* in the weeklies appeared on May 18 in the *Atlas.* The writer was sorry he had read the poem. He had long been looking for another work from the author of *Paracelsus* and *Bells and Pomegranates* and was prepared to find in it something new and excellent. His great faith in Browning was not enough to allow him to admire *Christmas-Eve and Easter-Day.* Power he found, but it was a "very peculiar and not very attractive kind." He did not know whether to be revolted or awed: "The sublime and the ultra-homely are . . . blended together — there is . . . a mixture of coarseness and solemnity. . . ." By summary and quotation the critic explained that *Christmas-Eve* was a "sort of exposition of the different phases of Christianity, as evidenced in the doctrines of different sects." He found less wilfulness, less bold experimentalizing in *Easter-Day,* which he did not discuss. The whole thing would disappoint those who had looked eagerly for new outpourings from one that had for many years been considered a true poet, one with a "rich poetic mind." Why should Browning destroy his reputation in "this wilful manner"?

In June a perfunctory three-sentence notice of *Christmas-Eve and Easter-Day* appeared in the *New Monthly Magazine.* It had nothing about the poem except part of a statement lifted from the *Athenaeum* concerning the discordant doggerel. Like many other reviewers, this one granted Browning's poetic ability but did not find his poetry palatable: he was a "genuine poet" with "great peculiarity and eccentricity."

The tide had already begun to change with a criticism in May in the *Prospective Review,* a Unitarian quarterly. R. H. Hutton, critic and theologian, discussed *Christmas-Eve and Easter-Day* along with Philip Bailey's *The Angel World and Other Poems.* There was "no contest at present with Mr. Browning's views." *Christmas-Eve* was written to show that "Christ blesses by his presence all the churches that earnestly and in truth desire to follow and love him . . . and yet that the eclectic principle in religion is spurious and worthless, since the true faith lies in one view and in one only." *Easter-Day* was written to show that doubts of the Incarnation arise from the feebleness of man's love, which makes it difficult, sometimes impossible, for him to believe that "divine love could ever have been so infinite as to lead God to put on for our sakes man's imperfect nature, and submit to the sufferings and the sorrows of a mortal lot." The critic stressed that Bailey's poem had more of the poetic nature than Browning's, though *Christmas-Eve and Easter-Day* exhibited a "higher intellectual power, a keener moral sensitiveness, and altogether a far more spiritual nature." The only passages that were poetic, according to the critic, were the description of the lunar rainbow and the vision of Christ in the first poem and the description of the Aurora Borealis in *Easter-Day*. Browning's poetry was "altogether of a hard description"; it showed "more appreciation of the picturesque, than of the essentially beautiful and sublime." This was evident in his "ungraceful versification, which is totally devoid of melody and even smoothness, and yet is not ill adapted to bring out sharp distinctions and pointed contrasts."

The *Prospective Review* marked a turning point in the history of the reception of *Christmas-Eve and Easter-Day*. More and more, reviewers subordinated attention to diction and verse to consideration of *Christmas-Eve and Easter-Day* as a religious poem and Browning as a religious poet; or, like the critics for the *Examiner* and the *Leader* (with some exceptions), they looked approvingly at the style. If there was objection to Browning's expression and tone, the critics were not irritated to the point of rejecting the argument or if they were irritated further thought changed their attitude. In time, the religious import seemed to them far more important than the expression.

In June 1850, two months after the publication of *Christmas-Eve and Easter-Day*, *In Memoriam* was published. In September the High Church *English Review* had an article on *Christmas-Eve and Easter-Day*, *In Memoriam*, and a play by Henry Taylor. Taylor was far from being ranked as high as Tennyson and Browning — the "undoubted chiefs of their poetic era." The *English Review* had carried discussions of Browning's work in 1845 and in 1849, and in both the critic surpassed some others of the day in acuteness and understanding. Even their objections to Browning on moral grounds had not made them irritable and had not blinded them to the outstanding qualities of Browning's writing. The assessment of this latest publication was unequivocal: "On the whole . . . this contribution of Browning's to our poetic literature is a great work, and is gladly hailed by us as such. Essentially different as it is in all respects from 'In Memoriam,' they are both destined to an earthly immortality."

Unlike a number of earlier critics of *Christmas-Eve and Easter-Day*, the reviewer never quarrelled with what seemed strange; sometimes he

even showed admiration for it. He considered the work a "wildly fantastic composition, powerful, earnest, in part devotional, yet audacious, and Hudibrastically satirical." Along with the extremely "bold"
speculations and the *"bizarre"* groundwork, he found "deep thought
and genuine feeling," "quiet yet earnest scorn for the mythical school
of unbelievers," "concentrated power, and originality of execution."
The expression impressed him as "strangely grotesque," yet he did not
object to it. After making introductory remarks, he concentrated on
Christmas-Eve, in which Browning indicated "his faith in Christianity
as a fact." Through five pages of summary and analysis, supported by
quotations, the critic presented the description of the Dissenting
chapel as "most admirable" and the realism, "touched with a master-
hand," as scarcely surpassed. Browning had described the vision and
mystical flight "strangely but grandly" and the professor "most graphically." The critic was sympathetic with the treatment of rationalism,
the lecture being a "perfect epitome of the common-places of the now
fashionable transcendental infidelity." What puzzled him was the
poet's preference for Dissent. "And yet we believe, we almost know,
that our author has been throughout life a member of our Church
Communion." (Browning was not an Anglican communicant.)

There was less than a page of discussion of *Easter-Day,* which the
reviewer found far less satisfactory though more poetic and grander
than *Christmas-Eve.* For one thing, he disapproved of the degree of as-
ceticism which it seemed to him the poem endorsed. But Browning
had powerfully demonstrated "that earth without the hope of heaven
would only be a wilderness."

After the year of its publication, whenever reviewers mentioned
or discussed *Christmas-Eve and Easter-Day* they were more interested in
the thought than in the style. Reviews of the collected edition that appeared in *Fraser's* and in the *Christian Remembrancer* in 1851 (their pronouncements on the collected edition have been discussed in Chapter
XIII) included commentaries on *Christmas-Eve and Easter-Day.* As a result of reading the poem, both critics revised their opinion of Browning's religious feelings. Charles Kingsley was probably the writer of
the review in the February issue of *Fraser's.* After commenting unfavorably, even severely, on Browning's earlier works, some with a "lurid
and unhealthy tone" which Browning's muse seemed to find most congenial, Kingsley turned to *Christmas-Eve and Easter-Day.* After the first
reading he was aware of the old "levity and irreverence," "curdled
style," and obscurity. Then he reread and reread the work until he fan-

cied that he had arrived at something of the general idea, which he left to his readers to find for themselves. He admitted that the rereading had caused him to change his mind about Browning.

This shift is the noteworthy aspect of the review. Kingsley was convinced of the "intense earnestness," which was reason enough for excusing the "artistic faults." Even though he disapproved of Browning's style, he softened his objections to it in this work; if the reader took the message as coming, not from the poet, but from the poet's Lord, the manner of writing became more acceptable. Browning threw into the conveyance of the message "all his peculiar talents, all the force of his peculiar personality" because only thus could it become "real and palpable." Other critics, too, accepted the style of Christmas-Eve and Easter-Day because of the appeal of the religious content.

In April 1851, two months after the critic for *Fraser's* had changed his mind, the *Christian Remembrancer,* a High Church periodical, which in a few years would make a general reassessment in Browning's favor, reviewed *Christmas-Eve and Easter-Day* as well as the collected edition. In the first part of the review the critic attacked Browning for his subject matter on moral and spiritual grounds. Although he objected to *Christmas-Eve and Easter-Day* and felt that the first impression of most readers would be that it was written "in intentional irreverence," he said he believed that Browning regarded religion as a "real and important thing" and that he would willingly strengthen his faith. "But it [*Christmas-Eve and Easter-Day*] betrays the workings of a coarse, rude, though powerful mind, incapable of spiritual elevation, and despising flights because it cannot attain to them. In all systems it seeks the visible, the gross, the earthy; without this element religion seems to possess to him no body."

In May 1853, two years after the review in the *Christian Remembrancer,* George MacDonald contributed a highly favorable discussion of *Christmas-Eve and Easter-Day* to the *Monthly Christian Spectator.* He gave ten pages to summary and analysis with ample quotation, most of it dealing with *Christmas-Eve.* He hoped to aid the reader's comprehension of a poem that would initially seem obscure. He explained the "central point" of *Christmas-Eve:* "The life of a man here . . . is a continual attempt to find his place, his centre of recipiency, and active agency." Man needs to find the position "which, while it answers best the necessities of his own soul with regard to God, will enable him to feel himself connected with the whole Christian world, and to sympathize with all." The lesson of both parts of the poem, which is taught more directly in *Easter-Day,* is "that the business of a man's life is to be a Christian."

Like the critic for the *English Review,* MacDonald praised the poem's style. He thought the rhymes contributed to the "humorous charm" and often found the double and triple rhymes pleasing, even in solemn parts of the poem. At first sight the verse might seem unfitted to the thought, but being "full of life and vigour, flagging never," it was well chosen because any other kind of verse for so much argument would have been dull. MacDonald praised the realism in the description of the chapel and justified the proximity of the humorous and the serious by reminding his readers that this proximity occurs in life and all that is human is admissible in art. "A work of this kind must . . . be taken as a whole and in regard to its design." The praise at the end of the review is indicative of the critic's receptiveness. "The argumentative power is indeed wonderful; the arguments themselves powerful in their simplicity, and embodied in words of admirable force. The poem is full of pathos and humour; full of beauty and grandeur, earnestness and truth."

Favorable references to *Christmas-Eve and Easter-Day* were to be included in several reviews that appeared after the publication of *Men and Women,* reviews of *Men and Women* or of it and other works as well.

We have seen that the early reviewers for the weeklies, with two exceptions, followed the usual pattern of allowing their irritation to augment their dislike or misunderstanding of a new work by Browning. They were puzzled as well as irritated by the style, which seemed unsuited to the religious subject matter. Since they felt that Browning had poetic ability, they thought he was wilful. The censure of style tended to disappear when religious periodicals turned their attention to *Christmas-Eve and Easter-Day;* more of them were taking a closer look at Browning, and for the first time there was a definite interest in him as a writer of religious poetry. In seeing the stamp of a poet of faith in this poem, one with powers of thought and argument, the critics accepted his manner of writing, some even praising the sections given to the Dissenting chapel and the lecture hall.

It is not surprising that there were inadequate interpretations and misinterpretations of *Christmas-Eve and Easter-Day.* What is striking is that when the religious periodicals did turn to it both a High Church and a Nonconformist critic accepted it wholeheartedly. Each found something to satisfy him, evidence for the existence of an intellectual poet who was interested in religion. A poet who presented different beliefs and asserted faith in Divine Love was welcome in a decade of increasing religious concern, when the liberal minded raised questions and the orthodox brought forth strong defenses, a period characterized by Charles Kingsley in his review as "these intellectual-worshipping times." Though Darwin's *Origin of Species* was not published until 1859, signal fires had been appearing in such works as Charles Lyell's *Principles of Geology* (1830–3), David Friedrich Strauss's *Das Leben Jesu* (1835), and Robert Chambers' *Vestiges of the Natural History of Creation* (1844). By the fifties Biblical scholarship and scientific discoveries were upsetting old beliefs.

Christmas-Eve and Easter-Day might not have stirred and quickened thought in all of its readers, as Forster had prophesied it would, but it brought about a wider interest in Browning as a serious poet, this being particularly noticeable in religious periodicals. It laid the foundation for his reputation as a religious poet and would become an important poem for this reason. According to the *Christian Spectator* (Jan. 1865), it was the first of Browning's works to make the circulating libraries. When critics encountered it in the sixties they either accepted it silently or praised it.

The first report of the sale of *Christmas-Eve and Easter-Day* was favorable. According to Elizabeth, two hundred copies "went off" in the first fortnight.[19] But the ripple of encouragement was followed by an ominous calm. The publisher still had copies on his hand in 1864.[20] In spite of the poor sale, not long after publication *Christmas-Eve and Easter-Day* began to influence the direction which Browning's reputation was to take. He was to be thought of as a poet of elevated thought who was interested in matters that concerned serious Victorians.

CHAPTER XVI

Prose and Finances

Essay on Shelley, 1852

At the end of *Bells and Pomegranates,* Browning was able to look back upon his repeated failures as experience that he would profit by in his new life with Elizabeth. He was confident that in the future he would do "quite other and better things" and that his works would sell. During the courtship his concern was the responsibility that he would have immediately after marriage. When the matter of money came up, Browning, who had not earned his livelihood before his engagement to Elizabeth, expressed his readiness to turn his "talent" (which he said he had as well as what Elizabeth called his "genius") into moneymaking.[1] But Elizabeth would not agree to "an exchange of higher work for lower work,"[2] not being of the same mind as Mrs. Procter, who thought it a pity that Browning "had not seven or eight hours a day of occupation."[3] Diplomatic service was a possibility,[4] but during months of quieting Elizabeth's doubts of the wisdom of his marrying her and of overcoming her inclination to postpone the final step, the problem of finding employment was pushed into the future. Browning wanted to believe — and did believe — that the produce of his pen would yield sufficient income for the simple life that he and Elizabeth planned to lead. Elizabeth had an income of her own;[5] and after talking back and forth about the use or disposition of it, Browning recognized the practicality of having her money as a safeguard.[6]

During the time that Robert and Elizabeth spent in Pisa following their marriage, Browning approached Monckton Milnes in an effort to obtain a secretarial post in an embassy to Pius IX that was being considered. It never materialized.[7] Eventually finances became a real problem. Even if, as Elizabeth pointed out, living in Italy was inexpensive, their expectations of income from various sources were not fulfilled. In 1850 there was a decrease in Elizabeth's income from the ship *David Lyon,* and Browning was defeated in his hope of making money by his writing. Elizabeth wrote in December, ". . . we have had not a sou from our books for a year past, the booksellers being bound of course to cover their own expenses first. Then this Christmas account has not yet reached us."[8]

A shortage of income was one of the causes for the postponement of a visit to London. Kenyon wanted to send the Brownings money in 1850, probably for a trip to England. After writing two letters and then tearing them up, Browning sent what he called an "awkward attempt" at declining the offer and showing appreciation.[9] In 1851 and 1852 Browning and Elizabeth repeatedly expressed gratitude to Kenyon for monetary assistance.[10] It seems that by associating a transfer to them of £100 a year with the birth of their son[11] Kenyon had succeeded in overcoming Browning's reluctance to receive help. Finally they decided to let their apartment in Florence instead of giving it up entirely. Elizabeth told Kenyon his assistance would help them with an experiment: she was going to "try hard to be able to stay in Paris,"[12] so that they could live nearer their families. Quite obviously she doubted that she would be as well there as in Italy. With some hesitancy on Browning's part because of their low finances (even with the £100 from Kenyon), they started for Paris in May of 1851, with England as their goal. They were not to return to Florence until November in the following year.

During a stay in Venice, Robert was uneasy because no news had come of Elizabeth's shares in the *David Lyon.* He wrote his uncle Reuben Browning, who was with the London branch of the Rothschilds, about arrangements to be made for getting funds.[13] The Brownings resumed their journey and arrived in Lucerne with ten francs. There they received money to relieve their immediate want but also the grim news that Elizabeth's income from the *David Lyon* was even less than in the preceding year. They were left with only eighty pounds to spend in the next six months.[14] Even after arriving in Paris at the end of June they were not sure that financially they would be able to go on to England.[15]

Elizabeth wrote Arabel that Browning's "anxious temper . . . vexed him terribly throughout this journey," that he had been "in a horrible fright all the way" and let "his imagination master him"; "house-letting as well as everything else in the world" had made him despondent.[16]

Elizabeth, who had come from a family of considerable means and had never thought much about money one way or the other, wrote to Arabel after discussing Browning's distress. "It's impossible to fret me about money-matters. If we can't live on bread & cheese, we must live on bread alone. . . ."[17] Browning did enough worrying for both of them. He was always meticulous in financial affairs. Elizabeth's letters reveal the effect of debts, even of short standing, upon him.[18] She said that he should have five thousand a year to meet the "exigencies of his nature," that he let "his imagination buffet & torment him in the small uncertainties of life."[19]

They did go on to London towards the end of July 1851 for their first visit to their homeland since leaving England in 1846. Their busy life of seeing family and friends, of being caught in a social whirl that at times overwhelmed them, did not prevent Browning from attending to matters of professional concern. He had a potential involvement with the *Westminster*. It was for this quarterly (then the *London and Westminster Review*) that Mill, its proprietor, had intended to write a review of *Sordello* but did not. Soon thereafter, Mill gave up the *Review* and it resumed its original title. Later it and the *Foreign Quarterly Review*, in which Browning's article on Tasso and Chatterton[20] had appeared earlier (1842), were united. In 1851 the *Westminster* was again passing from one management to another, and talent was being lined up for promotion of the venture.

Browning's name was suggested to the new editor, who invited the poet to call on him, presumably to be made an offer. Browning saw him on August 26, 1851.[21] One of the persons who had recommended Browning to the editor was Carlyle. Having advised Browning, as well as other poets to write in prose, Carlyle encouraged him to contribute to the *Westminster*. "There you are in Paris, there you were in Florence, with fiery interest in all manner of things, with whole Libraries to write and say on this and the other thing! The man means to pay, handsomely. . . ."[22] In October Browning, by this time settled with Elizabeth and their son in Paris for the winter of 1851–2, answered Carlyle, "I conceive your kindness in pointing out a way to him [the new editor], had I wanted it."[23]

Browning turned down the offer. His well-known reluctance to publish poetry in periodicals probably extended to contributing prose to them. Later in life he wrote: "I cannot bring myself to write for periodicals. If I publish a book, and people choose to buy it, that proves they want to read my work. But to have them turn over the pages of a magazine and find me — that is to be an uninvited guest."[24] In the forties he had written at least two prose essays for publication without his name. The authorship of the one beginning with Tasso and passing on to Chatterton in the *Foreign Quarterly Review* (1842) remained unknown until Donald Smalley published his study and edition of it under the title of *Browning's Essay on Chatterton* (1948). There is evidence that Browning wrote another essay with the understanding that the authorship would be kept secret. When it was revealed, he destroyed his manuscript.[25] This deep-seated reluctance to be the "uninvited guest" of magazine readers throws light on his refusal to write for the *Westminster* even though he was much concerned about the state of the family finances and the failure of his writing to bring in money; it also says something about his pride and sensitiveness.

In September of 1851, near the time when Browning rejected the offer of the *Westminster* editor, he wrote Chapman: ". . . I am vexed at the ill luck of *Christmas-Eve* etc. Was the price too high? Could anything be done by judicious advertizing at the seasons the book treats of? Could one put in some illustrations, even now?"[26] As if the slow sale of the collected edition and of *Christmas-Eve and Easter-Day* were not enough, Browning had another setback.

While he was still in London, Moxon, his former publisher, asked him to write an introduction to twenty-five Shelley letters that he had bought at Sotheby's. With copies or proofs of the letters in hand, Browning wrote an introductory essay after he and his family went to Paris for the winter of 1851–2. He first explained the differences between two classes of poets, the objective and the subjective, and then made use of this distinction in his discussion. Browning of course considered it more important to know the biography (which includes letters) of the subjective than of the objective poet.

The essay commands our attention because of Browning's distinction between the two kinds of poet and his allowance for a poet who combines objectivity and subjectivity and also because of his defense of Shelley, whom he had long been concerned with and whose life was undergoing public scrutiny at this time. He had relatively little to say of the particular letters that were being published by Moxon. Apparently he thought that they were not a significant addition to the previously known Shelley correspondence. They were "not offered as presenting any new feature of the poet's character." Browning reinforced this opinion at the last of the essay when he spoke of his "few, inadequate words upon these scarcely more important supplementary letters of Shelley." Elizabeth confessed that she found the letters "by no means interesting."[27]

Browning appended the date of December 4, 1851, to the introductory essay; on the 5th Elizabeth said the work was off his hands on that day.[28] Moxon sent payment for the essay, a "very liberal remittance," said Browning. "I do hope that you will be no loser by your very handsome behavior. You gain my best thanks, at all events, for it — whatever they may be worth. I will spare no pains with the proofs, or anything else I can do in connection with the matter."[29] Here was a narrow ray of light in the dismal picture of Browning's earning power, but that ray soon vanished. The little book of twenty-five letters with Browning's introduction was published in February. Not long after publication it was found that twenty-three were forgeries and two were copies of genuine letters.[30] Moxon had to withdraw the Letters of Percy Bysshe Shelley.

Before the forgery was detected four weeklies gave attention to the letters and the prefatory essay. Like Browning, the critics for the Athenaeum (Feb. 21, 1852), the Spectator (Feb. 21), and the Guardian (Mar. 3) thought that the correspondence was of no real importance. The Athenaeum and Guardian objected to the length and obscurity of Browning's introduction, but found that it contained something of interest. According to the Guardian, it was "not without some striking thoughts and a good many striking expressions."

The fourth weekly, the Literary Gazette (Feb. 21) had the longest review in the weeklies — eight columns covering nearly three pages. The critic "lamented that so well-intentioned a publisher should fall into the hands of so incoherent a dreamer." He was annoyed that "Mr. Browning should have taken such unprofitable pains to display his own singular powers of writing, instead of confining himself simply, exclusively, and heartily to the necessary work he had heroically undertaken." He complained of Browning's "very indifferent English and most questionable grammar" and the "pervading obscurity of style and thought." Seemingly the critic did not make an effort to represent the essay fairly. He ignored Browning's sympathetic attitude to Shelley the man and wrote a spirited support of Shelley as if he were refuting an attack by Browning.

The publication of the letters and the essay, of course, prompted remarks on Shelley, whose conduct and opinions were in the spotlight. The comments of the reviewers reflected differing opinions in the literary world. The *Spectator* spoke of Browning's just and charitable view of Shelley's life and opinions; on the other hand, the *Guardian* found Browning's approbation of Shelley's conduct "startling and offensive." The reviewer for the *Literary Gazette* expressed himself more vehemently. After a long drawn-out defense of Shelley from the attacks that had been made upon his personal life, he stated that if he had ever had any doubts about Shelley's character the new letters would remove them. He quoted from the letters at length and wrote in glowing terms of them and what they revealed of Shelley. His assertiveness came to nothing when all but two of the letters were found to be spurious.

F. T. Palgrave raised questions about the genuineness of the purported Shelley letters and wrote to the *Literary Gazette.* His letter, with details to substantiate his doubts, was published on February 28. On March 6 the *Athenaeum* gave an account of the discovery of the forgery and the acquisition of the letters.[31] The *Atlas* (Mar. 13), *John Bull* (Mar. 13), and the *Critic* (Mar. 15) carried the news and quoted from the *Athenaeum.* The *Critic* went further. The volume was "not all worthless"; Browning's essay was of permanent value. Therefore the *Critic* would place before its readers portions of a review written by "an author of note" before the forgery was discovered. The reviewer said that Browning's essay contained "some interesting and profound remarks upon poets, considered with regard to their subjectivity and objectivity" and upon the importance of having reliable information about the life of a subjective poet like Shelley. He accepted Browning's assessment and defense of Shelley.

Browning's introductory essay to the spurious Shelley letters received still further attention in the *Westminster Review* of April 1852 in an article written by George Henry Lewes. The title "Shelley and the Letters of Poets" indicated that it embraced more than a discussion of the collection of Shelley's letters. Lewes demonstrated by reference to other writers that what the man is as shown in his letters may or may not be in harmony with what we find in his works. Though the discussion was long, Lewes did not lose sight of Browning and he defended him against those who made merry with him for having written a preface to letters that turned out to be forged. A careful reading of the essay, he said, would show that it was not specifically an introduction to these letters but to the whole of Shelley's correspondence. Lewes did not entirely approve of the style of the essay, but he liked the content and regretted that circumstances "checked the influence of a loving but wise appreciation of him [Shelley] recorded by such a man as Browning."

Although Browning did not think very highly of his essay, according to statements made by Elizabeth before the forgery was known,[32] his efforts were not entirely in vain. Objections to style did not play an important part in the reception. The content made a good impression on all the critics who reviewed the work except the one for the *Literary Gazette,* so captious that Horne defended Browning in a letter that was published in the same periodical on March 13. The essay was again to be made available to readers by the Browning Society in 1881 and by the Shelley Society in 1888, and it has been reprinted from time to time in the present century. Browning's discussion is of interest today for its reflection of his own position as poet.

Browning received praise for his work from a familiar quarter, one in which his prose was welcome. He had written and sent a copy of the little book to Carlyle, who replied on March 8, 1852, before the forgery was widely publicized. "I liked the Essay extremely well indeed; a solid, well-wrought, massive, manful bit of discourse; and interesting to me, over and above, as the first bit of *prose* I had ever seen from you; — I hope only the first of very many." Carlyle's view of Browning's essay was somewhat in keeping with that of the critics:

> This Essay of yours, and another little word by Emerson are the only new things I have read with real pleasure for a great while past. I agree with what you say of Shelley's moralities and spiritual position; I honour and respect the weighty estimate you have formed of the Poetic Art; and I admire very much the grave expressiveness of style (a *little* too elaborate here and there), and the dignified tone, in which you manage to deliver yourself on all that.[33]

Carlyle's words helped to alleviate the disappointment of the unfortunate business of the letters. After the exposure Browning's mind must have gone back to another forger, one whom he was closely associated with during his earlier career — Thomas Powell.[34] Nor was Browning's involvement with forgers at an end. The time was yet to come when T. J. Wise was to pass off as first editions falsely dated pamphlets containing individual poems, Elizabeth's as well as Browning's. When Browning knew him in the eighties, he was suspicious on one occasion but he did not live to see the exposure of this most productive of the three forgers.[35]

Browning completed his essay on Shelley in Paris in December 1851. On successive days — January 1, 2, 3 of 1852 — he wrote three poems that were later published in *Men and Women*. He was to write no more during this time away from Italy. He and Elizabeth were again in London from July 6 to October 12, 1852, and returned to Paris for only a short time before starting for Italy. Browning saw many old friends and made new ones. These visits, traveling and settling temporarily in a number of places, and changing his father and sister's residence from London to Paris (to evade a legal entanglement) left him little time or peace for composition.

Whether in London or Paris or in Florence after his return later in 1852, Browning was concerned about professional and business matters. He insisted that Chapman provide semiannual accounts; he wanted one for his and one for Elizabeth's poetry. His publisher's haphazard way of doing business was vexatious to one as careful as Browning in financial matters. Often he had to remind Chapman that accounts were overdue. Furthermore he had to encourage him to push his works. Browning's suggestion of September 1851 to use advertisements and illustrations was one instance of his efforts to stir Chapman into action. Living at such a great distance from London placed Browning in a disadvantageous position for promoting his works, which were to all appearances having little success and needed to have attention drawn to them.

When early in 1853 Helen Faucit, now Mrs. Theodore Martin, asked Browning for a renewal of the permission he had given her to play in *Colombe's Birthday,* he considered the good effect that successful performances of the play would have on the sale of his poems. He wrote Chapman of the possibilities: ". . . if there were to be any sort of success, it would help the poems to fetch up their lee-way, I suppose. Hadn't you better advertise, in that case?"[36] It seemed that the Brownings' chief interest in the seven performances in April and May of 1853 was their possible effect on the sale of his poetry. Elizabeth wrote,

"What I hope is, that the poetical appreciation of 'Colombe' will give an impulse to the sale of the poems, which will be more acceptable to us than the other kind of success. . . ."[37] Browning by now might have felt that *Christmas-Eve and Easter-Day* would do little to advance his reputation; he could hope for further recognition chiefly through his collected edition of 1849. In telling Kenyon of Helen Faucit's request, he indicated that having the play acted would be gratifying in itself and its success would call attention to other works in the collected edition. "I said 'yes,' gladly enough — for the play having been in print these ten years, the players dealing with it can be but a compliment, at worst, — while a very little success would advertise the volumes it stands in — do, look out next month for the Haymarket's doings — & wish me well, as you will!"[38] It is not surprising that Browning was pleased with the prospect of the staging of the play that Kean had taken little interest in.

For the time being apparently there was no surfacing of the deep-seated disappointment that Browning had felt because of the failure of his plays. In telling Forster of the coming appearances of *Colombe's Birthday*, he looked back with detachment to the earlier frustrating years, "How odd the remembrance of the playgoing seems now . . . ."[39] We have already seen (in the chapter that traces the history of *Colombe's Birthday*) that critics of 1853 found the play praiseworthy but not as a stage play. Browning seemed satisfied — perhaps relieved — that Helen Faucit's production went over as well as it did. He thanked Reuben Browning for sending him news of its success — "for such, on the whole, it may be called," he added.[40] Elizabeth said the play succeeded but it was a *succes d'estime*.[41]

On July 16, 1853, after the performances of *Colombe's Birthday*, there appeared in *Chambers's Edinburgh Journal* a sympathetic review of Browning in which a number of works were briefly but perceptively introduced. The critic praised Browning's originality, found his poetic genius to be of no common order, thought he deserved wider recognition than he had received, and predicted that he would become better known. His faults would be pardoned "for the sake of the true and sometimes lofty poetry." The critic recognized that dramatic force was the outstanding quality of Browning's poems, and he felt that the short pieces were best fitted to serve as an introduction to him. The review ended with a brief discussion of *Christmas-Eve and Easter-Day*, which the critic thought perhaps had a fuller measure of originality than any other of Browning's writings, though it was "too full of close and subtile reasoning ever to be popular."

All of the reviews — including those of *Christmas-Eve and Easter-Day*, of Browning's introductory essay to Shelley's letters, and of the performances of *Colombe's Birthday* in 1853 — kept Browning's reputation in a low simmering state during the early part of the decade. The appearance of *Christmas-Eve and Easter-Day* at a time when the unsettled religious climate was threatening a change in Victorian thinking caused the critics to see Browning in a new light. But, concerned as he was about the present, he could not see that *Christmas-Eve and Easter-Day* was leading to his being accepted as an outstanding writer of religious poetry. Nor could he see that the praise of *Colombe's Birthday* as closet drama was an extension of the initial recognition in the later forties of his plays as suitable for reading and would lead to a better perspective of his dramatic genius in the sixties.

What he could see was that while he was vainly struggling to reach a wide public, others were succeeding. Alexander Smith, a poet of the spasmodic school, was somewhat of a sensation as the result of his first volume of poems, *A Life Drama*. Elizabeth's comments reflected the interest taken in him.[42] A worthier poet than Alexander Smith, Tennyson, had already gained the ear of the public. The Brownings were staunch supporters of the man and his poetry, and no doubt as they observed the reception of his works they wondered about the future of the poetry of their own making. When Elizabeth was advancing the notion in December 1850 that in the long run poetry paid better than the novel (not, she said, that they spoke out of "golden experience"), she referred to "Tennyson's returns from Moxon last year," which, she understood, "amounted to five hundred pounds."[43] She continued, "To be sure, 'In Memoriam' was a new success, which should not prevent our considering the fact of a regular income proceeding from the previous books."

In 1842 Browning had written to Domett of his work, "But the time of figs is not yet."[44] It still had not come in the early fifties. After receiving half a year's report from Chapman, he wrote him late in March of 1853: "I condole with you about my own bad job — I'll be bound you haven't sold a copy of *Christmas Eve;* yet I heard only last week about its success in America. Things may mend, however."[45] In a letter to Forster in the following month Browning referred to "that poor *Christmas Eve* which hasn't paid printing yet" and added, "Who cares, after all!"[46] Elizabeth's works fared better, a fact of which Browning was well aware — of course he felt proud of her and took pleasure in her success. After the receipt of an account in March 1854 Browning wrote Chapman, ". . . my books will creep on, perhaps, and my wife's run on, no doubt."[47] It was a few days after acknowledging receipt of Chapman's account that Browning wrote Forster of the seventy copies of the collected edition sold in the preceding half year and at last a balance of seven pence. He would see, he added, if he could do any better with his new book of poems.[48]

Browning was discouraged because he had not had the success that he had foreseen before his marriage, but he could be optimistic about the poems he was preparing for *Men and Women*. In the earlier letter to Chapman in which he referred to his "own bad job," he had said, "Meantime, I shall give you something saleable, one of these days — see if I don't."[49] The sympathetic reader who has followed the story of Browning's struggles, defeats, and confidences can look forward with the poet to the saleable work to come. Would it be his next publication — *Men and Women?*

CHAPTER XVII

Newer Manner Than Matter

Men and Women, 1855: Form and Technique

In acknowledging receipt of the supposed Shelley letters with Browning's introductory essay, Carlyle had some advice to give:

> Seriously, dear Browning, you must at last gird up your loins again; and give us a right stroke of work: — I do not wish to hurry you; far the contrary: but I remind you what is expected; and say with what joy I for one will see it arrive. — Nor do I restrict you to Prose, in spite of all I have said and still say: Prose or Poetry, either of them you can master; and we will wait for you with welcome in whatever form your own *Daimon* bids. Only see that *he* does bid it; and then go with your best speed. . . .[1]

Browning had already written several poems that would go into his next publication when he received Carlyle's letter in Paris in March 1852. The "best speed" started, however, late in the year, after the Brownings had gone back to Florence. The irregular life of a year and a half away from Italy, especially wearying in London, was past. Browning was no longer "slipping out of waistcoats and friends at once — so worn and teased he was" with trying to fulfill social commitments.[2] In Florence, where Robert and Elizabeth were settled for the winter of 1852–3, there was time for writing.

Browning returned to the kind of poetry that he first wrote in 1842 "for popularity's sake." Although *Dramatic Lyrics* had attracted little favorable criticism, the second and better collection of short poems, *Dramatic Romances and Lyrics,* had fared well enough for him to be encouraged. Now that he had tried his hand at another kind of poem in *Christmas-Eve and Easter-Day* without attracting the desired number of receptive readers, he reverted again to the shorter poem. He wrote Joseph Milsand on February 24, 1853, during his winter of work in Florence: "I have not left the house one evening since our return. I am writing, a sort of first step toward popularity (for me!), 'Lyrics' with more music and painting than before, so as to get people to hear and see. . . . "[3] He was making an attempt to reach more readers.

Escaping the heat of Florence grew to be routine for the Brownings; they went to the Baths of Lucca for the summer of 1853. They intended "to buy" their holiday by working,[4] Robert on his new collection and Elizabeth on *Aurora Leigh.* In August Elizabeth said that she had seen only a few of the poems he had written; "those seemed to me as fine as anything he has done."[5] There was no longer a suggestion of his addressing readers directly. By now Elizabeth was saying, "I want him to write dramatic poems for the world, and not dramas for the players."[6] In October she made another progress report: "We have been very happy here & not idle either. Robert especially has done a great deal of work, & will have his volume ready for the spring without failure he says."[7]

The Brownings, who had looked forward to being in Rome, spent their first winter there in 1853–4. At the beginning illness and death in the W. W. Story family, with whom they had become friends, gave them much concern,[8] and later Browning was involved in time-consuming social activities. He had been in an "advanced state"[9] in composing poems for his new collection before he went to Rome, but while he was there he did not write as much as he had intended to. After his return to Florence in the first part of June 1854, he applied himself to his work. "I am trying to make up for wasted time in Rome and setting my poetical house in order," he wrote Story.[10] At about the same time he informed Forster of the necessity of going to "London, or Paris at farthest" to get his poems printed. He explained:

> This is what I have written — only a number of poems of all sorts and sizes and styles and subjects — not written before last year, but the beginning of an expressing the spirit of all the fruits of the years since I last turned the winch of the wine press. The manner will be newer than the matter. I hope to be listened to, this time, and I am

glad I have been made to wait this not very long while. . . . I shall
be ready by the Autumn. . . .[11]

By July the Brownings' plans for going to England had to be
given up because of a severe shortage of money. Even the customary
summer trip away from the heat of Florence was not possible. In the
autumn the financial situation was better, but it was too late to go
north. By virtue of the delay, the number of poems for Browning's collection increased. The projected work that he wrote of to Forster in
June 1854 and that Elizabeth had written of in the spring of that year[12]
was the one originally planned. Its length can be surmised by a reference Browning made in August to a collection of 5000 lines that
he expected to bring out.[13] The Brownings were settled in Casa Guidi
for the winter of 1854–5 and did not receive visitors before three
o'clock.[14] By April Browning had increased the number of lines to
8000, which were being transcribed by their friend Isa Blagden from
his dictation.[15] In June they left for England, Browning with a completed manuscript except for the dedication poem that was to be written in London — *One Word More* — and Elizabeth with a manuscript
that would be completed before they returned to Italy.

They arrived in London on July 12 after a stop in Paris. This summer of 1855 in England, like the ones in 1851 and 1852, was agitat-
ing. The first order of business with Browning was to see about the
printing of his new poems, which were to come out in two volumes.
There was much to take his attention away from the last details of
preparation for the press, including many pleasurable visits with
friends and an upsetting experience with D. D. Home (or Hume), the
American medium (Elizabeth was a believer in spiritualism and
Browning a skeptic).[16] Elizabeth had looked forward to being with her
sisters, but she was able to see one only for a while and the other not at
all, partly because of limited funds. Browning was suffering agony
from pecuniary difficulties, as Elizabeth indicated to her sister Arabel.

. . . and as to money-matters, the idea of being in a difficulty is absolutely horrible to him. Now he thinks that the change from one
house to another, entails expense, (besides the journeying) — and he
has set it down as certain (which he has done a hundred times before
since we have been together) that we are all going down a precipice
for want of pecuniary means. Say nothing of it — but he has seriously proposed to me to go straight off to Florence to avoid these
northern expenses which we are unequal to meet, he holds.[17]

Robert Browning

One particularly bright spot during the summer was having Tennyson visit them on successive days, September 26th and 27th. Among their experiences it was a "top jewel" added to their crown, Browning wrote Kenyon.[18] Both Elizabeth and Robert were touched by Tennyson's manner. He wanted to discuss how all three of them as "brother-poets" worked. On one evening he read the recently published *Maud* aloud, and Dante Gabriel Rossetti, who along with others was present, made a sketch of him. His reading — "between a song and a recitation" — quite haunted the Brownings. He stopped now and then "to comment on his own work with an adorable naïveté — calling attention to this and the other nicety."[19] Browning also read a poem. He chose *Fra Lippo Lippi,* which would soon appear in the collection that he felt would be a success.

Not long before Tennyson's visits, Browning had written *One Word More,* the dedication poem to Elizabeth, which became the fifty-first and last poem in *Men and Women.* When the "first half volume" was in proof, Elizabeth observed, ". . . the work looks better than ever in print, as all true work does brought into the light."[20] Fox, who had heard Forster read *Christmas-Eve and Easter-Day* in proof, now became acquainted with *Men and Women* while it was in the same stage. This time the poet himself read to Fox, who thought that the poems were "at the top of art in their kind."[21]

There is evidence, as there was in earlier years, that Browning was considering public taste, soliciting criticism from friends, and working hard to make improvements as long as he had proofs in hand. Comments that he made to Kenyon in 1853 and in 1855 allow us glimpses of him during the process of planning, writing, and revising before the publication of *Men and Women.* While he was working on the poems, Browning told Kenyon, as well as Forster and Milsand, that he was attempting to write poems that would attract readers. "I am trying if I can't take people's ears at last, by the lyrical tip; if they have one; and make songs & such like at a great rate — *that* being your presidency in my 'work,' — at all events, I do my best & think I may have found out and set right some old cranks & hitches which used to stop my success so cruelly."[22]

While Browning was preparing his poems for the press in 1855, Kenyon as well as Fox and also Lytton and Forster became acquainted with them in proof. Browning wanted to profit by their criticisms. Apparently Kenyon, who had always appreciated Browning's genius but had been concerned because he did not write so as to reach a wider public, read proofs that Browning sent him for part of *Men and Woman* and made critical remarks indicating the same concern. On October 1 Browning sent him proof sheets for the last part of Volume II along with a reply to his observations on the earlier portions. Browning assured him that he had done his very best and had really believed he would have his approval this time. His letter shows that his own confidence in the poems had been supported by the opinion of others, support that did not entirely obliterate the disappointment he felt in receiving Kenyon's unpromising opinion.

> But why should not I tell you what will give you the pleasure you would give me were this in your power — that Fox and Forster, — and I will associate with them Lytton, young as he is, — these three and yourself being my sole referees hitherto, with one exception, — well, these three take one's breath away with their — not sympathy merely — but anticipations of success — of "a sale" in short: and Chapman, shrewd as he is, makes no scruple of declaring that he expects the same. My exception — my fourth critic is the fine fellow of the Revue des Deux Mondes — who writes of the first volume (to me) "il y a là du colossal!" I put all this down impudently on paper to please you, as I say — for I know whether you will grieve or no to find your dark auguries met by some blue bits in various parts of my poor horizon.[23]

As we shall see in a subsequent chapter, Lytton's high praise of the poems did not preclude his prediction of a limited audience. It was the brighter part of his comment that impressed Browning. Yet the poet's realistic attitude toward the public and his tendency to heed advice in order to improve his readability and appeal prompted him to take Kenyon's criticisms seriously. He was going to alter places in *Saul* according to his suggestions, he told Kenyon. Furthermore, he had gone over "the preceding portion of the two volumes perhaps half a dozen times or more very carefully, making minute improvements which 'tell' on the general effect."[24] William S. Peterson has studied a set of proofs of *Men and Women* and found "considerable evidence of Browning's painstaking craftsmanship, which extended to even the finest nuances of punctuation," and Allan C. Dooley has added to Peterson's observations.[25] Browning's letters and these studies show that the efforts he had made in the forties to improve his poetry continued into the later periods of writing.

At length the revising and proofreading came to an end. Robert and Elizabeth, with their son, were to follow the procedure of their earlier visit in the North — staying in Paris for the winter and then spending another summer in England before returning to Italy. They left London for Paris in the middle of October. Soon after their arrival Browning wrote his publisher about errors he had found in the printed poems. After some hesitation he decided that it would be advisable to correct them in a later edition rather than call attention to them by appending a list of errata. He did, in fact, send a list of corrections to Dante Gabriel Rossetti, including ones for two poems on art that Rossetti would be especially interested in.[26]

In a month the critics would start making their pronouncements on *Men and Women*. Since Fox, Forster, and Lytton had praised the poems highly and Milsand had called them "superhuman,"[27] Browning could well feel that his own confidence in the poems was justified. Thirteen years earlier he had published his first collection of short poems and since that time he had been going through a period of experimentation with the revelation of character. Even though *Christmas-Eve and Easter-Day* was an interruption in the direct line of development toward the maturity of the dramatic monologue, he had been storing up impressions for *Men and Women*. When Browning told Forster that the poems were of "all sorts and sizes and styles and subjects," he was preparing him for the extensive ground he had covered. In length they went from 13 lines (*My Star*) to 1013 lines (*Bishop Blougram's Apology*). Love, art, music, religion; the medieval, the renaissance, the contemporary; the emotional, the casuistical — the cloth could be stretched in many ways.

The two volumes of *Men and Women* were published on November 10, 1855, at the price of twelve shillings. In writing the poems Browning had gone beyond the stereotyped approach of other writers to Christianity by examining it through the eyes of widely different characters. He surpassed others in placing love in a variety of lights. Who before this time had so effectively used musical terms and forms or a knowledge of art and artists to unfold ideas and feeling in poems? Browning's technique had reached a high level of maturity. In going through the experimental stage of writing short poems and the last plays of the *Bells and Pomegranates* series, he had learned to fashion the elements of poetry into harmonious, meaningful, and highly individualized poems.

Men and Women attracted more reviews than any other work of Browning's since *Strafford,* and the collection had neither the stage nor Macready as a drawing card. Periodicals that had ignored Browning earlier now took notice, and periodicals just beginning to be published considered him important enough to warrant their attention. If there was faultfinding and intolerance in the reviews, there was considerable praise, though sometimes it was weakened by reluctance or self-contradiction, and much of the criticism foreshadowed that which marked the establishment of Browning's fame in the sixties. Lines of criticism present in earlier reviews continued, some merging and anticipating later attitudes.

We cannot say that after *Men and Women* was published the reviews tended during the succeeding few years to become progressively more understanding as they had after the publication of *Pippa Passes* and the short dramatic poems, with the passage of time giving opportunity for digestion. Coping with such a multiplicity of unconventional poems was a demanding intellectual task, and not until the sixties was there to be a noticeable increase in critical understanding and appreciation. The earlier works had not prepared the critics for the large number of poems bearing the stamp of Browning's mature genius. It was in the presentation of his characters — that is, his way of placing them before his readers — that he made the most decided advancement. In that area lay the greatest problems for the reviewers.

As we have seen, Browning wrote Forster that his forthcoming poems would be newer in manner than matter. Having often been told that his difficult manner turned readers away, Browning seemed to have been promising to make some kind of change with that in mind. His distinction between "manner" and "matter" parallels the ordinary one expressed by the pairs "style and content" and "form and substance." Though "manner and matter" are not entirely separable, they may be distinguished for convenience of discussion, especially since many of his critics observed this distinction. The present chapter will consider the varying degrees of approval or disapproval of Browning's "manner" in *Men and Women*, and the following chapter will deal with the more uniform and favorable response to his "matter." Before we go on to the reviews it should be said that the manner was newer only in the sense that Browning had brought his technique to a higher level of artistry. He could hardly alter his manner basically. In both manner and matter his poetry had undergone enrichment.

So much of the criticism concerning manner or style (preferable as the usual word) was persistently negative and ranting that the more positive and receptive side might go unnoticed without a rather full examination. The reviews fall into certain categories that allow an advantageous analysis of the professional criticism, especially that touching upon poems of individual character study now recognized as among the best of Browning's creations. In this chapter the reviews are divided into three groups according to their attitude to Browning's style and its influence principally on the evaluation of five dramatic monologues — *Cleon, An Epistle Containing the Strange Medical Experience of Karshish, Bishop Blougram's Apology, Andrea del Sarto,* and *Fra Lippo Lippi.* In the first group the reviewers found the style so obscure that they could see little or no merit. In the second group they were critical of Browning's style but they set apart some or all of the monologues for favorable comment. The third group accepted Browning's style for what it was and accorded high praise to these poems. Variations in the degree of approval or disapproval are present within each group. Eight reviews belong to the first group, six to the second, and nine to the third.

By their tone two reviews in the first group successfully blurred the little credit given Browning — a flippant one in *Blackwood's* and a supercilious one in the *Saturday Review.* The virulence of the early days of *Blackwood's* had by now abated, but the old recklessness remained in a discussion entitled "Modern Light Literature — Poetry," in which Browning appeared. It was written by Mrs. Margaret Oliphant, a popular and prolific novelist of the day. She grouped Browning with Tennyson, Mrs. Browning, and a few minor poets, who together resembled a family; Browning was the wild boy of the household, with his "boisterous noisy shouting voice." He was succinctly dismissed as a writer having a dramatic gift and sincerity of mind who produced obscure poetry of "rent and tortured fabric."

The recently established *Saturday Review* was more damaging because it was attracting much attention and because Browning later harbored the embitterment that it aroused in him. In the nearly three columns given to *Men and Women* in its fourth issue, obscurity was the chief target. The offensive tone of the first two sentences prepared the reader for the strictures on style that followed.

> It is really high time that this sort of thing should, if possible, be stopped. Here is another book of madness and mysticism — another melancholy specimen of power wantonly wasted, and talent deliberately perverted — another act of self-prostration before that demon of bad taste who now seems to hold in absolute possession the fashionable masters of our ideal literature.

In his harangue on obscurity, the critic condemned the unintelligibility of such "stuff" as he found in By the Fireside and concluded that
Browning was obscure because he lacked genius. Even when the reviewer admitted that there was something worthwhile in Browning's
poetry, he could not let his readers forget his objections. We shall see
that this review was still on Browning's mind in the sixties.

In this first group there were reviewers who more solemnly set
about their task of judging Browning's poems. They objected primarily to his unpoetic quality and obscurity, specifying characteristics that
made him hard to read and castigating his perverseness in holding fast
to his faults. They were so intent upon pointing out faults of style that
they were blinded to the outstanding poems portraying character.

The Guardian was typical. The critic thought the poems difficult
to read and understand. "In some cases the transitions are so brusque,
the train of ideas so difficult to follow, and grammatical structure of
the sentences so involved, that most readers will be fain to pass on in
contented ignorance of their aim or object." Trying to follow the idea
was hard enough; "to catch the rhythm of the various metres" was no
less taxing. Browning's elliptical mode of expression, occasional inappropriate use of diction, and abrupt transition from one thought to another contributed often to make the attempt to understand a "very
weariness." If Browning would only realize that the primary object of
poetical language was to convey the poet's idea to the reader and that
meter should be pleasing to the ear, he might take a high rank among
living poets.

In the same group with the Guardian were the Literary Gazette,
Irish Quarterly Review, Christian Remembrancer (Apr. 1856), and Athenaeum. The Critic belonged to this group also, although at the end of the
discussion the reviewer did encourage readers to turn to the poetry because they would find enough to atone for the faults. The reviewers exercised little restraint in their attacks. In designating Browning as
preeminently "the King of Darkness," the Irish Quarterly Review saw in
Men and Women "sufficient crudities, contortions, and dissections of
the language, to ruin the reputation of fifty poets." The Christian Remembrancer wrote of "stitches, cramps, and spasms, grinding cart-
wheels, clanking chains, Charivaris, shrieks, insane utterances." The
Christian Remembrancer as well as others resented the "toil of perusal."

Most of the criticisms in this group indicated that the inclination
of some poets to ignore established norms was a foolhardy and disastrous one; according to the Athenaeum, Browning indulged in license

instead of following traditional standards. However "great his intellectual power or fertile his invention," a poet must avoid obscurity and discord by following conventional rules of composition in order to reach his readers, said the *Literary Gazette*. Browning, like others who were not conventional, would pass into oblivion. One after another, like the critic for the *Irish Quarterly*, the reviewers accused Browning of clinging to his vices with dogged pertinacity. They recognized that he possessed qualities that could make a good poet, but their objections crowded out an open-minded consideration of these qualities.

These are samples of the prevailing irritable complaints of Browning's wilfulness in writing harsh, obscure, unconventional, and difficult poetry. That Browning did exercise care; that each poem criticized needed to be considered in its entirety, not just by its poetic line and diction; and that the critical measurement of traditional poetry was not appropriate — such points seemingly did not occur to the critics of the first group. They did not find many poems in *Men and Women* that would sufficiently fit into their preconceived notions of what poetry should be. A few votes were cast for *One Word More, The Statue and the Bust, In a Balcony,* and *Up at a Villa*. The *Saturday Review* found *Bishop Blougram's Apology* and *Cleon* worth reading, and *Blackwood's* found *Andrea del Sarto* and *Bishop Blougram's Apology* intelligible. The critics for these two periodicals barely mentioned these poems, and the other critics, with the exception of the one for the *Guardian* (who called attention to the content of *Blougram* and wrote more of *Lippo* by way of summary), either objected to or did not refer to them at all. Since Browning did not take the trouble to write like the established poets of the past, the critics thus far discussed felt it their business to say that he was at fault, especially in the mechanics of his poetry.

Less blind critics in the second and third groups praised outstanding poems of character revelation. They observed and appreciated Browning's interest in character and his special way of dealing with it. Since the publication of *Paracelsus* there had been comments on Browning's concern for humanity — his awareness of the problems of man's existence, his strength in revealing the emotions and passions of the heart, his penetration of the mind — and there had also been recognition of his peculiar literary methods and procedures. The understanding by the end of the forties that Browning's genius was preeminently dramatic, though not suitable to the stage, had anticipated a more persistent appreciation in the reviews of *Men and Women* of the poems in which a speaker indirectly reveals his inner self and some facet of his life. The critics of the fifties ranged all the way from those who let Browning's failure to conform to traditional poetry becloud their acceptance of his poems to those whose liberal view of his nonconformity resulted in an advance toward appreciation of the totality of his art.

The second group of reviews recognized Browning's skill in the presentation of character, but found fault with his style. They gave a fair amount of favorable attention to *Andrea, Lippo, Karshish, Cleon,* and *Blougram,* whereas reviews in the first group, with the exception of those in *Blackwood's,* the *Saturday Review,* and the *Guardian* either objected to these poems or said nothing about them. In the second group the reviewers for the *London Quarterly Review,* the *Dublin University Magazine,* and *Fraser's* observed and commended Browning's interest in man and his behavior, though their objections to his manner of writing outweighed their commendation. They felt that Browning was a poet of unusual ability and they paid lip service to his originality; but their severe complaints showed that they were not capable of readjusting their traditional notions of poetical technique. They could not see that the very aspects of his poetry which they inveighed against were part of his originality. In a confused mixture of praise and blame, these critics tended to be querulous in their accusations against Browning for being obscure, for not conforming to the conventional manner of writing, and for not trying to improve. Although they praised at least some of the five dramatic monologues, they gave considerable attention to other poems that they disapproved of.

The critic for the *London Quarterly Review* recognized Browning as "a student of men, and a sketcher of character and costume." Early in the review he said that he was disposed to doubt the utility of "prelusive canons" in judging Browning's works, that defects and beauties were almost inseparable by the time of *Men and Women,* and that Browning must be accepted for what he was. Yet such an acceptance demanded more critical flexibility than the reviewer possessed. He was not altogether consistent in his attitude. In one place he complained of the hard work necessary for understanding Browning's poetry and in another assented to the needed expenditure of time and study. He commended Browning and acknowledged his originality with recognition of *Andrea* and *Blougram,* but he did not comprehend some aspects of the poetry which marked it as original. The hold of traditional standards on his mind is clearly shown in the following:

> The fact is, that Mr. Browning is too proud for anything. He disdains to take a little pains to put the reader at a similar advantage

with himself, — to give a preparatory statement which may help to make his subsequent effusion plain and logical. He scorns the good old style of beginning at the beginning. . . . leaves out (or out of sight) a link here and another there of that which forms the inevitable chain of truth, making a hint or a word supply its place. . . . He abandons himself to a train of vivid associations, and brings out some features of them with remarkable effect; but he gives you no clue whereby to follow him throughout.

The *London Quarterly Review* was impatient in its treatment of *Men and Women*, and *Fraser's* was quarrelsome in its more extended criticism. They strongly objected to Browning's obscurity and perversity. They both perceived that he was an original poet, but, in their disorderly and inconsistent discussions, they could not applaud his performance. According to George Brimley, the writer for *Fraser's*, Browning wandered pretty much at will "through God's and the Devil's world," and looked about him "with his own eyes, and not through the spectacles of school, or sect, or party." He had that "combination of curious and extended observation of mankind, with a subtile power of analysing motives and a vivid imagination, which is necessary for the great dramatist." His originality was defeated by lack of clarity. His art was as "awkward and rude and ineffective" as it ever was. He had not tried to improve his style; he was wilful and careless.

That Brimley was disconcerted by odd phrases, disregard of straightforward narrative sequence, unusual or imperfect rhymes, and abrupt transitions of thought is not surprising, for such uncommon aspects of poetry as these that the critics often faced in reading the poems of *Men and Women* were formidable ones. But the carping tone is hardly to be condoned. When we read of "insane kicking up of heels, meaningless braying, and sportive breaches of asinine manners, in the rich pasturemeadow of poetry," we can only say that such irritation often accompanied misunderstanding and confusion.

After singling out poems to demonstrate Browning's vices of style at their worst, Brimley named others which he exempted from his strong disapproval and to which he accorded a degree of praise — "compositions in which the exhibition of character is effected by a single discourse — soliloquy, conversation, or epistle." These included the five outstanding monologues of *Men and Women* and also *My Last Duchess* and *The Bishop Orders His Tomb* (both published earlier). In explaining why he thought that Browning's faults did not stand out so much in these poems, he called attention to the laxity of style "not unfitting the colloquial character of the subject," the discursiveness admissible in the framework of the poems, and the appropriateness of the blank verse to the "facility of execution which he [Browning] affects." He could see that the two volumes of *Men and Women* were a "treasury of beauty, and sense, and feeling" compared with "ninety-nine of a hundred volumes of contemporary poetry." Yet this praise lay buried in an overwhelming quantity of irritable faultfinding.

In its two pages of comments on character analysis, originality, and style, the shorter and less stringent review in the *Dublin University Magazine* exhibited the same pattern of criticism as that in the *London Quarterly Review* and *Fraser's*. The critic thought that Browning stood alone in "style, in mode of expression, in an abrupt careless strength of thought, in often times an acute analysis of supposed states of existence, and the action of the mind therein." He was impressed by three of the five dramatic monologues. He thought that Browning's originality did not always serve him well. There was needless obscurity and lack of finish. With a little trouble, Browning could observe the ordinary rules of art, and the critic wished that he would concern himself about his careless strength, which was his idiosyncrasy.

The remaining reviews in the second group — those in the *Spectator, Bentley's,* and the *Atlas* (a single review in two parts) — were distinguished from the others in this group only by being somewhat less severe in condemning what they considered Browning's faults. These critics also gave favorable attention to the dramatic monologues. They were ready to attack Browning's obscurity and consider the individual characteristics of his style as due to a lack of discipline. They vented their displeasure at having to work hard to understand the poems, though these three had more feeling than others in the second group that the effort was repaid in the end. What emerged, however, is brought out in the following paragraphs — that the reviewers realized they must not be so obsessed by what they considered faulty and so opinionated or impatient that their objections would overshadow the truly praiseworthy in *Men and Women.*

According to the *Spectator, Men and Women* contained "more genuine poetry than ninety-nine out of a hundred volumes pretending to that venerable title." The general characteristic of the collection was the quantity and high quality of thought — not abstract and scientific, but real thought, "embodied in persons and things, learnt from life or from living study of books," and Browning was most successful "in his character-poems — what may with some latitude of meaning be called dramatic sketches — conversation-pieces, fictitious epistles, and the like."

The reviewer for *Bentley's* thought that Browning should be exalted for his gifts and not judged by his faults. "Nobly endowed is Robert Browning with gifts superior not only in degree but in kind to more than two or three, among contemporary poets, who are read and applauded to the echo by thousands, where he is read and musingly beloved by tens." The gifts included "subtle intellect, deep searchings of heart, shrewd experience, genial spirits, aesthetic culture, lyrical expression." The critic said that the reader would be repaid for "time-taking perusal" of *Cleon* and suggested that he would be rewarded for time expended on other poems.

The reviewer for the *Atlas* felt that after hostile criticism had done its worst there were pieces in *Men and Women* that the higher class of readers would be thankful to receive. Browning, "for depth of meaning, range of illustration, and psychological anatomy," stood unrivalled among modern poets. "To enter into delicate and subtle thoughts, to paint character and depict passion exhibited and acting under extraordinary circumstances, is Browning's prerogative. . . ." The critic said that at first sight much was unintelligible and much seemed trivial in the poems; "but they are well worth the pains to understand, and contain matter which no living writer could have produced or rivalled in its peculiar way."

The critics for *Bentley's,* the *Spectator,* and the *Atlas* (of the second group) saw Browning as a poet of unusual gifts; among his distinguishing characteristics they admired his intellectual cast and his human quality. Although they expressed but little disapproval of the poems which they singled out for discussion and although they felt that the poetry was superior in spite of its faults, like the others in this and the first group they were incapable of sympathetic response to much in Browning that did not conform to traditional techniques of poetic composition.

The third and last group to be discussed contained the most promising reviews. It included those in the *Examiner, Leader* (a single review in successive issues), *New Quarterly Review* (running from 1852 to 1862, not to be confused with the *New Quarterly* of the forties), *British Quarterly Review, Westminster, Oxford and Cambridge Magazine, Christian Remembrancer* (Oct. 1857, a second review of *Men and Women* in the same periodical), *Rambler,* and *Jersey Independent.*[28] (From the time of *Men and Women* separate reviews of a certain work occasionally appeared in the same periodical. In such a case the date of the review being mentioned or discussed is shown in parenthesis.) On the whole, in this group nontraditional poetic techniques were sympathetically examined and aspects of Browning's poetry were to some extent related to each other. Involved in his dramatic method were the peculiarities of rhythm and diction, which if not understood at least did not blind the critics to Browning's genius. The reviewers saw that his wide range of observation supplied a rich source of character investigation and that his dramatic genius provided the successful medium for such investigation. The qualities that critics had in the past praised in isolation, the critics in this group recognized in Browning's manner of presenting characters in the poems in *Men and Women*. In order to inform their readers of Browning's varied contribution, they tended to discuss a considerable number of poems, including *Cleon, Karshish, Andrea, Lippo,* and *Blougram,* all of which they commended highly.

The critics of this third group considered Browning's unorthodox technique with open minds. The position they assumed helped to place his reputation on its proper basis. Browning's originality turned readers away, they said, and his obscurity was especially troublesome; but objections had often been too severe. They pointed out that although the difficulty was sometimes caused by a manner warranting criticism, it often arose from the high quality of Browning's thought and the poetry was worth the effort expended to understand it. Like a few critics of the later forties, they took seriously the function of the critic as a middleman: to explain the characteristics that made the poetry difficult and to show the qualities that rewarded the reader for his pains. The *Christian Remembrancer* expressed the guideline that others followed. According to the critic, giving an account of the poems unfamiliar to readers and an opinion of their value might prove useful to many "if they are thereby led to the study of an unduly neglected bard, and find the path to the comprehension of his difficulties in any degree smoothed and facilitated." In their tractable and sympathetic critical approach the critics did not insist, as others had insisted, that Browning did not not trouble himself to help his readers.

Specific statements that these critics made about obscurity show how much they were trying to put down the ogre that had caused much harm. Forster, the critic for the *Examiner,* said he quoted at length "to establish beyond dispute" that the volumes were not exclusively obscure and mystical. There were, he admitted, too many pieces that did have obscurity in the meaning and "perverse harshness" in the meter. He did not wish to defend indisputable faults but to explain why they disfigured the work of a true genius. He felt there was danger in carrying the strictures too far. The obscurity came from a full mind; it was inseparable from a cast of thought imparting its pervading excellence and flavor. More precisely, Forster explained that among the chief causes of Browning's obscurity were a distinctive quaintness, a concentration of expression, and dramatic verse effects. But he reminded the readers of the *Examiner* that these were part of Browning's individuality and it was by virtue of his individuality that he would live.

The *Leader* explained that it was Browning's originality that kept him from being popular. There were unfamiliar accents and an abrupt and needlessly obscure manner. The critic did not wish to dwell on the topic of obscurity. It was enough, he said, to indicate the difficulty in passing and warn the reader not to be impatient but give time and thought to the pages in hand, for the poetry that distressed him was not without value. The critic's laudatory remarks and the long quotations demonstrated its high quality. George Eliot, in the *Westminster*, said that much of the obscurity in Browning was a "majestic obscurity," which repelled the ignorant and the idle. The reader would find no conventionality, no melodious commonplace; he must exert himself to understand the elliptical and pithy verse, but grasping the meaning was always worth the effort. She gave less attention to another kind of obscurity, a whimsical mannerism, which she found objectionable and sometimes even irritating.

David Masson, the critic for the *British Quarterly Review,* acknowledged that critics as well as other readers would find much of *Men and Women* obscure because of the content and the style, and gave specific reasons for the difficulties. He found that for himself the final judgment was still "immensely more on the side of admiration than on that of dissatisfaction or criticism." In the *Rambler,* Richard Simpson, emphasizing that Browning wrote for the few, asked whether we can say that obscurity and true poetry are incompatible. "If the poet is to be allowed to write on obscure subjects, he must be allowed to write obscurely; if he is to state the enigma of life, we must be content to let an enigma remain an enigma."

The *Christian Remembrancer* thought that Browning might be very recklessly accused of being obscure. The critic conceded that the accusation was just in some instances but went on to say, ". . . it is only fair to admit, in *his* case, palliations which are freely accepted for poets of past time." He named other poets who were excused for obscurity

and claimed the same privilege for Browning. William Morris, in the
Oxford and Cambridge Magazine, wrote a spirited defense of Browning
on this score. That there was some obscurity in Browning's verse he
did not deny, but he asserted "fearlessly" that seldom was it so prominent as to be damaging. What was called obscurity was difficulty, and
it resulted "from depth of thought, and greatness of subject, on the
poet's part, and on his readers' part, from their shallower brains and
more bounded knowledge" and also from their idleness. James Thomson, in the *Jersey Independent,* wrote of *Men and Women* "that no person
of fair intelligence and enough love of poetry to be willing to expend
study on it, will be baffled in this work by obscurity."

Though they had open minds, the critics of the third group were
not able to get very far beyond their times in understanding Browning's accomplishment in creating new effects in his verse. His ability
to harness speech into poetic rhythm in order to achieve the desired
impression of the monologuist produced undeniably daring lines for
that day. This in addition to the choice of diction to accord with the
speaker's character resulted in an unorthodox poetic line that caused
uneasiness in even the sympathetic critics of this group.

In the *Westminster* George Eliot said that the greatest deficiency in
Browning's verse was its lack of music. This criticism was applicable
primarily to the dramatic lyrics. As for Browning's blank-verse poems,
she said, ". . . it is remarkable that in his blank verse, though it is
often colloquial, we are never shocked by the sense of a sudden lapse
into prose." Other critics of the third group took no strong stand on
the poetical quality of the verse except in their discussions of the lyrics.
In fact, there was a playing down of what had so often been objected
to. These critics, like those who came after the early derogatory ones of
Christmas-Eve and Easter-Day, were foreshadowing the lessening concern in the sixties for the technique of Browning's verse.

Masson, in the *British Quarterly Review,* devoted more space to
Browning's technique than the other reviewers in group three. Although he defended Browning against other objections to his poetry,
he said he was not able to support his "mechanical execution." He did
offer some explanation.

> It may be, indeed, that he has framed for himself higher and more
> complex notions of literary harmony than those by which simple
> folks judge. What seems rough discord to the common reader may
> be to him but a phrase of richer music. What is called harshness,
> crabbedness, or even coarseness in his words and allusions, may seem

to him only the assertion of healthy, manly taste, against a feeble
and insipid conventionalism.

After this independent but cautious advance, the critic retreated to a
safer position: "We do not think that it is quite so, however." And he
referred to others who saw Browning's imperfections as an artist. Yet
he was not satisfied to dismiss the topic negatively. "To us it seems
that his art is more perfect the nearer he keeps to blank verse, and the
other kinds of verse suited to narration, description, and exposition,
and the less he ventures on purely lyrical measures, except for a bold or
grand occasional purpose." This critic, like George Eliot (and also
Brimley of the second group), appreciated Browning's blank verse,
which was limited almost entirely to the five major dramatic monologues.

Masson's remarks indicated how sympathetic critics of *Men and
Women* could struggle with the problem of Browning's poetic line. He
and Simpson of the *Rambler* both thought that Browning's verse deserved serious consideration. Simpson suggested, "The application of
the rules of musical rhythm will often solve the problem of an apparently halting verse." This seems like a promising approach to his discussion of the verse of *Men and Women,* but Simpson actually made little headway beyond having a feeling for Browning's metrical dexterity.
Some of the reviewers seemed to realize that conventional standards
were inapplicable to Browning's rhythm. George Eliot, in thinking of
other poetry and formulating her ideas of Browning's distinctive line,
said that he seemed "by his commanding powers to compel language
into verse."

Morris, in the *Oxford and Cambridge Magazine,* gave no evidence of
having had trouble with or lacking appreciation of Browning's lines;
he praised the rhythm of particular poems. His participation in readings of various writers that he and his friends held, writers that first included Tennyson and then Browning, might have served as his guide.
Reading aloud was important. That Browning dictated his *Men and
Women* for his final copy instead of having someone make a fair copy
from his script indicates that he was checking the poems by hearing
the lines. He also read the poems aloud to Fox before they were published. In reading poetry, we are told, he approximated a natural style
of speaking.[29]

Masson thought it strange that Browning, though a musician,
wrote unmusically. Critics did not see that Browning's keen ear
prompted him to shape the variety of speech into a rhythmic pattern,

to go to the limit of flexing the rhythm but not beyond in order to make the speech suitable to the character. When critics said that Browning's poetry lacked music, they did not take into consideration his understanding of the technique of music as it could be applied to the writing of poetry. He — not the critics — knew what he was doing in avoiding what he called "sing-song." An American published an article called "Browning and Music" and sent him a copy. Browning's reply indicated his appreciation, included an account of his musical studies, and closed with an illuminating comment: "All this will show that I have given much attention to music *proper* — I believe to the detriment of what people take for 'music' in poetry, when I had to consider that quality. For the first effect of apprehending real musicality was to make me abjure the sing-song which, in my early days, was taken for it."[30]

Forster, who in the *Examiner* had repeatedly observed that Browning's choice of rhythm was in keeping with the thought, now referred to the "inborn dramatic feeling which is often apt to suggest breaks of phrase, and making interruptions to a train of thought." The observation that Browning's line was appropriate to his poetic intention had been made in the past by a few critics besides Forster (usually those who had examined his work more than once) and it would be made again in the following decade.

It is obvious in their discussions of individual poems that the critics recognized Browning's skill in using a variety of language, but they did not give much specific attention to the character of his diction. The *Rambler*, seeing his "facility of expression," wrote of *Old Pictures in Florence* as "outrageously dishevelled in rhyme and language" and of the "beautifully descriptive" words in *Love Among the Ruins*. When there was objection to the diction it was not harsh. The *Westminster* thought there was "sometimes eccentricity of expression," and the *British Quarterly Review* asserted that a very sensitive person would find instances throughout the poetry of "slovenly and untasteful expressions." The *Christian Remembrancer* felt that Browning was "not so consummate an artist" as Tennyson, and continued, "But then it must be said, that the apparently rough and unconventional phrase of the poet before us, has constantly a force and point peculiarly its own." In its discussion of Browning's works as a whole, the *Remembrancer* spoke of his language as "terse, vigorous, flowing, and almost always admirably *en rapport* with his subject."

The reviewers of the third group indicated a reticence to criticize Browning's monologues for faults of syntax, rhythm, and diction. They had a feeling for his poetic manner, but they could not praise it by ordinary critical standards, which some realized were inapplicable. They were most outspoken in their attitude toward the lyrics, in which they expected the smooth and melodic verse of traditional poetry.

If there was little comment in the reviews on correlation of verse with the particular effect Browning wished to give, more of the third-group critics in their awareness of his keen observation of character commented on the dramatic quality of his poetry and his dramatic method. Forster began his review in the *Examiner* by saying that the dramatic character of Browning's genius, familiar to his readers, was displayed in the poems of *Men and Women.* Others agreed with him. Simpson commented in the *Rambler* that the poems seemed "meritorious in direct ratio to their dramatic form or intention." George Eliot gave praise to what she called the "dramatic-psychological." She wrote in the *Westminster:* "His keen glance pierces into all the secrets of human character, but, being as thoroughly alive to the outward as to the inward, he reveals those secrets, not by a process of dissection, but by dramatic painting."

The reviewers were interested in Browning's dramatic method. In speaking of his abilities as a poet, the critic for the *Leader* found in *Men and Women* "the same dramatic power of going out of himself, and speaking through his characters." The *British Quarterly Review* observed, "In the art of character painting, . . . in the power of throwing himself into states of mind and trains of circumstance the most alien from our present habits, in the intuitive faculty of reconceiving the most peculiar and obsolete modes of thinking, he ranks as a master." Browning could deal not only with "aliens" but also with ordinary people, said the *New Quarterly Review:* he needed only ordinary circumstances and the feelings of ordinary people to allow his genius to throw itself into innumerable conditions of human existence with "an almost Protean power of reproduction." Simpson, in the Catholic *Rambler,* saw a danger in Browning's power to project himself into a wide variety of characters, the bad as well as the good. "Mr. Browning has such a perilous facility of putting himself into the place of the most horrible men, of uttering their thoughts and expressing their feelings, that a religious person reading his works runs great risk of being shocked at each page."

In evaluating Browning's dramatic achievement, the critics called attention to his power, originality, and intellect — qualities that had been repeatedly recognized in isolation. At the beginning of his criticism in the British Quarterly Review, Masson attributed these qualities to Browning — and others that would contribute to the making of an ideal poet.

> That, among the English authors of our day, very few, indeed, could be compared with Mr. Browning for power and originality of mind, has long been the settled opinion of all acquainted with his writings, and capable of judging of them. To an intellect of extraordinary natural force and subtlety, it was plain that he added many of those other qualifications not always combined with this, which help to make an author distinguished, and to give body and character to his works — a large store of acquired ideas, the results of his previous thinking on a variety of subjects; no mean amount of learning in tracks not commonly explored, even by scholars; keen powers of observation, wit, and sarcasm, and a shrewd acquaintance with the world and its ways. . . .

The critics in the third group not only praised Browning's power, originality, and intellect but to an appreciable extent they saw the relationship of them to each other and to his dramatic presentation and the technique of his verse.

Looking back, we can see how the degree of open-mindedness to the individuality of Browning's technique influenced the three groups of critics in their reception of his portrayal of character. Those of the first group were completely blinded by the untraditional in his poetry. Those of the second recognized Browning's superiority in character presentation, but their inability to readjust their conventional ideas of style muddled their evaluation. The critics in the third group moved a step forward. They saw that harangues on obscurity blocked out appreciation of Browning's genius. They had a feeling for the relationship of various aspects of his poetry. Since they were not truculent and did not allow their minds to drag in traditional grooves, their reviews were unmarred by the impatient rejection of the first group of critics and the confusion of the second group. The result was a receptivity that enabled them, in comparison with the first two groups, to achieve a fuller appreciation of Cleon, Karshish, Andrea, Lippo, and Blougram.

With the exception of the open-mindedness of critics in the third group, the prospect for acceptance of the technical aspects of Browning's poems is not at first sight promising. But in the inconsistency in the reviews of group two lay an encouraging note. The simultaneous querulous objections to Browning's technique and the acceptance, even praise, of poems created by that technique seemed to grow out of a confused groping toward understanding rather than a mind set on total rejection. It would take time to cope with the problems presented by the poems in *Men and Women*. As we shall see in the following chapter, the critics' attitude toward the content of *Men and Women*, which they often treated separately from technique, showed definite signs of change for the better.

CHAPTER XVIII

Limited Recognition

Men and Women, 1855: Values and Substance

Besides assuming certain positions with regard to Browning's style and the literary worth of five outstanding monologues in *Men and Women,* the reviewers paid a great deal of attention to Browning's subject matter in the two volumes of poems. The spiritual significance of Browning's poetry that was stressed after the publication of *Christmas-Eve and Easter-Day* continued to appeal to critics. That they had made progress in their attitude toward his presentation of a broad range of human nature and of remote areas of knowledge shows up in their general comments and in their approbation of individual poems in *Men and Women,* though they still had trouble when what was less familiar obstructed their understanding. The poetry attracted some critics because they saw in it a reflection of the time and some because they recognized Browning's voice in certain poems. His standing with his critics comes out indirectly in the censure that some of them made of others for harsh treatment of him.

One line of criticism, scarcely referred to in the preceding chapter, was being brought into the discussion of the poems in *Men and Women* — their spiritual value and the related moral value. This aspect of the criticism, which had become noticeable in connection with *A Blot,* was eventually to have such a powerful influence on Browning's reputation that a few words are needed by way of recapitulation and introduction to the present chapter.

The Victorian code of morality and respectability in conduct and thought was generally accepted by professional critics. Many observed it either because of personal conviction or because of editorial policy that took its cue from public opinion, though some judged literature without deference to a straitlaced standard. In a time when bowdlerized texts were frequently used and when Thackeray, editor of the *Cornhill,* rejected (though reluctantly) a poem of Elizabeth's because it would offend readers of his magazine,[1] reviewers of literary works often played the role of guardian. They did not always succeed. Sometimes poetry attracted readers though it did not conform to Victorian standards of propriety. Although Elizabeth's *Aurora Leigh* with its liberal treatment of the behavior of Victorian women (in showing problems they faced) was denounced by leading periodicals, it went into its second edition two weeks after publication and into its fifth four years later.[2] Its popularity was to some degree due to its timeliness. That critics were not always inhibited by the moral sanctions of the age in judging literature had been evident in their appreciation of Browning's fine passage from *Pippa Passes* beginning "Buried in woods we lay." It was offensive to a few critics during the forties, but more often the first lines were quoted and praised.

The most concentrated objections to the immoral in Browning's poetry had appeared in the reviews of *A Blot* when it was published in 1843. A dual strain of criticism showed up strongly in the reviews of *Dramatic Romances and Lyrics* (1845), in which there were poems to censure and poems to praise. This double strain continued in the reviews of the collected edition (1849), when religious periodicals were beginning to take an interest in the moral and religious aspect of Browning's poetry. After most of the weeklies had severely criticized *Christmas-Eve and Easter-Day* (1850), centering their attention mainly on its style, periodicals representing different denominations showed their approval of an intellectual poet who examined what was of serious concern to his contemporaries. They were shifting the interest to Browning as a religious poet. More and more *Christmas-Eve and Easter-Day* persuaded critics, including ones that were not writing for denominational periodicals, that the spiritual quality of Browning's poetry was to be taken seriously. The pointed treatment of religion in *Christmas-Eve and Easter-Day,* the spiritual concerns of the time, a consideration of Browning's latest work along with a reconsideration of the earlier ones — these contributed to the change taking place in the perspective of the critics.

By the time of *Men and Women* the critics were in a better position to deal with Browning's subject matter. When objections to the content of *Men and Women* were raised, they were usually moderate. The exception was the denunciatory review in the Anglican *Guardian;* the critic was disturbed because Browning, like Fra Lippo Lippi, could not get "the value and significance of flesh" out of his mind and because Browning's philosophy left an impression that "God and man, faith and virtue" were delusions "used by knaves to compass their selfish ends." Two reviews with somewhat contradictory opinions fell in between the *Guardian's* negative attitude and the eulogistic attitude that was becoming more frequent. The critic for the *Dublin University Magazine* objected to the gross irreverence of *The Heretic's Tragedy;* he quoted with approval eighteen lines in *Fra Lippo Lippi* asserting the inseparability of the spiritual and the material in painting. *Fraser's* approved of Browning's strength in exhibiting the intellectual and moral characteristics of a man or an age but found fault with him for not solving moral problems that "a wide experience of men presents to him." Richard Simpson's criticism of Browning in the *Rambler* was a strange mixture of approval and disapproval. As a liberal Catholic, to some degree he extended his liberalism to his criticism. His adverse criticism of Browning on the score of religion was qualified by praise of the poet's dramatic genius and his serious thought. Simpson disapproved of Protestant notions that he found in the poetry, but he saw a great deal that appealed to him. "When one sees how much Mr. Browning must have thought and reflected, and how near he comes to Christianity, one wonders why he has stopped, why he is not a Catholic."

Others anticipated the attitude of the sixties. One of Browning's gifts, according to *Bentley's,* was "a lofty moral earnestness, . . . a pervading religious tone, jarred only, not drowned, by mocking-bird discords and 'accidental sharps' (exceptions by which some would triumphantly prove the rule)." Several reviews were in agreement. There was often the "purest spiritual feeling" in the poems, said the *Examiner;* the Nonconformist *British Quarterly Review* referred to "a certain rigid determination of his genius towards the noble and elevated." In the *Jersey Independent* the disbeliever James Thomson pointed out Browning's "profound unsectarian Christianity" as one of the "leading characteristics" of the praiseworthy *Men and Women.* The *New Quarterly Review* foreshadowed the realization of the sixties that Browning was able to show the spiritual in depicting a broad range of humanity.

The most remarkable characteristic of the present work is that, with an indomitable and unbaffled instinct for the spiritual beneath its manifold material disguises, it reveals to the thoughtful reader how much of the immutable, the holy, and the awful hourly escapes our common observation in the trivial emotions and passing impulses — the wandering lights and shadows of the soul — that chequer and agitate our daily life.

The best way to see what was happening is to note the change of attitude toward Browning's thought in denominational periodicals. The *English Review* (High Church), *Eclectic Review* (Nonconformist), and *Christian Remembrancer* (High Church) carried several criticisms of Browning's works. In every one of these an indeterminate or disapproving opinion recorded in the mid-forties was eventually superseded by one of approval. The reviews of 1846, 1851, 1856, and 1857 in the *Christian Remembrancer* exemplify the change taking place. It expressed strong disapproval of Browning in the first three and shifted opinion in the last. In 1846 the reviewer thought that *Dramatic Romances and Lyrics* could not be read freely and without reserve. In the reviews of 1851 (of the collected edition of 1849 and *Christmas-Eve and Easter-Day*) and 1856 (of *Men and Women*) the critic attacked Browning for the low quality of his tastes, morals, and religion. Even his feminine characters did not escape censure in 1851. "His women are forward, and often immodest; qualities, however, which very little affect their admirers, who are enchained solely by personal charms: 'great eyes,' 'smooth white faces,' 'coiled hair.' " Such forwardness had no place in the make-up of the standardized Victorian ideal of woman. "Nothing can be less intelligent than their love; no reserves are kept up, and the ladies generally make the first advances."

According to remarks on *Men and Women* in the review of April 1856, our nature has high instincts and aspirations as well as low propensities, but Browning found the only interesting part of humanity to be its "fallen earthly elements," which he fastened upon and gloated over. Much of the review was a tirade against the unwholesomeness and immorality of the poetry. The critic left no doubt about his opinion.

The subjects are various, but the mode of treating them tolerably uniform — themes of small interest, acted on by men and women of low ideas, and resulting in some grovelling end. A sort of chemical process may be observed throughout, by which the dregs of each feeling and passion remain, the purer emotions having vanished we know not whither. His pictures of love are coarse passion, or at best a subjugation of conscience and reason to passion; his idea of beauty is sensual, his religion bigotry or hypocrisy, his patriotism selfishness, his philosophy scepticism.

Eighteen months later, in October 1857, the *Christian Remembrancer* carried a second article headed *Men and Women;* in this one *Christmas-Eve and Easter-Day* and the collected edition were also discussed (as in the review of 1851). The conclusion in 1857 was that Browning was a religious teacher in spite of "somewhat too much of self-reliance, too much of making every one his own instructor and priest" and "an occasional coarseness of thought and expression (never, however, uttered in the author's own person, but meant to be in character for a Lippo Lippi and the like)." There was a noticeable change of opinion from that expressed in 1856. Whereas the 1856 review had discerned in Browning a "doubt as to our future destiny and an uncertainty as to any eternal consequences accruing to men from their actions," the 1857 review discovered in Browning a quite different attitude to life after death. "In no other secular poetry of our day do we perceive so full a recognition of another life." And "we know not of any poetry (not professedly sacred) wherein is so deeply pondered and strikingly proclaimed the mystery of the holy Incarnation."

The impression of Browning that *Christmas-Eve and Easter-Day* left upon J. G. Cazenova, the critic of 1857, marks the change of opinion. To the critic of 1851 the writer of the poem portrayed himself as one who "would willingly strengthen his faith," but he had a mind "incapable of spiritual elevation." Browning was severely taken to task because he was "without reverence, without ready sympathy for the unseen," who ill discriminated between the pure and the base, and who confessed himself more than others to be tied down to earth and incapable of looking beyond it. In the 1857 review Browning was designated as a "religious poet," so revealed by the "remarkable" *Christmas-Eve and Easter-Day.* There was no more talk of Browning's depiction of undesirable passions nor of his incapability of strengthening his faith.

Before the fifties critics had observed Browning's morality or immorality, spirituality or irreverence, high aim or wantonness. As the fifties advanced, approval increasingly overshadowed complaint; the critics for both religious and secular periodicals became aware of his spiritual intention in the dramatic revelation of character.

The critics were undergoing change not only from their earlier feeling against what had been considered a lack of spiritual and moral values but also from their objection to the unusual in human nature or to whatever else they considered unfit subject matter for poetry. In their exposure to Browning's broad range of observation and knowledge with much that was alien to conventional poetry, the critics had not found the process of adjusting their opinions easy, but they were making headway.

The *Athenaeum* could not understand why Browning used his poetic ability to advance the "pleadings of a casuist, or the arguments of a critic, or the ponderous discoursings of some obsolete schoolman." The *Christian Remembrancer's* survey (1857) of all of Browning's poetry, which appeared under the heading of *Men and Women,* did not allow much space to the poetry of these two latest volumes. In his general remarks, the critic said of Browning, ". . . he is fond, perhaps almost too fond, of exhibiting the weaknesses, inconsistencies, and meannesses of human nature." But the critic wrote favorably of works with such content. The fact that he, like others, praised specific poems with subject matter pronounced objectionable elsewhere in the review was an indication that resistance to Browning's choice of the unusual was breaking down.

Simpson of the Catholic *Rambler* thought Browning's poetry included more of human nature than was conventionally allowed: ". . . he makes no bones of uttering from the housetops that which the decent conventionality of society generally agrees to cover and to forget." Simpson, who did not think that Browning's unlimited use of human nature was acceptable to all, indicated his own approval of what could be classed as unconventional. "He expresses things, of which those who are ignorant had better remain so, but which those who know of them will be glad to find so well expressed, so well prepared for dissection and study." Elsewhere in the review Simpson gave approval to the conception of a poet as a "representer" of the realities of life and of human character and thought, and he classified Browning as such a poet. He leaned considerably more to the side of praise than blame.

As we have seen, *Fraser's* condemned Browning extensively, but the critic, who complained because Browning did not solve moral problems, did not indicate aversion to his unlimited use of human nature in presenting these problems.

He shrinks from no facts, does not pick his path with delicate step along the world's highway, fearful of dirtying his feet, is startled at nothing, peers with scrutinising glance into byeways, alleys, and noisome dens, and what he sees he can record, not with the cold natural-history voice of a speculator, but the living tones of a man who enters into the human and passionate element in all the varied world of suffering and enjoyment, of virtue and of crime, of good and evil.

Several reviewers gave passing recognition to the psychological in Browning's poetry — those for *Bentley's*, the *Dublin University Magazine*, and the *Atlas* — without approbation or censure. George Eliot, in the *Westminster*, indicated her approval.

Browning's drawing upon material from foreign countries, especially Italy, instead of England and from the remote past had elicited condemnation earlier. Now the critic for the *Irish Quarterly Review*, in his harsh and irritable treatment, attacked Browning's choice of subjects.

> Besides these sad facts, the subjects of the poems themselves are the most tasteless, and the most unmeaning it is possible to conceive: the Author would appear to have sedulously searched the most dusty shelves of the most antiquated book cases; to have taken therefrom the most musty tomes, and like a veritable bookworm of the Dominie Sampson school, to have selected the most trifling quips and quiddities of the schoolmen for public parade, and as fit stalking horses, for his ponderous and drowsy amplification.

This attitude was becoming rare. David Masson in the *British Quarterly Review* defended Browning's choice of "side-regions of technical art or knowledge" and "foreign garb for his thoughts"; he did not see why a poet need present his thoughts "in a plain tissue of British associations." Although Masson referred to other critics who had objected to foreign topics and out-of-the-way history, in the reviews of *Men and Women* there was little objection. The *Irish Quarterly Review* condemned the use of remote history. The *Christian Remembrancer* (1856) criticized Browning for preferring Italy to his native land. When the same quarterly said in 1857 that Browning was too fond of showing the bad side of human nature in his poetry, he added, ". . . thus Italy comes in for her share of blame." The *London Quarterly Review* recognized, without praise or blame, his drawing upon Italy. Two of the critics who wrote generally unfavorable reviews of *Men and Women* — those for the *Literary Gazette* and the *Guardian* — went so far as to rank the poems taken from Italian life above others.

In their approval of some poems and disapproval of others, the critics revealed the extent of their progress in evaluating Browning's poetry. Preference for certain poems indicated that they were in some respects shifting their attitude toward Browning's subject matter and in others holding on to the familiar. *Fra Lippo Lippi* and *Andrea del Sarto* were among the poems that received the most favorable attention; others were *Cleon, Karshish,* and *Bishop Blougram's Apology*. *Andrea* and *Lippo* placed high because the critics appreciated Browning's knowledge of art and even more his ability in characterization. He was not taken to task because the artists belonged to the Italian Renaissance. The meditations of an Arab physician and of a Greek philosopher of the first century, respectively in *Karshish* and *Cleon,* were not objectionable to the reviewers. They indicated their approval of Browning's concern with the problems of faith and doubt, of his intellectual and religious speculation, and of his portrayal of the state of feeling of each of the characters in these two poems.

Bishop Blougram's Apology attracted more favorable attention than any other poem in the two volumes; even the captious critic for the *Saturday Review* considered it and *Cleon* "well worth reading and thinking over." Reviewers were attracted to *Blougram* for several reasons. Browning was dealing with the timely problem of belief and unbelief and Victorians were searching for answers in an unsettled spiritual world. A prominent churchman of the time served as model for the speaker. Although the critics saw Bishop Blougram in different lights, most of them were impressed by the subtlety and force of the argument. They had no trouble with the blank verse. It has been shown that even in the generally negative reviews in the first group (in the preceding chapter) *Blougram* received brief attention by three critics and *Cleon, Andrea,* and *Lippo* each was accepted by one critic.

Other poems appealed to the critics because the reading was facilitated by familiarity in some way and by reduced requirement of mental strain. *In a Balcony* was one of the most frequently discussed, and the criticism was generally favorable. Accustomed by now to seeing Browning's plays as closet drama, with few exceptions the critics made no comment on its not conforming to stage drama. The two remaining popular poems were *One Word More* and *The Statue and the Bust. One Word More,* which dedicated *Men and Women* to Elizabeth Barrett Browning, was pleasing in its sentiment. The narrative of *The Statue and the Bust,* written in terza rima, moved quickly and clearly, and, as two reviewers said, with grace. In fact, the critics were so pleased with the ease of reading it that only a few saw the poem as objectionable from a moral standpoint.

The difficulties of the critics were apparent in their marked objection to poems with subject matter requiring a technical knowledge of music. A number of critics at least attempted to read *A Toccata of Galuppi's* and *Master Hugues of Saxe-Gotha*, but these poems were formidable and frustrating to those who lacked a knowledge of thirds, dominants, sixths, and sevenths and of the construction of a fugue. In writing of *A Toccata*, the *London Quarterly Review* said the very title was enough "to frighten or perplex the untravelled reader." Even the sympathetic and flexible *New Quarterly Review* had difficulty; the titles of the poems misled the reviewer into thinking that they were "as far removed as can be from all '*human*' interest, or the emotions of real life." Critics of *Men and Women* who welcomed Browning's poetic utterances on religion failed to understand his use of the fugue-figure in *Master Hugues:* the complexities of the movements of the voices of the fugue, an intellectualized musical form, like the spider web covering the "gilt moulding and groining" of the church in which the organist is playing, represent "man's usurpature" (by means of "comments and glozes," "traditions, inventions"), under which truth and nature, "God's gold," are palled.

Another stumbling block was the grotesque. Some critics were still having difficulty in getting accustomed to Browning's use of it for serious purposes. Besides objecting to the grotesque in rhymes and diction here and there in the poetry, the critics who did not silently pass over two poems with grotesque substance — *Holy-Cross Day* and *The Heretic's Tragedy* — were reluctant to praise them or did so only with caution. The strength of this particular form of art in *Holy-Cross Day* did not go unnoticed by the *British Quarterly Review*. A not wholly uncomplimentary comment was made by Simpson in the *Rambler*.

> Here [in *Holy-Cross Day*] is a real Hogarth-like picture of the frowzy saturnalia of the votaries of the nauseous mythological triad, Old Clo', Cloaca, and Cloacina. . . . In fact, abundant evidence might be produced that in one phase at least of his character our poet is, so to say, a Saxon swine. But this phase of his powers may only serve to enhance other sides of his character. . . . And it may be that the poet gives evidence of other faculties besides mere power, when he can wave one hand in the pure regions of the ether above the mountaintops, and with the other grub for offal among the mud of a duckpond. . . .

Simpson claimed for Browning the same privilege that we accord Shakespeare.

Who blames Shakespeare for Falstaff? and why refuse to acknowledge Robert Browning's right to disport himself in the same re-
gions? If the style of [the] thing was wrong, by all means condemn
it in Shakespeare, and in better men than he; but if it is only contrary to present etiquette, it is mere conventionalism and dandifica-
tion to turn up your nose at it.

A number of critics, including the more perceptive ones, thought
that Browning's lyrics were inferior to his dramatic poems, and they
explained why. After Masson said in the *British Quarterly Review* that he
did not think Browning's lyrics as good as the other poems, he gave his
explanation: Browning's intellect mitigated against lyricism.

He does not seem at home in such brief and purely lyrical effusions,
requiring, as they do, an instant gush of feeling, a cessation for the
time of all merely intellectual activity, and a clear and flowing tune
. . . . In his case, the head is constantly intruding its suggestions
where the heart alone should be speaking; we have strokes of the
hard imagination where we expect nothing but unconscious melody
and cadence; and hence a roughness and constraint incompatible
with the simple beauty and warmth of the lyric.

The critics thought that Browning's intellectual vigor was not suitable
to the lyric, in which they wanted a refinement of form without the
pronounced exercise of thought. The critic for *Fraser's* said that we ask
for no more than the vigor of a sketch in Browning's character pieces;
we get that, but in his lyrics we do not get the necessary perfection of
form. Simpson wrote in the *Rambler* that Browning's lyric power was
far inferior to his dramatic vigor; he said that Browning was too energetic to produce perfectly pleasing images. According to the *Spectator*,
looseness of execution did not jar so much in the character poems as in
the lyrics, which were less effective in freshness and range of thought.

George Eliot, in the *Westminster*, said that in the lyric, "where he
[Browning] engrosses us less by his thought, we are more sensible of
his obscurity and his want of melody." For her the lyrics "seem to be
struggling painfully under a burthen too heavy for them; and many of
them have the disagreeable puzzling effect of a charade, rather than the
touching or animating influence of song." The critics did not see with
Browning that "lyrics may be dramatic also in the highest sense."[3]
They showed that they had advanced in their appreciation of Browning's individuality in the dramatic monologue, but they did not approve of the lyrics in which he also used a style to suit his subject. A

few critics — including those for the *Athenaeum, Oxford and Cambridge Magazine,* and *Examiner* — commented favorably on specific lyrics.

When critics were on unfamiliar territory they frequently stumbled. When, however, subject matter they did not associate with poetry was presented in the light of their own time, they felt more secure. In the fifties they were beginning to relate Browning's poetry to concerns which they themselves considered important. Some critics pointed out that Browning was a poet sensitive to the intellectual and spiritual problems of his own day. *Christmas-Eve and Easter-Day* had indicated this line of development, and *Men and Women* contained a number of poems relevant to contemporary thought. At a time when materialism and advances in science were causing consternation, the *Christian Remembrancer* (1857) called attention to their effect on Browning as well as on other poets. "The work-day tendencies of our own age, and the rapid strides of physical science, are, not unnaturally, thought to have led by reaction to the poetry of mysticism; among whose votaries may be named Wordsworth, the present laureate, and Robert Browning." Later in the review the critic said that Browning's voice and lot were "with the central dogma of the Christian faith against the vague pantheistic dreamings of the day." The *Examiner* saw in *Men and Women* "touches in abundance" that indicated Browning's freedom from materialistic teaching.

Masson, writing for the *British Quarterly Review,* was aware of the appeal of certain timely poems in *Men and Women,* though he thought that this appeal was felt by the few rather than the many.

> In not a few of the finest poems, as may have been seen, such as *Transcendentalism, Bishop Blougram's Apology,* and others in the semi-expository vein — the thought is of a kind so high and subtle, so inwound with the topics of the deeper philosophy and metaphysics of the time, that, though perfectly intelligible to those who are already competent in such matters, it can have no interest for the many who like only what may be called nice fire-side poetry. . . .

A great body of readers did prefer light literature, but scientific and historical studies were changing the reading and thinking habits of others, who were often ready to turn from the shallowness of fireside poetry to a higher level of thought. In the *Jersey Independent* James Thomson wrote of the value that Browning's poetry had "in upholding the sway of Christianity over the minds of young and thoughtful persons who turn with contempt from the abounding trash of tracts, and find most clergymen's books vitiated by the special pleading of hired advocates, and scarcely meet with a minister liberal and wise enough to command their intellectual esteem, and know that modern erudition has beaten down and undermined many of what were once considered main bulwarks and buttresses of the Church." Browning had always been looked upon as an intellectual poet, and a number of critics welcomed the serious turn of his thought. When critics discussed *Cleon* and *Karshish* they did not label Browning's interest in the problem of faith and doubt as timely, but they did spotlight the speculative point of view toward Christianity and found that the poems would repay the reader for his time and effort. In the sixties critics would comment on the timeliness of Browning's poetry in subject and also in method.

Reviewers praised or commented on poems that in other ways reflected the spirit of the times. *Bentley's*, the *British Quarterly Review*, and the *Oxford and Cambridge Magazine* praised *A Grammarian's Funeral* with its emphasis on the pursuit of knowledge, which so strongly pervaded Victorian life. *Fraser's* and the *Examiner* wrote favorably of *The Statue and the Bust* and the *Oxford and Cambridge Magazine* of it and of *Childe Roland* for stressing the necessity of committing oneself to some significant choice and acting upon it. This has a relation to the Victorian gospel of work and desire for achievement. Some critics were impressed by Browning's advocacy of striving as having a spiritual connotation. Forster in the *Examiner* and the critic for the *Irish Quarterly Review* quoted his lines from *A Grammarian's Funeral* bearing on the popular Victorian philosophy of the Glorification of the Imperfect, as expressed by Ruskin in *The Stones of Venice*. But there was another side to the coin. The Catholic *Rambler* quoted lines from Browning's poems to illustrate his advocacy of action even though the action might be wrong. This the critic labeled as Protestant and lamented it and other indications of contemporary Protestantism in Browning's poetry.

In spite of his dramatic presentation reviewers sometimes thought that they could hear Browning's voice speaking through his characters. In his poems the *Rambler* discovered an expression of the author's beliefs. The *Guardian* could not help thinking that Browning was stating his own views in *Fra Lippo Lippi*. George Eliot fancied that he was describing himself in *How It Strikes a Contemporary*. And in reading *Transcendentalism* the *London Quarterly Review* thought that some parts sounded like his "own defence." Among his gifts *Bentley's* saw "a rare union of subjective reflectiveness with objective life and vigour, so that he can make his *personae* speak out his thoughts without prejudice to their own individual being." In examining some of the works, the *British Quarterly Review* recognized Browning's moral "judgment only vaguely appearing in the impression made by the total synthesis, or declaring itself more obviously in the manner in which justice and mercy were meted out, according to desert, at the close." The extent to which Browning's characters were voicing their thoughts or his own is a question which Browning addressed in correspondence with Ruskin, to be discussed in the next chapter. In the sixties there would be varied reactions to what Browning called his "idealization" of the characters.

In picking up reviews of *Men and Women* at random or looking over them in the order of their appearance, the reader who is attempting to trace the development of Browning's reputation might at first be more impressed by the blindness of some critics than by their effort to understand. The objections leave a strong impression partly because of their repetition in a large number of reviews and because of their irritable and impatient tone. In a close examination we have seen signs auguring a better future. The confusion, along with the inconsistencies, in some reviews is discouraging, but it indicates a struggling toward understanding instead of apathy and total rejection.

If the objections stand out, so does the recognition by the critics of Browning's high place among English poets. Some reviewers of *Men and Women* ranked him among the best of his contemporaries. Few poets of the day could be compared to him for power and originality of mind, said the *British Quarterly Review*. The *Oxford and Cambridge Magazine* was undecided whether to place him first or second. Frequent comparison with Tennyson, who was at this time generally considered the foremost Victorian poet, indicated Browning's rise in critical estimation.

But there was little or no optimism among the critics about the acceptance of Browning by readers generally. To be sure, he had devoted followers. That was recognized now as it had been even early in his career. The *Christian Remembrancer* (1857) took this view of the situation: "If Southey were right in pronouncing the popular fame a less happy lot for a poet, than to live in the hearts of his devoted admirers, that happy lot we venture to predict for Robert Browning." Although the *New Quarterly Review* predicted "no inconsiderable increase to the dignity of his poetical reputation," the general feeling was that *Men and Women* would not change the outlook; and the critics' recital of reasons for Browning's restricted audience accentuated that feeling.

Some reviewers blamed other reviewers for Browning's limited reputation. William Morris, in writing for the *Oxford and Cambridge Magazine*, dealt severely with professional critics for the damage they had done; he thought that their accusations of carelessness, roughness in rhythm, and obscurity had kept away readers who might otherwise have been sympathetic. Browning's critics had censured their fellows before; now the censure was stronger. A good part of the article of over twenty-nine pages in the *British Quarterly Review* by Masson was a strong defense of Browning's poetry against reviewers who felt that he was perverse and who objected to the "odd, recondite, and occult character of much of his thinking" and to his "correspondingly eccentric choice of subjects as vehicles for his thinking." Masson found fault with reviewers who considered Browning's style as something apart from other aspects of his poetry and hence saw it to be an obstruction to intelligibility. The remarks of critics in the process of defending Browning sometimes pointed to particular reviews. The *Examiner* seemingly had in mind the criticism of the *Saturday Review* and the *Athenaeum*. The *Rambler* vigorously supported Browning against objections made by the *Athenaeum;* and the *Oxford and Cambridge Magazine*, in a sharp reprisal, referred to criticisms made in *Blackwood's, Fraser's,* and the *Saturday Review*, without naming these reviews. The *Christian Remembrancer* (1857) criticized the *Guardian* for finding the first stanza of *One Word More* obscure.

The attack by comprehending and supportive critics on those who were less perceptive and more resistant to the innovative nature of Browning's art was a healthy sign. This attack would continue into the sixties. Other tendencies that have been discussed (some just appearing) were to continue also: growing realization that Browning's dramatic strength lay in his character-revealing poems; recognition of his dramatic method of assuming the identity of his characters; breaking down of earlier aversions to unconventional subject matter; emphasis on the spiritual quality of his poetry and awareness of the relationship of his insight into man and his sense of the divine; observation of his purposeful use of verse and feeling for the total design of his poems as various aspects of his poetry were drawn together; notice of his timeliness; recognition of his own voice in his verse; endeavor to advance appreciation of the poetry by explaining the difficulties, by showing that what was not approved of was sometimes inherent in Browning's individuality, and by persuading readers that the poetry was worth the effort necessary for understanding it.

As the critical statements about the style and content of the poems in *Men and Women* and *Christmas-Eve and Easter-Day* have been discussed here and in preceding chapters, now and then something has been said about the influence and the class of the periodicals in which the reviews appeared. A few more observations should be made. Recognition that the harm of an obtuse or otherwise offensive review in an influential periodical might well not be offset by a discerning review in a periodical of much less importance leads to discouraging conclusions. The good achieved by the favorable reviews in the *New Quarterly Review* (1852–62) and the *Oxford and Cambridge Magazine* (Jan.–Dec. 1856) — both short-lived and restricted in influence — could not make up for the harm done by the flippancy of *Blackwood's* and the nagging and confusion of *Fraser's* — both more important and longer established periodicals.

As has been indicated earlier, the periodicity, or frequency of the publication, of a periodical might well have an effect on reviews of Browning, and the majority of the earlier ones appeared in weeklies. It was of course desirable that a review be perceptive as well as prompt. But unless a critic for a weekly had an advanced copy or was sympathetic with Browning as the result of prior familiarity with his poetry, he did not have sufficient time to digest the new work. Before the fifties Browning had gained little benefit from the immediacy of reviews. With some limitation most of the reviews in the *Examiner* satisfied both requirements; except for a few favorable ones in the *Athenaeum* there was more hindrance than help in the rest of the weeklies.

Nor did he get much help in the fifties. The five weeklies that had started reviewing Browning at the outset of his career — the *Literary Gazette, Atlas, Athenaeum, Examiner,* and *Spectator* — lost no time in reviewing *Christmas-Eve and Easter-Day* and *Men and Women;* with one exception for each work the reviews in the weeklies were among the first to appear after publication. Only the *Examiner* had a beneficial review. Three weeklies that reviewed *Men and Women* as promptly as the long-established ones were the *Leader,* which contained some discussion of faults but more of the strong points in Browning's writings and praise for *Men and Women;* the *Critic,* which made little headway in comprehension of *Men and Women;* and the *Saturday Review,* which carried its devastatingly offensive criticism of the poems. The *Saturday Review* far outstripped the other two in influence.

In spite of the discouraging aspects of the reviewing in the fifties, encouragement came in the extension of interest in Browning to the non-weeklies. The weeklies no longer predominated. The total number of monthlies and quarterlies reviewing *Christmas-Eve and Easter-Day* and *Men and Women* slightly exceeded the number of weeklies that reviewed these works. The most perceptive and sympathetic reviews appeared in monthlies and quarterlies, in which more space was alloted to the critics. Also encouraging was the fact that among the periodicals reviewing the publications of the fifties there were a number that had ignored Browning earlier, and only a few of these were totally unreceptive to the merits of his works and some had considerable understanding, including the *Westminster,* the third of the three great quarterlies. Extended interest was evident in another way, which should be mentioned here. In earlier years the favorable reviews were written principally by men who were Browning's friends or acquaintances and who moved in the circles he frequented; certainly to some extent Browning had talked of his works to these men. Besides those who knew him personally apparently there were now other reviewers who took an interest in his poetry and helped to advance his reputation.

One important aspect of Browning's reputation that was already noticeable in the late forties became more significant in the fifties — interest in him by the sectarian periodicals. Three reviewed him for the first time in the fifties. The Methodist *London Quarterly Review* (started in 1853) concerned itself impatiently with the style of Browning's poetry. The Catholic *Rambler* (started in 1848) and the Unitarian *Prospective Review* (started in 1845) — both favorably inclined toward Browning — fell in with others in commenting on his spiritual quality. The High Church *English Review,* which had carried two reviews of Browning in the forties, continued its attitude toward Browning as a Christian poet (expressed in 1849). The Nonconformist *British Quarterly Review,* in which Lewes in 1847 had concentrated disapprovingly on the manner of Browning's writing, now had a perceptive discussion of both his style and elevated thought; and the High Church *Christian Remembrancer,* as has already been pointed out, turned from denunciation of Browning's degraded taste to praise of him as a religious poet. Only the High Church *Guardian* retained its negative attitude. So much attention to Browning's elevated thought in the religious press was a strong directive force in the shaping of his reputation, and it came from periodicals of various denominations.

A consideration of the influence, the periodicity, and the character of the periodicals, like the examination of what the reviewers said, shows that in spite of the discouraging aspects of the reception by the press, there were definite signs of progress.

When Browning was thinking of the disappointing reception of his poems in the fifties, a reception contrary to all of his expectations, he could not see that there were tendencies foreshadowing gratifying developments in the sixties. Notwithstanding his behavior toward Macready and the sporadic flare-ups against critics, Browning had exercised a remarkable fortitude during some twenty years of attempting to reach the public. In 1842 he had written Domett that he did not "expect to do any real thing" for ten or twelve years.[4] Twelve years and more had passed and through hard work and costly experience he had at last produced poetry that deserved recognition. The critics had had enough time also to make progress, and there were signs of advancement among those who exerted effort in dealing with the fifty-one poems of great variety in the rich and original collection of 1855.

Robert and Elizabeth and their son were in Paris when *Men and Women* was published. On November 15 Elizabeth reported to her sister Henrietta on the immediate reaction. "Though the book was only published on saturday [*sic*, Nov. 10] we hear good news of the promise of success, 'the trade' having 'subscribed' (as they call it) largely — that is — having made large orders — so that the expenses were covered after three days."[5] Browning could well be pleased by the promise of success, but he was waiting for what he had always considered of most value to wide acceptance: beneficial criticism in the press, which would encourage sale after the trade subscription.

He went to Galignani's and read the reviews of *Men and Women*. His hopes, which had been so high, were dashed. Browning saw in the criticism that which would impede immediate appreciation of his poems. On December 17 he wrote to Chapman:

> Meanwhile don't take to heart the zoological utterances I have stopped my ears against at Galignani's of late. "Whoo-oo-oo-oo" mouths the big monkey — "Whee-ee-ee-ee" squeaks the little monkey and such a dig with the end of my umbrella as I should give the brutes if I couldn't keep my temper, and consider how they miss their nut[s] and gingerbread![6]

Reviews in seven periodicals had already appeared, and the outcry against Browning's faults was conspicuous in most of them. When Forster, in the *Examiner,* wrote that there was "some danger at present . . . of the objection being carried too far," he was right. Although the favorable comments made by the *Leader* and the *Atlas* were not over-shadowed by their unfavorable remarks on the poems, the very little good that the critics for the *Literary Gazette, Athenaeum,* and the *Saturday Review* had to say was obscured by their nagging and assured condemnation, and the *Critic* was almost as damaging. The four left the impression that Browning had perversely set out to be obscure.

These reviews were enough to set Browning on edge. As he continued his letter to Chapman he referred to a forthcoming review of his works in France, written by his friend Joseph Milsand. "He would no more suffer me to see a word of his performance, to correct a syllable of his version, than do a far meaner thing, being altogether a noble fellow, but judge whether *he* finds the writing unintelligible, — he, a Frenchman!"

On the same day that Browning wrote Chapman, Elizabeth wrote Mrs. William Burnet Kinney: "Robert's poems are prospering among the claps of hands, & the barkings of dogs. They have produced a sensation — and the haters do us nearly as much good as the lovers. Half the edition was gone after three days. Still, the poetry is so much too good for a rapid success, that I cannot quite believe in it."[7] Elizabeth, with her knowledge of critics and criticism, felt that it would take time for the poetic accomplishment of *Men and Women* to be accepted and appreciated.

A month later Browning again took up the subject of reviews in a letter to Chapman: "I have read heaps of critiques at Galignani's, mostly stupid and spiteful, self-contradicting and contradictory of each other." His adjectives were to a considerable extent justified, as the discussion of the reviews has indicated. Browning was concerned for his reputation. "What effect such 'rot' would have on me, in the case of the book being somebody else's, I know exactly, but how it works with the reading public, you must tell me if I am ever to know."[8] Browning, as we have seen, had written to Elizabeth in 1846 about the difference in the way a derogatory review would strike him and the way it might well affect other readers.[9]

Browning was not yet ready to give up hope entirely. "I suppose we are not at the end of them [reviews], and the best comes last, it is to be hoped." Actually the majority of the best reviews had already appeared. Certainly he had seen the one whose writer had taken the most trouble to defend and praise him. In acknowledging four reviews that Chapman had sent him, he singled Masson's out for comment. *"The British Quarterly* was just what I had not seen and would have lost most by missing." [10] Judging from the early history of some of his works, he could expect more understanding reviews after time had passed for digestion. But in this case his publication was not a single poem like *Pippa Passes* or a small collection like *Dramatic Romances and Lyrics*. Even the additional time of a few weeks or months was not enough for critics who were defeated by the overwhelming number of original poems in *Men and Women*. It was the persevering critic with the open and flexible mind who appreciated the two volumes.

During this time when Browning was distressed by the reception of his poems, he did have good news from America. He had written James T. Fields of Ticknor and Fields in August 1854[11] and again in September 1855[12] to interest him in the sheets of *Men and Women* to be gathered and bound for American issue. Mr. Fields, who had met Browning in 1851, accepted his offer; after an exchange of letters Fields agreed to pay him £60 for the sheets.[13] Late in 1855 the American edition, in one volume, was published, and in January and February and then in April of 1856 Browning wrote Chapman from Paris that he had had good news of its reception.[14] Louise Greer, in her book *Browning and America*, made a comparison: "This work did not attract so much attention among reviewers, or inspire so much favorable comment, as the *Poems* [an unauthorized reprint of the collected edition published by Chapman and Hall in 1849]."[15]

As the months passed after his letter to Chapman in January, Browning continued vainly to try to get information from him about the demand for *Men and Women*. On April 12, 1856, he wrote, ". . . I don't tell you much but you tell me nothing at all, — so, reform."[16] Later in the month the silence was broken, and the report was not good. Browning answered, "As to my own Poems — they must be left to Providence and that fine sense of discrimination which I never cease to meditate upon and admire in the public: they cry out for new things and when you furnish them with what they cried for, 'it's *so* new,' they grunt."[17] The critical lament that he did not write traditional poetry was ringing in his ears.

During this winter of 1855–6 in Paris — the period of defeated hopes and bitterness — Browning was working on the revision of *Sordello*, which the critics had hung like an albatross about his neck. Soon after his marriage Browning had talked of his plan to revise the poem.[18] The topic came up again when, just before the appearance of *Men and Women* in England, Browning was writing Fields about publication of the collection in America. More than once he wrote him of his intention to revise *Sordello* and *Strafford*, both of which had been omitted in the collected edition of 1849 (reprinted by Ticknor, Reed, and Fields), and of his offer to allow them to be republished in America a year before their appearance in England. Obviously Browning was particularly interested in bringing out a revision of *Sordello*, his "best performance hitherto," he told Fields.[19]

Browning wrote optimistically of effectively revising *Sordello*, but as the months passed the difficulty of the task and the memory of its failure were added discords to the disappointing reception of *Men and Women* in England. Could they ever be resolved? A good public response to the two works that he considered his best seemed impossible. By May of 1856 Browning had taken to drawing, which gave him only temporary relief from the gnawing sense of failure. On June 10 he wrote to William Allingham, in answer to a comment on *Men and Women*, "I have heard a rare cackle whenever I looked London-wards this winter, and shall probably miss something if, next time I lean over the rail of the literary pond, Goosey *Fraser,* and Gander *Blackwood* don't give me their opinion of my outward man."[20] On June 18 he wrote Fields, " 'Sordello' takes a weary time to do thoroughly — but I hope to complete & give it you in the course of the year. . . ."[21] We hear no more of *Sordello* at this time. It was not republished in 1857, as Browning had suggested it might be, but in 1863 in England and, along with *Strafford* and *Christmas-Eve and Easter-Day,* in 1864 in America.

Following the winter in Paris, the Brownings spent several months in England. During this time Elizabeth completed the poem that she had brought with her from Florence — *Aurora Leigh* — and after it was printed she and Robert turned to the proofs. They were out of London for a month or more, during which they continued the work. Elizabeth was able to be near one sister and go to see the other, and she and Robert visited Kenyon, who, now seriously ill, was staying in his home in West Cowes on the Isle of Wight. Back in London Elizabeth was inclined to droop in the early autumn atmosphere, but they remained in England until they had taken care of all the proof sheets. Late in October they left for a brief sojourn in Paris before starting for their home base in Florence.

After they were again settled in Casa Guidi, Browning continued to be rankled by criticism. He was in no mood to accept stoically Chapman's failure to include a message when he sent a copy of Elizabeth's *Aurora Leigh* after its publication in November. Although he was accustomed to their publisher's slowness of communication, the arrival of her book without an accompanying word seemed ominous after the disappointing reception of *Men and Women*. The reviews of *Aurora Leigh* that he had already examined gave Browning concern, and on the day when Elizabeth's book arrived he wrote Chapman, releasing some of the venom against critics that had been accumulating:

> I saw the *Athenaeum, Globe,* and *Daily News,* that's all, hearing of eulogy from the *Lit. Gaz.* and blackguardism from the "Press"; all like those night-men who are always emptying their cart at my door, and welcome when I remember that after all they don't touch our bread with their beastly hands, as they used to do. Don't you mind them, and leave me to rub their noses in their own filth some fine day.[22]

Kenneth Knickerbocker has shown how Browning's letters to Chapman after the publication of *Men and Women* served as "the antecedent action for the dramatic outbursts in *Pacchiarotto,*" written and published twenty years later.[23] In the remaining time that the Brownings lived in Italy, however, seemingly only a few friends were aware of the extent of his suffering from defeated hopes. One of these was Isa Blagden, who became close to the Brownings during the fifties. In a letter written to her while he and Elizabeth were staying two months on the French coast in 1858, Browning revealed something of his discouraged state of mind. "I go mechanically out & in, and get a day through — whereof not ten minutes have been my own — so much for your 'quantities of writing' (in expectation) — I began pretty zealously — but it's no use now: nor will the world very greatly care."[24] Outsiders could easily misunderstand the poet who during these years presented a lively and optimistic face to the world. At about the time Browning wrote Isa, Thackeray, in a conversation with Allingham about the poet, said: "He has a good belief, in himself, at all events. I suppose he doesn't care whether people praise him or not."[25] That he had confidence in himself was fortunately true; that he was indifferent to praise was a misconception that Thackeray shared with others. Allingham corrected him on this point.

Recognition of his works was important to Browning not only as an indication of his standing in the literary world but also as an influence on his breadwinning ability. The *Athenaeum* had written in a review of *Pauline,* his first work, that the day was past "for either fee or fame in the service of the muse." Twenty years of devoted service had brought him neither fee nor fame. He knew that his own feeling about the worthiness of his work had been confirmed by men of discernment, but their belief was not tantamount to the wide recognition that he felt would produce financial reward.

Before their marriage Browning told Elizabeth it "would be horrible to have to come back" to the world and "ask its help."[26] In their life together his anxiety was evident in his meticulous records of expenditures and in his self-torture when their financial situation was precarious. Now he faced the reality that even his *Men and Women,* his ultimate hope for gain, was a failure. Elizabeth had written, "I·. . . am ready to die at the stake for my faith in these last [poems],"[27] but copies of *Men and Women* (and *Christmas-Eve and Easter-Day* as well) were still unsold over eight years after publication.[28]

Browning's customary resilience following a failure with the public deserted him after the discouraging reception of *Men and Women.* The decline of Elizabeth's health also marked the years from 1857. Winters, as well as summers, in Florence were no longer advisable. To have the right climate for Elizabeth, the Brownings spent the last three winters of her life in Rome and the last two summers in Siena; they were in Florence only in passing to and from these places. Besides tenderly and attentively caring for his wife, Browning devoted considerable time to drawing and modeling in clay, and he indulged in social life in Rome. Apparently only during the winter of 1859–60 did he apply himself to writing.

During that period he and Elizabeth again planned a joint publication. Browning's part came to nothing, according to Elizabeth's report to Sarianna Browning:

> Robert and I began to write on the Italian question together, and our plan was (Robert's own suggestion!) to publish jointly. When I showed him my ode on Napoleon he observed that I was gentle to England in comparison to what he had been, but after Villafranca (the Palmerston Ministry having come in) he destroyed his poem and left me alone, and I determined to stand alone. What Robert had written no longer suited the moment. . . .[29]

But something was retained. Browning later explained that during this Roman period of composition he had started his poem on Napoleon, *Prince Hohenstiel-Schwangau.* In the early seventies he alluded to "a little sketch begun in *Rome in '60,* that I have occasionally fancied I should like to finish, or rather expand. . . ."[30] And at another time he thus referred to beginning the poem, "I really wrote — that is, conceived the poem, twelve years ago in the Via del Tritone — in a little handbreadth of prose, — now yellow with age and Italian ink. . . ."[31]

Elizabeth praised Browning for the work he had done during the winter. "Robert deserves no reproaches, for he has been writing a good deal this winter — working at a long poem which I have not seen a line of, and producing short lyrics which I *have* seen, and may declare worthy of him."[32] The long poem is generally supposed to be *Mr. Sludge, "The Medium."*[33]

Elizabeth was grateful for this oasis of work in an otherwise comparatively barren period; she understood the despair that weighed upon Browning during these years. She was anxious about him and his work and early in 1860 lamented to Sarianna Browning the public's neglect:

> I don't complain for myself of an unappreciating public — *I have no reason.* But, just for *that* reason, I complain more about Robert, only he does not hear me complain. To *you* I may say, that the blindness, deafness, and stupidity of the English public to Robert are amazing. . . . Robert *is.* All England can't prevent his existence, I suppose. But nobody there, except a small knot of pre-Raffaelite men, pretends to do him justice. Mr. Forster has done the best in the press. As a sort of lion, Robert has his range in society, and, for the rest, you should see Chapman's returns; while in America he's a power, a writer, a poet.[34]

Elizabeth wrote this in March, the month in which her collection *Poems before Congress* was published. During these years Browning harbored resentment against the critics, who, he felt strongly, had the power to sway opinion against writers. His patience was tried again when Elizabeth's collection was denounced in the press.[35] With one exception her poems had grown out of the Italian situation, and the critics found Elizabeth's political attitude objectionable. The one exception, *A Curse for a Nation,* was also condemned by the reviewers, who mistakenly interpreted it as a criticism of England though it was written as an attack on slavery in the United States. Chorley, a close friend and reviewer of both the Brownings, made this mistake in the *Athenaeum.* "Robert," wrote Elizabeth, "was *furious* about the 'Athenaeum'; no other word describes him. . . ."[36] and later in the letter she said, "I never saw Robert so enraged about a criticism." After other severe criticisms appeared, she reported a change: "It was only the misstatement in the 'Athenaeum' which overset him, only the first fire which made him wink. Now he turns a hero's face to all this cannonading."[37]

Browning restrained himself because uppermost in his mind at this time was his desire to protect Elizabeth. She was more disturbed by the reviews of this work than was usual with her. Since her ardent sympathy with the Italian movement prompted her to write the poems, she equated the attack upon them with opposition to the good of Italy. Her spiritual involvement with the Italian crisis amounted to a feverish obsession, and Browning knew the danger to her of further distress.

In June of 1860, a few months after the upsetting reviews appeared, the Brownings saw Frederic Chapman, the nephew of their publisher, in Italy. He reported that in spite of the unfavorable press reception of *Poems before Congress,* Elizabeth's poetry was selling well. Browning wrote to friends, ". . . he talks about new editions & other encouragement. Aurora Leigh: *Fifth* is getting ready & the second of 'Before Congress' is imminent."[38] Elizabeth recalled another aspect of the interview, "Also Chapman junior . . . smoothes me down a little about Robert, and says that the sale is bettering itself, and that a new edition of the 'Poems' will soon be wanted."[39]

A later comment of Browning's on the financial situation of his poetry in 1860 raises questions about Frederic's report. "These very poems, the last year but one that I was in Italy, did not sell — one single copy in six months. . . ."[40] The fact that not a single copy of the *Poems* of 1849 had been sold in a six-months' period during the last of Browning's Italian years and that copies of *Christmas-Eve and Easter-Day* and *Men and Women* were still on hand as late as 1863 makes it very unlikely that the publisher was considering a new edition of his poetry. Perhaps this was a conciliatory suggestion because the firm did not want to lose the sale of Elizabeth's books, which during her lifetime far exceeded that of Robert's.

It was no wonder that Browning could not shake off his sense of futility. He had felt that the failures in his early career provided the experience needed to make him successful in the future, and he had been confident that *Men and Women* would be well received by the critics. He now felt the uselessness of trying in the face of indifference to his works. After the 1859–60 winter of work he reverted to the state of poetic inactivity into which he had lapsed following the extremely depressing reception of *Men and Women.* He turned his great energy into various channels, one of which was now particularly satisfying to him. A few months before her death Elizabeth wrote to his sister: "And as to the modelling — well, I told you that I grudged a little the time from his own particular art — and that is true. But it does not do to dishearten him about his modelling." Browning could not conceal from Elizabeth the sense of failure that left him no peace. She was aware of the danger of his fretting:

> As long as I have known him he has not been able to read long at a time — he can do it now better than in the beginning of time. The consequence of which is that he wants occupation and that an active occupation is salvation to him with his irritable nerves, saves him from ruminating bitter cud, and from the process which I call beating his dear head against the wall till it is bruised, simply because he sees a fly there, magnified by his own two eyes almost indefinitely into some Saurian monster.

All she could do was to watch and try to restrain him from saying what she felt would be better left unsaid. "At the same time his treatment in England affects him naturally — and for my part I set it down as an infamy of that public — no other word. He says he has told you some things you had not heard, and which, I acknowledge, I always try to prevent him from repeating to anyone."[41]

At least, Browning no longer felt the pressure of providing funds sufficient for the care of his family. Kenyon had died late in 1856. In his will (on record in Somerset House) he bequeathed Elizabeth £4000 and Robert £6500. Henceforth the combined income from Kenyon's bequests and Elizabeth's investments relieved Browning from anxiety about finances.

But the deep hurt from his failure remained. Browning was reticent to speak to William Rossetti about his work in 1860,[42] which was strange, for at other times he talked freely about it to the Rossettis, as well as to others. In this period of disappointed hopes he probably dared not risk a discussion that would arouse his emotions. Holding a tight leash on them may have seemed desirable in the last part of Elizabeth's life; but inward seething could eventually exact a price, as it had done in the past. The period of professional unrest was coming to an end. Elizabeth, who had borne with him the "infamy" of the English public and whose belief in his genius had never wavered, did not live to see him win the acclaim that established him as a foremost poet. She died on June 29, 1861. Fifteen years earlier Browning had started his married life in Italy full of hope for recognition of his works. Now he was to return to England with his son, still without the success he had been confident he could achieve.

CHAPTER XIX

Nonprofessional Opinion in the Fifties

In the preceding four chapters very little has been said about the opinions of Browning's poetry in the fifties other than those expressed by reviewers. In the first half of that decade, as in the thirties and forties, he was given recognition in print by people who knew him personally. In 1851 Talfourd published a *Sonnet to Robert Browning; Suggested by a Sunset of Unusual Beauty*.[1] In the same year there appeared another poem addressed to Browning, this one by Bryan Waller Procter, who published it under his pseudonym Barry Cornwall. It was *A Familiar Epistle to Robert Browning* (in 186 lines) and appeared in a collection made up of reprinted and new poems.[2] *The Epistle* was divided into two parts, the first dated 1839. In it were lines that remind the reader of the older man's advice to Browning to "shun brain fever," given in the letter of March 21, 1844.

> Leave learned volumes: leave the sharp goose-quill:
> Leave perilous thinking, and all kinds of ill.
> Waste not thy soul on books! If Learning be
> That delving, toiling, struggling Thing we see,
> Abandon it.

The last part, dated 1846–50, made an appeal in closing.

> Therefore I call on *Thee*, a Spirit bold,
> And able to maintain the poet's gage,
> To stamp thy fame, in lines of burning gold,
> Upon the page

347

Of everlasting adamant, where lie
The few great names which Memory
Has rescued from the oblivious deep Abyss!
— Spurn not good counsel, even in verse like this.
Summon thy spirit! Grasp thine arms, — (the best);
Plunge in the strife, — and Fate will do the rest.

Near the time when this poem was published, James T. Fields was surprised to hear Procter, who had known many poets, declare Browning to be the "peer of any one who had written" in the century. "Mind what I say," Procter insisted, "Browning will make an enduring name, and give another supremely great poet to England." Others learned of Procter's high opinion.[3]

Besides being the subject of poems, Browning was discussed in books that appeared in the early fifties. *The Living Authors of England* by Thomas Powell, after its appearance in America in 1849, was published in England in 1851 under the title *Pictures of the Living Authors of Britain*. Though some of the chapters were omitted in the 1851 edition, the one on Browning remained with some changes in punctuation and a few other revisions.[4] It is not surprising that Powell, who was careless of the rights and desires of others, retained the short paragraph on *Pauline,* despite the fact that Browning still did not wish the public to know that *Pauline* was his.

In 1849 Miss Mitford, who had already clearly indicated her disapproval of Browning's poetry, made an admission. "I am just reading Robert Browning's 'Poems;' there is much more in them than I thought to find. . . ." She continued, "He ought to be forced to write journey work for his daily bread (say for the 'Times') which would make him write clearly." In her *Recollections of a Literary Life,* published in 1852, she commented on several plays and poems with unqualified praise,[5] probably as the result of her love for Elizabeth and of persuasion from others to see good in Browning's poetry. The commendation of *Paracelsus* in Anna Jameson's *A Commonplace Book of Thoughts, Memories, and Fancies* (1854)[6] was a manifestation of her general interest in Browning. Recognition by Procter, Talfourd, Mitford, and Jameson — all well-known — helped to keep Browning's name before the public in the early fifties, when his progress was indeterminate and he was living away from England.

A good sign of Browning's standing was the appearance of his poems in anthologies — two in Robert A. Willmott's collection *Poets of the Nineteenth Century* (1857) and five in William Allingham's *Nightingale Valley* (1860).[7]

Besides appearing in a favorable light in works by people who knew him, Browning was discussed unfavorably in two works on contemporary writers, both published in the early fifties and both echoing past opinions. Even though the authors concentrated on the undesirable qualities in his poetry, Browning was now of sufficient stature in the literary world not to be ignored in a consideration of well-known poets of the day. In their condemnation of Browning's manner of writing, the authors joined in the hue and cry of many reviewers, even as they recognized him as an outstanding poet.

In a series of lectures on the social, literary, and scientific history of the first half of the century, sponsored by the Edinburgh Philosophical Association, D. M. Moir gave six lectures on poetical literature (published in 1851), in the last of which he commented on *Paracelsus, Sordello,* and *Bells and Pomegranates.* He thought that whatever good there was in *Paracelsus* and *Bells and Pomegranates* was overshadowed by the incomprehensible and that *Sordello* was nothing but incomprehensibility. Seemingly Browning had blinded himself to conventional poetical art.

> The truth is, that with an ill-regulated imagination, Mr Browning has utterly mistaken singularity for originality — the uncommon for the fine. Style and manner he despises; indeed, he may be said to have none — for these are with him like the wind blowing where it listeth; or, as extremes meet, he may be said to have all kinds, from the most composite and Arabesque to the most disjointed and Doric.[8]

Browning had plenty of materials, Moir said, but he left them like cairns rather than buildings. "Genius of some kind — it may be of a high kind — Browning must have; but, most assuredly, never was genius of any kind or degree more perversely misapplied." Moir supposed that Browning might attract a small band of worshippers who would have to search for a thread to lead them through his mystical labyrinth.

Nicholas J. Gannon, who discussed characteristic errors of distinguished living poets, readily found imperfections in Browning's writing. After acknowledging that some of the plays contained beauties of one kind or another, he asserted that these excellencies were more than counteracted by faults, particularly unintelligibility. To show Browning's characteristic errors, he gave five pages of his six on Browning to the "great and glaring defects" of *Sordello,* "a most melancholy embodiment" of obscurity.[9] Three years later, in 1856, Gannon was to write the unfavorable review of *Men and Women* in the *Irish Quarterly Review*. In it he emphasized Browning's obscurity.

In other comments on Browning, ones not designed for publication, we find a variety of opinion. One general remark on Browning's poetry made by Tennyson's brother Frederick in a letter of 1854 is worth quoting because it represents the attitude of those who admired Browning the man but could not bring themselves to accept the individuality of his poetry.

> Though I have the highest esteem for Browning, and believe him to be a man of infinite learning, jest and bonhomie, and moreover a sterling heart that reverbs no hollowness, I verily believe his school of poetry to be the most grotesque conceivable. With the exception of the *Blot on the Scutcheon* [sic], through which you may possibly grope your way without the aid of an Ariadne, the rest appear to me to be Chinese puzzles, trackless labyrinths, unapproachable nebulosities. Yet he has a very Catholic taste in poetry, doing justice to everything good in all poets past or present, and he is one who has a profound admiration of Alfred.[10]

Besides comments on Browning's works, there are other gauges of his standing with the reading public. The tendency to link the names of Browning and Tennyson that was appearing in the fifties showed that Browning's reputation was moving forward. Both professional and nonprofessional critics came to appreciate Tennyson earlier than they did Browning. *In Memoriam* (1850) secured Tennyson's place in the Victorian world of poetry, and he was hailed by many critics as the greatest poet of the time.[11] Browning was compared with Tennyson occasionally at first and more and more often as the fifties advanced.

Remarks by Carlyle and Landor show the inclination to associate the names of these two poets. Carlyle, in lamenting in 1851 that Tennyson and Browning expressed their thoughts in verse, said, "Alfred knows how to jingle, but Browning does not."[12] The mention of one often brought to mind the other. When Landor, whose literary judgments could be surprising, in 1850 named Browning and Aubrey de Vere as the two greatest poets in England, he gave Browning the preference and went on to link his name with Tennyson's — "Browning the greatest — more power than Tennyson."[13] After the recognition of Browning had passed beyond the bounds of a comparatively restricted number, the question of who was the greater — Tennyson or Browning — would bring forth an outpouring of sentiment rather than sense.

We shall see as we now turn to comments on specific works published in the fifties that those who were not under professional obligation to read Browning's poetry read it because they were acquainted with him, because his poetry was sufficiently well known to attract their interest, or because someone persuaded them to read it. If they did not approve of what he had written and expressed their disapproval, they usually dismissed him with a statement or two. Among those who liked his poetry a number warned Browning that its difficulty was a barrier. Standing out above all was the enthusiasm of certain young people. One thing noticeably absent from the nonprofessional criticism was the nagging frequently indulged in by the reviewers.

Among the earliest to read Browning's first new work after his marriage, *Christmas-Eve and Easter-Day,* were Forster and Chorley, old friends of his and reviewers of his works. When Forster, according to Fox's daughter, read *Christmas-Eve* to the Fox family from the proof sheets, they revelled in the humor of the opening passages; and Forster's "melodious voice did justice to the grand vision."[14] Arnould wrote Browning that he had never known Chorley to be so enthusiastic about anything of Browning's as he was about *Christmas-Eve and Easter-Day;* he especially liked the grotesque "from the vigorous contrast it lent to the 'strains of higher mood' which abound in the Poem."[15]

But the enthusiasm of Forster and Chorley seemed to be the exception to other private reactions to *Christmas-Eve and Easter-Day* at the time of its publication. Arnould, in his letter to Browning about Chorley's enthusiasm for the poems, frankly stated that he did not share it. The reason he gave was sequential to part of his earlier attitude. Like others he had admonished Browning to consider the hoi polloi. In his verse epistle praising *Dramatic Lyrics* he had said, as we recall, that in writing *Sordello* Browning had half forgot the readers he wished to attract. When he later heard from Browning that he was revising his poems for a collected edition, Arnould advised him to "run the risk of all things for the sake of being clear; sacrifice the private boxes to the gallery, the coteries to the multitude." At the same time he assured Browning that he did not want him to give up the "characteristic features or well known hues" of his poetry.[16] With this kind of advice in mind, it is no wonder that Browning, during a period of revising for his collected edition, told Fanny Haworth that he would gladly never write another line of poetry. Was it possible to retain the characteristic features of his poetry and produce what could be understood by the multitude?

The first new work that Browning published after receiving Arnould's advice was *Christmas-Eve and Easter-Day*. His friend read it and wrote within the month of publication. "As to the superb magnificences of your poem — your moonrise, your night-rainbow, your St. Peter's, your visioned Form, your theory of Christian Art — they are in the memories and filling the hearts of hundreds of your true admirers." Arnould, like others, praised these individual aspects of *Christmas-Eve and Easter-Day*, but in the sincerity of friendship he asked Browning to think twice before again allowing his "wondrous facility for all the ingenuities of Hudibrastic verse" to carry him "so far aloof from the sympathies of readers of severer taste." Although he expressed approval as well as disapproval, Arnould made it clear that *Christmas-Eve and Easter-Day* was "less satisfactory" to him than some of Browning's "earlier inspirations." He did not favor the grotesque, inventive and ingenious as it was, not so much because of his own dislike, he said, but because it might be a "stumbling block to so many weaker brethren in the critic world." [17] By the time Browning read the letter he could see that Arnould's anticipation had been correct; the grotesque element had already proved to be a stumbling block to early critics of *Christmas-Eve and Easter-Day*.

Macready, as well as Arnould, objected to Browning's new work, but he expressed his opinion in his *Diaries* instead of to Browning. Forster took him a copy of *Christmas-Eve and Easter-Day*. On the next day, April 8, with Forster's favorable review in hand, he recorded the results of his efforts: "I am willing, quite willing, to concede a want of taste and quickness of apprehension, but I *cannot* go with it, or relish it — it does not touch me; on the contrary, I object to the juxtaposition of vulgar and coarse images and high religious thoughts." Twice more he tackled the poem with no more success. "I *cannot* relish it. I cannot approve it. . . . I *cannot* like it." [18]

Considering Macready's past criticism of Browning's plays, we might brush aside his opinion as a continuation of a set state of mind were it not that it resembles the reaction to *Christmas-Eve and Easter-Day* of Arnould and others who had enthusiastically read Browning's earlier poetry. When *Christmas-Eve and Easter-Day* presented itself for consideration, Robert Lytton and some of the Rossetti circle were vague or silent. Was this a mask for disapproval or indecision?

Lytton, who had become acquainted with *Bells and Pomegranates* in the forties, went into diplomatic service; in 1852 he was in Florence, to which he had been sent as an unpaid attaché. Soon after his arrival he went to Casa Guidi with a letter of introduction from Forster, and before long he was on a friendly standing with the Brownings. Association with them seemingly nourished his aspiration to become a poet. After the Brownings went to Bagni di Lucca for the summer of 1853, Lytton, in a letter dated July 26, indicated the high value that he placed on Browning's criticism and encouragement.

> Any scrap from you would be prized by me, for to have a place in the mind of a great man is indeed a noble privilege. But this letter, so full of kindness — I cannot say how I am touched and gladdened by it. Believe me I am *most* grateful. No criticism, no encouragement, c^d affect me so much as that which comes from you, for I have been for years your constant, hearty, and *reverent* admirer.[19]

A month before he wrote these words to Browning, Lytton had sent a letter to his father which, as Aurelia Brooks Harlan has pointed out, indicates that he was a disciple of the author of *Bells and Pomegranates*.[20] It does not seem, however, that Lytton was impressed by *Christmas-Eve and Easter-Day;* at least in his letters to Browning that we have he expressed no particular opinion. In August he wrote to Browning that he had lent the work to friends. "So that you see you leave us 'gentle words and use your influence on the mind.' "[21] We wonder whether Lytton, who was to write at length to Browning about *Men and Women,* had no more to say to him about *Christmas-Eve and Easter-Day.*

We might look expectantly to the Pre-Raphaelites and their friends for a definite commentary on *Christmas-Eve and Easter-Day.* The earlier admirers were eager to read Browning's latest work, and on the day of publication, April 1, 1850, F. G. Stephens obtained a copy. By the eighth William Rossetti had read it, and then he read it again, this time aloud to Walter Deverell. William recorded this information in his diary without citing anyone's opinion. According to his entry of October 27 Coventry Patmore had just read *Christmas-Eve and Easter-Day* and was "evidently deeply impressed with it, more than with any other of the great man's works, tho' he does not exactly know 'what to make of it.' "[22] All in all the reception of the poem by the Pre-Raphaelites appears lifeless beside their early vigorous promotion of Browning's cause. Although, as we have seen, two of them did give him public support in the Pre-Raphaelite *Germ* (May 1850), Stephens' article contained no reference to *Christmas-Eve and Easter-Day* and William Rossetti's article (primarily on the test of style) served only as an introduction to a forthcoming review of the poem, a review which never appeared because of the demise of the *Germ.*

We may not know what Lytton and the Pre-Raphaelites actually felt about *Christmas-Eve and Easter-Day,* but ample evidence exists that they, as well as other young men, saw *Men and Women* as an outstanding contribution to literature. The comments that Lytton made after reading part of the proofs of *Men and Women* suggest that Browning asked for his opinion; and it was sincerely given. The poems, Lytton said, surpassed even his most ardent hopes. He was haunted by all that he had read; ". . . new sensations of beauty, new thoughts of power from immeasurable depths well up through my recollections of poem after poem. . . ." He regarded what he had seen of the new work "as the quintessential flower of all that has preceded it." Earlier Lytton had hoped "to be permitted" to review the forthcoming *Men and Women* in the *Dublin University Magazine.* Since the imperceptive remarks in the *Dublin* (1856) were far removed from Lytton's opinion, we can assume he did not write the review. In a poem to be published in 1858 he did pay public tribute to Browning,

> . . . who dwells among
> The Apennine, and there hath strung
> A harp of Anakim;
>
> Than whom a mightier master never
> Touch'd the deep chords of hidden things;
>
> Nor error did from truth dissever
> With keener glance; nor made endeavour
> To rise on bolder wings
>
> In those high regions of the soul
> Where thought itself grows dim with awe.[23]

Whatever Lytton and other admirers of Browning thought of the poems, there was still the question of public reception, and in his letter Lytton was not reassuring on that point. Browning had told Forster and Milsand that he had written the poems to get people to hear — that is, to make a broad appeal, to reach beyond his limited audience. Lytton's comments after he read the proofs foreshadowed the reception and the dashing of Browning's hopes. The poems, Lytton wrote, would place Browning *"immediately* in more friendly relations with the public" than he had yet cared to seek and ultimately add the "greatest dignity" to his position among the "greatest English Poets." But many of the so-called reading public, the ones for whom the book manufacturers provided, would approach the poetry with puzzled face. Doubting Browning's rather than their own capacity, they would think, "By what other names and under what other forms do I already know that w^h, under forms so singular, Browning w^d express to me?" Lytton had the answer, "You know it not at all, and never will know it; and if you ever did come to know it, you w^d perceive it as clearly under this form as any other." Browning had made his poetry difficult, Lytton said, but he had won a following of superior readers with whom he had established a claim to immortality.

> You have of course — here as elsewhere — thought fit to place about the Hesperian fruit such spiked fences and quickset hedges that I cannot but foresee that many will go away with scratcht hands; and those that enter the enchanted garden will still be a society select and reverend — but the question is how will these fare? And with these, I prophesy that you have herein establisht the loftiest title to immortality.[24]

Browning's supporters acknowledged that he was difficult. So said Lytton and so said many others who were sympathetic, more and more of whom were stating that persistence of the reader meant gain in the long run. According to Mrs. Andrew Crosse, Frances Power Cobbe said that reading Browning's poetry was like "riding in a hansom cab, with a lame horse, over a rough road." The description continued, "The road is rough, and the horse may be lame, but there is a glorious landscape beyond the hedge, if you are tall enough to look over, or can find courage to grasp the blackthorn and gain a standpoint for the view."[25]

When he became acquainted with Browning's poetry, James Thomson, who was later to publish favorable criticisms of it and whose poems were to be influenced by it, observed the gain from making a real effort to comprehend. In the fifties, when he was giving intellectual encouragement to the daughter of an older friend, he sent the two volumes of *Men and Women* with persuasive words in their behalf. "The author, Robert Browning, is about the strongest and manliest of our living poets." He warned her that she would probably not care for the poems at first; "but," he continued, "they are worth your study, and you may find, as I did, that they improve much with longer acquaintance." After giving her instructions about reading the poems, he offered further assistance: "Should you care enough for Browning to wish thoroughly to comprehend him, I shall of course be happy to render you what little assistance may be in my power towards the clearing up of obscurities."[26]

The urge of those already won over to Browning's poetry to help others understand and appreciate it came to be recognized as peculiar to many of his admirers. Mrs. Crosse was one of those who realized that with the passing of time its stimulating power increased. "Out of every three who read him, two at least are seized with the desire of explaining him to the rest of the world."[27]

This proselytizing, as we have seen, was characteristic of members and friends of the Pre-Raphaelite Brotherhood in the late forties. Though the ideals of Pre-Raphaelitism continued to exist in diminishing force, the Brotherhood itself came to an end before *Men and Women* was published. But earlier enthusiasms were still alive. When Browning was in London in 1851, Dante Gabriel Rossetti met him for the first time. After *Men and Women* was published Rossetti's reaction to the poems came out in a correspondence he was keeping up with William Allingham.

According to Browning's instructions, Chapman sent a copy of *Men and Women* to Rossetti, who received the two volumes the day before he left London for Paris late in 1855. He was "hard at work" before his departure, but he felt he must become acquainted with the poems at once. While he worked, his brother William read from the two volumes to him. Allingham learned this and more from a letter he received from Rossetti, begun on November 25 after his return from Paris. On the journey he read the poems himself and then read some of them again; "but they'll bear lots of squeezing yet," he wrote. The letter was not completed until January 8, 1856. Browning's poetry, as well as the man himself, whom he had seen in Paris, was still occupying Rossetti's mind. He told of "drenching" himself with *Men and Women* at intervals, of friends borrowing his copy, and of his longing for Allingham's comments. He craved a "speedy" answer, to fire his own opinion. His brother William agreed with him too much on Browning to bring his own thoughts into activity, wrote Gabriel; therefore, he had been "bottled up" ever since the poems were published. In reality, he had not been so bottled up that he could not decide which were his favorites. He named them to Allingham — *Childe Roland, Bishop Blougram, Karshish, How It Strikes a Contemporary, Lippo Lippi, Cleon,* and *Popularity.*[28]

The sculptor Alexander Munro had accompanied Rossetti to Paris, and among his "wonderful and grand remembrances" was the great one of passing "a most delightful evening" with Browning. He enjoyed the new volumes "very much — and immensely more than

Maud,"[29] which had been published shortly before this time. William Bell Scott, poet and artist, thought *Men and Women* contained "more wonderful lights than any books" he knew; he felt that *Karshish* and *Bishop Blougram's Apology* were beyond all "inventions" that Browning had yet created.[30] After the publication of *Men and Women,* Thomas Woolner, sculptor and writer of verse, wrote to Mrs. Tennyson of his admiration for all of Browning's books except one and to Allingham of rejoicing in the praise he had heard of the "great Robert," who deserved "the best that can be bestowed." In 1859 he wrote Mrs. Tennyson of a "majestically beautiful" lady whose "established poet was Tennyson" and who preferred Longfellow to Browning; his "sense of fitness was violated in knowing that such an imperial looking creature should have anything like serious admiration for Longfellow, and yet turn from Robert Browning as from a thing of not much importance."[31] Woolner, like Thomson, was trying to make a convert.

Rossetti's influence was not by any means restricted to the Pre-Raphaelite circle. He was an expansive man with a magnetic personality, and his active support of Browning was not at an end when his path converged with that of two students from Oxford who were becoming liberalized in their thinking and tastes. William Morris and Edward Burne-Jones met in the early fifties in Exeter College; and, along with others, had the visions and independence of youth and the desire to dream and talk with sympathetic peers. The result was the formation of what they called "the Brotherhood" (not to be confused with the Pre-Raphaelite Brotherhood). A participant in some of the evening sessions recalled, "It was a new world into which I was brought. . . . The subjects I had always heard discussed were never discussed here, while matters on which I had never heard any one speak formed here the staple of the talk."[32] With various interests, including literature and art, these Oxfordians had to have their own magazine. Friends from Cambridge were drawn into the undertaking, and the first number of the *Oxford and Cambridge Magazine* came out in January of 1856. Like the *Germ,* it was destined to have a short life in spite of the enthusiasm and faith with which it was launched. By the end of the year the magazine had run its course.

For a while the group thought that Tennyson was the ultimate in poetry, unsurpassed in fresh poetic diction. One of them wrote of Tennyson in later years, ". . . we all had the feeling that after him no farther development was possible: that we were at the end of all things in poetry."[33] Then came the reading of Browning — a new area of poetry to be explored. *Bishop Blougram's Apology* was eagerly discussed by the set. Morris wrote the review of *Men and Women* for their magazine. Burne-Jones called Browning "the greatest poet alive."[34] He found him "too different from anyone else to be liked at first sight by most, but he is the deepest and intensest of all poets — writes lower down in the dark heart of things — rises up to the seemingly clear surface less often." His works were "sung out" as if the poet "sat continually at the roots of human life and saw all things."[35]

Some of the men who made up the Brotherhood were reevaluating their former objectives in life as the result of new intellectual experiences. The plans that Burne-Jones and Morris had made for their future became unsettled, and in redirecting them they were influenced by Rossetti. They became acquainted with the *Germ,* in which they read his poems, and they saw a book illustration and a water-color of his as well as paintings by other Pre-Raphaelites that excited their attention. Then each was granted the much-desired opportunity of becoming acquainted with Rossetti. On the night of meeting him for the first time, Burne-Jones heard Rossetti rend someone "in pieces" for speaking disrespectfully of *Men and Women.*[36]

As young men Morris and Burne-Jones first thought of taking holy orders, then of becoming church architects, and finally of devoting themselves to art. In the middle fifties they moved to London, where they were caught up in a friendship with Rossetti and met other artists. In August 1857 they became part of the group associated with Rossetti in the well-known project of the wall-painting for the debating hall of the Oxford Union, carried out to the accompaniment of much talking and fun-making, but destined to fade away.

There was no losing sight of Browning among his ardent supporters. Morris was writing poems, which were published in 1858. When someone asked him about *The Defence of Guenevere,* one poem in his collection, he answered that he supposed it was more "like Browning than any one else."[37] Before the wall-painting adventure was at an end for Rossetti and his companions, there would cross their path a member of still a third group whose attention was turning to Browning — Swinburne.

The young men of this group called themselves the Old Mortality Society. It was started in Balliol College, Oxford, in 1856. Maurice Cramer, in his article on Browning's reputation at Oxford, has written in detail of the personnel of the group and of their interest in Browning.[38] Here something needs to be said about the general character of the Society and about three men of the group, whose reaction to Browning's poetry has been left on record.

John Nichol, poet and biographer, proposed the institution of the Society, which was to have as its object "stimulating and promoting of the interchange of thought among its members, on the more general questions of Literature, Philosophy, and Science, as well as the diffusion of a correct knowledge and critical appreciation of our standard English authors."[39] Years later one of the group spoke of the meeting as "the very salt of their university life for some of its members," with its "free discussion of everything in heaven or earth, the fresh enjoyment of intellectual sympathy, the fearless intercommunion of spirits."[40] *The Undergraduate Papers* was an outlet of expression for members of the Society.[41] In retrospect this magazine takes its place beside the *Germ* and the *Oxford and Cambridge Magazine*.

According to his biographer, Nichol was "one of the earliest in his generation to discover the philosophical merits of the poetry of Browning, and he seems at this period of his life to have been addicted to proselytism on the subject." This claim of very early discovery may stretch the truth, but certainly Nichol deserves credit for his promotion of Browning. He praised the poet to Benjamin Jowett, eloquently asserting the "psychological subtlety, the vigour of his dramatic characterization, etc."[42] In the 1850's he made favorable references to Browning in literary articles;[43] in 1860 he wrote to his future wife that he had not been able to persuade her father that Browning was a greater poet than Elizabeth Barrett Browning; and after he became a professor of literature in the University of Glasgow in 1862 he proclaimed Browning's greatness.[44]

Another Old Mortality member, George Birkbeck Hill, in later years wrote a delightful account of his own experiences, in which he told that he entered Oxford "as ignorant of the new School of Poetry as anyone well could be." He sat at dinner beside someone very much his senior who thinking him "worth taking in hand" proposed reading from *In Memoriam* every evening over a cup of tea. The lesson was productive; after becoming acquainted with the whole of the poem, Hill was an ardent convert. He did not stop with Tennyson. "I went on to read Mr. Browning, and as my admiration for him increased, so increased my scorn for the poets who were of a widely different school."[45]

In the crisscross pattern of intersecting groups, Swinburne, the third Old Mortality member to be discussed here, became acquainted with Rossetti during the time of the Oxford fiasco. He was apt to be more susceptible to influences outside rather than within the academic regimen, and he was easily attracted to the carefree artists decorating the walls of the debating hall — some of whom were poets as well. The promotion of Browning by Nichol and Rossetti encouraged Swinburne's interest in a poet whose works he continued to read and comment on in succeeding decades.

Swinburne read Browning's introductory essay to Shelley's letters, *The Heretic's Tragedy, Bishop Blougram's Apology,* and *The Statue and the Bust* to the Old Mortality Society.[46] He took to *Sordello* with considerable zeal after meeting Rossetti and his companions. In writing to a friend in February 1858, Swinburne called it one of his canonical scriptures and spoke of Palma and Sordello in paradise with verbal aesthetic treacle that would have astounded Browning.[47] Doubtless Rossetti was still about his business of promoting *Sordello* as he had been earlier when he was reciting twenty pages at a time from memory. Swinburne proved to be his match, for when he was nineteen he memorized the whole of it, as he indicated in a letter written to Browning in 1875.[48]

The young men in the three groups had characteristics in common. On the whole they had strong and high-spirited personalities; a desire to explore the unprescribed in one area or another existed in their ranks; and they had a love for literature and were familiar with past and contemporary works. As is not unusual with youth, they welcomed what they found for themselves outside the establishment, and they were stimulated by fresh approaches. When they read Browning's poetry, it appealed to them. *Bishop Blougram's Apology* was mentioned most often, and it was, we know, one of the favorites of the reviewers. There is no indication, however, that this or any other poem of Browning's had for them the religious or spiritual attraction that was beginning to be felt by others. These young men belonged rather with Browning's supporters who valued his poetry for its vigor, psychological subtlety, revelation of humanity, and originality without condemning the qualities that made these possible. This acuter criticism had appeared occasionally in Browning's earlier career, picked up momentum in the fifties, and was to thrive in the climate of the sixties.

Of what value was all this enthusiasm to Browning's reputation in the fifties? The Pre-Raphaelites who had lauded Browning in the forties had little literary influence outside their circle. In the fifties they as well as the other young men who were interested in Browning were in no position to bring about a considerable change in the evaluation of his work. The periodicals sponsored by the three groups had a life too short and a circulation too limited to reach many readers not already familiar with his poetry. It is true that criticism by word of mouth was the forerunner of critical approaches in the sixties and that some who were exposed to the fervor for Browning would speak out to good effect after the fifties.

One person, however — one associated with Rossetti and other Pre-Raphaelites — did speak out to good effect in the fifties, though not on *Men and Women*. This was John Ruskin. Fortunately, those who were favorably influenced were unaware of the irony of the situation. Although what Ruskin wrote for public consumption attracted others to Browning's poetry, he himself found the poems hard to comprehend. David DeLaura has published letters for the first time that add considerably to the account of the relationship between the Brownings and Ruskin.[49] They include sixteen from Ruskin to Browning. We can examine exactly what Ruskin wrote to Browning of his poetry and set several of his letters against ones of Browning's published earlier that significantly show his reaction to Ruskin's comments. What Ruskin said in his letters contrasts with what he said in his published works, which had a very favorable influence on the critics. The correspondence of the two men from December 2, 1855, to October 3, 1856, is particularly illuminating.

Ruskin, who broke new ground himself, was defeated in his effort to appreciate Browning's originality. The unrestrained remarks in his letters to Browning suggest the struggle of other intelligent contemporaries who sensed Browning's superiority without understanding it. Probably as the result of Ruskin's qualified praise of Browning's earlier poetry in a letter to Elizabeth,[50] Browning sent Ruskin a copy of *Men and Women* when it was published in November of 1855. Dante Gabriel Rossetti wrote Allingham of its immediate effect. "Ruskin, on reading *Men and Women* (and with it some of the other works which he didn't know before), declared them rebelliously to be a mass of conundrums, and compelled me to sit down before him and lay siege for one whole night; the result of which was that he sent me next morning a bulky letter to be forwarded to B[rowning] . . . ."[51]

The letter, written on December 2, 1855, was filled with complaints. The little credit that Ruskin gave Browning was qualified. Like others, he emphasized the power as he regretted the misuse of it. He mixed praise with blame. "There is a stuff and fancy in your work which assuredly is in no other living writer's, and how far this purple of it *must* be within this terrible shell; and only to be fished for among threshing of foam & slippery rocks, I don't know. There are truths & depths in it, far beyond anything I have read except Shakespeare. . . ."[52] This last comment surely grew out of the discussion of *Men and Women* with Rossetti, who hoped that Ruskin in his letter had told Browning "he was the greatest man since Shakespeare."[53]

Ruskin's chief intention in writing the letter was to tell Browning how much he failed to understand and approve of his poetry. For every line that he made out there were two that he could not understand; he sent detailed queries and comments on *Popularity* to show how many puzzles it presented and expressed other objections as well. He did think, however, that Browning's earlier poem *The Bishop Orders His Tomb* was "very glorious"; Rossetti had pointed it out.[54]

In the following week, on December 10, Browning answered Ruskin's letter, beginning with tactful remarks. He was faced with questions on nearly every stanza of *Popularity*, including ones that Browning surely must have felt no intelligent man of imagination should be asking. For the most part he ignored these; the reply that he did give was brief and spirited. "So could I twit you through the whole series of your objurgations," he wrote. He chose instead to declare his "own notion of the law on the subject," which will be presented at the end of the section on Ruskin, in a discussion of Browning's reaction to Ruskin's objections.[55]

Late in January of 1856 Ruskin wrote Browning that he had just sent a copy of Volume III of *Modern Painters* (recently published). He added that Browning would be surprised because his poems were not spoken of. In extenuation he said, ". . . you know that I admire them." But he did not know "what to think or say" about Browning's poetry or his position among poets. What he said would be about his "wonderful understanding of painting & mediaevalism, unique among poets, and some reference to St Praxeds under coloured stones."[56]

On February 1 Browning sent a long reply. He discussed Volume III at length and answered specific questions about his poetry that Ruskin had asked in a postscript to the letter of late January. More importantly he was concerned about Ruskin's statement that the "most startling fault of the age" was the "faithlessness" of its writers.[57] Browning's reply will be discussed along with his reaction to Ruskin's objections to *Men and Women*.

Volume IV of *Modern Painters* appeared in April 1856 and it contained the promised commentary, a discussion of *The Bishop Orders His*

Tomb, with the well-known passage about the poem. Ruskin did not send Browning a copy of the volume until August. He wrote on the 29th, "I was so ashamed of the way I had mangled that poem of yours that I dared not look you even by letter in the face for some time afterwards. . . ."[58] In trying to understand Browning's poetry, he recognized his own deficiency, and his frustration came out in his remarks. Although in the preceding year he had written Browning of the usefulness of poetry,[59] he now floundered to the point of saying, "I don't see any use in poetry. I recollect you have written something nice about figs, somewhere — but that is all I do recollect."[60] On October 3, a few days after Browning returned to London (following a month's sojourn out of the city) and found Ruskin's letter and Volume IV of *Modern Painters,* he acknowledged the book and alluded to the letter. Besides writing a few sentences on his immediate family plans and situation, Browning, schooled as he was in adroit letter writing, made some innocuous remarks related to Ruskin and his work and, in expressing appreciation for the book, referred to the commentary on *The Bishop Orders His Tomb* in *Modern Painters,* "I think I can afford to say that it is pleasant indeed to see my name among good names. . . ."[61] As laconic as this acknowledgment was, Browning, as we shall see, was grateful for the published recognition with its ring of confidence, and it was to have a favorable and far-reaching influence.

Part of Ruskin's passage on *The Bishop* has often been quoted, but we need to consult all of it in order to round out the whole picture of his struggle to comprehend Browning's poetry. In chapter 20 of Volume IV of *Modern Painters* Ruskin made the point that Shakespeare wrote in the spirit of the sixteenth century and not in that of earlier centuries. In Victorian England, which Ruskin thought was "emptied of splendour," great men might have to bring to life the past. Among poets, several had "put more vitality into the shadows of the dead than most others can give the presences of the living." One such poet that Ruskin named was Robert Browning, "unerring in every sentence he writes of the Middle Ages; always vital, right, and profound; so that in the matter of art, with which we have been specially concerned, there is hardly a principle connected with the mediaeval temper, that he has not struck upon in those seemingly careless and too rugged rhymes of his." After further comparison with Shakespeare, Ruskin quoted from *The Bishop* and then pronounced the following well-known commendation:

> I know no other piece of modern English, prose or poetry, in which there is so much told, as in these lines, of the Renaissance

spirit, — its worldliness, inconsistency, pride, hypocrisy, ignorance of itself, love of art, of luxury, and of good Latin. It is nearly all that I said of the central Renaissance in thirty pages of the *Stones of Venice* put into as many lines, Browning's being also the antecedent work.

Just as Ruskin did not compliment Browning on his representation of the Middle Ages without raising the question of his rhymes, he did not stop with his praise of Browning's representation of the Renaissance. He continued in a sentence that has been neglected:

> The worst of it is that this kind of concentrated writing needs so much *solution* before the reader can fairly get the good of it, that people's patience fails them, and they give the thing up as insoluble; though, truly, it ought to be to the current of common thought like Saladin's talisman, dipped in clear water, not soluble altogether, but making the element medicinal.[62]

Both in the Victorian Age and in our time critics have usually passed over the sentence in Ruskin's comment that reflects the difficulty he had in understanding Browning. Contemporary reviewers had written so much about "rugged rhymes" and the "insoluble" in his poetry that the unfavorable side of Ruskin's remarks made little imprint on their mind. What impressed them was his fresh and invigorating comment on *The Bishop Orders His Tomb* and his high opinion of Browning's fidelity to the Renaissance. They often echoed Ruskin's praise in their reviews, though it said nothing about Browning's skill as a creative artist.

In 1858 Ruskin again quoted from *The Bishop* — this time in an address, as one of several examples showing how poetical power increased "according to the extent and emotional power of the facts stated, and on the penetration of the writer into the movements of the soul. . . ."[63]

Ruskin's published opinion is not to be taken lightly. His place as an art critic was assured. About the time when he made his comments on *The Bishop,* the following *Poem by a Perfectly Furious Academician* appeared in *Punch* (May 24, 1856):

> I takes and paints,
> Hears no complaints,
> And sells before I'm dry;
> Till savage RUSKIN
> He sticks his tusk in,
> Then nobody will buy.

The furious academician had evidently felt the power of Ruskin's word. Once a statement of his that no one had painted the "delicate pink of apple blossoms against the soft clear blue of a spring sky" brought a deluge of apple blossoms at the next exhibition at the Royal Academy. One critic remarked, "From Millais (who paints blossoms as big as babies' heads, growing on trees in full leaf) down to the sorriest scrub who seeks a teacher's certificate from the Department of Art, all appear to have taken the apple-blossom fever, and to have painted the blossoms when at the height of their delirium."[64] It was during this period of influence that Ruskin's comments on *The Bishop* caught the attention of literary critics who relayed his opinion of Browning's accurate reflection of the Renaissance to their readers.

Aside from the ironical situation of the fillip given to reviewers as the result of the published remarks by Ruskin, who himself lacked insight into Browning's poetical genius, there is the other important aspect of the criticism — Browning's reaction to Ruskin's comments. It comes out in the letter Browning wrote on December 10, 1855, in answer to Ruskin's criticism of *Men and Women,* particularly of *Popularity,* and in the letter he wrote on February 1, 1856, as the result of a commentary of Ruskin's on the lack of faith among modern poets in Volume III of *Modern Painters* (both letters already referred to). Browning's remarks serve as answers to Ruskin and to related criticisms appearing in the reviews and also as a revelation of some of his poetic intentions.

In his letter of December 2, 1855, in which he stated his objections to *Men and Women,* Ruskin criticized Browning for his ellipses: ". . . before one can get through ten lines, one has to patch you up in twenty places, wrong or right, and if one hasn't much stuff of one's own to spare to patch with! You are worse than the worst Alpine Glacier I ever crossed. Bright, & deep enough truly, but so full of Clefts that half the journey has to be done with ladder & hatchet."[65] According to Browning's answer of December 10, his art required that the reader make some concessions:

> For the deepnesses you think you discern, — may they be more than mere blacknesses! . . . We don't read poetry the same way, by the same law; it is too clear. I cannot begin writing poetry till my imaginary reader has conceded licences to me which you demur at altogether. I *know* that I don't make out my conception by my language, all poetry being a putting the infinite within the finite. You would have me paint it all plain out, which can't be; but by various artifices

I try to make shift with touches and bits of outlines which *succeed* if they bear the conception from me to you.

He upheld his method; it was not the same as that for writing prose, which Ruskin (or any other reader) needed to recognize:

> You ought, I think, to keep pace with the thought tripping from ledge to ledge of my 'glaciers,' as you call them; not stand poking your alpenstock into the holes, and demonstrating that no foot could have stood there; — suppose it sprang over there? in *prose* you may criticise so — because that is the absolute representation of portions of truth, what chronicling is to history — but in asking for more *ultimates* you must accept less *mediates,* nor expect that a Druid stone-circle will be traced for you with as few breaks to the eye as the North Crescent and South Crescent that go together so cleverly in many a suburb. Why, you look at my little song as if it were Hobbs' or Nobbs' [imaginary characters in *Popularity*] lease of his house, or testament of his devisings, wherein, I grant you, not a 'then and there,' 'to him and his heirs,' 'to have and to hold,' and so on, would be superfluous. . . .[66]

This explanation probably failed to influence Ruskin, who wanted more "mediates." Ten years earlier Browning had written Elizabeth something of the difficulty facing a dramatic poet. He must choose all that his character does or says in order to make the desired impression upon the reader, who must perceive for himself. The poet cannot stand by and direct the reader as can the novelist with his explanation.[67] Ruskin was one of those who expected direction.

Ruskin had another objection. ". . . I entirely deny & refuse the right of any poet to require me to pronounce words short and long, exactly as he likes — to require me to read a plain & harsh & straightforward piece of prose."[68] Browning again defended his manner of writing. "The other hard measure you deal me I won't bear — about my requiring you to pronounce words short and long, exactly as I like. Nay, but exactly as the language likes, in this case."[69] By the examples he gave, Browning showed that he turned his observation of speech to good account by shaping versification to serve his needs instead of being a slave to the conventional notion of its use in poetry.

Still another objection of Ruskin's was that as a poet of his "real dramatic power" Browning ought not let himself come through in various characters, as in Pippa.[70] Browning's answer was brief. "The last charge I cannot answer, for you may be right in preferring it, however unwitting I am of the fact. I *may* put Robert Browning into Pippa and other men and maids. If so, *peccavi:* but I don't see myself in them, at all events."[71] Browning did not think he was writing directly to his reader if he lent his mind to his characters when they spoke.

This was not Browning's last word to Ruskin on the question of his speaking directly to his reader. On February 1, 1856, he wrote him, "Of all my things, the single chance I have had of speaking in my own person — not dramatically — has been in a few words in the course of 'Sordello' . . . ."[72] The remark grew out of the statement that Ruskin had made, in Volume III of *Modern Painters*, that modern poets lacked faith.[73] Browning — erroneously, according to Ruskin — thought he was included among those who did "not apprehend distinctly any Divine being." To show that he was free of this "reproach," he quoted passages with an expression of his faith in and apprehension of God.[74]

Browning's seeing the passages in *Sordello* as the single chance he had had of presenting his own thoughts directly is of a piece with his insistence to others that his poetry was not self-revelatory. He probably did not have in mind the thoughts themselves but his dramatic presentation of them. He might not have put himself in toto into Pippa or Lippo or the Corregidor, but as any present-day reader knows and some critics of his time asserted, his own ideas were often expressed through his characters. As a matter of fact, in the same letter in which he professed not to see himself in his characters (Dec. 10, 1855) he stated a belief that he had asserted more than once elsewhere: "A poet's affair is with God, — to whom he is accountable, and of whom is his reward; look elsewhere, and you find misery enough."[75] Ruskin had only to turn to *Men and Women* to see the reflection of Browning's attitude toward his art in *How It Strikes a Contemporary*. Like the Corregidor, he should forget the people and keep the Lord "all the more in mind."

In the quoted sentence Browning made it clear that reward did not come from people. He explained why to Ruskin. It was not the business of a poet to tell people what they already knew, for that they accepted easily and approved of. Poetry had another use. "It is all teaching, on the contrary, and the people hate to be taught." This sentence succinctly referred to Browning's belief in the didactic function of poetry, which he expressed from time to time. It as well as the rest of his defense and explanation of his poetry to Ruskin belongs with remarks which he made about his art throughout his life, a number of which have already been pointed out.

Ruskin's comments to and on Browning in the fifties stand out because they prompted Browning's animated and revealing defense of himself and because the published ones were influential.

Browning's explanation might not have made a difference to others like Ruskin if they had read it. Apparently Clough did not find anything in *Men and Women* to approve of except *Fra Lippo Lippi.*[76] Thackeray admitted in the early fifties that he did not read Browning because he could not comprehend him, and after *Men and Women* was published he said he could not "manage" his poetry; he wanted "poetry to be musical, to run sweetly."[77] The poems in *Men and Women* presented problems even to Edmund Lushington and Mrs. Jameson, who were more receptive to Browning's work. Lushington wrote to Tennyson in 1856: "Have you seen Browning's new volumes? I have been trying to construe them, and no gold had ever to be digged out through more stubborn rocks. But he is a poet as well as good fellow."[78] Mrs. Jameson, who had placed *Paracelsus* high on her list of favorite poems and seemingly had read it with ease, was greatly impressed by *Men and Women* but evidently had difficulty. She wrote Elizabeth that her idea of Browning's power was raised after reading the new poems and that she was struck "with absolute wonder by the depth and reach of intellect they display." She made an observation similar to a few others that we have noted. "I could complain of that singularity of form and expression which renders them difficult reading but then if it were quite otherwise it would not be R. B." She continued, "The diction has individuality as well as peculiarity . . . only I wish one could have pleasure unmixed with perplexity the first time of reading — on the whole, my idea of the Poet's *power* is raised."[79]

Browning had more than a little evidence that the readers of his poetry wanted him "to paint it all plain out." Not even the longer acquaintance with it that James Thomson had thought would help readers was always effective. Carlyle had been reading Browning for a number of years and he had never ceased to admonish him to write with "articulate clearness." The young poet had been a welcome guest in the older writer's home in Chelsea. To a man in the journeyman stage the interest of an established and respected person is of the highest value. It is easy to imagine what it meant to Browning when Carlyle wrote and spoke to him with honesty and generosity. There had been no danger of deriving false hopes from his criticism. Carlyle had recognized in Browning no mere poetaster; he saw Browning's rare gift, but reflections on his good qualities were accompanied by anxieties, chiefly because of his lack of clarity.

As grateful as Browning was for Carlyle's interest, he was apprehensive of his opinion. He did not at once send him a copy of *Men and Women*. Even without the presentation copy that he had habitually received in the early years, Carlyle read *How It Strikes a Contemporary* and told Browning that the old Corregidor was a "diamond." He had had a glimpse of *Men and Women* and would not, he said, rest until he had read it.[80] This led to a presentation copy for Carlyle and Browning's confession to him of his lack of courage to send one earlier.

> I hold so to what kind feeling for me you express, and which I cannot have a right to doubt, therefore — that it seemed foolish to hazard this by sending you poems to read you might like me none the better, or somewhat the less for. But that fear seems stupid on reflection; for you have written, beside the word now, many words, once on a time, the best I ever got for my pains.[81]

Before Carlyle received his copy of *Men and Women*, he had further acquaintance with the Corregidor. He wrote Browning that during a visit in a friend's home "the entertainment of two evenings, much the best that turned up," was hearing the hostess read from *Men and Women*. She chose *How It Strikes a Contemporary* and *Bishop Blougram's Apology*, and the guests "sat (being intelligent creatures, all) in rapt attention . . . and understood everything." Carlyle expressed his continued faith in Browning's genius: "I have never been in doubt about the noble spiritual outfit I discovered in you from our first acquaintance, many years back now; and my faith still is, you have got a great deal to tell your poor fellow creatures contemporary and future."[82]

After Carlyle received the presentation copy and read *Men and Women* carefully and understood most of the poems, he wrote to Browning at considerable length — he sent "honest words, rough and ready, from a fellow-pilgrim."[83] In one of his letters to Ruskin, Browning referred to "gold words" that Carlyle had sent him (on the Corregidor) and said "he looks to what suits his own sight in what I show."[84] The statement is borne out by the qualities that Carlyle praised after he read all the poems in *Men and Women*.

> It is certain there is an excellent opulence of intellect in these two rhymed volumes: intellect in the big ingot shape and down to the smallest current coin; — I shall look far, I believe, to find such a pair of *eyes* as I see busy there inspecting human life this long while. The

keenest just insight into men and things; — and all that goes along
with really good *insight:* a fresh valiant manful character, equipped
with rugged humour, with just love, just contempt, well carried and
bestowed; — in fine a most extraordinary power of expression; such
I must call it, whether it be "expressive" *enough,* or not. Rhythm
there is too, endless poetic fancy, symbolical *help* to express; and if
not melody always or often (for that would mean finish and perfection), there is what the Germans call *takt,* — fine *dancing,* if to the
music only of *drums.*[85]

Carlyle saw genius *"worth* cultivating, worth sacrificing oneself to
tame and subdue into perfection; — none more so" in any man he
knew of men living, in fact apparently the *"finest* poetic genius, finest
possibility of such" vouchsafed in that generation. The genius had
grown — but there was a "shadow side of the Picture." Browning was
"dreadfully difficult to understand"; most of the pieces were "too hard
of interpretation" and more than one "a very enigma." Carlyle did not,
like others, attribute Browning's lack of clarity to perversity. Because
of a kinship in this difficulty Carlyle felt that the cure was not easy and
that the sin was not wilful. "It is the effort of a man with very much to
say, endeavouring to get it said in a not sordid or unworthy way, to
men who are at home chiefly in the sordid, the prosaic, inane and unworthy. I see you pitching big crags into the dirty bottomless morass,
trying to *found* your marble work. . . ." Even if Carlyle did not — as
we can see — have a very clear notion of Browning's method he appreciated the poems enough to repeat what he had said in his letter to
Browning on his prefatory essay to the Shelley forgeries. "I do not at
this point any longer forbid you *verse,* as probably I once did. I perceive
it has grown to be your dialect. . . ."[86]

Carlyle and the others whose opinions have been presented in this
chapter were in considerable agreement with the reviewers. There were
common elements in both groups: praise for the thought, originality,
strength, and interest in human nature; complaints of obscurity; recognition of compensation for the effort of understanding; and a wish to
explain Browning to others. As in the periodicals, *Men and Women* had
more support than *Christmas-Eve and Easter-Day.* One difference is noticeable. Consideration of Browning as a religious teacher that was appearing more and more in the press was not present. Also absent from
the comments of the nonprofessionals were the irritability and nagging
often present in the reviews. With the exception of Ruskin, the ones
who disapproved of Browning privately were inclined to dismiss his

works with little or no discussion. The ones who approved had the desire to say something about his poetry.

A few comments besides those already cited fill out the picture of
Browning's relationship with private critics and his reaction to their
criticisms in the fifties. The bitterness that Browning expressed to
Chapman about the reviews of *Men and Women* is absent from his responses to the objections expressed by his friends. Though he looked
upon many of the reviews as impediments to his success, he appreciated the criticisms from friends whose judgments he valued and even
sought the opinions of some of them. Their attempt to help him by
personal communication was quite different from a public harangue
that turned readers away from his poetry.

As Browning continued to hear in the fifties the complaints that
he had been hearing for many years, he went all the way from polite
restraint to expressions of sincere appreciation in answering the criticism, and on occasion he defended his method to others as well as to
Ruskin. In reply to Mrs. William Kinney's "few kind pats of encouragement" and "occasional lift of an admonitory finger," Browning
promised to become as smooth and as plain as he could be.[87] He might
have written perfunctorily to Mrs. Kinney, but he wrote with sincerity
and feeling to Carlyle and Leigh Hunt of his intention to improve his
clarity. He assured Carlyle of continued efforts. "As I believe no man a
real poet or genius of any sort who does not go on improving till eighty
and over, I shall begin again and again as often as you set me right."[88]
When Hunt praised *Men and Women,* Browning replied, ". . . you put
a flower in my breast which I hardly dare look at, much less finger."
Hunt must have brought up the matter of obscurity, according to
Browning's answer: "Of my books — I dare only reply to your 'third'
note on them, that I know they err in obscure and imperfect expression, — wishing it were not so, and trying always for the future it may
be less so."[89]

When Kenyon read *Men and Women* in proof and sent Browning
his opinion, Browning replied that he had made use of some of the
criticisms, and he thanked him "heartily." In referring to others, he
defended his use of the dramatic.

> In your remarks on the little or no pleasure you derive from dramatic
> — in comparison with lyric — poetry . . . I partake your feeling to
> a great degree: lyric is the oldest, most natural, most *poetical* of po-
> etry, and I would always get it if I could: but I find in these latter
> days that one has a great deal to say, and try and get attended to,

which is out of the lyrical element and capability — and I am forced
to take the nearest way to it. . . .[90]

Browning responded wholeheartedly to the interest that the two
Rossettis and their friends took in his works. In a letter to Dante Gabriel dated May 16, 1870, he was still thinking of his extended support when he wrote of the "twenty years' accumulation of the sympathy" that Rossetti had given him when there were "few enough gifts of
the kind."[91] In the fifties he mentioned to Rossetti the gratifying review of *Men and Women* in the *Oxford and Cambridge Magazine* (written
by William Morris).[92]

Browning was a good business man as well as a good poet. He had
now and then prepared the way for the publication of reviews and for
the understanding of his poetry before reviews were written. When
Ruskin sent Volume III of *Modern Painters* to him and wrote that he did
not know what to say about him but planned to say something,
Browning did not let much time pass before he replied. Besides answering the charge which Browning mistakenly thought Ruskin had
intended for him as well as other modern poets, he made a plea that
Ruskin try to understand him before he spoke of his work in the future. "You know whether I should be proud or no to be recognized by
you, as you propose: also, despite your entire goodness and sympathy,
whether I suppose you will say one word that you do not think." The
sentence that followed may have been lost on Ruskin but would have
been meaningful to Elizabeth or anyone else who knew Browning's
desperate hope of being understood. "I can only speak to that goodness
and bid you try and know me before you make up your mind — I aim
widely and want more than a glance to take in all I endeavor at, hit or
miss."[93]

Ruskin's promised comment did not concern *Men and Women*,
which Browning so much wanted to be recognized. Even though
Browning found it strange as well as pleasant, he was grateful. Rus-
kin's name carried weight. On April 22, 1856, Browning wrote to
Rossetti, who first made him acquainted with Ruskin's remarks on *The
Bishop Orders His Tomb*:

> The extract from Ruskin was strange and pleasant, — I thank
> you altogether for sending it and so making it more pleasant and a
> little less strange. I value a word from him at its worth, I venture to
> believe, — I know at least how I should regard any Brown or Jones
> with a "passed muster, J. Ruskin" — stuck on the front of his cap:

the praise, in itself, is quite above this mark, of course — but in this world judgments are made by overpayments here & underpayments there, from the same paymaster often. . . .[94]

It was as a good business man that Browning considered how such favorable publicized statements would help promote his product. In complaining to Chapman about the public that would "grunt" when he produced new works they had cried out for, he suggested the counteracting influence of comments like the one of Ruskin's on *The Bishop Orders His Tomb*.

> The half-dozen people who know and could impose their opinions on the whole sty of grunters say nothing to *them* . . . and speak so low in my own ear that it's lost to all intents and purposes. Now, is not Ruskin a layer-down of the law in matters of art? Then, see what he says of a poem of mine, printed twelve years ago and more, in this fourth volume, but nobody will snip that round into a neat little paragraph, and head it "Ruskin on Browning," and stick it among the "News of the Week," "Topics of the Day," as the friendly method is![95]

Browning was probably thinking of Carlyle among those who did not but "could impose their opinions" on the "grunters." If only Carlyle would speak out publicly in favor of his works! The stamp of approval of the established writer would have been invaluable; despite the objections that he made to Browning's poetry, Carlyle had a high regard for his ability. In later life Browning indicated regret that Carlyle had never made public the feeling he expressed in private to him and to others.[96] His voice added to Ruskin's would have helped to silence the detractors that Browning referred to in his letter of April 1856 to Rossetti, ". . . while Ruskin pays me a great gold piece for a poor little matter, some Grimley, or whatever is the name, is sure to be picking my pocket and putting a bad fourpenny 'bit' into my hand."[97] (Grimley was George Brimley, author of the review in *Fraser's*, a review that even Brimley's friends disapproved of and that Rossetti wrote of as "the cheekiest of human products."[98])

Sometimes it may seem that Browning valued the good opinion of influential friends only when it was published. That was not true. Although he felt disappointment that Carlyle did not comment publicly in his interest, more than once he referred to Carlyle's "gold words." He continued to love and honor him and never forgot the older man's interest in his writing, as his continuing attentiveness to the aged Carlyle indicated. Often Browning expressed gratitude for the sympathy of others with his work. In response to his friends' communications of interest and concern, many times he resolved to try to improve his writing, and his future attempts would bear out the seriousness of his intention. After the hiatus in his professional life during the later fifties, Browning was to resume his old habits of working hard, with due consideration of criticism and public taste, and exerting efforts for the promotion of his works.

CHAPTER XX

Attracting Readers

*Selections from the Poetical Works
of Robert Browning, 1863*

In 1861, after Elizabeth's death, Browning returned with his son to London, which became his home for the rest of his life. He had lived in Italy for fifteen years. Before he reached England Carlyle sent him a message through John Forster. "Tell him . . . that I expect a *new epoch* for *him,* in regard to his own work in this world, now that he is coming back to England at last; and that, in my poor opinion, wh[h] I have never changed, a noble victory lies ahead for him, if he stand to it while time yet is." Carlyle's regret was "that a soul like R. B.'s was kept weltering, in a *hobbled* condition" in Italy.[1]

It is true that Browning had been handicapped in being far away from the place where his works went through the press and were reviewed by critics who complained of his being in Italy. His reputation may well have suffered by his absence from his homeland. But hobbled he had not been in writing poetry, for his genius had flowered during the years away from England. Many of his greatest poems were written in Italy, and *The Ring and the Book* was the product of his life there.

Not since the disappointing reception of *Men and Women* following its appearance in 1855 had Browning returned to a course of poetic activity with his usual resilience and determination. In the sixties two significant new publications were to appear — *Dramatis Personae* (1864) and *The Ring and the Book* (1868–9). *Dramatis Personae,* because of its timeliness, attracted much attention, and *The Ring and the Book* was recognized as his magnum opus. Besides these there was a steady run of works that had already appeared — in both selections and collected editions. The republications were important, since they provided an opportunity for a needed reevaluation of Browning's poetry and kept his name before the public.

The first work of the sixties was a volume of selections, silently edited by two of Browning's friends — Bryan Waller Procter (pseud. Barry Cornwall) and John Forster. On October 25, 1861, less than a month after Browning came back to London, Procter expressed his view to Forster that the projected volume should consist of shorter poems. "Concerning Browning — *I* have picked out (also) a list of the smaller poems, which I think likely to serve his popularity — and which indeed I think the best. . . . Any selection from the greater (or longer) poems would be difficult. The object of course is to induce readers of the Selections to read all his works."

Procter's long-standing admiration of Browning was not unqualified. He found "extreme subtlety and deep sympathy with his personages (great pathos and great characterization — so to speak)." But some of the poems did not move him, perhaps because, as he confessed, he did not entirely understand them. Tennyson, he thought, was much more polished but much inferior in "pathos, dramatic character, and depth of sentiment." If only Browning would take a quarter of the pains that Tennyson took! "Yet — I don't know — one might lose a good deal of gold in the process."[2]

Two weeks later Procter repeated his opinion. "I doubt whether it be advisable to extend the Selection beyond the smaller poems. They will I think make their way the best." When he had heard people speak of Browning, they had generally referred to *My Last Duchess* and "others of the Lyrics." Of the longer poems he admitted that he did not know *Paracelsus* well. As fine as parts were in *Luria* and other dramas, they would require some explanation and it would be difficult to extract samples.[3]

Forster, who had clung tenaciously to the idea that Browning was potentially a successful dramatist, probably did not agree with Procter, but in the published book twice as many pages were given to the shorter poems as to excerpts from the plays and longer poems. According to the Preface, *Paracelsus, Sordello,* and *Christmas-Eve and Easter-Day* "appear by such portions only as could be so detached that they should possess an independent and intelligible interest" and the dramas "are represented each by separate acts or scenes constituting pictures of character in themselves complete." The editors included noth-

ing from one play — *A Soul's Tragedy,* which could not be
advantageously represented by a detached portion and in addition was
too far removed from conventional drama to be easily appreciated.
They quoted the whole of the well-favored scene of Ottima and Sebald
from *Pippa Passes,* and a number of the shorter poems they selected
were ones that had received approval by the critics. Their guideline
was to choose poetry that would win readers. They made their purpose
explicit in a persuasive sentence at the end of the Preface.

> It is believed that this little book, by the range and variety of power
> it brings at once under view, will arrest, without overstraining, the
> attention of many readers; and, by making less novel and unfamiliar
> to them the style of a thoroughly original poet, will open to them
> sooner the full enjoyment of a series of writings as remarkable as any
> that have enriched the literature of our time.

While preparation of the *Selections* was in progress, Browning
began his new life. He resumed writing and turned to the task of reis-
suing his earlier works. He also attended to the publication of new and
republication of old works of Elizabeth's. In addition, he was putting
into effect plans for his son's education. Just as Forster and others had
given him the assistance needed to get his works published when he
was not in London, he helped his friend William Wetmore Story in a
similar situation.

Browning had much to keep him occupied in this transition period. But outside the fulfillment of the professional and family demands during the first months in England, his life in its bareness was
in sharp contrast to that of the past. In the shadow of grief he took long
solitary walks and saw but few friends. Isa Blagden and W. W. Story,
who had been close to him during his Italian years, urged him to par-
ticipate in social life, which had been so much a part of his existence
and which he had always considered profitable to him as a writer. Early
in 1862 he began emerging from his seclusion. He had kept up many
friendships from the first part of his career and had made new ones during his marriage. As a socially inclined poet with a great store of information, an ease of conversation, and a broad experience in foreign
lands, he readily became a welcome addition to a variety of circles in
London.

Encouragement to broaden his activities came in various ways
during the difficult period of readjustment. Not long after his return
to England, certain friends, including Edward Twisleton, were inter-

ested in his being "introduced to the Athenaeum [Club] by the expe-
ditious method." Browning was pleased with the idea of becoming a
member, and after his election he thanked Monckton Milnes, who was
on the committee, and Twisleton. "You must," he wrote to Twisleton,
"make me aware of the decencies of the position to which your kindness has exalted me."[4] On February 6, 1862, he wrote to Isa that he
had learned the day before of his election and a week later he informed
Story of it, expressing in both instances his resolution to call on friends
and take part in social life.[5] He did it all "with a purpose," he wrote
to Isa.[6]

Early in 1862 he also had the satisfaction of being offered the editorship of the *Cornhill Magazine* when Thackeray resigned. Browning
probably never seriously considered accepting it any more than he had
considered writing for the *Westminster* in 1851, though just as he had
not rejected the proposal from the editor of the *Westminster* without
talking to him, he did not at once dismiss this offer. The *Cornhill* was
published by George Smith, who had been financially unable in 1849
to risk the publication of the collected edition. That Browning relished
the idea of being considered for the editorship was clear from his letter
to Story.

> . . . the Editorship has, under the circumstances . . . been offered
> to — *me!* I really take it as a compliment because I am, by your in-
> dulgence, a bit of a poet, if you like — but a man of the world and
> able editor, hardly! They count on my attracting writers, — I who
> could never muster *English* readers enough to pay for salt & bread!
> My first answer was prompt enough — that my life was done for &
> settled, that I could not change it & would not — but the conveyer
> of the message bade me consider, in a flattering way & I took the
> [week] to do so accordingly. . . .[7]

Browning saw reasons for accepting the position: "first to get the sal-
ary, which Pen might find something to do with, — next to figure as
a man actually capable of choosing better articles from the quantity always on hand than have illustrated the Cornhill, — and last, to try
what the business is like." One aspect of the offer was of particular importance. "It requires *merely editing* — no line of my own writing —
(*that* would be another matter.)"

But there were reasons for not accepting. Browning decided to
"diplomatize." He did not decline at once, and before giving a final
decision he said he should like to have a precise statement of duties and

recompense. He reported that there was a silence after he asked for a definite statement.[8] This admittedly flattering but really unwanted offer faded away. Whatever the outcome, in his period of grief and after the professionally depressing years from 1855 to 1861 the offer had a salutary effect.

Such attention came at a particularly propitious time. Browning was returning to his writing with his former determination to succeed, now strengthened by the remembrance of Elizabeth's faith in his genius and her desire that he should continue his efforts. Although he felt a particular need to apply himself to the limits of his ability, he still, as he had made clear to Elizabeth and Fanny Haworth in earlier years, found writing itself an arduous task. "I . . . mean to keep writing, whether I like it or no," he said in a letter to Isa.[9] Browning's son later reported that his father had always been relieved to have his morning's work completed; ". . . he really hated to write."[10] Browning was probably never completely able to divorce the actual writing from the thought of his many failures to reach the public and his need to make concessions. In the sixties as in the rest of his life the work had its reward: he always fulfilled his duty and did his best.

Sometimes there was an attempted concealment of his real feelings. The poet who had always desperately wanted recognition wrote to the Storys in March:

> Seriously, now that I care not one whit about what I never cared for too much, people are getting goodnatured to my poems. There's printing a book of "Selections from RB" — (SCULPTOR & poet) which is to popularize my old things: & so & so means to review it, and somebody or [other] always was looking out for such an occasion, and what's his name always said he admired me, only he didn't say it, though he said something else every week of his life in some Journal. The breath of man![11]

For a man professing such indifference to the reception of his works, Browning always showed a remarkable interest in the determination of the most favorable time for their presentation to the public. On October 1, 1862, in writing Story about the "season" for publishing, he said that the *Selections* had been ready for two months but Forster would not let the book appear before the middle of November, a better time for publication.[12] The Preface was dated November 1862. On December 22 Browning wrote George Barrett, ". . . they publish to-day a little selection of my things, containing nothing new, but a pretty little book enough. . . ." [13] The work appeared as *Selections from the Poetical Works of Robert Browning* with the year 1863 on the title page, the year that will be used in later citations.

The reviews were not numerous, but they were generally favorable. Earlier dissenting notes were replaced by a more harmonious acceptance of Browning's poetry, even in the *Saturday Review* and the *London Quarterly Review,* both of which had formerly been faultfinding. One noticeable aspect of the reviews was the effect on the critics of having only portions of *Paracelsus, Sordello,* and *Christmas-Eve and Easter-Day* and of the plays (*A Soul's Tragedy* was omitted altogether).

Earlier critics had acknowledged that much was lost when they quoted parts of Browning's works. Now more than one reviewer of the *Selections* saw the disadvantage of trying to do justice to a literary whole by considering only excerpts from it. *Chambers's Journal* said, "The great majority of these Selections are so complete in themselves, that to extract any portion of them is as barbarous as to make a torso of a statue in order that it may fit a niche on one's staircase." The critic specified three such poems: *Pippa Passes* (only the Ottima-Sebald scene appeared in *Selections*), *Fra Lippo Lippi* (in full), and *The Bishop Orders His Tomb* (in full). He did not quote from the first two but he could not resist quoting from the last one. According to the *Saturday Review,* with one exception (the scene from *A Blot*) the selections from the plays lost much of their power by being detached from their context. ". . . Mr. Browning is a poet who works so entirely under the guidance of a far-seeing and preorganizing intellect, that everything he completes is . . . woven without seam. . . ." His work did not "readily admit of being cut into samples." The *London Review* and the *London Quarterly Review* objected to the extracts taken from the plays. The critic for the *London Quarterly Review,* who moreover was not pleased with the excerpts from other works, pointed out that fragments should not be considered apart from the artistic whole.

Since most excerpts could not well be read out of context and the critics probably lacked time to turn to the originals, they said little about the plays. *Pippa Passes* received most attention. The few remarks on the other plays indicated far less interest in them than in the shorter poems. The critic for the *Saturday Review,* who had read *Colombe's Birthday, Pippa Passes, Luria,* and *A Blot in the 'Scutcheon* many years before with "great delight," said that perhaps the plays were Browning's chief efforts but made no definite reference to the excerpts given in the *Selections* except to the one from *A Blot.* The reviewer of *Chambers's Jour-*

nal passed over the plays, he explained, because he could give no "example" of them (no adequate quotation), but he did not regret the omission since two at least — *Colombe's Birthday* and *A Blot* — were known by stage representations. In a general statement about Browning, the *Eclectic Review* referred to *The Return of the Druses* with its "tropical passion" and to *Luria*, the "highest of all his dramatic efforts." The *London Review* seemed to feel justified in ignoring the plays, since, according to the critic's statement, Browning indicated in the dedication to his last drama his "abandonment" of the "dramatic form." What the reviewer did say was in part as much a comment on the dramatic monologues as on the plays. Each character was "prone to the same searching introspective habits, the same hesitating self-analysis." The speeches were "often skilful monologues in disguise: the poet answering the poet through the long procession of subtle and well-elaborated verses."

The wind was blowing in the right direction. *Pippa Passes* continued to fare well since the barriers for understanding it had broken down in the forties. The low-keyed discussion of the other works included under the head of "Drama" in *Selections* was to Browning's advantage. His reputation also gained by the moderate notice of *Paracelsus;* in the past the considerable space given to it had diverted attention from works promising more for the understanding of his genius. *Pauline*, not represented in the *Selections* and not yet publicly acknowledged by the author, was mentioned by the *Eclectic Review*. Since *Pauline, Paracelsus*, and *Sordello* were largely ignored, Browning's mature poems stood a better chance of serving as standards by which his artistry might be judged. Unfortunately *Sordello* was mentioned several times and the Jerrold story lingered on. *Christmas-Eve and Easter-Day*, which had been gaining approval, was highly praised by the critics for the *Eclectic* and the *London Quarterly Review*, though they were not satisfied with the extracts chosen to represent the poem.

Procter was justified in thinking that Browning's reputation would profit by emphasis on the shorter poems. With the exception of *Pippa Passes* and *Christmas-Eve and Easter-day* the critics took little or no interest in the excerpts from the plays and the longer poems. The shorter works that received the most favorable attention were, in order, first, *The Bishop Orders His Tomb* and, next, *Bishop Blougram's Apology, Saul, Fra Lippo Lippi*, and *How They Brought the Good News*, followed by *My Last Duchess, Cleon, An Epistle . . . of Karshish, Soliloquy of the Spanish Cloister*, and *Andrea del Sarto*. The preference for *The Bishop Orders*

His Tomb may be accounted for by Ruskin's comment on the poem,
which was referred to in half of the reviews. He was one influential
friend among the nonprofessional literary critics who had spoken out to
good effect.

A dissenting note in the reviews of *Selections* was remarkably pronounced: doubt about Browning's preoccupation with internal states,
particularly those poetically unacceptable. Several critics of the forties
had made passing mention of the psychological aspect of Browning's
works. Although some critics of *Men and Women* had called attention to
his interest in the psychological, criticism of the unconventional treatment of character was not outstanding. Among the few who spoke out
was the *Rambler;* it questioned the search below a surface that many
Victorians thought should be left undisturbed. The task of going
through such a great number of highly original poems and writing
about them might have left little room for particular consideration of
Browning's psychological bent. Some critics of the *Selections* showed reluctance to accept in theory what was outside poetic conventions of
their day, but nevertheless they found Browning's treatment of the
psychological satisfying in its total effect or in individual poems.

According to the *Saturday Review,* Browning's special intellectual
province lay in "an extraordinary power of psychological analysis"
rather than in "what is usually regarded as poetical inspiration." He
spent too much time on "subtle reproductions of characters not generally interesting"; he would not attain as much acceptance as competi-
tors who aimed at "broad and simple effect." Yet the critic praised
poems distinguished "by great originality of conception, by a subtle
insight into the secret springs of action, and by a power of reproducing
modes of thought and feeling the most remote from those of the poet
himself" — *Blougram, Lippo, Karshish, Cleon, The Bishop Orders his
Tomb,* and *My Last Duchess.* The reviewer was convinced that the genius producing these was extraordinary, but he did not know whether
it was poetical or metaphysical. Clearly he was tottering on his traditional base, yet not prepared to change to another.

Acceptance and rejection moving side by side evidenced hesitancy
in the *London Review* also. Browning's poems were "finished works of
art in their way"; the poet possessed not only power, "but an intensity
of power rarely exceeded." It was, however, "power exercised upon
subjects more remote from the ordinary experience of men" than those
found in the work of any other true poet known to the critic. Browning
succeeded in presenting with "lucid keenness" the passions, intrica-

cies, and dark corners that most men could not sympathize with and few even penetrate. Instead of going beyond the bounds of convention, he should deal with "elementary human sentiments." Browning's excellence was "as much archaeological or psychological as poetical." The characters and situations in such works as *Lippo, Andrea, The Bishop Orders His Tomb, Cleon,* and *Blougram* probably could not provide matter for poems that would be more than "literary curiosities" — even if shaped by the highest poetical genius. That this disapproval was not wholehearted was shown by a later concession: "But taking them within their peculiar limits, for what they aim at, several of those [poems] named in the earlier part of our essay are perfect."

The critic for the *Eclectic Review* said that Browning removed himself from "what is ordinarily conceived of the character of the poet." He dwelt on "psychological analogies and distinctions" too much; they so predominated that they made him "comparatively unreadable by the ordinary crowd." The subtlety of such poetry, he said, demanded effort which most readers were not willing to expend. The reviewer himself was impressed by Browning's particular kind of writing and considered him a great poet.

> How he delights to work and worm and wind his way to the subtlest places of the soul, and to the mazy problems which the soul is perpetually seeking to solve! . . . He is a dramatist in all that we usually imply by that word, entering into the innermost arena of the being. . . . He transfers the circumstances of our being from the *without* to the *within*. In this way they [the poems] all become noble pictures of the striving and the attaining soul.

Another prominent topic besides Browning's propensity for the psychological was his inclination towards remoteness in time and place, which had been condemned in earlier reviews, especially his use of Italian scenes and subjects. In their appreciation of *Lippo, Andrea,* and other dramatic monologues when *Men and Women* was published, the critics had shown a weakening in their resistance to poems with remote settings. This shift continued in reviews of the *Selections.* In citing obstacles to Browning's popularity, the critic for *Chambers's Journal* said that he alienated his English readers by selecting subjects having to do with Italy and, moreover, going back several hundred years in the past. The reviewer seemed not to be emphasizing his own reaction as much as that of readers in general (he found "application enough to modern and home matters" in many poems). The critic for the *Eclectic*

Review thought that these practices made the poet unfit for English readers, but he did not himself object to Browning's recondite knowledge — his use of out-of-the-way "magnificent scenes" and "great historic incidents and historical characters" — to exhibit "the greatness of souls."

Others also were inclined to accept Browning's use of the remote in time and place. The reviewer for the *Critic* felt that his choice of foreign subjects contributed to his unpopularity; he might have wished, he said, that Browning would concern himself with his countrymen, but he concluded, "It is probably best as it is." In the mind of the writer for the *London Review* there was no objection to foreign material or remote history, only a question of popular appeal and historical accuracy. He went so far as to say, "The reproduction of the past is generally excellent, the details especially marvels of sharp, decisive handling." The *London Quarterly Review* gave undiluted praise to Browning: ". . . he has, more than any other dramatic writer we know, the faculty of throwing his mind into another age and country, and reproducing in a marvellous way the modes of thought which were then and there prevalent." The critics themselves were inclined to accept the foreign and historical in Browning, but they were not always sure that his readers could go beyond the insular.

There were signs that much of the critical struggle was passing. Although Browning's psychological probing was not fully sanctioned as material for poetry, it was not rejected. The use of remote sources was more expressly accepted by the reviewers of the *Selections* than by the reviewers of *Men and Women*. They could see more clearly the nature of Browning's intellectual force. The critics were now primarily concerned with the effect of the subject matter on readers in general; they themselves appreciated Browning's extraordinary accomplishments. What of the other targets — rough prosody, unpoetical diction, irregular syntax, and the accompanying accusations of obscurity and wilfulness?

The reviewers of the *Selections* showed little of the former hostility to Browning's diction and his poetic line. The *Saturday Review* found too much "merely mechanical skill" in his rhyming. In stating reasons for his lack of popularity, the critic for the *London Quarterly Review* said that Browning's failure to use the "simplest and most intelligible forms" made the reading of his poetry a "toil" instead of a pleasure and pointed out the defects of "a quaint and outlandish dress of words," "want of music in the versification, and a habit of breaking a verse or a line at any point, no matter where, and beginning a new and totally different sentence." But when he turned to a discussion of Browning's talents, he spoke of the "occasional force and vividness of the language" — one of the great beauties of his poems — and quoted passages in illustration. Though in general the verse seemed "deficient in music and in flow" to the critic for the *London Review,* he praised Browning for adapting it "with rare skill to the expression of the thought."

A tendency of the more perceptive critics of *Men and Women* continued: with the acceptance of Browning's dramatic monologue as a literary form came an increased willingness to accept all that went into the making of it. The *Critic* explained that as the "most intensely dramatic and realistic poet of the day" Browning worked "from within outwards, entering, as by some subtle sympathy, into the very nature of his subject, his metrical embodiment of which will be simply a growth from roots thus struck." To the *Eclectic* the "frequently involved tortuousness of his versification" that seemed at first to contradict the dramatic quality, on second thought appeared natural to Browning's peculiar genius. He had "measureless command over versification and language." All of this was certainly an advancement over the early position taken by most critics.

One further sign that the impediments of the past were disappearing was evident in the tone of the reviews. The critics were not querulous. The only one who alloted space to Browning's obscurity and perversity was the reviewer for the *London Quarterly Review,* and instead of letting the objections color his general discussion he brought them in to explain Browning's unpopularity and then turned to the more "welcome task" of pointing out great talents "for the sake of which all, and much more than all, his faults should be overlooked." On the whole, the reviewers showed considerable sympathy. They took trouble to explain wherein Browning's poetry had power, originality, and intellect — the qualities that had been assigned to his works since the beginning of his career — and they assured readers that their hard work would be repaid.

It was no longer said that if Browning did this or that he would become a good poet. He was one — a poet with a dramatic vigor "equalled by no poet living," "a true Poet" *(Chambers's Journal);* a man of "certain great talents" *(London Quarterly Review);* "the second of our great English living poets," far beyond any other in "light" *(Eclectic Review);* one among the few who would stand out as "bright particular stars" *(Saturday Review)*. But the critics felt that their own opinion of Browning and especially of the *Selections* was not necessarily an indication of the public's response. They agreed that Browning was not popular, though he was known and appreciated by a limited number of readers. It was the opinion of the *London Review* that even the next generation would probably not be able to understand him. Although reasons given earlier for Browning's unpopularity were repeated — obscurity along with disjointed expression, unpoetic diction, faulty rhymes, irregular lines, and a preference for remote settings — another reason emphasized was his use of the psychological for poetry. Only the *Critic* and *Chambers's Journal* felt that the *Selections* might improve Browning's standing with the public.

Two substantial retrospective reviews that made a strong case for Browning's achievement appeared in the early sixties — one before and one not long after the *Selections*. The first one was published in the *North British Review* in May of 1861, several years after the last of the reviews of *Men and Women;* it was written by Gerald Massey. The second came out in *Fraser's* in February of 1863; it was by John Skelton, a regular contributor to *Fraser's*, under his pseudonym Shirley. At some time before Easter of 1862 Skelton wrote James Anthony Froude, who was then editor of *Fraser's*, that he would like to send him an article on Browning. Although Froude told him to send it, he did not publish it until February of the following year, and then he did so, as he said, only for Skelton's sake. He explained that he did not like Browning's poetry; furthermore, the length of the article created a problem. He warned Skelton that his praise would be in vain.[14] Since the review of *Paracelsus* in 1836, this was the first discussion of Browning in *Fraser's* with a sympathetic attitude to his poetry.

Both critics noted Browning's unpopularity and observed that the poet was not for the run-and-read sort of mind, a mind which, according to Massey, was natural in the present life of haste. Like other reviewers, they discussed the subject matter and characteristics that made Browning's poetry difficult and that kept him from being widely read. Massey expressed disapproval of the foreign element and questioned the use of the peculiar instead of the familiar (yet he praised poems with foreign settings and unconventional subject matter); Browning, he said, loved "to worm his gnarly way to the dark heart of a good knotty problem." Skelton, on the other hand, was inclined to assert his approval of subjects that would deter the average reader, such as grave issues instead of trivialities and "byeways of the imagination" instead of stock passions. He was impressed by Browning's philosophy with its strong human orientation, his study of the human mind with its "delicate works and complicated springs," and his fidelity of observation.

The two critics did not see eye to eye on Browning's style. According to Massey the quick way of leaping to conclusions, the gaps that needed to be filled in, the hurried manner that prevented understanding, and the meaning that was not brought into sufficient relief placed an undue burden on the reader. Too much of the hammer was heard; this was a natural impediment. Another impediment was one Browning wilfully practiced by "twisting words into grotesque rhymes" when the subject demanded a serious treatment. Skelton, in discussing the difficulties of style, said the question was one of degree; the intended audience must be considered. He defended what others had been objecting to: ruggedness, whimsical or grotesque rhymes, abruptness, and intricate meters. He thought that Browning's defects had been exaggerated and that they were not wilful. "The occasional obscurity of his language, and the irregularity of the poetic forms which he uses, cannot be attributed to affectation. They are the natural and appropriate garniture of a peculiar and complex genius." With a "true dramatic conception of the whole," Browning let nothing "interfere with the life that he seeks to create or to restore."

Both critics had much to say in behalf of the individual poems, including ones that had found favor in the sight of other critics of the early sixties. They echoed Ruskin's pronouncement on *The Bishop Orders His Tomb*. In particular, they saw that Browning excelled as a dramatic, intellectual, original, and religious poet. The dramas alone ought to be "sufficient to build up the fame of a true and great poet" (Massey); Browning was one of England's greatest dramatists (Skelton). They discussed the plays not as products for the stage but as character studies. It was the inner life, not the meaning on the surface, that concerned Browning in play and in dramatic poem. He identified himself with his characters; he entered into their secret thoughts and hidden feelings and looked through their eyes in order to reveal what they felt.

If Skelton was in advance of Massey in not objecting to the foreign subject matter and the style of Browning's poetry, Massey projected more clearly and specifically the acceptance of Browning as a religious poet. Browning possessed the clearest of all seeing faculties — religious faith, said Massey.

The poet's nature, of all others, most needs that high reverence
which is to the spirit what iron is to the blood. . . . The poet's nature, of all others, most needs the revelation of Christianity, by virtue of its own peculiar temptations, doubts, and fears, obstinate
questionings, and yearnings for the bosom of rest. Mr Browning has
this reverence, and accepts this revelation. He is not, like some
poets, half ashamed to mention God or Christ, though he never
takes the name of either in vain. . . . His poem of "Christmas Eve
and Easter Day" is passionately alive with an intense desire for the
most personal relationship, lowly of heart as it is lofty in awe.

These two long and sympathetic surveys ushered in the fruitful sixties.
They kept the corpus of Browning's poetry before the public when no
new works were making their appearance. After the depressing reception of *Men and Women,* Browning could well have been pleased.

More than likely, he read both of the reviews — certainly the one
in *Fraser's* during the month when it appeared. In fact, he had already
read it when Skelton sent him a copy. In an accompanying note Skelton said he had attempted "in a weak way" to express something of his
admiration. He added, ". . . the article only inadequately expresses
the deep & genuine feeling with which I have read your works." [15]
Browning's answer showed his appreciation.

I find your note, on returning to London after a fortnight's absence;
you will have guessed the reason of any delay in answering it. I read
your article last month. I am glad indeed of the opportunity your
kindness gives me of saying that I do not think it "weak" or "inadequate" — but assuredly generous, and in that respect not unworthy
of you, however it may be undeserved by me. I do not often speak
about myself, but I think I feel your sympathy as gratefully as you
could desire. [16]

Browning's answer was not a perfunctory one, for later he wrote to
someone else of the article, "I think it a very generous piece of criticism and have no doubt that it exercised much influence on the for-
tunes of my poetry." [17]

After Browning resumed writing in the early sixties, he sent
Story and Isa news of his works in progress and of other facets of his poetic life. Two comments to Isa are noteworthy for their characteristic
quality — one showing his antagonism toward a periodical that had
been hostile to his work — this time the *Saturday Review* — and the
other showing his attitude toward socializing. In answering Isa's re-

mark on a criticism in the *Saturday Review* of one of her novels, Browning, in May 1863, gave her advice that he did not heed himself. He was doubtless thinking of the *Saturday's* flippantly arrogant attack on his obscurity in its review of *Men and Women*.

> . . . I thought you knew the trick of the superfine "Saturday," which I saw through long ago: you don't suppose they ever want to do anything but look fine themselves at everybody's expense, — what good would they get from honestly putting all the good of your book prominently forward, — animadverting, if you please, on any blemishes, but doing justice on the whole to the real worth there? All they hope for is that people will never think of the book but as the text whence they preached so clever a sermon. I read the article at the Club, thought it poor & ungenerous enough — but you are a woman doing her best & they enjoy putting down such impertinence as *that*.[18]

Then he admonished her, "But don't mind them — how young you must be, in the craft, to mind what one forgets in a week!" But even after the *Saturday Review* began to write favorably of his own works, Browning remembered its failure to do justice to *Men and Women* in its review of 1855. In fact, when he wrote Isa the "superfine" *Saturday* had already become more sympathetic with his poetry. Recently (Feb. 7, 1863) the critic of the *Selections* had soberly approached his task; he granted poetic gifts and appreciated the revelation of character in the *Selections*, though his remarks indicated that he was mystified by Browning's originality. Since Browning promptly read reviews of his works, especially those in the major periodicals, he had surely already examined the criticism, but obviously it had not cleared away his first impression. In 1864 he would still be referring to the captious criticism of 1855, but when not long afterwards the *Saturday Review* defended him against the *Edinburgh Review* he was gratified.

The other advice that he gave Isa was on socializing. It reflected his own practice. In January of 1863 he expressed pleasure in her going to balls, for she would "find the good of them" in the novels she wrote. In February he explained more particularly why she as a writer should attend such functions: ". . . you can describe what you have seen capitally."[19] He felt, as he had written Elizabeth in 1845, that some unknown good might escape him if he kept to himself.[20] He confided to Henriette Corkran, "I am not ashamed to confess that I do enjoy being with cultured folk, besides I find that mixing with others and the frictions of ideas are necessary to a writer."[21] So much did he move in society after he settled in London that numerous Victorians commented on his social life and Alfred Austin saw Browning as seeking fame by means of it (*Temple Bar,* June 1869).

In the early sixties, when Browning's works began to attract more and more readers and his social contacts were widening perceptibly, misconceptions started to increase. Comments on and by Browning in the sixties and later often need to be corrected or modified. A point to be remembered is that it is necessary to make a broad examination of available sources in order to test the accuracy of a questionable report or statement. It was not easy for Victorians to see the whole Browning. With their facile pens, many recorded limited impressions of him after a brief encounter, often in a social setting. If he belied the impression they had formed by having read his works, there was sometimes an element of surprise or occasionally of consternation in their description of his behavior and his appearance. The dedicated poet, who had left an unfavorable opinion when he called for the first time on Carlyle in a fashionable green riding coat and who had impressed Eliza Flower as a bit of a dandy when wearing lemon-colored gloves,[22] appeared to people in later life to be a well-dressed man of the world — perhaps a banker, a successful man of affairs, or a prosperous and cultivated merchant. His gloves still attracted attention, appearing to one observer as if they had grown on his shapely hands.[23] Some were disillusioned, as was Mrs. Thomas B. Aldrich, by Browning's *"savoir-faire."*[24] She and others did not, like Carlyle and Eliza Flower, have the opportunity to see beyond the appearance to the substance.

Browning the famous poet had much in common with Browning the ambitious young poet. During his early career he moved in circles that were made up almost entirely of professional men, such as Chorley, Forster, Macready, Domett, and others already referred to. He talked of his work to these friends who were engaged in pursuits related to his. After gaining wide recognition Browning also displayed freely the spirit and feelings of the poet; on occasion he did not hesitate to talk of his work.

In his years as an established poet, Browning's social life was broader and more varied. Many gatherings did not have the character of professionalism that had prevailed earlier. Professional men might be present, but the atmosphere was primarily social, and he was at ease. For conversation he could draw on his extensive storehouse of knowledge. Considered an outstanding conversationalist in his younger years, he was admired later for his spontaneous overflow of talk, his fund of anecdotes, and his knowledge of a great variety of subjects. Dante Gabriel Rossetti in the fifties found Browning's knowledge of early Italian art beyond that of any one he had ever met, and the pianist Charles Hallé later paid tribute to his wide and unusual knowledge of the literature of music and also to his "unfailing" judgment in musical matters.[25] As a sophisticated man of the world, he could without personal reference enter easily into conversation with people of diverse interests.

With a mobile existence that included gatherings in great houses in London, country estates, the universities — gatherings that were formal and informal, large and small — Browning, not surprisingly, impressed people in different ways. In his *Reminiscences* Justin McCarthy said, ". . . I do not know that I have ever met a talker more brilliant or who could, when he pleased, go more deeply into the heart of a subject than Robert Browning." In the same passage he criticized another writer who described the poet "as a mere chatterer in society, and a devotee of rank and fashion."[26] Each of these contradictory opinions was expressed by others who had rubbed shoulders with Browning.

One mistaken view was expressed by Wilfred Meynell, who thought that Browning possessed a detachment "which made him so tolerant, which left him unmoved by an individual or a public ignorance or neglect of him, and which, above all, made him equally indifferent to private appreciation or public praise."[27] Evidently Meynell had little or no knowledge of Browning's attitude toward the critics' harsh treatment or neglect of his works.

Meynell's impression of Browning's detachment and indifference is no more accurate than lingering half-truths that cloud the picture. One is that Browning was hostile to critics and criticism indiscriminately, but in reality he was hostile to critics who he thought made no effort to understand and represent his work fairly and he was appreciative of critics who sympathetically approached it, even though perhaps with some misunderstanding. Another is that in the act of composing Browning was indifferent to professional criticism, whether favorable or unfavorable, but in reality he disregarded criticism that might stifle his artistic impulse and he also gave due consideration to whatever might prove beneficial.

Half-truths and total misconceptions die hard. Now and then a contemporary of Browning's left on record an impression so arresting for its dramatic quality that a surprising number of modern commentators have allowed themselves to be misled by it. Mary Gladstone's

early opinion that Browning was disagreeable in manner, recorded in
her diary, has been referred to over and over without consideration of
her later opinion of him as he talked about his poetry. Henry James's
picture of a compartmentalized Browning in his book on William
Wetmore Story is an example of overstatement that has held on with
the tenacity of a limpet. He thought that Browning in his London period had a double identity. "The poet and the 'member of society' were
. . . dissociated in him as they can rarely elsewhere have been. . . ."[28]
James could have known little of Browning's habits. Or was he formulating a neat and striking contrast in order to produce an effect?
Such statements as these made by Mary Gladstone and Henry James
make good copy and invite repetition, but they should not be taken seriously unless all of the related evidence is considered.

Browning walked abroad, made his contacts, absorbed ideas; the
outer world flowed into his study. When he sat down to write he was
not sharply separated from the man who shared his life with others and
who considered the friction of ideas beneficial to him as a poet. In his
associations he must have reflected at least as much of the poetic mind
as most of our great writers. He had no need and no desire to discuss
his own art when this subject was out of place. Browning's reported response to a statement that Wordsworth was the "best talker in England" is revealing: ". . . he was certainly not at all so in latter years; he
spoke little, and only on subjects that interested himself, without respect to the taste of his audience."[29] Browning himself respected the
interests of others and the decorum of social intercourse. When it was
appropriate to do so, on social occasions he spoke of his works, especially to one person. Others besides Mary Gladstone heard him talk of
his poetry.

In general Browning did speak or write willingly and considerably about his poetic existence. He explained lines, allusions, the
meaning of his poems, and the circumstances of their composition or
publication. His letters to Furnivall and Julia Wedgwood show how
unhesitatingly he replied to their questions or comments and volun-
teered information about his art.[30] He wrote as readily but not as often
or as much to Buxton Forman, Dowden, and others.[31] In his correspondence with Reverend Williams there was an easy exchange of comments. Browning wrote of improving his poetry, of answering questions through Furnivall as intermediary, and of the reception of his
work; and he replied to Reverend Williams' questions. It was apparent
that he gave information spontaneously and generously; in one letter

he told Reverend Williams that he had given Mrs. Orr "whatever explanations she chose to consider necessary" for her "Primer" *(Handbook)*.[32] Rudolf Lehmann wrote, "He would freely speak of his published writings."[33] Records left by Victorians testify to that. Admirers even came to his home to ask questions, and he answered them.[34] And Sidney Colvin was one of the number of contemporaries who told of Browning's willingness to read his poetry to friends.[35] There is no shortage of evidence that Browning helped others profit by his poetry. Ian Jack, in his article " 'Commented It Must Be': Browning Annotating Browning," illuminates this aspect of his life.[36]

Browning was not indifferent to the needs of his readers, as was often said in his lifetime. There are plenty of instances of his willingness to answer questions or make explanatory comments on his poetry. Moreover, to some works he added prefaces intended to guide the reader. As we shall see, in the *works* of 1863 he arranged the poems so as to bring out his special qualities and smooth the reader's path. And in the *Works* of 1868 he adopted a chronological arrangement in order to show his poetic development, which he felt should be taken into account for a just and comprehensive appreciation. His efforts were praiseworthy responses to the needs of his readers.

Occasionally mistaken notions arose from a misrepresentation by Browning, and again an in-depth view is desirable. When he reacted to circumstances that aroused the memory of painful experiences, his response could misrepresent the real situation. Now and then he was on the defensive against a critical world. When he talked or wrote to someone about subjects that deeply concerned him, he sometimes displayed characteristics that need to be weighed and evaluated in the light of the complex make-up of a sensitive, confident, and ambitious poet facing a public that must be convinced of his worth. His reaction to the belated reception of his works, the early ones in particular, brought out in the first chapters of this study, shows how his sensibility and pride could impel him to make a defensive or self-deceptive statement. Some of his contemporaries took his words at face value. Others could see beyond them. Story knew Browning well enough not to take seriously his assertion, quoted above, of indifference to criticism.

We read with interest — and caution — his statement to Mrs. Thomas Fitzgerald, "I have desired Mr F.[Furnivall] to thank the author, if he has occasion, for the great pleasure he has given me — but I never myself on any occasion thank a critic for his criticism. . . ."[37] He modified this position when he wrote Skelton a letter of appreciation on November 15, 1878. "I cannot generally bring my mind to thank a judge when he lays down the law, and it favours me; but I may say that the points wherein you pronounced for my poetry were precisely those which I should wish made conspicuous."[38] He did thank critics — after his own fashion — as is clear from remarks of his quoted in this book, including his expression of gratefulness to Skelton cited earlier in this chapter.

In our desire to present Browning as he really was we should read his statements about himself in the light of all that we know. The need for doing so is evident from his words to Mrs. John F. Corkran, as quoted by her daughter. He told her he had just completed his plan for *The Inn Album*. "I am another man to-day — my poem is planned." The hard part, he said, was planning the story and conceiving the characters; after that he would resolve to write so many lines a day and then carry out his resolution. "I never re-write," he said. "I always find that I have chosen the right word at first. I know that my critics would say my writing could be clearer if I made more erasures in the manuscript, but it is not so. I write with my whole mind, and at a high tension of concentration — and I could not find more fitting words to express my thoughts."[39] If Browning made the comment as it was reported, it does not entirely accord with what we know about his working habits. It is true that to him rewriting seemed to mean changing his conception. It is also true, however, that in revising he definitely did find and use better words than those he had first written. We learn from De-Vane that in fact the manuscript for *The Inn Album* (which seemingly he had in mind when he said he never rewrote his lines), though "written smoothly and easily" otherwise, did show "considerable blotting, scratching, and rewriting" towards the end of one section and indicated trouble with the concluding lines.[40] In the exhiliration of having completed the plan for his poem, with characteristic confidence he spoke of his ability to carry it out. Perhaps we should not take literally a creative artist's comment on the process of his writing.

Enough has been said of Browning's social life as it was related to his poetic existence to show the importance of attempting to separate fact from fancy and drawing valid conclusions from a large body of comments. Misconceptions once formed are tenacious; only time and repeated effort can correct false notions that had their inception many years ago.

After returning from Italy Browning went through a period of concentration on personal and professional matters. He resumed contact with friends and began to extend his social activities at about the time when *Selections* was published. Critics took a fresh interest in his poetry. With the progress they had made in the fifties, limited though it was, they could advantageously reconsider the whole of his works. They would soon do so, for even before the last of the reviews of the *Selections* appeared the first volume of *the Poetical Works* of 1863 was published.

CHAPTER XXI

A Broad View

The Poetical Works of Robert Browning, 1863

Browning, who had considered frequent publication important, did not produce many works during his fifteen years in Italy. Besides his first collected edition (1849), he published *Christmas-Eve and Easter-Day* (1850) and *Men and Women* (1855); his introductory essay to the forged Shelley letters appeared briefly (1852). Soon after his return to England in 1861 friends prepared *Selections from the Poetical Works of Robert Browning* (with 1863 on the title page but 1862 in fact); he republished earlier works in *The Poetical Works of Robert Browning* (3 vols., 1863) and published new poems in *Dramatis Personae* (1864). Thus he resumed his custom of steady publication, as in the forties. He also took up his old practice of having more than one work in hand at the same time and of looking ahead to still other writing. Even while the *Selections* and *The Poetical Works* were in progress, he was composing poems for *Dramatis Personae* and making plans for *The Ring and the Book* (1868–9).

Browning was in a position to perceive very quickly the effect of his publications; he was no longer handicapped, as he had been while living outside of England, by not having ready access to oral opinion and, more importantly, to the reaction of periodicals. After the appearance of his *Selections* he saw signs of change in the critical response to his works. During the fifties and into the sixties his publisher, Edward Chapman of Chapman and Hall (d. 1847), had not gained financially from his association with Browning, though Elizabeth's works had been profitable. On the other hand, Browning had had to endure — not without making known his objections — Chapman's slipshod manner of caring for both his and Elizabeth's interests.

From the standpoint of the firm, the poet's return to England would obviously bring no drastic change. Chapman offered Browning £120 for *the Poetical Works* of 1863,[1] which to a publisher without the gift of prophecy would seem adequate. Though the attitude of readers toward Browning's poetry showed a marked change by the middle of the decade, Chapman's careless way of doing business remained. Since being in England gave Browning the advantage of taking better stock of the situation and since he was not one to let matters drift if it was in his power to improve them, a change to a more businesslike publisher seemed inevitable.

The fact that Browning was on the ground had a good effect on the reviewing. The critics who had complained about his being away from his own country could do so no more; and the well-intentioned ones wishing to get in touch with him found him to be approachable. Moncure D. Conway, an American Unitarian clergyman and writer who lived in England for many years, had earlier written an article on Browning. In spite of some misrepresentation,[2] Browning appreciated the good will that prompted Conway's interest in his poetry. When Browning was away from London on a holiday he answered a request from Conway for information about the collected edition.[3] This information was of some assistance to Conway as he prepared a review which was to appear in the *Victoria Magazine* in February 1864. As usual, Browning, who welcomed effort in his behalf, was ready to give help that would be instrumental in promoting his works.

In considering the presentation of his works, he decided to make a bid for readers by following the procedure that he and Elizabeth had suggested to Chapman in 1856 for Elizabeth's poems — publication "volume by volume, so as to allow people to buy by degrees."[4] He also considered the effect on the reader of the order of the poems. Seemingly he kept in mind what he would like readers to be most impressed by, what he knew critics had liked best and understood, and also what he felt needed to be deemphasized to assure the desired impressions. This accounts for the arrangement of the pieces in the collection of 1863.

Volume I of *The Poetical Works of Robert Browning*, Third Edition (so labeled on the general title page — each volume also had a separate title page), appeared in May of 1863, subtitled *Lyrics, Romances, Men, and Women*. In it the poems from *Dramatic Lyrics* of 1842, *Dramatic Ro-*

mances and Lyrics of 1845, and *Men and Women* of 1855 were redistributed. Volume II, subtitled *Tragedies and Other Plays,* was published in June of 1863. Volume III was published in September of 1863 and bore the subtitle *Paracelsus, Christmas-Eve and Easter-Day, Sordello.* This last poem, which Browning had revised during the winter of 1855–6, carried a dedication to Joseph Milsand. The *Works* as a whole was dedicated to John Forster.[5] Once the volumes began to appear, Browning had to wait for reviews, always a difficult time for him.

The order of presentation was helpful and the interval between publication dates allowed time that was needed for reading or rereading the works in each volume. The dramatic poems, the ones that had appeared first as parts of the *Bells* series (republished in the 1849 collected edition) and the ones in *Men and Women,* were given the leading position. Repeated exposure to the works that best exemplified the stamp of Browning's genius was beneficial. They would receive the emphasis they deserved as the critics saw the suitability of Browning's particular dramatic quality to them rather than to the plays.

Browning's selection for the second volume was also advantageous. With the poems of the first volume in mind, the critics could see that the technique of character revelation Browning had used to good effect in the poetry had not been suited to plays written for the stage and that they should not be judged by the standard of contemporary drama. In the later forties complaints about the plays had decreased and critics tended either by implication or by incidental remarks to classify them as plays to be read. With the exception of *In a Balcony* (a "playlet" published in *Men and Women*) and *Colombe's Birthday* (performed in 1853, though first published in 1844), no play of Browning's had been publicly brought to the attention of his readers in the fifties. The next appearance of his plays in print had been only fragmentary, in the *Selections.* The tendency had been to dismiss them, and that was good at the time. When the plays appeared again in the second volume of the 1863 collection, their subordinate position was fairly well settled and they could be examined in this light. The critics now explained why they could not be successful on the contemporary stage.

The plays — which had caused Macready much trouble, brought frustration to the poet, and nettled the critics — were now dispassionately evaluated. No longer was the account of their deficiencies as stage plays accompanied by intemperate accusations of carelessness and wilfulness. Instead of condemning them for failing as stage plays, the critics evaluated them for the characteristics common to his plays and short poems. According to the *Saturday Review*, Browning's plays possessed qualities that made them unsuitable for stage presentation, but the reviewer praised them as closet drama; they afforded the "delight which melodious verse, brilliant fancy, analysis of the passions, and earnest ethical purpose always command." The *National Review* said that Browning never entered into the practical forces that constituted the life of great drama; at most conflict was indicated to illustrate character.

By recognizing the dramatic quality present in the shorter poems as well as in the plays, some critics were led to express preference for the poems. The *Spectator*, which in its early severe and irritable criticisms of the plays had accused Browning of cultivating his weeds, now served as explicator: Browning painted the "*tendencies* of a character, but not its action"; the march and procession of events were lacking. Since Browning cared only "to make his 'men and women' explain themselves, not to see how they acquit themselves in the battle," the dramatic sketches were more satisfying than the regular dramas. The *London Quarterly Review* had a similar comparison of play and poem: the plays adapted for performance were "far below the average of his shorter dramatic poems"; it was not the outward bearing that Browning chiefly revealed but instead the hidden centers. The *Guardian* (Aug. 5, 1863) saw the superiority of the poems in a somewhat different light: "He [Browning] can compress the spirit of a period into a single character; he cannot animate a whole group of moving figures with the glow of life, incident, and adventures." In time this view came to be accepted by Browning critics.

Pippa Passes, included in Volume II *(Tragedies and Other Plays),* and *Paracelsus* and *Sordello,* included in Volume III, were examined for their dramatic qualities. *Pippa Passes,* more secure than ever as one of the most admired of Browning's poems, had more favorable attention than any other work in Volume II. The *Guardian* (Aug. 5, 1863) considered it excellent as a "series of effective tableaux." The critic for the *Saturday Review,* who thought Browning had mistitled the second volume, said that *Pippa Passes* would be more aptly called a "scenic vision." The *London Quarterly Review,* which expressed along with some objection real praise for *Paracelsus,* called it and *Pippa* the best of Browning's dramas but the least suitable to the stage. (*Paracelsus,* with its divisions into scenes and its dialogue, gave the impression that it was a play, though Browning labeled it "a poem, not a drama.") All of

Browning's earliest long poems were considered as drama by one critic: Conway, in the *Victoria Magazine*, said *Pauline* (not included in the *Poetical Works*), *Paracelsus*, and *Sordello* were dramas no less than *Colombe's Birthday* and quoted a passage from *Paracelsus* as being "a fine instance of that dramatic representation of the inmost states of mind, in which Mr. Browning is *facile princeps*." It was obvious now that all of Browning's works were cut from the same cloth.

As the critics discussed the dramatic aspect of Browning's poems, they also had much to say about another prominent aspect, the intellectual. In reviewing the *Selections* they had called attention to it in connection with Browning's use of the psychological for poetry. Now as they were observing its function in the totality of Browning's art they were moving toward a more liberal standard of criticism, though some of them were still concerned about the demands that Browning's technique made on his readers. He understood men chiefly on their intellectual side; a "more dramatic *intellect* than Mr. Browning's it would not be easy to find" *(Spectator)*. As a dramatic poet, he identified himself with his characters, scarcely revealing his own thoughts, and became a "keen and searching analyst" *(London Quarterly Review)*. In setting his men up "as he conceives them to have acted and spoken in the crisis of their existence," he demanded an imagination scarcely feasible on the part of his readers *(London Review)*. In starting in the middle, he left the reader to find his "bearings" *(Spectator)*. Browning's method, which we are accustomed to today, could be startling to his contemporaries. Just how much so comes out in the following quotation from the *National Review:*

> Instead of fascinating you with his harmony of movement, and gradually insinuating the drift and spirit of the poem into your imagination, Mr. Browning rushes upon you with a sort of intellectual *douche*, half stuns you with the abruptness of the start, repeats the application in a multitude of swift various shocks from unexpected points of the compass, and leaves you at last giddy and wondering where you are, but with a vague sense that, were you but properly prepared beforehand, and warned as to its laws of approach, you might discern a unity and power in this intellectual water-spout, though its first descent only drenched and bewildered your imagination.

The peculiar character of Browning's mental activity became more significant than ever. The critic for the *Reader* paid high tribute to his intellectual quality, in which the "imagination or creative faculty is paramount." His poetry was not lacking, as some had maintained, in the "deep, permanent, elemental song," but the intellectual did predominate. There was a special need of the time for a "poet whose manner it is to involve the melodies that move the heart in such florid profusion of curious intellectual harmonies." The critic, primarily interested in Browning's inquisitiveness and the restlessness of his quest, saw that he went below the surface, explored the byways, and represented various fields of knowledge.

After a long stretch of rejection, critics of *Men and Women* had begun to accept Browning's liking for Italian or historical subjects. They had expressed their own acceptance in the reviews of the *Selections* but felt that readers in general would not approve of his predilection for the remote. Now some saw his wide range as an asset. He was English in mind and genius, but he went outside England and contemporary life for themes and details, for history and art *(Reader)*. To depict "the course of life in the past and present ages" was desirable in a time of lopsidedness and fragmentation *(London Review)*. The tendency of modern English poets "to raise the local and social characteristics of this one country into a more universal light than they will bear" was regrettable; but Browning, who could deal sympathetically and convincingly with a German or Italian or Oriental of another day and age, deserved high praise for his "vast range" *(Victoria Magazine)*.

In recognizing the expanse of Browning's interests and sympathies the critics could say that he had a "balanced, rounded intellect, which loves nature without despising man" and admits within his vision the worldling as well as the pietist *(London Review)*. Representing the baser side of human nature had militated against Browning earlier; this was no longer true. His "skill in depicting vice no more implies actual vice than skill in depicting virtue necessarily implies actual virtue"; Browning's works as a whole show the "marks of an earnest and religious spirit" *(London Quarterly Review)*. According to the *Spectator* there was "something peculiarly powerful about most of Mr. Browning's treatment of theological or semi-theological subjects." The critic was impressed by his "strong intellectual imagination in dealing with the attitude of the mind towards naked truth." The critics saw the serious and lofty intent in the depiction of evil as well as good, and, like Conway in the *Victoria Magazine,* they gave Browning a high place as a religious thinker and poet.

Foreshadowing modern commentaries, these critics observed Browning's drawing together the real and the ideal and relating man's imperfect world to the world beyond, to perfection. The *National Review* emphasized and applauded Browning's interest in the "borderland between the supernatural and the worldly wisdom" and his "study of some striking conflict or some still more striking combination between the craft of the visible world and the craft of the invisible, and of the many threads of connexion between the two." The critic for the *London Quarterly Review* said that the poet concerned himself with "the complication, the strife, and the aspiration" in life. Browning believed that humanity was working out "God's own plan" — it could not fail to be true that "God's in His Heaven, / All's right with the world!" Browning the optimist was emerging.

As the critics discussed poems involving religious questions and became increasingly aware of Browning's religious thought in general, some observed that he was reflecting concerns of his day. In the fifties the pertinence of *Christmas-Eve and Easter-Day* to current beliefs had aroused interest in Browning as a religious poet, and the relation of *Men and Women* to the Victorian climate of opinion had been noted with approval. Now according to the *London Quarterly Review* Browning caught the spirit of the time by revealing "the inner life of men, the world of thought and feeling," which was more prominent than action.

In the *Victoria Magazine,* Conway pointed out the seasonable concern evident in Browning's poetry: "He has, indeed, a fine philosophic insight into the workings of the human mind and heart, and is a fair analyst of the forms in which they are best represented in the present age." In speaking of Browning's acquaintance with the "philosophical and religious systems" of the time, Conway reminded his readers, "Long before Darwin gave to the world his theory of the transmutation of species by natural selection, Mr. Browning [in *Paracelsus*] had traced a similar law working in human society. . . ." Browning, he said, had given this law varied expressions in his later poetry. Conway recalled that a distinguished thinker (not named) had called *Paracelsus* "the wail of the nineteenth century." In the early sixties, as in the fifties, some critics saw the contemporary relevance of Browning's poetry — this before the publication of *Dramatis Personae* (1864), in which the relevance was more apparent.

Among the poems most often discussed and favored were those reflecting the interests of the time, especially the engrossing problem of religion. In the reviews of the *Poetical Works* several critics referred approvingly to *Christmas-Eve and Easter-Day (National Review, London Review, Victoria Magazine)* and to *Bishop Blougram's Apology (Reader,*

London Review, National Review, Spectator) in relation to religion or to other aspects of contemporary life. It must be said, however, that the *National Review* did not consistently praise *Blougram.* The critic for the *London Review* said that the poems he named "and a score more, illustrate our own times." *Cleon,* though thoroughly Greek in tone, bore a "trace of the nineteenth century" here and there, according to the *London Quarterly Review.* Remarks made in some of the reviews indicate that the different presentments of religious thought in Browning's poetry contributed to the critics' interest in it. Other poems most often and most favorably discussed included *Saul, Karshish, The Bishop Orders His Tomb,* and *Fra Lippo Lippi.* Three other poems should be named for the attention they received. *Pippa Passes,* as has been said, was still a favorite with the critics, and the comments on *Good News* and *Soliloquy of the Spanish Cloister* indicated an interest in them. Of the plays, *Colombe's Birthday, Luria,* and *A Soul's Tragedy* were the most attractive to reviewers, not as conventional stage plays but as poems exhibiting the author's intellectual qualities.

The majority of critics were far more concerned with the intellectual character of Browning's poems and his seriousness of purpose than with their poetic quality. A few of them admitted that his style might be a deterrent to his popularity, but they were not stating their own objections to it. The *Spectator* and *National Review* did have complaints, which were more or less the same inasmuch as R. H. Hutton wrote both of the reviews. In the *National Review* he criticized particularly the diction, rhyme, and meter of the lyrics, but he had something favorable to say about the poems devoid of lyrical content. "In the dramas, where Mr. Browning's dramatic genius corresponds to the *form* of his thought, and in the confessedly dramatic fragments called 'Men and Women,' where there is no effort to be lyrical, nothing can be more lucid and simple than his style, so soon as you have once found your true latitude and caught the spirit of the situation."

The critic for the *London Quarterly Review* saw that objections to Browning's style could justly be raised, but it seemed to him that the blame should not be placed on the poet alone. At times faults appeared to be so to readers whose shortcomings made them incapable of coping with Browning's poetry. His power of conveying the results of his keen and searching analysis of character "in a dramatic form, by the aid of language, and of language almost exclusively, is, so far as we are aware, a new thing in literature." The critic thought that we should take Browning's works as they are, "without too much grumbling at their failings."

As the critics commended monologues like *Karshish*, *Fra Lippo Lippi*, and *The Bishop Orders His Tomb*, they were adjusting their taste to Browning's nontraditional method. But they still were not ready to accept the originality of the lyrics. Browning's characterization of the *Dramatic Lyrics* in his Advertisement to that publication — that though they were "for the most part Lyric in expression," they were "always Dramatic in principle" — had never meant much to the critics. There had been unfavorable criticism of the lyrics in *Men and Women*, and the two critics of the *Poetical Works* — Conway and Hutton — that did comment on them indicated trouble with Browning's originality in that form. Although the receptive Conway did not fail to praise Browning's lyrical efforts, he said, "Mr. Browning's style of expression is to be admired for the very quality which forbids its being a complete vehicle of lyric poetry, — namely, its exactness" (*Victoria Magazine*).

The other critic, Hutton, rated Browning's lyrics as failures, and he used considerable space to make his point (*National Review*). He quoted Browning's Advertisement to the *Dramatic Lyrics* and then said that the poems tried to be "lyric in expression" but failed; they "show, by the rasping and the friction of the style that they have somehow got embodied in a wholly unsuitable poetic organism." His discussion shows that he was trying to make Browning's poems fit into his set idea of what lyrics should be. Just as the dramatic monologues had suffered from being judged according to traditional patterns, the lyrics were not being accepted on their own artistic terms.

The publication of the *Poetical Works* was a good test of Browning's standing with the critics. For the first time they had a collection that included *Christmas-Eve and Easter-Day* and *Men and Women* with its treasure of original poems; hence, they could reexamine all — or almost all — of Browning's works. Of the twelve reviews of *Poetical Works* appearing in the separate list of reviews, the one in the *Critic* was merely a reprint of two short comments from other reviews, and the three in the *Guardian* and the one in *Weldon's* had little more than a few sketchy comments, though *Weldon's* quoted all of four poems and a considerable portion of two others. The seven remaining were substantial discussions; only Hutton's reviews contained an appreciable amount of questioning along with favorable recognition of some of the dramatic monologues to illustrate Browning's strength. (More will be said in greater detail about Hutton's criticism in the *National Review* when we come to Browning's reaction to it.)

The seven substantial reviews show a continuation of the steadily increasing perceptiveness of Browning's special qualities. The critics no longer had trouble in recognizing that his genius as a dramatic writer was best suited to character revelation in a monologue. The originality which they once had merely pointed out generally they now identified specifically in the form, content, and style of his poetry. His intellectual force was stressed, as it always had been; but the perception of his intellectuality in relation to his other qualities that was present in the reviews of the *Selections* was extended and intensified in the reviews of *Poetical Works*. The critics saw that besides leading Browning to a broader view of knowledge and the study of man's behavior this intellectual impulse led him to reflect the realities of life and associate them with spiritual values in character dramatization. Even Hutton, who exhibited some of the shortcomings of earlier critics, while contradicting himself and objecting severely to Browning's style went to great lengths to discuss and praise the extent of Browning's intellectual imagination.

One of the most encouraging aspects of the criticism of the *Poetical Works* was the near absence of hesitancy and inconsistency. This confidence was accompanied by a belief that the public was becoming more receptive to Browning's poetry or might well become more receptive as the result of reading the *Poetical Works*. The *National Review* began with a discussion of Browning's failure to make a broad appeal but closed by saying, ". . . these poems cannot fail to win for him slowly a substantial and an enduring fame." Though Browning was still caviar to many, especially to young people, said the *Reader,* his poetry was finding its way to new readers by the efforts of admirers or even more probably by "mere continued percolation . . . through society."

There was a feeling that in itself the publication of the *Poetical Works* indicated a change in the reading public toward Browning. The fact that a collected edition was called for showed "that a great singer, if not the greatest of those amongst us, is gaining acceptance, which we may hope is all the surer since it has been somewhat slow" (*London Review*). Although not a popular poet, Browning was steadily gaining readers; there was reason to believe that the complete edition was published in response to a sufficient demand of the reading public (*Victoria Magazine*). The republication of his poems surely indicated a gradual increase of admirers and readers (*London Quarterly Review*). It looked as if there was no longer need for hesitancy in pronouncing a gain in public appreciation.

Browning watched for and read reviews of the *Poetical Works*. None had appeared in the *Athenaeum* of the first two volumes when he wrote Isa, in September of 1863, that the criticisms of poetry in the *Athenaeum* were "beneath contempt," and then described its review of a collection of sea songs and ballads "as full of stupidity as an egg is of meat."[6] As we have observed, Browning had had a similar reaction years before when he had been expecting a review of *Dramatic Romances and Lyrics* in the same weekly; it did not appear at once. During the waiting period, a trying time for Browning, he found fault with another review that did appear.[7] Whatever discredit the two criticisms the *Athenaeum* deserved, we suspect that it was the absence of a review of his own works that disturbed Browning.

One review of the *Poetical Works* left such a strong impression on Browning that he discussed it when he wrote Isa on November 19 and when he wrote Mrs. Story a week later. It was the one by Hutton in the *National Review* of October 1863. We have already pointed to Hutton's remarks that are related to the topics that have been discussed in this chapter. Here we are concerned with the aspects of the review that aroused Browning to express his objections and at the same time reveal something of his artistic intentions and his consternation at pronouncements upon aspects of his poetry that the critic failed to understand or that he was not sufficiently familiar with.

Hutton began his discussion by asserting that Browning, instead of being a celebrated poet in Europe or even in his own country, was the poet of an "intellectual sect." The reason for this, he said, was "the almost complete absence of that atmosphere of fascination about his verse, that melody of mind and speech, which is the main attraction of poetry to ordinary men." To develop this point, Hutton quoted Coleridge's definition of a poem (in *Biographia Literaria*, chap. XIV), according to which a poem is differentiated from other species of composition that have pleasure rather than truth as their *immediate* object, "by proposing to itself such delight from the *whole* as is compatible with a distinct gratification from each component *part*." Hutton thought this was a bad definition, one which would exclude Browning's works from the realm of poetry; he felt sure that Coleridge would have appreciated Browning's power and insight. Nevertheless, Hutton used the definition to make two generalizations about Browning's poems: they "give scarcely any immediate sensitive pleasure" and they "are not so organised that the parts have any gratification for you at all, till you catch a view of his whole." Browning does not lead his readers along pleasurably and smoothly, but forces them to form a notion of the whole before they can grasp the significance and function of the parts — in other words, they have to reread and study.

Complaints of this kind were nothing new to Browning, but Hutton stung him by stating the case very vigorously. Hutton made it seem that he spoke with the authority of Coleridge. Using Coleridge's terms, he said that Browning placed too much emphasis on the whole and not enough on the parts. To Browning it was the central effect that was important and the parts lent themselves to the production of that effect. Hutton thought that Browning should give "an *independent* interest and attractiveness to the component parts of his poems."

The review was not devoid of favorable comments, even discerning ones, but that it stopped short of being a perceptive review becomes evident in the following discussion of Browning's reaction to it. Hutton said that in range of thought Browning surpassed all of his poetic contemporaries. Yet in discussing his intellectual qualities as a dramatic poet Hutton exhibited a shortsightedness that particularly vexed Browning. Browning's genius "for sketching character *in position*" was, the reviewer said, probably the secret of the poet's lyrical failures and also of his defective powers of poetical expression in general. This genius, he reasoned, "implies an intellectual basis for his dramatic power, and suggests that Mr. Browning is rather a highly intellectual actor, throwing himself into a new part, and feeling its characteristic points. . . ."

Hutton pointed out that Browning's keen intellect was overpowering — that

> *his* style . . . is fatiguing and destitute of lower tints and undertones, and that when he is pictorial, as he very often is, he crowds and accentuates the striking points, so as to miss the harmony of poetry. It gives one the impression of a vigilant intellect noting all the principal features of the scene acutely, and concentrating his perceptive faculties so completely in the gaze of attention as to miss those numberless under-growths of half-dreamy observation which constitute so great a charm of poetic insight.

Browning wrote Mrs. Story that the review was "noticeable for its mixed nature, — over-laudatory, perhaps, and candid in the main point of giving to me the exact canon of composition whereby I live, move & have my being."⁸ We learn what the canon is. "He says, I seek a central effect, and only wish the details to be subordinate and seen by a reflected light from the whole: exactly! simply, it is wrong, he holds — and 'right,' I maintain." Browning's claim for this principle should be set beside his defense of his art in his letter to Ruskin of February 1, 1856. There, in metaphorical language, he said that he did not "paint it all plain out" as Ruskin would have him do, but used "touches and bits of outlines" to convey his conception to the viewer.

Browning had a further complaint of Hutton.

> Then he overlooks whole poems & plays written to exemplify the very things he says I never even try to do: people used to ignore *all* I had done, — now they recognize a bit and ignore the rest — "pazienza"! And the "bit" is absurdly accounted for — "my long acquaintance with Priests & the Confessional" — I who never spoke to any other priest than our little Abbé for two minutes in my life!

We can turn again to the review for explanation of Browning's comment. Hutton wrote of the poet's "long residence in the country of Machiavelli and Cavour, and a close study of the ecclesiastical wisdom, craft, and subtlety produced by the system of the confessional." And he discussed favorably at length Browning's poems dealing with ecclesiastical persons and different phases of religious thought.

Browning had made a comment to Isa which was in part an anticipation of the one to Mrs. Story, but he wrote Isa more specifically of what, according to Hutton, he had never even tried to do.

> That critique was fair in giving the right key to my poetry — in as much as it *is* meant to have "one central meaning, seen only by reflexion in details" — "our principle," says the critic — "mine and good" say I: he is more than fair in praising one portion of my works at the expense of all the rest, — unfair in saying I have never even *tried* to do, what I have done, well or ill, in long poems he is pleased — not to call failures but pass clean over: thus, I never describe ("Flight of the Duchess") — never delineate the quieter female character ("Colombe") & so on.⁹

Let us see what Hutton said about Browning's women and his descriptive powers. The basis of Browning's genius, he wrote, was not meditatively intellectual, but speculatively intellectual, "of which we may see one great proof in the far superior character of his masculine than of his feminine sketches, of his 'men' than of his 'women.'" Women's characters, Hutton continued, are best depicted "by essence and indefinite tone." Browning "throws his feminine characters into as strongly-defined attitudes as his masculine, and the consequence is, that they are not nearly so effective; and also that, half-conscious of this intellectualising mould of his mind, he attempts them very much less often." Ottima did not entirely please Hutton; she was too strongly delineated. Of Browning's other feminine pictures the only ones that impressed him were those in *In a Balcony,* and they were "not perhaps overdrawn, but drawn on the stretch, and not in the way in which women most naturally express themselves."

What was said about Browning's descriptions? According to the review, it was the restlessness of Browning's intellect that kept his poetry from having the excellent descriptive power of Tennyson's poetry, with its "undergrowth of perception" that came from a "brooding, silent, receptive mind." According to Hutton, Browning's intellect did not always serve him well.

Ironically, Hutton stated that he would be satisfied if by having written the review he could "diminish in any degree the obstacles to a true appreciation of his [Browning's] genius." Hutton was serious; he had doubtless worked hard to prepare for the thirty-page review of a writer whose poems, he thought, would surely bring fame. Browning appreciated his efforts, but it was upsetting to see censure of the "exact canon of composition" by which he worked. Hutton, who showed critical ability in evaluating the content of Browning's poetry, fell short when he needed to judge it according to the individuality of its artistry. It was also disquieting for Browning to see Hutton ignore certain poems when he took him to task for lacking adequate descriptive power and being unable to portray quieter feminine characters. Browning conceded, however, at the end of his comments on the review in the letter to Isa, "The fact is, there is more in my works than a new comer can take in at once — or by next month, when the article ought to be ready."

In the same letters that Browning wrote about the *National Review* to Isa and Mrs. Story he told them that his new poems (*Dramatis Personae*) were delayed because of the success of his *Poetical Works;* he did not wish to run the risk of detracting from the favorable attention being paid to this collection by bringing out another book too soon. At last, in the reception of the *Poetical Works* we can see some results of Browning's own steadfast efforts and of the laborious struggle for understanding that had been taking place in the minds of many critics.

CHAPTER XXII

Timely Topics and Wider Acceptance

Dramatis Personae, 1864

After Browning's return to England two retrospective collections of his works appeared — *Selections* (chosen and arranged by two friends) and *The Poetical Works*, both in 1863. The poems in his next book, *Dramatis Personae*, were new, except for several that (in whole or in part) had appeared earlier or were appearing simultaneously in America. While he was still in Italy Browning wrote some of the poems for *Dramatis Personae* and began adding to them in 1862. At the end of the year he informed Isa, ". . . I write a good deal & mean to do more."[1] He worked while in London and also during his vacations away from home in 1862 and 1863. There were noticeable differences from *Men and Women*. No longer prominent was the rich background of Italian life. Browning continued to write love poems, but now the ones concerning unfulfilled love stood out sharply. In the completed volume a greatly increased proportion of poems were concerned with religious affirmation, and specific topics of controversy came through more often and more definitely than ever before.

Being in the midst of the intellectual stir of London accounted to some extent for the greater attention that Browning paid to timely topics, but not entirely. He had probably started *Mr. Sludge* while he was still in Italy. In considering the extent to which he turned to contemporary life as he wrote the poems for *Dramatis Personae*, we must remember that he read reviews carefully and that earlier in his career his work had changed in some respects in accordance with the criticism he had received. From reviews he had learned that *Christmas-Eve and Easter-Day* had more and more, as time passed, called attention to him as a poet interested in matters of Christian import. Of the poems in *Men and Women*, the most popular was *Bishop Blougram's Apology*, and high on the list were *Cleon* and *Karshish*, all three dealing with the problem of faith and doubt, which was of much concern to the Englishman of the fifties and sixties. Since according to his own words Browning wished to attract readers, it is not surprising that, after seeing how *Christmas-Eve and Easter-Day* affected his reputation and which poems in *Men and Women* received favorable attention, he continued to examine what was of interest to him — spiritual matters — now with a varied and striking pertinence to religious thought of the day.

He had written Edward Chapman that he would have lost most had he not read the criticism of *Men and Women* in the *British Quarterly Review*.[2] The writer of it saw in "not a few of the finest poems" high and subtle thought inwound with topics of "deeper philosophy and metaphysics of the time," though he did add that such poems would have no interest for the many, who preferred "nice fire-side poetry." The statement of approbation might well have impressed Browning and the remark on limited interest might not have discouraged him because enough critics were drawn to his timely poems to indicate a likely source of appeal. In addition to the probable effect of the reviews on Browning, there was, of course, the memory of Elizabeth's predilection for topics of contemporary concern and of the popularity of her *Aurora Leigh*, which dealt with problems faced by women of the nineteenth century. It was, as we shall see, the timeliness of a few of the poems in *Dramatis Personae* that was the main attraction.

Browning kept Isa and W. W. Story informed of his plans for publication. Originally *Dramatis Personae* was to appear before his *Poetical Works* of 1863. In November of 1862 he wrote Isa, "Early in Spring, I print new poems, a number: then, a new edition of all my old things, corrected."[3] Later he decided to allow the old works to be reevaluated before advancing the new. He wrote Story in March 1863, "My old books are getting printed, and so slowly that I shall not be able to bring out the new book till Autumn. . . ." He wanted "to draw a distinct line between past & present."[4]

But the new poems were not published in the autumn. In September the last volume of his collected edition of 1863 appeared, and, according to a letter to Story, Browning was still thinking of the new poems as belonging to the future. "I bring out two volumes of new things (men & women — but under some other name, to please the publisher)."⁵ As already indicated, in November 1863 he wrote both Isa and Story that the book would be delayed in order to benefit from the success of *The Poetical Works*. In his comment to Story he added that there were reviews in preparation that should come out before the appearance of the new poems.⁶ (Two substantial reviews of *Poetical Works* were still to appear: one in the *Victoria Magazine* in February 1864 and another in the *London Quarterly Review* in April of the same year.)

During the writing of poems and the making of plans for his books to reach the public, the effect of his resolve to take part in London life is noticeable in reports of his activities. Isa learned that he was made a member of the Cosmopolitan Club,⁷ whose members included certain distinguished men of the day. The Royal Academy, whose exhibitions Browning took an interest in for the rest of his life and whose future president Frederick Leighton was a friend of his (he designed Elizabeth's monument), had its banquet on April 30, 1864. Browning was listed among the principal guests. The *Times* included the following on May 2 in its account of the affair:

> The President. — The toast which I will next beg to propose is "The Interests of Literature." In paying our respects to the gifted writers . . . I select a name . . . Mr. John Forster. . . .
>
> Mr. Forster . . . returned thanks. After alluding to the disadvantage he felt in interposing before men with higher claims than himself to represent literature . . . he continued . . . I see poetry in some pleasant forms known to you all, and especially in that of Mr. Browning, one of the most original thinkers as well as one of the first poets of his time. [Cheers.]

In a letter to Story written a few days later, Browning mentioned the banquet and added information about the publication of *Dramatis Personae:*

> I shall send you my Poems when they appear — on the 21ˢᵗ. They have been delayed thus long to suit the requirements of Mr Fields, who made such an offer as induced me to conquer my repugnance and let him print some of the things in his Magazine before publication here: when he got them safe, he informed me that the money (stipulated to be in English pounds) should be forthcoming — in better times! Suppose I had reversed the process, required the money *first,* and then announced that when my invention was better, I would remit the owing verses with five percent interest, — meanwhile praising extremely the quality of his cheque!⁸

James T. Fields was the American publisher whom Browning had approached in 1855 and whose firm had published the American edition of *Men and Women*. Browning's irritation with Fields does not come as a surprise. He himself was always prompt and meticulous in business matters. Furthermore, with the exception of *Men and Women* Browning had not received any compensation for poetry published by Fields,[9] a remissness that Browning did not forget.[10] Strangely enough, he consented to the publication of several of his poems in the *Atlantic Monthly*, which Fields edited. The advance sheets of *Dramatis Personae* were sent to Ticknor and Fields and publication in London was postponed in order to allow for the appearance of *Gold Hair, Prospice*, and section VI of *James Lee* in the *Atlantic* (May, June 1864).

Throughout the years Browning had objected to the appearance of his poems in periodicals. Four years earlier he had, according to his well-established practice, turned down an invitation from Thackeray[11] to contribute, along with recognized English writers, to the *Cornhill Magazine*. Why then did he conquer his repugnance in this case? Browning said in the letter in which he agreed to Fields' terms that he had to think of his son's interests,[12] and to others he spoke of the money needed for his son, who was being prepared for Oxford. It is likely that the explanation, at least in part, lies there. It might have been easier for him to appear in a magazine in a country far from his own, especially since many readers in that country had been receptive to his and Elizabeth's works.

Browning seemed pleased with the terms. He talked about them to Procter, who then informed Forster of the transaction. "Browning . . . [is] enriched by his having received from Fields (of Boston) £153 for the Dramatis Personae. . . . Such are the returns which flow into poets' pockets nowadays."[13] Louise Greer thought the sum of £153 might have included payment for the poems in the *Atlantic*. "If this was the case, Browning would have received £103 for the three pieces in the *Atlantic Monthly*, since, according to the records of the publishing company, £50 was the price paid for the advance sheets for the book."[14] We can set these figures against the ones Browning gave in his acceptance letter to Fields: "With respect to your offer of '£60 for the sheets of my new volume, one month in advance of publication, — or £100 for the additional right of printing one or two of the pieces (not printed elsewhere) in your magazine' — I accept it. . . ."[15] If we assume that "or £100 for the additional right" means "*and* £100 for the additional right, the figures pretty well agree with those that

Louise Greer gave. The payment of £100 for the pieces in the *Atlantic* could well have given Browning satisfaction at this time when he was encouraged by the reception in England of the 1863 collected edition but before the decided success of *Dramatis Personae*.[16]

Moncure D. Conway, to whom Browning had sent information for his review of *The Poetical Works*, said that he gave assistance in the arrangements for publication of Browning's poetry in America (possibly *Dramatis Personae*) and that the poet, to show his gratitude, presented him with one of the remaining copies of *Pauline*.[17] Knowing that Conway wanted to write a review of *Dramatis Personae*, Browning sent him the proofs, which, he said, with one exception no one had seen. And later he warned Conway not to let his review appear before the book.

> With respect to the early sheets, they are of course only for American use — if one "favoured" (as they politely call it) an English Journal at the expense of its fellows, author and publisher would have to pay for it. You can, of course, get your article ready and manage that it appear *almost* simultaneously with the book's self — and I am sure I shall be happy to see and profit by it.[18]

Dramatis Personae was published on May 28, 1864, in a printing of probably two thousand copies,[19] and Conway's review of June 2 in the *Morning Star* was the earliest criticism of the poems to appear.

This was the first time a collection of new poems by Browning had appeared under favorable conditions. More and more, his critics had achieved some understanding of his dramatic method of presentation (except in his lyrics), they had pretty much overcome objections to his use of remote places and history, and they were well on their way to accepting the psychological and the unusual in his poetry. Some of them had already related his poetry to the movements and spirit of the times. Now in the perplexity following recent publications that had challenged conservative religious values, they could look to a poet whom they had already accepted for the intellectual and religious quality of his work.

The signal fires that had appeared earlier had not prepared most Victorians for Darwin's *Origin of Species* in 1859, which was followed in rapid succession by other alarming publications, including *Essays and Reviews* by seven authors in 1860, the first part of J. W. Colenso's *The Pentateuch and Book of Joshua Critically Examined* in 1862, and Ernest Renan's *La Vie de Jésus* in 1863. Darwin based his theory of evolution on the operation of natural selection; *Essays and Reviews,* by six clergy-men of the Church of England and one layman — called the Seven Against Christ — supported free discussion so that Darwinism could be reconciled with rather than destroy religion; Colenso, Bishop of Natal and a former Cambridge mathematician, found flaws in the Pen-tateuch by the use of arithmetic; Renan, a great French scholar trained originally for the priesthood, accepted Christ as an ethical teacher but denied his divinity. Instead of being benign and benevolent, nature was now seen to involve ruthless competition and survival of the fit-test, miracles were challenged, the fourth gospel was the subject of controversy, revelation was doubted.

Advances in the study of history and science had already dis-turbed old habits of thinking among educated men, and now the pub-lic did not take lightly the import of these works by men of scholarship and moral seriousness. The spread of new ideas within as well as with-out the Church was upsetting. Attacks and counterattacks and at-tempted compromise between the old and new spread the disturbance to greater and greater numbers of people. It would take time to recon-cile the old and new attitudes. Critics, who reflected the widespread anxiety, were receptive to Browning's concern in *Dramatis Personae* with topics of paramount interest.

They saw the author of *Dramatis Personae* as one who faced the current problems of religious belief. According to the *Times,* Brown-ing's profoundest works were "records of religious experience and at-tempts to unveil the mystery of a faith that has to encounter miracle on the one hand and evil on the other." The critic for the *London Review* saw in *Dramatis Personae* a treatment of certain subjects most worthy of attention, among them "the ever-renewed contest in the human mind between faith and doubt, — the yearning of the soul towards the un-seen world." In a review in the *Quarterly,* Gerald Massey said of Browning, with *A Death in the Desert* in mind: "It is evident that he takes great interest in the stir of our time, the obstinate questionings of doubt, which will yet make the flame of faith burn up toward heaven more direct and clear than ever. And he says his say emphati-cally on the side of belief."

As the critics pointed out Browning's participation in the strife between faith and doubt, they confirmed their earlier recognition that his poetry was moral and religious, with commendation coming from various classes of periodicals. From the *Saturday Review:* "Of all vices, Mr. Browning appears especially to abhor the ingrained falsehood of successful charlatans, and although the morality of a poem has little to do with its value, the marvellous astuteness with which hypocrisy is traced through its remoter windings is essentially imaginative and poetic." From the *Christian Spectator:* ". . . he is the most moral, as he is the most metaphysical and the most Christian, of our modern great poets." From the *Times:* Mr. Browning is "pre-eminently a religious poet, and . . . his greatest efforts have been directed to the setting forth of some phase of religious thought." From the *Englishwoman's Domestic Magazine:* ". . . Mr. Browning is the most devout of English poets, not excepting even Herbert." These comments and others in the same vein give assurance that Browning had attained the stature of a poet of high seriousness.

The critics pointed up the moral and religious aspect of Browning's poetry by singling out earlier favorites that showed his interest in religion and associating them with new poems in *Dramatis Personae*. *A Death in the Desert* reminded the critics of the *Morning Star*, the *Athenaeum*, and the *Eclectic and Congregational Review* (July 1864) of *Karshish*. The *Times*, reviewing *The Poetical Works* and *Dramatis Personae*, thought that *A Death in the Desert* and *Caliban*, as well as *Bishop Blougram's Apology*, *The Bishop Orders His Tomb*, *Fra Lippo Lippi*, and *Karshish*, showed how Browning's muse hovered about "the doubts, difficulties, and dangers" of contemporary religious life. The *Saturday Review* associated *Blougram* and *Mr. Sludge* as poems showing "wilful falsehood" blending with "half-conscious self-deception" and associated *Karshish*, *Cleon*, and *A Death in the Desert* as poems set in the early Christian period and belonging to a cycle that Browning "first discussed or applied to the purposes of poetry." The *Quarterly Review*, also reviewing *The Poetical Works* and *Dramatis Personae*, felt that no one could understand Browning who had not examined two poems related by their religious significance: *Easter-Day*, for its powerful proclamation of the mystery of the Incarnation, and *A Death in the Desert*, for its "close *grapple* of thought with the Subject of Subjects."

The critics called attention to Browning's awareness of evil and imperfection and to the part they played in his religious thought. At the same time they saw that he recognized the operation of a divine power. A sermon was present in *Rabbi Ben Ezra*, and the speaker was an "optimist," said the *New Monthly Magazine*. Browning, observed the critic, did not look upon the worst side of character and life; bad men he described but they had their good points, misery he depicted but it would not last, imperfection may be but perfection hidden. That

Browning saw evil was obvious to the critics. When the reviewer for
St. James's Magazine said that Browning was not an optimist though he
was "always trying, unsuccessfully, to be one," according to the context he meant that in searching for the good and finding it Browning
also saw the bad, which he refused to disjoin from a divine power. The
critic for the *Christian Spectator* could understand why Browning so
often dealt with evil when he read the end of *Gold Hair,* including the
lines:

> Evil or good may be better or worse
> In the human heart, but the mixture of each
> Is a marvel and a curse.

The problem of evil became a prominent one when Victorians
asked questions about God and Christianity. Could the coexistence of
God and evil be reconciled? Did the doctrine of eternal punishment
contradict the idea of a loving and merciful God? The critics for the
Christian Spectator, the *Times,* and *St. James's* were interested in Browning's acknowledgment of the existence of evil. *St. James's* and the *New
Monthly Magazine* saw that with the recognition of evil there was an
expression of faith in the last lines of *Apparent Failure,* which closed an
account of three men lying in the morgue at the end of wasted lives. It
was Browning's hope

> That what began best, can't end worst,
> Nor what God blessed once, prove accurst.

The critic for *St. James's* not only saw that Browning was not a
blind or superficial optimist; he also saw that *Dramatis Personae* would
help greatly "to disperse the fogs of materialistic theory." Throughout
his review he had in mind and was deploring the recently published
History of the Intellectual Development of Europe, by J. W. Draper, an
American scientist. This work purported to show how science had con-
quered religion, and to the reviewer it represented skepticism in the
worst sense of the word. He did not think that all skepticism was of
the kind represented by Draper. It could lead to a good end, as Browning had demonstrated. "Mr. Browning has shown elsewhere, in former
volumes, how useful scepticism is in promoting the good growth."
Whatever might be said in the future of Browning as an easy optimist,
there were critics of *Dramatis Personae* who perceived in him a poet who
could acknowledge the existence of evil and doubt and still maintain an
optimistic position.

The three poems that elicited most attention in the reviews were
concerned with controversies of the day involving belief — A Death in
the Desert, Caliban upon Setebos; or, Natural Theology in the Island, and
Mr. Sludge, "The Medium." The critics found in A Death in the Desert a
reply to Strauss and Renan. Strauss, who saw in the Christ story the
myth-making process, and Renan, who presented Christ as a superior
human being, unsettled or antagonized many an Englishman. Browning must have had in mind D. F. Strauss's Das Leben Jesu (2 vols.;
1835-6; tr. George Eliot, 1846) when he wrote Christmas-Eve and
Easter-Day and doubtless still had the work in mind when he wrote A
Death in the Desert. It is tempting to see also a response to Renan's La
Vie de Jésus (1863) in the later poem since Browning in the Epilogue to
Dramatis Personae answered the French scholar and in a letter to Isa
Blagden denounced his book.[20] A connection can only be conjectured,
for the date of composition of A Death in the Desert is unknown.
Whether or not Renan's work had appeared before Browning wrote all
or part of A Death in the Desert, it had appeared by the time the poem
was published and reviewed. The critics associated Renan's life with
the one by Strauss, more than likely not with Strauss's rewritten version, which was not published in German until 1864 and not in an
English translation until 1865. Both Strauss and Renan raised questions about the authorship of the gospel of St. John, a topic of much
controversy, and challenged the orthodox view of miracles.

In their reviews the critics explicitly mentioned Strauss and
Renan in connexion with A Death in the Desert. According to the Athenaeum, the poem came as an answer to the "Frenchman's 'Life of
Jesus,'" and according to the Saturday Review, "St. John delivered his
last oracular warning against heresies which perhaps border on the theories of Strauss and Renan." In July the Eclectic and Congregational
wrote: "In the Death in the Desert, Mr. Browning sets himself to reply,
with happy point and with a pathos which thrills to the very core, to
the flippancies of Strauss and Renan. . . ." This periodical thought
that no other living poet "could have approached this great delineation." In October it carried another review, in which the critic, after
quoting the passage on miracles from the poem, explained why he did
so: "because it contains such an excellent protest against sensational-
ism, and such a lucid statement of . . . Mr. Browning's own view on
the vexed question of miracles." St. James's Magazine also approved of
the view expressed by St. John in A Death in the Desert that miracles
were no longer needed: the dying apostle had an answer to the doubt-

ing man's request for more miracles, "which should reach the souls of those who admire M. Ernest Renan."

Historical and scientific inquiry had undermined the belief in miracles, and much attention was being given them in religious controversy. St. John's view, as stated in *A Death in the Desert,* coincided with that of Baden Powell, a contributor to *Essays and Reviews* (1860), who argued that the power of miracles to support religious belief is relative to the climate of thought: ". . . all evidential reasoning is essentially an adaptation to the conditions of mind and thought of the parties addressed, or it fails in its object."[21] It is interesting to note that in the sixteenth century Martin Luther had said, "External miracles are the apples and nuts which God gave to the childish world as playthings; we no longer have need of them."[22]

The critic for the *Christian Spectator,* as well as other reviewers, saw *A Death in the Desert* as "a 'word in season' amid many of the conflicts and bewilderments" of the time. According to the *New Monthly Magazine,* ". . . the doubts and difficulties of our day are answered and overcome." Browning made a strong impression on the critics in having St. John foresee the doubts of the future. In the *Athenaeum* Massey said of the poem: "Very startlingly does it put the fact that when St. John was speaking many in the world were asking each other about Christ's second coming, seeing signs of promise all around them; and now possibly there are as many asking, did Christ ever come at all?" Massey, in writing more of the poem in the *Quarterly,* said of St. John's prophecy: "The dying man rises and dilates . . . whilst in solemn vision his spirit ranges forward into the far-off time, when in many lands men will be saying, 'Did John live at all? and did he say *he saw* the veritable Christ?' "

Like the other reviews, the *Eclectic and Congregational* (July 1864) and the *Reader* saw the relevance of Browning's poem to the time of doubt, when Revelation and the authenticity of the fourth Gospel were being questioned. And the *London Review* wrote of Browning's St. John:

> Then he proceeds to speak as one who, looking far into the future, beyond the simple faith of the earliest Christian era, and the subtle controversies which endangered its existence, had seen the doubts and fears of the present day, the unwilling distrust, the reluctant disbelief, the mournful surrendering of early hopes and severing of ties endeared by a thousand associations. . . . And indeed it is to our generation he speaks; the difficulties with which he grapples are such

as present themselves to the men of our own times, not to the disbelievers or heretics of his own.

Only a few of the critics disapproved of Browning's treatment of St. John. The one for the *Edinburgh* objected to seeing "St. John on his death-bed made a medium for a writer to philosophise upon the Gospel in Platonic strains, and to add an apocryphal chapter to the New Testament." In a longer discussion the High Church *Guardian* maintained that Browning should have presented St. John "in the utmost simplicity of spirit"; instead he was given words unsuitable to him. These remarks are not surprising; both of the reviews were generally unfavorable to *Dramatis Personae*. The third negative attitude, however, stood out in an almost entirely laudatory review in the *Morning Star*. In it Conway (a Unitarian minister) said that *A Death in the Desert* was not so fine a poem as *Saul,* because of its "too obvious bearing upon the religious discussions of the present day." Besides, St. John reminded him of "an Anglican defender of the faith." Conway did concede that the poem was "replete with vigour, and one cannot read it without being moved, for it is written from perfect conviction."

Although the critics in general spoke of such matters as the noble lines and symmetrical beauty in *A Death in the Desert,* they were most struck by the thought or content of the poem. The same interest in substance, especially as it reflected the concerns of the time, was apparent in the discussions of *Caliban* and *Mr. Sludge.* Even though the reviewers did not apprehend all the subtleties of *Caliban,* some approved and others admired Browning's accomplishment. These subtleties did not need to be emphasized, said the critic for the *Athenaeum* — they must be felt. He continued, ". . . the reader will hardly fail to make out a good deal of the satire which Caliban's theology reflects upon ours." The *Guardian* and *St. James's* suggested that the subject was unsuitable for poetry, yet the *Guardian* admitted to the good use of Caliban "as a means of attacking the conceptions which far more developed intellects than that of the son of Sycorax have allowed to mingle with their ideas of a Being infinitely higher than Setebos."

Both religious and secular periodicals were pleased with the subject. A number of critics indicated the content, and a few, without commentary, relied upon the full title (*Caliban upon Setebos; or, Natural Theology in the Island*) and the quotation from Psalms ("Thou thoughtest that I was altogether such an one as thyself") to convey a notion of what the poem was about. Some of the critics made remarks that in varying degrees of specification pointed to contemporary religious concerns. In this "wonderful poem," said the *Christian Spectator,* "we have a reflected light upon our own 'Natural Theology.' " *Caliban* was seen by the *London Review* as a "sketch of an abject superstition, not entirely confined to the narrow range of Caliban's island"; by the *Reader* as the metaphorical use of Caliban in Browning's grim view of "the Natural Theology of a race of beings that do not consider themselves of the type of Caliban." The *Guardian* said that Caliban was "a stalking-horse from behind which the writer shoots at higher game." The critic for the *New Monthly Magazine* referred to this statement and said he did not wish to inquire into the number of Browning's targets or the correctness of his aim. "Each for himself, as his need is, may surely learn a lesson from the dark gropings of Caliban."

In expressing the attitude of Dissent, the *Eclectic and Congregational* (July 1864) was more specific: ". . . Caliban discourses upon that which he is able to see, and describes that which he is able to believe — a most edifying chapter to innumerable gentlemen of our acquaintance, Darwinians, believers in force and matter, and other such divine and worshipful deities." In October the reviewer for the same periodical found a strange fascination in the poem. But admittedly it was with a feeling of intense melancholy that he read the poem: he saw in it the anthropomorphism that he understood all religions necessarily have and thought the potter-and-clay figure presented in *Caliban* with terrible cynicism. He ended his discussion with a note of dismay that was characteristic of the time:

> Very sad the feelings with which we rise from these wild fancies of the delicate monster. To think that, so many thousand years after Christ is come in the flesh, the God of such a vast number even of so-called Christians is more like to Setebos than to the Father of Lights, in Whom is no variableness, neither shadow of turning [James 1:17].

The theory of evolution caused a change in attitude toward natural theology, which to most Victorians meant the formulation by William Paley. His *Natural Theology* (1802), or his ideas if not his book, must have been well known to English men of letters. Paley's proof of the existence of God rested upon the old argument from design, that as from a watch we infer a watchmaker, so from nature we infer a divine artisan. He went further in asserting that nature provides evidence for God's goodness. While Darwin's case for natural selection as the chief cause of evolution was gaining ground, nature's benevolent aspect was fading. The *Spectator* thought that perhaps the most subtle touch in the "striking and original" *Caliban upon Setebos* was the similarity between Paley's and Caliban's theological reasoning to arrive at different concepts of God: "The very same points which Paley insists on in his argument from design, this fanciful Caliban insists on also, but as telling in favour of *malicious* design."

The third poem that attracted the critics for its contemporary relevance was *Mr. Sludge, "The Medium,"* which had for its subject spiritualism. In writing of doubt and uncertainty in the Victorian period, Elliott-Binns, a twentieth-century historian of religion, said, ". . . man's need for something outside himself takes strange forms when it ceases to find satisfaction in what the Christian believes to be the revelation given by God Himself."[23] An age of unbelief, he thought, readily becomes an age of superstition. One current superstition, he explained, was the cult of spiritualism. The *Christian Spectator* estimated how many had turned to it: "Some mythical number of converts — generally ten thousand, we believe — is reported from time to time. . . ."

Most reviewers of *Mr. Sludge* found spiritualism repugnant. The denominational periodicals especially saw in the movement a real danger to the faith they upheld. The *Eclectic and Congregational* (Oct. 1864) thought that as the "bands of true faith" were being relaxed, spiritualism was growing stronger. "Confuted it must be, and no one could have done the work better than Mr. Browning," said the reviewer. The critic explained that he was giving a full analysis of *Mr. Sludge* with quotations from it (over six pages) "chiefly, because, in Mr. Sludge, the poet is enforcing a much-needed lesson." The *Christian Spectator* was alarmed because supporters of spiritualism presented claims that rivaled those of Christianity; having been won over from infidelity, the spiritualists believed in a future state as revealed by supernatural manifestations.

The *Athenaeum,* in one of the first reviews of *Dramatis Personae,* stated, "The subject is not pleasant to dwell upon, but the way in which patronizing credulity leads into temptation those who have a love of tampering with human wonder, and opens its mouth and shuts its eyes so invitingly that it would be almost a sin not to deceive it, is exquisitely pictured." Then one after another of the critics commented on Browning's condemnation of the people who were gullible enough to fall prey to the Sludges of society. Although a third of the reviewers found the poem distasteful or its subject inappropriate for poetry, most who discussed *Mr. Sludge* merely indicated approval or expressed high praise. Conway made a glowing statement in the *Morning Star:* "It might hardly be anticipated that even Mr. Browning could evoke a great poem from such a subject; yet he has done so. In some regards, this is the most notable work he has ever produced: in some it is the most notable written by any poet."

Elizabeth's interest in spiritualism caused Browning lasting distress. Lurking in his mind as he wrote *Mr. Sludge* was Daniel Dunglass Home (or Hume), the popular spiritualist whose manifestations deeply impressed Elizabeth for a period of time. The poem grew out of a séance (referred to in Chapter XVII) at which Robert and Elizabeth were present. Browning's ensuing hostility was well known. Some reviewers had wind of Browning's antagonism toward Home and alluded to it. Was not the *London Review* aiming at Home in this statement, ". . . Mr. Browning seems to have constructed his effigy rather with the passion of a personal foe than with the self-control of an impartial artist"? *St. James's* was surely pointing to Home: ". . . it strikes us forcibly that we know who sat for the portrait." According to Conway, few would have any difficulty in "fixing the identity of Mr. Sludge." The *Englishwoman's Domestic Magazine* went further in relaying rumors — "true or false" — of Browning's personal hostility to "a certain medium" to explain his poetic attack.

A representative of spiritualism spoke out. In July 1864 the *Spiritual Magazine,* using the excuse that the press had identified Sludge with Home, carried a defense of the medium. The article, "Mr. Robert Browning on Spiritualism," by Robert Cooper, consisted of a caustic denunciation of Browning's attack on Home in *Mr. Sludge,* a rough summary of the poem, and unrelated remarks designed to insult Browning. Following the article was "Mr. Home's Account" of Browning's reaction to the séance at which Robert and Elizabeth had been present.[24] Home wrote the account apparently in response to *Mr. Sludge.* Since Browning examined many periodicals, it is not surprising that Cooper's article and Home's account came to his attention,[25] even though the very name of the magazine might have turned him aside. The *Spiritual Magazine* touched one of Browning's sensitive spots by publicizing Elizabeth's interest in spiritualism, to say nothing of the offense offered by insolent and inconsiderate remarks on himself.

One more association of Browning with spiritualism occurred in the press, this time in his favor. In the *Examiner* of June 4, 1864, the reviewer of a work called *Spirit-Rapping in Glasgow in 1864* referred to *Mr. Sludge* as "a worthy study of our time." Seemingly this was the last of the immediate comments on *Mr. Sludge.*

Caliban, A Death in the Desert, and *Mr. Sludge* received most of the critics' attention. The reason for this response could be explained to some extent by a statement that appeared in the *Reader.* "These poems, being either in part narrative or at least accompanied by a sufficient suggestion of the story or set of circumstances they suppose, are perfectly intelligible . . . to such readers . . . as Mr. Browning can have meant to address in them." The critics were drawn immediately to *Mr. Sludge, "The Medium"* by the spiritualistic craze and to *Caliban* by their familiarity with Shakespeare's character. There were additional reasons why their first glance at *Caliban* would lead them on: the religious implications of the second part of the title and the quotation from Psalms and also the interest in primitive man stimulated by reports brought back to the mother country from the far colonies. Early in *A Death in the Desert* there were clues to its religious import. After the three poems of major concern, next in approval came *Rabbi Ben Ezra* and *Abt Vogler.* There was little discussion of them though they were often mentioned favorably and quoted from freely, being singled out for such qualities as their expression of the religious man's loftiest aspirations and their inculcation of high trust.

In the four remaining poems with religious significance — *Gold Hair, Apparent Failure, Prospice,* and the *Epilogue* to *Dramatis Personae* — we have an expression of some of Browning's own religious beliefs or feelings. Yet even with the references to *Essays and Reviews,* Colenso, and Original Sin in *Gold Hair* and with Renan as one of the speakers in the *Epilogue,* the majority of critics ignored or could not understand these poems. It is strange that *Prospice,* which could be read easily and was to become a favorite poem, did not attract more attention at the time of its first appearance. Its shortness allowed the whole of it to be quoted in several reviews. For the most part it was dismissed succinctly as "intelligible" and as having "noble lines," though the *Athenaeum* gave it three sentences of extremely high praise. *Gold Hair* received more attention than the *Epilogue* and *Apparent Failure,* probably because of the story with the combination at the end of what the critics called the moral or lesson and the naming of *Essays and Reviews* and Colenso. Even though Renan was one of the speakers in the *Epilogue,* it did not arouse much interest; the critic for the *Athenaeum* said that he was in doubt as to whether the Face was Mrs. Browning's or Christ's.

It is somewhat strange that only two critics gave any attention to *Apparent Failure,* which expressed Browning's disbelief in everlasting damnation and which could not be misunderstood. This relative silence might be accounted for. In the midst of the current heated controversy over eternal punishment and atonement, Browning expressed confidence in a future life for the three sinners who had committed suicide. In the minds of many the idea of a benevolent God conflicted with the notion of future punishment, which was still being supported vigorously by its adherents. If there were critics receptive to Browning's position and inclined to comment on *Apparent Failure*, they might well have refrained because they were reluctant to become involved in a discussion having to do with traditionally accepted belief.

We have not yet examined the nonreligious poems. They were either labeled obscure or ignored. Of these *Too Late* and *James Lee* (changed to *James Lee's Wife* in 1868) were most often singled out for their unintelligibility. The *Worst of It* and *Dis Aliter Visum* met this objection to a lesser extent. The majority of the critics had nothing at all to say about *A Face, Confessions, A Likeness, Youth and Art*, and *May and Death*. One reviewer, Conway in the *Morning Star*, was exceptional: he gave as much attention to shorter poems as to the three major ones, and he wrote favorably of all but one that he discussed. With the proof sheets in hands, sent in advance by Browning, Conway apparently set out to write a very full review. He started by discussing the first seven poems in the volume — four on love and *Gold Hair, Abt Vogler*, and *Rabbi Ben Ezra*. The eighth was *A Death in the Desert;* but at this point he had used up more than half of his space, so that he was somewhat cramped in his discussion of this and the two other major poems — *Caliban* and *Mr. Sludge* — and had no room for the remaining shorter poems.

Apart from the comments on the difficulty of some of the shorter poems, complaints of Browning's obscurity were negligible with the exception of the discussions in the *Edinburgh Review* and the *Guardian*, whose reproofs were reminiscent of those in earlier uncompromising reviews. Of the *Edinburgh* more will be said in the following chapter. The *Guardian* had been reviewing Browning since 1851; unlike other periodicals at this time it had scarcely gained in flexibility of perception. For the critics of other periodicals Browning's prosody and syntax, which had long drawn unfavorable comment, were no longer a major concern. As always, a few could not resist bringing in *Sordello* as an example of Browning's obscure manner *(Victoria Magazine, Times, Edinburgh Review, Dublin University Magazine)*. The *Quarterly Review* had something to say about those whose criticism was warped by their knowledge or hearsay knowledge of *Sordello:* "The current opinion of his poetry, outside the circle of the few who have thoroughly studied the subject, and met with their reward, would be somewhat nearer the mark, supposing the poet had only written his poem called 'Sordello.' "

Objections appeared chiefly in the discussion of the poems concerning love, which were generally classified as lyrics or dramatic lyrics. The critics had complained earlier because Browning's lyrics did not follow the established practices of lyric composition. The *Quarterly Review* explained that Browning was dramatic "down to his smallest lyrics," and *St. James's* said, "He has not written a line which, however lyrical in form, is not essentially dramatic in expression." Many reviewers were disinclined to accept the originality of method in the lyrics, though they had learned to accept it in the favorite dramatic monologues, such as *My Last Duchess* or *The Bishop Orders His Tomb*. It was clearer than ever that they found the lyrics too strenuous to be enjoyed. According to Massey in the *Athenaeum,* most bewildering to many was the poetry that Browning had labeled as dramatic in principle and lyrical in expression. Massey explained:

> When the poetry is purely subjective, a writer can hint and leave much to the imagination. A slight breathing of meaning is sufficient to send the most delicious ripples over the mind . . . but Mr. Browning carries this mode of suggesting into the objective domain, where we require much more "making out," more visible grounds, in order that we may obtain a satisfactory foothold.

The reader could not immediately grasp the story in *Too Late,* said the reviewer.

The critic for the *Reader* thought that it was the short pieces, "lyrical in form," that would revive the old complaint of obscurity. He said that in not a few of the short poems some explanation was needed at once to facilitate understanding. After struggling with *James Lee,* the reviewer for the *Eclectic and Congregational Review* (Oct. 1864) was still in doubt about its meaning as well as that of *Too Late:* "since . . . he [Browning] does not stop to tell you the beginning of his thought, you often get hopelessly lost amid an intricate maze of fancies and conceits." The critic for the *Christian Spectator* pretty well summed up the predominating attitude toward the dramatic lyrics. He stated that the obscurity in such poems as *Too Late* and *James Lee* arose from their incompleteness; the reader had to piece the story together in order to understand the poem. The strangeness of the emotions complicated the problem: when "we add the strange exceptional character of the emotions with which he [Browning] deals, it will appear no wonder that it is often hard, sometimes impossible, to follow him."

Far removed from this characteristic objection to Browning's lyrics was the critical flexibility demonstrated by Massey in the *Quarterly Review*. Though his general criticism of 1861 in the *North British Review* (discussed in Chapter XX) had been favorable, as he continued to read Browning he became more perceptive in several ways in assessing his technique. In the *Quarterly* (a review of *Dramatis Personae* and the collection of 1863) he arrived at an important guideline: "We must understand the principles of Mr. Browning's art . . . before we shall be on the way for interpreting his poems rightly." He saw the difficulty of the poetry in a new light. "The complaint often made is that readers do not at once catch the idea, which is the root of vitality to the poem." The question, he said, was not whether obscurity is a fault but whether there is something "worth getting at" in the poetry. His increased awareness that traditional notions must be set aside was exhibited in his appraisal of the lyrics.

> We cannot compare Mr. Browning's lyrics with those of any subjective poet; he has called them *Dramatic Lyrics* for the very purpose of distinguishing them from such. Nor may we judge him as a lyrical poet by comparison with any subjective lyrist. We must in both cases appraise them on their own grounds; and if we applaud the subjective lyrist because the movement of his verse felicitously corresponds to the thought or emotion, then we must at least estimate the fitness or beauty of the movement in the Objective Lyric by its correspondence with the speaker's character, or the nature of the action.

Instead of a "pleasant ripple of emotion that passes away, or a mere play of feeling," characteristic of the conventional lyric, the reader of Browning gains an original and permanent "picture of life, of intricate character, of uncommon manners, which has been almost engraved upon the mind by the process of getting at it. . . ."

Massey, himself a poet of some standing, discussed at length the effect of Browning's feeling for music on the quality of his verse. "With Mr. Browning it would seem that his sense of music served to put into his verse a greater use of *accent* than flow of melody. . . ." The readers' judgment had to be exercised, had to become flexible, for they might not have heard any poetry like it before. That it did not fit the standard notions of rhythm was unimportant. The point was whether the music and movement of the verse receive "their impetus and government in any sensible way from the character [in the poem], so as to become its natural expression." As the "supple, fluent movement, the low-toned suavity and colloquial ease give an insinuating grace of manner to the Italian Noble" in *My Last Duchess,* the "coarse, blunt, gutteral sounds, and dogged stiffnecked movement of the 'Soliloquy in [of] the Spanish Cloister' . . . aid materially in embodying the imaginary speaker."

Unfortunately Massey could not sustain his forward look. He was beset by the doubt and the hesitation felt by a critic who sees old patterns broken down and new life infused into poetry but cannot totally surrender old standards of judgment. "Still the question remains whether such harsh, abrupt sounds can be legitimately introduced into poetry. We do not think them well suited to the English language." Later Massey said that the character of Karshish likewise informed the movement of the verse. "We have no hurry, no gasps of utterance, but a work perfect in manner as in matter, grave and staid, the pauses answering to the pondering, and altogether fine in expression as it is weighty in thought." Massey's discussion of Browning's rhythm was an amplification of Forster's early comments and a forerunner of present-day analysis.

By now others were looking more sympathetically, sometimes more perceptively, at Browning's versification. His old manner of writing persisted, said Hutton in the *Spectator,* but at times he felt that "a gentler and more musical tone charms the ear." In keeping with this was the observation of the *Eclectic and Congregational* (Oct. 1864) that Browning's "studied roughness" at rare intervals gave way to a "bit of exquisite melody"; Browning, a many-sided poet, was a "sort of mocking-bird among the bards." The same periodical had exclaimed in July, ". . . what music there is in Mr. Browning's verse!" There was no music like it, "only that it needs a certain education in life; a certain ear-experience and culture not merely to appreciate it but even to apprehend it." The importance of ear-experience was brought out in a similar observation made by Massey in expressing his approval of Browning's originality. "His music is not as the music of other men. He frequently strikes out something nobly novel; but it is not to be quickly caught, for we have not heard the like before, and at first the mind of the reader finds it difficult to dance to the beat of the time." This appeared in 1864 in the *Athenaeum,* the weekly that in its review of *Men and Women* in 1855 had decried the license Browning took instead of following traditional versification.

Limited though it was, praise of Browning's language came out more strongly than it ever had after the publication of a new work. The *Times* commented on his "resources of diction." Massey said in the *Athenaeum*, "Mr. Browning's art is chastened, his expression only rich now in the most precious plainness of speech. Rare, telling English language he speaks in." In the *Quarterly* he observed "the commonest forms of speech"; though the diction was not always acceptable, the poetry was full of "hearty English character." Here was a test of the critics' progress and some of them passed it, for if there were grounds for seeing Browning's language as unsuitable to poetry — that is, traditional poetry — they were present in *Dramatis Personae*.

Except in the lyrics Browning's revelation of character was acceptable to the critics. His strange subject matter was no longer disturbing. Nor did the critics dwell on the difficulties caused by his originality; some even welcomed the effort required for comprehension. Their attention to *Mr. Sludge*, which they sometimes related to *Bishop Blougram's Apology* (Blougram was another imposter), showed their approval of Browning's manner of portraying man. The *Saturday Review*, which called Browning a close psychological observer, wrote, "The recondite sophistries and oblique impulses which he delights to trace are always embodied in a dramatic impersonation"; the imposters whose characters Browning analyzed, it continued, were compelled "to tell their own story with involuntary candour." In reading *Mr. Sludge*, the critic for the *Christian Spectator* saw "the sly specious argument, wonderfully sustained by Mr. Browning, in which the impostor, half a dupe himself, tries to show that after all there may be something in his science." The critic for *St. James's* went further as he explained Browning's revelation of Sludge and Blougram. "He does justice to everybody, even the most vicious, and discovers that even Mr. Sludge, the medium, has his good points; he won't be too hard even upon sophistry, so he shows glimpses of the divine even through the portly waistcoat of Bishop Blougram." This statement takes us back to Browning's remark to Elizabeth in 1845 about Luria's wicked adversaries, ". . . I sympathize just as much with these as with him."

The critics had mentioned earlier the poet's projection of his own mind into that of his characters, and now they looked at his method more closely. The *Spectator* remarked: "One sees clearly enough from this [a quotation from *Mr. Sludge*] that Mr. Browning does not object to magnify a little the intellectual powers of his *'dramatis personae'* in order to help them to paint themselves. . . . It is Mr. Browning dwarfing himself, in all *but* intellect, to Sludge, transforming himself in all but intellect into Caliban, who writes, not Sludge and Caliban themselves." In the *Morning Star,* Conway made the point that Browning's power of projection could occasionally obscure his moral attitude: ". . . he is so merged in some person his imagination has evoked that there is an impression at times of the absence in the poet of any moral standard." A few critics were to realize later in the sixties that a problem of distinguishing Browning's voice from that of the speaker existed, but they did not address it deliberately, as have some scholars today.

Critics commented on the strangeness of the poetry. Massey wrote in the *Quarterly Review* that Browning "produced things sometimes totally unlike anything called 'poems' hitherto, but remarkable works of art nevertheless." Hutton wrote in the *Spectator* of some of the poems, ". . . it is hard to call them poems, and harder still to call them anything else. . . ." Strange as the poems were, however, most reviewers of *Dramatis Personae* had reached the point of being able to appreciate Browning's highly individual artistry as they came to see in his poetry a combination of the religious, the timely, and the intellectual. If we recognize this advancement, we can see why the grotesque in *Caliban* was generally acceptable.

Along with earlier objections to the difficulty of reading Browning's unusual poems, here and there had appeared a note of acceptance of the effort necessary for understanding them, a note that was now more sustained. "He delights in a class of subjects, which in their very nature are dark and difficult to deal with, but which, nevertheless, will ever attract the study of thoughtful minds," said the critic for the *Times.* For the most part the difficulty, according to the now more perceptive *Saturday Review,* was inherent in the subject matter. "The mysteries of thought and the paradoxes of human nature are not to be apprehended without an effort even by the aid of masterly exposition . . . ." The *New Monthly Magazine* had no wish that Browning's work should be compared with that of weaker contemporaries; he required careful study that is necessary for anything good. "To say that his thoughts are quickly fathomed is indeed no compliment to him; and saying it will send no earnest reader to his pages." The critic for the *Christian Spectator* quoted and agreed with a statement Elizabeth had made in a preface to one of her works: "I never mistook pleasure for the final cause of poetry; nor leisure, for the hour of the poet." Some critics, like those for the *Times* and the *Quarterly Review,* said Browning's thought was worth reaching for.

Though the critics still pointed out the difficulty of reading Browning's poetry, except in writing of the lyrics they no longer expressed strong objection. Intellectual effort was in keeping with the spirit of the time. The critic for the *Saturday Review,* in a forthcoming attack on the *Edinburgh's* unfavorable review of Browning, was to write, ". . . poetry, especially in an age like ours, hardly fulfils its purpose better than when it makes us enter vividly into the past or the remote — when it leads us to exercise our minds, and gives us that best and highest of pleasures which involves self-exertion." The concept of what poetry should be was undergoing a change.

In the sixties, when the questioning of traditional religious values caused widespread and distressing uncertainty, the critics could find in Browning reassurance for religious affirmation that was welcome to many Victorians. The reviewers for *St. James's* and the *Quarterly* thought that the poet's dramatic method itself was conducive to his support of faith. In *St. James's* the critic said that the subjective poet lacked the weapons to combat materialistic reasoners. "But when the dramatist steps forward to do battle on the side of faith, the case is widely different; he is armed at all points, and is not to be laughed down." In the *Quarterly* Massey, who thought that the "excessive subjectiveness" of modern poetry would likely lead to decay, saw advantages for the dramatic poet who had no stage.

> He is able to make points in various directions where he could not have shaped out complete plays. He can thus portray much that is of intense interest to us in our modern days. There are dramas of mental conflict, such as could not be shown on the stage in action; tragedies and farces that occur in the intellectual sphere, as well as in the world of feeling, to be witnessed by God and his angels rather than by men. Mr. Browning has taken advantage of this liberty.

With their appreciation of his dramatic method, power of intellect, moral and religious spirit, and discernment of man's nature, the critics welcomed, as we have seen, Browning's presentation of topics of concern in England at this time. Although undoubtedly they were not in total agreement on their religious views, there was scarcely a disapproving word about the religious and spiritual content of the poems. Perhaps the very fact that Browning did not unreservedly embrace or-

thodoxy was to his advantage. Note what the critic for *St. James's* said
about orthodoxy and individual judgment: "More than most men does
he believe in the ever-present stimulation of divine agencies. Nor is he
a mere torpid acceptor of the respectable, the orthodox; he has reasoned
out the matter entirely to his own conviction." A statement overlapping this was made in the *Quarterly Review:*

> He has the true reverence for the Creator of all that beauty on which
> poetry is fed — the clearest of all the seeing faculties — and recog-
> nises the Master of the feast. His poetry, however, is not religious in
> a vague general way, nor dry through being doctrinal; it is, as in
> 'Christmas Eve' and 'Easter Day,' passionately alive with the most
> intense yearning for a personal relationship.

The increase in the number of critics who had some grasp of
Browning's genius was the result of the progress they had made, even
though it had been slow and they had often been frustrated in evaluating the unusual in his works. The gradual process of approaching an
understanding of how the particular qualities of Browning's poetry
were interrelated had helped prepare critics for *Dramatis Personae*. The
wider range of human experience represented in *Men and Women* had
been beneficial. The reflection of contemporary religious interests and
beliefs in *Christmas-Eve and Easter-day* and *Men and Women* had encouraged critics to consider the seriousness of Browning's thought. After
they read the three longest poems in *Dramatis Personae* (*A Death in the
Desert, Caliban, Mr. Sludge*) and associated the current religious and
moral concerns expressed in them with those presented in earlier
poems, they no longer had any doubt that Browning was one of their
own. Once criticized for being apart from his country and his time, he
was now established as a poet who faced problems created by shifting
intellectual standards and religious values. Various aspects of his writing were considered in the reviews, but clearly the specific application
of his poetic thought and technique to existing problems exerted the
strongest appeal. The critics like the one for the *New Quarterly Review*
of January 1846 who had said that Browning was unpopular because he
did not write of his time could say this no longer.

Most of the reviewers and critics who have been discussed thus far
were relatively free from the restrictive standards used earlier for judging Browning's poetry, though there were objections to the technique
of the lyrics and a failure to understand some of the shorter poems. The
favorable reviewers carried the day. It is clear that they had made an

appreciable advancement in coming to terms with Browning's poetry. Though they pointed out the difficulty of it, they did not object to the effort required (except for the lyrics). What effect did they think the poems would have on Browning's reputation? They had felt that publication of the *Poetical Works* was the response to an increased demand for his poetry. Though they approved of the new work, particularly the long poems, most of those who discussed the probable reception of *Dramatis Personae* did not think that it would attract new admirers. They were wrong. On August 19, three months after the publication of *Dramatis Personae*, Browning wrote Isa that a "new edition" was nearly ready,[26] on September 24 Chapman and Hall advertised it in the *Examiner*, and on October 8 the *Athenaeum* announced the "second edition." It was a slightly revised printing. It could not be denied that Browning was attracting a wider range of readers. The sale of so many copies, though not phenomenal, was in itself enough to show that his readers included more than the devoted few that critics had long referred to.

There remained, however, a dwindling number of critics whose adherence to current standards of judgment made it hard for them to evaluate *Dramatis Personae* fairly. They were inclined to slight the new offerings and to repeat earlier charges brought against Browning. Their limitations drew comments from some of their more open-minded fellows. Browning's reaction to this uncomprehending criticism was expressed in letters to friends. These matters will be dealt with in the following chapter.

CHAPTER XXIII

Critics Against Critics

Dramatis Personae, 1864

The critics who were negative to the merits of *Dramatis Personae* were in the minority. Two of them were emphatically rebuked by fellow critics. This was a new development in the history of Browning criticism — some critics openly attacking others for their limited and unfair representation of Browning's art. As we shall see, agreement existed between the more liberalized ones and Browning in specifying the shortcomings of those who were narrow-minded. This meant that to a greater extent Browning was now being judged with reference to his own artistic assumptions and intentions.

Although in the shifting assessment of Browning by the majority there were signs that critics were taking a more relaxed view of the proper function and qualities of poetry, the earlier standards of judgment had not entirely disappeared. The *Edinburgh Review, Guardian,* and *National Review* could not accept poetry that did not fulfill the requirement of being pleasing and beautiful in the traditional sense. Their strictures were out of line with the general opinion expressed by critics after the publication of *Dramatis Personae.* Throughout the review of Browning's poetry in the *Edinburgh,* the critic insisted upon one thing: "Tried by the standards which have hitherto been supposed to uphold the force and beauty of the English tongue and of English literature, his [Browning's] works are deficient in the qualities we should desire to find. . . ." The critic for the *Guardian* complained that Browning chose "the complex, grotesque, and *bizarre* rather than the simple and beautiful" and was "much too fond of prying curiously into those unpleasant recesses of our nature."

In his article "Wordsworth, Tennyson, and Browning; or, Pure, Ornate, and Grotesque Art in English Poetry," published in the *National Review,* Walter Bagehot singled out the grotesque in Browning, which had not particularly concerned reviewers in the early sixties, as the basis for an extended criticism. Of grotesque art he said, "It deals, to use the language of science, not with normal types but with abnormal specimens," with types *"in difficulties."* Although Bagehot expressed an admiration for Browning's mind, for his applying a "hard strong intellect" to real life and to the problems of the age, he wrote, "His mistake has been, that . . . he has forced his art to topics on which no one could charm, or on which he, at any rate, could not; that on these occasions and in these poems he has failed in fascinating men and women of sane taste." Browning's flair for the grotesque (which attracted him to the medieval) was not justifiable. Bagehot maintained that "though pleasure is not the end of poetry, pleasing is a condition of poetry." It was characteristic of Browning to choose "out-of-the-way and detestable subjects." His works demand more than can be taken in by most readers; the persistent reader will find "a sort of quarry of ideas . . . in such a jagged, ugly, useless shape that he can hardly bear them." As one of his examples of how Browning had gone wrong, Bagehot named *Caliban.* Here was the description of a *"mind in difficulties";* a type "less likely to find truth" could scarcely be imagined.

After the publication of *Men and Women* some critics came to Browning's defense against others who had censured him unjustly, and some now spoke out after the publication of *Dramatis Personae.* The reviewer for the *Christian Spectator* took exception to Bagehot's approach to Browning's art. He admitted the difficulty of the poetry, but he defended it as he challenged Bagehot's criticism. He referred to *Caliban* as a "wonderful poem" and explained that Browning's poetry dealt with "unfamiliar phases of thought and feeling" and with new combinations of characters and circumstances. Browning presented familiar scenes from new points of view and affections strangely displaced and "chanted in new keys." The reviewer continued with a counter to Bagehot's failure to see choice of the grotesque as a means of arriving at truth.

> Yet, as we listen, we recognise the profound truth. A critic whom we have quoted [Bagehot] calls these new combinations "grotesque." He is welcome to the word. Only, it should be remem-

bered, that a keen appreciation of the incongruous not only co-exists with, but even depends upon, the quick sense of proportion and harmony. Mr. Browning's genius is "mediæval," it is said [by Bagehot]. Yes: but if the mediaeval architect in his play carved the grinning gargoyle, he planned in his serious mood the cathedral from which it projects.

Some of Bagehot's statements could apply to *Christmas-Eve and Easter-Day*. More than likely with these in mind Gerald Massey of the *Quarterly* wrote of *Christmas-Eve:*

> The casual reader may possibly set the 'Christmas Eve' down hastily as a strange mixture of grave matter and gay manner; a religious subject loosely treated with quips and cranks of irreverent rhyme. But this would be a mistake. The author has a sardonic way of conveying certain hints of the truth when no other way would be so effective. In this poem we have a contrast such as furnished a hint of the true grotesque in art.

Massey's review of *The Poetical Works* and *Dramatis Personae* in the *Quarterly*, which appeared in July of 1865, defended qualities of Browning's poetry that had been criticized earlier, a defense reminiscent of David Masson's long review in the *British Quarterly* in 1856. Critics were showing signs of progress in their own sympathy for Browning's poetry when they took up the cudgels against others for their restricted views. The strongest and most revealing expression of disapproval came in replies to William Stigand's discussion in the *Edinburgh Review* of October 1864. During the fifties and earlier sixties when many critics were step by step approaching a new point of view, the *Edinburgh* ignored Browning's poetry. Now with emphasis on his obscurity in a criticism mainly of the old works, this quarterly raised dust that had generally been laid as critical insight became more penetrating; four critics rose in the poet's defense. Their replies in the *Examiner, London Review, Reader,* and *Saturday Review* showed the extent to which the critical judgment of the *Edinburgh Review* had lagged behind.

Whereas the defense of Browning by critics in the fifties lay somewhat obscured in their reviews of *Men and Women*, these attacks in the sixties on the *Edinburgh* stood out prominently — two (*London Review, Examiner*) in columns that carried commentaries on particular recent issues of periodicals and two (*Reader, Saturday Review*) whose headings indicated that the entire discussion concerned Browning and the *Edinburgh*. The *London Review* could accept the *Edinburgh's* pronouncement on the "oddities and wilful obscurity" of *Sordello*, but not the general severity of the criticism, which did not do justice to the "singular genius and great powers of the poet." The *Examiner* said that the *Edinburgh Review* dealt with Browning's poems somewhat harshly. Though conceding the fairness of censuring Browning's obscurity, the *Examiner* thought that the critic for the *Edinburgh* pushed the case against Browning to the extreme. He failed to take everything into consideration and was not sound on all points.

Massey signed a spirited letter of over two columns to the editor of the *Reader,* in which he attacked the "tawdry twaddle" of the *Edinburgh Review*. He piled up examples of lapses of good English, especially of obscure writing, in a review making severe criticism of obscurity and bad English in Browning's poetry, and he cited evidence of the critic's lack of careful reading of the poems. The critic for the *Edinburgh* did not have the "faculty or fitness" to review a great genius of originality and intellectual vigor. The *Saturday Review* in over three columns of discussion also found Stigand "totally incapable" of understanding Browning. This weekly, which had denounced *Men and Women* ten years earlier (1855) and had become more receptive in two subsequent reviews (in 1863), took the *Edinburgh* to task for finding indecencies and irreverence in certain poems, for not judging the poet's genius as a whole, for making unjustified criticisms of obscurity in certain passages, and for creating "four palpable blunders" in two sentences. It ended by calling the review in the *Edinburgh* "the most complete literary *fiasco* which any of our Quarterlies have perpetrated for very many years" and by making the point that the time was past when after the fashion of the *Edinburgh* and the *Quarterly* of earlier years a review could make or break a poet's reputation.

Browning was not likely to miss this stir in the press since he must have been watching for criticisms of *Dramatis Personae*. As we read letters to his friends we see again his attitude toward reviews that retarded understanding of his works and something of what he wanted the critics to be aware of. We also see in this instance how much his censure of disparaging reviews was in keeping with that of some critics who defended him.

Browning wrote of the criticisms in the *Saturday Review, Edinburgh Review,* and *Dublin University Magazine* in his early letters to Julia Wedgwood, a Victorian bluestocking with whom he carried on a correspondence from 1864 to 1870. As we proceed from one remark to another on these periodicals and their reviews and bring in remarks which he made to others, we can observe Browning's extreme sensitiveness to criticism. It is necessary to say something about the contents of the reviews in order to understand his reaction to them. The attack on *Men and Women* by the *Saturday Review* in 1855 (on the grounds of obscurity), which has already been discussed, was sufficiently severe and offensive to affect a writer less impressionable than Browning. Just as in 1863 a reference by Isa Blagden to this weekly had moved Browning to a caustic criticism of the "superfine" *Saturday*, in 1864 a comment of Miss Wedgwood's again stirred up his memory of the *Saturday's* critical incompetence in the past. By way of analogy he told her a story going back to the Talmud.

> Rabbi Perida took such great care of his scholars, who from appearances were as promising as my own, that he made it a general rule to read and explain the same thing four hundred times over: but such was his fortune, that on a particular occasion, one of his hopeful pupils, either through stupidity or inattention, was at the end of the lecture as wise as he was at the beginning: whereupon the Rabbi gave a specimen of his patience by repeating the same lecture over four hundred times more.[1]

In answer to the prayers of his scholars heaven granted the Rabbi a life of four hundred years. Browning wrote at the end of the story, "I keep trying to be quite intelligible, next poem: what if the 'Saturday Review' should get me four hundred years more of rendering-intelligible, by general outcry to heaven?" Thus Browning showed that the *Saturday Review's* attack on his obscurity in 1855 was still lurking in his mind some nine years later. He was called Perida in subsequent letters that he and Miss Wedgwood exchanged.

In October 1864, less than two months after Browning's reference to the *Saturday Review's* insistence on his unintelligibility, Stigand's unfavorable criticism of his *Poetical Works* and *Dramatis Personae* appeared in the *Edinburgh Review*. Two days after reading the review Browning wrote one sentence about it to Isa Blagden, "Do you see the 'Edinburg' that says all my poetry is summed up in 'Bang whang, whang, goes the Drum?' "[2] He had more to say to Julia Wedgwood. On the day when he read the review, October 17, he expressed his irritation forcefully in a letter to her.

> The clever creature rummages over my wardrobe of thirty years' accumulation, strips every old coat of its queer button or odd tag and

tassel, then holds them out, "So Mr. B. goes dressed now!" — of the cut of the coats, not a word. I had fancied that the bugholes of that crazy old bedstead [where bedbugs could hide] were plugged-up at this time of the day, — but no, here is the nastiness on one again! or rather off already, for to smash it would make things worse.[3]

When Browning spoke disparagingly of his critics to Julia Wedgwood, she did not openly find fault, nor did she profess sympathy with him; sometimes she questioned his severity. So it was in this instance, and he did not let the topic drop. What, he countered on October 31, if under the pretense of reviewing Tennyson's recent works, she referred to his early poems as representative of what he was at the present doing and scarcely mentioned the latest volume? Browning ended the discussion by revealing just how sensitive he was to the *Edinburgh's* criticism and how little he restrained his feeling.

> You don't, of course, confound one's classing a creeper definitely as *Cimex Edenburgensis* (graveolens Reevii) — for mere science's sake, — with being put out of temper by the thing: there happens to be a spice in me of the snuff-taker's vice, love of sub-irritation, — mild pugnaciousness. But I don't want to degrade God's creatures and bid them scratch and so far amuse me.[4]

Henry Reeve, the object of Browning's abuse, was the editor of the *Edinburgh Review*, but not the author of the criticism.

When the offensive criticism in the *Edinburgh Review* appeared in October 1864, Francis Turner Palgrave, poet and critic, fearing that Browning would think he was responsible for the review, wrote with little delay to deny his authorship. In his prompt answer of October 19 Browning again showed how much the review had affected him.

> *You* write the article? No, indeed! Were you minded to review me, you might easily have much to say against the general cut of my coat, but would not — I fancy — go grubbing among my old wardrobe of thirty years' accumulation, and, picking off here a quaint button, there a queer tag and tassel, exhibit them as my daily wear. Bless us! in the course of my musical exercises, and according to the moods of many a year, I may have treated myself to an occasional whistle, cherrup, and guffaw, besides the regular symphonies — and even in these, it's not unlikely that 'Strafford,' written twenty-eight years ago, is far from perfect; whereupon . . . but see the Review and then smash it! I had supposed that the ramshackle old 'Edin-

burg,' under a succession of sleepy editors, was cleaned in the crannies; but — body o' me! here's a bug again![5]

In Browning's figurative language to Miss Wedgwood and Palgrave, queer, quaint buttons and odd, queer tags and tassels stand for out-of-date, relatively insignificant aspects of his poetry and the general cut of his coat for the characteristic and constant aspects — the real achievement by which he should be judged. There was justification for his response to a revival of old objections which he felt were no longer applicable and to a passing over of the considerable merits which he felt he had demonstrated again and again in his years of writing poetry.

It is true that Stigand, the author of the review in the *Edinburgh*, had read many of Browning's poems and liked some of them; and he said very early in his discussion that every reader must see Browning as "a man of rare accomplishments, with a singularly original mind capable of sympathising with a multiplicity of tastes and characters very far removed from every-day experience." But when Stigand made a statement that displayed a glimmer of sympathy with Browning's contribution to poetry, he at once dispelled that bit of light by his accompanying remarks. The negative quality of his attitude toward the poetry and an obsession with its obscurity overshadowed what he could find to praise. With a limited point of view, he called attention to works to show his objections to Browning's undesirable characters, his choice of indecent, irreverent, or unpleasant subject matter, his obscure diction and grotesque rhymes; and he mentioned a few plays, which, he said, were failures on the stage. In proportion to the discussions of other poems he gave too much attention to *Paracelsus* and *Sordello*, and for his illustrations he sometimes leaned on quaint buttons and queer tags and sometimes reproduced lines exemplary of Browning's better writing but undervalued them.

Stigand neglected the general cut of the coat that other critics of the *Poetical Works* had shown their readers: how Browning used his originality in combining his dramatic genius, his intellectual versatility, and his spiritual concern for man in the world of reality. He failed to see what other critics of *Dramatis Personae* were also pointing out: that Browning filled a need by facing specific problems of the time. Stigand's relative inattention to *Dramatis Personae* contributed much to Browning's reaction to the article. Although it was supposed to be a review of this latest work as well as of the *Poetical Works* of 1863, the discussion scarcely touched upon the poems in *Dramatis Personae*. To Stigand it was clear that Browning had "so wedded himself to what is quaint and obscure in his forms of expression and choice of subject" that no change was to be hoped for. There was hardly a fault, he said, that Browning had ever been charged with that was not present in *Dramatis Personae*, "intensified to an extravagant degree."

Stigand's criticism stands out by contrast with that in two other periodicals which also reviewed the *Poetical Works* of 1863 as well as *Dramatis Personae* — the *Quarterly Review* and the *Times*. The critics were far more aware than Stigand of the relative importance of individual poems in revealing Browning's genius and establishing the characteristic features of his poetry. Though they did not discuss *Dramatis Personae* at length (the critic for the *Quarterly Review* had already reviewed it in the *Athenaeum*), they were favorably disposed toward the volume; each thought that some of the poetry in it demonstrated Browning at his best.

As we take leave of Stigand and his review, we can empathize with Browning in his pleasure that his earlier decrier, the *Saturday Review*, was one of those who attacked the *Edinburgh Review*, among other things for its unfair comments on his obscurity. Assuming the name of Rabbi Perida, whose story he had told Miss Wedgwood to emphasize the weekly's early harangue on his obscurity, he added in a postscript to his letter to her of January 9, 1865, two days after the *Saturday Review's* censure of the *Edinburgh*, "Hasn't Perida just got some nice tall fellow to take his part in this 'Saturday review!' "[6]

A little while after Browning had denounced the criticism in the *Edinburgh* he wrote Miss Wedgwood that an "infinitely viler" review had come out to divert his attention from the *Edinburgh*. The writer, Browning said, begins "his performance by apprising us that we find 'the imaginative faculty' in this man and that, and — 'here and there a little of it in———Coleridge!' Then he goes on to laud me, — and him. . . ."[7] The review was in the *Dublin University Magazine* (Nov. 1864), and it was written by T. C. Irwin, an Irish poet. In imagination he placed Browning in the class with the highest names in English literature, and in dramatic power combined with other qualities, including the poetic, he considered him endowed to a greater degree than any other dramatic poet since the Elizabethan period. Browning, however, "great as a poetic conceiver and dramatic artist," was "far from always being a poetic one." There was a lack of finish in his poetry: most of his pieces appeared to be "rather sketches thrown off in the first heat of the mind and never revised . . . hardly one of them can be called a finished composition." Irwin lessened the effect of a complimentary opinion by proceeding to a disparaging one. "His primary purpose is to give nature and dramatic force to his subjects [which, he said, Browning did], and this is of course the highest object a poet can have in view; but in working them out he is often so obscure as to be well-nigh unintelligible."

Although the heading to the *Dublin University Magazine* promised only a review of *Dramatis Personae*, Irwin, like Stigand, rummaged through Browning's early poetic wardrobe and pulled off a few quaint buttons. And he brought in *Paracelsus* and *Sordello*, even repeating the tiresome Jerrold story. He then turned to Browning's latest work. Like other critics, he labeled some of the shorter poems in *Dramatis Personae* obscure (they partook too much of the obscurity of *Sordello*, he said) and praised *Abt Vogler, Rabbi Ben Ezra, A Death in the Desert*, and *Caliban* and quoted at length from them. These favorable remarks were followed by praise of the "power and beauty" displayed in earlier volumes — enough, in spite of obscurity, to insure Browning a high place in posterity. At this point we might suppose that commendation of Browning will take us to the end of the review. Irwin, however, reverted to *Dramatis Personae*, which he pronounced "inferior to his [Browning's] previous poetic essays, with the exception of his most characteristic poem, the Soliloquy of Caliban." This statement seems to belie Irwin's high praise of individual poems in *Dramatis Personae*. Throughout the review he gives the impression of not knowing his own mind. Browning, who had been welcoming increased critical perception, did not find it in the *Dublin University Magazine*. It is not easy to see why he thought Irwin's review "infinitely viler" than Stigand's: both reviewers praised Browning on certain points but weakened their praise by qualifications and both concluded that *Dramatis Personae*, instead of evidencing a further development of Browning's art, fell below his previous effort. Stigand was the more severe.

The time had come when Browning and his sympathetic reviewers were looking at his detractors in the same light. There is agreement between Browning's complaints and the attacks that the *London Review, Saturday Review, Examiner*, and *Reader* made on the *Edinburgh:* the dissenting critics had not taken a broad view of Browning's poetical output, had overemphasized his weaknesses while underestimating his strength, and were incapable of a comprehensive assessment of his work. An accusation that the *Christian Spectator* made against Bagehot of the *National Review* coincides with Browning's reaction to the *Edinburgh*. Bagehot, said the *Christian Spectator*, was guilty of unfairness when, to illustrate Browning's genius, he quoted *The Pied Piper* at length and said nothing of *A Death in the Desert*. Here is an echo of Browning's complaint that the *Edinburgh* had sacrificed the more representative poem to the queer tag and tassel, and this time Bagehot chose a tag and tassel that Browning never considered worth publishing in the first place.[8]

Browning knew well that he had written poems that did not equal his best efforts, and he had not intended for some of them to be taken too seriously; as he said to Palgrave, he had treated himself to "an occasional whistle, cherrup, and guffaw, besides the regular symphonies." He had written Elizabeth in 1845 that he was placing some "easy" poems in between the others, to "break the shock of collision."[9] He felt that they served a purpose among the poems that could not be so readily understood. In the sixties, he hoped that critics would not give undue attention to the lighter poems and to his serious but less mature works and that they would base their estimate principally on the more significant ones and on the character and development of the distinctive qualities of his poetry.

As more criticism appeared that at last helped to break down the barriers to a recognition of his poetic contribution, Browning had difficulty in resigning himself to the critics who continued to maintain the barriers. In his remarks to Julia Wedgwood on the effect of criticism on Keats, the significance of one statement stands out in relief: ". . . don't believe a man of average sensibility is ever insulted by a blackguard without suffering enough: despise it? yes, but you feel the slap in the face, too. . . ."[10] With the fresh hopes for recognition in the sixties, Browning felt the sting of the damaging slaps in his face, even though at times he indicated that he was invulnerable to the pain.

CHAPTER XXIV

Republications and Comprehensive Reviews

The Poetical Works of Robert Browning, 1865;

A Selection from the Works of Robert Browning, 1865;

The Poetical Works of Robert Browning, 1868

On August 19, 1865, after the favorable reception of *Dramatis Personae,* Browning wrote Isa Blagden a letter in which he revealed his attitude toward his past and present reputation and toward the reviewers and the character of the reviewing. He took into consideration the possible effect of social activities on his poetic career.

> I suppose that what you call "my fame within these four years"
> comes from a little of this gossiping and going out, and showing
> myself to be alive: and so indeed some folks say — but I hardly think
> it: for remember I was uninterruptedly (almost) in London from the
> time I published Paracelsus — till I ended that string of plays with
> Luria: and I used to go out then, and see far more of merely literary
> people, critics &c — than I do now, — but what came of it? There
> were always a few people who had a certain opinion of my poems,
> but nobody cared to speak what he thought, or the things printed
> twenty five years ago would not have waited so long for the good
> word. . . .[1]

He was right in saying that he had had considerable social life before he married and moved to Italy, just as he had after his return to England. But he was inaccurate in saying "nobody cared to speak what he thought" of the writings, just as he had been wrong in making a similar complaint to the Storys in his letter of March 19, 1862, when he was referring to the printing of the *Selections.* He had had devoted

444

champions, if not many, who had spoken out, a few of them repeatedly. Whatever support he had was limited, but he was ignoring the uneven quality of his publications (which resulted in some obscuring of his genius), the departure of his work from conventional poetry, the successive plays that misled the critics, as well as other barriers that delayed recognition. To some extent Browning himself had intellectually recognized these obstacles and furthermore had shown appreciation for support that he now minimized. This statement to Isa is the kind that should not be taken in isolation as representative but should be considered with other statements that did show appreciation of his critics.

Although on the whole Browning faced life squarely, the frustration that he had suffered from delay of recognition sometimes caused him to distort reality; and it must be remembered that he wrote as much out of his heart as out of his head to Isa. His outburst in the same letter gave evidence of the bitterness that arose from the past inadequate reception of his work and the anxiety that came from examining current reviews.

> I observe that some of my old friends don't like at all the irruption of *outsiders* who rescue me from their sober and private approval and take those words out of their mouths "which they always meant to say", and never *did*. When there gets to be a general feeling of this kind, that there must be *something* in the works of an author, the reviews are obliged to notice him, such notice as it is: but what poor work, even when doing its best! — I mean, poor in the failure to give a general notion of the whole works, — not a particular one of such and such points therein.

The comment on the failure to give a fair idea of the whole of his works is interesting because Browning had approximated it in other passages that have already been discussed — complaints of unfair criticism in the *Edinburgh Review* of October 1864 to Miss Wedgwood and to F. T. Palgrave, in which he objected that the general cut of his coat was ignored and a queer button and odd tag and tassel were pointed to as if they were his daily wear. In writing of the criticism in the *National Review* of October 1863, he had previously complained to Mrs. Story and to Isa that only part of his work was recognized, the rest ignored. At that time his letter to Isa indicated that critics were confronted with more in his poetry than they could grasp in the limited time they had to prepare their reviews, just as he had written Ruskin in 1856 that more than a glance was needed to take in all that he attempted to do.

In July 1865, shortly before Browning made his complaint to Isa, the *Quarterly Review* had published its 29-page favorable criticism of *Dramatis Personae* and *The Poetical Works* of 1863, in which various aspects of his works were discussed with supporting examples. Had Browning not seen this review by August 19, when he wrote of the "poor" reviews? He did become familiar with it at some time between July and the end of the year, according to a comment that he made to Procter.[2] Although Browning left London at the end of the month in which the review appeared and was away until October, as a rule he kept up with at least the leading reviews of his works, usually reading them soon after they appeared. If he had seen the *Quarterly*, which was likely, and put it in the back of his mind, here was another occasion in the sixties when good reviewing was obscured in his memory. After the encouragement that came from the 1863 republications and the decided step forward that followed the new poetry of *Dramatis Personae*, Browning, with his perfectly justifiable desire for continued recognition, was more than ever alert to whatever might obstruct a better understanding of his poetry. As he read each "poor" review, he became inescapably aware of the possible detrimental influence on the now increasing public acceptance of his works.

While reading and evaluating the reviews, Browning was a wideawake guardian of his reputation. He was republishing his works between the appearance of *Dramatis Personae* and *The Ring and the Book*, thinking of what he could do in order to attract more readers. In early 1865, when the reviews of *Dramatis Personae* were coming to an end, he published *The Poetical Works of Robert Browning*, Fourth Edition. (For many years mistakenly called a reprint of the 1863 *Poetical Works*, it is now established as a revised edition.[3]) Also in 1865 a second selection from his works appeared; it was one of the series of Moxon's Miniature Poets.

There was talk of a third book of selections. In February of 1865 Alexander Macmillan wrote Browning about the possibility of a volume in the Golden Treasury series. Macmillan had already talked to Chapman twice about such a possibility, and in his letter to Browning he went so far as to make a tentative proposal for a joint publication of his and Elizabeth's poems: ". . . I will very gladly do this: — print and publish at my own risk, and give you and him a royalty for every 1000 copies I printed. This, of course, to be fixed when I knew precisely what the volumes would make."[4] There seems to be no record of Browning's answer.

The subject of a selection of poems, this time seemingly of Robert's only, was again brought up when Browning and Macmillan were at a friend's house in July. Macmillan's move in that direction within a week indicates that publishers, as well as critics, were becoming aware of the attraction of Browning's poetry. Macmillan wrote him on Thursday, July 20, 1865, "I think I see my way to a quite new Selection which should not interfere with any existing one, and which might be of use to the public by making them better acquainted with a great poet, and which also would do no harm to the said great poet." Macmillan asked Browning to call on him. On Saturday Browning sent Chapman the communication and promised to let him know what Macmillan proposed at the meeting set to take place on Monday.[5]

Although, according to Macmillan, Browning had expressed in their discussion a "willingness" to come to an agreement and both men had acted promptly, nothing came of the meeting. In Browning's letter of August 19 to Isa he told her of Macmillan's proposal and added, ". . . but *three* [*Selections* of 1863 and *A Selection* of 1865, with Macmillan's as the third] seemed too absurd."[6]

The collected editions of 1863 and 1865 had not included the poems in *Dramatis Personae,* and Browning was turning his thoughts to a new collection. Because of Edward Chapman's negligent business habits, he thought he should find a publisher who could and would handle his works to greater advantage, especially since they were attracting more and more attention. On July 5, 1867, apparently before the final break, he wrote to Frederic Chapman, by now in charge of the firm, "I think the best way will be for you to apprise me whenever the sale of the Poems reduces your stock to 50: I will then make up my mind about what is to be done."[7] Browning considered the volumes in the editions of 1863 and 1865 oversized (Vol. I, pp. 432; II, 605; III, 465); with the addition of the poems from *Dramatis Personae* he wanted to do something about the size. One solution that appealed to him would be to reduce the number of pages in each volume and so increase the number of volumes, each available by itself to his readers. He continued his letter to Chapman: "I think the great size of the volumes, and the number of them, as they are now, a great disadvantage, — and should be inclined to try what breaking up the thing into separate poems would do. People buy one volume at a Railway Station, — for instance, — and would not be encumbered with three bulky books." He concluded, "But I avoid coming to any determination at present."

By November Browning had made up his mind to leave Chapman and Hall. On the 11th he wrote George Smith, of Smith, Elder and Co., to see if he was interested in publishing the new edition. In his letter he again explained his preference for thinner volumes, which would be accomplished by having six instead of three volumes. "I should also prefer the six volumes as distinct each from the other, purchasable by itself, and in a lighter and cheaper form."[8]

He wished also to change the order of his works. In 1863 he had thought it best to place in the first volume of his *Poetical Works* the poems that had been published in *Dramatic Lyrics, Dramatic Romances and Lyrics,* and *Men and Women;* in the second, the plays; and in the third, *Sordello, Paracelsus,* and *Christmas-Eve and Easter-Day.* This order would place immediately before readers the works most representative of Browning's genius, and the others could be seen in perspective. As we know, according to his comments to Palgrave, Mrs. Story, Isa, and Julia Wedgwood, when he read reviews of his works that were published in the first half of the sixties he became concerned because some of them emphasized certain poems without giving a notion of his whole poetical effort; in other words, they did not recognize the different aspects of his contribution and the development of his art. The critics would be in a better position to see the development if they could consider all of his works in the order in which they were published.

With Browning's desire for his readers to evaluate his entire production came his decision to republish his unacknowledged first poem. He began to realize the need of protecting himself by including it in his 1868 collection when, as he told William Rossetti,[9] someone "contemplated" publishing a "considerable part" of the anonymous *Pauline* (this was early in 1867; see Chapter I). It could best appear as his first work in a collection designed to show the advancement of his poetic efforts. He had already realized that it should be republished before receiving encouragement from his new publisher to do so.[10] Since he now saw the expediency of publicly acknowledging a work from which he had disassociated himself for thirty-five years, it seemed of great importance that the critics not isolate *Pauline* or *Sordello* or any other work for discussion but instead see the lines along which his writing had developed. He decided, therefore, to arrange the works in his new edition in the order in which they had first been published.

In 1868 Smith, Elder published *The Poetical Works of Robert Browning* in six volumes and identified the author as "M. A., Honorary Fellow of Balliol College, Oxford." In his Preface Browning said that the poems were "in the order of their publication," and they were almost in that order. The places of *Luria* and *A Soul's Tragedy* were interchanged. *In a Balcony,* which had originally been one of *Men and Women* (now in Volume V) was placed at the beginning of Volume VI as a separate work and was followed by *Dramatis Personae.*

When Browning sent the material for the last two volumes to Smith he said that he felt they gained considerably by the new arrangement: ". . . it stands to reason that the sequence which seemed natural to the writer of these pieces should be natural also to the reader of them; and that, as there was some original cause for passing from one to the other attempt, by way of a change, — so there must be an advantage in giving them just as they were produced."[11] This statement should be read with Browning's comment on the new arrangement as recorded by William Rossetti after talking to him about the inclusion of *Pauline* in his collection. "His new edition, now just coming out, is on a strictly chronological scheme: he says that he finds the heavier works, such as dramas, read much the most agreeably thus arranged."[12] Whether the change of order was beneficial is a moot question. One thing is sure: Browning continued to consider how best to present his poetry to the public.

Browning was throwing himself wholeheartedly into his professional life. The fifties had been a disheartening period; in the sixties his professional activities began to bear fruit. He occupied himself with republication of his works in collected editions, giving attention to the best ordering of his poems and plays for reading, and he found a more satisfactory publisher. He was also making plans for *The Ring and the Book.* During this time the critics and reviewers were looking back on his work.

Little needs to be said of the reception of the *Selection* in *Moxon's Miniature Poets.* As Browning stated in his preface, none of the poems in it had appeared in the collection arranged by Forster and Procter in 1863. In its notice of the book, the *Fortnightly* explained the purpose of the series: "The series is not meant for the readers of the poets: they want the works and not selections. But it is charmingly adapted to the large class who wish to have 'a taste,' many of whom will be lured by that taste into more serious acquaintance with the poets; and it is just the sort of series to place in the hands of the young." The *Selection* might have served this purpose; but appearing as it did between Browning's more considerable publications, it was given only cursory attention by a few professional reviewers.

More important are four long reviews that appeared in 1867 and
1868; each one covered a wide range of Browning's poems. The *Contemporary Review* carried a 31-page review in two parts in January and
February 1867; the *Free Churchman and Christian Spectator*, a 26-page
review in two parts in October and November 1868; the *Eclectic and
Congregational Review*, a 29-page review in December 1868; and the
North British Review, a 56-page review in the same month. The breathing space between the publication of *Dramatis Personae* (May 1864) and
the publication of the first volume of *The Ring and the Book* (Nov.
1868) allowed the critics to make a long and thorough examination of
Browning's works.

With little deviation these reviews were in line with the favorable
criticisms of *The Poetical Works* of 1863 and *Dramatis Personae* of 1864.
Three of the critics commented on the intellectual quality in the unusual subject matter and in the method of presentation; they considered that herein lay to a marked degree the originality and strength of
Browning's writing. To follow his poetry required effort, they said,
but the works were not to be condemned because of the study involved
in understanding them. The fourth was J. H. Stirling, a Scottish philosopher, who wrote for the *North British Review*. He was not as perceptive as the others in evaluating the qualities of Browning's writing
though he discussed many poems and praised some of the best ones.
He criticized the poems by groups, beginning with a group characterized by "obscurity and other disappointing strangenesses" and continuing in an ascending sequence to a final group labeled "supreme."

With increased understanding of Browning's originality, the critics could see the value of characteristics that had earlier been censured.
Abrupt beginnings, according to the *Contemporary Review*, should not
deter a reader; if he persisted he would be rewarded. Augustus S. Wilkins, a classical scholar, defended Browning in the *Free Churchman* on
points of style that made his works difficult to read. Both the *Eclectic*
and the *Free Churchman* discussed the appropriateness of Browning's
verse to the content. In reply to those who found no artistry in Browning, E. P. Hood, who was reviewing his works for the third time,
could now write in the *Eclectic*, "To us there seems an exact and most
harmonious fitness between the thoughts of the poet and the measure
in which he expresses himself. . . ." In the *Free Churchman* Wilkins explained a principle in Browning's verse that should, he said, clear away
numerous criticisms. "The rhythm in many cases has almost as much
to do with the revelation of the character to be depicted as the words

he uses." Both of the reviews also approved of Browning's employment of the grotesque; Hood, who objected to representing Browning as exclusively a poet of the grotesque school, used Bagehot's general classification of poetry in the *National Review* ("Wordsworth, Tennyson, and Browning; or, Pure, Ornate, and Grotesque Art in English Poetry") as an introduction to a discussion of the place of the grotesque in the totality of Browning's work. Though the critic for the *Contemporary Review* did not wholeheartedly approve of the grotesque, he saw Browning as a master in the use of it.

The critic for the *Contemporary Review* (formerly identified as Henry Alford, the editor, now doubtful) took the earlier conservative view of Browning's subject matter, emphasizing the repulsive and objecting to the foreign element — two criticisms not made in other reviews during the time span from 1865 to 1868. Though the subject matter was offensive to him, this critic did admit the powerful effect that Browning created by the use of it in his comprehensive and truthful depiction of man. This view was not entirely removed from that of Wilkins in the *Free Churchman,* who was representative of those who approved of Browning's subject matter. Wilkins said that condemnation of Browning's poetry as unwholesome was based on a few poems in which repulsive ideas are seemingly dwelt on. "But these are introduced only when dramatically needful, and bear no manner of proportion to the simpler, purer pictures that are painted for us everywhere." There was far more difference in the pronouncements made by these two reviewers on Browning's use of Italian life and character. The critic for the *Contemporary Review* thought that no poet possessing power equal to Browning's, with the possible exception of Byron, had done "so little to represent and to ennoble English thought and life." He found many poems "thoroughly Italian"; and he regretted that Browning had been "so far denationalized." Wilkins expressed a contrary view: "But passionate as his love for Italy is, Mr. Browning is above all an Englishman. . . ."

In the four long reviews there was the usual emphasis on Browning's character analysis and dramatic method. According to the *North British Review,* his works were not to be labeled dramatic in the sense of exhibiting action. "Browning's characteristic, in fact, were, perhaps better named by the phrase psychological analytico-synthetic reproduction than by the word drama or dramatic." Besides the plays, excellent for their study of character, Browning used another form of composition for analysis of characters in poems such as *Bishop Blou-*

gram's Apology and *Mr. Sludge,* explained the *Free Churchman.* "We hardly know by what name to describe it, or where to find a parallel instance." As psychological studies they were unique. *Blougram,* said Hood of the *Eclectic,* was "a remarkable illustration of the manner in which the nicest and most refining idiosyncrasies of a character are made to render up every nerve, and vein, and pore of the moral skin to the searching knowledge of the poet."

Not only the psychological aspect of such poems but also Browning's projection of himself into the mind of the monologuist continued to elicit comment. Hood wrote of Browning's "throwing himself completely into the personality of the actor he describes"; in *Blougram* he "winds himself through all the pathways of mingled sophism and logic." The question was how much Browning was revealing his own beliefs. This might be asked appropriately since Browning's poetry concerned bewildering problems of the day — since, as the *Eclectic* said, the reader of Browning's poetry would find "every variety of painful thought of our times touched upon."

We can see from the *Free Churchman* how one critic applauded Browning's dramatic approach and from the *Contemporary Review* how another felt that his approach could have the unfortunate effect of concealing Browning's own views. Although the critic for the *Free Churchman* hesitated to use the overworked terms "objective" and "subjective," he found that the word "objective" best described the quality of Browning's lyrics as well as his plays. It was a good sign, he said, that poets like William Morris and Browning were reacting to the "sickly subjectivity" of many modern poets with "variations on melodies . . . whose key-note is always 'ego.' " Instead of confining themselves to their own emotions and experiences, poets were again engaged in the nobler task of showing "the essential oneness of human nature in every time and land, the fundamental similarity in the soul's sorrows and aspirations." Most reviewers of Browning's works in the sixties, like this one, appreciated his dramatic method and were scarcely conscious of a problem in identifying Browning himself in his poetry.

It was, however, the suppression of the subjective that concerned the critic for the *Contemporary Review.* Like Hood of the *Eclectic* and Wilkins of the *Free Churchman,* he saw Browning as a religious poet. The following passage, which leads off from one on Keble, points out the difficulty of determining the extent to which Browning was revealing his own position with regard to religious matters.

> Mr. Browning's influence, we need hardly say, is of a very different character. His creed is less definite, his temper less submissive, his handling of sacred themes bolder and more free, and the essentially dramatic character of most of his poems makes it difficult for us to determine how far he is speaking in his own person, or representing some phase of the great drama of man's religious life.

Although the reviewer welcomed the Christian thought, Browning's method was not entirely satisfying. His "intensely dramatic power," a "great and wonderful gift," carried with it the subtle and perilous danger of hiding the poet's own thought. "Asking himself what he himself believes, and uttering the answer which we hope he is prepared to give, in no faltering voice, he may come to be the greatest Christian poet that England has yet seen in this century or in all the past, and leave a name to live with those of Dante and of Milton."

The critic for the *Contemporary Review* was posing the problem that concerned him and the readers of his Review, that of ascertaining Browning's religious beliefs. He thought that the dramatic presentation, though praiseworthy, did not make possible a defining of Browning's position, which was desirable. A few reviewers had discerned Browning's opinion in certain poems in *Men and Women,* and after *Dramatis Personae* was published the reviewers had read enough of his poetry to feel confident that he was speaking through his monologuists against immorality and unbelief. They felt no need to question whether the opinions in the dramatic poems were Browning's, though a few were mildly aware of the possibility of such an inquiry. In general they simply appreciated the moral, religious, and philosophical value of the poetry and felt that Browning was saying something of importance to his contemporaries.

By summary, quotation, or limited analysis, the writers of the long general reviews that appeared between *Dramatis Personae* and *The Ring and the Book* gave attention to individual poems that showed Browning as a Christian and a philosophical poet, and three of them paid high tribute to him. He was, according to the *Free Churchman,* above all "a philosophical poet" who grappled in verse "with the highest problems of life and destiny"; his words were instinct with "deep Christian conviction." The *Eclectic* spoke of the philosophy that his works taught, of the "indestructible existence of soul" that seemed ever to be present with him, of the teaching that showed "evil in the world . . . to be less absolute an entity than theologians usually like to make it." The critics saw that Browning, as a Christian poet, did not ignore the reality of life — the bad along with the good. Thinking of Browning's broad consideration of religious practice and thought, the critic for the *Contemporary Review* wrote, "No living writer — and we do not know any one in the past who can be named in this respect, in the same breath with him — approaches his power of analyzing and reproducing the morbid forms, the corrupt semblances, the hypocrisies, formalisms, and fanaticisms of that [religious] life." This reviewer saw that with the "sense of the reality of the mystery of evil" in Browning's poetry there was also "a clear and vivid apprehension of the glory of the 'mystery of godliness.' "

Apparently these four reviewers set out to survey all of Browning's works. The critic for the *Contemporary Review* did not know about *Pauline* since his article appeared before the publication of the 1868 *Poetical Works*, in which it was first reprinted. But Browning's first poem was scarcely noticed in the three other long reviews that appeared after this publication. Each critic gave only one sentence to it. Although ostensibly the critics set out to discuss the 1868 edition, it is possible that they wrote with the 1863 or 1865 *Poetical Works* in hand and later inserted their sentence on *Pauline*. The critic for the *North British Review*, in fact, said that the most recent collection came "too late for general use" in his article. The *Guardian*, in its one paragraph on the *Poetical Works* of 1868, repeated Browning's explanation for the republication of *Pauline*.

Something should be said about the comments on *Paracelsus* and two other poems in the long reviews. Particular interest in *Paracelsus* had subsided during the early and middle sixties, but the writers of all four of the long reviews published in 1867 and 1868 praised it; three discussed the poem (one of them gave six pages to it); the fourth, who could not say as much as he wished to of a number of poems that he introduced at the end of his review, gave the remaining space to a long summary sentence of *Paracelsus*. Other than this and two other exceptions preference given to individual poems was generally in agreement with opinions stated in reviews of the *Selections* (1863), *Poetical Works* (1863), and *Dramatis Personae* (1864). The exceptions should be pointed out. The critic for the *North British Review*, blind to the merits of *Pippa Passes*, had much to say that was unfavorable. The one for the *Contemporary Review* thought that *A Death in the Desert*, though worth study, was "dramatically . . . among the least successful of Mr. Browning's portraits"; he questioned the imaginative projection of St. John's thoughts into the troublesome Victorian time — a projection that had been generally welcomed by the reviewers of *Dramatis Personae*.

Several poems were singled out in the later sixties for special examination, though not always in the four long criticisms just discussed. In *St. James's* (June 1865) T. Frederick Wedmore, an art critic, summarized *Fra Lippo Lippi* and *Andrea del Sarto* and discussed the artists as historical characters. The favorable attention that *Sordello* received is noteworthy. Although this poem had generally been maligned from the time of its publication, a few critics had been sympathetically inclined toward it. As has been pointed out, Forster (1841) and Horne (1842) had felt that *Sordello* should not be summarily condemned, and several reviewers of the 1849 collected edition instead of ridiculing it had recognized it as an extraordinary poem.

In the generally propitious early sixties *Sordello* profited by the renewed interest in Browning's poetry, though some critics could not restrain the cry of unintelligibility. After the *Poetical Works* of 1863 (in which it was first republished) appeared, the *Victoria Magazine* (Feb. 1864) and the *London Quarterly Review* (Apr. 1864) expressed admiration for the poem in spite of its faults. Following the publication of *Dramatis Personae,* three reviewers who commented on *Sordello* did so not to find fault but to consider it seriously as the early and difficult work of a great poet — the ones for the *Eclectic and Congregational Review* (July 1864), *Quarterly Review* (July 1865), and *Saturday Review* (Jan. 7, 1865, in answer to the *Edinburgh Review*).

When Browning included a revision of *Sordello* in his *Poetical Works* of 1863, he wrote in his dedication to Milsand, ". . . my stress lay on the incidents in the development of a soul: little else is worth study." Attention was more and more focused on that statement. Conway, in the *Victoria Magazine,* saw in the poem the failures and triumphs of the soul. The reviewer for the *Eclectic and Congregational* commented, "It is certainly a succession of great studies fetched from history and from life — a very fine, if as surely a very strange, picture of the ways and means of a human soul in the accomplishment of its purposes."

The remarks of 1864 and 1865 were prefatory to three tributes paid to *Sordello* in 1867 and 1868. The "First Paper" of a discussion of the poem appeared in *Fraser's* in October 1867; it ran to more than twelve pages and was signed by Edward Dowden. The editor of the monthly, J. A. Froude, was away when Dowden's contribution was accepted by the temporary editor (possibly Charles Kingsley). As we have seen, Froude, who disapproved of Browning's poetry, had reluctantly included a general review of his works in *Fraser's* of February

1863 (written by John Skelton and published under his pseudonym Shirley). Now, in 1867, he refused to print in *Fraser's* the remainder of Dowden's article on *Sordello*. (The whole article appeared in Dowden's *Transcripts and Studies* in 1888, with a few changes.)

In his discussion in *Fraser's,* Dowden stated that he wanted to "indicate the place of *Sordello* amongst the poems of Mr. Browning, and to make clear its purport as a whole." Its place was with a number of short poems as well as with *Paracelsus* and *Easter-Day,* all of which illustrated Browning's idea that the imperfect state of man on earth gives scope for progress. Man "must perpetually grasp at things which are just within, or almost without his reach, and, having attained them, find that they are unsatisfying; so that by an endless series of aspirations and endeavours, which generate new aspirations and new endeavours, he may be sent on to God and Christ and heaven." To show how the poet unfolded this idea in *Sordello,* Dowden planned to summarize the story by tracing "the incidents in the development of a soul." In the part of his long article that was published in *Fraser's,* he summarized two books of *Sordello* and related a number of Browning's poems to it.

In the *Eclectic and Congregational Review* (Dec. 1868) Hood gave over seven pages to *Sordello.* He also associated its thought with that of other works by Browning. To him it was "one of the wealthiest poems" in the English language, even if perhaps the hardest to read; it was an "eminently great poem." By commentary and quotation he explained its high aim and teaching. "It is remarkable that in 'Sordello' stands out pretty complete the chief revelation of all Browning's poetry; viz., the doctrine of the value of every soul, and the relation of all the work of every soul for its own sake. . . ." Browning, he said, had repeated this lesson in many ways and places. "To live is indeed to strive. . . ." The striving may result in what seems to be failure, but "all real work tells somehow on the assured being, the eternal inheritance, the immortality. . . ." Hood realized the inadequacy of a few pages for a work "every word of which is a nerve palpitating and thrilling with such lofty living hopes." Remarkable as the poem was, he wondered "that so tardy and begrudging a praise" had been given to it. He wondered all the more because besides having loftiness of thought it was "crowded with small exquisitely cut cameos, delicate miniatures, sweet little etchings and landscapes, more or less completely finished."

The third tribute does not, strictly speaking, belong in a consideration of press reviews, but as the lengthiest discussion of *Sordello* up to this time it cannot be passed over here. J. T. Nettleship, an animal painter who later became a member of the Browning Society (founded in 1881) and a contributor to its *Papers,* published in 1868 the first book on Browning — *Essays on Robert Browning's Poetry.* In it he included two essays on *Sordello.* The first contained summary, commentary, and historical background; the second treated the "digression" at the end of Book III. Browning's great object was the "analysis of a soul." (The book was reprinted with additional essays in 1890 as *Robert Browning: Essays and Thoughts.*)

Comments in the sixties, astute or otherwise, showed an increased receptivity to *Sordello.* Dowden, Hood, and Nettleship demonstrated that its obscurities were not so complete a deterrent to reading the poem as earlier critics had maintained. That *Sordello* was considered at least worthy of a close examination was one measure of Browning's standing; his position as a poet was too important for a work so much ridiculed in the past to escape scrutiny now. And since his high place depended to a great extent on the spiritual and ethical import of his works, his remark in the 1863 dedication to *Sordello* that he had intended to stress the development of a soul was bound to carry directive force for some critics. Hood, Dowden, and Nettleship responded by giving particular consideration to the spiritual growth of Sordello.

The poem that had cost Browning so much travail during the process of composition as well as after its publication was an attempt to express much that was of vital importance to him as a poet. Its difficulty had caused many critics to treat it as a laughing matter, and even after the publication of the products of his mature efforts it had often been discussed as if it were representative of his style. Browning was pleased that various critics in the sixties attempted to reveal the significance and merits of the poem to those who wished to know and understand him.

Always fully aware of the effect of helpful reviews, Browning particularly welcomed the sympathetic treatment of *Sordello.* Years earlier, in 1844, he had expressed his appreciation to R. H. Horne for the attention he gave it in his *New Spirit of the Age;* in 1858 he had indicated his gratification to William Rossetti for his contemplated exposition of the poem; and he was not silent when others spoke out in the poem's behalf in the sixties.

He wrote two gracious letters of appreciation to Dowden.[13] The first one had to do with the publication of his discussion of *Sordello* in

Fraser's. "I hardly dare be sure you describe me, as the writer, properly, and not too generously. Anyway, I cannot but wholly sympathise with such an one as you describe; will *that* seem too Jesuitic?" The other letter was prompted by the "mystery of the rejection" of the second part of the discussion. He wrote, "I wish with all my heart I may yet see that phenomenon registered beyond the reach of incredulity, and that I may be honoured by the publication, as you seem to think possible." In this letter Browning referred to another study of *Sordello,* which had been sent to him in manuscript and was going to be published soon; it was the discussion in Nettleship's *Essays.*

Browning was happy to learn that students in universities were reading his poetry. In his letter to Isa of August 1865, in which he blocked out of his memory the help that his peers and a few older men had given him in the past, he focused his attention on the interest that young people were taking in his work. He wrote to Isa, ". . . but at last a new set of men arrive who don't mind the conventionalities of ignoring one and seeing everything in another: Chapman says, 'The orders come from Oxford and Cambridge', and all my new cultivators are young men. . . ."

Browning's poetry did appeal to the young — quite naturally. They more easily open their minds to what is new and different, sometimes happy to accept something beyond the comprehension of their elders. As we have seen, even before the sixties young people were usually more attracted to Browning's works than were older readers. Among others, Forster and Chorley, near his own age, were his early supporters; and the youthful Pre-Raphaelites responded enthusiastically to his poetry. Edward Bulwer Lytton wrote of Browning's poetry to his son Robert Lytton in 1861: "But there must be a force and originality about him more perceptible to a younger man than myself, because I recognize in him a great deal that has served to form your own theories and influence your own style." [14]

At the time when Browning was writing Isa about "a new set of men," it was not only in Oxford and Cambridge that the students were drawn to him; in at least one more academic institution, and there were possibly more, students in the midst of traditionalism felt the attraction of a fresh poetic mind. At Marlborough College two of the young men who were reading Browning's poetry wrote independently about him in their magazine, the *Marlburian.* [15] The writer of the first article recognized Browning's "defiance of all the received canons of poetical criticism" and because the literature current at Marlborough was disposed to be "somewhat conventional" he felt the need to direct readers of the magazine to "a mine of acknowledged depth of thought and richness of imagination." After admitting the difficulties of Browning's poetry, he pointed to its outstanding qualities, with the hope that readers who "have not already made his acquaintance . . . will at once proceed to do so." Eight months later the *Marlburian* carried a second article on Browning, which was largely a defense of Browning's obscurity on the grounds that his poetry was of the highest kind.

J. Comyns Carr, an art critic, who was more attracted in his youth than in his later years to Browning's poetry, explained why this was true for him and for other young people: ". . . I believe . . . it is the intellectual quality in verse that first most strongly attracts the younger student of poetry . . . . The complexity of thought, even the obscurity of expression which marks so much of Browning's work, had for me then the strongest fascination." He was pretty much in agreement with the Marlburians. "That half-rebel note in his style, with its defiant scorn of all accepted models of musical form and rhythmical expression, was in itself an added allurement to the poet's untiring intellectual agility of which the rugged verse was but the chosen garment." [16]

At the time when young people were at a loss in the spiritual confusion of the world around them, there were some who turned to Browning's poetry, as R. W. Church, Dean of St. Paul's, indicated. "Then I had young people round me who read, and loved, and defended Browning, and found in him what their souls longed for; and they showed me such poems as *Ben Ezra* and *Saul* and the *Death in the Desert*, and *Abt Vogler;* and various things from *Men and Women;* and *Christmas Eve and Easter Day*, and *Bishop Blougram*, and *Mr. Sludge the Medium. . . .*" [17]

But the increasing recognition of Browning is not to be explained merely by pointing to the young people's interest in his poetry or to his active social life. The explanation is not as simple as that. We have seen that other influences as well were at work in various combinations: an effort, at least on the part of some critics, to understand the poet and the gain made by their repeated reading of his works; the timely appeal of his poetry, especially that of certain poems in *Dramatis Personae*, and the relation of these poems to earlier ones; the critics' continued exposure to the mature products of Browning's genius in the fifties and sixties; and shifts in poetic tastes along with a decline in resistance to difficult poetry as a result of the stressful intellectual atmosphere of the times. Reviewing itself was undergoing changes that noticeably affected Browning's standing; new periodicals with writers drawn from academic ranks and signed reviews produced a more open-minded and responsible kind of criticism.

The increasing number of published discussions of Browning's poetry outside the reviews testified to the growth of his reputation. Nettleship devoted a whole book to Browning; other books contained sections of varying length treating him as an outstanding poet. A Compendious History of English Literature and of the English Language by George L. Craik (1861); Portraits of Men of Eminence in Literature, Science, and Art with Biographical Memoirs, edited by Lovell Reeve (1863); A Course of English Literature by James Hannay (1866) contain instances of the respect paid in the sixties to Browning's works.

A few more remarks should be made about Browning's change of publishers, which was advantageous to him professionally and personally. Edward Chapman, who had followed Moxon as Browning's publisher in 1848 when others were not ready to accept a poet whose works were a risk, continued to irritate Browning with his all-too-casual way of doing business. K. L. Knickerbocker, who has traced the relationship between Browning and Chapman in the sixties, included among the causes for Browning's leaving Chapman and Hall his wish for a better financial return. [18] At times Browning had raised questions about Chapman's responsibility in handling his and Elizabeth's poetry. After examining their account early in 1852 he pointed out to Chapman what seemed to him an insufficient financial return for 700 copies of one of her works. [19] In 1866, after Elizabeth's death, Browning faced Chapman with the question of his own situation: ". . . a publication from which we were entitled to expect considerable results had proved a comparative failure, and it did strike me that my trees of this sort would gain by changing the soil." [20] The publication that did not bring a proper financial reward was Dramatis Personae, even though it reached a second edition in four months. Browning was probably also looking back on the payment of £120 for the Poetical Works of 1863 as insufficient.

Belatedly Edward Chapman and his nephew Frederic saw the handwriting on the wall. In 1865 they acknowledged to Aubrey de Vere that Browning's works had recently gained popularity. [21] After thanking Frederic for a check in January of 1867 Browning wrote, "I am glad the books (I mean my own) are selling better: your advertisements ought to help this, for you supply them liberally." [22] Browning no longer had to press his publisher to advertise; it was apparent that promotion of his poetry was a good investment. His eagerness to talk to others of *The Ring and the Book* served as advanced publicity for the poem, and Edward and Frederic became aware of the interest aroused in it. After Browning wrote them late in 1867 that he was breaking with the firm, Frederic answered, probably in all sincerity, that they were sorry to lose him. In the last of the exchange of letters in 1868, after Browning's break with Chapman and Hall, Frederic was to mention a report that must have brought cold comfort to the firm, "I think that we have been doing pretty well with your books this half year, considering how dull business has been."[23]

After settling in London, the scene of literary production, Browning could provide better conditions for the promotion of his works. When he decided to leave Chapman and Hall, he no longer had to go from one publisher to another. Besides Macmillan there were others who considered him an asset. One of them was Christian Bernhard Tauchnitz, who wrote him on March 11, 1867, "Long has it been my wish to write your name, so highly esteemed also on the Continent, with my series. . . ." He had heard that Browning was now "disposed to this publication." Although Tauchnitz was happy to see his "long nourished wish fulfilled" and hoped for publication "in a time not too far," he had no desire to cause Browning any inconvenience. "Please therefore to do it quite at your leisure," he wrote.[24] The Tauchnitz edition was published, but not until later — Volumes I and II in 1872 and III and IV in 1884.

It was in the year that Tauchnitz approached him, 1867, that Browning asked George Smith if he was interested in publishing his collected poems. We know that he had wanted Smith, Elder to take over his works when he was preparing them for the 1849 collected edition and that Smith was unable to do so. A severe crisis in his firm at that time did not allow him to risk publication of a work that his literary adviser warned him against as a "pecuniary speculation." After he did become Browning's publisher in the sixties Browning never during the rest of his life had to think of a change. Smith became not only his publisher but his staunch friend and sometimes his general adviser as well.[25] When the agreement was made for the 1868 collected edition, Browning had good reason to begin this new relationship with appreciation for his publisher's generous terms. Whereas, according to Browning's statement, Chapman had paid £120 for the collected edition of 1863, Smith paid him £600 for the edition of 1868.[26] Browning indicated his gratitude in a letter to Smith. He hoped, so he wrote, that Smith would be as satisfied with him in their association as he was with Smith's kindness and help.[27]

Browning felt justified in leaving Chapman and confident that both he and his poetry could profit by the change. And they did when he turned to Smith, Elder. His letters to Chapman, many of them written when he was struggling vainly to increase the number of his readers, had been colored by suggestions or outright complaints of negligence, carelessness, and tardiness as well as entreaties for more attentiveness. His letters to Smith, written when he was a famous poet, contained many indications of confidence and expressions of gratitude for what Smith was doing for him and his works.[28]

Another fillip to Browning's healthy ego came in the later sixties. Benjamin Jowett, who helped train the intellect of many of England's future distinguished men, had done what he could toward the preparation of Browning's son for Balliol College. But Pen, who did not take to academic studies, was unable to qualify. Jowett could not do the impossible for Pen, but he did have something to do with bestowing Oxfordian honors on Browning. Browning kept Isa informed of developments. First came the consideration early in 1867 of his becoming a candidate for the Professorship of Poetry at Oxford; there would be three lectures a year — a formidable matter for Browning, who thought they "would take as much trouble to write as three tragedies." The professorship did not materialize because Browning did not have the requisite M.A. degree. In June came the news that he was to be given an M.A. degree by Diploma — "a very rare distinction," he told her, "said to have only happened in Dr Johnson's case!" In October he was elected Honorary Fellow of Balliol. "I really don't know what makes folk so kind all at once," he confided to Isa. This so pleased Browning that when his six-volume edition appeared in 1868, he added below his name on the title page "M.A., Honorary Fellow of Balliol College, Oxford." He explained to Isa: "I put it on the face of my new edition, this same dignity, M.A. & all, having received a hint so to do: it is a pretty piece of respect, after all, and I like it better than tokens from nobody at all, — Oxford is a more fit foundation of honour."[29] Certainly the honors from Oxford, as well as an invitation from St. Andrews in November to be Lord Rector,[30] indicated the stature Browning had achieved among poets even before the publication of *The Ring and the Book.*

CHAPTER XXV

The Masterpiece:
Inception to Publication

The Ring and the Book, 1868–9

At the end of the criticism of *Men and Women* that Carlyle gave Browning in 1856, he had a suggestion. "If you took up some one *great* subject and tasked all your powers upon it for a long while, vowing to Heaven that you *would* be plain to mean capacities, then — !"[1] In the *North British Review* (Dec. 1868) James H. Stirling wrote of Browning's 1868 *Poetical Works,* ". . . we would fain still have, at the hands of Browning, one great and comprehensive work, which, adequate to his genius, we might set beside the 'Princess' and the 'Idylls' and the 'In Memoriam.' " In 1860, four years after Carlyle made his suggestion, Browning found the Old Yellow Book, the primary source for *The Ring and the Book,* the work he tasked his powers upon for a long while; and eight years later, shortly before Stirling's review appeared, the first volume of the poem was published.

One June day in 1860, as Browning was going across the Piazza San Lorenzo in Florence, he found a "square old yellow Book." In it were documents concerning a murder trial that took place in 1698 in Rome. In the beginning of *The Ring and the Book* Browning tells how he saw the "Small-quarto size, part print part manuscript" among odds and ends of ware at one of the booths, cried "Stall!" and paid a lira, "eightpence English just." Attracted at once to it, he started reading. Never taking his eyes off his prize, he went from "written title-page / To written index, on, through street and street. . . ." By the time he reached Casa Guidi he "had mastered the contents, knew the whole

463

truth / Gathered together, bound up in this book. . . ." That night as he paced the "lozenge-brickwork sprinkled cool" of the balcony of Casa Guidi he surrendered his imagination to the contents of the Old Yellow Book.

Elizabeth "never took the least interest in the story, so much as to wish to inspect the papers," Browning said after her death.[2] If at first he had any notion of using the Old Yellow Book, he gave up the idea temporarily, for he offered it to other writers.[3] But even while he was offering the material to others and was seeing about the publication of his and Elizabeth's works in London in the early sixties, it kept its hold on him. In November of 1862 he expressed his resolution to "begin on his murder-case" as soon as his *Poetical Works* of 1863 and *Dramatis Personae* were out of the way.[4] All three volumes of the collected edition were in print by September 1863 and *Dramatis Personae* was published in May 1864.

We learn from William Rossetti's diary that Browning arrived at the plan of *The Ring and the Book* during his vacation in 1864. After talking to Browning of the poem in 1868, Rossetti recorded the following under the date of March 15. "He began it in October '64. Was staying at Bayonne, and walked out to a mountain-gorge traditionally said to have been cut or kicked out by Roland, and there laid out the full plan of his twelve cantos, accurately carried out in the execution."[5]

We can set this against Browning's own statements made to Julia Wedgwood in 1864. On August 20, he wrote her from "Cambo, près Bayonne" that he had gone that morning to the Pass of Roland. Later, on October 3, he wrote from Biarritz that he had well in his head the whole of a poem she had asked about and indicated it would be in twelve books. (He had written Isa Blagden on September 19 that the whole of his poem was "pretty well" in his head.)[6] These statements of Browning's are consistent with Rossetti's report of what Browning had told him. Both sources tell us that Browning went to the Pass of Roland in 1864. Rossetti specifies that there the plan of his poem came to him. We learn from Browning's letters to Miss Wedgwood that he went to the Pass in August and that he had the whole of the poem in his head by October, the month that Rossetti gave for beginning the poem. Rossetti said that Browning was at Bayonne and Browning's letter to Julia Wedgwood showed that he was at Cambo, which he located for her as being near Bayonne; this difference is not significant inasmuch as Browning had gone to Cambo, a village sixteen miles from the city, after failing to find suitable accommodations there.

(Browning probably said Cambo, near Bayonne, to Rossetti — as he had written to Julia, Isa, and also Mrs. Story in August of 1864 — and Rossetti recorded Bayonne.)

Rudolf Lehmann, who had drawn and painted Browning's portrait and was a longtime friend of his, related that Browning settled upon the plan of *The Ring and the Book* just after buying and reading the old quarto. (In giving his information Lehmann quoted Browning.) Browning said that he went for a walk and laid out pebbles on a parapet bordering a road to represent the twelve chapters into which he would divide his poem.[7] In Lehmann's account there is no indication of a lapse of time between the reading of the quarto and the walk on which Browning laid out the twelve pebbles, but in fact there was a lapse of some four years. Where the walk took place is not specified — no mention is made of the Pass of Roland. A modern scholar has argued that Lehmann's account is trustworthy and that Rossetti's is not. He denies that the Pass of Roland had any connection with the conception of *The Ring and the Book*. A principal point in his argument is that as early as 1862 Browning was working hard on "a long poem to be something remarkable." This statement he found in a letter of Browning's to Isa Blagden first assigned to 1862 but later shown to belong to 1865.[8] There is no reason for questioning the reliability of Rossetti's report of what Browning had told him about when and where he determined the plan for his poem — in 1864 at the Pass of Roland. The details of Rossetti's report correlate very well with the information in the letters to Julia and Isa referred to in the preceding paragraph.

Once his poem was started, Browning's progress — which can be charted from statements to Isa, Miss Wedgwood, and W. W. Story — shows how elastic his projected time of completion was. First he said the poem would be ready in April 1865; later he said it would be finished by the summer of that year.[9] The time continued to change: 1866; May 1867 or later; probably September of 1867; October or November of 1867.[10] The last estimate recorded was that he hoped it would be out by May 1868 — that is, six months before the publication of the first volume.[11] As the time for completion stretched out, Browning indicated the increase in the number of lines: 8,400 in July 1865; 16,000 in May 1866.[12] The figures have to be taken somewhat loosely, for Browning again reported 16,000 lines in April 1867; then 18,000 in May 1867, and the poem, he said, was not "altogether done yet, nor by a good deal."[13] He was still to write over three thousand lines to reach a total of 21,116.

Not since *Sordello* had Browning expended so much time and effort on a work. He said to Allingham, ". . . a builder will tell you sometimes of a house, 'there's twice as much work underground as above,' and so it is with my poem."[14] From time to time echoes of this underground work were heard. According to Browning, he was on the scent of related material even before he left Italy.[15] At some point after his return to England, for the sake of accuracy he obtained from the Astronomer Royal knowledge of the phases of the moon in the year 1697, knowledge used in writing a few lines.[16] In September of 1862 he wrote Isa Blagden to ask someone they knew in Italy if he could borrow a manuscript account of the trial of Count Francesco Guidi (known as the Secondary Source of *The Ring and the Book*), which he wanted to collate with his own material.[17] When Frederick Leighton was in Rome in 1864, Browning asked him to go to the church in which the bodies of Pompilia's adoptive parents had been exposed, San Lorenzo in Lucina (identified by its location to distinguish it from other churches in Rome named for San Lorenzo), and examine the interior "attentively" in order to describe it on his return to London.[18]

Browning continued to collect information. In March of 1866, two months before he first reported that he had completed 16,000 lines, he wrote to the Keeper of the British Museum (now the British Library) for assistance in getting details.

I would gladly be put in the way of getting, through any memoirs or letters of the time, at the *gossip* of Rome during the reign of Innocent XII — or between 1690 and 1700: — any particulars of the Pope's private life, the persons, resident or foreign, remarkable at Rome: the Jubilee of 1694 or 5: anything illustrative of the social life there, in short.

I wish also for any notices of the like kind respecting Arezzo from 1650 to 1700: but more especially, an exact account of the city, a plan of its streets and neighbourhood, the genealogy of its chief families, any old prints of costumes &c.[19]

Two days later Browning received an answer from the Keeper, who indicated that searches had been made and invited Browning to his study, where he might provide him with some knowledge of the state and topography of Arezzo.[20] Soon after that, Browning's father sent him from Paris information for his poem, probably on Pope Innocent XII.[21] Other indications of Browning's research have come to light but only one more instance of his effort will be given. In January 1867 Browning wrote George Barrett, who was in Italy, that should he come across, without going to any trouble, "any old postal map of the road between Arezzo and Rome, via Perugia, — containing the names of *all* the little villages by the way, — of the year 1700, a little earlier or later," he should be glad to have it.[22]

"Work, be unhappy but bear life, my son!"[23] These words from the Pope to Caponsacchi, reflecting Browning's grief and his resolution to make the most of his life, fell into place in a labor strongly supported by the memory of Elizabeth's belief in his poetic genius. He worked with tremendous effort: gathered information, read his documents eight times over, and after beginning the poem in couplets changed to blank verse.[24] He observed a regular schedule of writing; when he had completed over two-thirds of the poem, he told Isa that he had given the "precious *earlier* hours of the morning to it . . . which take the strength out of one."[25] It had been a "particularly weary business," he admitted to Julia Wedgwood. He had not had the help of an amanuensis, with a not surprising drawback: ". . . I cannot clearly see what is done, or undone, so long as it is thru' the medium of my own hand-writing — about which there is nothing *sacred* — imperative for, or repellent of — change. . . ."[26]

It was not the weariness but a sustained energy that came through the lines of the poem until the very end. Browning's zeal no doubt impressed others. The work was "to be something remarkable"; "good luck to my great venture," he wrote to Isa in the early stages of composition.[27] He said to the novelist Margaret Hunt, with whom he sometimes had tea, "I should be sorry to think that anyone was in advance in any way of me in my new poem."[28] He told Allingham that the poem was "admirable."[29] After he had completed the whole of it and Julia Wedgwood had found fault with it, he replied with subdued confidence. "But I 'buckled to,' and the thing is done, ill or well: *well* I think, on the whole."[30] Jowett wrote with admiration of Browning's fervor. "I like to hear my friend Mr. Browning say, 'I have just finished a poem (I am ashamed to tell you the length — about 20,000 lines): I am sure that it is by far the best thing which I have yet done, and when I have done that I shall try to do something better still, and so on as long as I live.' "[31]

The Browning at work on *The Ring and the Book* was the poet we have observed for a span of thirty-five years. He had kept the subject in mind over a period of time before the actual composition, a procedure which, as we know, he had followed in the past. He told William Rossetti that such was often the case with him except in the production of

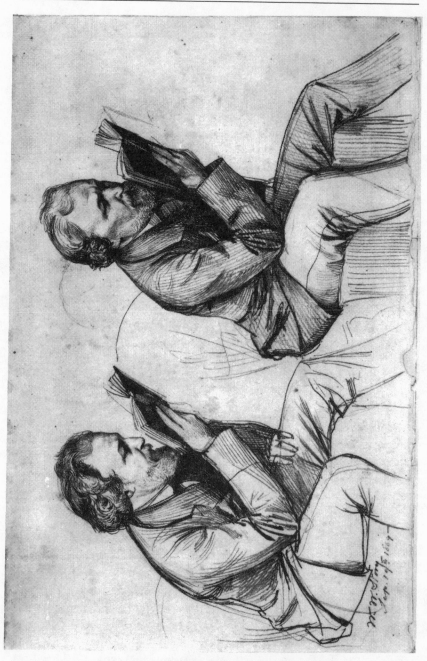

Robert Browning reading The Ring and the Book.

brief poems.[32] He also continued to be the conscious innovator, to be mindful of criticism in his planning, writing, and revising, and to talk of the work in progress.

He described *The Ring and the Book* as *"new* in subject, treatment and form."[33] Browning, with his experimental inclination, stressed the new here as he had when he had written Forster of *Men and Women,* and in both instances his claim was justified. The raw materials would readily lend themselves to the use of a series of monologues, and Browning saw that he could give them a precise arrangement. The poem was divided into twelve books. There were nine speakers; one, Guido, was given two monologues. Three speakers represented Rome, three were the principal figures in the tragic action, and three represented the law (one of these, the spiritual law). The first book would serve as introduction and the last as epilogue. Browning was careful not to let the number of lines vary greatly from book to book. When he was still in the stage of revising, he wrote his publisher that Volume III was thin in comparison with other volumes and that he planned to increase the number of lines in the monologues of the lawyers for the sake of conformity.[34]

By "new" Browning did not mean that he was departing completely from past poetic practices. He built on what he had done well in the past and what his readers had appreciated. The poem was the consummate exhibition of his knowledge of human nature and deep insight into motivation; it also reflected something of his own beliefs and of the spirit of his time. Critics were prepared for Browning the psychologist and for the personal and the timely in his poetry. They appreciated his kind of monologue but knew it only as an independent poetic form. It was what Browning was able to achieve in the combination and interdependence of the monologues that was new. The reader is introduced to the story and characters in the first book and as he progresses from one monologue to another he is presented with different details, attitudes, and points of view. One set of facts presents many faces, and the conflicting evidence must be considered before a satisfactory judgment can be given.

Browning facilitated the understanding of his readers by his precise planning and careful revision. Hints or outright statements of his continued efforts to improve the poem occur in comments to a number of people, including Isa Blagden, Julia Wedgwood, W. M. Rossetti, and George Smith. As Browning worked out the plan and put it into execution, he felt that it gave no grounds for the oft-repeated charge of obscurity and difficulty made against his work. Time after time he had seen complaints by the critics that they had to read through the whole of a work before they could get the drift of it. That would not be the case with *The Ring and the Book,* for in the first book they would be given a preliminary notion of what was to follow. Browning's words to George MacDonald when he showed him the manuscript of his poem indicated his intention. "People say I am obscure. Now there is nothing difficult here; this is a simple story."[35]

Although we shall say more elsewhere of Browning's intentions and objectives in relation to his professional life in the sixties, we can say briefly here that in commenting freely and enthusiastically to MacDonald and others on the work in hand he was following his practice of earlier years. He reacted generously to W. M. Rossetti's interest during the writing of *The Ring and the Book,* and we shall see that he overwhelmed Allingham with his exuberant confidence in it and firmly defended it to Julia Wedgwood. He spoke of it to the Hunts and to Jowett. The list of those to whom he talked of the poem could be easily extended, though now as in earlier times only a few close friends were permitted to read any of his work before publication.

If Browning postponed the time of completion, he did not extend his work because of having to shift his direction as when he was writing *Sordello.* He followed his first and only plan and was willing to take whatever time and effort needed for the proper execution of it. Observing a regular schedule during his periods of work was not a new procedure; he had done so when he was writing the poems for other publications, including *Men and Women.*[36] The business of living caused interruptions; they impeded his progress, to be sure, but he did not feel the urgency of publication that he had felt in the forties or in the early sixties. The final state of the poem was a matter of paramount importance. In November of 1867 he wrote Isa, ". . . it won't appear a day before it is ready if I wait another two or three years . . .," and on March of the following year W. M. Rossetti recorded that Browning said he would defer publication if he found that doing so was "more conducive to the satisfactory completion of the work."[37] With the confidence that he had always had and that since the fifties had been justified by the maturity of his powers, he knew full well the greatness of his achievement. And the critics were soon to recognize it also.

Browning wrote Isa that booksellers were making him "pretty offers" for his poem. "One sent to propose . . . to publish it at his risk, give me *all* the profits, and pay me the whole *in advance* — 'for the incidental advantage of my name.' "[38] One of the offers came from Alexander Macmillan,[39] who had talked to Browning in 1865 about publishing a book of selections for the Golden Treasury series. In the end it was Smith, Elder and Co., publishers of *The Poetical Works* of 1868, who brought out the poem. George Smith, head of the firm, offered Browning £400 for *The Ring and the Book,* the highest he had been paid for any of his works. "This offer," wrote the author of *The House of Smith Elder* (no comma in title), "was afterwards amended by the publisher to £1,250 for the right of publication for five years."[40] In July 1868, Browning accepted "with hearty thanks" the "very generous offer of terms."[41] Nearly six months later, in sending Smith a receipt for a remittance, he wrote, ". . . I enclose . . . the receipt, with sincere thanks for that & all the other kindness you have shown my book: if it fail to repay you in the long run, the fault will be purely its own, — you have helped, as nothing of mine was ever helped before."[42]

The presentation of his poem had to be considered. There was an even greater problem now than when he had published earlier works. The number of lines in *The Ring and the Book* — over 21,000 — was formidable. "Why the Paradise Lost and Regained (two poems) are of less length," wrote Procter to Forster.[43] It had to be decided whether it was better to place the volumes before the public all at once, two at a time, or one by one. Browning discussed the problem when Allingham visited him on May 26, 1868:

> And now! can you advise me? I'm puzzled about how to publish it. I want people not to turn to the end, but to read through in proper order. Magazine, you'll say: but no, I don't like the notion of being sandwiched between Politics and Deer-Stalking, say. I think of bringing it out in four monthly volumes, giving people time to read and digest it, part by part, but not to forget what has gone before.[44]

In 1867 the plan had been to publish the work in two volumes.[45] It is not surprising that Browning came to favor four monthly volumes because seemingly earlier he had been aware of the advisability of not giving readers too much to master at once.[46] After examining the manuscript early in July of 1868, George Smith saw that publication in four volumes would be preferable. Browning wrote him in July, "I am wholly in favour of your notion of publishing at the interval of a month between each volume: it is what I always wanted to do. . . ." This was the arrangement that Browning had talked about to Allingham in May. Smith liked what he had read, which gratified Browning, especially since he thought that the work was still "very rough and admits of plenty improvement of the minuter kind,"[47] an improvement sure to come.

The choice of the title, as well as the manner of presentation, had to be settled. Before the publication of *Dramatis Personae* in 1864 Browning was still writing of men and women but, he said, "under some other name, to please the publisher."[48] In 1868 he was inclined to show in the title that he had again written about men and women. In a letter to Smith, he rejected the title *The Book and the Ring* as "too pretty-fairy-story-like" (he was thinking of Thackeray's *The Rose and the Ring*) and considered *The Franschini,* which "includes everybody in the piece, inasmuch as everyone is for either Franceschini or his wife, a Franceschini also."[49] Browning's final choice of title was relevant to the design and primary source that he had used, as critics would readily see while reading Book I.

The decision to have the poem appear in four installments caused trouble in the arrangements for publication in America. The whole transaction showed that as a good businessman Browning did not hesitate to protect his interests and that publishers could not, without being challenged, undervalue the right to bring out his poem. Browning had offered Ticknor and Fields, the American firm that had published *Men and Women* and *Dramatis Personae,* the sheets of *The Ring and the Book* for £200, and the offer was accepted in May 1867.[50] A letter from Ticknor and Fields, written in June, specified details of the "transmission of the early sheets" of the poem. "We shall desire the sheets of the entire work to be in our hands one month at least before the day of publication in England — to ensure which, it will be necessary to send two Sets — the first seven weeks before the English publication, and the duplicate by the following steamer."[51] In July Browning sent his thanks to the firm and gave information about the poem, which included the statement that it would be published in two volumes. He also said that his English publishers did not want to send anything seven weeks before publication as the American publishers had requested.[52]

On July 12, 1868, a few days after Browning learned that George Smith favored bringing out the poem in four volumes, he wrote to Fields that the poem would be published in four volumes (not two as he had earlier stated) and that the first volume would appear about the 25th of October.[53] Browning heard from the American publishers that they wanted the poem to come out in two volumes; and they reduced their offer from the £200 agreed upon earlier to £50. We learn this from Browning's answer. He was indignant, but he did not declare an end to the negotiations without giving explanations that he felt the Americans should have.

> I am very sorry that you find the arrangements of my publishers inconsistent with such as you wished to make, and that you break our bargain in consequence; so, let it be broken by all means! No doubt my first notion was to print the poem in two volumes! but the publisher, on reading the MS., thought so well of the thing as to believe it would bear, indeed be advantaged by, printing in four volumes, one a month. I rather thought of proposing, with his leave, to send you *two* volumes at once (they are here in type), but I like just as well making no further appeal to a liberality which has been munificent indeed, and would make my acceptance of your new offer of £50 for my twenty thousand lines altogether inexcusable.

Remembering Fields' unauthorized publications of his first collection of poems, Browning warned the partners that, since the negotiations were at an end and he was free to turn to another American publisher, they had no right to print his poem.[54] The next letter from Fields did not improve the situation. Still desiring to publish the poem in two volumes, he suggested that "four bites at such a masterful cherry . . . will puzzle the American appetite." Browning answered that instead of what Fields considered "four bites of a cherry" he would have "an apple, which you will eat unchoked, if you decently quarter it."[55] In spite of being preoccupied with financial and other difficulties, Fields bestirred himself at this point to restore the original offer. Finally, Fields, Osgood & Co. (a new partnership had been set up) agreed to pay Browning £200; the poem was to be brought out in two volumes in America, Volume I in December 1868 and Volume II in April 1869.[56] When the sheets came to hand Fields read enough at once to be able to report to Browning his favorable impression of the work. He added, "I cannot tell you what a satisfaction it is to me personally, to have the opportunity of putting my name on the title-page with yours in this new venture."[57]

Browning, who had felt the pulse of his reading public in England in the sixties and knew something of his following in America, was no longer in the position of having to accept the whims of a publisher and having to bide his time until his readers began to catch up with him. Now with reason to think that critics were better prepared to appreciate his poetry and with the feeling of elation over his poem, he could look forward to the publication.

The title page of the first volume read: *The Ring and the Book*. By Robert Browning, M.A., Honorary Fellow of Balliol College, Oxford. In Four Volumes. Volume I. London: Smith, Elder and Co., 1868. In the completed work the contents of each volume were as follows:

Volume I (November 21, 1868)
  Book I   The Ring and the Book
      II   Half-Rome
      III   The Other Half-Rome
Volume II (December 26, 1868)
  Book IV   Tertium Quid
      V   Count Guido Franceschini
      VI   Giuseppe Caponsacchi
Volume III (January 30, 1869)
  Book VII Pompilia
      VIII Dominus Hyacinthus de Archangelis,
             Pauperum Procurator
      IX   Juris Doctor Johannes-Baptista Bottinius, Fisci
             et Rev. Cam. Apostol. Advocatus
Volume IV (February 27, 1869)
  Book X   The Pope
      XI   Guido
      XII   The Book and the Ring

CHAPTER XXVI

The Masterpiece: Assessments

The Ring and the Book, 1868–9

The critics' acceptance and appreciation of Browning that had moved forward slowly but more or less steadily since the middle forties was put to the test by a unique poem of some 21,000 lines — *The Ring and the Book*. By their comments on the length and plan, on the characterization, on Browning's thoughts as well as the contemporary appeal of the poem, we can see that they persisted remarkably well in the formidable task. It is true that they could not keep pace with the monthly publication of the volumes. There were twelve reviews of Volume I; four of them came out before and seven after the appearance of Volume II and one after Volume III. By the time of Volume IV a few critics had managed to review Volume II (along with Volume I if they had not already reviewed it) and no one had considered Volume III. The majority of the reviews appeared after the publication of Volume IV.

Before the critics had the whole poem in hand, how did they react to the plan revealed in Book I? At the outset did they think the unprecedented form suitable to the special kind of dramatic revelation of character which they had come to expect of Browning and which they had learned to appreciate? After finishing *The Ring and the Book,* did they think that by means of his design Browning had been able to present his characters with the dramatic subtlety that he had earlier demonstrated? Let us attempt to answer these three interrelated questions.

In the early reviews there was marvel at this poem of such magnitude and the feeling that though the plan seemed to threaten repeti-

475

tion Browning thus far was holding the attention of his readers. The critic for the *British Quarterly Review* (Jan. 1869) confessed his initial amazement. (When two or more reviews of a certain work appear in the same periodical, my practice is to specify in parenthesis the date of the review being cited.)

> When . . . we find the same weird, fearsome little story told, at least four, if not five times over in this first quarter of the poem, and . . . we are promised some six more repetitions of the wild romance from different points of view, and by different actors in the tragedy, we confess to something like awe at the prodigality of the force which is lavished on these pages.

In a discussion of Volume I and part of Volume II Frederick Greenwood, the writer for the *Cornhill,* was enthusiastic. "Everybody has heard by this time what the plan is of this wonderful story, and knows how original and how daring was the attempt." Greenwood said that he had followed every turn of the story with suspense.

The critics felt that in spite of the danger of monotony, as far as they had read their interest had not flagged. The critic for the *Press and St. James's Chronicle* was not able to stop reading until he had completed the first volume, because of the absorbing story, the "magnetic force of the successive series of *tableaux vivants,*" and the "masterly anatomy of motive" with which Browning had dissected the minds of the leading characters. Browning had planned to get and hold his readers' interest and had succeeded, said J. A. Symonds in *Macmillan's* (Jan. 1869).

> For, although we are informed pretty plainly of the general conclusion at which we ought to arrive, and though our sympathies are enlisted on one side from the first, there are so many perplexities in the story, that our curiosity is fully whetted and kept alive by watching the mere movement of the intricate machinery which has been explained to us.

After reading the first two volumes, the critic for the *Guardian* (Jan. 20, 1869) said that the work repeated itself greatly, ". . . yet, wonderful to say, *The Ring and the Book* is not dull and tedious. . . ." Browning gave variety to the same facts by "looking at them at different times through different media," and consequently sustained attention. The reviewer was looking forward to the remaining two volumes.

Some of the earlier critics felt that circumspection was advisable until the appearance of the whole poem. Two of these — the ones for the *Athenaeum* and the *Saturday Review* — indicated that interest was being sustained, but they were careful not to venture too far in their approval. The problem was to avoid wearying the intellect by repetition of the same details, Robert Buchanan pointed out in the *Athenaeum* (Dec. 26, 1868). Browning had "so to preserve the dramatic disguise as to lend a totally distinct colouring to each circumstance at each time of narration," and thus far he had been successful within the limitations of his genius. Like earlier critics for the *Athenaeum,* Buchanan felt it expedient to exercise caution in his pronouncements. He said he was not called upon, nor was it scarcely his duty, "to determine in what degree the inspiration and workmanship of 'The Ring and the Book' are poetic as distinguished from intellectual: far less to guess what place the work promises to hold in relation to the poetry of our time."

In spite of the early revelation of the story and the repetition entailed by the plan, the vivid conflicting evidence and different movements of the Roman popular mind made the critic for the *Saturday Review* (Dec. 26, 1868) eager at the end of Volume I to know how the "real fact will develop itself out of the maze of conjecture and inconsistency." Though he looked forward to reading the rest of the poem, he was uneasy about expressing his opinion. "We are disposed to think that nothing in the present volume equals some of his former pieces; but we may be mistaken. . . ."

Other critics were also reluctant to commit themselves too strongly until they had read the whole poem. The one for the *Fortnightly,* (Jan. 1869), with only a mention of variety of presentation and strength of fiber, gave his reason for writing a short discussion of Volume I: ". . . there is as yet no adequate material for criticism." Although the reviewer for the *Westminster* (Jan. 1869) thought from reading Volume I that *The Ring and the Book* promised to be the greatest of all of Browning's works, he felt it best to comment on "particular passages without any regard to the scope of the poem" since publication had just begun.

It occurred to several critics that the murder case might provide the plot for a tragedy, but they did not say that Browning had chosen the wrong form. Their statements should not mislead us. They were not lamenting that he did not write a drama based on the story. If they said that he could not write successfully for the stage, they did so not to deplore a shortcoming but rather to preface their explanation and praise of the peculiar dramatic quality of his poetry. Symonds, in *Macmillan's* (Jan. 1869), thought of the possibility of turning the tragic story into a drama and rejected the idea. "But ours is not a dramatic age." He explained that the intellectual process that Browning used to study character was of more interest. Though Browning was not a master of action, said the critic in the first review in the *Illustrated London News* (Jan. 16, 1869), he was unsurpassed by any modern poet in portraying the inner workings of the mind. In the second review (Mar. 27, 1869) he said a dramatist could have used the story to create characters for dramatic effect but not for such psychological study as only Browning was capable of.

Others praised Browning's use of the monologue. In the *Athenaeum* (Dec. 26, 1868) Buchanan said that the monologue — even perfectly done — could never "rival the 'scene.' " He granted that Browning's monologues are imperfect if it is demanded that the author's "*manner* of thought" (including his values) not be evident at all, but he expressed "wonder" and "admiration" for what Browning had done. "The drama is glorious . . . but we want this thing [presentation by monologues] as well. . . ." Other critics, including H. Buxton Forman in the *London Quarterly Review,* saw Browning's use of a series of monologues in a unified whole as a great contribution to dramatic art.

In their awareness of the suitability of the design to Browning's genius for character revelation, the critics saw the possibilities of exercising to the fullest three of Browning's qualities that they had recognized from the beginning and had emphasized throughout his career — power, intellect, and originality — and their spotlight played on these in various combinations. The reviewer for the *Press and St. James's Chronicle* preceded his discussion of Volume I by specifying qualities that had already established Browning's reputation:

> His power is manifested in many ways, and under many forms — he is original, the most original of all our Victorian poets: he sings a strain we never heard before, and sings it in a way equally original. Subtle, too, is he in thought, mighty and many-sided in his large and generous humanity, sounding depths in the human heart, and soaring to heights of imagination. . . .

The critic for the *Daily Telegraph,* in reviewing Volume I, wrote of these qualities when he said that Browning "spoils you for other singers; he takes the taste out of your mouth for writing less intense, analytical, surprising, vigorous, and master-like. . . ." The plan of *The Ring and the Book* offered greater possibilities than ever for Browning's genius, according to *Macmillan's* review of Volume I:

> In nothing is the vigour of Mr. Browning's imagination, the delicacy of his perception, the subtlety and ingenuity of his invention, more remarkable than in the different colour which he has given to the same series of facts and the different inferences which he has drawn from the same premises, according as the speaker represents the one or the other prepossession.

If stress was placed anywhere in the early criticisms of *The Ring and the Book*, it was on the motivating power of Browning's intellect in the conception and execution of the poem. *St. James's Magazine* saw the poem as a Browningesque piece of mental dissection. "The story is thus told over and over again, each section of society taking a different view, and thus the crime is analysed and dissected with a minuteness and subtlety very characteristic of Mr. Browning." Here was the "anatomist laying bare with searching scalpel the innermost root and fibre of the matter." The *Daily Telegraph* said this of the poem: "Its analysis is more piercing than ever: its easy hold of motive, its living reproduction of life, its hard, sure grasp of character, its infinite variety, its burning colour, its various and copious erudition, its spontaneity, sweep, and literary muscle, are of the author's very best."

The *Cornhill* praised the subtlety which created the distinct characters and even more the finer subtlety which showed the play of minds over the same circumstances. According to R. H. Hutton of the *Spectator* (Dec. 12, 1868), in "fertility of intellectual resource" there was no other poetry like Browning's and in the "brilliancy of his descriptions of character" he had no rival; and it was almost impossible to speak too highly of the power with which the subject was treated. *Tinsley's Magazine* was impressed by the intellectual analysis, which, the critic said, produced valuable results. In his review for the *Athenaeum* (Dec. 26, 1868), Buchanan wrote, "Everything Browingish is found here, — the legal jauntiness, the knitted argumentation, the cunning prying into detail, the suppressed tenderness, the humanity, — the salt intellectual humour. . . ." He said that Browning had the "*secretive* habit of all purely intellectual faculties"; he was like a magpie who finds glittering objects in unpleasant and unlikely places, hides them away, and then swaggers about chuckling to itself. Buchanan did not mean this to be uncomplimentary; the poem as a whole, he said, is not obscure. On the day following the appearance of the review, Browning told Allingham that it was good. As usual Browning was prompt in reading reviews of his works.

The first two questions asked at the beginning of this chapter have now been answered. The critics who had read only part of the poem were impressed by its plan, and they did foresee the possibilities for Browning's exercise of his particular qualities in his presentation of character. The third question can be answered as we examine what the critics said after the appearance of the final volume in February 1869. We can see from their remarks whether the early interest was sustained and expectations were fulfilled.

In the reviews appearing after the publication of Volume IV the plan continued to be discussed. Some reviewers objected to it but praised parts of the poem. The critic for the *Guardian* (Mar. 24, 1869) said that Browning made so many beginnings that he could not attain a satisfactory ending; his poem, like any other long work of imagination, should go in a definite direction until the end is reached. "This serious defect . . . must not blind us to the great power displayed in separate parts." Hutton, the critic for the *Spectator* (Mar. 13, 1869), saw the truth of the picture as being too entirely on one side to justify the pleadings on so many different sides; yet he thought it not easy to express "too highly" his admiration for the monologues of Guido, Caponsacchi, Pompilia, and the Pope.

A few critics raised questions about the plan, sometimes with objections to the consequent length, though they recognized Browning's accomplishment by means of his procedure. J. R. Mozley, who also wrote the review for the *Quarterly,* said in *Macmillan's* (Apr. 1869) that the great length of the poem, based as it was on a subject of such little importance, might keep it from enduring, but the plan allowed for a widening and deepening of the characters — "the very texture of their natures is altered by their mutual influences." This produced a "natural unity" that some other long poems did not have, including *Don Juan* and *The Excursion.* According to the *British Quarterly Review* (Apr. 1869) the construction was faulty: ". . . to give eight versions of the same story, yet nowhere to tell the story in its true and direct form, is of course original, but is certainly inartistic." The effect resembled "that which results from reading through a long trial in the newspapers." Yet the plan brought Browning's special faculty into play — his ability to throw himself "with marvellous skill" into many characters — and by virtue of this skill the poem was not wearisome. *St.*

Paul's objected to revealing all the story at first, which allowed no room for suspense, and objected even more to the redundancy that came in the working out of the plan; but the poem was "profoundly interesting by its great compensating merits." Browning was "triumphant at the goal."

Other reviewers who objected to the length, by outright statement or implication, differed in their opinions of the plan. The *Month* and the *Athenaeum* (Mar. 20, 1869) praised it; the *Dublin Review* and the *Saturday Review* (Apr. 3, 1869) raised objections. The *Edinburgh Review* did not specifically discuss the plan as such but clearly was impressed favorably by the results which it made possible. In the short discussion of *The Ring and the Book* in the *Quarterly Review* Mozley disapproved of the length, but did not consider the plan directly. As we have seen, in the criticism he wrote for *Macmillan's* (Apr. 1869) he questioned the survival of a poem with the plan Browning had adopted.

Quite naturally if critics objected to the length they might consider what could or should be omitted, though some of them realized that the omissions would detract from the value of the poem. Since the monologues of Caponsacchi, Pompilia, Guido, and the Pope were the favorites with relatively little dissent, no one wished to lose any of them. The *Athenaeum* (Mar. 20, 1869) could have done without "about a fourth of the whole work," which would include the second Guido only because of its "extreme and discordant pain," yet the critic recalled that "one of the noblest touches in the whole work" came at the very end of the book. Pompilia's monologue could have been shorter, according to several reviewers — the *Guardian* (Mar. 24, 1869), *Macmillan's* (Apr. 1869), and *St., Paul's*. The *Edinburgh Review* and *Macmillan's* (Apr. 1869) would gladly have had part of the final book omitted. The reviewer for the *Spectator* (Mar. 13, 1869) thought that if Browning had restricted the poem to the monologues of the Pope and those involved in the tragedy, he would have had "five times as many eager and interested students." Yet he saw that the other monologues had "a large share of Mr. Browning's peculiar genius."

The lawyers' speeches came in for the greatest share of criticism. *Macmillan's* (Apr. 1869) and the *Saturday Review* (Apr. 3, 1869) expressed their objections. The *Examiner and London Review, St. Paul's,* and *Chambers's Journal,* as well the *Athenaeum* (Mar. 20, 1869), thought they could well have been omitted, though the *Athenaeum* was not completely negative. "These, of course, are extraordinarily clever;

but cleverness is a poor quality for a man like Robert Browning to parade." The *Illustrated London News* (Mar.27, 1869) praised Browning's inclusion of the lawyers' monologues. A preference for one or the other of the lawyers was sometimes stated. The *Guardian* (Mar. 24, 1869) thought that Arcangeli, the advocate for Guido, was tediously presented and that Bottini, the lawyer for Pompilia, came in a more finished shape, though his repulsive insincerity made his monologue seem overlong. Reversely the *Month* thought that Bottini was "feebly drawn beside the vigorous and hearty description" of Arcangeli.

Other reviewers, six in all, indicated a greater appreciation of the design. Richard Simpson, the critic for the *North British Review*, devoted considerable discussion to the plan, which, similar to that of Chaucer's *Canterbury Tales* though with "a more compressed unity," was "cousin-german to a series of newspaper articles." The interest lay in the "ambiguous character" of the story, which allowed for various interpretations of the acts and motives of the characters. Thinking along the same lines, John Morley wrote in the *Fortnightly* (Mar. 1869) of the "striking human transaction" with its diverse threads "wrought into a single rich and many-coloured web of art." Answering critics who had objected to being told the story all at once, Morley said that such knowledge did not impair the interest of the poem, which consisted in the development and presentation of character and in the "many sides which a single transaction" offered to various minds.

John Skelton (writing under his pseudonym Shirley), who had supported Browning in 1863 and now reviewed *The Ring and the Book* in *Fraser's*, saw the poem as "in effect a criminal trial." He thought that the interest was sustained until the end by the investigation into the why and wherefore of the crime; by a disclosure of each speaker's individual idiosyncrasy; by presentation of the motives of the characters in every conceivable light; and by each speaker's "enlarging on one particular episode of the story, which is not mentioned, except in passing, by the others."

Three more critics showed appreciation for the plan. The one for the *Times* expressed his approval: "With Mr. Browning's genius the story has emanated in a form characteristic, experimental, and peculiar, but successful." One feature of the poem, he said, which might at first sight seem to nullify the interest of the whole "but which in reality supplies the tension of the narrative" was the repetition of the same story. Each was told "from a separate point of view," and over each the author knew "how to throw that exquisitely subtle film of human motives." The reviewer for the *Scotsman* also explained the merit of the treatment: ". . . as your familiarity with the incidents grows, so does your interest in the revelations that are continually being made — revelations not of new events but of fresh conceptions of character and of the mysterious limits set on human knowledge and the equally mysterious triumphs of human love." Forman in the *London Quarterly Review* saw that the "series of monologues which, while each stands perfectly by itself and makes clear its own speaker and situation, are all so welded together as to constitute an indivisible unity." He said, "The mere arrangement of these monologues is strikingly strong and effective."

None of these six critics wished that the lawyers had been omitted. However tedious, they were comic and burlesque personages and, along with the major characters, were dramatically brought out, according to the *North British Review*. *Fraser's* and the *Fortnightly* (Mar. 1869) pointed out the value of the portraits. The reviewer for the *Scotsman* would not "willingly have missed" either of the lawyers. The *Times* appreciated Browning's "dry humour" in the two monologues. There was no specific expression of approval in the laudatory criticism in the *London Quarterly Review,* but Forman clearly appreciated the function of the "special-pleadings of the men of law."

Among these six critics, however, the wish to shorten the poem was not entirely absent. The reviewer for the *Scotsman* thought that it would have gained by compression of the three sections entitled "Half-Rome," "Other Half-Rome," and "Tertium Quid" into one section. Skelton thought that the poem would make a much more "permanently powerful" impression if the four volumes were condensed into two. He granted that it would be difficult to do this without losing a great deal that one would wish to keep — as a matter of fact Browning had avoided monotony only by the "exercise of really consummate art." Nevertheless Skelton had a suggestion to offer: the whole of the three Roman monologues as well as a considerable portion of the introductory section might "without much injury" be omitted. Of Guido's first monologue he said, "There is a Guido in volume two which . . . *might* be dispensed with, — I am far from saying *should* be, for this Count Guido is a marvellously clever rascal, at once plausible and savage. . . . Still the first Guido is not the real Guido. . . ." This seesawing is an example of the problem that the length of the *Ring* presented to sympathetic critics, who hardly knew how to deal with it.

The third question asked at the outset of this chapter has now been answered. Despite dissatisfaction with consequences of the plan such as repetition and length, the reviews of the whole poem reinforced the opinion expressed in the early reviews that Browning's plan had indeed proved to be a means of exercising his ability in the portrayal of character. Though the design was not specifically discussed by a number of laudatory reviewers, they alluded to its originality or they implied their approval in assessing the impressive accomplishment which it made possible.

With great appreciation for a design that permitted varying interpretations of the same set of events, the critics were interested mainly in the monologues of the three principal characters and the Pope's pronouncements in passing judgment. Before we turn to the critical treatment of these four characters and the techniques of characterization, something should be said of the minor figures with their varying degrees of individuality. The critics of *Christmas-Eve and Easter-Day* had complained in the weeklies of the realism of the Dissenting chapel. Now the critics of *The Ring and the Book* praised the vividness of Browning's pictures of minor as well as major personages amidst the teeming activity of Rome in 1698.

Even before all of the monologuists appeared and the discussion was focused on them, the writer for the *Illustrated London News* (Jan. 16, 1869), who thought that the poem was "a miracle of imaginative genius" in its "positive resurrection of the characters," called attention to what others also saw about the realism of Browning's characters.

> He is an uncompromising realist, who strives to represent mankind in detail precisely as he finds them. He will produce every one in his actual shape, with his own peculiar gesture and accent, in the very same habit in which he has lived, and with the identical stains and patches his garments have contracted before the poet met him. Few writers of fiction, even in prose, can bring us so close to the stark, staring, personal individuality of the characters whom they seek to describe.

After all of the volumes were published, similar comments were made about the characters. "Above all, they are every one of them frankly men and women, with free play of human life in limb and feature, as in an antique sculpture." Morley, who said this in the *Fortnightly* (Mar. 1869), pointed out

> a long procession of human figures, infinitely various in form and thought, in character and act; a group of men and women, eager, passionate, indifferent; tender and ravenous, mean and noble, hu-

morous and profound, jovial with prosperity and half-dumb with misery, skirting the central tragedy, or plunged deep into the thick of it, passers-by who put themselves off with a glance at the surface of a thing, and another or two who dive to the heart of it. And they all come out with a certain Shakesperian fulness, vividness, directness.

The broad prospect of a variety of accessory human beings was impressive. Julian Fane, the writer for the *Edinburgh Review*, noted the "men and women throbbing with life and passion" and the assemblage of characters. "These characters range, we may almost say, through the entire scale of human nature." And he discussed characters besides the major ones that stood out clearly on the great canvas. Buchanan, too, in the *Athenaeum's* first review (Dec. 26, 1868), directed attention to the "exquisite *portraits*, clear and sharp-cut, like those on antique gems" — portraits of the Confessor, the aged Luca Cini, the dull brainless clods at Arezzo. "Everywhere there is life, sense, motion — the flash of real faces, the warmth of real breath." The *Examiner and London Review* praised the picture of the Comparini, which was "drawn with marvellous skill and boldness." The *Illustrated London News* (Jan. 16, 1869) was appreciative of the array of figures. "The accessory persons, the witnesses, spectators, and contemporary judges of their conduct and fate, are brought . . . prominently before us, and are compelled to reveal their own particular characters, their sentiments and habits of thought, as plainly as if they were our next neighbours at the present day." The critic for the *Scotsman* observed the skill with which Browning enabled his readers to see the people of Rome of two centuries earlier.

Although reviewers recognized the variety of minor figures, they discussed in detail only the principal characters; in them Browning was able to bring to its highest point his particular technique of portraying human experience and the study of the human mind. The writer of the second review in the *Illustrated London News* (Mar. 27, 1869) represented the viewpoint of many critics. He saw in *The Ring and the Book* a "very striking example of that rare power of displaying individual characters in the attitude of self-disclosure . . . which is the most original capacity of his [Browning's] genius." With the exception of the plays of Shakespeare the critic thought that no dramatic writer had given such a complete representation of character as Browning did in his special kind of dramatic poetry.

It is the endeavour . . . of a poet and moral philosopher like Browning to set before us, at the cost of any amount of protracted monologue — for dialogue will not serve his turn and does not suit his talent — the entire concrete reality of the individual consciousness,
with its habitual sensations, reflections, and volitions; the characteristic personality, the mind and soul of this or that human being, as
an object of supreme interest for its own sake.

Critic after critic appreciated the portraiture of Caponsacchi,
Pompilia, and Guido and praised the monologue of the Pope. "We feel
that we should know them if we met them anywhere else, under a different guise, and with new occasions to act upon," wrote the *Illustrated
London News* (Mar. 27, 1869) of the major participants in the tragedy.
"In Count Guido, Caponsacchi, and especially in Pompilia, we have
distinct creations, characters which stand forth in clearness and completeness like Macbeth, Hamlet or Cordelia," said the critic for *Chambers's Journal.*

The major characters were often coupled for the purpose of contrast or sometimes for a statement of preference or for praise. Caponsacchi and Guido were Browning's "most signal triumphs," said the critic
for the *Saturday Review* (Apr. 3, 1869). He continued, "We question
if, since the greatest dramatists of the Elizabethan age, English poetry
has ever produced characters so solid, so complex, so carefully thought
out." Their speeches were "by far the best and most dramatic in the
whole poem," according to *St. Paul's.* Contrast was often observed: between Guido and Caponsacchi *(Saturday Review,* Apr. 3, 1869; *Macmillan's,* Apr. 1869; *St. Paul's);* between Guido and Pompilia *(Dublin
Review; Illustrated London News,* Mar. 27, 1869); and between Guido on
one hand and Pompilia and Caponsacchi on the other *(North British Review).*

The critic for the *Spectator* (Jan. 30, 1869) knew "scarcely anything in modern poetry" finer than the contrast of Guido and Caponsacchi, and he discussed it at length. The reviewer for the *Examiner and
London Review* thought that the powerful effect of the characters might
be due in part to the force of contrast. "Pompilia is so fair in her juxtaposition to Guido's evil blackness; Caponsacchi so chivalrous in comparison with Guido's meanness; and the Pope, enlarged by the dignity
of his age and office, hearkening with an air of grand abstraction to all
the turmoil of crime and suffering, . . . is so striking a contrast to the
puppet-hearted Violante." The interrelationship of the characters did
not go unobserved. *Macmillan's* (Apr. 1869) noted that the main char-

acters acted and reacted upon one another; and the *Illustrated London News* (Mar. 27, 1869) said they complimented each other ethically. The critic for the *Athenaeum* (Mar. 20, 1869) wrote of Caponsacchi, "What we miss in the psychology Pompilia herself supplies."

Browning's treatment of Caponsacchi impressed the critics in various ways. When the reviewer for the *Guardian* (Jan. 20, 1869) discussed the first two volumes, he thought that Caponsacchi's case was "indeed a curious psychological study." In the change from a lighthearted priest to a serious knight-errant, the reviewer saw a greater consistency than in Guido, who in his plea before the judges first appeared ironical and bitter and at the end rose to the height of "a philosophical morality." Because the critic for *St. Paul's* saw the other major figures as simple rather than complex — the Pope and Pompilia dazzling white and Guido dark — he was attracted most strongly to Caponsacchi, with the more ordinary intermixture of good and evil.

Some critics saw Caponsacchi's monologue as unusual in Browning's writing. The *Saturday Review* (Apr. 3, 1869) made such an observation. "His [Caponsacchi's] speech is of a kind which is a novelty in Mr. Browning's writings; there is in it so much of straightforward description, so little of argumentative subtlety." In keeping with this, Mozley in *Macmillan's* (Apr. 1869) was impressed by "pages together of forcible and simple narrative" revealing Caponsacchi's character, and he felt that the monologue would probably be the one most frequently read. Thinking of the Guido of both monologues (which he had praised), Mozley remarked on the difference between him and Caponsacchi. "The character of Caponsacchi is much simpler than that of Guido, and so affords less scope for the exercise of Mr. Browning's peculiar powers." Though less peculiar than that displayed in Guido, the power shown in the conception of Caponsacchi was "very great." Nevertheless Mozley observed dramatic errors in Caponsacchi's speech. After expressing admiration for the simple narrative he concluded that so "passionate a man would surely have been more inclined to plunge in *medias res*" rather than detain his judges with an account of his early life, and he could not reconcile himself to the beginning of Caponsacchi's monologue. "It is full of abrupt jerks, spasmodic incoherences, and extreme levity." Unfortunately, he said, beginnings in such "crude and abrupt manner" were characteristic of Browning, who "glides afterward into smoothness and eloquence."

Forman in the *London Quarterly Review* also called attention to the direct manner of the narration, different from Guido's "argumentative eloquence" as long as Caponsacchi was calmly giving evidence. He noted that when the priest was deeply moved Browning's manner of writing was "modified to the occasion." Other critics also praised Caponsacchi's monologue. Morley in the *Fortnightly* (Mar. 1869), for example, considered it "as noble alike in conception and execution as anything that Browning has written."

A few derogatory remarks were mixed in with the praise of Caponsacchi's speech, but there was no real objection except in two periodicals with Catholic leanings. The picture of Caponsacchi was drawn in Browning's "graphic and vigorous style," conceded the *Month*. "If, however, it is intended for a Catholic Priest, it is very far from the mark." According to the *Dublin Review*, the depiction of Caponsacchi was a failure. The critic thought that there was something lacking in him which would have been present in a real priest.

> If the author meant to make a hero of him, he ought to have been less like a young English parson. That is probably the highest type of the churchman — at least the young churchman — which Mr. Browning can conceive; but a good young priest, such as one can imagine in Caponsacchi's place, though not less than a brave, true, and honourable gentleman, would also be something more.

A number of critics admired the originality of Browning's portraiture of Pompilia and enthusiastically praised her simplicity, maternal love, and saintliness. They seemed to be most impressed by the simplicity of her character. Like a leitmotif, this quality was noted in highly laudatory discussions of Pompilia: "simple as truth" (*Examiner and London Review*); "simple alike in her religious maternal love . . . and in the confession of the pure depth and intensity of her devotion to the young priest" (*Spectator*, Mar. 13, 1869); whose tale "runs in our ear like a strain of soft and simple music" (*Illustrated London News*, Mar. 27, 1869). "Pompilia's character is one which makes analysis a superfluity by reason of its mere simplicity and purity" (*London Quarterly Review*). The critic, Forman, reverted to the topic of simplicity at the end of his discussion of her: "Pompilia will take rank among the highest of the great women of art. Never was a character of greater solidity and clearness built of materials so simple. Complex enough are the surrounding characters and scenery; but nothing in healthy psychology can be less complex than this absolute piece of feminine integrity. . . ." *Chambers's Journal, Fraser's,* and the *Dublin Review,* as well as others, noted her simplicity.

On the other hand, complaints were made by two reviewers that more simplicity was needed — a foreshadowing of some modern criticism. One was in *Macmillan's* (Apr. 1869): "Pompilia is drawn with studied simplicity; and yet, perhaps, not with simplicity enough. . . . [She] is too acute in her observation, too thoughtful, sometimes even too satirical, for so young a girl. Yet her speech is very beautiful and touching; and through the defects of the execution the genuineness of the conception may be not doubtfully seen." Elizabeth J. Hasell, the critic for *St. Paul's,* regretted that in her monologue Pompilia did not seem to be the ideal of simplicity and piety that she had appeared to be in Book I, and she suggested omissions that to many other critics would have restricted the revelation of her character. An objection of a different kind occurred in the *Saturday Review* (Apr. 3, 1869). Pompilia was hardly so perfect a figure as the other major speakers: ". . . a wife, however estranged from her husband, however much she had suffered at his hands, would scarcely have been able to regard him in so purely indifferent a manner, from so external a point of view, as Pompilia takes up with respect to Count Guido." On the whole, however, these notes of adverse criticism of Pompilia's characterization were all but inaudible in the full chorus of praise.

Of the three main characters in the tragedy, Guido in his two monologues received the lion's share of attention from Browning. Guido had the advantage over the others as the most striking personage in the poem and the critics responded to the subtleties of his character. Few found fault with the portrayal. Two points of disapproval have already been cited: the *Guardian's* (Jan. 20, 1869) complaint of a lack of consistency in Browning's first presentation in Volume II; and the *Athenaeum's* (Mar. 20, 1869) objection to the "extreme and discordant pain" of the second monologue. The *Times* thought that this monologue was the objectionable part of the whole poem.

Beyond these objections there was fair agreement among the reviewers in praising the depiction of Guido, as in his first monologue with his true self cunningly concealed in an effort to save his life, and then as in his second monologue with his evil fully exposed and his desperation unbounded. The plenitude of praise in the *Saturday Review,* the *London Quarterly Review,* and *Macmillan's* gives a notion of the critical approval of the characterization of Guido. Following Guido through the shift in his behavior, the reviewers saw the complexity of his character and furthermore recognized in him a man not to be entirely despised.

In its second criticism the *Saturday Review* (Apr. 3, 1869) compared Guido with Shelley's Count Cenci and found Browning's creation superior. Unlike Count Cenci, Guido was a man with characteristics similar to those possessed by people we know in everyday life — though not in the same combination, explained the critic. "The union of his cold sceptical nature with the heat of his fierce revenge might have seemed contradictory if portrayed by an inferior master; but in Mr. Browning's hands the apparent inconsistency proves to be one of nature's contrasts, the more veritable because so unexpected."

In an extended analysis the *London Quarterly Review* praised Browning's skill. "It is such a character as this Count that yields a fine subject for a violent transition from outspoken, fearless hate, to terrible, heartrending pleading for life; and in the whole range of literature, probably, such a situation has never been so powerfully handled as here." Forman, the writer of the review, pronounced Guido a creation of "almost unrivalled finish." *Macmillan's* (Apr. 1869) expressed what others felt: ". . . it is impossible not to admire the skill, the fulness, and the energy with which the character of Guido is drawn." The critic, Mozley, thought him in most respects portrayed "with greater skill even than Bishop Blougram," who up until this time was Browning's "greatest exploit" in the same kind of technique.

There was an extra dimension to the self-revelation of character: Browning projected his mind into the thinking of each major character — to "better their thoughts and instruction," he said to Julia Wedgwood. The critics made two observations: he achieved a sympathetic understanding of the characters and at times he allowed his own voice to come through to his readers. It was his "special faculty," said the *British Quarterly Review* (Apr. 1869), to add himself to each of his characters; he was "acting" Guido, he was "with all his subtlety and strength" in the monologues of the Pope and of Pompilia. *Macmillan's* (Apr. 1869) found that although Guido, Caponsacchi, and Pompilia were "distinguished from each other by broad lines," in many parts of their speeches they talked "like three Mr. Brownings." Simpson wrote instructively in the *North British Review* of Browning's identifying himself with his characters:

> With a secondary sympathy for creeds which he does not profess, and for habits which he disallows, he takes a special pleasure, and shows an extraordinary facility in throwing himself into the states of mind of the professors of such creeds, or the thralls of such habits, groping tenderly his assumed conscience, explaining and defending to him-

self his hypothetical position, and making out the best case he can in the assertion, or defence, or palliation, or simple exposition, of the mental and moral situation.

The *Month* observed that Browning had "the power of throwing himself out of himself, and gleaning from the minds he enters trophies such as they themselves would be utterly unable to lay bare."

The critics readily recognized Browning's voice in the monologues. There was a "strong undercurrent of subjective power" in his poem, according to the *Times*. Browning was "at once intensely subjective and intensely dramatic," observed *Tinsley's*. The *Guardian* (Jan. 20, 1869) said that the reader is aware of the poet, who is dramatic writer and critic at once. Agreeing with this, the *Spectator* in its first review (Dec. 12, 1868) saw Browning as "never quite dramatic, for we never lose sight of the critical eye of the poet himself." The *North British Review* emphasized Browning's presence in the poem.

> . . . he always tried to be a dramatist; but he is, and ever will be, a critical poet. The author is never off the scene. Like Thackeray, he is always commenting on the sayings and doings and meanings of his dramatic personages. And when he is not formally doing so his readers feel that the process is still going on underground. He is his own chorus, the ideal spectator of his own dramas; and the chorus is often, perhaps generally, more important than the dialogue.

For the most part the reviewers of *The Ring and the Book* did not concern themselves with the problem of identifying Browning's voice. *Tinsley's* review of Volume I pointed out, ". . . Browning so wholly identifies himself with the persons whom he brings upon the stage that not a few worthy people have been staggered by the impossibility of finding out what shadow of the poet's personal opinion may lie behind these dramatic utterances." If the critics were staggered by such a problem, they seldom showed it. The critic for the *Guardian* (Jan. 20, 1869) recognized that the question existed. He felt that it was often hard to understand Browning's characters, who were expressing thoughts of their own as well as thoughts of the poet, though the difficulty was not so pronounced in *The Ring and the Book* because it was constructed on a larger scale. The *Dublin Review* disapproved strongly but not on the grounds of uncertainty. "The 'subjective-objectivity' of the characters is well brought out on the whole, but 'the voice of Jacob' is too distinguishable everywhere." At the other extreme Buchanan wrote in his first review in the *Athenaeum* (Dec. 26, 1868), ". . . we get Mr. Browning masquing under so many disguises, never quite hiding his identity, and generally most delicious, indeed, when the disguise is most transparent." Somewhere between this enthusiastic approval and the disapproval of the *Dublin Review* lay the general acceptance, stated or implied, that Browning's own thoughts show through his dramatic presentation of the characters.

The moral and spiritual values implied by Browning's characters when they seemed to be speaking for him were such as would be accepted by most critics. In the monologues of the three principal characters and of the Pope the critics recognized the voice of the poet who had already won their approbation by speaking out on matters relevant to contemporary thought. The experiences of the participants in the action provided grounds for the operation of ideas that warranted the consideration of serious people of the time. According to the *Edinburgh Review* no English poet had produced three characters more beautiful or better for man's contemplation than Pompilia, Caponsacchi, and the Pope; "and if the ethical teaching of Mr. Browning were confined to the profound moral which underlies these characters, he would deserve the study which his writings exact at our hands."

Since critics saw that these three characters and also Guido served as vehicles of Browning's teaching, they pointed out certain of his views. One that the *North British Review* and the *London Quarterly Review* called attention to was the value of intuition as set over against reason. After saying that each speaker in *The Ring and the Book* was a mask "to conceal the poet's face, not his voice," the critic for the *North British Review* observed: "In contrast with the cold reason and active conventionality of Guido, we have the nature and passion of Pompilia, his wife, and Caponsacchi, her deliverer. Each, either devoid of education or ill-educated, puts to shame the artificial power of education by the natural flow of right feeling and instinct."

One of Browning's aims as a dramatic poet, according to the *London Quarterly Review,* was "to depict a wide variety of character without palpable bias, and yet to leave the moral bearings of the product not only uninvolved, but strongly self-evident." The critic showed how characters in *The Ring and the Book* illustrated the misuse of the intellect as opposed to the right guidance of the intuition. There was Guido:

> No clownish, dull-witted piece of mere brutality is this Count; but
> a clear-headed man of the world, far above the average in abilities —
> a man who lives, and has lived for "the world," in the conventional

acceptation of that term, and whose ideas all centre round worldly advantage — a man to whose *heart* religion is unknown in any form, but whose *intellect* has yet appraised and considered it in many forms, and finally cast it out, choosing that worse part which he is never able to make as entirely his own as he would wish.

Caponsacchi demonstrated the value of intuitive reaction when it was needed in an authoritative religious world.

In matters of debate he regards the inward voice which asserts the greatest sway over his feelings; and, being of a manly, unselfish nature, the result, under due stress of circumstance, is sure to be great and noteworthy. . . . The natural proneness to accept authority save under strong emotional conviction comes back when, for this escapade, he is relegated: he submits calmly; and, when summoned to give evidence on the trial, he obeys; but, as he warms to the discussion of the murder, his whole soul boils over in eloquent vendication of Pompilia and execration of Guido.

Consideration of the moral decisions of the characters led to the examination of another concern of Victorians besides the guidance of the heart — the problem of salvation. Of the many critics who quoted the Count's dramatic last words some saw in them an expression of belief in ultimate salvation. The *Athenaeum* (Mar. 20, 1869) typified their reaction.

We are made to feel that the "damnable blot" on his soul is only temporary, that the sharp axe will be a rod of mercy, and that the poor, petulant, vicious little Count will brighten betimes, and be saved through the purification of the very passions which have doomed him on earth. No writer that we know, except Shakespeare, could, without clumsy art and sentimental psychology, have made us feel so subtly the divine light issuing at last out of the selfish and utterly ignoble nature of Guido Franceschini.

Although these ideas — the place of feeling in determining right conduct and ultimate salvation — were not always labelled as Browning's when they were associated with Pompilia, Caponsacchi, or Guido, they were, as we shall see, definitely identified as his when they were projected into the Pope's monologue.

Browning's reputation as a philosophical and religious poet was strongly supported by the reflections of the Pope. The *Saturday Review* (Apr. 3, 1869) expressed the general attitude: ". . . the meditation of the Pope displays that intensity of thought on religious problems which is more continual in Mr. Browning than in any other poet of the same eminence." Critics readily identified the thoughts expressed by Pope Innocent XII as Browning's. The Catholic *Month* pointed out his use of the Pope to express his own views, which were "out of joint" with the character of the Pope and the age in which he lived. The critic wrote, ". . . if we carefully examine the piece, we shall discover so many crotchetty and poetical reasons for Papal manners and justice, so many strange 'philosophic' views of life and its ends, that we cannot be mistaken in seeing here a good picture of the writer himself rather than of any wearer of the tiara."

What those strange philosophic views were came out in the criticisms written by others who discussed Browning's use of the Pope to address himself to topics that were of interest to himself and to his contemporaries, which in part overlapped those dealt with in other monologues.

The most satisfactory monologue on the whole was that of the aged Pope, said Simpson in the *North British Review,* and it was the poet himself who spoke behind the mask. "In this canto of the poem, consequently, Mr. Browning's whole circle of teaching, feeling, and criticism may be most conveniently studied." The critic thus defined Browning's cast of mind:

> He exhibits a general scepticism, not about the observed laws, but about deduced precepts and conventional rules of morals, politics, and economy. He includes in the same condemnation premeditated proofs, prepared speeches, made-up marriages, codified rules, regulated education, and routine in general. He enforces his argument by examples of the failure of special contrivances.

The *Guardian* (Mar. 24, 1869) called attention to the fact that the Pope, himself an old man, regarded with sympathy the operation of the "nobler natural impulses" usually distrusted by older men. Though this picture might not be true to Innocent XII, Browning was free to follow his own imagination. It might also be questioned whether the Pope could foresee that the approaching eighteenth century would usher in an age of doubt to challenge the age of faith, but the critic thought that Browning was standing on safe ground and was not guilty of "poetic anachronism." According to the critic for the *Scotsman,* who recognized the success with which Browning conveyed high moral lessons artistically in *The Ring and the Book,* the Pope in justifying his judgment turned from "details of evidence" and to the "true nature" of those who were to be judged; he saw the value of "noble instincts." Thoughts in the Popes's monologue had been expressed elsewhere by Browning. Of his treatment of doubt, the critic said, "[It] shapes itself into an able chapter of Christian apologetics, in which Mr Browning's readers will recognise a close likeness to that contained in his 'Death In The Desert.' "

St. Paul's felt that in much of his monologue the Pope disappeared and Browning took his place. "The Pope's disregard of external as compared with internal evidence, his admission of the possibility that revealed truth may be, not absolute, but regulative, his dimly-expressed hope for Guido, strike us as very modern indeed, and as wholly unsuited to the Vatican." *St. Paul's* shared the observation of the *Guardian* on the reflection of the high value placed by Browning on natural impulses. It also shared the observation of two quarterlies — the *British Quarterly Review* and the *Edinburg Review* — on Browning's belief in the possibility of salvation for even great sinners as manifested in the Pope's consideration of Guido, a belief, as we have seen, that several critics called attention to in their discussion of Guido's monologue.

The critic for the *British Quarterly Review* (Apr. 1869) said that though Browning threw himself with marvelous skill into many characters, he never forgot himself. "You hear the poet's voice behind the mask. The idea, for example, wherewith Pope Innocent ends his soliloquy — that Guido Franceschini may be saved from eternal torment by a revelation of truth in and through his punishment — is surely more poetic than papal." Similarly the *Edinburgh Review* wrote, "The readers of Mr. Browning's works know how large is the hope which his philosophy cherishes of the final pardon and purification of the guilty soul." In the following words of the Pope the critic saw a sequence to Browning's earlier expression of the same thought:

> So may the truth be flashed out by one blow,
> And Guido see, one instant, and be saved.
> Else I avert my face, nor follow him
> Into that sad obscure sequestered state
> Where God unmakes but to remake the soul
> He else made first in vain; which must not be.

Critics had previously observed that Browning brought together the visible and the invisible world, the human and the divine, and as they continued reading *The Ring and the Book* they saw more clearly that it transcended the realism of pain, sorrow, and evil. Out of these arose moral and spiritual values that were of importance to readers. The critics varied in showing the effect that the poem would produce on readers according to their needs and cast of mind. Mozley in *Macmillan's* (Apr. 1869) felt it would be for the thoughtful. Buchanan in the *Athenaeum* (Mar. 20, 1869), who considered the intellectual greatness of the poem "as nothing compared with its transcendent spiritual teaching," believed that the true public of the poem lay outside the literary circle — that inferior men and feeble women would be most beneficiently affected by it. Simpson in the *North British Review,* who gave Browning an exalted position in the realm of serious thought, suggested to what extent Browning's poetry reached his contemporaries: ". . . in spite of his theological bias and undeniable Christianity, he is acceptable to the materialistic and positivist thought of the day." Clearly, the critics were convinced of the widespread value of the poem. Just as R. W. Church, the Dean of St. Paul's, pointed out that young people turned to Browning's poetry in a time of trouble, Skelton in *Fraser's* indicated the dependence of many on Browning the poet in matters of serious import. Skelton placed him above a mere metaphysician who confines himself to an analysis of nature and human nature:

> All of us, more or less . . . desire to obtain some authentic information about this strange existence in which we so unaccountably find ourselves — external and internal — nature and human nature. The analysis of human nature by the metaphysicians who are schoolmen only — of the soul on its formal or technical side — has always seemed to me to be barren. But an analysis by a metaphysician who is also a poet or *seer* . . . is a far different matter.

Before *The Ring and the Book* appeared, the poet of character revelation had been looked upon as being also a philosopher and a spiritual and moral teacher, and his masterpiece reinforced this valuation. To the *Examiner and London Review,* Browning, a keen and sympathetic portrayer of every type of humanity, was "a profound thinker, a large-hearted philosopher." As we have already observed in a discussion of the critical pronouncements on Browning's portrayal of character, the critic for the *Illustrated London News* (Mar. 27, 1869) thought of Browning as "a poet and moral philosopher" trying to display individual consciousness in the fullest manner. More will be said of Browning as a moral teacher, particularly of his method of inculcating morals.

By this time others agreed with Mozley, who said of Browning in the *Quarterly Review*, ". . . he feels deeply with the men of his own generation." The moral and spiritual force of Browning's poetry was related to contemporary interests, and so was his concern with man. In a period of scientific progress, man — as an individual and as a member of a collective body — had come under scrutiny, and the study of man in the realities of his existence accorded with contemporary interests. The *Fortnightly* (Mar. 1869), *Athenaeum* (Mar. 20, 1869), and *Quarterly* saw *The Ring and the Book* as being striking for its great human drama, "human fibre," and meditation on human action.

Forman in the *London Quarterly Review* discussed the modernity of Browning's study of man. In an article which carried at its head a list of Browning's publications (twenty-four in all) Forman identified the Idyllic and Psychological Schools as "intimately connected with modern ideas" and proceeded to discuss Browning as the poet of the psychological monologue. From his review of a collection of W. W. Story's poems, published in the *Fortnightly* of January 1869, he quoted in a footnote a passage on the change that had been taking place in poetry.

> Whoever has followed out the history of poetry during the last thirty years, must have observed a great change in the subjects selected for treatment, as well as the manner of treating them. The entity 'nature,' which before the present era of poetry absorbed so large a proportion of our aesthetic energies, has in its turn been absorbed by the real being, man; and the great bulk of poetic force is now brought to bear on the treatment of man, and of man alone — for whatever our poets now find to say about inanimate nature is not of an apostrophic kind, but of an order having reference to nature merely in its bearings on man. Under these auspices, the Psychological School of Poetry has been forming. . . .

Forman acknowledged Browning as "the foremost of our time in knowledge of the human heart, and insight into human motive," and he considered *The Ring and the Book* the "Epic of Psychology." The following passage shows the high rank that he gave *The Ring and the Book* as a modern epic.

> Breadth of mind and width of heart come first now, and the largest action is not that which covers the greatest area and deploys the largest aggregate of physical powers, but that which involves most disinterestedness, philanthropy, purity of heart, power of thought — in short, the maximum of intellectual and moral force. For such a dis-

play, one act of modern men and women serves as well as another for types; and the Roman murder case of 150 years ago, which has so strongly taken hold of Browning, was the germ of what is more essentially modern than any great poetic production of these latter centuries.

A sentence in Morley's review in the *Fortnightly* (Mar. 1869) falls into the same pattern.

The truth is that nothing can be more powerfully efficacious from the moral point of view than the exercise of an exalted creative art, stirring within the intelligence of the spectator active thought and curiosity about many types of character and many changeful issues of conduct and fortune, at once enlarging and elevating the range of his reflections on mankind, ever kindling his sympathies into the warm and continuous glow which purifies and strengthens nature, and fills men with that love of humanity which is the best inspirer of virtue.

According to Morley, instead of the grandeur that readers might expect in such a long poem there is a compensating quality: "a certain simple touching of our sense of human kinship, of the large identity of the conditions of the human lot. . . ." These statements, and also others to be quoted below on the nondidactic nature of Browning's poetry, show that it was evident to the critics how Browning's intellectual strength provided the means for his presentation of the large area of human feeling and behavior and how from this presentation arose the pursuit of moral truth. Both Forman and Morley recognized in Browning the alliance of intellect, moral force, and interest in man.

Browning's intellectual strength resided not only in the breadth and choice of his material but also in the manner of presenting it, and that, too, the critics pointed out, was in accordance with contemporary tastes. The reader of *The Ring and the Book* was put into possession of the various points of view of the characters, and he was caught up in the effort to determine, in the midst of conflicting testimony and arguments, the morally right judgment. The required expenditure of effort, which had at one time aroused a war cry against Browning, was now seen to be in his favor. For many, in a time of spiritual restiveness and abundant intellectual energy, the placing of a matter of interest in a position to be examined for its validity was more acceptable than a conclusion that showed no signs of the effort by which it was reached.

Symonds, who said in *Macmillan's* (Jan. 1869) that Browning's monologue was suitable to the age, explained, "We want to get behind the scenes, to trace the inmost working of motives, to weigh the balance of conflicting evidence, to hear every side of the question and to study the tissue of facts in their complexity, with all the scientific accuracy of an anatomist." Skelton, in *Fraser's,* asserted the desirability for Victorians of this involvement of intellectual energy: ". . . we require to grapple strenuously with this poetry, as Jacob grappled with his angel, before we learn how rich and wonderful it is; and the struggle itself is a delight, a keen excitement to the intellect. . . ."

Along with the desire for involvement in the intellectual movement of the poem came the wish not to be told outright what to think. Browning's dramatic method kept him from appearing to be what Morley called in the *Fortnightly* (Mar. 1869) "directly didactic" — an undesirable quality. "It is a commonplace to the wise, and an everlasting puzzle to the foolish, that direct inculcation of morals should invariably prove so powerless an instrument, so futile a method," said Morley. He wrote further, "Given a certain rectitude as well as vigour of intelligence, then whatever stimulates the fancy, expands the imagination, enlivens meditation upon the great human drama, is essentially moral."

Chambers's Journal felt that in *The Ring and the Book* there was "no putting aside the poet for the didactic teacher; no thrusting forward of the author's individuality to speak for the characters, or to interpret them to his reader." *Chambers's* approved of Browning's not scattering moral reflections over the drama; he let the characters "speak for themselves, without coming forward like a chorus to explain the situation." The critic, like others, welcomed relief from poets of the subjective school, "who view the universe of men and things through a medium supplied by their own idiosyncrasies, and whose poetry comes to us savouring strongly of the mind and heart of the individual poet." The *Scotsman* remarked upon "the success with which it [*The Ring and the Book*] conveys high moral lessons artistically . . . . It is none of the poet's business to teach morals except by implication."

Two more passages that laud the absence of didacticism should be quoted to show the strong appeal of *The Ring and the Book.* Each brings into focus several aspects of Browning's poetry. Like Morley, Buchanan pointed out in the *Athenaeum* (Mar. 20, 1869) the effect of Browning's method upon the reader.

> The one great and patent fact is, that, with a faculty in our own time
> at least unparalleled, he manages to create beings of thoroughly
> human fibre; he is just without judgment, without pre-occupation,

to every being so created; and he succeeds, without a single didactic note, in stirring the soul of the spectator with the concentrated emotion and spiritual exaltation which heighten the soul's stature in the finest moments of life itself.

Mozley was also among the critics who applauded Browning's effectiveness as a moral leader by means of a method that excluded didacticism. In his brief discussion of *The Ring and the Book* in the *Quarterly Review*, he wrote of Browning's accomplishment.

> Like all that Mr. Browning writes, it bears the stamp of a rare sincerity; nothing in it is put forward to take the popular ear, nothing without the manifest search after truth, and the conviction that the sentiments put forward are needful to be known and weighed. A distinct moral purpose runs through the poem; not a moral, not an obtrusive excrescence, not anything that can be expressed in a few neatly compacted sentences at the end; but a course of deep meditation on human action and the problems of life. Few poets have been able to deliver arguments and judgments without being didactic.

We have seen that the critics appreciated the originality of the plan of *The Ring and the Book* and the possibilities it provided for a realistic backdrop of a variety of minor characters and of life and for the energetic exercise of Browning's psychological ingenuity in characterizing individuals with differing points of view. They were impressed by his entering sympathetically into the minds of his characters, by his use of major characters as a mouthpiece for his own thoughts on moral and spiritual questions, and by the timely appeal of both his ideas and methods. One noteworthy feature of the reviews of *The Ring and the Book*, when taken together, was the more complete merging of lines of criticism that had been gradually moving closer together since the forties. We shall see the full import of that merging in the next chapter.

CHAPTER XXVII

The Masterpiece: Comprehensive Appraisal

The Ring and the Book, 1868–9

Attention has not yet been given to specific comments of the critics on the poetic suitability of the material chosen by Browning for *The Ring and the Book* and on diction and metrics along with comprehensibility. At the first of his career these were the areas in which critics saw faults that they criticized as unrelated to the commendable qualities that he possessed — intellect, power, and originality. Obsessed with the notion that Browning should observe tradition, the critics too often lacked the flexibility of judgment necessary for fair consideration of his individuality. The gradual and beneficial merging of various lines of criticism began in the forties and moved slowly in the direction of a more complete understanding of Browning's art. The reception of *The Ring and the Book* shows how far the integration of these lines had changed the attitude toward the subject matter and the technique and led at last to an evaluation of the poem as a whole composed of interrelated elements and to the recognition of Browning's high place as a poet. This advancement will be discussed in some detail in this chapter. At the end something will be said about shifts in the history of the periodical press and about some distinguishing qualities of reviewing, which played an important part in the appreciation of *The Ring and the Book,* as well as of Browning's other works in the sixties.

In the preceding chapter we discussed the critical response to plan and length, character portrayal, questions of moral and spiritual import, and contemporary relevance in *The Ring and the Book.* A closely related topic is selection of subject. Instead of declaring that a trial for a violent crime could not be a fit subject for a poem aspiring to greatness, the critics were inclined to consider whether Browning's creative genius was equal to the task of transforming the raw material into a work of high art. It is the reviewers' pronouncements upon this question that we shall now examine. The Old Yellow Book provided Browning with three figures related to each other through a crime. Similarly, for the major poems of *Dramatis Personae* he had found preexisting figures in the apostle John, a contemporary charlatan, and a primitive monster from Shakespeare.

The choice of a sensational murder that took place in Rome in 1698 was a bold stroke, even after Caliban and Mr. Sludge. Browning, who had learned to observe the pulse of his readers, must have thought that they would now accept his use of such a subject for his ambitious poem; at any rate he was confident of the successful outcome of his efforts. He was right in thinking that they were prepared. For the most part they did not dismiss it in isolation as unfit for poetry. If they did not approve of the distasteful elements at first, as they read more of the poem they looked beyond the bare facts to Browning's treatment and recognized the achievement resulting from his presentation through a number of monologuists speaking from different points of view.

The story itself, "a hideous tale of sordid crime," seemed of no value to the *Illustrated London News* (Mar. 27, 1869); it was the use that Browning as psychological poet had made of it that was important. The *Times* said that a murder trial, especially one laid in seventeenth-century Italy, might not seem a poetical or manageable story, but the poet's "strong sense of humanity has stood him in good stead." As we have already observed, Forman in the *London Quarterly Review* approved of the Roman murder story for Browning's epic. In it were "all the hidden beauties to be found in any complex human subject," which was one "rich in characters, replete with vivid variety of life, teeming with complexities of intellect and emotion, full of dark unexplored mental places."

Seeing the high seriousness of the poem caused some critics to reconsider their first opinion of the subject as they continued to read later volumes. Morley, in the *Fortnightly* (Mar. 1869), referred to the lamentation from various quarters over the subject matter of the poem when the first volume was published. He observed that censure on this score tended to diminish or vanish as publication progressed.

When the second volume, containing *Giuseppe Caponsacchi*, appeared, men no longer found it sordid or ugly; the third, with *Pompilia*, convinced them that the subject was not, after all, so incurably unlovely; and the fourth, with *The Pope* and the passage from the Friar's sermon, may well persuade those who need persuasion, that moral fruitfulness depends on the master, his eye and hand, his vision and grasp. . . .

The *Saturday Review's* (Dec. 26, 1868) objection in its review of Volume I that the "intrinsic disagreeableness acts rather as a hindrance to the expression of lofty and noble sentiments" changed in its second review to praise of Browning as a religious poet. Mozley, who wrote the second review of *The Ring and the Book* in *Macmillan's* (Apr. 1869), could say, ". . . it has become more and more apparent what the ultimate purpose was, in much that seemed at first insignificant or repulsive. . . ." (Mozley did, however, object to the "slight" subject and "so many ignoble elements," as well as the length, in his otherwise favorable brief commentary on *The Ring and the Book* in the *Quarterly*.)

As some continued to read, whatever their questioning of the choice of material, they perceived Browning's successful exercise of his poetic gifts and his accomplishment. According to *St. Paul's*, on artistic grounds it might be doubted whether the general effect of the story was not too distressing and whether the eye had not been kept too long fixed on the catastrophe. Guido in his second appearance was "too much beyond the pale of human sympathy and experience for legitimate art." Unquestionably, however, he was drawn with great power and consistency; if critics find fault with Browning, "they cannot refuse to crown him for his courage, nor can they fail to admire the power of thought and profound knowledge of human nature which have sustained him in the performance of his unexampled feat." The critic for the *Edinburgh Review* found moral audacity in the "occasional outrages of thought and language . . . which he assigns to male characters," but he had high praise for a poem whose conception bore the impress of a preeminently pure mind. Browning's temerity resulted from his desire to be true to nature. Though the critic for *Chambers's Journal* condemned Browning's choice of subject, he gave high praise to the use he made of it: ". . . there is no mark of great and lofty poetry wanting in the elaboration of this noble masterpiece."

A few periodicals with religious leanings were more severe in their judgment. According to the *Dublin Review*, the poem was not "for all hands." Although the writer of the first review in the *Guardian*

(Jan. 20, 1869) made allowances for the "incidental violence of language and coarseness of thought" in a "story of actual murder and possible adultery," the writer of the second review in the *Guardian* (Mar. 24, 1869) said the good that was apparent in the undesirable did not erase the impression that Browning would have done better "if he had bestowed his persevering labour, his marvellous insight into character, his keen observation of details, and his united strength and subtlety of touch, on a somewhat purer subject."

According to the *Month,* with its strangely mixed censure and praise of the poem, nature herself "teaches us to throw round some things the veil of silence." The very scenes that called for this silence — "if for no other motive, out of regard, at least for the young and tender conscience" — Browning had described most "graphically and minutely." The critic could not sanction Browning's "tearing away the veil from what conscience and common decency conspire to hide." Yet with his "disgust" at the "most glaring moral blot" he did not place Browning in a class of poets "whose glory it is to trample under foot Christian modesty." The critic for the chiefly religious *British Quarterly Review* (Apr. 1869) did not think Guido's murder of Pompilia a worthy theme for a great poem. He seemed not to be concerned about indecency or impurity so much as about what constituted a proper subject for poetry. Echoing Arnold, he wrote, "It is a primary canon of criticism that a great poem can be based only upon a great human action. . . ."

The kind of remark made in the religious press was the exception; it represented the earlier tendency to isolate subject matter for condemnation. There was relatively little objection to the presence of much vice and evil and of exploring the dark corners of the mind, which at one time would have raised questions about poetic suitability. Now on the whole there was justification of Browning's choice of material or incidental remarks or no comments at all as Browning's accomplishment was discussed — an indication of how much the subject was accepted as a means to an artistic and moral end.

Nor was the Italian background isolated for adverse criticism. Instead, the use of details peculiar to life there was praised. Hardly any objection was made to the remote setting in late seventeenth-century Italy. The *North British Review* saw that although Browning was attracted by the story he was not completely Italianate; ". . . if he goes to Italy and studies there, he paints Italian subjects in the Dutch manner, and is most attracted by the deposits of the Teuton admixture in the strata of the Italian mind." The critic for *Tinsley's*, who attributed Browning's unpopularity partly to the Italian coloring of his mind and work and who himself seemed to prefer English to Italian subjects, thought Italy and Italian characters best suited to Browning's genius and on that basis did not object to his choice for *The Ring and the Book*.

The remaining aspect of Browning's poetry that had formerly prompted severe criticism was its unusual and difficult style, with obscurity drawing especially heavy fire. Before *The Ring and the Book* was published the critics had soft-pedalled their attacks, including those on Browning's carelessness and wilfulness. The more they accepted other aspects of his poetry, the more inclined they were to reconsider his manner of writing verse. After the publication of *The Ring and the Book*, however, some critics reverted to the old complaints.

The severest censure of the poetic line of *The Ring and the Book* came in four reviews unsympathetic with the poem otherwise — those in the *Westminster* (Apr. 1869), *Month, Dublin Review,* and *British Quarterly Review* (Apr. 1869). We shall turn to them first. The tone of all but *The British Quarterly Review* bore a strong resemblance to that of early criticisms in which irritation rather than an effort to be fair prompted the evaluation. The *Westminster's* single paragraph on the poem in the Belles Lettres section, unlike its earlier brief discussion, was disparaging. There was impatience with the monologues of the lawyers along with accusations of wilfulness and obscurity. Browning had "returned to his old faults." The majority of readers would see much of the poem "as a puzzle, if not a positive stumbling-block."

The other three reviews found fault with the subject matter. Objections to Browning's representation of Catholicism that were expressed in the *Month* and the *Dublin Review* overflowed into other areas, including that of style. The writer for the *Dublin Review*, who admitted at the first of his article that as a Catholic he did not approach his task "with the perfect calmness and temper of judicial indifference," and complained of "monstrous perversions of history and reason" in the Pope's monologue, quoted and castigated "prose run mad" and "deliberate offences . . . against rhythm, good taste, and even the English language. . . ." The *Month* found no harmony and rhythm, disapproved of Browning's diction, and deplored his obscurity. The tone echoed the early unrestrained criticism of many reviews. "In diction it [the poetry] is downright prose, made unintelligible by an attempt to throw it into or rather label it as blank verse." And there was more on obscurity. "For most people no small portion of the four volumes will be nothing more or less than an enigma. And they had better let them remain an enigma for any good they will get by trying to solve them, or any good they will miss by not trying." Yet the critic who made these remarks alluded in the same review to others "who have vented their ill-humour on the obscurity of the author by a wilful blindness to the much sterling and genuine poetry that is scattered in wild profusion through this remarkable work."

The last of the reviews with severe criticism of the poetic line was in the *British Quarterly Review*. Like the *Month* and the *Dublin Review*, it carried objections to the subject matter. The writer, however, in a rather short discussion of the poem in a review of all of Browning's works called attention to Browning's "great qualities" as well as his defects. Although he regarded *The Ring and the Book* as a "work of enormous power, of unique originality," he lamented "power defiant of Art, and original thought hidden in difficult language." He complained of obscurity, ruggedness, and unfit diction.

The reviewer for the *Times,* gave more space to an unfavorable discussion of Browning's style than those who disapproved of *The Ring and the Book* in general. He did see, however, improvement in Browning's latest effort, which was "in whatever way it be regarded, an event of no small importance," a poem he praised and placed among the highest of the time in "original power and importance." Although the critic began by saying that in *The Ring and the Book* Browning's faults were less glaring and his power less crude, he discussed at length the prosiness of quoted passages, good and bad usage of language, and crude rhythm. He labelled Browning as "the prophet of modern realism" and condemned this quality in his verse. Realism had "hardly yet become properly fused and malleable for purposes of art"; in Browning's poetry it accounted for "a deficiency in that sense of harmony and feeling for beauty which go for so much in the making of a poet." The critic's conservatism blinded him to Browning's skill, which others were now aware of.

In contrast to these comments, the majority of criticisms pointed up the progress that had been made in the general attitude toward Browning's style. It is not that there were no other unfavorable criticisms but rather that others were not belabored. A few reviews contained objections to obscurity as well as other faults, but their controlled and balanced critical evaluation carried no sting. The *Examiner and London Review, Press and St. James's Chronicle, Morning Star,* and *Chambers's Journal* gave passing notice to obscurity and other faults of a poem that they highly praised. Sometimes praise balanced, sometimes outweighed, faultfinding. The prolixity, obscurity, and harshness that Symonds in *Macmillan's* (Jan. 1869) found in the first book, when Browning was narrator in his own person, he did not find when Browning spoke through the mouths of his monologuists; and those who put forth effort to understand the "most profound of living artists" would be repaid. The *Westminster* (Jan. 1869) in its first review, *Fortnightly* (Mar. 1869), and *Edinburgh Review* felt that if Browning wrote rugged verse he also wrote lines of beauty. For others, including the *Saturday Review* (Apr. 3, 1869) and *Cornhill,* the poem improved as it advanced. At the first of his article in *Macmillan's* (Apr. 1869) Mozley wrote of the difficulty of *The Ring and the Book,* but at the end he could say of Browning, "All his works, and this not the least, grow on the reader of them; the difficulty dies away, the sense of power increases."

Most significant were the discussions in which the reviewers associated Browning's choice of various kinds of lines with his intended effect. Earlier critics had advanced this notion, though sometimes timidly. There were critics now who spoke with confidence, among them two who were reviewing the first volume. One, the reviewer for *St. James's Magazine,* appreciated the relationship of Browning's thought and verse.

> He is a sternly logical and argumentative poet, not given to mere prettinesses and sonorous lines, but preferring rather rugged versification than to abate one jot or tittle of the full development of the thesis he advances. That he can be infinitely musical when he chooses, no one . . . can for a moment doubt. But his specialty is the pure crude thought in his work rather than rhythmic subtleties, and he makes everything subservient to that.

The other reviewer made a similar criticism in the *Daily Telegraph.*

> Prose of the most work-a-day sort is hammered into ten or eleven feet of strong, uncouth stuff, for whole pages; and then, into this metallic work, like the finest inlaying of Florentine gold, or soft *appliques* of Limoges enamels, come lovely passages of perfect harmony — showing that this blacksmithery in speech is for subtle purposes, and never for lack of precious metal, nor of skill to work fine.

After all the volumes were published, critics commented further on Browning's artistic skill. By lines that Elizabeth J. Hasell quoted in

St. Paul's she demonstrated that in spite of occasional carelessness Browning was a "master of dramatic blank verse"; the music of many lines was "alike perfect in itself and most harmonious with the feeling they express." And Skelton (pseud. Shirley) observed in *Fraser's,* "Determined at whatever cost to embody the conception in his mind, the poet not unfrequently treats the garment of words with apparent severity and harshness."

Other comments that stood out were those on the improvement in Browning's writing, especially its greater clarity. Critics saw improvement in the first volume: it was as "clear and lucid as glass" *(St. James's)* and had "fewer . . . wilful extravagances, crabbedness verging to obscurity" (*Westminster,* Jan. 1869). According to the *London Review,* Browning, who had sometimes puzzled his readers, laid down the basis for his new poem "as clearly as good printer's type could do it." The *Guardian* (Jan. 20, 1869) thought Browning's writing in Volumes I and II was "more easily intelligible than usual."

Later reviewers continued to write of Browning's achievement. In discussing Volumes II, III, and IV, the *Athenaeum* (Mar. 20, 1869) said, ". . . every fibre of the thought is clear as day. . . ." Others wrote of all four volumes. The *Edinburgh Review,* which had in 1864 dwelt on Browning's obscurity and had been called to account for its severe criticism, found less obscurity in *The Ring and the Book* than in Browning's earlier works. Then followed a further discussion of the matter of clarity, with mixed approval and disapproval. (The editor might have been responsible for inserting harsh criticism accompanied by such derogatory phrases as "occasional outrages of thought and language" and "mental and verbal garbage." These are not in keeping with the tone of the article. Julian Fane, the author, complained of changes made in his manuscript that detracted from the favorable impression he had intended to give, as we shall see in the next chapter.)

To Simpson, the critic for the *North British Review,* Browning was a "poetical philosopher, though it may be a question whether his philosophy does not tend to strangle his poetry." Even so, there was something to be said for the improved clarity of his style. Realizing the difficulty his poetry presented, the poet had "set himself . . . to repeat what he had to say in a tongue more comprehensible" and he had succeeded. Forman wrote in the *London Quarterly Review,* "Though he has certainly done no violence to his genius, by adopting aught from the popular style of the day, he has evidently laboured much to make his meaning perfectly clear in this last work."

The full impact of the change that had been taking place in the critical approach to Browning's poetry comes when we see that the critics no longer tended to isolate and find fault with the subject matter or the quality of the verse without regard to other aspects of Browning's poetry that they thought praiseworthy. The increased awareness of the interrelationship of the elements in a poem of Browning's brought together lines of criticism which had formerly remained separate. The result was that the critics with a more receptive frame of mind could now see *The Ring and the Book* as an artistic whole instead of emphasizing one element to the point of distortion.

The critics now saw how Browning could effectively use the account of a sensational murder and at times employ a style once considered too unpleasing to be acceptable as a means of achieving the high purpose of literature. Furthermore, whatever appeared to them as a flaw was placed in an enlightening perspective. For example, take the length. In discussing the plan, a number of critics said that the poem was too long, but in spite of this objection they could see the value of the design. So it was when they discussed faults that they saw in other aspects of the poem.

Two quotations forcefully indicate that perceptive critics were succeeding in considering the poem as a unified entity. According to Morley in the *Fortnightly* (Mar. 1869) whatever the reader thought of this or that part, he felt that the poem fully satisfied the conditions of artistic triumph. "Are we to ignore the grandeur of a colossal statue, and the nobility of the human conceptions which it embodies, because here and there we notice a flaw in the marble, a blemish in its colour, a jagged slip of the chisel?" The same strain of laudation is evident in Buchanan's review in the *Athenaeum* (Mar. 20, 1869). "Faultfinders will discover plenty to carp at in a work so colossal. For ourselves, we are too much moved to think of trifles, and are content to bow in homage, again and again, to what seems to us the highest product of modern thought and culture." A large portion of the critics had matured enough to judge *The Ring and the Book* by its virtues instead of condemning it for its shortcomings. When critics could maintain that the flaws did not invalidate the greatness of the poem, it is evident that they had indeed made progress.

Along with praise for *The Ring and the Book* there appeared much comment on the place of the poem among Browning's works and among other works of the time. When the critic for the *Westminster* (Jan. 1869) said that it promised to be Browning's greatest, he was expressing the opinion of others besides himself when they reviewed the first volume. It "bids fair to be one of the most original, startling, and brilliant of all his poems," said the *British Quarterly Review* (Jan. 1869). The *Press and St. James's Chronicle* judged it "his most brilliant, original, and transcendent flight in the poetical firmament," and according to *Tinsley's*, "Mr. Browning had never written anything more powerful. . . ." Similar assertions continued as the volumes appeared. The last two books of Volume II, according to the *Spectator* (Jan. 30, 1869), "constitute . . . what seem to us Mr. Browning's greatest poetic achievement."

When all four volumes were out, this high recognition continued. The *Fortnightly* (Mar. 1869) hailed the entire work as Browning's "masterpiece," as did the *Spectator* (Mar. 13, 1869), *Morning Star*, and *North British Review*. Beyond this, it was ranked very high among the outstanding poems of the time. The *Saturday Review* (Apr. 3, 1869) called it one of the most considerable poems of the century and the *Athenaeum* (Mar. 20, 1869) the *opus magnum* of the generation. One further quotation will suffice to show how high the critics ranked *The Ring and the Book*. It comes from *Chambers's Journal*. "But it is in the work now before us that Mr Browning's genius reaches the culminating point. Henceforth, his place in the very first rank of English poets must be conceded without a murmur or a doubt. He has added a new lustre to English literature, and enriched our language with a possession for ever."

Recognition in varying degrees was given to *The Ring and the Book* in four articles that included discussions of other works of Browning's. These have already been cited on specific points. Another general article by Alfred Austin in the *Temple Bar*, well known but not yet referred to here, argued tenaciously throughout approximately fifteen pages that Browning was no poet at all, that favorable adjectives could be used to describe what he wrote but it was impossible to call it poetry. Browning, he said, would not find in small London literary coteries and large fashionable London salons the fame he sought. After this and additional insulting personal remarks to end the review, Austin added a "P.S." In it he explained that he did not discuss *The Ring and the Book* because it threw no new light on the subject of Browning's attempts to write poetry.

The other general criticisms of Browning's works are quite different from Austin's. The critics for three of them — the *Quarterly Review*, *British Quarterly Review* (Apr. 1869), and *St. Paul's* — admired Browning for his intellectual and moral qualities and for his originality and knowledge of human nature; they pointed out and praised highly works that possessed these qualities. Even though they had not entirely thrown aside conservative standards of measurement, their objections were overshadowed by their attention to compensating merits. They found fault with Browning's subject matter and style more in theory than in reality, as is demonstrated by their favorable comments on individual works.

Mozley in the *Quarterly Review* and Mortimer Collins in the *British Quarterly Review* gave comparatively little space to *The Ring and the Book*, and there was not much elaboration of what the critics considered its good and bad qualities. Elizabeth J. Hasell, in writing for *St. Paul's*, devoted about the same number of pages to Browning's latest poem as to a discussion of the preceding works, and she related it to them, explaining that in it as in his other poems he did not control his great powers of thought and artistic conscience. But she gave considerable praise to *The Ring and the Book* and was grateful to a poet with a "perfectly original mind" for his contributions throughout his long career.

Forman, who wrote the remaining overall discussion of Browning's works, traced in the *London Quarterly Review* the "development and perfection" of Browning's psychological monologue of the soul from its beginning in *Pauline* to its crowning achievement in *The Ring and the Book*, which he said afforded "a great lesson on the adaptability of the strict monologue form for epic uses." *The Ring and the Book* could be "fitly termed the Epic of Psychology" because modern man's primary involvement is with intellectual and moral forces rather than with physical action covering a great area in geography, as in the traditional epic.

Would the many critics who recognized at once and continued to recognize the high position of *The Ring and the Book* among Browning's works go so far as to assert, before knowing how readers in general would respond, that it would assure an enduring reputation for Browning? We must remember that the critics had always tended to be circumspect until it was clear how a new work fared with the public. Not until the second printing of *Dramatis Personae* and the repeated appearances of the collections indicated a substantial increase in the demand for Browning's poetry did they speak with confidence of his growing reputation.

For about a year and a half before the publication of *The Ring and the Book* critics were writing of Browning as an established poet. Never in the past had they approached a new work of his with such high expectations. By January 1867 the *Contemporary Review* wrote of Browning's fame as already being secure: "The strength of one who is not impatient for popularity and can afford to wait, while others of far inferior power catch the clamorous applause of the day, had at last done its work." The critic referred to the recognition that came to Browning after *Dramatis Personae*. "The more authoritative Reviews, which are supposed to constitute the highest critical tribunal in our courts of literature, at last, with various degrees of heartiness and discernment, recognized the fame which had been won without them. . . ." The republication in 1868 of all of Browning's works in six volumes indicated to the *Guardian* (Aug. 5, 1868) and *Free Churchman* that he was making substantial progress with the reading public.

Two reviews that came out after the first volume of *The Ring and the Book* was published but were not occasioned by it were optimistic about Browning's reputation. According to the *Eclectic Review* (Dec. 1868) Browning was "destined for future regard as, since Wordsworth, incomparably the chiefest and most representative poet" of the time. The *North British Review* (Dec. 1868) wrote: "The uncertain chisel of fitful hope, he, no longer, — bowed and broken in undeserved neglect, — plies slackly: he has received the freedom of the estate, and can do nought unwelcome."

In spite of these reassuring remarks, critics did not uniformly predict that *The Ring and the Book* would enhance Browning's reputation. There was variation in the earlier comments (in reviews of either Volume I or of Volumes I and II) on its possible effect. When Volume I was published, the *Spectator* (Dec. 12, 1868) said, ". . . no one of Mr. Browning's works is likely to take a stronger hold on the public mind . . . ." The critic who wrote the first review in the *Westminster* (Jan. 1869) thought that Browning, though still limited to a restricted audience, had gained readers and felt that the poem would "do much to make him popular." Caution was still exercised. As in the past, some critics who themselves appreciated what Browning had written supposed that it would not be popular; it did not fit into the established channels of poetry. The critic for the *Daily Telegraph,* who could see that the poem was "a marvellous, exquisite, and precious thing of art," said, "Judged by the usual canons of art, 'The Ring and the Book' is a rebellion, a heresy, a verbose monstrosity. . . ." The first volume would, he conjectured, distress the average reader and delight the elect. The critic who wrote the first review in the *Illustrated London News* (Jan. 16, 1869) felt that the poem would not please a great multitude of readers, though he himself had a high regard for it.

Browning's reputation, according to some, had been established before the publication of *The Ring and the Book*. The *Saturday Review* (Dec. 26, 1868) said that at present Browning was certainly not unhonored. "It is now some years since the keenness of his satire, and the subtlety of his appreciation of character, have forced themselves upon the notice, not merely of a few select adherents, but of all educated men." Others indicated a similar opinion: Browning had an established reputation, according to the *Press and St. James's Chronicle;* he had a pretty complete universal recognition, asserted the *Cornhill*. Still others were sure of a confirmed reception of Browning's poetry but it would come in the future. The critic for *St. James's* thought Browning could never be popular; yet he predicted that succeeding generations would read him "with delight" and then wonder how his contemporaries had so little appreciated him. The merits of his poetry though not yet "in accordance with the poetical taste and fashion of the age," would, said *Chambers's Journal,* with certainty have "ultimate appreciation."

There was more agreement in the reviews that considered the entire poem. It is true that Hutton, writer for the *Spectator* (Mar. 13, 1869), felt that the length would endanger the fame of *The Ring and the Book,* and the *Month* and *Westminster* (Apr. 1869) did not think the poem would increase the number of Browning's readers. But others agreed with Simpson in the *North British Review,* who wrote that it had gained the "success of pleasing his revilers and turning them into admirers," and with Skelton in *Fraser's,* who could discern an audience as wide as the dominion of the English language.

Critics liked to explain Browning's reputation, tracing its progress or speaking, as they had often done in the past, of the deterrents to wide recognition. More and more they realized the value of a fresh examination of his works, and they recognized the favorable impression that Browning made on younger readers. One of the more interesting comments on this topic occurred in the *Edinburgh Review.*

> Indeed, the best proof of the force and authority of his genius is the fact that in spite of the obscurity of his thoughts, the subtlety of his allusions, and the habitual rudeness of his versification, he has, after thirty-five years of persevering labour, caught the ear of the public,

and won the sympathy of the most cultivated portion of the younger generation. It is idle to attribute this sort of success — which is a real influence — to the caprice of fashion, or the whims of perverted taste and judgment. Even those who are insensible to Mr. Browning's merits as a poet, must acknowledge that he has produced on his time some of the effects which are commonly attributed to great poets; and that perhaps the greatest of his achievements is to have caused the world to take an interest in his own works.

In considering Browning's reputation, Elizabeth J. Hasell in *St. Paul's* saw signs that the younger generation, the second since Browning's first work had appeared, would grant him the favor that their fathers had refused him, and she hoped that prospective poets would not copy Browning's defects and overlook his perfections. The *Cornhill* said the new generation opened its eyes even before the time of *Dramatis Personae,* and the critic spoke of "more confident and outspoken opinion in college coteries, in 'society' and elsewhere, as to the author's merits. . . ."

In our discussion of the critics' attitude toward Browning's reputation we face a topic that cannot be passed over inasmuch as it serves as a guage of opinion — the comparison of Browning with Tennyson. Early in Browning's career his work had been linked with that of various writers, including Charles Mackay, R. M. Milnes, Henry Taylor, Ambrose Philips — and Tennyson. As time passed, names other than Tennyson's tended to disappear in the comparisons. In August 1849 the *Eclectic Review* considered Browning "worthy to claim brotherhood with his contemporary, Alfred Tennyson," and in September 1850 the *English Review* called the two the "undoubted chiefs of their poetic era." The critics began seriously to associate them in the fifties, the decade in which Tennyson achieved fame — this was one sign of the increasing recognition of Browning's poetry regardless of how they were seen in relation to each other. In the reviews of *Men and Women,* Brimley in *Fraser's* and Thomas McNicoll in the *London Quarterly Review* definitely favored Tennyson; William Morris, in writing for the *Oxford and Cambridge Magazine,* scarcely knew whether to place Browning first or second among the poets of his time; Simpson in the *Rambler* discussed the merits of each without stating a preference. Then in 1861 Gerald Massey said in the *North British Review* that Browning narrowly missed being the greatest living poet.

Such opinions continued to be expressed with more frequency on into the sixties. When the two poets were set side by side, as a rule

Tennyson was given the place of superiority in poetic — that is, melodic — expression; Browning gained ground by virtue of his power deriving from subtlety of intellect. How far the comparisons were carried was shown in a series of letters that appeared in 1865. In October a short discussion of Browning's 1865 *Selection* appeared in *Public Opinion,* in which the writer, who confessed that he himself considered Browning the superior poet, wrote an introductory paragraph on this question that concerned many readers of poetry. In the next month the same periodical carried a letter signed by W. J. Metcalfe. He was to open a discussion at a Young Men's Mutual Improvement Society "upon the question whether Browning or Tennyson be the greater poet" and he invited comments. They came readily — with such signatures as Common Sense, B. A. Oxford, Justita, De Gustibus non est Disputandem. One liked Tennyson, another Browning; a third said that they could not be compared; still another that neither was good. The opinions stretched through five issues before the editor called a halt.

Significantly, after *The Ring and the Book* was published the contention that Tennyson was the more popular all but disappeared. It seems that in the minds of many Browning had risen to Tennyson's place of eminence. Two critics, one who had long supported Browning and one who considered him no poet at all, pointed to the position he had won by this time. Skelton, Browning's champion, wrote for *Fraser's:* ". . . the critics who guide the mob are, I see, dethroning the laureate, and placing the long-neglected poet in the vacant chair." According to Alfred Austin, whose discussion in the *Temple Bar* contributed to Browning's later attack in *Pacchiarotto,* "the Poet Laureate was beginning to totter on his throne" and certain critics wanted to place Browning there instead. Austin begged the public to return to its original low opinion of Browning.

Austin's entreaties went unheeded. The hopeful notes — appearing in the late forties and repeated by perceptive critics in the next decade — increasingly prevailed in the sixties. This account of the reception of *The Ring and the Book* may be closed by an apt comment in the *North British Review:*

> Criticism, indeed, is hardly to be trusted in appraising novelties; nor is it quite its business to announce to the world the advent of the poet of the future. It can see the revolution, can perceive the negation, but cannot determine the positive worth of the new phenomenon. It is not criticism, but sympathy, which catches at once the whispers of genius, and readily recognises a new poet in the bud.

Such an apparition appeals to the critic, not on the critical side of his nature, which proceeds by rules and precedents, but on the side of his feelings, which it is his business to control and prune. The plodding critic sees too little; the enthusiastic critic sees too much; the genuine critic is suspected of enthusiasm. Amongst them the new poet remains unacknowledged, and has to make his way by his own weight.

Browning had made his way by the strength of his genius, and there had been a sufficient number of sympathetic critics who ignored precedents to assert opinions that led to better understanding.

The course of Browning's reputation was influenced by the importance, audience, frequency, circulation, and span of life of the periodicals in which the criticisms appeared. In the sixties there were developments in the history of journalism which contributed to the enhancement of Browning's reputation. Periodicals increased in number after the abolition in 1861 of the duty on paper, the last of the three so-called "taxes on knowledge." In this decade many reviews began to show an intensified intellectual impetus. And there was a trend toward signed and hence more responsible reviews.

As the content of the reviews of the sixties has already indicated, the unfavorable comments stood out not because they were predominant but because they were unusual. For the first time in Browning's career that a new work was published, definite as well as immediate praise appeared in the weeklies. The earlier frequent disapproval or wavering in the *Athenaeum* and the almost entirely negative attitude of the *Spectator* changed to praise of *Dramatis Personae* and *The Ring and the Book*. In the sixties these (the *Athenaeum* retained its strong influence and the *Spectator* had achieved new importance) were second only in influence to the more recently established *Saturday Review*, which by now had dropped its initial swaggering attitude to Browning and considered him seriously and approvingly. Through these and other weeklies Browning's poetry was being reviewed favorably for various kinds of readers. Three weeklies that should be mentioned fall into different categories. The *Reader*, which had a low circulation with an appeal to the educated class, reviewed Browning several times in its short life (1863–6). At the other extreme was the highly popular weekly — the *Illustrated London News* — to set its stamp of approval on Browning's *The Ring and the Book* for the many thousands of its readers. The third, the *Guardian*, considered the most influential of the religious weeklies, after a long period of disapproval highly praised *The Ring and the*

Book in its first review though it expressed some objections in the second review.

Browning also fared well in the monthlies. For the first time the influential ones accorded him strong approbation. *Fraser's* had not given him just consideration since the publication of *Paracelsus*. Though Froude, its editor in the sixties, did not care for Browning's poetry, he could not ignore the recognition it was receiving in the sixties. He accepted Skelton's encouraging review in the early sixties and his later review of *The Ring and the Book,* though he rejected the second part of the article of 1867 on *Sordello* by Dowden after the first part had been published in his absence by the temporary editor. The greatest benefit that Browning's poetry received from the monthlies did not come from long established ones but from those that were springing up and bringing new life to the press. *Macmillan's* (started in 1859), the *Cornhill* (in 1860), and the *Fortnightly* (in 1865, changed to monthly in 1866) carried reviews in the early months of 1869. The *Contemporary Review* (started in 1866) reviewed Browning's collected works in 1867, and *St. Paul's Magazine* (started in 1867) discussed *The Ring and the Book* in a review begun in December 1870 and concluded in January 1871. All were edited for the kind of readers most likely to be attracted to Browning's works, and all were favorable. Monthlies of lesser importance to Browning's reputation that started in the sixties also reviewed his publications of this decade; of them only the Catholic *Month* (started in 1864) was derogatory.

Most variance came in the oldest of the quarterlies. The *Edinburgh* and the *Quarterly* had lost much of their weight but were still to be reckoned with. The *Edinburgh's* failure to keep abreast of the progress that had been made in understanding Browning did — unintentionally — some service to him: the vigorous attack made upon its harsh review of 1864 by other periodicals emphasized more than ever the increasing regard for Browning's poetry. Its next review of Browning, that of *The Ring and the Book* by Julian Fane, was favorable. When in the sixties the *Quarterly* broke its silence on Browning of over thirty years, fortunately the two critics involved, Gerald Massey and J. R. Mozley, had not lagged behind the growing appreciation of Browning. The *Westminster,* which had carried the perceptive review of *Men and Women* during the time when George Eliot and John Chapman were raising its standards, ingloriously turned its back on the wide acclaim given to *The Ring and the Book* when it changed from approval in its first to disapproval in its second review.

Three religious quarterlies reviewed Browning's works in the six-ties. Although their circulation was not the highest among quarterlies, they carried some outstanding criticisms. After a short enthusiastic discussion of Book I of *The Ring and the Book,* a longer and more inclu-sive criticism in the *British Quarterly Review* indicated a limited under-standing of Browning's works. The *London Quarterly Review* and the *North British Review* (with a weakened denominational stand) each car-ried several reviews in the sixties, all sympathetic and some particu-larly instructive. By now the endorsement of the spiritual and moral in Browning's poetry, in both denominational and nondenominational periodicals, had become the practice. One exception was the *Dublin Review,* high in influence among Roman Catholics.

Besides pertinent observations on the periodicals in which the re-views were published there are noteworthy aspects of the authorship of the criticisms. If we look into the lives of the identifiable reviewers of Browning's works published in the sixties, we can point to a few who were not devoted exclusively to literature in the ordinary sense but pos-sessed knowledge and interests in other fields besides. John Skelton *(Fraser's),* who was trained for the legal profession and became an ad-ministrator of the laws pertaining to public health and the poor in Scotland, was beginning to write on the subject of political history. J. R. Mozley *(Quarterly, Macmillan's)* was a professor of pure mathe-matics at Owens College in Manchester. James H. Stirling *(North Brit-ish Review),* a Scottish philosopher, who started his career as a medical practitioner, wrote his most important work in 1865, *The Secret of Hegel.* Julian Fane *(Edinburgh)* had already advanced in his career as a diplomat.

We can also point to some critics who reviewed Browning's works repeatedly. Instead of Fox, Horne, Chorley, and Forster of the early years there were Hutton, Massey, and Skelton as well as others who re-viewed Browning more than once in the sixties. When these later crit-ics persisted in their sympathetic reading and evaluation of Browning they could well gain in perspective. Doubtless some profited by the general shift of opinion in his favor. Massey, for example, wrote two reviews of Browning, and though the criticisms were in considerable agreement, a few differences in the second reflected the increasing ac-ceptance of certain aspects of Browning's works, such as his choice of remote subject matter.

Changes that were taking place in the world of journalism in-cluded a movement from anonymity to signed articles. In the early

Victorian period the value of signature had not gone without some recognition, but not until the 1860's was there a strong movement toward signed articles. *Macmillan's* and the *Contemporary Review,* as well as others, made use of signature, and the *Fortnightly* adopted it as a policy. Although there were arguments for and against anonymity, Browning profited by the signature of men well known and respected in their areas of knowledge. John Addington Symonds, with his brilliant record at Oxford just behind him and his active literary life already started, subscribed his name to a favorable review of Volume I of *The Ring and the Book* in *Macmillan's.* T. F. Wedmore, the up-and-coming art critic, signed his article on Filippo Lippi and Andrea del Sarto (biographical sketches making use of Browning's poems) in *St. James's Magazine* and he also signed his favorable review of *Dramatis Personae* in the *New Monthly Magazine.* By signature Mozley (*Macmillan's*) acknowledged Browning as a poet of intellect and power. Edward Dowden, already appointed to the chair of English literature in Trinity College, Dublin, publicized his support of *Sordello* in *Fraser's* by signing his name. John Morley, the editor of the *Fortnightly Review* and an advocate of signature, subscribed "Editor" to his high praise of *The Ring and the Book.* The articles in *Fraser's* signed "Shirley" were recognized by many as John Skelton's.

It is obvious that the changes taking place were propitious. By the time of Browning's first publication in the sixties, the three "taxes on knowledge" had all been abolished, with a resultant increase in the number of periodicals, including outstanding ones for educated readers and, because of lowered rates, an increase in circulation of some of the established periodicals. The new climate of thinking and discussion, stimulated by widened areas of investigation in science, history, and religion, had a liberalizing influence on literary criticism. Judgment of literature narrowed by sectarianism had disappeared to some extent. Provincialism that a few earlier critics deplored was giving ground to greater breadth of outlook. Since critics were now more open-minded, their comments showed a deeper insight and a better balance. More reviews were being signed, so that the identity of the author of a favorable review could be known to all and be of particular value wherever the name carried weight. Browning's achievement was recognized by men of stature not only in professional journalism but in other areas of activity also. Some of the standards of measurement that had been deeply entrenched could hardly survive in the general atmosphere of inquiry. There was a definite weakening or virtual disappearance of the old insistence by professional critics that Browning should observe the canons presumed to govern poetic composition. In the eyes of many commentators Browning's disregard of these canons was offset by the moral and spiritual significance of his poetry and its relevance to important questions of the day. *The Ring and the Book,* the great product of Browning's innovative genius, appeared at an opportune time.

CHAPTER XXVIII

Nonprofessional Opinion in the Sixties

As Browning's poetry of the sixties acquired new dimensions and attracted a wider audience, the nonprofessional criticism resembled a patchwork quilt. Some of the older generation who had supported Browning were not appreciative of the new flights and others who as his peers had been enthusiastic earlier about his works grew cold to them; at times attitudes were seemingly influenced by personal matters. Some who earlier had found nothing to accept in his poetry continued to reject it. Then there were those who still approved, either with or without reservations, and others whose eyes were opened for the first time. Quite naturally in the broad range of Browning's works his sympathetic readers, who were of varying professions and levels of literary endowment, saw them from different points of view.

The present chapter begins with a sampling of opinions before the appearance of *The Ring and the Book,* some regarding *Dramatis Personae,* and then continues with a more extended examination of the remarks of Dante Gabriel Rossetti and Swinburne about Browning's poetry of the sixties, including *The Ring and the Book.* This leads to miscellaneous criticisms of *The Ring* and then to an evaluation of Browning's poetry by two outstanding writers not yet considered — Matthew Arnold and Alfred Tennyson. The last part of the chapter presents opinions of others that are of particular interest because we have Browning's response to them. These include Julia Wedgwood's observations on *The Ring and the Book* in her letters to Browning, whose gift of the first two volumes had the effect of renewing their correspondence after a lapse of two years. In the exchange of comments on *The Ring* her remarks, mostly severe, led Browning to state and defend his intentions and to indicate his efforts to make improvements after receiving the proofs. From his statements to her and to others the already established pattern of his poetic endeavors emerges more clearly.

The spontaneity of the remarks and the variety of interests of those who were speaking of but not reviewing Browning accounts for the absence of more or less definite lines of criticism that have been noted in the reviews. It becomes evident, however, that both professional and nonprofessional attitudes have something in common.

From comments made before the publication of *The Ring and the Book* we can see pieces that went into the patchwork quilt. Readers of various professions recognized the merits of Browning's poetry even as they called attention to the difficulty of reading it. Francis Power Cobbe, a theological and social writer, thought of Browning as the poet of the future, "wonderfully wise and scientific and suggestive no doubt" but not very harmonious and requiring much cultivation and study to be understood.[1] J. Llewelyn Davies, an Anglican clergyman (Broad Church), who early recognized and admired Browning's genius, wrote in 1864: "Few studies are more exciting, to my mind, than that of Browning. His obscurity I admit and feel to the utmost. But such estimates as those of the *Edinburgh* and Bagehot are the estimates of men insensible to the noblest qualities of poetry. . . ."[2] Alexander Macmillan, the publisher, wrote Browning of the difficulty that two poems in *Dramatis Personae* presented. After the second reading of *A Death in the Desert* (he read it aloud to his wife and sister) things became clearer, "as they do when the dimmed eye gets used to stronger light." The "early pictures" he pronounced "marvellous." After one reading of *Caliban* he "somewhat guessed" the drift. "But you do read us all riddles. 'Doth he not speak in parables?' Still we are thankful he does speak."[3] In only a few months after he expressed this opinion he was writing Browning of his wish to publish a selection of his works — a possibility hardly to be considered by a publisher without the expectation of attracting readers at once, not in the future.

When *Dramatis Personae* was published in 1864, Edward Dowden read it and thought it was very good. If he wanted "strong new wine" he went to Browning.[4] In letters written in 1868 Octavia Hill, a social worker, indicated the appeal of Browning's poetry. "Now Browning, with all his dramatic power, and turning it upon such various (and

often such low) people, has yet distinct love or scorn, has definite grasp
of some positive good." She thought that *Rabbi Ben Ezra* was "one of
the truest things" he or anyone else had ever written.[5]

In the earlier sixties unfavorable remarks seemed to be in the minority. Some months after *Dramatis Personae* was published Ruskin
wrote a letter to Browning in which he commented on only one poem
in the volume. We miss the indication of expended effort to understand Browning's poems, the few favorable remarks, and the spirit of
inquiry that characterized his comments in the fifties. He singled out
Mr. Sludge for severe criticism:

> I was provoked by that poem of yours on table rapping — for this
> reason. If it be jugglery — one does not write poems against jugglers
> — you might as well have written against Morison's Pills. But if it
> be not jugglery — there is no use in raving about it — and you only
> hinder the proper investigation of facts. . . . If tables turn — it is
> the part of a man of sense to know why — and if not — to say so in
> plain prose — and have done with it. I am violently grieved and an-
> gered by the abuse of a talent like yours on such a matter, while the
> passions of the nation are allowed to run riot in war and avarice,
> without rebuke. . . . I love you always though I'm in a rage at you
> just now.[6]

David DeLaura has discussed Ruskin's interest in spiritualism, which
began in the sixties and continued into the seventies. Of his reaction to
Mr. Sludge, DeLaura said, "It seems likely that the 'rage' he expressed
in this letter arose precisely from his inability to decide whether 'table
rapping' was indeed jugglery or not — especially in a period when his
earlier religious convictions were under the severest scrutiny."[7]

A more general comment was made by Anthony Froude in the
early sixties. After explaining why he as editor of *Fraser's* had not yet
published Skelton's sympathetic criticism of Browning, he wrote,
"But Browning's verse! — with intellect, thought, power, grace, all
the charms in detail which poetry should have, it rings after all like a
bell of lead. . . . To this generation Browning is as uninteresting as
Shakespeare's Sonnets were to the last century. In making the comparison you see I admit that you may be right."[8]

Froude could not foresee the acclamation that Browning would
receive before the end of the decade. Indications of better understanding that had appeared in the press in the late forties had gradually increased, and by the middle of the sixties acceptance had stimulated an
unprecedented sale of Browning's works. In 1865 Aubrey de Vere

wrote to Allingham, "One of the most remarkable turns that literary things have taken of late is the sudden popularity of Browning's poems. His publishers told me that in fifteen years he had hardly sold fifteen copies of them: and all at once they have leaped up into popularity so great that I hear the young men at the Universities run after him more than Tennyson."[9] The approval of these young men was part of the broader acceptance of Browning in the sixties.

By 1866 William Rossetti was indicating the opinion that would become more and more prominent among both professional critics and other readers as the decade advanced — that Browning, even with his shortcomings, was to be ranked along with the greatest living poets. This opinion was stated in Rossetti's study of Swinburne's *Poems and Ballads,* published in 1866, and it illuminates the change taking place. First there was laudation.

> We regard Browning's natural wealth of workable poetic perceptions and ideas as the richest entrusted to any English poet of our time, if not even of any time since Shakespear's; marvelously varied and pungent, and thoroughly and essentially human. On this splendid stock he works with luminous flashes of intellect, and strangely captivating though too fleeting felicities of art.

Then came a comment on the defect of Browning's poetry.

> Unfortunately, Browning is gifted, along with this lavish fund of poetic material and aptitude, with another endowment which is radically prosaic — ingenuity. . . . This ingenuity is a heavy drawback to his freedom, consistency, and greatness, as a poet: it is the bar sinister on his poetic shield — it is the false note which menaces several of his astonishing works with final relegation to that category of art which, as some one said of certain ear-battering music, one would wish to be "not only difficult, but impossible."

Even with this drawback Browning's place as a foremost poet was secure.

> For all this, we recognise Browning as so superb and exceptional a poetic genius that no superiority of art, whether displayed by a Tennyson, a Swinburne, or whosoever else, no obliquity of direction in his own powers, can oust him from a seat second to none in the ranks of our living singers.[10]

We should keep this comment in mind as we examine further the heterogeneous comments of the sixties.

In this decade there was among those who had earlier supported Browning as much variation in opinion as their was among those new on the scene. Two past admirers, though now somewhat less ardent, thought well of *Dramatis Personae* and were highly appreciative of *The Ring and the Book* — Swinburne and Dante Gabriel Rossetti. Swinburne, though subjected to the enthusiasm of the persuasive Rossetti during the fifties, was fully capable of forming an independent judgment of Browning and he did so, as we have already seen in the account of his earliest expression of appreciation and will further see in his later remarks. His letters, his works, and to a lesser degree the reports of contemporaries reveal his appraisal of Browning's poetry. With the exception of a brief introductory statement of his general opinion, we shall stay within the time limitations of this study. A remarkable commentary he made on Browning in his eassy on the dramatist George Chapman (1875), many scattered comments on Browning's works in his letters after the sixties, and sonnets on Browning written after his death will not be included in the following discussion.

After his initial acquaintance with Browning's works Swinburne read the individual volumes as they appeared and often recorded his impressions. Some of his remarks show that he considered Browning the "dreariest of playwrights" and that he disapproved of works of the seventies for which Browning turned to the literature of ancient Greece, especially the drama. Though not consistent in his opinion of Browning's lyrical poems, at times Swinburne saw "the charm and grace and sweetness of some of the shorter and simpler lyrics," and he had great praise for the qualities that gave Browning superiority as an analytical poet.[11] We have no evidence that any other Victorian poet of considerable standing read Browning's works more promptly and more carefully. Remarks in Swinburne's letters indicate how sharply they impressed him.

With a headstrong temperament, an agile mind, and a facile pen, Swinburne on occasion expressed his anger without giving quarter. There were two such occasions in the history of the association of Swinburne and Browning, though it is to Swinburne's credit that his outbursts did not turn him away from a close and eager reading of Browning's poems.

One outburst came in the sixties,[12] and in the heat of his anger Swinburne wrote a criticism of Browning that was inconsistent with the expressions of respect that he usually used in speaking to or of the older poet. At a dinner where both Swinburne and Browning were present, Swinburne recited some of his own poems, which Browning considered, according to a statement in a letter of July 7, 1863, to Richard Monckton Milnes, "moral mistakes, redeemed by much intellectual ability." At some time after the dinner Chapman, who was Browning's publisher and who was considering publishing Swinburne, called upon Browning for an opinion of the poems. Browning was thus caught up in the complex circumstances prior to the publication of Swinburne's *Poems and Ballads,* which aroused widespread condemnation when it finally appeared in 1866. Browning's report of the scene with Chapman, given in his letter to Milnes, shows that he felt compelled to be candid in spite of wishing not to injure a young poet.

> When I was abruptly appealed to, some days after, for my estimate of Mr. Swinburne's powers, — I don't know what I could do but say "that he had genius, and wrote verses in which to my mind there was no good at all."
>
> If I referred, — as I probably did, — to a similarity of opinion on the part of others present, it was from the reluctance I had to stand forward and throw even this cherry-stone at a young poet. . . . Unluckily the truth is the truth, and one must speak it now and then. It was a shame in this case for Chapman to quote my blame of two or three little pieces — given on a demand for unqualified praise which was impossible — as the reason for rejecting a whole bookful of what may be real poetry, for aught I am aware. . . .

Swinburne must have learned of Browning's criticism. *The Chaotic School,* a devastating attack on Browning's poetry, was probably his spontaneous reaction.[13] Fortunately the fiery young poet did not publish his diatribe.

Cecil Y. Lang, who edited *The Chaotic School* on its first publication in 1964, has pointed out that it was written between May 1, 1863, and May 28, 1864 (May 28 was the publication date of *Dramatis Personae*), or soon thereafter.[14] Writing the essay did not effect a complete purging of Swinburne's emotions. To Milnes, who played a prominent part in the unfortunate episode, he wrote on March 31, 1864, of "the Brownings and other blatant creatures begotten on the slime of modern chaos."[15] In reaching out here and there in *The Chaotic School* to Browning's works for illustration, Swinburne, as Lang pointed out, made no reference to the poems in *Dramatis Personae,* which seems to confirm that his satire was composed earlier.

Although Swinburne had been "interlarding his discourse with ferocious invectives against Browning,"[16] within three weeks of the publication of *Dramatis Personae* he had read it. He wrote to John Nichol of the pleasure that two poems gave him.

> I have read all Browning's new book since we parted; and while quite holding to all I said and say about his work as a poet I must also say — I have even had the candour to say to Rossetti — that I fully recognize the unique and most admirable power of 'Sludge' and 'Caliban.' I want to send you my full acknowledgment of this: because we talked enough about the matter, and because I have really derived such rare and keen pleasure, in the teeth of all personal or artistic feelings of dislike, from these two poems (if poems they are to be called) that I don't want you to suppose me insensible to their delightful qualities.

Swinburne still bore the marks of the recent experience, but he had sufficiently regained his balance to praise where he thought praise was due. He continued by comparing *Caliban* and *Mr. Sludge* with *Blougram,* bringing in other writers in his comparison, and criticizing *A Death in the Desert.*

> I class both these [*Caliban* and *Mr. Sludge*] above Blougram — not as intellectual exercises, but as samples of good work done. They are as good as Swift — i.e. not so good here, and better there; incomparably above Thackeray — and I think only a little below Chamfort and Stendhal. This last with me is higher praise than all the rest. Not less noble is the opening of St. John — but long before the end the poem is swamped in controversial shallows, and the finer features effaced under a mask of indurate theological mud. In all the rest of the book I see much that is clever and nothing that is good — much that is ingenious and nothing that is right.[17]

Despite signs of damage to his vanity that persisted for a time,[18] Swinburne's recognition of Browning as a poet of great merit survived the pique. On December 2, 1868, soon after Volume I of *The Ring and the Book* was published, he wrote to a friend, "You should read the first volume (all yet published) of Browning's new poem; if it is not poetry proper, it is quite wonderfully interesting as a story and a study. I devoured it with the old boyish enjoyment."[19] On January 12, 1869, after Volume II had appeared, William Rossetti recorded that Swinburne was "excessively enthusiastic" about the poem.[20]

Swinburne also indicated his enthusiasm to Milnes.

> What a wonderful work this is of Browning's. I tore through the first volume in a day of careful study, with a sense of absolute

possession. I have not felt so strongly that delightful sense of being mastered — dominated — by another man's imaginative work since I was a small boy. I always except, of course, Victor Hugo's which has the same force and insight and variety of imagination together with that exquisite bloom and flavour of the highest poetry which Browning's has not: though it has perhaps a more wonderful subtlety at once and breadth of humorous invention and perception.

As for interest, it simply kills all other matters of thought for the time. This is his real work — big enough to give him breathing-space, whereas in play or song he is alike cramped. It is of the mixed-political composite-dramatic order which alone suits him and serves him.[21]

Swinburne referred to Guido in an article ("Notes on the Text of Shelley") published in May of 1869 in the *Fortnightly:* "The wonderful figure so cunningly drawn and coloured by Mr. Browning is a model of intense and punctilious realism." In a letter to William Rossetti (Oct. 1869) he called Alfred Austin's remarks on Browning in the *Temple Bar* "astoundingly and personally insolent." He continued, "You know I do *not* count Browning a lyric poet proper, nor properly a dramatic, as he breaks down in dialogue; but his greatness as an *artist* I think (now more than ever) established to all time by his *monodramas*. I say *artist,* or poet, as well as thinker."[22] This passage reflects for the most part Swinburne's fairly consistent attitude toward Browning.

Words of praise in the sixties came from the other enthusiastic admirer of the past — Dante Gabriel Rossetti. Browning sent him copies of the *Selections* (1863), *Dramatis Personae, The Poetical Works of Robert Browning* (1865), and *The Ring and the Book.* Rossetti's letters of acknowledgement, published in 1972 by Rosalie Grylls, provide some account of his reaction to Browning's poetry in the last decade of their friendship.[23] Rossetti wrote (Jan. 5, 1863) of his satisfaction in receiving a copy of the *Selections* and acknowledged (June 8, 1864) *Dramatis Personae* in a brief note with a reference to *Rabbi Ben Ezra, A Death in the Desert,* and *Caliban* as "all of your most glorious work to my thinking." After receiving his copy of the 1865 *Poetical Works* he recalled (Nov. 6, 1865) his early delight in Browning's works in the time "when one makes choice of one's gods."[24]

The first comment we have of Rossetti's on *The Ring and the Book* was made not in a letter to Browning but in a postscript to a letter to Allingham. With Volume I in hand, Rossetti raised a question about the rest of the poem.

How do you like the *Ring and the Book?* It is full of wonderful work, but it seems to me that, whereas other poets are the more liable to get incoherent the more fanciful their starting point happens to be, the thing that makes Browning drunk is to give him a dram of pro-saic reality, and unluckily this time the "gum-tickler" is less like pure Cognac than 7 Dials gin. Whether the consequent evolutions will be bearable to their proposed extent without the intervening walls of the station-house to tone down their exuberance may be du-bious. This *entre nous.*[25]

Rossetti's favorable reaction to *Men and Women* had been instan-taneous. He had extended his ecstatic praise of the poems and their au-thor throughout two installments of a letter to Allingham. Reading each volume of *The Ring and the Book* as it was published was not the same, and the praise did not come at once. Whatever he thought of Volume I, the man who had earlier defied public opinion in his sup-port of *Sordello* would certainly read further and make his own judg-ment. His letters to Browning indicate his warm and discerning appre-ciation of the poem.

Within a month after the appearance of each of the remaining volumes Rossetti wrote Browning with enthusiasm for the monologues of the major characters and with admiration for the monologues of the lawyers (in particular of Dominus Hyacinthus), which most readers found distasteful. After reading Volume II he wrote (Jan. 19, 1869), "The way in which the ideal element is at last infused into the book without sacrificing one tittle of its supreme reality, is a triumph of Art such as no Englishman but yourself could venture to hope for." He read *Caponsacchi* three times. He thought it was the "very greatest thing" Browning had yet done and *Count Guido* as great in its own way. "You have made him [Guido] assume so far the impulsive tone of self-belief as really to awaken sympathy for the issues of such a case as he feigns, and so make the mind recoil upon him with double abhor-rence when the truth already known recurs to it. . . ."

After receiving Volume III he indicated (Feb. 22, 1869) his fur-ther admiration. He read and reread *Pompilia* and, like others whom he had talked to about it, thought it "as noble and lovely as Caponsac-chi." He was impressed by the gradual unfolding of the inmost truth, by what Browning had achieved in spite of the revelations at the first of the poem. "The surprises of the book are infinite, where, by its plan, surprise seemed almost excluded." Rossetti was longing for the moment when Guido would have to tell the truth, and when he read

Volume IV he was not disappointed. He wrote (Mar. 13, 1869) enthusiastically of Browning's "supreme master-stroke" at the end of Guido's second monologue. He also wrote in the superlative about the
Pope's monologue. "In itself I suppose it must be admitted as the
grandest piece of sustained work in the whole cycle of your writings."

According to these excerpts, any doubt that Rossetti had felt after
reading Volume I disappeared long before he reached the end of *The
Ring and the Book*. After completing the last volume, he wrote,

> I feel as if we were in communication now even before I put pen
> to paper: for is not your completed thought now filling me? — in
> how many ways, at what strange junctures, to recur to me forever?
> Such function I have long acknowledged as yours; but now most
> strongly, by this confirmed and controlling impression of your
> greatness at a time when judgment should be mature in me.[26]

These comments on *The Ring and the Book* were Rossetti's glowing tribute to Browning's genius, his last such words written to him before a
shadow fell across their friendship.

The remaining nonprofessional criticisms of *The Ring and the
Book*, most of them expressed by friends, were fairly divided as favorable and unfavorable. Browning received high praise for the poem from
John Forster, whose years of reviewing were past. He read the first two
volumes and wrote Browning (Jan. 13, 1869) that he found the "master hand" everywhere. He saw it nowhere so much as at the end of the
second volume (*Caponsacchi*), "where one hears the beginning swell of
the full and final music." He continued, "It would be difficult to say
how much affected I was by the flight to Rome. It is a wonderful piece
of writing." That the reactions to the poem would vary widely, he felt
sure. "But time will be on your side." A few days after Forster read the
third volume, he thanked (Feb. 4, 1869) Browning for *Pompilia*. "You
have written nothing more — well, I will say, *so* beautiful; so profoundly affecting; higher in its order of poetry, or reaching down to
such depths of wisdom and humanity."[27]

Although Forster was no longer active in the journalistic world,
we learn from a letter of his to Browning (July 28, 1869) that he had
taken up his pen once more in Browning's behalf. Julian Fane, after
writing his criticism of *The Ring and the Book* for the *Edinburgh Review*,
asked Forster for suggestions. They were given for the "more complete
expression of what he [Fane] desired to say in regard to the great poem
he was anxious to write of not unworthily." When the article appeared

Fane, as well as Forster, was "startled" to see the changes that had been made by the editor, changes that detracted from the favorable impression Fane had wished to give readers and that would misrepresent to Browning his intention.[28] Though he was a supporter of Browning in the early years, Forster had sometimes assumed a patronizing manner. Now he disapproved of an editor's doing so — Browning's ability as a poet was not to be questioned.

Others besides Swinburne, Rossetti, and Forster welcomed *The Ring and the Book*. Among them was the former Helen Faucit, who had performed in *Strafford*, *A Blot*, and *Colombe's Birthday*. As Lady Martin, she maintained her early admiration of Browning the poet and the man, and she and her husband kept up an active friendship with Browning until his death. While she was in the process of reading, with deep satisfaction, *The Ring and the Book,* she met him in the park and was gratified when he said, "Ah, if I could have had you to *act* my Pompilia!"[29] After she completed her reading, she wrote Browning a long letter of detailed eulogy of the poem, in which she remarked: "You show in it clearly and so decisively that art is not what I have so often had to hear it called an imitation of nature, but the medium, the one way possible for communicating its truth and beauties to man."[30]

Two eminent Anglican clergymen, both historians, one High Church and the other Broad, praised *The Ring and the Book*, notwithstanding its difficulties. Richard William Church, Dean of St. Paul's, who had not taken to Browning's works earlier, was strongly attracted to the poem because it satisfied a longing he had had "to have the *same set* of facts told and dealt with . . . as they appear to all manner of different people" and because he found in the work "such piercing insight into human realities of thought and feeling, into the depths and heights of the soul, such magnanimity, such pervading sense of the awfulness and certainty of Divine judgment."[31] He was one of those who thought that the difficulties were as nothing to the greatness of the poem. Connop Thirlwall, Bishop of St. David's, had to read some passages several times before he could understand them. "It is not, however, necessary for the enjoyment of the story to stop at these knotty points, but if it was there would be ample compensation for the exertion in the amazing ingenuity of the invention and beauty of the execution, though a little marred by occasional negligences, which such a poet can well afford, as they rather produce the effect of conscious power. . . ."[32] We might add what a Unitarian minister said to Browning himself. From a mutual friend Browning had already heard about T. W. Chignell, a Goethe and Spinoza scholar, when he called at Westbourne Terrace in 1869. Chignell, who had read Browning since he was twenty years old, told him that he had been "loyally studying 'The Ring and the Book' " and that his writings were "a glorious stimulant to preachers."[33]

George Meredith, whose interest in Browning had begun in the forties, encouraged a friend to read the principal monologues in *The Ring and the Book*. "If you have not read Browning's *The Ring and the Book*, I recommend the 'Caponsacchi' — 'Pompilia', 'the Pope' and the two 'Guidos'. Browning has his faults, but at least they are not those of a mannered trickster airing a leg with love-knots."[34] Benjamin Jowett gratefully acknowledged Browning's gift of the first volume — he could hardly put it down. "I was wholly taken up with the poem while reading & perceive that it shows the highest dramatic power and is full of noble thoughts, of wisdom & humour & knowledge of the world; — also that it is a very curious work of art & (with the exception of a very few lines), perfectly intelligible." He later told Swinburne that the second Guido monologue was "too dreadful."[35]

The Ring and the Book had its detractors in the midst or on the fringes of contemporary English literature. Edward Fitzgerald, whose biographer said he appreciated "small, felicitous effects" but underestimated "large authors with definite mannerisms such as Milton, Browning, Victor Hugo, and Thackeray,"[36] railed against *The Ring and the Book*. After making three vain attempts at Volume I, he pronounced it "an audacious piece of [Browning's] defiance to the Public whom he had found so long blind to his Merits." He wrote W. F. Pollock three letters vigorously denouncing the poem, the third one expressing strong indignation because the *Athenaeum* compared the relative merits of Tennyson and Browning. To consider Browning, in whom Fitzgerald could see little but "Cockney Sublime, Cockney Energy, etc.," a rival to Tennyson was beyond his comprehension. He heard that at Oxford and Cambridge Browning was considered the "deepest." Such regard for Browning, he felt positive, would pass away.[37]

Fitzgerald wished for the power to spread propaganda — noisy propaganda at that — against *The Ring and the Book*. He wrote to his friend Tennyson that he abused Browning and got others to abuse him. He could not understand why the critics belauded him; none of the men that he knew, in no wise inferior to the critics, could endure or even read the poem at all. He quoted two of his friends, Pollock and

Carlyle, who shared his dislike. Fitzgerald was both puzzled by the critics and chagrined.

> Who, then, are the people that write the nonsense in the Reviews? I believe the reason at the bottom is that R. B. is a clever London diner-out, etc., while A. T. holds aloof from the newspaper men . . . . But I don't understand why Venables, or some of the men who think as I do, and wield trenchant pens in big places, why they don't come out, and set all this right. I only wish I could do it: but I can only see the right thing, but not prove it to others.[38]

Frederick Tennyson had a decided dislike for Browning's poetry, but he did not try to turn others from it, and he took care to separate the poet from the man Browning, always honoring the man. When *The Ring and the Book* was published he said he did not have the courage to read it. "He is a great friend of mine. . . . But it does not follow that I should put up with obsolete horrors, and unrhythmical composition. What has come upon the world that it should take any metrical (?) arrangement of facts for holy Poesy?" Alfred's brother thought that all of Browning's "performances" were "pure *brain-work.*" He found nothing but the "inextricably hard and the extravagantly fantastical." He added, "On such diet I cannot live."[39]

Some who had enthusiastically supported Browning's poetry in the past did not care for *The Ring and the Book.* Oscar Browning (not related to Robert) confessed that he was not an admirer of the poem.[40] Allingham, a lesser poet and an aggressor in his friendships with greater writers, had been in earlier years, according to William Rossetti, "most fully sensitive to the great claims of Browning."[41] In 1868, before the appearance of *The Ring and the Book,* Allingham indicated an uncertainty of opinion concerning Browning. "He has been and still is very dear to me. But I can no longer commit myself to his hands in faith and trust. Neither can I allow the faintest shadow of a suspicion to dwell in my mind that his genius may have a leaven of quackery. Yet, alas! he is not solid — which is a very different thing from prosaic."[42]

According to his *Diary,* Allingham had lunch with Browning in May and again in December of 1868. On the first occasion, before any of *The Ring and the Book* was published, Browning's talk ran "chiefly" on the poem before and during lunch. On December 27, the day after Volume II was published, he again talked of his poem. He asked Allingham point-blank, "How do you like it?" Allingham confided to his *Diary* that he answered with nothing but praise — and with uneasy conscience. "[I] don't know how to set about criticism, especially with but half of the Poem as yet seen." Later Allingham recorded his comment to Carlyle on the poem: "I said that B. had neither given us the real story as he found it, nor, on the other hand, constructed a poem out of it, and in reading *The Ring and the Book* I felt (as I told B. himself) like a creature with one leg and one wing, half hopping, half flying; at which C. laughed."[43]

M. L. Howe, in an article on Browning and Allingham, has suggested that Allingham's falling off of interest in Browning's poetry went hand in hand with a feeling that the poet had grown indifferent to him. With Browning's increasing fame, it was inevitable that his crowded life, in particular the social part, would find disfavor with some of his older friends. Browning, who had never been the seeker in the Allingham relationship, was probably scarcely aware, as Howe pointed out, that he had offended Allingham.[44] In writing of the seventies William Holman Hunt made an observation on a change among Browning's friends. "Some of his original champions were confessedly displeased in that he seemed to approve the fashionable admiration of London society rather than their own, and words were wafted about expressing indifference to his later poems."[45] This attitude toward Browning's social life seems to have had its origin in the sixties.

The relationship between Robert Lytton and Browning also suffered a change. For a few years after Elizabeth's death the correspondence between them retained its warmth, and they continued to write of poetical pursuits.[46] Then Lytton's earlier glowing interest and esteem faded as the sixties advanced. Lytton did not like *The Ring and the Book*. He wrote to his father, "I have read Browning's first volume, and think it positively bad," and later added, "I have just finished with great difficulty and weariness the fourth volume of Browning's enormous poem. I see it is immensely praised, but retain my opinion that it is a mammoth failure and marvellously unreadable."[47]

Lady Balfour, Lytton's daughter, interpreted the shift in his attitude that became evident with the appearance of *The Ring and the Book* as the "decline of a personal hero-worship," the end of the Browning glamour. She explained that the two men no longer kept in touch and little social circumstances helped to estrange them. "Now . . . that Robert Browning was applauded by all the critics who had formerly run him down, and had become the darling of London society, Robert Lytton felt that any diminution of intimacy or admiration on his part would not be noticed or regretted by the master whose popularity was now widespread and unquestioned."[48] But eventually Browning did notice and did regret a lessening of warmth on Lytton's part; he called Lytton's attention to it and wrote to his friend Isa Blagden of the pain which his change in manner gave him.[49]

Whatever caused the breach in their association, two excerpts from Lytton's reply to Browning indicated how the vicissitudes that attend fame can affect the feelings of early supporters and friends. Lytton referred to the situation that followed their earlier close relationship.

> . . . when you ceased to send me your books, I shrank from sending you mine, lest I should put upon you a constraint to notice them in some more formal and troublesome way than the old way was, when I had still my boy's place in your workshop — at your elbow, as it were — and my boy's privilege of bringing you, as a matter of course, my own toy-work to look at.

He then noted the "ever widening recognition" of Browning's genius and the new following that came with it.

> Nor watching only, but claiming full share in the triumph of all this; for I look on new proselytes with the pride of an old disciple, and sniff with no little self-satisfaction each fresh whiff of incense offered by others on the altar of my early faith — where my own bits of parsley were strewn long ago, whilst the new worshippers were still unregenerate heathens.[50]

By this time Lytton himself was a man of importance; he already had claims to achievements in the field of diplomacy and would in a few years become the Viceroy of India. He, as well as others, felt that the expanding circle of Browning's friends, personal and professional, was responsible for a change in their relationship.

Procter, who had encouraged Browning in various ways, wrote of him in 1866, "Surely he is somewhat changed within the last two or three years."[51] We do not know that Procter was influenced in his opinion of Browning's work by any change that he had observed in the man. He commented on the length of *The Ring and the Book*. "Browning has a poem in progress which will consist of twenty thousand lines. I — who am merely one of the *oi polloi* — should never have ventured on so voluminous an experiment of course."[52] It must be remembered that it was Procter who argued for the inclusion of the shorter poems of Browning's in the *Selections* that he and Forster were editing. Procter's opinion of *The Ring and the Book* is not known. It is known, however, that Browning's feeling for Procter never changed and that after Procter's death he continued to see Mrs. Procter at the Sunday afternoon gatherings in her home.

Another contemporary who was also, like Procter, older than Browning did not withhold his opinion of *The Ring and the Book* — Carlyle. For many years he had recognized Browning's genius, and he had singled him out as one of the few literary men in England from whom it was possible to expect something.[53] The accounts that have already been given of his response to Browning's poetry show that although he was concerned about its lack of clarity, he recognized its spiritual and intellectual quality. Browning had valued Carlyle's criticism and wanted whatever he wrote to please him. As he had worked on *The Ring and the Book,* according to his own lights he had taken seriously the older man's advice (written at the end of his long commentary on *Men and Women*) to give his best for a long while to a great subject, with the determination to make himself clear. When, therefore, Browning met Carlyle after his poem was published, he hoped — perhaps even expected — that he would like it. Carlyle intended to say something to please Browning, according to a report that he gave to Dante Gabriel Rossetti.[54] If so, he failed. He spoke of the encounter on several occasions. On one Charles Eliot Norton of Harvard was present. He later recorded Carlyle's account in his journal. Carlyle is speaking:

> I met Browning, indeed, in Piccadilly the other day, and I told him I'd read his poem from the first word thereof way to the last, and he said to me, quickly, 'Well! Well?' and I replied that I thought it a book of prodigious talent and unparellelled ingenuity; but then, I suppose trusting to the sincerity of my own thoughts, I went on to say that of all the strange books produced on this distracted airth, by any of the sons of Adam this one was altogether the strangest and the most preposterous in its construction; and where, said I, do ye think to find the eternal harmonies in it? Browning did not seem to be pleased with my speech, and he bade me good morning.[55]

Browning's reaction is understandable. In the past he had had strong encouragement from Carlyle along with some corrective criticism. Here the adverse criticism stood out in sharp relief. In this and other reports of Carlyle's opinion of *The Ring and the Book* we find considerable agreement. To Fitzgerald he said, "It is full of talent, energy, and effort: but actually without *Backbone* or Basis of Common Sense. I think it among the absurdest books ever written by a gifted man." He told Allingham that it was "not poetry at all." Instead of appreciating the design that was intended to insure clarity (the quality that Carlyle said Browning needed), he said to Conway that the plan was like "bawling into the ear of a deaf man."[56] But he praised Browning's talent and energy, and he commended the picture of Italian society more than once. In time he was able to see high merit in certain parts of the poem.[57]

The warmth accompanying the early criticism was lacking in later years. During this time Browning once told Carlyle that he would rather trust him with his body than with his work.[58] But he never forgot what Carlyle had meant to him. In his years of fame Browning still visited the house where he had found encouragement as a young man, and after Carlyle's death he spoke out for him in the controversy that began with the publication of Froude's edition of Carlyle's *Reminiscences* (1881). That Carlyle had not expressed his good opinion publicly in earlier years did cause Browning disappointment but did not obscure his gratefulness for his association with and love for the older man.[59]

The Ring and the Book perplexed some readers. They realized that undoubtedly the poem had merit but in varying degrees their praise came with reservations. Browning's friend Francis T. Palgrave, who respected his genius, was one of these. After reading the entire poem to his wife he said,

> Within a rather narrow range it has amazing power and subtlety. What I do not find are charm and delicacy. . . . Tennyson seems to me ten times the greater poet, and ten times the wider and deeper thinker. But Browning's individuality is of course his own. . . . However, the whole poem certainly adds some marvellously living figures to our gallery of English poetry, and is excellent *sui generis.*[60]

It is true, as we have seen, that some rejected *The Ring and the Book* summarily, but more realized that it as well as other works of Browning's in the sixties had extraordinary qualities. Passing doubts or even decided objections did not contradict the underlying assumption that Browning had achieved a permanent and high place as a poet. The feeling in the decade of *Dramatis Personae* and *The Ring and the Book* that Browning's position was established despite his faults was expressed by D. G. Rossetti at the beginning of the seventies. "Browning seems likely to remain, with all his sins, the most original and varied mind, by long odds, which betakes itself to poetry in our time."[61] The remarks of nonprofessionals on Browning's poetry and the criticisms made by the spokesmen for periodicals had two common points: there were lingering objections to the lack of harmonious verse and ease of reading (even with the appreciable changed outlook of many critics of *The Ring and the Book*), yet there was a strong tendency to recognize Browning's greatness in spite of objections that could be made to some aspects of his works. The opinions of two Victorian writers of stature whom we have not discussed in earlier chapters provide an instructive gloss on these responses to Browning's poetry.

Since Matthew Arnold wrote so forcefully of what he considered the proper nature of poetry, it is interesting to turn to his statements on the poems of Browning, a man with whom he had cordial relations and whom he respected. Arnold would have gladly had Browning follow him as Professor of Poetry at Oxford, but Browning did not possess the requisite M.A. degree. In the late 1840's Arnold wrote to Clough of Browning:

> As Browning is a man with a moderate gift passionately desiring movement and fulness, and obtaining but a confused multitudinousness, so Keats with a very high gift, is yet also consumed by this desire: and cannot produce the truly living and moving, as his conscience keeps telling him. They will not be patient neither understand that they must begin with an Idea of the world in order not to be prevailed over by the world's multitudinousness: or if they cannot get that, at least with isolated ideas: and all other things shall (perhaps) be added unto them.

In a letter of 1853 to Clough he referred to Alexander Smith's poetry. "This kind does not go far: it dies like Keats or loses itself like Browning."[62]

It must be remembered that when these statements were made Arnold and Browning were in the plastic stage of their literary careers. Browning had not yet published his *Men and Women* and his works of the sixties, and Arnold, who suppressed his *Empedocles on Etna* after its publication in 1852 (later reprinted at Browning's request), had not yet written his well-known Preface to the *Poems* of 1853, in which he explained why he was not including *Empedocles* and discussed the principles of poetic composition.

Two remarks that Arnold made in the sixties provided a mature expression of his opinion. He was asked to review Browning and he declined, as he had declined other such requests. He explained why: Browning was a "real man of genius, with a reach of mind compared to which Tennyson's reach of mind" was petty, but in the duty of a modern poet to be pellucidly and absolutely clear, to "use plainness of speech," Browning fell very short indeed. Arnold concluded: "I could not in conscience review him without saying this, and the public would inevitably seize upon this, and neglect all one said about Browning's genius — so that I should do his vogue no good, and should run the risk of annoying a man whom personally I know and like, and whose genius, as I have said, I most fully recognise."[63]

Arnold made the second remark to his mother in speculating on the future of his own poetry. He thought that it represented, on the whole, "the main movement of mind of the last quarter of a century," and would have its day as people became conscious of what that movement of mind was and took an interest in the literary productions which reflected it. It might be fairly urged, Arnold added, that he had "less poetical sentiment than Tennyson, and less intellectual vigour and abundance than Browning." He concluded his prediction: ". . . yet, because I have perhaps more of a fusion of the two than either of them, and have more regularly applied that fusion to the main line of modern development, I am likely enough to have my turn, as they have had theirs."[64]

In accordance with his own poetical credo and practice Arnold approved of Browning's reach of mind and disapproved of his deficiency in clarity, as we have seen by his general statements. In one particular poem Browning did strike a favorite chord of Arnold's: he considered *Artemis Prologizes* one of the "very best antique fragments" that he knew.[65] Arnold, like a number of others, looked for qualities in Browning that he valued in general and strove for in his own poetry. Also he, like others, felt that whatever Browning's faults were, he was undeniably a genius.

These same tendencies are obvious in Tennyson's attitude toward Browning. Some of his criticisms of poets were recorded by his son Hallam, including his criticism of Browning.

> Browning never greatly cares about the glory of words or beauty of form: he has told me that the world must take him as it finds him. As for his obscurity in his great imaginative analyses, I believe it is a mistake to explain poetry too much, people have really a pleasure in discovering their own interpretations. He has a mighty intellect, but sometimes I cannot read him. He seldom attempts the marriage of sense with sound, although he shows a spontaneous felicity in the adaptation of words to ideas and feelings.[66]

The date of this remark is unknown, but seemingly Tennyson consistently praised Browning's intellect and criticized the obscurity and ruggedness of his verse. According to Hallam, he even spoke to Browning of his faults. "On rare occasions my father would rally Browning playfully on his harshness of rhythm, the obscurity and length of his poems." Tennyson would state and metaphorically emphasize his own notion of a poet's aim: "An artist should get his workmanship as good as he can, and make his work as perfect as possible. A small vessel, built on fine lines, is likely to float further down the stream of time than a big raft."[67]

But if Tennyson felt that the length lessened the chances for mending the obscurities and improving the sound, he appreciated the intellectual quality of Browning's verse. He would cite *Rabbi Ben Ezra, A Death in the Desert, Caliban, The Englishman in Italy,* and *A Grammarian's Funeral* as poems of "fine thought." He would give *Mr. Sludge* as an example of "exceeding ingenuity of mind," though, as he told Browning, it was "two-thirds too long."[68]

If *Mr. Sludge* was far too long, what about *The Ring and the Book?* In 1865, three years before it was published, Tennyson said to Allingham, "His new poem has 15,000 lines — there's copiousness! I can't venture to put out a thing without care."[69] The 21,000 lines of the finished poem gave Tennyson even more cause to think that Browning did not exercise care in writing. On the day before Volume I was published Browning read the first part of the poem to Tennyson, who recorded the impression it made on him: "Browning read his Preface to us last night, full of strange vigour and remarkable in many ways; doubtful whether it can ever be popular."[70] At another time when he was following his usual pattern in discussing Browning, he spoke of *The Ring and the Book.* "Robert Browning has no music. He is force with a vengeance! but a poet has no right to defy music. Parts of 'The Ring and Book' are poetry and beautiful. If he would condense. No one like him!"[71] When Fitzgerald was fulminating against the poem, Tennyson told him he found greatness in it.[72]

Victorians commented on the fine feeling that existed between the two leading poets of the time. When Tennyson was in London Browning habitually saw him, they exchanged warm and affectionate letters, and each dedicated a work to the other. As the years went by, the friendship — based as it was on generosity, sincerity, and mutual appreciation — remained firm and gratifying. Tennyson said of Browning, "If the pronunciation of the English language were forgotten, Browning would be held the greatest of modern poets, having treated the greatest variety of subjects in a powerful manner."[73]

The Laureate was frank about what he liked and what he disliked in his friend's poetry, and he readily asserted his high regard. His grandson said that he did not "spare strong language when he felt that the situation deserved it." He gave as an example what happened at an evening party when Tennyson was surrounded by questioning admirers: ". . . he silenced one questioner, who asked whether Browning or Blank were the greater poet, by thundering out with all the emphasis at his command: 'Compared with Browning, Blank is as the DUNG BENEATH MY FEET!' "[74] He never felt that the faults he saw in Browning's poetry destroyed its greatness. One of his statements succinctly summarized his opinion of Browning: "A true genius, but wanting in art."[75]

With the breadth of his genius Browning appealed to different people for different reasons. We have seen that his poetry affected, for the most part favorably but sometimes unfavorably, poets, historians, and classical scholars as well as people in other areas of activity. A number of fields, including those of religion, the arts, and social welfare, have been represented in our sampling of criticism. The variety should not be surprising. In general it does not arise from contradictory remarks but from reflections of different interests and tastes. Though expressed spontaneously in a conversation or a personal letter, the favorable opinions coincide in a number of points with the deliberations of professional critics (intellect, high seriousness, originality, character revelation) and there is agreement in the final estimate: Browning had achieved a place of eminence as a poet.

Julia Wedgwood's remarks on *The Ring and the Book* in her letters to Browning constitute a commentary that is different from all others in its combined severity and specificity and in the revelatory response that it elicited. The correspondence as a whole reflects the poet who took advantage of, even sometimes sought, an occasion for talking of his work and who welcomed criticism if it came from someone whom he considered sympathetic with his efforts. After a break in the friendly exchange (brought about by Miss Wedgwood), the correspondence started again with the subject of *The Ring and the Book,* and the remaining letters consisted principally of a discussion of that poem. In the letters from October 30, 1868, to March 8, 1869, and in the letter dated June 14, 1870, there is a cluster of revealing statements on *The Ring and the Book* from Browning's own pen. We shall first look at his defense against Miss Wedgwood's specific criticisms of the poem. Additional statements in the correspondence as well as in other sources of information provide a view of Browning's workshop in the sixties.

Over twenty years earlier Elizabeth had criticized, at Browning's request, poems of his both in manuscript and in proofs. Now Browning sent the first two printed volumes of *The Ring and the Book* to Julia Wedgwood with an explanation that "hindrances" had prevented his sending any part of the manuscript for the "help" of her opinion. With the volumes came a request.

> Now, I shall have your sympathy, whatever be the appreciation my work meet with; also, if you please to criticise it, I shall be as sure of your honesty: but I may beg — not so much for your courage, as your confidence in my own somewhat stiffish texture of mind, and my ability to bear banging, if you see cause to bestow it. I will endeavour to let you have the remainder of the poem in time to make immediate use of whatever correction of yours I may wish to adopt.[76]

As a result of Miss Wedgwood's own "stiffish texture of mind" Browning had to bear considerable "banging" because in the poem she saw a "superfluity of detail in the hideous portraits," "so much ugliness in the picture," and his "unduly predominant" interest in evil.[77] Browning defended the presence of evil in his poem: he included fact as he found it in the source; the white could not have come out as clearly without the black; evil existed in life itself.[78] When she insisted that circumstances could call for a change of facts, he repeated his conviction that facts needed to be explained, not altered; his pride in this poem was to invent nothing.[79] She considered it an artistic defect to depart from the framework of a basically dramatic poem by "lending" so much of himself to the contemptible characters.[80] Browning had answered a similar objection from Ruskin thirteen years earlier. His defense of his method to Miss Wedgwood was more positive.

> I don't admit even your objections to my artistry — the undramatic bits of myself you see peep thro' the disguised people. In that sense, Shakespeare is always undramatic, for he makes his foolish people all clever. I don't think I do more than better their thoughts and instruction . . . up to the general bettering, and intended tone of the whole composition — what one calls, idealization of the characters.[81]

After the interruption in the correspondence the letters lost the relaxed tone of the early ones. Miss Wedgwood's letters suffered more from the change of mood than Browning's did. With her continuing battering of the poem that he had confidence in, he turned from his request for criticism to a comment of gratefulness for her reading so much of what she did not altogether like and then to a statement that he would try to please her better another time.[82]

While defending his poem from her specific criticisms, Browning was revealing something of his intention in *The Ring and the Book* and of his general tastes and practices. Partly to explain and perhaps partly to forestall her criticism, he told her that the lawyers in the third volume served an artistic purpose: they let the reader breathe a little before the final appearance of Guido.[83] He wrote of turning to something else "in a different way," now that the poem was completed.[84] Here appeared his old impulse to try something new, not necessarily because he was dissatisfied with what he had done — undoubtedly not in this instance — but because he wished a different employment of his genius.

Innovator though he was, certain compelling forces of his genius were inclined to remain. He might pay homage to what she wished him to do — write poetry that spoke directly to the reader and use subjects that did not explore the dark corners of the soul — but it was clear where his interests lay. Miss Wedgwood urged him to fulfill her condition of poetry — a "direct utterance of some congenial feeling"; to represent so much evil was not the function of art.[85] There was in his poem, Browning insisted, an utterance of congenial feeling, protest against evil and approbation of the good — "all the louder that it is not *direct.*"[86]

One remark to her on the other compelling poetic tendency — exploring dark corners of the soul — was in part defense of a particular interest and in part admission of a weakness.

> In this case, I think you do correctly indicate a fault of my nature — not perhaps a fault in this particular work, artistically regarded: I believe I do unduly like the study of morbid cases of the soul, — and I will try and get over that taste in future works; because, even if I still think that mine was the proper way to treat this particular subject, — the objection still holds, "Why prefer this sort of subject?" — as my conscience lets me know I do.[87]

In other places Browning upheld his interest in the workings of the soul. When Ruskin objected to *Mr. Sludge* as a futile waste of talent — whether table rapping was or was not jugglery — Browning answered: "I don't expose jugglery, but anatomize the mood of the juggler, — all morbidness of the soul is worth the soul's study; and the particular sword which 'loveth and maketh a lie' is of wide ramification. What I present, thus anatomized, would have its use even were there a veritable 'mediumship' of which this of mine were but a *simulacrum.*"[88] After Tennyson published *The Holy Grail and Other Poems* in 1869, Browning wrote Isa Blagden:

> We look at the object of art in poetry so differently! Here is an Idyll about a knight being untrue to his friend and yielding to the temptation of that friend's mistress after having engaged to assist him in his suit. I should judge the conflict in the knight's soul the proper subject to describe: Tennyson thinks he should describe the castle, and effect of the moon on its towers, and anything *but* the soul.[89]

These convictions that Browning had about his poetry were as firmly rooted in his mind as his desire to improve his work and benefit by the criticism of it. From his remarks cited in Chapter XXV we learned something of the care he exercised in writing *The Ring and the Book* and of his feeling that as a result his readers would have no difficulty in understanding it. After Miss Wedgwood read the first two volumes, she said that he was "hardly, if at all, liable in this work to the stock reproach" made against him.[90] Browning's statements to her reflected the effort he expended in revision. Since he could not "clearly see what is done, or undone" in his own handwriting, the poem had scarcely been readable until the proofs came back to him; he had thrown away much that he had written; he had "very reluctantly" left out one "prime passage."[91] The manuscript Browning sent to the printers is now in the British Library. Changes he made before publication of the poem indicate his concern for improvement. He was grateful when Miss Wedgwood called attention to one faulty passage, which he said he would take care of.[92] When Browning sent her the first two volumes, he said he would try to send the rest of the poem in time to profit by her remarks. He welcomed helpful criticism.

But the intelligent and moralistic, as well as inflexible, Miss Wedgwood, with the exception of her statement on the clarity of his writing, favorable comments on the Pope's monologue, and qualified praise for Pompilia's monologue, gave little indication that she appreciated the results of Browning's long and fruitful labor. In spite of her severe criticism, several times he expressed to her his good opinion of *The Ring and the Book,* just as he had indicated it to others before the poem was completed. Once he wrote to her, "Accept the willingness

on my part to be wrong, if I could but get to think myself so. . . ."
Near the end of the correspondence, he wrote, ". . . I consider that
your estimate of the poem, — which is below my own estimate, —
ought to rise a little: . . . you have in many other respects done me
more than justice out of the warmth and goodness of your heart."[93]

Browning did have, however, one friend whose criticism he welcomed and made use of during these years — Joseph Milsand, a
Frenchman of literary acumen, sensitivity, and generosity. Their
friendship had started in the early fifties after Milsand published a
sympathetic review of Browning's poetry. During one of the visits that
Milsand often made to Browning in his home in London, this friend
read the first and second books of Volume I of *The Ring and the Book*.
Though we do not have a record of his remarks, we know, from a letter
that Browning wrote him after sending proofs of *Red Cotton Night-Cap
Country* in 1872 and receiving his comments, just how *"inestimable"* he
considered Milsand's assistance. "There is not one point to which you
called attention which I was not thereby enabled to improve — in some
cases essentially benefit." In spite of the differences in English and
French punctuation, Browning found Milsand's suggestions in that
area serviceable and resolved that one day he would repunctuate all of
his earlier works on Milsand's principle. The other "changes and elu-
cidations" were of "vital importance." Browning recognized that writers may need someone to read their manuscripts, and he was deeply
grateful for Milsand's help. "The fact is, in the case of a writer with my
peculiarities and habits, somebody quite ignorant of what I may have
meant to write, and only occupied with what is really written — ought
to supervise the thing produced. And I never hoped or dreamed I
should find such an intelligence as yours at my service."[94]

During the sixties, as in earlier decades, Browning wanted sympathetic criticism and he often heeded it. When errors in his writing
were called to his attention, he might explain, as in letters to Dowden,
how they came about but he was grateful, gave assurance of correction,
and invited further criticism.[95] As a result of a point made by George
Eliot during a call of Browning's, he added three stanzas to *Gold Hair*
between the first and second printing.[96] He continued to revise his
works before they were first printed and before they were republished.[97] Clearly his statement to Tennyson that he could not change,
that his readers would have to take him as they found him is in accord
with his comment that he seldom revised,[98] but these remarks are not
to be accepted at their face value. They, as well as similar ones both be-

fore and after Browning achieved fame, came from a poet whose words and behavior often indicated that he wanted to be read and that he exerted a real effort to help his readers without giving up his distinctive art. He could not have become another kind of poet even if he had wanted to, but he was willing to make improvements if he thought them appropriate. Like many other writers, he could not easily assume a detached point of view, could not anticipate just how his composition might strike a reader. For this reason he appreciated those few whom he trusted implicitly to look over his manuscript before publication.

A statement (made late in life as the result of the old complaint of obscurity) that he had gone carefully through his work twice without finding a single obscure expression[99] is related to what was brought out in early chapters — his resolution to make his work clear in spite of his surprise that others had difficulty in understanding it. At one time he said, "I have too much respect for my trade to be wilfully careless about anything I write."[100] Frederick W. Farrar repeated a comment of Browning's that reflected his lifelong position. He said that he had not designedly tried to puzzle people, as some of his critics had supposed. "On the other hand," he continued, "I never pretended to offer such literature as should be a substitute for a cigar or a game of dominoes to an idle man; so perhaps, on the whole, I get my deserts, and something over; not a crowd, but a few I value more."[101]

Browning certainly did not offer *The Ring and the Book* as light or easy reading. It required sustained attention to the narration of the basically same events by different persons, to their long speeches in defense of their actions and motives, to the intricate arguments of the opposing lawyers, and to the finely reasoned judgment of the Pope. Nevertheless many persevering and discerning readers followed all of this through with interest and admiration. Browning, always confident of his ability, was justified in thinking that he had created an excellent work. He once admitted to Gosse that he always suffered from puerperal fever immediately after the publication of a work of his,[102] and we have observed periods of anxiety between the publication and reception of his works. But there were no signs that he went through the usual period of emotional strain while he waited for reviews of *The Ring and the Book*. In December of 1868 he told Allingham that the first criticism of it in the *Athenaeum* (its reviews, or the absence of them, had been a matter of grave concern in earlier years) was good.[103] In February of 1869 he wrote Miss Wedgwood of his satisfaction with the immediate effect of the poem.[104] Frederick Pollock recorded

Browning's reaction to the favorable reception after a talk with him in April.

> He said that he had at last secured the ear of the public, but that he had done it by vigorously assaulting it, and by telling his story four times over. He added that he had perhaps after all failed in making himself intelligible, and said it was like bawling into a deaf man's trumpet [reminiscent of Carlyle's remark], and then being asked not to speak so loud, but more distinctly. [105]

By this time there had been the most highly convincing evidence of the eminence he had achieved. In March 1869 Browning and three other outstanding men were presented to the Queen. One other person present was Carlyle, who overheard the Queen ask Browning if he was writing anything. Browning reported the event and its aftermath to Miss Wedgwood.

> Yes, the British Public like, and more than like me, this week, they let their admiration ray out on me, and at sundry congregations of men wherein I have figured these three or four days, I have seen, felt and, thru' white gloves, handled a true affectionateness not unmingled with awe — which all comes of the Queen's having desired to see me, and three other extraordinary persons, last Thursday: whereupon we took tea together and pretended to converse for an hour and twenty minutes; the other worthies, with the wives of such as were provided, being Carlyle, Grote and Lyell. This eventful incident in my life — say, the dove descending out of heaven upon my head — seems to have opened peoples' minds at last. . . . [106]

The high position that Browning had attained signified his success at last, after a long period of hard work, frustrations, and attempts to adapt his art to the reading public without stifling his genius. During the twenty remaining years of his life he continued to write and publish new works. Though their reception was not always favorable, he was looked upon as a great poet whose publications, however they might be ranked by various critics, always commanded serious notice. He received many honors and was respected by young and old, by people with various beliefs and interests. When he died in 1889 he was buried in Westminster Abbey among other illustrious men of England. He lies in the Poets' Corner near Chaucer and Tennyson.

Overview

The basic elements that determined Browning's reputation from 1833 to 1870 were of course his professional activities and the opinions of critics and others. To these should be added certain significant movements in the intellectual and spiritual milieu that encouraged relaxation of conventional poetic standards by widening the scope of subjects thought to be suitable to poetry and by liberalizing the manner of treatment. This was beneficial to Browning in the fifties and sixties and helped him advance to his position of security by 1870. The complexities of his career, present from the first, can hardly be reduced to simple statements and easy generalizations.

With considerable struggle Browning and his critics persevered in different ways until his reputation was established. Over a long period of time and with difficulty critics learned that they could not judge Browning's works by traditional standards. Repeated exposure to his individual dramatic method, a shift in their opinion of what constituted the province of poetry, an increasing awareness of the totality of his achievement, and a recognition of the timeliness of his work — these contributed to the process of growing acceptance and appreciation. Very early in his career Browning became aware of the gap between himself and the critics, who represented the poetry-reading public. Feeling that he had a sacred duty to attain his place as a poet, he was determined to protect the central force of his creative genius and at the same time narrow the existing gap. He was sensitive to whatever would help or hinder the achievement of his desired goal.

The highlights of the broad canvas with many details indicate the character and direction of the efforts of both Browning and his critics. In Browning's exercise of his innovative genius, his workshop habits, and the performance of the critics during the first period of his literary life (which ended with the publication of the collected edition of 1849) lie the clues for understanding the gradual progress that led to wide recognition. Browning's readers were frustrated in the beginning by his experimenting with genres. To recognize his movement toward the best medium of expression for his individual talent they would have needed superior judgment, with the ability to see beyond the early period of misleading efforts.

The four works after the unacknowledged *Pauline* included two that partook of the character of drama but were different from each other *(Paracelsus* and *Pippa Passes), one play (Strafford)* that was performed, and a poem that was primarily narrative *(Sordello).* All of them bore the mark of his originality and all were difficult for the critics to understand. In his continuing experiments in the forties Browning wrote six more plays, which seemed to type him as a dramatist. His interest in internal states and changes rather than external action kept his plays from being successful on the stage, though he wrote four out of the six to be performed. Best suited to his genius were the innovative *Pippa Passes* and such short poems as those in *Dramatic Lyrics* and *Dramatic Romances and Lyrics.* Unfortunately these were overshadowed by the sheer volume of works less indicative of his future accomplishments. The critics would need considerable exposure to his poetry to see the direction of his efforts.

Although they were not capable of adequately appreciating the value of Browning's efforts, early critics observed that he was better than the rank and file of poets. His interest in man and human behavior and his dramatic ability were noted, and qualities of his poetry that were later to be repeatedly praised were pointed out — intellect, originality, and power (variously called force, energy, or strength). In this awareness lay the bare rudiments of a better understanding. Though they recognized his poetic ability, even when they did not approve of the work they were reviewing, critics could not see that what they considered praiseworthy was involved in what they attacked. They were unable to relate lines of criticism. They perceived that Browning had originality, but their deeply ingrained conservatism impelled them to feel that he should follow conventional rules of art and avoid unwholesome or otherwise unacceptable subject matter for poetry. To them he seemed little concerned about the obscurity of his verse. Why not make an effort to be clear, pleasing, and easy to read? Since the critics thought that Browning could be better, they often indulged in irritable accusations of wilfulness. In their faultfinding they occasionally had a glimmer of his individual techniques without seeing their significance. These were years of frustration for both Browning and his critics.

Browning had confidence in his instinctive creative force, and he wanted others to understand his intentions. In an effort to guide readers and encourage acceptance he wrote introductory comments for three of his early works, but they did not serve the purpose he had in mind. He had not yet won over many readers when he made repeated but unsuccessful attempts to write plays for the stage, which provided an opportunity for attracting wide attention. After reviewers (and Macready) made clear the qualities necessary for a play to succeed, Browning tried in *A Blot* and *Colombe's Birthday* to tailor his creative ideas to the demands of critics, who represented the tastes of the general public. In spite of his failures in poetry and drama he was tireless in his efforts to advance his art as well as his reputation.

Browning paid attention to what critics and others said of his work. He was fully aware of the influence of reviews. The helping hand of explanation that he apparently extended to friends who were critics was intended to prepare the way for a better understanding of his artistic aims. He watched for reviews anxiously and took to heart particularly the important ones. Though at times he demonstrated rather noisily his sensitiveness to the detrimental effect of a review, at other times in general remarks he showed tolerance for shortsighted criticism. He expressed gratefulness for favorable reviews, even showing a remarkable appreciation for those by friends who wrote sympathetically but in some respects showed deficiencies in judgment. Alert to suggestions of ways to gain an audience, he not only attempted to adapt his own ideas to standard notions of playwriting; he also wrote short pieces at the suggestion of his publisher Moxon and acted upon Fox's criticisms in his review of *Pauline.* He heeded professional advice for the best time to publish, and he gave up the compact appearance of his works as in *Bells and Pomegranates,* which he personally favored, after critics as well as other readers called attention to the cramped, ill-printed pamphlets in the series.

He took criticism seriously, and even sought well-intentioned suggestions. In fact, in the early part of his career he leaned on his friends to a great extent, though he had difficulty in seeing the problems that his work presented to others. He turned to Fox, Fanny Haworth, Domett, and Harriet Martineau as well as to others and later to Elizabeth, sometimes pressing them for suggestions. Most disturbing was the obscurity of his writing. He repeatedly assured others that he was working to eliminate it. Clarity in expression of thought was the "whole problem" of the artist, he wrote Elizabeth. His works as well as the reviews, indicated that his efforts resulted in improvement.

Contrary to the impression that he occasionally left on critics and others that he produced his works rapidly and did little or no revision, Browning put forth much effort in planning, writing, and revising his works. There is evidence that he withheld certain works, sometimes for a considerable period, so that he could better revise them, and then he examined them in proof for further revision. The early habits which he formed as a part of his literary life continued except as they had to be modified because of changes in his situation.

At the end of Browning's first period he was not satisfied. He looked upon his past efforts as experience that would result in better poetry. With a fundamentally optimistic nature, Browning sometimes suffered states of dejection that gave place to confidence in the future. The artistic ego that had prompted him to talk to Macready of his eventual celebrity, of *Sordello* with "obstinate faith" in it, and of the wisdom of putting his plays on the stage enabled him to continue his work. As strong as his ego, was a sense of humility in his dedication and his dependence on others for help.

After choosing a subject and deciding upon a plan for treating it, Browning applied his great energy and creative force to the task in hand, even before completing one work looking ahead to possible subjects and different genres. His unyielding application was not in vain. By the later forties signs of a departure from the earlier hidebound critical approach to his poetry began to appear. Indications of better understanding in the reception of the second collection of shorter dramatic poems continued through the criticism of the collected edition. Browning had drawn on his varied intellectual resources and critics were beginning to be impressed by the versatility of his genius and his interest in dramatic portrayal of character. In looking back on his total production, most of them were able to see the dramatic quality that characterized both poetry and plays. Instead of condemning the plays as unfit for the stage they were considering them as closet drama.

Complaints of the unwholesome and immoral were still present, but it is noteworthy that in religious periodicals, which were giving increasing attention to Browning, complaints were replaced by a marked duality of opinion. In both the sectarian and the nonsectarian press there were objections to the immoral and degrading. There also arose, with the recognition of Browning's intellectual range and interests, an awareness of the high seriousness with which he dramatically presented variety in life. These more definite perceptions of the qualities of Browning's poetry gave evidence of some attempt at drawing together hitherto separate lines of criticism with, in a few instances, clear and definite relations of lines. When the collected edition was published in 1849, the long poems, *Pippa Passes,* and the plays attracted most attention because they occupied the bulk of the two volumes. Since the shorter poems occupied less space the impression was given that they were of minor importance and hence they did not receive the recognition that the reviews of *Dramatic Romances and Lyrics* had promised.

The limitations of the critics when they were faced with unconventional writing had often contributed to their irritability. By the later forties Browning's manner of writing was not as disturbing as it had formerly been. Faultfinding because of obscurity had decreased. In fact, there was either acceptance of his manner or less emphasis on its shortcomings as attention was directed to the dramatic method and the subject matter. This and a very positive effort on the part of a few critics to explain the individuality of Browning's style and to persuade others that his poetry was worth the exertion needed to read it foreshadowed a critical position of the fifties and sixties.

The attitude of the critics toward Browning in the later forties seemed to predict an advance in the understanding of his genius upon the appearance of his next work. But instead of continuing his experiments with the dramatic revelation of character, which the critics had begun to appreciate, Browning, now living in Italy, wrote *Christmas-Eve and Easter-Day* (1850), which dealt with contemporary religious beliefs in a poem unlike any he had previously written. There was an outcry in the first of the reviews against the grotesque element and Hudibrastic style as unbefitting a religious poem. Passage of time could bring better understanding of a work of Browning's, as in the case of *Pippa Passes,* and now there was a shift in the appraisal after the major weeklies (with the exception of the *Examiner*) railed against *Christmas-Eve and Easter-Day.* In the second month after publication, criticism of the style weakened as approval of the religious import began to appear in denominational periodicals, which had already given signs of seeing Browning as a poet of high seriousness. This shift in emphasis led to the view that Browning was a religious poet, which did much to shape his reputation. The realization that Browning, an intellectual poet, was concerned with contemporary religious questions took root in the fifties, when old beliefs of the Victorians were already being questioned.

In *Men and Women* (1855) Browning reverted to the mode of dramatic poetry that he had initiated in *Dramatic Lyrics* (1842) and continued in *Dramatic Romances and Lyrics* (1845). Instead of profiting by the gains which they had made in the late forties, many critics were overpowered by the wealth and number of original poems in the two volumes of 1855. Some were completely blind to the value of the great dramatic poems in this collection, and they as well as others who had a glimmer of light were so vociferous and querulous in their objections primarily to the style that it is difficult to see the progress that was in fact taking place. A cursory look at the reviews can easily result in a sweeping condemnation of the critics.

A more thorough examination shows that the lines of criticism favorable to Browning that began to emerge in the late forties, as well as new ones, received support in the fifties — even in the confusion, contradictions, and struggles that were present. These prepared the way for the effectiveness of critical appraisal in the sixties. Browning's employment of his wide range of knowledge and interest in the varied experience of man as shown by his dramatic revelation of character was impressive, and some critics called attention to his manner of projecting himself into the mind of the characters. The more liberal tolerance of different kinds of knowledge, characters, and mental states, especially those traditionally considered not fit for poetry, resulted in part from seeing Browning not only as an intellectual but also as a religious poet. Recognition of him as a poet of high intent went hand in hand with an awareness of the relevance of his poetry to the religious movements and spirit of his day, an awareness that had followed the publication of *Christmas-Eve and Easter-Day*. The critics' changing attitude toward remote and unusual subject matter was noticeable in their discussions of poems with moral or religious significance and of other poems as well.

The conventional attitude toward Browning's style that characterized many earlier reviews and a number of reviews of *Men and Women* was giving way in the more perceptive reviews. This was especially demonstrated in the discussion of obscurity. The discriminating critics spoke out in defense of Browning on that score, with the implication that too much emphasis had been placed on it. Though their understanding of his technique was limited, especially in the dramatic lyric, they appreciated the blank verse of his great dramatic monologues and a few seemed to realize that his poetry was not to be judged by ordinary standards. Objective and poised criticism characterized these reviews, which made up more than a third of the total number dealing with *Men and Women.* Other critics were querulous in a confusion of praise and blame while attempting to understand Browning, whose genius they recognized without clearly comprehending it. Guided by preconceived notions of poetry, the remaining were completely blind to Browning's merits and were blatantly impatient.

Browning could not see that the encouraging notes foreshadowed the advancements to be made in the sixties. What he did see was that the poems he and others had justifiably thought would bring recognition were received with much irritable condemnation. He wrote his publisher in strong language to express his anger with critics, who he thought were threatening his financial and professional success. As a result of the greatest professional disappointment of his life, Browning felt the futility of further attempts. Earlier he had been able to continue his efforts in spite of poor reception; now he wrote little and that little he pushed aside.

On his return to England after Elizabeth's death in 1861, following his fifteen years of married life in Italy, Browning ended his long period of nonproductivity as he again took up old professional habits. Following the earlier trials and errors in his attempts to gain an audience, the first publications could not have been better planned and presented as a means of advancing his reputation. The *Selections* (1863), arranged by friends to attract readers, and his *Poetical Works* (1863), published volume by volume with his most distinctive works first to emphasize their importance, achieved the desired effect. Browning further advanced and secured his reputation when he published two new works, successful because of their contemporary relevance and their position in the sequence of his works — *Dramatis Personae* (1864) and *The Ring and the Book* (1868–9).

After the publication of the *Poetical Works* and *Dramatis Personae* a new note appeared in the reviews. The critics were aware that Browning had gained sufficient recognition from readers to warrant the republication of his works and a second edition of *Dramatis Personae.* No longer, as after the publication of *Selections* (1863), did critics need to fear that readers failed to share their high opinion of Browning. The deterrent to their assertive recommendation was removed. There was another sign of forward-moving independence. Critics had already reproached other critics for their damagings reviews: in the forties blame was incidental and after the publication of *Men and Women* it was more noticeable, usually either general or clearly directed against specific but unidentified reviews. After *Dramatis Personae* there were pronounced attacks. No less than four on the *Edinburgh Review* appeared, all effective in discrediting the identified offender.

Browning had not advanced in one area. His dramatic lyric failed to gain approval. He had first used the conventional lyric (in *Paracelsus*) as the result of Fox's advice. Later appeared the lyric that bore the stamp of his originality, but critics were too much blinded by their own traditional notion to accept Browning's individuality. Outspoken criticism began in the fifties and continued in the sixties. Except when they were discussing lyrics, the critics had grown less severe in their objections to style. In fact, there were encouraging signs in the reviews of the *Poetical Works* and *Dramatis Personae*. Among them was the continuation of recognition (which had appeared from time to time) that Browning's verse harmonized with the intended effect, that it could not be judged independently of the thought. Irritability had weakened as acceptance increased. Obscurity was no longer a main target. The attacks on it that had started with *Sordello* had lost force. When critics began opening their eyes in the forties, they realized that *Sordello* was not to be summarily rejected and in the sixties they discussed it on a new level.

The critics' opinion of what Browning said and how he said it should be examined with reference to the Victorian frame of thought. In the early sixties religious beliefs were being questioned in a climate of uncertainty. The second edition of *Dramatis Personae* was called for largely because of the attraction to the emphatic moral and religious pertinence of Browning's poetry. Changes in the intellectual milieu, such as the questioning of old assumptions and the appearance of new interests, contributed to the relaxing of hidebound standards of literary evaluation. Unusual or peculiar subjects, psychological probing, stylistic traits that made the poetry difficult — the general acceptance of these attested to the increasing appreciation of the range and employment of Browning's genius and at the same time to the intellectual forces at work. With more freedom in thinking came the acceptance of realism and the grotesque for serious purposes — both earlier denounced. The various dramatic presentations of a broad perspective of human behavior was welcome. Browning's projecting his mind into that of the characters provided not only the intellectual quality for better character revelation; it also allowed acceptable moral and spiritual values to emerge. In support of faith, the dramatic method was more effective than the subjective approach, said several critics of *Dramatis Personae*.

With *Dramatis Personae* out of the way and well received, Browning directed his energy to the great poem that he could now write and critics could appreciate. In *The Ring and the Book* he turned the account of a murder, abhorrent in itself and remote in time and place, into an epic of human behavior with profound thought such as appealed to the Englishman of the time. He translated experience into moral and spiritual truths by going beyond the single monologue, which had already gained approval, to a series of related ones. The result was compatible with critical values, which had been undergoing changes not only as the result of the uprooting of settled religious beliefs and the search for new footings but also as the result of the shifting away from insularity, the intellectual stir in the study of history, and interest in the importance and complexities of the individual.

The general habits of thinking, expansive in the search for new outlooks, had already been reflected in the more liberal critical position. Browning had employed the ruminations of a brute in *Caliban* and the roguery of an imposter in *Mr. Sludge* to point up matters of contemporary moral and spiritual concern of special importance to Victorians. In *The Ring and the Book* he turned to a Roman murder story. Now instead of expressing a desire for a simple subject and inoffensive elementary human emotions for the sake of mere pleasure in reading as in earlier years, the great majority of critics did not object to the sordid story. It was the use made of the subject that had become the test for value, and the use of it involved the interrelation of the various aspects of Browning's poetry that critics had once considered separately. The continuing process of merging lines of criticism prompted them to see the whole of the poem in a better light.

Changing habits of thinking were further reflected in the criticism of Browning's manner of writing in *The Ring and the Book*. The earlier frequent cry, "We want poetry that is easy to read," challenged by relatively few, was now subdued. At first Browning's poetry had been considered too difficult; then appeared the notion that the poetry was difficult but worth the effort required for understanding it; then out of the new intellectual movements grew attitudes that further modified the early complaint. In the intellectual climate readers desired meaningful poetry, and many preferred poetry that brought before them serious topics in such a way as to exercise their thinking. The preference was for dramatic poetry, which — unlike subjective poetry with its restriction to the thought and feeling of the writer — extended to a great variety of human experiences. The process of analyzing the working of the mind of man in the totality of life — seeing reality as related to the ideal, the earthly to the divine — was welcome in a time when questions were being asked and values weighed.

That Browning was not completely orthodox and did not impose his judgments didactically upon his readers appealed to those who wanted the benefit of his thought but also the chance at the same time to follow through the process of arriving at a belief, an opinion, or a judgment. Critics of various faiths or no faith at all were receptive to Browning's poetry. They saw that searching for the truth and arriving at personal convictions was important. Browning's stress on the value of individualism was appropriate in a time when many had lost faith in orthodoxy. The shaping of his source material in *The Ring and the Book* made a special appeal; readers were involved in the conflicting evidence in the search for truth just as they were involved in the conflict of new knowledge and old convictions in their search for a solution to their problems in a changing world.

Critics were more interested in what Browning said in *The Ring and the Book* and the way he approached his subject than in his poetic line. In chiefly the unfavorable reviews there were severe complaints about the verse. In the rest there was, relatively speaking, a modicum of faultfinding, which was well controlled. In fact, what stands out in the criticism is that instead of isolating and exaggerating the faults the critics stressed the greatness of the poem. They had arrived at an attitude that Browning, in a letter to Isa Blagden had advocated for critics: "animadverting, if you please, on any blemishes, but doing justice on the whole to the real worth there."

Pertinent to the evaluation of a review was the character of the periodical in which it appeared — its life span, kind and extent of audience, and periodicity. Besides the value of each review according to the character of the periodical, important in a study of Browning's reputation is the effect of reviews in certain groups of periodicals. The first group consisted of weeklies falling between 1833 and 1845. The majority of reviews of Browning's works were published in them and they were generally unfavorable. To some extent the value of a review in a weekly was its immediacy after publication, but to prepare a review of Browning's poetry on short notice meant that the critic did not have enough time to cope with difficult and original writing. Most of the reviews in weeklies that were favorable as well as other receptive ones in nonweeklies were written by men who moved in Browning's social-professional circles, some of them close friends to whom he probably talked of his poetry.

The second significant group was composed of reviews in the sectarian periodicals of the late forties and the fifties. The nonweekly periodicals increased in number in the late forties, and among them were sectarian periodicals whose critics turned their attention to Browning as a poet of high seriousness. Then after *Christmas-Eve and Easter-Day* they saw him as a poet interested in religious beliefs. This awareness was significant because it gave direction to Browning's reputation.

Changes taking place in the multiplicity of periodicals of the sixties influenced the reception of Browning's poetry. For the first time he benefited by reviews in weeklies. Two of the long established weeklies that had formerly disapproved of him and ones reviewing him for the first time placed their stamp of approval on his works. Some of these commanded a wide readership, either general or literary, and others appealed to restricted audiences of different kinds. The most significant change came in reviews in monthlies making their first appearance. These monthlies manifested a lively interest in varied aspects of Victorian life and appealed to readers who were capable of appreciating Browning.

He profited by the high caliber of many critics of the sixties. In the widening vistas of thought, intellectual and openminded men were attracted to critical expression, including reviewing. Generally the critics of Browning no longer felt subservient to restrictive principles. Besides those who were receptive to new standards, though in some respects timidly rejecting the old, there were those who by virtue of training or profession (some were recognized in fields other than literature) had little difficulty in following their own critical dictates. The practice of signing articles, as it came into increasing use, was beneficial to Browning; his poetry had a head start when reviews favorable to him were signed by men from various areas of thinking whose names carried weight.

It is instructive to set the opinions of professional critics against the opinions of those who did not review Browning in the course of earning their livelihood. On the negative side they both denounced or lamented the obscurity and difficulty of his verse. Agreement existed in the praise of Browning's thought, originality, strength, and interest in human behavior and also in the conclusion that whatever might be the faults of *The Ring and the Book* its greatness assured Browning's place as a foremost poet. Some of both groups wished to serve as explicators and thus convince others that the poetry was worth the effort required to understand it. In both groups there were enthusiastic readers who, being members of the younger generation, welcomed Browning's individuality for its fresh departure from the conventionally acceptable. Two differences stand out. The irritable faultfinding that was prominent in the negative and unsympathetic reviews was the exception in the comments of the nonprofessionals who did not like Browning's poetry. The complaint of Browning's immorality and unwholesomeness was absent from private assessments, but it often appeared in the earlier professional criticism, which was influenced by public opinion. Taken all in all, there was considerable agreement between the professional and nonprofessional attitude toward Browning's poetry.

After Browning's early period of experimentation, criticism by both reviewers and friends continued to play an important part in his life. He turned to Fox, Lytton, Kenyon, and Milsand for criticism of *Men and Women.* The surviving acknowledgments of his comments to Kenyon and other friends indicated that the most frequent complaints had to do with obscurity and difficulty. Since he could not escape the fact that his readers did have trouble, throughout his life he assured his friends that he made an effort to improve. There were times when he defended his manner of writing, but knowing that his friends had his interests at heart he was not indignant as he often was when he thought professionals were severe or obtuse.

Although after the forties Browning did not so openly show his desire to have his works reviewed — even to the point of soliciting reviews in earlier years — his letters to Conway indicated his willingness to help smooth a reviewer's path. After the publication of a work of his he continued to watch for reviews; that he felt their power is shown by his tenseness during the waiting period and his remarks after their appearance. When one was expected in an influential periodical and was delayed or did not appear at all he could be unduly disturbed. He was sometimes inclined to strike out against a critic who abused or misunderstood the work under consideration. His early frustration might be overcome temporarily and then, after going underground, reappear when activated by some reminder; harbored feelings gathered force and then erupted into an exaggerated account of what he considered an unfair or unjust reception. Unfortunately after the passage of years he could easily mix facts and fancies in defending his poetry. Throughout his life discordant notes tended to accompany the recall of a disappointing reception of one of his early efforts. Browning's reactions are best explained in the light of his strong impulse to foster his works and resist impediments to their acceptance.

Browning greatly appreciated those reviews that were written to further his cause and readily and generously gave credit where it was due. Long after the deed itself he was not forgetful of what others had done in his behalf. He acknowledged indebtiness to them in various ways and told others of the help he had received. A response that should be brought out as well as his gratefulness was his recognition, in the face of critical misunderstanding and inadequacy, of the difficult task of sympathetically inclined critics who could not, in a limited time, see his works as a whole. He also knew that they were sometimes subject to an editor who would diminish their degree of appreciation or otherwise alter their text for the worse. To his credit Browning maintained a high regard for Macready and Carlyle, who he felt had failed him professionally; he was capable of divorcing the lasting acute disappointment from the perpetrator of it, the professional pain from the friend.

Browning paid close attention to reviews and his consequent actions suggest their influence on him. He had turned from the confessional in *Pauline* after critics called attention to it and made changes in plays according to some of the complaints of his critics. He turned to contemporary English life in *Dramatis Personae* after objections to his use of the remote in time and place, especially Italy. The first part of *The Ring and the Book* was more than likely the consequence of repeated urging that to encourage ready understanding Browning should add an introductory explanation of what was to follow, and he said the simplicity of the story was an answer to the complaint of obscurity. His arrangements of the works in his collected editions of 1863 and 1868 were influenced by his desire to prevent critics from repeating mistaken evaluations made in the past and to guide them in the future. After the critics had difficulty as the result of coping in a limited time with the great wealth of subject matter and the individuality of poetic treatment in the two volumes of *Men and Women,* Browning published *Poetical Works* and *The Ring and the Book* in installments to allow time for understanding. And after being advised of the cramped effect of the pamphlet format of *Bells and Pomegranates* on his readers, he decided that the collection of 1868 should have six rather than fewer volumes, to make for easier reading and handling. Even after the failure of his early Prefaces, written to guide readers, he tried other means of forestalling misunderstanding, as in his lines at the end of *Christmas-Eve*.

Browning did not hesitate to talk of the means he used to attract readers. He talked to Allingham, Dante Gabriel Rossetti, George MacDonald, and others. During the years of his active professional life in England he talked with freedom of his writing and with enthusiasm for the finished product. He talked of his poetic life to one person or to a few in intimate gatherings in his ever-widening social life of the sixties. When serious discussion of his poetry was out of place, he was adept at making remarks to suit the occasion. Out of his social aplomb grew misconceptions of his attitude toward his works. A broad examination of his behavior shows that when communication was appropriate he did not hesitate to refer to his works, and he wrote to friends and sometimes to strangers of matters of importance to his poetry. He even went so far as to admit that socializing was beneficial to his writing.

In early years Browning revealed notions basic to his writing to Domett, Horne, Fanny Haworth, Macready, and Elizabeth, and later to Ruskin, Isa Blagden, W. W. Story, Julia Wedgwood, Kenyon, and Milsand as well as others. Besides stressing the importance of originality and clarity, he indicated his preference for conciseness and emphasized the worthiness of the study of the soul and the duty of the poet to teach, to advance truth, and to show evil as well as good in representing life and revealing spiritual insights. He admitted his sympathy with undesirable characters and his propensity for exploring dark corners of the soul. He talked of his aim to preserve the integrity of his art and of the responsibility of readers and audience. As a dramatic writer he talked of the degree of self-revelation that he sanctioned, of his principle of creating a central effect with subordinated details, and he called attention to the difference between the work of a dramatic poet and that of a narrative writer. He also indicated the change he had made in his prosody and his right to adapt verse to the rhythm of speech.

Both Browning and his critics, with frustration, confusion, and irritation throughout years of struggle, contributed to the gradual narrowing of the distance that lies between a great original poet and those who judge him. Browning followed and developed the bent of his creative impulse and observed critical response, and the critics by virtue of exposure and effort, supported by general changes in thinking, arrived at different standards of measurement. In *The Ring and the Book* Browning's genius — its integrity always safeguarded — reached a high level of expression, and his critics had attained a degree of appreciation that enabled them to recognize his achievement. Because of his confidence in his *daemon* and his determination to persevere, Browning produced poetry that in spirit and presentation contemporaries related to their time and in expression recognized as individual. He had attained a secure place as one of England's great poets.

Reviews of Browning's Works in British Periodicals, 1833–70

The entries in this list are arranged in chronological order. They are of two kinds interspersed: the titles of Browning's works (in capitals) and the titles of periodicals (in italics) in which reviews of his works appeared. Most of the reviews concern the work below which they occur, but some may have to do with works published earlier. Mere notices are included only when they are of particular significance.

An entry for a work consists of information from the title page, followed by an abbreviation used for reference to that work and, when possible, a more precise date of publicaiton. For plays I give the dates of performance. I have followed DeVane's dating without citing him as my authority; there are notations only when I have discovered evidence for a more precise fixing of the day of the month. In this and other instances when I have supplied or amended dating, I have indicated my sources of information in parentheses. Sometimes I have cited what must have been DeVane's unspecified source for a date that has not been questioned.

After the title of the periodical in which each review appears, there follow volume number (if there is one), date, and page or pages. In this sequence there may be disagreement with corresponding information in Litzinger and Smalley's collection of criticisms or in Broughton's bibliography or in both. Since these are at present regarded as standard sources of information concerning reviews of Browning, I have attempted to make doubly sure of my facts whenever my details differ from theirs. Sometimes I have supplied an omission or omissions in one or both.

After the volume, date, and page of the periodical, I indicate the work or works which the review concerns. Whenever a review is general rather than specific, I make a notation to that effect. It is not my practice to quote the title of a review (if it has one); I quote only a few especially revealing titles. If a review includes a discussion of several poets, as a rule I cite only the pages that relate to Browning.

If it is known, the reviewer's name is given, and the information pertinent to the assignment of authorship is provided in parentheses. When writers signed their names in full or used the signature of Editor or of a well-known pseudonym or when their reviews (sometimes with changes) were later reprinted under their names, identification is clearcut. It is safe to conclude from statements made by Browning and other contemporaries of John Forster that he wrote the reviews appearing in the *Examiner* until his retirement in 1855. And his recent biographer, James A. Davies, told me that this is a dependable assumption. I have greatly profited by the volumes of the *Wellesley Index,* in which the editors cite evidence for their assignment of authorship. Tener's extensive work on R. H. Hutton has been particularly helpful. Unless otherwise specified, I have accepted the attributions in the studies of individual periodicals by Marchand, Bevington, and Thrall. Some unverified attributions in *BSP,* Nicoll and Wise, Broughton, and Litzinger and Smalley that I have not been able to verify I have usually accepted without comment. The *Wellesley Index* will lead the way to a further increase in the establishment of authorship heretofore unknown, uncertain, or unverified. I have cited evidence for attributions for which I am responsible. When an explanation rather than a citation alone was required, I have referred to an entry in the general index that will direct the reader to an explanation in the text.

The following abbreviations are used in this headnote and in the bibliography of reviews.

Bevington. Merle M. Bevington, *The Saturday Review, 1855–1868.* New York: Columbia Univ. Press, 1941.
Broughton. *Robert Browning: A Bibliography, 1830–1950,* comp. Leslie Nathan Broughton, Clark Sutherland Northup, and Robert Pearsall. Ithaca, New York: Cornell Univ. Press, 1953. "New ed.," 1970. (Pearsall says that "updating and some correcting" may be found in the articles on the Brownings.)

BSP. "Trial-List of Criticisms and Notices of Browning's Works" and "Fresh Entries of Criticisms," *The Browning Society's Papers.* Vol. I. London: N. Trübner & Co., 1881.

Kaminsky. Alice R. Kaminsky, *George Henry Lewes as Literary Critic.* Syracuse, New York: Syracuse Univ. Press, 1968.

DeVane. William C. DeVane, *A Browning Handbook.* 2d ed. New York: Appleton-Century-Crofts, 1955.

Letters, Hood. *Letters of Robert Browning Collected by T. J. Wise,* ed. T. L. Hood. New Haven: Yale Univ. Press, 1933.

Litzinger and Smalley. *Browning: The Critical Heritage,* ed. Boyd Litzinger and Donald Smalley. New York: Barnes & Noble, 1970.

Marchand. Leslie A. Marchand, *The Athenaeum: A Mirror of Victorian Culture.* Chapel Hill: Univ. of North Carolina Press, 1941.

Morison, *The Times.* Stanley Morison, *The Tradition Established, 1841–1884.* Vol. II of *The History of the Times.* London: Written, Printed, and Published at the Office of the *Times,* 1939.

Nicoll and Wise. "Browningiana," a list of reviews of Robert Browning, in *Literary Anecdotes of the Nineteenth Century,* ed. W. Robertson Nicoll and Thomas J. Wise. Vol. I. London: Hodder & Stoughton, 1895.

PC. Publishers' Circular and Booksellers' Record of British and Foreign Literature.

RB. Robert Browning.

RB and AD. Robert Browning and Alfred Domett, ed. Frederic G. Kenyon. New York: E. P. Dutton & Co., 1906.

RB and EBB. The Letters of Robert Browning and Elizabeth Barrett Barrett, 1845–1846, ed. Elvan Kintner. Two vols. Cambridge, Mass.: Belknap Press of Harvard Univ. Press, 1969.

Rossetti to Allingham. Letters of Dante Gabriel Rossetti to William Allingham, 1854–1870, ed. George Birkbeck Hill. New York: Frederick A. Stokes Co., 1897.

Tener. Robert H. Tener, "R. H. Hutton: Some Attributions," *Victorian Periodicals Newsletter,* no. 20, June 1973, pp. 14–31.

Thrall. Miriam M. H. Thrall, *Rebellious Fraser's.* New York: Columbia Univ. Press, 1934.

W Index. The Wellesley Index to Victorian Periodicals, 1824–1900. Five vols. Vols. I–IV, ed. Walter E. Houghton with Esther R. Houghton et al.; Vol. V, ed. Jean H. Slingerland. Toronto: Univ. of Toronto Press, 1966, 1972, 1979, 1987, 1989. (Page numbers are followed by item numbers in brackets.)

PAULINE; A FRAGMENT OF A CONFESSION. London: Saunders and Otley, 1833. *Paul.* Ca. Mar. 7.
Literary Gazette, Mar. 23, 1833, p. 183. *Paul.*

Monthly Repository, n.s. VII, Apr. 1833, 252–62. *Paul.* William J. Fox. (See index under Fox.)

Athenaeum, Apr. 6, 1833, p. 216. *Paul.* Allan Cunningham. (Marchand, p. 286.)

Atlas, VIII, Apr. 14, 1833, 228. *Paul.*

Monthly Repository, n.s. VII, June 1833, 421. *Paul.* "Local Logic." William J. Fox. (See index under Fox.)

Tait's Edinburgh Magazine, III, Aug. 1833, 668. *Paul.* Christian Johnstone. *(W Index,* IV, 498 [301].)

Fraser's Magazine, VIII, Dec. 1833, 669–70. *Paul.* William Maginn? *(W Index,* II, 340 [636] and 338 [562]); cf. Thrall, p. 297, Maginn? and Thackeray?)

PARACELSUS. By Robert Browning. London: Published by Effingham Wilson, MDCCCXXXV. *Par.* Aug. 15.

Spectator, VIII, Aug. 15, 1835, 780–1. *Par.*

Atlas, X, Aug. 16, 1835, 520. *Par.*

Weekly Dispatch, Aug. 16, 1835, p. 298. *Par.*

Athenaeum, Aug. 22, 1835, p. 640. *Par.*

Examiner, Sept. 6, 1835, pp. 563–5. *Par.* John Forster.

Metropolitan Magazine, XIV, Oct. 1835, 39. *Par.*

Monthly Repository, n.s. IX, Nov. 1835, 716–27. *Par.* William J. Fox. (See index under Fox.)

Tait's Edinburgh Magazine, n.s. II, Nov. 1835, 765. *Par.* Christian Johnstone. *(W Index,* IV, 508 [644].)

Leigh Hunt's London Journal and the Printing Machine, II, Nov. 21, 1835, 405–8. *Par.* Probably Leigh Hunt. (Nicoll and Wise, I, 579.)

Fraser's Magazine, XIII, Mar. 1836, 362, 363–74. *Par.* J. A. Heraud. With William Maginn? *(W Index,* II, 351 [925]; Thrall, pp. 273–4, 285; cf. *BSP,* p. 89, Heraud only [for probable source of information, see *Letters,* Hood, p. 195, RB to Furnivall].)

New Monthly Magazine and Literary Journal, XLVI, Mar. 1836, 289–308. *Par.* John Forster. *(W Index,* III, 233 [2336]; *Letters,* Hood, p. 195, RB to Furnivall.)

Metropolitan Journal, Apr. 16, 1836, pp. 19–20; continued Apr. 23, 1836, pp. 35–6. *Par.* Signed O[rd]. (Supplement is signed John Walker Ord, who was the editor.)

STRAFFORD: AN HISTORICAL TRAGEDY. By Robert Browning, Author of "Paracelsus." London: Printed for Longman, Rees, Orme, Brown, Green, & Longman, 1837. *Straf.* May 1. (RB to Fox, May 1, 1837, in Mrs. Sutherland Orr, *Life and Letters of Robert Browning,* rev. F. G. Kenyon [Boston: Houghton Mifflin Co., 1908], p. 84.) Performed May 1, 3, 5, 9, and 30, 1837, at the Covent Garden Theatre. (The dates are from the playbills.)

Constitutional, May 2, 1837, p. [3]. *Straf.* Probably Douglas Jerrold. (W. H. Griffin and H. C. Minchin, *The Life of Robert Browning,* 3d ed. rev. [London: Methuen & Co., 1938], p. 109.)

Morning Chronicle, May 2, 1837, p. [3]. *Straf.*

Morning Post, May 2, 1837, p. [3]. *Straf.*

Times, May 2, 1837, p. 5. *Straf.*

True Sun, May 2, 1837, p. [3]. *Straf.* William J. Fox. (See index under Fox.)

Morning Herald, May 4, 1837, p. [3]. *Straf.* Possibly [no first name] Conan. (Macready recorded in his *Diaries* on May 4, 1837, that Conan wrote the review of *Strafford* in the *Morning Herald;* see the entry for this date in *The Diaries of William Charles Macready, 1833–1851,* ed. William Toynbee, 2 vols. [London: Chapman and Hall, 1912].)

Athenaeum, May 6, 1837, p. 331. *Straf.* Possibly George Darley. (Marchand, p. 287.)

Court Journal, May 6, 1837, p. 281. *Straf.*

Literary Gazette, May 6, 1837, pp. 283–4. *Straf.* Also p. 292, discussion of the acting.

Parthenon, May 6, 1837, p. 29. *Straf.*

Spectator, X, May 6, 1837, 423. *Straf.*

Atlas, XII, May 7, 1837, 293–4. *Straf.*

Bell's Life in London and Sporting Chronicle, May 7, 1837, p. [2]. *Straf.*

Examiner, May 7, 1837, pp. 294–5. *Straf.* John Forster.

John Bull, XVII, May 7, 1837 (Sunday), 225, and reprinted May 8 (Monday). *Straf.*

Weekly Dispatch, May 7, 1837, p. 224. *Straf.*

Casket, May 13, 1837, pp. 289–93; continued May 20, 1837, pp. 307–10; concluded May 27, 1837, pp. 329–30. Retelling of story of *Straf.*

Casket, May 13, 1837, pp. 297–8. *Straf.*

Examiner, May 14, 1837, p. 310. Notice of withdrawal of *Straf.* John Forster.

Court Journal, May 27, 1837, pp. 329–30. Announcement of May 30 performance of *Straf* and long extract from play.

Metropolitan Magazine, XIX, June 1837, 50–1. *Straf.*

New Monthly Magazine and Humorist, L, June 1837, 296. Comment on *Straf* and on Macready's performances. Probably John Forster. (See index under Forster.)

Edinburgh Review, LXV, July 1837, 132–51. *Straf.* Herman Merivale. (*W Index,* I, 483 [1620].)

Dramatic Spectator, Sept. 30, 1837, pp. 77–9. *Straf.*

SORDELLO. By Robert Browning. London: Edward Moxon, MDCCCXL. *Sord.* Mar. 7. (Announced in *Literary Gazette,* Feb. 29 and Mar. 7. On Mar. 7 Browning inscribed a copy for his mother [Sotheby's Catalogue of Auction, p. 81, Lot 477] and wrote a dated note to accompany a copy which he was sending to Alfred Domett [*RB and AD,* pp. 27–8].)

Spectator, XIII, Mar. 14, 1840, 257. *Sord.*

Bell's Life in London and Sporting Chronicle, Mar. 15, 1840, p. [4]. *Sord.*

Atlas, XV, Mar. 28, 1840, 203. *Sord.*

Metropolitan Magazine, XXVII, Apr. 1840, 108–9. *Sord.*

New Monthly Belle Assemblée, XII, Apr. 1840, 214. *Sord.*

Dublin Review, VIII, May 1840, 551–3. *Sord.* Probably George Irvine. *(W Index,* II, 30 [180].)

Monthly Chronicle, V, May 1840, 476–8. *Sord.* George Henry Lewes. *(W Index,* III, 130 [268].)

Monthly Review, n.s. II, May 1840, 149. *Sord.*

Athenaeum, May 30, 1840, pp. 431–2. *Sord.* T. K. Hervey. (Marchand, pp. 287–9.)

BELLS AND POMEGRANTES. No. I. — PIPPA PASSES. By Robert Browning, Author of "Paracelsus." London: Edward Moxon, MDCCCXLI. *B&P. PP.* Apr.

Spectator, XIV, Apr. 17, 1841, 379. *PP.*

Metropolitan Magazine, XXXI, May 1841, 15. *PP.*

Monthly Review, n.s. II, May 1841, 95–9. *PP.*

Atlas, XVI, May 1, 1841, 287. *PP.*

Tait's Edinburgh Magazine, n.s. VIII, June 1841, 405. *PP.* Christian Johnstone. *(W Index,* IV, 530 [1313].)

Morning Herald, July 10, 1841, p. 6. *PP.*

Examiner, Oct. 2, 1841, pp. 628–9. *PP* and a comment on *Sord.* John Forster.

Athenaeum, Dec. 11, 1841, p. 952. *PP.* T. K. Hervey. (Marchand, pp. 289–90.)

BELLS AND POMEGRANATES. No. II. — KING VICTOR AND KING CHARLES. By Robert Browning, Author of "Paracelsus." London: Edward Moxon, MDCCCXLII. *KVKC.* Mar. 2–5. (DeVane dated it Mar. 12, but the first review was on Mar. 5; *PC* placed it between May 2 and 16.)

Spectator, XV, Mar. 5, 1842, 233–4. *KVKC.*

Examiner, Apr. 2, 1842, pp. 211–2. *KVKC.* Reprinted in *London and Paris Observer,* Apr. 10, 1842. John Forster.

Athenaeum, Apr. 30, 1842, pp. 376–8. *KVKC.* Reprinted in *London and Paris Observer,* May 15, 1842. [No first name] Hemans. (Marchand, p. 290.)

Metropolitan Magazine, XXXIV, June 1842, 49–50. *KVKC.*

Atlas, XVII, July 16, 1842, 458. *KVKC.*

Church of England Quarterly Review, XII, Oct. 1842, 464–83. *Par* through *KVKC.* Richard H. Horne. *(RB and AD,* pp. 45, 50, 97.)

BELLS AND POMEGRANTES. No. III. — DRAMATIC LYRICS. By Robert Browning, Author of "Paracelsus." London: Edward Moxon, MDCCCXLII. *DL.* Nov. 21–6. (Browning wrote Moxon on Thursday, Nov. 17, that Forster did not want the publication to appear before

Nov. 21 [Monday] so that he could have his review in the *Examiner* on Nov. 26 [Saturday]. In *New Letters of Robert Browning,* ed. W. C. De-Vane and K. L. Knickerbocker [New Haven: Yale Univ. Press, 1950], pp. 29–30.)

Examiner, Nov. 26, 1842, pp. 756–7. *DL.* John Forster.

Spectator, XV, Dec. 10, 1842, 1191–2. *DL.*

Morning Herald, Dec. 20, 1842, p. 5. *DL.*

BELLS AND POMEGRANATES. No. IV. — THE RETURN OF THE DRUSES. A Tragedy. In Five Acts. By Robert Browning. Author of "Paracelsus." London: Edward Moxon, MDCCCXLIII. *RD.* Jan.

Metropolitan Magazine, XXXVI, Feb. 1843, 55. *DL.*

Spectator, XVI, Feb. 4, 1843, 116. *RD.*

BELLS AND POMEGRANATES. No. V. — A BLOT IN THE 'SCUTCH-EON. A Tragedy, In Three Acts. By Robert Browning, Author of "Paracelsus." London: Edward Moxon, MDCCCXLIII. *Blot.* Feb. 11. Performed Feb. 11, 15, and 17, 1843, at the Drury Lane Theatre. (These dates are from the playbills.)

Morning Post, Feb. 13, 1843, p. 3. *Blot.*

Times, Feb. 13, 1843, p. 5. *Blot.*

Athenaeum, Feb. 18, 1843, p. 166. *Blot.*

Atlas, XVIII, Feb. 18, 1843, 104–5. *Blot.*

Examiner, Feb. 18, 1843, p. 101. *Blot.* John Forster.

John Bull, XXIII, Feb. 18, 1843 (Saturday), 108–9, and reprinted Feb. 20 (Monday). *Blot.*

Literary Gazette, Feb. 18, 1843, pp. 107–8. *Blot.*

Spectator, XVI, Feb. 18, 1843, 159–60. *Blot.*

Era, Feb. 19, 1843, pp. 5–6. *Blot.*

New Monthly Belle Assemblée, XVIII, Mar. 1843, 183. *Blot.*

Athenaeum, Apr. 22, 1843, p. 385. *DL.* T. K. Hervey. (Marchand, p. 290.)

Westminster Review, XXXIX, May 1843, 603–4. *Blot.* Signed G[eorge]. H[enry]. L[ewes]. (Kaminsky, p. 157 and n. 66; *W Index,* III, 599 [930].)

Athenaeum, July 1, 1843, pp. 608–9. *RD.*

Gentleman's Magazine, n.s. XX, Aug. 1843, 168–9. *B&P,* Nos. I–IV, and a reference to *Par.*

Foreign and Colonial Quarterly Review, III, Jan. 1844, 202, 209–15. *RD* and one paragraph on *Blot.* Richard H. Horne. (See index under Horne.)

BELLS AND POMEGRANATES. No. VI. — COLOMBE'S BIRTHDAY. A Play, In Five Acts. By Robert Browning, Author of "Paracelsus." London: Edward Moxon, MDCCCXLIV. *CB.* Ca. Apr. 20.

Examiner, June 22, 1844, pp. 388–9. *CB.* John Forster.

New Quarterly Review; or, Home, Foreign, and Colonial Journal, IV, Oct. 1844, 563–4. *CB.* Probably Richard H. Horne. (See index under Horne.)

Athenaeum, Oct. 19, 1844, pp. 944–5. *CB.* Probably Henry F. Chorley. (Marchand, 291.)

New Quartelry Review; or, Home, Foreign, and Colonial Journal, V, Apr. 1845, 354, 368–84. Browning's plays from *Straf* through *CB.* Probably Richard H. Horne. (See index under Horne.)

Theologian, II, June 1845, 276–82. *Par.* Archer T. Gurney. (See index under Gurney.)

BELLS AND POMEGRANATES. No. VII. DRAMATIC ROMANCES & LYRICS. By Robert Browning, Author of "Paracelsus." London: Edward Moxon, MDCCCXLV. *DRL.* Nov. 6. *(RB and EBB,* I, 258.)

Examiner, Nov. 15, 1845, pp. 723–4. *DRL.* John Forster.

Douglas Jerrold's Shilling Magazine, II, Dec. 1845, 565–6. *DRL.* Probably Douglas Jerrold. (Nicoll and Wise, I, 581.)

English Review, IV, Dec. 1845, 259, 273–7. *B&P, Par,* and a reference to *Sord.* Bartholomew E. G. Warburton. *(RB and EBB,* I, 279, 301 and 302 n. 1.)

Critic, n.s. II, Dec. 27, 1845, 701–2. *DRL.*

New Monthly Belle Assemblée, XXIV, Jan. 1846, 33, 36–7. *DRL.* Signed Camilla Toulmin.

New Quarterly Review; or, Home, Foreign, and Colonial Journal, VII, Jan. 1846, 141, 152–7. *DRL* and references to *Paul, Par,* and *Sord.* Possibly J. A. Heraud and Thomas Powell. *(RB and EBB,* I, 380. In the bound volume Apr. is shown as the month of this issue, but RB and EBB discuss it in January.)

Oxford and Cambridge Review, and University Magazine, II, Jan. 1846, 102. *DRL.*

Athenaeum, Jan. 17, 1846, pp. 58–9. *DRL.* Henry F. Chorley. (Marchand, p. 291.)

Christian Remembrancer, n.s. XI, Apr. 1846, 316, 324–6, 329–30. *B&P,* Nos. I–VII.

Eclectic Review, 4th ser. XIX, Apr. 1846, 413, 421–6. *B&P,* Nos. I–VII.

BELLS AND POMEGRANATES. No. VIII. and Last. LURIA; and A SOUL'S TRAGEDY. By Robert Browning, Author of "Paracelsus." London: Edward Moxon, MDCCCXLVI. *L&AST.* Apr. 13 *(RB and EBB,* II, 619.)

Examiner, Apr. 25, 1846, pp. 259–60. *L&AST.* John Forster.

New Monthly Magazine and Humorist, LXXVII, May 1846, 124, 125. Brief general comment on *B&P* and one sentence on *L&AST.*

Douglas Jerrold's Shilling Magazine, III, June 1846, 573–4. *L&AST.* Probably Douglas Jerrold. (Nicoll and Wise, I, 582.)

Fraser's Magazine, XXXIII, June 1846, 715–6. General comment on Browning's poetry and specific remarks on two poems in *DRL.*

New Monthly Belle Assemblée, XXIV, June 1846, 370–2. *L&AST.* Probalby Camilla Toulmin. (See index under Toulmin.)

People's Journal, II, July 18, 1846, 38–40. *PP* and references to other works in *B&P.* Signed Henry F. Chorley.

Hood's Magazine, VI, Aug. 1846, 179–84. *L&AST.*

People's Journal, II, Aug. 22, 1846, 104–6. *CB.* Signed Henry F. Chorley.

New Quarterly Review; or, Home, Foreign, and Colonial Journal, VIII, Oct. 1846, 331, 332, 335, 350–2. According to the heading, a review of *L&AST,* actually of plays and long poems, including reference to *Paul.* (The issue containing the review was dated Jan. 1847; it should have been Oct. 1846. Dating the issues three months in advance persisted from the beginning of 1846. My dating agrees with that in Broughton.)

British Quarterly Review, VI, Nov. 1847, 490–509. *B&P* and comments on *Par, Sord,* and *Straf.* George Henry Lewes. (Kaminsky, p. 199; *W Index,* IV, 131 [127].)

Sharpe's London Magazine, VIII, Nov. 1848, 60–2; continued Dec. 1848, 122–7. *PP* and comments on *Par, Sord, Straf,* and *RD.*

PERFORMANCE OF A BLOT. *Blot* 48. Nov. 27, 28, 29; Dec. 7, 8, 9, 1848; Feb. 2, 3, 1849, at the Sadler's Wells Theatre. (These dates are from the playbills.)

Athenaeum, Dec. 2, 1848, p. 1217. *Blot* 48.

Literary Gazette, Dec. 2, 1848, p. 794. *Blot* 48.

Theatrical Times, Dec. 2, 1848, pp. 459–60. *Blot* 48.

Era, Dec. 3, 1848, p. 11. *Blot* 48.

Weekly Dispatch, Dec. 3, 1848, p. 584. *Blot* 48.

Examiner, Dec. 9, 1848, p. 789. *Blot* 48. John Forster.

POEMS by Robert Browning. In Two Volumes. Vol. I. [Vol. II.] A New Edition. London: Chapman & Hall, 1849. *Poems* 49. Dec. 15–23, 1848. (Dec. 15–29, 1848, according to *PC;* announcement on Dec. 2, 1848, by Chapman & Hall in *Athenaeum* of forthcoming publication and advertisement on Dec. 16 and 23 of publication.)

Atlas, XXIV, Jan. 13, 1849, supp., 33–4. *Poems* 49.

Literary Gazette, Mar. 3, 1849, p. 148. *Poems* 49.

English Review, XI, June 1849, 354–86. *Poems* 49.

Eclectic Review, 4th ser. XXVI, Aug. 1849, 203–14. *Poems* 49 and *Sord.* Cyrus Edmunds. *(BSP,* I, 91.)

Examiner, Sept. 8, 1849, p. 565. *Poems* 49. John Forster.

CHRISTMAS-EVE AND EASTER-DAY. A Poem. By Robert Browning. London: Chapman & Hall, 1850. *CEED.* Apr. 1.

Athenaeum, Apr. 6, 1850, pp. 370–1. *CEED.* J. Westland Marston. (Marchand, p. 291.)

Examiner, Apr. 6, 1850, pp. 211–3. *CEED.* John Forster.

Spectator, XXIII, Apr. 6, 1850, 329. *CEED.*

Literary Gazette, Apr. 13, 1850, pp. 260–1. *CEED.*

Critic, n.s. IX, Apr. 15, 1850, 193–4. *CEED.*

Leader, I, Apr. 27, 1850, 111. *CEED.* George Henry Lewes. (Kaminsky, p. 202.)

Germ (title changed to Art and Poetry with no. 3), no. 4, May 1850, pp. 169–73. "Modern Giants." Includes commentary on Browning's poetry. Frederic G. Stephens. (Laura Savage, given as author in table of contents, is identified in William Rossetti's handwriting as F. G. Stephens in the British Library copy; also in Rossetti's introduction to the facsimile reprint of the *Germ,* 1901.)

Germ (now *Art and Poetry*), no. 4, May 1850, pp. 187–92. *CEED.* William M. Rossetti. (Attributed to Rossetti in table of contents.)

Prospective Review, VI, May 1850, 267, 271–9. *CEED.* Probably Richard H. Hutton. (Tener, p. [16]; *W Index,* III, 353 [144].)

Atlas, XXV, May 18, 1850, 314–5. *CEED.*

New Monthly Magazine and Humorist, LXXXIX, June 1850, 268. *CEED.*

English Review, XIV, Sept. 1850, 65, 84–90. *CEED.*

Fraser's Magazine, XLIII, Feb. 1851, 170–7. *Sord, Poems* 49, and *CEED.* Probably Charles Kingsley. *(W Index,* II, 411 [2819].)

Guardian, VI, Mar. 12, 1851, 184. *Poems* 49 and reference to *Sord.*

Christian Remembrancer, n.s. XXI, Apr. 1851, 346–70. *Poems* 49 and *CEED.*

LETTERS OF PERCY BYSSHE SHELLEY. With an INTRODUCTORY ESSAY, by Robert Browning. London: Edward Moxon, 1852. *Essay.* Feb. 14–21. (Feb. 14–28 according to *PC.* First review was on Feb. 21.)

Athenaeum, Feb. 21, 1852, pp. 214–5. *Essay.*

Literary Gazette, Feb. 21, 1852, pp. 173–5. *Essay.*

Spectator, XXV, Feb. 21, 1852, 182–3. *Essay.*

Literary Gazette, Feb. 28, 1852, p. 205. Letter from Q (F. T. Palgrave) raising doubts about the genuineness of the Shelley letters.

Guardian, VII, Mar. 3, 1852, 147–8. *Essay.*

Athenaeum, Mar. 6, 1852, pp. 278–9. Account of the purchase of the letters and discovery of the forgery. Reprinted in *Atlas,* XXX, Mar. 13, 1852, 171–2; and partly quoted in *John Bull,* XXXII, Mar. 13, 1852, 173.

Critic, XI, Mar. 15, 1852, 152–3. Quotation from *Athenaeum,* Mar. 6, and discussion of the *Essay.*

Westminster Review, o.s. LVII, n.s. I, Apr. 1852, 502–11. *Essay.* George Henry Lewes. (Kaminsky, p. 206; *W Index,* III, 617 [1294].)

PERFORMANCE OF COLOMBE'S BIRTHDAY. *CB* 53. Apr. 25, 27, 28, 29, and May 2, 6, 11, 1853, at the Haymarket Theatre and once in Manchester in June. (These dates are from the playbills.)

Daily News, Apr. 26, 1853, p. 6. *CB* 53.

Morning Post, Apr. 26, 1853, p. 6. *CB* 53.

Times, Apr. 26, 1853, p. 6. *CB* 53.

Morning Herald, Apr. 27, 1853, p. 5. *CB* 53. This review also in *Standard* of same date, p. [3].

Athenaeum, Apr. 30, 1853, p. 537. *CB* 53.

Atlas, XXXI, Apr. 30, 1853, 283–4. *CB* 53.

Court Journal, Apr. 30, 1853, p. 279. *CB* 53.

Examiner, Apr. 30, 1853, p. 278. *CB* 53. John Forster.

Illustrated London News, XX, Apr. 30, 1853, 327. *CB* 53.

John Bull, XXXIII, Apr. 30, 1853, 285. *CB* 53.

Literary Gazette, Apr. 30, 1853, p. 435. *CB* 53.

Spectator, XXVI, Apr. 30, 1853, 414. *CB* 53.

Monthly Christian Spectator, III, May 1853, 261–73. *CEED.* Signed G[eorge]. M[ac]. D[onald]. (Reprinted in his *Orts,* 1882.)

Chambers's Edinburgh Journal, n.s. XX, July 16, 1853, 39–41. General review.

MEN AND WOMEN. By Robert Browning. In Two Volumes. Vol. I. [Vol. II.] London: Chapman and Hall, 1855. *MW.* Nov. 10. *(Elizabeth Barrett Browning: Letters to Her Sister, 1846–1859,* ed. Leonard Huxley [London: John Murray, 1929], p. 233; advertisement in *PC;* Ian Jack, "Browning on *Sordello* and *Men and Women:* Unpublished Letters to James T. Fields," *Huntington Library Quarterly,* XLV, Summer 1982, 191.)

Athenaeum, Nov. 17, 1855, pp. 1327–8. *MW.* Henry F. Chorley. (Marchand, p. 292.)

Saturday Review, I, Nov. 24, 1855, 69–70. *MW.* (That Joseph Arnould was possibly the author [see Bevington, pp. 332–3] can be ruled out. See index under Arnould.)

Atlas, no. 1542 (this replaces the customary vol. number), Dec. 1, 1855, pp. 771–2; continued in no. 1545, Dec. 22, 1855, pp. 819–20. *MW.*

Critic, XIV, Dec. 1, 1855, 581–2. *MW.*

Examiner, Dec. 1, 1855, pp. 756–7. *MW.* John Forster.

Leader, VI, Dec. 1, 1855, 1157–8; continued Dec. 8, 1855, 1182–3. *MW.*

Literary Gazette, Dec. 1, 1855, pp. 758–9. *MW.*

Spectator, XXVIII, Dec. 22, 1855, supp., 1346–7. *MW.*

Bentley's Miscellany, XXXIX, Jan. 1856, 64–70. *MW.*

British Quarterly Review, XXIII, Jan. 1856, 151–80. *MW.* David Masson. *(Rossetti to Allingham,* p. 160; *W Index,* IV, 144 [475].)

Fraser's Magazine, LIII, Jan. 1856, 105–16. *MW* and references to some earlier poems. Signed G[eorge]. B[rimley]. — T[rinity]. C[ollege]. C[ambridge]. *(Rossetti to Allingham,* p. 160; *BSP,* I, 92; *W Index,* II, 430 [3435].)

New Quarterly Review, V. Jan. 1856, 17–20. *MW.*

Rambler, o.s. XVII, 2d ser. V, Jan. 1856, 54–71. *MW.* Richard Simpson. *W Index,* II, 767 [732].)

Westminster Review, o.s. LXV, n.s. IX, Jan. 1856, 290–6. *MW.* George Eliot. *(W Index,* III, 624 [1452].)

Guardian, XI, Jan. 9, 1856, 34–5. *MW.*

Blackwood's Edinburgh Magazine, LXXIX, Feb. 1856, 135, 136–7. *MW.* Margaret Oliphant. *(Autobiography and Letters of Mrs. M. O. W. Oliphant,* ed. Mrs. Harry Coghill [New York: Dodd, Mead & Co., 1899], pp. 160–1, 445; *W Index,* I, 101 [3450].)

Irish Quarterly Review, VI, Mar. 1856, 1, 21–8. *MW.* Signed N. J. G. Probably Nicholas J. Gannon. (Signed "N. J. G.," a series of articles on "The Characteristic Errors of Our Most Distinguished Living Poets" appeared in the *IQR.* Under his name, Nicholas J. Gannon published them as a book, with the same title. See Index under Gannon.)

Oxford and Cambridge Magazine, no. 3, Mar. 1856, pp. 162–72. *MW.* William Morris. (Reprinted in vol. I of *The Collected Works of William Morris,* 1910.)

Christian Remembrancer, n.s. XXXI, Apr. 1856, 267, 281–94. *MW.*

Dublin University Magazine, XLVII, June 1856, 673–5. *MW.* (Robert Lytton was the author according to *W Index,* IV, 299 [2678]. The attribution is doubtful. See index under Robert Lytton.)

London Quarterly Review, VI, July 1856, 493–501. *MW.* Thomas McNicoll. (Reprinted in his *Essays on English Literature,* 1861.)

Christian Remembrancer, n.s. XXXIV, Oct. 1857, 361–90. General review. J. G. Cazenova. (Archives of the *W Index* at Wellesley College.)

North British Review, XXXIV, May 1861, 350–74. General review. Gerald Massey. (See *W Index,* I, 685 [639], and III, 998 [639].)

Jersey Independent, Feb. 20, 1862. *MW.* Signed T[homson]. J[ames]. (I have used the reprint in *The Speedy Extinction of Evil and Misery: Selected Prose of James Thomson* [B.V.], ed. William Schaeffer [Berkeley: Univ. of California Press, 1967], pp. 208–13.)

SELECTIONS FROM THE POETICAL WORKS OF ROBERT BROWNING. London: Chapman and Hall, 1863. *Sel.* 63. Dec. 22, 1862. *(Letters of the Brownings to George Barrett,* ed. Paul Landis and Ronald E. Freeman [Urbana: Univ. of Illinois Press, 1958], p. 283.)

Fraser's Magazine, LXVII, Feb. 1863, 240–56. General review. Signed Shirley, pseud. for John Skelton. (Reprinted in his *A Campaigner at Home,* 1865.)

Chambers's Journal, 3d ser. XIX, Feb. 7, 1863, 91–5. *Sel* 63.

Saturday Review, XV, Feb. 7, 1863, 179–80. *Sel.* 63. W. B. Donne. (Broughton, p. 101; Litzinger and Smalley, p. 303. No attribution by Bevington.)

Critic, XXV, Mar. 1863, 273–4. *Sel.* 63. (The *Critic* became a monthly in 1862 and thereafter was dated by the month.)

London Review, VI, Mar. 21, 1863, 310–2. *Sel* 63.

THE POETICAL WORKS OF ROBERT BROWNING. Volume I. *Lyrics, Romances, Men, and Women.* Third Edition. London: Chapman and Hall, 1863. *PW* 63 I. May 1–14. *(PC.)*

Eclectic Review, 6th ser. IV, May 1863, 436–54. *Sel* 63 and a reference to *Paul.* Edwin P. Hood. *(BSP,* I, 135; Nicoll and Wise, I, 586.)

Reader, I, May 30, 1863, 523–4. *PW* 63 I.

London Quarterly Review, XX, July 1863, 527–32. *Sel* 63. F. T. Marzials. (Broughton, p. 101; this assignment of authorship was adopted by *W Index,* IV, 393 [415].)

THE POETICAL WORKS OF ROBERT BROWNING. Volume II. *Tragedies and Other Plays.* Third Edition. London: Chapman and Hall, 1863. *PW* 63 II. June 15–30. *(PC.)*

Guardian, XVIII, July 15, 1863, 671. *PW* 63 I.

Weldon's Register, Aug. 1863, pp. 521–3. *PW* 63 I.

Guardian, XVIII, Aug. 5, 1863, 742. *PW* 63 II.

Saturday Review, XVI, Aug. 15, 1863, 222–4. *PW* 63 II. W. B. Donne. *(William Bodham Donne and His Friends,* ed. Catharine B. Johnson [London: Methuen & Co., 1905], p. 343; Bevington, pp. 211, 309, 340.)

Spectator, XXXVI, Sept. 5, 1863, 2460–2. *PW* 63 I–II. Probably Richard H. Hutton. (Tener, p. [19].)

THE POETICAL WORKS OF ROBERT BROWNING. Volume III. *Paracelsus, Christmas-Eve and Easter-Day, Sordello.* Third Edition. London: Chapman and Hall, 1863. *PW* 63 III. Sept. 1–14. *(PC.)*

London Review, VII, Sept. 19, 1863, 310–1. *PW* 63 I.

Critic, XXV, Oct. 1863, 476. *PW* 63 I–II.

National Review, XVII, Oct. 1863, 417–46. *PW* 63 I–III. Richard H. Hutton. (This and parts of his three reviews of *The Ring and the Book* in the *Spectator* [Dec. 12, 1868; Jan. 30, 1869; Mar. 13, 1869] were reprinted, with a number of changes, as one of his *Essays Theological and Literary,* Vol. II, 1871.)

Guardian, XVIII, Dec. 9, 1863, 1155. *PW* 63 III.

Victoria Magazine, II, Feb. 1864, 298–316. *PW* 63 I–III and a reference to *Paul.* Signed M. D. Conway.

Reader, III, Feb. 27, 1864, 264. On the rumor of a forthcoming work by RB.

London Quarterly Review, XXII, Apr. 1864, 30–47. *PW* 63 I–III. F. T. Marzials. *(W Index* assigned the review in the *London Quarterly* of July 1863 to Marzials, and on the basis of similarity of content and wording also assigned this one to him. See IV, 393 [435].)

DRAMATIS PERSONAE. By Robert Browning. London: Chapman and Hall, 1864. *DP.* May 28.

Morning Star, June 2, 1864, p. 3. *DP.* M. D. Conway. (Moncure Daniel Conway, *Autobiography: Memories and Experiences* [Boston: Houghton, Mifflin & Co., 1904], II, 21.)

Athenaeum, June 4, 1864, pp. 765–7. *DP.* Gerald Massey. (Marchand, p. 292.)

Examiner, June 4, 1864, p. 360. *DP.*

Reader, III, June 4, 1864, 704–5. *DP.* Julia Wedgwood? (See p. 39, n. 1, in *Robert Browning and Julia Wedgwood,* ed. Richard Curle [New York: Frederick A. Stokes Co., 1937].)

Saturday Review, XVII, June 18, 1864, 753–4. *DP.*

Spectator, XXXVII, June 18, 1864, 711–2. *DP.* Probably Richard H. Hutton. (Tener, p. [20].)

London Review, VIII, June 25, 1864, 683–5. *DP.*

British Quarterly Review, XL, July 1864, 264. *DP.*

Eclectic and Congregational Review, 6th ser. VII, July 1864, 62–72. *DP.* Edwin P. Hood. *(BSP,* I, 136; Nicoll and Wise, I, 587.)

Englishwoman's Domestic Magazine, n.s. IX, July 1864, 139–40. *DP.*

St. James's Magazine, X, July 1864, 477–91. *DP.* Signed R. B. (Attributed by Litzinger and Smalley [p. 223] to Robert Bell, 1800–67; and by Broughton [p. 102] to R. B[ell], who is confused with R. A. Bell [an illustrator] in the index.)

Spiritual Magazine, V, July 1864, 310–7. "Mr. Robert Browning on Spiritualism." Robert Cooper. (Horace Wyndham, *Mr. Sludge, the Medium* [London: Geoffrey Bles, 1937], pp. 131–2.) Followed by "Mr. Home's Account" of a séance in Ealing in 1855 attended by Elizabeth and Robert.

Victoria Magazine, III, July 1864, 282–3. *DP.*

Guardian, XIX, July 20, 1864, 722. *DP.*

DRAMATIS PERSONAE. By Robert Browning. Second Edition. London: Chapman and Hall, 1864. *DP* 2d. Sept. 15–30. *(PC;* advertised by Chapman and Hall in the *Examiner* on Sept. 24 and in the *Athenaeum* on Oct. 8.)

Eclectic and Congregational Review, 6th ser. VII, Oct. 1864, 361, 372–89. *DP.*

Edinburgh Review, CXX, Oct. 1864, 537–65. *PW* 63 and *DP.* William Stigand. *(W Index,* I, 514 [2636].) Replies to this review appeared in *Examiner,* Oct. 15, 1864, p. 664; *London Review,* IX, Oct. 15, 1864, 440; *Reader,* IV, Nov. 26, 1864, 674–5, signed Gerald Massey; *Saturday Review,* XIX, Jan. 7, 1865, 15–7.

Dublin University Magazine, LXIV, Nov. 1864, 573–9. *DP* and references to earlier works. T. C. Irwin. *(W Index,* IV, 327 [3744].)

National Review, o.s. XIX, n.s. I, Nov. 1864, 27–67. "Wordsworth, Tennyson, and Browning; or, Pure, Ornate, and Grotesque Art in English Poetry." Signed W[alter]. B[agehot]. (Reprinted in *Studies by the Late Walter Bagehot,* ed. R. H. Hutton, II, 1879.)

Christian Spectator, n.s. VI, Jan. 1865, 44–57. *DP* 2d. Signed G.

Times, Jan. 11, 1865, p. 12. *PW* 63 and *DP.* Eneas S. Dallas. (Morison, *The Times,* II, 484.)

New Monthly Magazine, CXXXIII, Feb. 1865, 186–94. *DP* 2d. Signed T. Fred[erick]. Wedmore.

THE POETICAL WORKS OF ROBERT BROWNING. Vols. I–III. Fourth Edition. London: Chapman and Hall, 1865. *PW* 65. Mar. 15–31. *(PC.)* Each vol. has a subtitle corresponding with that in the 3d ed.

St. James's Magazine, XIII, June 1865, 363–72. Account of lives of Fra Lippo Lippi and Andrea del Sarto drawing on Browning's presentation. Signed T. Frederick Wedmore.

Quarterly Review, CXVIII, July 1865, 77–105. *PW* 63 and *DP.* Gerald Massey. *(W Index,* I, 747 [1492].) Discussed in *London Review,* XI, July 15, 1865, 74; *Spectator,* XXXVIII, July 15, 1865, 788.)

A SELECTION FROM THE WORKS OF ROBERT BROWNING. Moxon's Miniature Poets [first line on title page]. London: Edward Moxon & Co., 1865. *Sel* 65. Oct. 2–14. *(PC.)*

Reader, VI, Oct. 14, 1865, 427. *Sel* 65.

Public Opinion, VIII, Oct. 21, 1865, 434. *Sel* 65.

Public Opinion, VIII, Nov. 25, 1865, 563–4. A letter concerning the comparative merits of Browning and Tennyson. Signed W. J. Metcalfe.

Fortnightly Review, III, Dec. 1, 1865, 256. *Sel* 65. Signed Editor. (George Henry Lewes.)

Marlburian, I, Mar. 21, 1866, 91–3. General discussion of Browning's poetry. Signed V. E. P. N. (W. J. Greenwell, according to letter from Gerald W. Murray, Librarian of Marlborough College, 20 Sept. 1967.)

Contemporary Review, IV, Jan. 1867, 1–15; continued in IV, Feb. 1867, 133–48. General review. (According to *W Index,* I, 216 [98, 106], Henry Alford was probably the writer of this two-part review, but see *W Index,* II, 1191 [98, 106], for retraction of attribution.)

Fraser's Magazine, LXXVI, Oct. 1867, 518–30. "Mr. Browning's *Sordello.* First Paper." Signed Edward Dowden. (Part of the First Paper reprinted in "Tennyson and Browning" in his *Studies in Literature,* 1878, and another part, along with the unpublished Second Paper, in his *Transcripts and Studies,* 1888.)

Marlburian, II, Nov. 6, 1867, 173–4. Defense of Browning's obscurity. Signed V. P. V. D. (Unidentified.)

THE POETICAL WORKS OF ROBERT BROWNING. M.A., Honorary Fellow of Balliol College, Oxford. Vols. I–VI. Vol. I. *Pauline — Paracelsus — Strafford.* [Vols. II–VI with contents designated.] London: Smith, Elder and Co., 1868. *PW* 68. Vol. I, Mar. 2; II, Apr. 1; III, May 1; IV, June 1; V, July 1; VI, Oct. 1. (Each of the first five volumes was advertised in *PC* under the heading "Now ready" or "Ready this day," but there was no such heading covering the six volumes listed together in the advertisement for Oct. 1. It specified the contents of each volume including VI, which might actually not have been ready until a later date.)

Guardian, XXIII, Aug. 5, 1868, 892. *PW* 68.

Free Churchman and Christian Spectator, I, Oct. 1868, 888–97; continued Nov. 1868, 986–1002. *PW* 68 and *Essays on Robert Browning's Poetry* by John T. Nettleship. Signed Aug[ustus]. S. Wilkins, M.A.

THE RING AND THE BOOK. By Robert Browning, M.A., Honorary Fellow of Balliol College, Oxford. In Four Volumes. Volume I. London: Smith, Elder and Co., 1868. *R&B* I. Nov. 21.

Eclectic and Congregational Review, 6th ser. XV, Dec. 1868, 441–70. *PW* 68. Edwin P. Hood. *(BSP,* I, 139; Nicoll and Wise, I, 590.)

North British Review, o.s. XLIX, n.s. X, Dec. 1868, 353–408. *Sel* 63, *PW* 63, *DP, Sel* 65, *PW* 68, and *Essays on Robert Browning's Poetry* by John T. Nettleship. James H. Stirling. *(W Index,* I, 692 [894].)

St. James's Magazine, n.s. II, Dec. 1868, 460–4. *R&B* I.

Daily Telegraph, Dec. 4, 1868, p. 5. *R&B* I.

London Review, XVII, Dec. 5, 1868, 619–20. *R&B* I.

Spectator, XLI, Dec. 12, 1868, 1464–6. *R&B* I. Richard H. Hutton. (About one-fourth of this review was reprinted in his *Essays Theological and Literary,* Vol. II, 1871; see above, *National Review,* Oct. 1863.)

THE RING AND THE BOOK. By Robert Browning, M.A., Honorary Fellow of Balliol College, Oxford. In Four Volumes. Volume II. London: Smith, Elder and Co., 1868. *R&B* II. Dec. 26.

Athenaeum, Dec. 26, 1868, pp. 875–6. *R&B* I. Robert Buchanan. (Reprinted in his *Master-Spirits,* 1873.)

Saturday Review, XXVI, Dec. 26, 1868, 832–4. *R&B* I.

British Quarterly Review, XLIX, Jan. 1869, 248–9. *R&B* I. Mortimer Collins. (Litzinger and Smalley, p. 306; *W Index* names no reviewer for Jan. 1869 — it assigns the review in *BQR* of Apr. 1869 to Collins.)

Fortnightly, o.s. XI, n.s. V, Jan. 1869, 117–8. In the first part of a review of W. W. Story's *Graffiti d'Italia,* identification of Browning as the innovator and master of the psychological school of petry. Signed H. Buxton Forman. (This discussion of Browning, along with criticism of him in the *London Quarterly Review* of July 1869, was reprinted in Forman's *Our Living Poets,* 1871.)

Fortnightly, o.s. XI, n.s. V., Jan. 1869, 125–6. *R&B* I.

Macmillan's Magazine, XIX, Jan. 1869, 258–62. *R&B* I. Signed John Addington Symonds.

Tinsley's Magazine, III. Jan. 1869, 665–74. *R&B* I. Signed W. B. (Attributed to Walter Bagehot with a question mark by Broughton, p. 108; but see *The Collected Works of Walter Bagehot,* ed. Norman St John-Stevas [Cambridge, Mass.: Harvard Univ. Press, 1965), I, 20, for discreditation of the authorship.)

Westminster Review, o.s. XCI, n.s. XXXV, Jan. 1869, 298–300. *R&B* I. J. R. Wise. *(W Index,* III, 643 [1920].)

Illustrated London News, LIV, Jan. 16, 1869, 74. *R&B* I–II.

Guardian, XXIV, Jan. 20, 1869, 73–4. *R&B* I–II.

THE RING AND THE BOOK. By Robert Browning, M.A., Honorary Fellow of Balliol College, Oxford. In Four Volumes. Volume III. London: Smith, Elder and Co., 1869. *R&B* III. Jan. 30.
Press and St. James's Chronicle, Jan. 30, 1869, pp. 2–3. *R&B* I.
Spectator, XLII, Jan. 30, 1869, 139–41. *R&B* II. Richard H. Hutton. (Not quite a fourth of this review was reprinted in his *Essays Theological and Literary,* Vol. II, 1871; see above, *National Review,* Oct. 1863.)
THE RING AND THE BOOK. By Robert Browning. M.A., Honorary Fellow of Balliol College, Oxford. In Four Volumes. Volume IV. London: Smith Elder and Co., 1869. *R&B* IV. Feb. 27.
Cornhill Magazine, XIX, Feb. 1869, 249–56. *R&B* I–II. Frederick Greenwood. *(W Index,* I, 347 [919].)
Fortnightly Review, o.s. XI, n.s. V, Mar. 1869, 331–43. *R&B* I–IV. Signed Editor. (John Morley.)
Spectator, XLII, Mar. 13, 1869, 324–5. *R&B* III–IV. Richard H. Hutton. (Over half of this review was reprinted in his *Essays Theological and Literary,* Vol. II, 1871; see above, *National Review,* Oct. 1863.)
Morning Star, Mar. 15, 1869, p. 5. *R&B* I–IV.
Athenaeum, Mar. 20, 1869, pp. 399–400. *R&B* II–IV. Robert Buchanan. (Reprinted in his *Master-Spirits,* 1873.)
Guardian, XXIV, Mar. 24, 1869, 343–4. *R&B* III–IV.
Scotsman, Mar. 26, 1869, p. 6. *R&B* I–IV.
Illustrated London News, LIV, Mar. 27, 1869, 322. *R&B* III–IV.
British Quarterly Review, XLIX, Apr. 1869, 435–59. *PW* 63, *DP, R&B* I–IV. Mortimer Collins. *(W Index,* IV, 159 [1024].)
Macmillan's Magazine, XIX, Apr. 1869, 544–52. *R&B* I–IV. Signed J. R. Mozley.
Quarterly Review, CXXVI, Apr. 1869, 328, 340–8. *PW* [undated], *R&B* I–IV. J. R. Mozley. *(W Index,* I, 751 [1630].)
Westminster Review, o.s. XCI, n.s. XXXV, Apr. 1869, 577–8. *R&B* II–IV. J. R. Wise *(W Index,* III, 643 [1930].)
Saturday Review, XXVII, Apr. 3, 1869, 460–1. *R&B* I–IV.
Examiner and London Review, Apr. 17, 1869, pp. 244–5. *R&B* I–IV.
Temple Bar, XXVI, June 1869, 316–33. Extended denial that RB was a poet. Alfred Austin. (Reprinted in his *Poetry of the Period,* 1870.)
Times, June 11, 1869, p. 4. *R&B* I–IV. Blair Leighton. (Morison, *The Times,* II, 485.)
Dublin Review, n.s. XIII, July 1869, 48–62. *R&B* I–IV. John Doherty. *(W Index,* II, 80 [1277].)
Edinburgh Review, CXXX, July 1869, 164–86. *R&B* I–IV. Julian H. C. Fane. *(W Index,* I, 518 [2816].)
London Quarterly Review, XXXII, July 1869, 325–57. *R&B* and all earlier works. "Robert Browning and the Epic of Psychology." H. Buxton Forman. (Reprinted, along with part of his signed review of W. W. Story's

Graffiti d'Italia in *Fortnightly* of January 1869, in his *Our Living Poets*, 1871.)

Chambers's Journal, 4th ser. VI, July 24, 1869, 473–6. *R&B* I–II.

North British Review, o.s. LI, n.s. XII, Oct. 1869, 97–126. *R&B* I–IV. Richard Simpson. (*W Index*, I, 693 [920].)

Fraser's Magazine, LXXX, Nov. 1869, 670–8. *R&B* I–IV. Signed Shirley, pseud. for John Skelton.

Month, XI, Dec. 1869, 618–24. *R&B* I–IV.

St. Pauls [no apostrophe appears in title, but I insert it in my citations], VII, Dec. 1870, 257–76; continued in VII, Jan. 1871, 377–97. *PW* 63, *DP, R&B* I–IV. Signed E[lizabeth]. J. H[asell]. (*W Index*, III, 376 [303].)

Notes

Abbreviations

Allingham: A Diary	*William Allingham: A Diary*, ed. H. Allingham and D. Radford. London: Macmillan & Co., 1907.
Arnould	Letters from Joseph Arnould to Alfred Domett, belonging to the Arnould family.
Baylor	Armstrong Browning Library, Baylor University.
Berg	Berg Collection, New York Public Library.
British Library	British Library, British Museum.
Browning to American Friends	*Browning to His American Friends: Letters between the Brownings, the Storys, and James Russell Lowell, 1841–1890*, ed. Gertrude R. Hudson. London: Bowes & Bowes, 1965.
Brownings to George Barrett	*Letters of the Brownings to George Barrett*, ed. Paul Landis and Ronald E. Freeman. Urbana: Univ. of Illinois Press, 1958.
Dearest Isa	*Dearest Isa: Robert Browning's Letters to Isabella Blagden*, ed. Edward C. McAleer. Austin: Univ. of Texas Press, 1951.
DeVane	William C. DeVane, *A Browning Handbook*, 2d ed. New York: Appleton-Century-Crofts, 1955.
EBB	Elizabeth Barrett Browning.
EBB Letters	*The Letters of Elizabeth Barrett Browning*, ed. Frederic G. Kenyon. Two vols. London: Smith, Elder, & Co., 1897.
EB to Mitford	*Elizabeth Barrett to Miss Mitford*, ed. Betty Miller. London: John Murray, 1954.
EBB to Sister	*Elizabeth Barrett Browning: Letters to Her Sister, 1846–1859*, ed. Leonard Huxley. London: John Murray, 1929.
Forster and Dyce	Forster and Dyce Collection, South Kensington Museum.

582

Gosse	Edmund Gosse, *Robert Browning: Personalia.* London: T. Fisher Unwin, 1890.
Greer	Louise Greer, *Browning and America.* Chapel Hill: Univ. of North Carolina Press, 1952.
Griffin and Minchin	W. H. Griffin and H. C. Minchin, *The Life of Robert Browning,* 3d ed. rev. London: Methuen & Co., 1938.
Houghton	Houghton Library, Harvard University.
Irvine and Honan	William Irvine and Park Honan, *The Book, the Ring, and the Poet: A Biography of Robert Browning.* New York: McGraw-Hill Book Co., 1974.
Letters, Hood	*Letters of Robert Browning Collected by T. J. Wise,* ed. T. L. Hood. New Haven: Yale Univ. Press, 1933.
Litzinger and Smalley	*Browning: The Critical Heritage,* ed. Boyd Litzinger and Donald Smalley. New York: Barnes & Noble, 1970.
Lounsbury	Thomas R. Lounsbury, *The Early Literary Career of Robert Browning.* New York: Charles Scribner's Sons, 1911.
Macready	*The Diaries of William Charles Macready, 1833–1851,* ed. William Toynbee. Two vols. London: Chapman & Hall, 1912.
Maynard	John Maynard, *Browning's Youth.* Cambridge, Mass.: Harvard Univ. Press, 1977.
MLN	*Modern Language Notes.*
Murray	Mr. John Murray, holder of copyright on unpublished material by Robert and Elizabeth Barrett Browning.
New Letters	*New Letters of Robert Browning,* ed. William C. DeVane and Kenneth L. Knickerbocker. New Haven: Yale Univ. Press, 1950.
NYPL	New York Public Library.
Orr	Mrs. Sutherland Orr, *Life and Letters of Robert Browning,* rev. Frederic G. Kenyon. Boston: Houghton Mifflin Co., 1908.
PMLA	*Publications of the Modern Language Association of America.*
P.R.B. Journal	*The P.R.B. Journal: William Michael Rossetti's Diary of the Pre-Raphaelite Brotherhood, 1849–1853,* ed. William E. Fredeman. Oxford: Clarendon Press, 1975.
RB	Robert Browning.

RB and AD — *Robert Browning and Alfred Domett*, ed. Frederic G. Kenyon. New York: E. P. Dutton & Co., 1906.

RB and EBB — *The Letters of Robert Browning and Elizabeth Barrett Barrett, 1845–1846*, ed. Elvan Kintner. Two vols. Cambridge, Mass.: Belknap Press of Harvard Univ. Press, 1969.

RB and JW — *Robert Browning and Julia Wedgwood: A Broken Friendship as Revealed by Their Letters*, ed. Richard Curle. New York: Frederick A. Stokes Co., 1937.

Rossetti Papers, 1862 to 1870 — *Rossetti Papers, 1862 to 1870*, comp. William Michael Rossetti. London: Sands & Co., 1903.

Sotheby — *The Browning Collections. Catalogue of . . . the Property of R. W. Barrett Browning. . . .* (Catalogue of auction held by Sotheby . . . May 1913).

Texas — University of Texas.

Wellesley — Wellesley College.

Works of Browning, ed. Jack and Smith — *The Poetical Works of Robert Browning*, ed. Ian Jack and Margaret Smith. Oxford: Clarendon Press. Vols. I and II, 1983, 1984.

Yale — Yale University.

Notes

CHAPTER I: *A Boyish Work*

  1. *RB and EBB*, II, 998–9, [Aug. 25, 1846].

  2. For earlier accounts of Fox and of the Flower sisters, see the following: Moncure D. Conway, *Centenary History of the South Place Society* (London: Williams & Norgate, 1894); Richard and Edward Garnett, *The Life of W. J. Fox* (London: John Lane, Bodley Head, 1910). The association of Browning with Fox is discussed by his daughter in F. L. Bridell-Fox, "Robert Browning," *Argosy*, XLIX, Feb. 1890, 108–14. Browning's comment on Eliza's genius for musical composition is in Conway's *South Place Society*, p. 89. See Maynard, particularly pp. 179–92, for the most instructive recent account of Fox and of the Flower sisters.

  3. *Letters*, Hood, p. 20, to R. H. Horne, Dec. 3, 1848. Sarah's comment is as follows: ". . . you shall hear what a delicious treat you may expect when you have turned over a new leaf. . . . I do most positively forbid your reading that Genius's poetry tho' I grant it looks very tempting until you have waded thro' the prosy part. . . . shall I tell you whose *mine* these gems come from? — and yet I wish they were *mine* with all my soul — and I'm sure it would be worth all *my* soul if they were . . . . They are 'the boy' Browning's *aet.* 14 — and so they as well as he can speak for themselves." (Bertram Dobell, "The Earliest Poems of Robert Browning," *Cornhill Magazine*, n.s. XXXVI, Jan. 1914, 18.)

  4. In a letter to Fanny Haworth, printed in part by Orr, pp. 95–7, and in full by H. C. Minchin, "A Letter from Hanover Cottage," *Bookman*, LXXXVI, Apr. 1934, 6–7. The letter is dated ca. Aug. 1, 1837, by DeVane (p. 132).

  5. Orr, p. 33; also quoted in Griffin and Minchin, pp. 42–3.

  6. *Letters*, Hood, p. 20, to Horne, Dec. 3, 1848.

  7. In the copy of *Pauline* that Mill marked, in Browning's explanation following a criticism of Mill's at the end of the poem. See Maynard, pp. 210 and 434 n. 49, and p. 222, for a different dating of the conception. See also Gosse, p. 27.

  8. *RB and EBB*, I, 389, [Jan. 15, 1846]. See DeVane, pp. 40–1, for date of composition.

  9. Orr, p. 52, n.d.

  10. Ibid., pp. 52–3, n.d.

  11. Ibid., p. 53, [po. Mar. 29, 1833].

  12. The letter from which the excerpt was taken was published in part in R. and E. Garnett, *Fox*, p. 110, and in full in *The Earlier Letters of John Stuart Mill, 1812–1848* (vols. XII and XIII of *Collected Works of John Stuart Mill*), ed. Francis E. Mineka (Toronto: Univ. of Toronto Press, 1963), XII, 157–8.

  13. *Earlier Letters of Mill*, XII, 159.

14. Ibid., p. 133.

15. Ibid., p. 162.

16. Ibid., p. 174.

17. *Letters,* Hood, p. 195, to F. J. Furnivall, Aug. 29, 1881.

18. *Earlier Letters of Mill,* XII, 185.

19. See the following: M. A. Phillips, "John Stuart Mill and Browning's 'Pauline,' " *Cornhill Magazine,* XXXII, May 1912, 671–7; William Lyon Phelps, "Notes on Browning's *Pauline,"* MLN, XLVII, May 1932, 292–9; Lewis F. Haines, "Mill and *Pauline:* The 'Review' that 'Retarded' Browning's Fame," MLN, LIX, June 1944, 410–12; Masao Miyoshi, "Mill and 'Pauline': The Myth and Some Facts," *Victorian Studies,* IX, Dec. 1965, 154–63; O. P. Govil, "A Note on Mill and Browning's *Pauline,"* *Victorian Poetry,* IV, Autumn 1966, 287–91. My discussion was written before the publication of the article by Miyoshi. He and I have much the same contention concerning the widespread notion of the effect of Mill's criticism on Browning though I employ a different approach. Two more articles on the annotated copy were published in the seventies: William S. Peterson and Fred L. Standley, "The J. S. Mill Marginalia in Robert Browning's *Pauline:* A History and Transcription," *Papers of the Bibliographical Society of America,* LXVI, 1972, 135–70; Michael A. Burr, "Browning's Note to Forster," *Victorian Poetry,* XII, 1974, 343–9. I have depended on my own examination of the annotated copy and have drawn my own conclusions.

20. Those who have examined the handwriting of these notes have not agreed on the authorship. Phillips said that they were written by Forster and Mill; according to Phelps, the technical assistant at the Victoria and Albert Museum said in 1912: "The notes are by one consistent hand throughout. . . ." F. A. Hayek was the first to suggest that some of the notes were written by Harriet Taylor (*John Stuart Mill and Harriet Taylor* [London: Routledge & Kegan Paul, 1951], p. 43).

21. Orr, p. 66, to Fox, Apr. 16, 1835.

22. *RB and EBB,* I, 28, [Feb. 26]; 75, [May 24].

23. Ibid., I, 389, [Jan. 15, 1846].

24. See Betty Miller, *Robert Browning: A Portrait* (London: John Murray, 1952), pp. 38–9.

25. For the discussion of *Pauline,* see letters exchanged in Jan. 1846 in *RB and EBB,* I, 374–408.

26. *RB and AD,* p. 141.

27. Arthur A. Adrian, "The Browning-Rossetti Friendship: Some Unpublished Letters," PMLA, LXXIII, Dec. 1958, 538.

28. Thomas Powell, *The Living Authors of England* (New York: D. Appleton & Co., 1849); *Pictures of the Living Authors of Britain* (London: Partridge & Oakey, 1851).

29. *New Letters,* p. 157.

30. *Letters,* Hood, p. 251, July 6, 1886.

31. "Notes on Browning's *Pauline,"* MLN, XLVII, May 1932, 295.

32. "Intimate Glimpses from Browning's Letter File," *Baylor University's Browning Interests,* 8th ser., 1934, p. 37. Shepherd's letter was published after Phelps wrote his article on the Forster-Mill copy of *Pauline.*

33. *Rossetti Papers, 1862 to 1870,* p. 299.

34. *Memoirs of the Life and Writings of Thomas Carlyle,* ed. Richard Herne Shepherd, asst. Charles N. Williamson (London: W. H. Allen & Co., 1881), II, 271.

35. DeVane, p. 48, n. 23; Irvine and Honan, p. 42.

36. *The Earlier Poems of Elizabeth Barrett Browning, 1826–1833* (London: Bartholomew Robson, 1878). The *Athenaeum* expressed strong disapproval of the reprinting of the

early poems, and Shepherd brought a suit for libel against the publisher of the *Athenaeum*. See Park Honan, "Browning's Testimony on His Essay on Shelley in 'Shepherd v. Francis,' " *English Language Notes*, II, Sept. 1964, 27−31.

37. Browning wrote to T. J. Wise on July 6, 1886: "If it really *does* interest you to have my statement 'in black and white,' I willingly repeat that to the best of my belief no single copy of the original edition of *Pauline* found a buyer. . . ." *(Letters,* Hood, p. 251.) The account of Sarianna Browning, who reputedly had an excellent memory, varied slightly. A letter signed by Browning's son and printed in *Literature* (VIII, Apr. 6, 1901, 276) has the statement that according to Miss Browning "few copies had been sold."

38. See the letter in *Literature* of Apr. 6, 1901.

39. For an account of these as well as other copies, see Mary Dean Reneau, "First Editions of Browning's *Pauline,*" *Baylor University Browning Interests,* 2d ser., 1931, pp. 41−50; Fannie Ratchford, "Browning's *Pauline* Comes to Texas," *Southwest Review,* XXVIII, Spring 1943, 280−9; British Library MS, Ashley Collection B 2530.

40. *Letters,* Hood, pp. 248, to Furnivall, May 25, 1886; 253, to Wise, Aug. 8, 1886.

41. Ibid., pp. 286 and xiii.

42. Orr, p. 380, to George Murray Smith.

43. See DeVane, p. 40; *Pauline by Robert Browning, The Text of 1833, Compared with That of 1867 and 1888,* ed. N. H. Wallis (London: Univ. of London Press, 1931); *Works of Browning,* ed. Jack and Smith, I, 16−7.

44. *New Letters,* p. 360, to C. Butler, June 25, 1888.

45. In addition to Reneau and Ratchford, see "Pauline," *Athenaeum,* Apr. 29, 1905, p. 532; "Pauline," *Poet-Lore,* XIII, 1901, 315.

46. *Letters,* Hood, p. 195, Aug. 29, 1881.

47. Gosse, p. 28.

48. Frederick W. Farrar, *Men I Have Known* (New York: Thomas Y. Crowell & Co., 1897), pp. 64−5.

49. Oscar Browning, *Memories of Sixty Years* (London: John Lane, Bodley Head, 1910), pp. 119−20.

50. Frances Horner, *Time Remembered* (London: William Heinemann, 1933), p. 33.

51. See F. Parvin Sharpless, *The Literary Criticism of John Stuart Mill,* Studies in English Literature, vol. XXXIII (The Hague: Mouton, 1967), p. 105.

CHAPTER II: *Evidences of a New Genius for Dramatic Poetry*

1. The dedication reads: "Inscribed to the Comte A. de Ripert-Monclar, by his affectionate friend, Robert Browning." For a discussion of Monclar and the friendship between him and Browning, see Maynard, pp. 121−6.

2. See *Works of Browning,* ed. Jack and Smith, I, 110.

3. F. L. Bridell-Fox, "Robert Browning," *Argosy,* XLIX, Feb. 1890, 112. This description was written by the daughter of William Johnson Fox under her married name.

4. Orr, p. 64.

5. Ibid., p. 65.

6. Texas MS, RB to Mrs. William Bridges Adams (née Sarah Flower), undated.

7. Orr, p. 67. See also Bridell-Fox, "Robert Browning," p. 110.

8. Orr, p. 66, Apr. 16, 1835.

9. The letter to Mrs. Adams (see n. 6), which more than likely refers to *Paracelsus,* shows that finding a publisher and reading the poem to Mr. Fox were Browning's concerns of the moment. "By the way, I received a note from Miss Sturtevant the other day, in which among other matters she tells me something about Mr Fox's expecting me to go &

read my work to him & to Miss Flower — some mistake, I imagine; I was certainly to have that honor, but Mr F was to write & appoint time & place — & I only got Miss Flower's address last week at Camden Town. I called on Mr Fox at Finsbury last Sunday, & expect to hear from him soon about this business which I want to have over as soon as possible." Browning later wrote Fanny Haworth (ca. Aug. 1, 1837) that he had read *Paracelsus* in manuscript to Fox and that Fox had "got a publisher" for the poem (H. C. Minchin, "A Letter from Hanover Cottage," *Bookman,* LXXXVI, Apr. 1934, 6).

10. Orr, p. 54, Mar. 31, 1833; pp. 64–5, Apr. 2, 1835; p. 65, Apr. 16, 1835.

11. Minchin, "A Letter from Hanover Cottage," p. 6; *New Letters,* p. 17, to Fanny Haworth, [Apr. 1839].

12. *Sonnet* ("Eyes, calm beside thee"), n.s. VIII, Oct. 1834, 712; *The King* ("A King lived long ago"), n.s. IX, Nov. 1835, 707–8; *Porphyria,* n.s. X, Jan. 1836, 43–4; *Johannes Agricola,* n.s. X, Jan. 1836, 45–6; *Lines* ("Still ailing, wind?"), n.s. X, May 1836, 270–1. "A King lived long ago" was later used in *Pippa Passes,* and "Still ailing, wind?" was later used in *James Lee's Wife.*

13. Orr, p. 66, Apr. 16, 1835.

14. *The Autobiography of Leigh Hunt,* ed. J. E. Morpurgo (London: Cresset Press, 1949), p. 428.

15. Reference to Macready's *Diaries* is made by entry date, which is specified in either my text or a note.

16. *Harriet Martineau's Autobiography,* ed. Maria Weston Chapman (Boston: Houghton, Mifflin & Co., 1877), I, 314–5.

17. The copy, which is in Texas, bears the inscription: "Euphrasia Fanny Haworth given her by W. C. Macready at Elstree." In it are five illustrative drawings for the poem; Miss Haworth, who was an illustrator and a writer of verse, made them and signed each with her initials. Browning wrote on the flyleaf: "How the author wishes he had presented this book to Miss Haworth!"

18. Juliet Pollock, *Macready as I Knew Him,* 2d ed. (London: Remington & Co., 1885), p. 65.

19. Anna Jameson, *A Commonplace Book of Thoughts, Memories, and Fancies* (London: Longman, Brown, Green, & Longmans, 1854), p. 81.

20. Theodore Martin, *Helena Faucit* (Edinburgh: William Blackwood & Sons, 1900), p. 46. Although her husband and biographer preferred "Helena" and after her marriage the former actress signed her letters to Browning "Helena F. [or Faucit] Martin," I have hused her professional name, "Helen Faucit," in this study.

21. *EB to Mitford,* p. 10, [July or Aug. 1836].

22. Houghton MS. Orr (p. 97) and Griffin and Minchin (p. 140) date the meeting of Browning and Kenyon as 1839. This cannot be right since Browning's reply was written in 1837.

23. Henry Fothergill Chorley: *Autobiography, Memoir, and Letters,* comp. Henry G. Hewlett (London: Richard Bentley & Son, 1873), I, 113. For an account by contemporaries of the *Ion* performance and dinner, see also the following: Mary Russell Mitford, *Recollections of a Literary Life* (London: Richard Bentley, 1852), I, 284; *Henry Crabb Robinson on Books and Their Writers,* ed. Edith J. Morley (London: J. M. Dent & Sons, 1938), II, 494; Macready, May 26, 1836.

24. In Forster's *Lives of Eminent British Statesmen,* which appeared in Dionysius Lardner's *Cabinet Cyclopædia* (London: Longman, Rees, Orme, Brown, Green, & Longman, 1836), II, 104.

25. *Poems* (vols. XIII–XVI of *The Complete Works of Walter Savage Landor),* ed. Stephen Wheeler (London: Chapman & Hall, 1933–36), XVI, 1936, 218–9.

26. Forster cut the quoted portion from his letter and sent it to Browning. It is given in H. C. Minchin, *Walter Savage Landor: Last Days, Letters and Conversations* (London: Methuen & Co., 1934), p. 16. There are minor errors in the transcription from the originals, now in Baylor. I follow the MS here and in subsequent quotations from these letters.

27. *RB and AD,* p. 86.

28. *Mary Russell Mitford: Correspondence with Charles Boner and John Ruskin,* ed. Elizabeth Lee (London: T. Fisher Unwin, 1914), p. 64.

29. John Skelton, *The Table-Talk of Shirley,* 6th ed. (Edinburgh: William Blackwood & Sons, 1896), pp. 127–8.

30. Moncure Daniel Conway, *Autobiography: Memories and Experiences* (Boston: Houghton, Mifflin & Co., 1904), II, 22.

31. *P. R. B. Journal,* p. 22.

32. See *Works of Browning,* ed. Jack and Smith, I, 110, 119. Browning's letters are dated Mar. 2, 1835, and Aug. 9, 1837.

33. *RB and EBB,* I, 307, [Dec. 7, 1845].

34. Ibid., I, 312–3.

35. Lounsbury, p. 35. For his full discussion of *Paracelsus,* see pp. 22–44.

36. Gosse, p. 46.

37. *New Letters,* p. 231.

38. See, for example, ibid., p. 230, to John Forster, Dec. 2, 1875. See also *The Diary of Alfred Domett, 1872–1885,* ed. E. A. Horsman (London: Oxford Univ. Press, 1953), p. 55.

CHAPTER III: *First Attempt at Playwriting*

1. Orr, p. 29.

2. For Kean in Richmond, see Frederick Bingham, *A Celebrated Old Playhouse* (London: Henry Vickers, 1886), pp. 22–5; Harold Newcomb Hillebrand, *Edmund Kean* (New York: Columbia Univ. Press, 1933), pp. 316–24; Theatre Royal and Opera House, Souvenir, *The Theatres of Richmond, 1719–1899* (Richmond: "Times" Printing Works, Sept. 18, 1899). At Kean's death a green silk purse with steel rings was found in his pocket — empty. Kean's son gave it to Forster, who gave it to Browning, who in turn gave it to Henry Irving. "It was sold at Christie's at the sale of Irving's curios, with already an illustrious record of possessors." Bram Stoker, *Personal Reminiscences of Henry Irving* (New York: Macmillan Co., 1906), II, 90.

3. British Library, Add. MS, 45,563. For this and other notes I have drawn from the valuable collection of information on Browning that W. Hall Griffin obtained from Browning's son, his sister, and others.

4. *Reminiscences* (London: Chatto & Windus, 1899), I, 46.

5. For the visit, see also Orr, p. 80.

6. This was published in vol. II of *Lives of Eminent British Statesmen,* which appeared in Dionysius Lardner's *Cabinet Cyclopædia* (London: Longman, Rees, Orme, Brown, Green, & Longman, 1836). The extent of Browning's help has puzzled Browning students. Furnivall went so far as to publish the life as *Robert Browning's Prose Life of Strafford* for the Browning Society in 1892 and in the Forewords claimed that the *Life* was largely Browning's work. DeVane (p. 63) thought that Furnivall and others exaggerated Browning's share in the work. Browning's comments on the subject (see Preface to 1837 *Strafford; New Letters,* pp., 76, 353–4; and also Elizabeth's replies to Browning in *RB and EBB,* II, 721, 734, 748, 763) do not clear up the puzzle. DeVane's view is given weight by the acceptance of Forster's authorship by his contemporaries, even by Browning's family. Gosse wrote to W. Hall Griffin in May 1902, ". . . the invention (for I can call it nothing else)

that Browning wrote the 'Life of Strafford' — has given acute pain to the Forster and Browning family alike. It is utter fabb, unqualified falsehood . . ." (British Library, Add. MS, 45,563). For other contemporary acceptance of Forster's authorship, see Macready, Apr. 5, 1837; Percy Fitzgerald, *Memoirs of an Author* (London: Richard Bentley & Son, 1894), I, 38–41; letters from Carlyle to Forster in the Forster and Dyce Collection (one dated Apr. 13, 1860, and another undated), in which Carlyle wrote to Forster of "your *Strafford.*" For Pen Browning's strong statement against Browning's authorship, see his letter of 1893 to Mrs. Forster ("Browningiana" in *Literary Anecdotes of the Nineteenth Century,* ed. W. Robertson Nicoll and T. J. Wise [London: Hodder & Stoughton, 1895], I, 397). Modern scholars are not in entire agreement. James A. Davies, Forster's recent biographer, has a reasonable discussion of the problem. See his *John Forster: A Literary Life* (Leicester: Leicester Univ. Press, 1983), pp. 132–5. As he says, he and Sylvère Monod (in *John Forster as a Literary Biographer*), whose opinion on the debated authorship he agrees with, both have the advantage of being familiar with Forster's "style and procedures" (see pp. 133 and 277, n. 13). Some scholars, including W. S. Peterson ("A Re-Examination of *Robert Browning's Prose Life of Strafford,*" *Browning Newsletter,* no. 3, Fall 1969, pp. 12–22), have given Browning credit for a great share of the work on the life of Strafford published under Forster's name. It is true that at various times (in the later forties as well as in his years of fame) Browning gave the impression that he had more responsibility in preparing the biography than he was credited with, but whatever he said or was reported to have said must be examined in the light of his feeling that his early efforts had received less than their just recognition.

7. *New Letters,* p. 12.

8. Texas MS, July 23, 1836.

9. Griffin and Minchin, p. 109; British Library, Add. MS, 45,564.

10. *Autobiographical Notes of the Life of William Bell Scott,* ed. W. Minto (New York: Harper & Bros., 1892), I, 124.

11. Orr, p. 84.

12. P. 52.

13. Edward Fitzball, *Thirty-Five Years of a Dramatic Author's Life* (London: T. C. Newby, 1859), II, 89. I examined the playbills in the British Library.

14. P. 5.

15. P. 54.

16. *Autobiographical Notes,* I, 124–5.

17. T. Wemyss Reid, *The Life, Letters, and Friendships of Richard Monckton Milnes,* 2d ed. (London: Cassell & Co., 1890), I, 196.

18. *The Poems Posthumous and Collected of Thomas Lovell Beddoes,* ed. [according to the British Library catalogue] T. F. Kelsall, with a memoir by the editor and reminiscences by C. D. Bevan (London: William Pickering, 1851), p. ciii. The copy in the British Library has an additional title page to vol. I reading: *Poems by the Late Thomas Lovell Beddoes.*

19. *England and the English,* in *Works* (London: Saunders & Otley, 1840), pt. 1, p. 458.

20. *EBB Letters,* II, 436, to Sarianna Browning, [end of Mar., po. 1861].

21. Theodore Martin, *Helena Faucit* (Edinburgh: William Blackwood & Sons, 1900), p. 243.

22. Orr, p. 85.

23. Ibid., p. 84, to W. J. Fox, May 1, 1837; p. 85, in Eliza Flower's letter (see n. 22).

24. Ibid., p. 84, to Fox, [ca. May 2, 1837].

25. "A *Strafford* Manuscript in the Lord Chamberlain's Office Records," *Browning Institute Studies*, XII, 1984, 163–86.

26. *Weekly Dispatch*, May 7, 1837. In Baylor. Sarianna's hand is mistaken for Robert's in *The Browning Collections: A Reconstruction with Other Memorabilia*, comp. Philip Kelley and Betty A. Coley (n.p., Armstrong Browning Library of Baylor Univ., 1984), p. 205, Item A2436.

27. See *New Letters*, p. 356, to Mrs. Charles Skirrow, Feb. 8, 1888, and n. 1; *Letters*, Hood, p. 259; *Browning's Trumpeter: The Correspondence of Robert Browning and Frederick J. Furnivall, 1872–1889*, ed. William S. Peterson (Washington, D.C.: Decatur House Press, 1979), pp. 140–1 and 141, n. 1; W. S. Peterson, *Interrogating the Oracle* (Athens, Ohio: Ohio Univ. Press, 1969), pp. 41–3.

28. *Letters*, Hood, p. 259; *Browning's Trumpeter*, pp. 140–1.

29. Wellesley MS, Dec. 22, 1886.

30. See, for example, the *Athenaeum*, Dec. 25, 1886, p. 871; *Academy*, XXXI, Jan. 1, 1887, 17.

31. " 'Strafford' at Oxford," *Theatre*, n.s. XV, Apr. 1, 1890, 224.

32. Browning's answer with the desired information is in *Letters*, Hood, pp. 295–8. Archer used the information in writing his *William Charles Macready* (London: Kegan Paul, Trench, Trübner & Co., 1890). The section concerning *Strafford* is on pp. 99–100.

33. Pp. 44–6.

34. *RB and EBB*, II, 682, [May 6, 1846].

CHAPTER IV: *Frustration*

1. *Studies in Philology*, XXVII, Jan. 1930, 1–24. Jack and Smith *(Works of Browning*, II, 163) have detected flaws in DeVane's account of the composition of *Sordello*. In spite of these flaws, I found DeVane's distinction of four periods serviceable in dealing with the complicated history of the poem's composition.

2. *New Letters*, p. 12.

3. *Harriet Martineau's Autobiography*, ed. Maria Weston Chapman (Boston: Houghton, Mifflin & Co., 1877), II, 325.

4. *Letters*, Hood, p. 2, [July 24, 1838].

5. Orr, p. 66.

6. *Autobiography*, I, 315.

7. S. M. Ellis, *William Harrison Ainsworth and His Friends* (London: John Lane, Bodley Head, 1911), I, 289–90.

8. Ibid., I, 290. On July 26 Macready recorded that he, Browning, and Ainsworth dined with Forster.

9. *Autobiography*, II, 325.

10. Orr, pp. 88–9. See also Griffin and Minchin, p. 137; and Betty Miller, *Robert Browning: A Portrait* (London: John Murray, 1952), pp. 61–2.

11. Mill's letter to Robertson was published in C. Marion D. [Robertson] Towers, "John Stuart Mill and the *London and Westminster Review*," *Atlantic Monthly*, LXIX, Jan. 1892, 69. It was later published in *The Earlier Letters of John Stuart Mill, 1812–1848* (vols. XII and XIII of *Collected Works of John Stuart Mill*), ed. Francis E. Mineka (Toronto: Univ. of Toronto Press, 1963), XIII, 393–4.

12. *RB and AD*, p. 30, [Mar. 23, 1840]. The conjectured dating is mine. Browning headed the letter "Monday Morning" and in it he referred to the review of "yesterday week" in *Bell's Life*. *Bell's* published its criticism of *Sordello* on Sunday, March 15.

13. I, 315.

14. See Thomas Powell, *The Living Authors of England* (New York: D. Appleton & Co., 1849), p. 73. Powell might have been the first to get the story into print.

15. Louisa May Alcott learned of the comments made by Tennyson and Mrs. Carlyle from Browning himself. See Maria S. Porter, *Recollections of Louisa May Alcott, John Greenleaf Whittier, and Robert Browning* (Published for the Author by the New England Magazine Corporation, 1893), pp. 50–1.

16. *Conversations with Carlyle* (New York: Charles Scribner's Sons, 1892), p. 62.

17. See Moncure Daniel Conway, *Autobiography* (Boston: Houghton, Mifflin & Co., 1904), II, 23.

18. *P. R. B. Journal,* pp. 48–9.

19. British Library, Add. MS, 45,564. This letter was written by Kate Lemann to W. Hall Griffin.

20. Undated letter published in the *Emerson College Magazine,* XX, Jan. 1912, 131–2. It was probably written on Mar. 7, 1840. *Sordello* had "only come to hand this minute." It was on Mar. 7 that Browning sent a copy of the poem to Domett and wrote the date in a copy for his mother (see Sotheby, p. 81, Lot 477).

21. MS in my possession, Eliza Flower to R. H. Horne, [Apr. 27, 1840].

22. British Library, Add. MS, 45,564.

23. The letters from Arnould and Browning to Domett are in *RB and AD* and the letters from Arnould to Browning are in Donald Smalley, "Joseph Arnould and Robert Browning: New Letters (1842–50) and a Verse Epistle," PMLA, LXXX, Mar. 1965, 90–101. Information on the "set" may be found in the following: Griffin and Minchin, pp. 79–88; W. Hall Griffin, "Early Friends of Browning," *Contemporary Review,* LXXXVII, Mar. 1905, 427–46, and "Robert Browning and Alfred Domett," *Living Age,* CCXLIV, Feb. 18, 1905, 393–410; Introduction to *RB and AD;* Introduction to *The Diary of Alfred Domett, 1872–1885,* ed. E. A. Horsman (London: Oxford Univ. Press, 1953). A recent and comprehensive discussion of the set is in Maynard, pp. 96–112.

24. *RB and AD,* p. 27, [Mar. 7, 1840]; p. 28, [Mar. 23, 1840]. Earlier, Browning had given Domett a copy of *Paracelsus,* now in Texas. It has Browning's autograph, as does Domett's copy of *Sordello,* now in the British Library.

25. See Smalley, "Arnould and Browning: New Letters," p. 92. I have followed the punctuation of the transcription.

26. *New Letters of Thomas Carlyle,* ed. Alexander Carlyle (London: John Lane, the Bodley Head, 1904), I, 233.

27. H. C. Minchin, *Walter Savage Landor: Last Days, Letters and Conversations* (London: Methuen & Co., 1934), p. 17. I quote the MS.

28. John Forster, *Walter Savage Landor* (London: Chapman & Hall, 1869), II, 424.

29. Richard and Edward Garnett, *The Life of W. J. Fox* (London: John Lane, Bodley Head, 1910), p. 197.

30. *New Letters,* p. 18, [May 1840].

31. For Elizabeth Barrett's comments to Westwood, see *EBB Letters,* I, 254, Apr. 9, 1845; 254–5, Apr. 1845; 264, May 22, 1845.

32. R. and E. Garnett, *Fox,* p. 277.

33. Lounsbury, p. 84; Litzinger and Smalley, p. 63.

34. *The Browning Society's Papers* (London: N. Trübner & Co., 1881–91), II, 67* [so paginated].

35. *EBB Letters,* I, 255, to Thomas Westwood, Apr. 1845.

36. See Sotheby, p. 39, Lot 174. The original account is in Colorado College, Colorado Springs, Colorado. I thank Barbara L. Neilon, Special Collections Librarian, for sending me a copy.

37. *P. R. B. Journal,* p. 58.
38. *New Letters,* pp. 18–9, [May 1840].
39. *RB and AD,* pp. 28–30, [Mar. 23, 1840].
40. For this paragraph, see *RB and EBB,* I, 186–7, [Sept. 9, 1845]; 238, [Oct. 15, 1845]; 336, [Dec. 21, 1845].
41. Ibid., I, 439, [Feb. 6, 1846].
42. George William Curtis, *From the Easy Chair* (New York: Harper & Bros., 1892), p. 202.
43. Ian Jack, "Browning on *Sordello* and *Men and Women:* Unpublished Letters to James T. Fields," *Huntington Library Quarterly,* XLV, Summer 1982, pp. 187, 190, 196.
44. *EBB Letters,* II, 228, [po. Feb. 28, 1856].
45. For changes, see DeVane, p. 72; "Changed Rymes and Fresh Lines in *Sordello"* (in 1863 and 1868), *Browning Society's Papers,* I, 80–7; *Diary of Domett,* pp. 49–50 and n. 8. See, especially, *Works of Browning,* ed. Jack and Smith, II, 186–90.
46. P. 89.
47. *New Letters,* p. 157, Sept. 17, 1863.
48. *Letters,* Hood, p. 248, May 25, 1886; also *Browning's Trumpeter: The Correspondence of Robert Browning and Frederick J. Furnivall, 1872–1889,* ed. William S. Peterson (Washington, D.C.: Decatur House Press, 1979), p. 134.
49. *Rossetti Papers, 1862 to 1870,* p. 299.
50. *Letters,* Hood, p. 4, Mar. 9, [ca. 1840]; also Orr, pp. 102–3.
51. *Letters,* Hood, pp. 91–2, Mar. 5, 1866.
52. *Ruskin: Rossetti: PreRaphaelitism, Papers 1854 to 1862,* ed. William Michael Rossetti (London: George Allen, 1899), pp. 218–9.
53. *Autobiographical Notes of the Life of William Bell Scott,* ed. W. Minto (New York: Harper & Bros., 1892), II, 57–8. In a letter to EBB in acknowledgment of a gift of *Poems before Congress,* William Rossetti said he had not written the projected exposition of *Sordello* that he had told Browning about. He told EBB of others who were making prose versions of some of the "most knotty passages" of the poem. (Wellesley MS, Rossetti to EBB, Mar. 27, [1860].)
54. Houghton MS. The copy belonged to Thomas Woolner, one of the Pre-Raphaelites.

CHAPTER V: *Appeal to a Pit-Audience*

1. *Letters,* Hood, p. 4, Mar. 9, [ca. 1840]. The letter was first published by Orr; see pp. 102–3 and n. 2 for dating.
2. The letter was published by John Maynard in his "Robert Browning to Mr. Moxon: A New Letter," *Browning Newsletter,* no. 9, Fall 1972, pp. 34–7.
3. Gosse, pp. 52–3.
4. *RB and EBB,* I, 241, [Oct. 18, 1845].
5. The dedication, which ends the last sentence of the Advertisement, reads as follows: ". . . I dedicate my best intentions most admiringly to the Author of 'Ion,' — most affectionately to Serjeant Talfourd."
6. Park Honan, *Browning's Characters: A Study in Poetic Tehnique* (New Haven: Yale Univ. Press, 1961), pp. 87–8).
7. P. 111.
8. Alfred Domett, *Flotsam and Jetsam: Rhymes Old and New* (London: Smith, Elder, & Co., 1877).
9. *EB to Mitford,* p. 103, Jan. 20, 1842.
10. Ibid., p. 78, [po. July 16, 1841].

11. Ibid., p. 80, July 17, 1841.

12. Ibid., p. 136, Oct. 19, 1842.

13. *RB and EBB*, I, 22, Feb. 17, 1845; 97, [June 16, 1845].

14. *EBB Letters*, I, 264, May 22, 1845. This letter was written two days after Browning made his first call on Elizabeth and over four months after the beginning of their correspondence.

15. Richard and Edward Garnett, *The Life of W. J. Fox* (London: John Lane, Bodley Head, 1910), p. 194.

16. *New Letters of Thomas Carlyle,* ed. Alexander Carlyle (London: John Lane, Bodley Head, 1904), I, 233–4.

CHAPTER VI: *Two Plays Rejected, and Poems for Popularity's Sake*

1. For the dating, see DeVane, pp. 98–9, 104, 132, 137.

2. H. C. Minchin, "A Letter from Hanover Cottage," *Bookman*, LXXXVI, Apr. 1934, 7. I quote the MS, now in Baylor, which differs in slight details from Minchin's transcription.

3. This is the letter with Fox's opinion of *Sordello*, referred to in Chap. IV, which was published in the *Emerson College Magazine*, XX, Jan. 1912, 131–2. As already indicated in n. 20 of Chap. IV, it was probably written on Mar. 7, 1840.

4. *RB and AD*, p. 29. I have dated the letter in n. 12 of Chap. IV.

5. *New Letters*, p. 19.

6. Ibid., p. 20.

7. Ibid., pp. 20–1, [Aug. 23, 1840].

8. *Letters*, Hood, p. 5.

9. Ibid., [ca. 1840].

10. Ibid., p. 7, [ca. Dec. 30, 1841].

11. Park Honan, *Browning's Characters: A Study in Poetic Technique* (New Haven: Yale Univ. Press, 1961), p. 63.

12. See *Brownings to George Barrett*, p. 81, Mar. 30, 1842.

13. *New Letters*, pp. 25–6, [Apr. 26, 1842].

14. *RB and AD*, pp. 35–6.

15. Ibid., p. 45, Sept. 31 [*sic*], 1842; p. 50, Dec. 13, 1842.

16. Ibid., p. 45, Sept. 31 [*sic*], 1842. Browning's remarks can be read in conjunction with a comment written on a copy of the review that is now in Baylor. It is in Sarianna Browning's handwriting and is dated Oct. 4. "The writer of the very inadequate review of Mr Browning's poems in the Church Quarterly, begs to apologize for various errors in the quotations, and for the feeble absurdity of an interpolation to the effect that Sordello was 'not devoid of beauties.' For none of these things is the writer accountable. He could obtain no proofs till too late to compare them with M͏ʳ Browning's works; and as for the other errors, God knows how they occurred!" The "interpolation" that *Sordello* was "not devoid of beauties" was replaced in Horne's *New Spirit of the Age* by "abounds with beauties" (p. 181).

17. Ibid., p. 36, May 22, 1842.

18. Ibid., p. 97, Nov. 8, 1843.

19. *New Letters,* pp. 29–30, [probably Nov. 17, 1842].

20. *EB to Mitford,* pp. 153–4, Dec. 14, 1842.

21. Ibid., p. 170, Jan. 15, 1843.

22. *RB and AD,* pp. 87–8, [n.d.]; see also pp. 61–2, [n.d.].

23. Donald Smalley, "Joseph Arnould and Robert Browning: New Letters (1842–50) and a Verse Epistle," *PMLA*, LXXX, Mar. 1965, p. 91.

24. Ibid., pp. 92–3.

25. *RB and AD*, pp. 48, 49–50, Dec. 13, 1842.

26. Ibid., p. 87, [n.d.].

27. *Letters,* Hood, p. 285, to Robert Barrett Browning, Jan. 28, 1888.

28. See, for example, remarks in J. M. Cohen, *Robert Browning* (Longmans, Green & Co., 1952), p. 22; and a more detailed discussion of the two plays in Honan, *Browning's Characters*, pp. 57–68. The failure of *King Victor* and the *Druses* and also of other plays as works for the stage is discussed in the following: H. B. Charlton, "Browning as Dramatist," *Bulletin of the John Rylands Library*, XXIII, Apr. 1939, 33–67; and Arthur E. DuBois, "Robert Browning, Dramatist," *Studies in Philology*, XXXIII, Oct. 1936, 626–55.

29. Evan Charteris, *The Life and Letters of Sir Edmund Gosse* (London: William Heinemann, 1931), p. 332.

CHAPTER VII: *A Play Accepted*

1. *New Letters,* pp. 25–6; see also *RB and AD*, p. 36, May 22, 1842.

2. In this and the next chapter all of Arnould's statements are from his discussion of *A Blot* on pp. 62–7 of *RB and AD* unless otherwise specified.

3. John Forster, *The Life of Charles Dickens* (London: Chapman & Hall, 1873), II, 25.

4. *RB and AD*, p. 48.

5. *Bulwer and Macready,* ed. Charles H. Shattuck (Urbana: Univ. of Illinois Press, 1958), p. 212.

6. *Our Recent Actors* (London: Sampson Low, Marston, Searle & Rivington, 1888), I, 62–3.

7. *New Letters,* pp. 28–9, to Macready, Oct. 13, [1842].

8. John Coleman, asst. Edward Coleman, *Memoirs of Samuel Phelps* (London: Remington & Co., 1886), pp. 166–8, 185. Besides the *Memoirs of Phelps* I have used as sources for this paragraph Macready's *Diaries* (Feb. 1, 6, 10) and *RB and AD*.

9. On Feb. 16, 1843, Macready recorded that he had received a letter from the Lord Chamberlain (who censored plays), "demanding to know by what authority I had played *The Blot on* [sic] *the 'Scutcheon. . . .*"

10. *RB and AD*, p. 87, n.d.

11. *EB to Mitford*, pp. 171–2, [Feb. 14], 1843.

12. *Allingham: A Diary*, pp. 41, 174.

13. *My Life in Two Hemispheres* (London: T. Fisher Unwin, 1903), II, 258.

14. William Lyon Phelps, *Robert Browning*, new ed. (Indianapolis: Bobbs-Merrill Co., 1932), p. 430–1.

15. *RB and AD*, p. 56, May 15, 1843.

16. *New Letters,* pp. 31–2, [Autumn 1843].

17. MS in my possession, RB to R. H. Horne, [1843].

18. Sotheby, p. 125, Lot 1025, lists the following: Quarles (F.) Divine Fancies, *autograph signature of "Robert Browning, Nov. 19, 1837," on fly-leaf, old calf 12 mo.* 1723.

The title page of this edition reads:

Divine Fancies, Digested into Epigrams, Meditations, and Observations, By Francis Quarles, Esq; The Ninth Edition, Corrected. London: John Wilford, MDCCXXIII.

It is highly likely that Browning had this copy before him when he wrote Horne. He was quoting from poem LV "On Slander." He omitted lines at the beginning and end and modified the first line of his quotation. He altered some of the punctuation and spelling and changed capitalized nouns to the lower case.

19. *RB and AD,* p. 84, n.d.

20. *Letters,* Hood, p. 21, Dec. 3, 1848.

21. Orr, pp. 116–7.

CHAPTER VIII: *A Play Restaged and Recalled to Mind*

1. Gosse, pp. 15–74, first published as "The Early Writings of Robert Browning," *Century Magazine,* o.s. XXIII, n.s. I, Dec. 1881.

2. For a good discussion of the production and reception of the play in America, see Greer, pp. 194–202, 228–30.

3. The following statements from the superseding paragraph in the *Daily News* (Dec. 22, 1884) show just how the critic used Browning's explanation: "A Blot on [sic] the 'Scutcheon' was originally produced at Drury Lane Theatre during the close of Macready's unlucky management in February, 1843; but under such unfavorable conditions that Mr. Browning, we believe, has always considered that the 'experiment' afforded no fair test of its acting qualities. Macready, who was then, as he expressed it, 'harassed by business and various troubles,' was unable to carry out his original intention of playing the part of Tresham, which was therefore assigned to Mr. Phelps."

4. Dated Dec. 15, 21, 25, 29, 1884; Jan. 15, Mar. 7, Apr. 10, 1885. In his letters to Mrs. Hill (Mar. 7 and Apr. 10) Browning continued his defense of *A Blot.* The MS letters are at Yale. All of the first letter and most of the second were printed in Orr, pp. 110–6. Lounsbury made use of Orr.

5. *Frederick James Furnivall: A Volume of Personal Record* (London: Oxford Univ. Press, 1911), p. lxvi. This volume consists of a biography by John Munro and reminiscences by various contributors.

6. In response to a request from Archer for information to be used in writing his life of Macready, Browning sent his comments on the production of *A Blot.* (See *Letters,* Hood, pp. 295–8.) These comments were used on p. 136 of Archer's *William Charles Macready* (London: Kegan Paul, Trench, Trübner & Co., 1890).

7. Gosse, p. 4.

8. Baylor MS, Nov. 13, 1884.

9. *New Letters,* pp. 25–6.

10. *Furnivall,* p. lxvii, n.2 (Munro).

11. *Bulwer and Macready,* ed. Charles H. Shattuck (Urbana: Univ. of Illinois Press, 1958), pp. 207, 209.

12. *RB and EBB,* II, 730, [May 25, 1846].

13. *The Diary of Alfred Domett, 1872–1885,* ed. E. A. Horsman (London: Oxford Univ. Press, 1953), p. 301.

14. "Browning and Macready: The Final Quarrel," PMLA, LXXV, Dec. 1960, 597–603.

15. Ibid., p. 601.

16. *RB and AD,* p. 84. Arnould's letter is undated.

17. *EB to Mitford,* p. 173, Feb. 16, 1843.

18. See Gertrude Reese, "Robert Browning and *A Blot in the 'Scutcheon,*" MLN, LXIII, Apr. 1948, 237–40.

19. Orr, p. 118.

20. Ed. W. Robertson Nicoll and Thomas J. Wise (London: Hodder & Stoughton, 1895), I, 433.

21. *The Living Authors of England* (New York: D. Appleton & Co., 1849), p. 175; *Pictures of the Living Authors of Britain* (London: Partridge & Oakey, 1851), p. 112.

22. When Browning returned to England to live, Forster, with his domineering manner, sometimes became objectionable. Browning held himself in check until Forster, at a dinner party, questioned the reliability of the word of a lady whom Browning had quoted — a friend of his. Other guests restrained Browning when he lost control and attempted to throw a decanter of wine at Forster. This story has been told from time to time, without the name of the lady involved. In the W. Hall Griffin papers a letter from Pen Browning to Griffin refers to the "incident of the bottle" and to the lady as Lady William Russell (British Library, Add. MS, 45,564), a distinguished and valued friend of Browning's. In spite of the explosion and the interruption of the association, Browning never forgot Forster's professional assistance during the early years of his career. In an expression of gratefulness in 1875, Browning referred to the incident at the dinner party in recalling former days and a friendship which was "too vital to succumb at the interruption of *that*" *(New Letters,* p. 230, Dec. 2, 1875).

23. The following comments appear as evidence in Browning's letters to Hill.
". . . and a play, — not with himself as protagonist, and deprived of every advantage . . . proved — what Macready himself declared it to be — 'a complete sucess.' " (Dec. 21, 1884.)
"If 'applause' means success, the play thus maimed and maltreated was successful enough. . . ." (Dec. 15, 1884.)
"I would submit to anybody drawing a conclusion from one or two facts past contradiction, whether that play could have thoroughly failed which was not only not withdrawn at once but acted three nights in the same week, and, years afterward, re-produced at his own theatre . . . by Mr Phelps. . . . Why not enquire how it happened that, this second time, there was no doubt of the plays doing as well as plays ordinarily do? — for those were not the days of a 'run.' " (Dec. 21, 1884.)

24. Donald Smalley, "Joseph Arnould and Robert Browning: New Letters (1842–50) and a Verse Epistle," *PMLA,* LXXX, Mar. 1965, p. 98.

25. Elizabeth wrote of Chorley's attendance and his letter to them. See *EBB Letters,* I, 393, to Miss Mitford, Dec. 16, [1848].

26. W. May Phelps and John Forbes-Robertson, *The Life and Life-Work of Samuel Phelps* (London: Sampson Low, Marston, Searle, & Rivington, 1886), p. 374.

27. For this and other professional comments, see Greer, pp. 197–8, 201.

28. *Furnivall,* pp. 60–1 (Charles Fry's reminiscences).

29. *Diary of Domett,* p. 301.

30. *Letters,* Hood, p. 237, to Gosse, July 1, 1885. See also Roma A. King, Jr., "Robert Browning's Finances from His Own Account Book," *Baylor University Browning Interests,* 15th ser., 1947, pp. 17–8.

31. See Greer, pp. 195 and 293, n. 46. The MS letter is in her collection.

32. Ibid., pp. 195–6.

33. Texas MS, RB to Gustav Natorp, Apr. 25, 1885.

34. *Furnivall,* pp. 61–2 (Fry), pp. lxvii–viii (Munro, letter dated by RB Apr. 29 for Apr. 30); *Browning's Trumpeter: The Correspondence of Robert Browning and Frederick J. Furnivall, 1872–1889,* ed. William S. Peterson (Washington, D.C.: Decatur House Press, 1979), p. 112.

35. *Letters,* Hood, p. 235, Feb. 3, 1885.

36. *Alma Murray: Portrait as Beatrice Cenci with Critical Notice Containing Four Letters from Robert Browning* (London: Elkin Mathews, 1891), p. 8. The date of the letter is given as Mar. 1888. Later published (with the date of Mar. 16, 1888) in *Ten Letters of Robert Browning Concerning Miss Alma Murray* (Printed for Private Circulation, 1929), p. 15. For Browning's earlier letter (Oct. 11, 1887) on the projected performance of *A Blot,* see *Ten*

Letters, p. 13. Browning addressed the letters to Mrs. Forman. (Alma Murray was married to Alfred Forman.) It was his American friend Mrs. Bronson who learned of the revival of his playwriting urge late in life (Katherine C. Bronson, "Browning in Asolo," *Century Magazine*, o.s. LIX, n.s. XXXVII, Apr. 1900, 930).

37. *Ten Letters*, pp. 17–8. The letter is dated Aug. 11, 1888.

38. *The Bancrofts: Recollections of Sixty Years* (London: John Murray, 1909), p. 395. The letter is dated June 29, 1885.

39. Macready referred to the "regretful message" from Browning in the entry for Apr. 7, 1850; *New Letters*, p. 55, to Macready, Sept. 23, 1852; pp. 61–2, to Forster, Apr. 12, 1853.

40. Houghton MS, Oct. 1, 1855.

41. *EBB to Sister*, p. 244, Apr. 11, 1856; see also *New Letters*, p. 90, to Edward Chapman, [Apr. 12, 1856].

42. *Browning Newsletter*, no. 1, Fall 1968, p. 16. The letter is dated Aug. 14, 1856.

43. Baylor MS, Nov. 13, 1884. Anne Thackeray Ritchie said she had often heard Browning, despite "many differences and consequent estrangements," speak of Macready with "interest and sympathy," the last time being after Lady Pollock's book was published. "He said he had stopped at home all that winter's day reading it by the fire, and now that dinner-time was come he could quote page after page from memory." Anne Ritchie, *Records of Tennyson, Ruskin, Browning* (New York: Harper & Bros., 1899), p. 143.

44. Browning included his estimate in his letter to Archer, who used it with slight changes, mostly in punctuation, in his biography of Macready. See *Letters*, Hood, p. 296; and Archer, *Macready*, p. 214.

45. Quoted in William Lyon Phelps, *Robert Browning*, new ed. (Indianapolis: Bobbs-Merrill Co., 1932), p. 428. The letter is dated Jan. 3, 1884.

CHAPTER IX: *Farewell to the Stage*

1. *Letters*, Hood, p. 4, Mar. 9, [ca. 1840]; also Orr, p. 103.

2. *New Letters*, p. 23, [Aug. 23, 1840].

3. *RB and AD*, p. 67. This letter, undated, can be assigned by internal evidence to 1843.

4. *EB to Mitford*, p. 178, May 4, [1843].

5. *RB and AD*, p. 55, May 15, 1843.

6. MS in my possession, RB to R. H. Horne, [Oct. 5, 1843].

7. *New Letters*, pp. 30–5, to Horne, [Autumn 1843].

8. Cyril Pearl, *Always Morning: The Life of Richard Henry "Orion" Horne* (Melbourne: F. W. Cheshire, 1960), pp. 32–3, 42.

9. See *RB and EBB*, I, 62, [May 13, 1845], and 66, [May 15, 1845]; *Literary Gazette*, Mar. 16 and Sept. 7, 1844; S. M. Ellis, *William Harrison Ainsworth and His Friends* (London: John Lane, Bodley Head, 1911), II, 69. Also Arnould MS, Joseph Arnould to Alfred Domett, July 28, 1844.

10. For the kind of and extent of assistance that Elizabeth Barrett gave Horne, see Dorothy Hewlett, *Elizabeth Barrett Browning* (New York: Alfred A. Knopf, 1952), pp. 107–15; Gardner B. Taplin, *The Life of Elizabeth Barrett Browning* (London: John Murray, 1957), pp. 116–7. See also *Letters of Elizabeth Barrett Browning Addressed to Richard Hengist Horne*, ed. S. R. Townshend Mayer (London: Richard Bentley & Son, 1877), I, 132–272; II, 3–49.

11. *RB and EBB*, I, 66, [May 15, 1845].

12. *Letters*, Hood, p. 8, [ca. Dec. 1842].

13. MS in my possession, RB to Horne, Mar. 6, [1844]. Besides glimpses of Browning's warm regard for Horne in later years, there are two outstanding examples of his appreciative remembrance of Horne's early activities. When Horne applied for a Civil List pension Browning exerted effort in his behalf, and when Horne wished to publish letters of EBB (to him) Browning made an exception to his rule of denying permission for the publication of Elizabeth's letters. (RB to Horne, Aug. 11, 1872, and July 7, 1873.)

14. *RB and EBB,* I, 62–3, [May 13, 1845].

15. MS in my possession, RB to Horne, Mar. 6, [1844].

16. *New Letters,* pp. 22–3, [Aug. 23, 1840].

17. *RB and AD,* p. 41, July 13, 1842.

18. Ibid., p. 96, Nov. 8, 1843.

19. Ibid., p. 84. This letter, undated, can be assigned by internal evidence to 1843.

20. For the account Browning gave to Dowson of the Kean episode, see *Letters,* Hood, pp. 9–10; see also ibid., pp. 179–80, for the account he gave H. B. Forman on July 2, 1877.

21. *RB and AD,* p. 92, Oct. 9, 1843.

22. Ibid., p. 57, May 15, 1843; see also ibid., p. 113, Feb. 23, 1845.

23. Browning apparently thought of Thomas Powell as part proprietor of the *New Quarterly Review* who assumed editorial privileges. Arnould said that Browning had introduced him to the editor of the *New Quarterly* and thereby helped him gain entry into that periodical (Arnould MS, Joseph Arnould to Alfred Domett, July 28, 1844; W. Hall Griffin, "Early Friends of Robert Browning," *Contemporary Review,* LXXXVII, Mar. 1905, p. 429). Arnould was surely referring to Powell. According to Browning, Powell accepted an article from Arnould for the *New Quarterly* (*RB and EBB,* I, 380, [Jan. 11, 1846]).

24. Richard Willard Armour, *Barry Cornwall: A Biography of Bryan Waller Procter* (Boston: Meador Publishing Co., 1935), pp. 222–3. The dedication reads: "No one loves and honours Barry Cornwall more than Robert Browning; who, having nothing better than this play to give him in proof of it, must say so. March, 1844."

25. Hudson Long, "Helena Faucit Martin's Unpublished Letters to Robert Browning," *Baylor University Browning Interests,* 2d ser., 1931, p. 9.

26. Browning's answer, dated Jan. 31, 1853, to Helen Faucit's letter is in Theodore Martin, *Helena Faucit* (Edinburgh: William Blackwood & Sons, 1900), pp. 237–8. Part of the letter is quoted in Orr, p. 185.

27. *EBB Letters,* II, 112, to Mrs. Jameson, Apr. 12, [1853], and 115–6, to John Kenyon, May 16, [1853]. For Elizabeth's anxiety, see also Berg MS, EBB to Arabel, Apr. 30, [1853]; *Brownings to George Barrett,* pp. 183–4, May 2, [1853].

28. *EBB Letters,* I, 392–3, to Miss Mitford, Dec. 16, [1848].

29. Ibid., II, 112, to Mrs. Jameson, Apr. 12, [1853]; *New Letters,* p. 61, to John Forster, Apr. 12, 1853.

30. See *New Letters,* p. 59, to Edward Chapman, Mar. 5, 1853, and Wellesley MS, RB to John Kenyon, Mar. 17, 1853.

31. *New Letters,* p. 63, to Reuben Browning, July 18, 1853; Martin, *Faucit,* p. 239.

32. Samuel Phelps did not produce *Colombe's Birthday* at the Haymarket in 1853, as stated by Griffin and Minchin (p. 121). Nor did he take the leading role, as stated by Irvine and Honan (p. 111). At the time of Helen Faucit's performances J. B. Buckstone was the manager of the Haymarket and Phelps was at Sadler's Wells. See John Coleman, asst. Edward Coleman, *Memoirs of Samuel Phelps* (London: Remington & Co., 1886), pp. 199–200, 230–1; W. May Phelps and John Forbes-Robertson, *The Life and Life-Work of Samuel Phelps* (London: Sampson Low, Marston, Searle, & Rivington, 1886), pp. 64, 128; Martin, *Faucit,* p. 237.

33. See Martin, *Faucit,* p. 240. Henry Crabb Robinson saw the play on April 29, but since he recorded that he heard "little and understood less" and did not even get the name of the leading lady correct, we need not take seriously his pronouncement that the play was "very obscure in style." See *Henry Crabb Robinson on Books and Their Writers,* ed. Edith J. Morley (London: J. M. Dent & Sons, 1938), II, 724.

34. Browning's uncle Reuben went to the play. *(New Letters,* p. 63, to Reuben Browning, July 18, 1853.) Elizabeth's letter to Fanny Haworth of June [1853] suggests that Miss Haworth also went. *(EBB Letters,* II, pp. 118–9.)

35. MS in my possession, [1843].

36. *Letters,* Hood, p. 10, Mar. 10, [1844].

CHAPTER X: *Working in a New Light*

1. *RB and AD,* p. 106, July 31, 1844.

2. *Athenaeum,* Aug. 27, 1842, p. 759.

3. Elizabeth wrote to her brother George *(Brownings to George Barrett,* p. 81, Mar. 30, 1842) and H. S. Boyd *(EBB Letters,* I, 104, Apr. 2, 1842). For letter to Kenyon, see *EBB Letters,* I, 143, May 19, 1843. The poem was *The Dead Pan* (see Mrs. Andrew Crosse, *Red-Letter Days of My Life* [London: Richard Bentley & Son, 1892], I, 242).

4. *RB and EBB,* I, 271, [Nov. 16, 1845].

5. The ballad was a fortuitous addition to the collection. When Elizabeth's publisher saw shortly before publication that her two volumes were unequal in length, Elizabeth hastily completed a poem she had not intended to use — *Lady Geraldine's Courtship. (EBB Letters,* I, 176–7, to H. S. Boyd, [po. Aug. 1, 1844].)

6. *RB and EBB,* I, 271, [Nov. 16, 1845].

7. Ibid., I, 3.

8. Ibid., I, 39, [Mar. 11, 1845].

9. Ibid., I, 26.

10. Ibid., I, 56, [May 3, 1845].

11. Ibid., I, 63 [May 13, 1845].

12. Ibid., I, 95.

13. Ibid., I, 95, June 14, 1845.

14. *The Laboratory* (I, June 1844, 513–4), *Claret and Tokay* (I, June 1844, 525), *Garden Fancies* (II, July 1844, 45–8), *The Boy and the Angel* (II, Aug. 1844, 140–2), *The Tomb at St. Praxed's* (III, Mar. 1845, 237–9), the first nine sections of *The Flight of the Duchess* (III, Apr. 1845, 313–8).

15. Part of that time the work moved slowly because of a family crisis in Elizabeth's life that affected Browning as well as her. The unreasonable and adamant position Mr. Barrett assumed when Elizabeth sought his permission to go to a warmer climate for her health was a jarring blow to her affection for him, and Browning could do nothing to alleviate the suffering of the woman he loved.

16. *RB and EBB,* I, 135, [July 25, 1845].

17. Ibid., I, 190, [Sept. 11, 1845].

18. Ibid., I, 236.

19. Ibid., I, 149, [Aug. 10, 1845].

20. Ibid., I, 17–8, [Feb. 11, 1845].

21. Ibid., I, 150.

22. *Thomas Carlyle: Letters to His Wife,* ed. Trudy Bliss (London: Victor Gollancz, 1953), p. 209. In the late forties Carlyle told Duffy that Browning hoped to do something altogether different from *Sordello and Paracelsus.* See Charles Gavan Duffy, *Conversations with Carlyle* (New York: Charles Scribner's Sons, 1892), pp. 57–8.

23. *New Letters,* pp. 22–3, [Aug. 23, 1840]; *RB and AD,* p. 41, July 13, 1842.

24. *RB and EBB,* I, 46, [Apr. 15, 1845].

25. Ibid., I, 365, [Jan. 6, 1846].

26. See ibid., I, 244, [Oct. 21–2, 1845]; I, 173, [Aug. 27, 1845].

27. Ibid., I, 95, June 14, 1845.

28. Wellesley MS. A transcription of Elizabeth's notes for all of the poems except *The Flight of the Duchess* was published in *New Poems by Robert Browning and Elizabeth Barrett Browning,* ed. F. G. Kenyon (London: Smith, Elder, & Co., 1914) and reprinted in the Macmillan edition of Browning's works (New York: Macmillan Co., 1915). For an account of her remarks on *The Flight of the Duchess,* see Edward Snyder and Frederic Palmer, Jr., "New Light on the Brownings," *Quarterly Review,* CCLXIX, July 1937, 48–63.

29. *RB and EBB,* I, 135, [July 25, 1845].

30. Ibid., I, 251, [po. Oct. 27, 1845].

31. Ibid., I, 258, [Nov. 6, 1845].

32. In their "New Light on the Brownings."

33. If Elizabeth was swayed by the principles of prosody that served as her guide, she was not altogether oblivious to Browning's skillful employment of rhythm to create particular effects. In her letter dated July 26, 1845, she told Browning that she had been wrong to suggest the addition of *or* in the middle of the line "Was it singing, was it saying" (in *The Flight of the Duchess*). And she at once saw the superiority of *The Tomb at St. Praxed's.* She praised it in a letter to Browning and in her notes; her only suggestion for a change led to Browning's improvement of a line.

34. For the quotations in this paragraph, see "New Light on the Brownings," pp. 60, 54, 62. For similarities in the attitude of these writers and that of Harlan Henthorne Hatcher, see Chapter II, "Browning's Habits of Composition and Revision," in his *The Versification of Robert Browning,* Ohio State Univ. Studies, no. 5 (Columbus: Ohio State Univ. Press, 1928), pp. 9–22.

35. In *Saul* (11. 23–4) Browning wrote:

but soon I descried
Something more black than the blackness — the vast, upright. . . .

Elizabeth wanted *a* and *the* added, and Browning made the addition:

A something more black than the blackness — the vast, the upright. . . .

36. See the chapter "Spiritual Dogmatics" in his *The Bow and the Lyre: The Art of Robert Browning* (Ann Arbor: Univ. of Michigan Press, 1957), pp. 100–23.

37. *RB and EBB,* I, 19, [Feb. 11, 1845].

38. *RB and AD,* pp. 40–1, July 13, 1842.

39. See Edgar Finley Shannon, Jr., *Tennyson and the Reviewers: A Study of His Literary Reputation and of the Influence of the Critics upon His Poetry, 1827–1851* (Cambridge, Mass.: Harvard Univ. Press, 1952), p. 164.

40. *RB and EBB,* I, 222, [Oct. 4, 1845].

41. Ibid., I, 223, [Oct. 6, 1845].

42. See *RB and AD,* p. 29, [Mar. 23, 1840]. The dating is mine. See n. 12 of Chap. IV.

43. *RB and EBB,* I, 239, [Oct. 17, 1845].

44. Ibid., I, 241, [Oct. 18, 1845].

45. Ibid., I, 221, [Oct. 2, 1845].

46. Ibid., I, 143.

47. Ibid., I, 229.

48. Ibid., I, 235, [Oct. 14, 1845].

49. Ibid., I, 251.

50. The inscription reads: "Inscribed to John Kenyon, Esq., in the hope that a recollection of his own successful 'Rhymed Plea for Tolerance' may induce him to admit good-naturedly this humbler prose one of his very sincere friend, R. B. Nov. 1845."

CHAPTER XI: _A Step Forward_

1. P. 160.
2. See _RB and EBB_, I, 204, [Sept. 17, 1845].
3. Ibid., I, 236, [Oct. 15, 1845].
4. Ibid., I, 259, [Nov. 6, 1845].
5. See ibid., I, 276, [Nov. 17, 1845].
6. Ibid., I, 301, [po. Dec. 3, 1845], and I, 302, n. 1; see also I, 279, [Nov. 20, 1845], and I, 282, n. 2; I, 284, [Nov. 21, 1845].
7. Ibid., I, 369, [Jan. 7, 1846].
8. Ibid., I, 367, [Jan. 6, 1846]; I, 375, [Jan. 10, 1846].
9. Browning supposed that two-thirds of the article in the _New Quarterly Review_ was written by Heraud and the remaining third by Powell. (Ibid., I, 380, [Jan. 11, 1846].) Powell persistently and successfully sought the acquaintance of prominent men of letters, including Browning, who went so far as to help him revise some poems for a book. He was given to deceptive dealings and some of Browning's friends had been victims. While in the employ of a business firm he embezzled funds. Before the embezzlement was discovered and he fled to America, he bought part interest in the _New Quarterly_. That Browning's authorship of _Pauline_ was revealed in the review by Powell (along with Heraud) was a count added to those that Browning already held against him. Powell knew that Browning did not want the authorship known; yet he repeated the exposure in his _Living Authors of England_ (New York: D. Appleton & Co., 1849), p. 72, and in _Pictures of the Living Authors of Britain_ (London: Partridge & Oakey, 1851), p. 62. For Browning's comments on Powell to Elizabeth, see _RB and EBB_, I, 380–1, [Jan. 11, 1846]; I, 551, [Mar. 22, 1846]; II, 766, [June 8, 1846]. He made references to Powell in letters to various correspondents. See _Letters_, Hood, p. 21, to R. H. Horne, Dec. 3, 1848; pp. 224–5, to F. J. Furnivall, Oct. 15, 1883; pp. 256–7, to W. B. Slater, Nov. 6, 1886; p. 258, to J. H. Ingram, Nov. 24, 1886. See also Wilfred Partington, "Should a Biographer Tell?" _Atlantic Monthly_, CLXXX, Aug. 1947, 56–63.
10. _RB and EBB_, I, 398, [Jan. 17, 1846]; I, 401, [Jan. 18, 1846].
11. Ibid., I, 258, [Nov. 6, 1845].
12. For an account of the gathering at the home of Mr. Z, who, we know from the description, was Thomas Powell, see Mrs. Newton Crosland (Camilla Toulmin), _Landmarks of a Literary Life, 1820–1892_ (New York: Charles Scribner's Sons, 1893), pp. 147–51.
13. _RB and EBB_, I, 279, [Nov. 20, 1845].
14. Ibid., I, 284, [Nov. 21, 1845]; I, 397–8, [Jan. 17, 1846].
15. Ibid., I, 264, [Nov. 10, 1845], and 315, [Dec. 9, 1845].
16. Ibid., I, 267, [Nov. 12, 1845].
17. H. C. Minchin, _Walter Savage Landor: Last Days, Letters and Conversations_ (London: Methuen & Co., 1934), p. 18. I quote the MS.
18. _RB and EBB_, I, 278, [Nov. 20, 1845].
19. _New Letters_, p. 37, [Nov. 19, 1845]; _RB and AD_, pp. 124–5, Mar. 19, 1846.
20. _RB and EBB_, I, 279, [Nov. 20, 1845].
21. Ibid., I, 288, [Nov. 23, 1845]; _RB and AD_, p. 124, Mar. 19, 1846.
22. _RB and EBB_, I, 277–8, [Nov. 20, 1845].
23. Ibid., I, 19.
24. Ibid., I, 39, [Mar. 11, 1845].

25. W. L. Phelps, "Robert Browning as Seen by His Son," *Century Magazine,* LXXXV, Jan. 1913, 419.

26. *New Letters,* pp. 37—8, [Nov. 19, 1845].

27. *RB and EBB,* I, 347, [Dec. 27, 1845].

28. Ibid., I, 349, [Dec. 30, 1845].

29. Ibid., I, 381—2.

30. Ibid., I, 383, n. 11.

31. Crosland, *Landmarks,* p. 152.

32. *RB and EBB,* I, 367.

33. Kintner, ed. of *RB and EBB,* designates the three reviews: one of four volumes of Irish poetry, another of James White's *Earl of Gowrie,* the third of the anonymous *My Life,* Part the First. *(Ibid.,* I, 367—8, n. 3.)

34. Ibid., I, 401—2, [Jan. 18, 1846].

35. Ibid., I, 397—8, [Jan. 17, 1846]. Browning was probably aware of the difficulties Chorley faced as a reviewer. Arnould later wrote him of Chorley: ". . . I know that one of the main grievances of his critical life was his inability to get the reviewal of your work in the Athenaeum, which was done by an incompetent hand." (Donald Smalley, "Joseph Arnould and Robert Browning: New Letters (1842—50) and a Verse Epistle," PMLA, LXXX, Mar. 1965, 100.)

36. *RB and AD,* p. 125, Mar. 19, 1846. Kenyon inserted the *it.*

37. See *RB and EBB,* I, 345, [Dec. 27, 1845]; I, 455, [Feb. 13, 1846]; I, 512; I, 552, [Mar. 24, 1846].

38. Ibid., I, 248, [Oct. 24, 1845].

CHAPTER XII: *Plays for Reading*

1. *RB and EBB,* I, 18.

2. Ibid., I, 26.

3. For example, in *Prince Hohenstiel-Schwangau, Mr. Sludge,* and *Bishop Blougram's Apology* Browning, despite his antipathies, had each monologuist speak in defense or justification of his position. For comments made by Browning on the effect he intended to give in *Bishop Blougram's Apology* and *Prince Hohenstiel-Schwangau,* see Charles Gaven Duffy, *My Life in Two Hemispheres* (London: T. Fisher Unwin, 1903), II, 261; *Dearest Isa,* p. 372, Jan, 25, 1872; and *Browning to American Friends,* p. 167, Jan. 1, 1872.

4. *RB and EBB,* I, 55, [May 3, 1845].

5. Ibid., I, 223.

6. Ibid., I, 236, [Oct. 15, 1845].

7. See ibid., I, 22, Feb. 17, 1845; I, 29—30, Feb. 27, 1845.

8. Ibid., I, 251.

9. Ibid., I, 381.

10. Ibid., I, 406—7, [Jan. 21, 1846].

11. Ibid., I, 411, [Jan. 22, 1846].

12. Ibid., I, 445—6, [Feb. 10, 1846].

13. Ibid., I, 451.

14. Ibid., I, 551.

15. Ibid., II, 573, [Mar. 30, 1846].

16. Ibid., II, 579—80, [po. Apr. 1, 1846].

17. See DeVane, p. 190, for time of composition of *A Soul's Tragedy* and *RB and AD,* p. 36, for Browning's comment to Domett.

18. Macready rejected *King Victor and King Charles* in 1839 and *The Return of the Druses* in 1840 and held *A Blot* from April 1841 (or earlier) until its performance in February 1843.

19. *RB and EBB*, I, 451–2.

20. Ibid., I, 455, [Feb. 13, 1846].

21. Ibid.

22. Ibid., I, 493, [Feb. 25, 1846].

23. Ibid., I, 525, [Mar. 10, 1846].

24. Ibid., II, 569, [Mar. 29, 1846].

25. Ibid., II, 572, [Mar. 30, 1846].

26. Ibid., I, 551, [Mar. 22, 1846]; I, 546, [po. Mar. 18, 1846]; II, 579, [po. Apr. 1, 1846].

27. Ibid., II, 594, [Apr. 6, 1846]; II, 598, [Apr. 7, 1846].

28. For Elizabeth's comments on the plays, see *The Complete Poetical Works of Robert Browning*, new ed. (New York: Macmillan Co., 1915), pp. 1341–2, 1346–50.

29. *RB and EBB*, I, 548, [Mar. 21, 1846].

30. "Revision in Browning's *Paracelsus*," MLN, LV, Mar. 1940, 195–7.

31. *New Letters*, p. 157, Sept. 17, 1863.

32. *Robert Browning's Moral-Aesthetic Theory, 1833–1855* (Lincoln: Univ. of Nebraska Press, 1967), p. 119.

33. *RB and EBB*, II, 577, [Mar. 31, 1846]; II, 643, [Apr. 21, 1846].

34. Ibid., I, 439, [Feb. 6, 1846]. Browning referred to the comment Carlyle made in acknowledging the copies of *Sordello* and *Pippa Passes* that he had sent.

35. Ibid., I, 553, [Mar. 24, 1846].

36. The dedication reads: "I dedicate these last attempts for the present at dramatic poetry to a great dramatic poet; 'wishing what I write may be read by his light:' — if a phrase originally addressed, by not the least worthy of his contemporaries, to Shakespeare, may be applied here, by one whose sole privilege is in a grateful admiration, to Walter Savage Landor. March 29, 1846."

37. *RB and EBB*, II, 619, [Apr. 13, 1846].

38. Ibid., II, 623, [Apr. 14, 1846].

39. Park Honan, *Browning's Characters: A Study in Poetic Technique* (New Haven: Yale Univ. Press, 1961), pp. 94–5.

40. For the opinions referred to in this paragraph, see *RB and EBB*, II, 907, [July 27, 1846]; II, 650, [Apr. 23, 1846]; II, 642, [Apr. 21, 1846].

41. Ibid., II, 633–4, [Apr. 17, 1846].

42. Ibid., II, 652, [Apr. 24, 1846]; II, 707, [May 16, 1846]; II, 636, [Apr. 18, 1846]; II, 656–7, [Apr. 26, 1846]; II, 632, [Apr. 17, 1846].

43. Ibid., II, 641, [Apr. 21, 1846].

44. H. C. Minichin, *Walter Savage Landor: Last Days, Letters and Conversations* (London: Methuen & Co., 1934), pp. 21–2. I quote the MS.

45. John Forster, *Walter Savage Landor: A Biography* (London: Chapman & Hall, 1869), II, 425.

46. *RB and EBB*, II, 656, [Apr. 26, 1846].

47. Ibid., II, 659, [Apr. 27, 1846].

48. Ibid., II, 662, [Apr. 28, 1846].

49. Ibid., II, 946, [Aug. 9, 1846].

50. For the comment to Elizabeth, see ibid., I, 558, [Mar. 25, 1846]; to Domett, see *RB and AD*, p. 36, May 22, 1842.

51. *RB and AD*, pp. 127–8.

52. *RB and EBB,* II, 580, [po. Apr. 1, 1846].

53. Ibid., I, 271, [Nov. 16, 1845].

54. *RB and AD,* p. 37, May 22, 1842; p. 48, Dec. 13, 1842.

55. *RB and EBB,* I, 39, [Mar. 11, 1845]; I, 206, [Sept. 18, 1845].

56. Richard Willard Armour, *Barry Cornwall: A Biography of Bryan Waller Procter* (Boston: Meador Publishing Co., 1935), p. 223.

57. Sarah Norton and M. A. DeWolfe Howe, *Letters of Charles Eliot Norton with Biographical Comment* (Boston: Houghton Mifflin Co., 1913), I, 325.

58. *RB and AD,* p. 86, n.d.; p. 122, Nov. 24, 1845.

59. *RB and EBB,* I, 75, [May 24, 1845].

60. Arnould MS, Joseph Arnould to Alfred Domett, Nov. 24, 1845.

61. Wellesley MS, Jan. 30, 1846.

62. Ibid. Elizabeth and Robert exchanged comments on Domett's letter. See *RB and EBB,* II, 889, [July 19, 1846]; II, 890–1, [July 20, 1846].

63. *RB and AD,* p. 127, July 13, 1846.

64. *RB and EBB,* I, 95, June 14, 1845.

65. *RB and AD,* p. 35, May 22, 1842.

66. *RB and EBB,* I, 337, [Dec. 21, 1845].

CHAPTER XIII: *Further Encouraging Signs*

1. *RB and EBB,* II, 890, [July 20, 1846].

2. Ibid., II, 986, [Aug. 22, 1846].

3. Ibid., II, 1022, [Aug. 30, 1846].

4. *EBB Letters,* I, 314.

5. Berg MS.

6. *Letters,* Hood, p. 14, Feb. 24, 1847.

7. Ibid.

8. Ibid. For Browning's later opinion, see *New Letters,* p. 108, to Edward Chapman, Aug. 8, [1858].

9. *Frederick Locker-Lampson: A Character Sketch,* ed. Augustine Birrell (New York: Charles Scribner's Sons, 1920), pp. 102–3. The letter is dated Feb. 20, 1874.

10. Berg MS, Mar. 9, 1847.

11. *RB and EBB,* II, 1015, [Aug. 28, 1846].

12. Ibid.

13. [Leonard Huxley], *The House of Smith Elder* (London: Printed for Private Circulation, 1923), p. 155. See also Michael Meredith, "Browning and the Prince of Publishers," *Browning Institute Studies,* VII, 1979, 5–6.

14. *P. R. B. Journal,* p. 9.

15. Arthur Waugh, *A Hundred Years of Publishing: Being the Story of Chapman & Hall* (London: Chapman & Hall, 1930), pp. 27–8, 78. See also *Locker-Lampson,* p. 103.

16. *EBB Letters,* I, 364, May 1, [1848].

17. *EBB to Sister,* p. 94.

18. The article can be assigned to Archer Gurney. On March 10, 1846, Browning thanked him for sending "the Review" with two articles that gratified him. "Both pieces are admirably written, and the one which more immediately concerns me is amends for a great deal of the ordinary measure dealt out to the book since its appearance ten years back, praise or blame." (Hood, *Letters,* p. 12.) Gurney contributed to the *Theologian,* which was published every other month, and his two articles that gratified Browning appeared in that periodical in 1845. It carried in its issue for June one on *Paracelsus* (the article that "immediately" concerned Browning) and in its issue for October one on Thomas Powell's poems,

in which Gurney paid tribute to Browning and referred to the discussion of *Parcelsus* that had appeared in June.

    19. *The Browning Society's Papers* (London: N. Trübner & Co., 1881–91), I, 114.

CHAPTER XIV: *Retrospection*

    1. Donald Smalley, "Joseph Arnould and Robert Browning: New Letters (1842–50) and a Verse Epistle," PMLA, LXXX, Mar. 1965, 98, 99.

    2. British Library, Add. MS, 38,110, R. H. Horne to Leigh Hunt, May 8, 1843.

    3. *RB and EBB*, II, 883–4, [July 17, 1846].

    4. *The Blind Wife; or, The Student of Bonn* (London: W. E. Painter, 1843).

    5. *A Day at Tivoli with Other Verses* (London: Longman, Brown, Green, and Longmans, 1849).

    6. T. N. Talfourd, *Tragedies* (London: Moxon, 1844).

    7. Archer Gurney, *Love's Legends* (London: C. Mitchell, 1845).

    8. Mrs. Andrew Crosse, *Red-Letter Days of My Life* (London: Richard Bentley & Son, 1892), I, 226–7.

    9. *Henry Fothergill Chorley: Autobiography, Memoir, and Letters,* comp. Henry G. Hewlett (London: Richard Bentley & Son, 1873), I, 223.

    10. See *Henry Crabb Robinson on Books and Their Writers,* ed. Edith J. Morley (London: J. M. Dent & Sons, 1938), II, 591, 642, 658, 719, 654.

    11. Wellesley MS, Jan. 30, 1846.

    12. *Personal and Literary Letters of Robert, First Earl of Lytton,* ed. Betty Balfour (London: Longmans, Green, & Co., 1906), I, 42; Aurelia Brooks Harlan, *Owen Meredith: A Critical Biography of Robert, First Earl of Lytton* (New York: Columbia Univ. Press, 1946), pp. 47–8.

    13. Oscar Browning, "Personal Recollections of English Poets," *Empire Review,* XXVIII, Nov. 1923, 1243.

    14. Charles Gavan Duffy, *Conversations with Carlyle* (New York: Charles Scribner's Sons, 1892), pp. 56–7.

    15. M. E. Grant Duff, *Notes from a Diary, 1889–1891* (London: John Murray, 1901), I, 198.

    16. *The Letters of George Meredith,* ed. C. L. Cline (Oxford: Clarendon Press, 1970), II, 849. See also II, 830, and n. 1.

    17. Arthur A. Adrian, "The Browning-Rossetti Friendship: Some Unpublished Letters," PMLA, LXXIII, Dec. 1958, 538.

    18. William Michael Rossetti, *Some Reminiscences* (London: Brown Langham & Co., 1906), I, 233.

    19. W. Holman Hunt, *Pre-Raphaelitism and the Pre-Raphaelite Brotherhood* (New York: Macmillan Co., 1905), I, 145.

    20. Rossetti, *Some Reminiscences,* I, 233, 234.

    21. Maurice B. Cramer, "What Browning's Literary Reputation Owed to the Pre-Raphaelites, 1847–1856," *A Journal of English Literary History,* VIII, Dec. 1941, 305–21.

    22. Rossetti, *Some Reminiscences,* II, 233.

    23. Amy Woolner, *Thomas Woolner, R. A., Sculptor and Poet: His Life in Letters* (London: Chapman & Hall, 1917), pp. 5–6.

    24. *Letters to William Allingham,* ed. H. Allingham and E. Baumer Williams (London: Longmans, Green & Co., 1911), pp. 7, 41–2; *Allingham: A Diary,* p. 41.

    25. *Allingham: A Diary,* p. 36.

    26. *New Letters,* p. 43, June 29, 1847.

27. *Letters,* Hood, p. 21.
28. *EBB Letters,* I, 404, to Mrs. Martin, May 14, [1849].
29. Ibid., I, 399, to Miss Mitford, Apr. 30, 1849.
30. *RB and EBB,* II, 1006, [Aug. 26, 1846].
31. Smalley, "Arnould and Browning: New Letters," p. 99.
32. *New Letters,* p. 74, Apr. 1854.

CHAPTER XV: *A Religious Poem*

1. *Letters,* Hood, p. 14, Feb. 24, 1847.
2. Berg MS, Mar. 11, [1847].
3. *EBB Letters,* I, 422.
4. See, for example, DeVane, p. 197; Irvine and Honan, pp. 263–5; William O. Raymond, *The Infinite Moment and Other Essays on Robert Browning,* 2d ed. (Toronto: Univ. of Toronto Press, 1965), pp. 27–31; Kingsbury Badger, " 'See the Christ Stand!': Browning's Religion," *Boston University Studies in English,* I, 1955, 53–4, 63–8.
5. *RB and EBB,* I, 7, Jan. 13, 1845.
6. Ibid., I, 12, [Jan. 27, 1845].
7. Ibid., I, 14, Feb. 3, 1845.
8. Ibid., I, 17, [Feb. 11, 1845].
9. F. R. G. Duckworth, *Browning: Background and Conflict* (New York: E. P. Dutton & Co., 1932), pp. 183–6. Duckworth was discussing Browning's frustrated desire to speak in his own person to his reader.
10. *RB and EBB,* I, 31, Feb. 27, 1845. For an expression of her desire that Browning write directly to his reader, see ibid., II, 731–2, [May 25, 1846].
11. Ibid., I, 36, [Mar. 11, 1845].
12. Ibid., I, 43, Mar. 20, 1845.
13. *New Letters,* pp. 35–6, to F. O. Ward, Feb. 18, 1845. The poem was published in *Hood's* in March of 1845. It had probably been written late in 1844 (DeVane, pp. 166, 167). An awareness of the importance of the past that was prominent in the Oxford Movement brought about the formation of the Camden Society in 1838 in honor of William Camden (1551–1623), antiquary and historian of his time. It printed books and documents concerning the early history of England, some of which had an influence on the Oxford Movement. The Cambridge Camden Society was formed in 1839; it was later called the Ecclesiological Society.
14. See H. C. Minchin, "A Letter from Hanover Cottage," *Bookman,* LXXXVI, Apr. 1934, 6–7. The letter was written to Fanny Haworth in August of 1837.
15. *RB and EBB,* I, 26, [Feb. 26, 1845].
16. E. F. Bridell-Fox, "Robert Browning," *Argosy,* XLIX, Feb. 1890, 113.
17. *EBB Letters,* I, 446–7, to Miss Mitford, Apr. 1850.
18. See his introduction to a facsimile reprint of the *Germ* (1901).
19. *EBB Letters,* I, 447, to Miss Mitford, [end of] Apr. 1850.
20. *New Letters,* Appendix B, p. 392; Appendix C, p. 400.

CHAPTER XVI: *Prose and Finances*

1. *RB and EBB,* I, 200, [Sept. 16, 1845].
2. Ibid., I, 203, [Sept. 17, 1845].
3. Ibid., II, 615, [Apr. 12, 1846].
4. Ibid., II, 793, [June 17, 1846].
5. See ibid., II, 936, [Aug. 5, 1846].
6. Ibid., II, 906, [July 27, 1846].

7. See T. Wemyss Reid, *The Life, Letters, and Friendships of Richard Monckton Milnes, First Lord Houghton,* 2d ed. (London: Cassell & Co., 1890), I, 384–5.

8. Elizabeth wrote Miss Mitford of their inexpensive living in Italy and of their restricted means in 1850. See *EBB Letters,* I, 373, July 4, [1848]; I, 451, June 15, 1850; I, 471, Dec. 13, 1850.

9. *Letters,* Hood, pp. 27–30, July 29, 1850.

10. Wellesley MSS, EBB to Kenyon, May 1, [1851]; Nov. 23[–24], [1852].

11. See *Brownings to George Barrett,* p. 253, Apr. 2, [1861].

12. Wellesley MS, EBB to Kenyon, May 1, [1851].

13. *New Letters,* pp. 47–9, June 12, 1850 [for 1851].

14. Berg MS, EBB to Arabel, June 26, [1851].

15. Berg MS, EBB to Arabel, [po. July 10, 1851].

16. Berg MS, June 26, [1851].

17. Ibid.

18. *EBB Letters,* I, 301, 390, to Mrs. Martin, Nov. 5, [1846], and Dec. 3, 1848; *Brownings to George Barrett,* pp. 252–3, Apr. 2, [1861].

19. Berg MS, EBB to Arabel, [po. July 10, 1851].

20. See Browning's *Essay on Chatterton,* ed. Donald Smalley (Cambridge, Mass.: Harvard Univ. Press, 1948).

21. G. S. Haight, *George Eliot and John Chapman* (New Haven: Yale Univ. Press, 1940), p. 42.

22. "Correspondence between Carlyle and Browning," ed. Alexander Carlyle, *Cornhill Magazine,* CXI, n.s. XXXVIII, May 1915, 656.

23. *Letters,* Hood, p. 36.

24. Ibid., p. 244, to the editor of a Boston magazine, [ca. 1886].

25. MS in my possession, RB to Horne, Nov. 2, 1843.

26. *New Letters,* p. 52, Sept. 23, 1851.

27. Berg MS, EBB to Arabel, [Feb. 18, 1852].

28. *Brownings to George Barrett,* p. 159.

29. *New Letters,* pp. 52–3, [Dec. 17, 1851]. A later statement of Browning's (Feb. 20, 1874) to Locker-Lampson that was quoted in an earlier chapter should be repeated here. "Moxon was kind & civil, made no profit by me, I am sure & never tried to help me to any, he would have assured you." *(Frederick Locker-Lampson: A Character Sketch,* ed. Augustine Birrell [New York: Charles Scribner's Sons, 1920], p. 103.) Browning was probably forgetting the "handsome behavior" and remembering his experience with *Bells and Pomegranates* and Moxon's unwillingness to publish the collected edition of 1849.

30. See pp. 24–7 of Richard Garnett's Introduction to *Browning's Essay on Shelley* (London: Alexander Moring, De La More Press, 1903).

31. For a contemporary account of the forger, see *Letters of Mary Russell Mitford,* 2d ser., ed. Henry Chorley (London: Richard Bentley & Son, 1872), II, 130–1. For later discussions of the forgeries, see J. A. Farrer, *Literary Forgeries* (London: Longmans, Green, & Co., 1907), pp. 175–90; and Park Honan, "Browning's Testimony on His Essay on Shelley in 'Shepherd v. Francis,' " *English Language Notes,* II, Sept. 1964, 27–31.

32. *EBB Letters,* II, 53, to John Kenyon, Feb. 15, 1852; Berg MS, EBB to Arabel, [Feb. 18, 1852].

33. "Correspondence between Carlyle and Browning," pp. 659, 660.

34. At one time Powell was on friendly terms with Browning as well as other literary men in London. Browning became aware of his devious practices *(RB and EBB,* I, 380, [Jan. 11, 1846]) even before he exercised his skill in forgery on a large scale and had to

flee from England in disgrace. See Wilfred Partington, "Should a Biographer Tell?" *Atlantic Monthly*, CLXXX, Aug. 1947, 56–63.

35. See *Letters*, Hood, p. 298, to Thomas J. Wise, Aug. 1, 1888. For the exposure of Wise, see John Carter and Graham Pottle, *An Enquiry into the Nature of Certain Nineteenth Century Pamphlets* (London: Constable & Co., 1934).

36. *New Letters*, p. 59, Mar. 5, 1853.

37. *EBB Letters*, II, 116, to John Kenyon, May 16, [1853].

38. Wellesley MS, RB and EBB to Kenyon, Mar. 17, 1853.

39. *New Letters*, p. 61, Apr. 12, 1853.

40. Ibid., p. 63, July 18, 1853.

41. *EBB Letters*, II, 116, n. 1, to Miss Mitford, May 20, 1853; *Brownings to George Barrett*, p. 184, May 2, [1853].

42. *EBB Letters*, II, 134, 161, to Miss Mitford, Aug. 20 and 21, 1853, and Mar. 19, 1854; II, 138–9, to Thomas Westwood, Sept. [1853]; *Brownings to George Barrett*, p. 203, Oct. 7, [1853].

43. *EBB Letters*, I, 471–2, to Miss Mitford, Dec. 13, 1850.

44. *RB and AD*, p. 45, Sept. 31 [*sic*], 1842.

45. *New Letters*, p. 58, Mar. 5, 1853.

46. Ibid., p. 61, Apr. 12, 1853.

47. Ibid., p. 70, Mar. 30, 1854.

48. Ibid., p. 74, Apr. 2, 1854.

49. Ibid., p. 59, Mar. 5, 1853.

CHAPTER XVII: *New Manner Than Matter*

1. "Correspondence between Carlyle and Browning," ed. Alexander Carlyle, *Cornhill Magazine*, CXI, n.s. XXXVIII, May 1915, 660–1.

2. *EBB Letters*, II, 127, to H. F. Chorley, Aug. 10, [1853].

3. Th. Bentzon (pseud. for Marie T. de S. Blanc), "A French Friend of Browning — Joseph Milsand," *Scribner's Magazine*, XX, July 1896, 115. The passage, along with more of the letter, is also published in *Revue Germanique*, XII, July–Sept. 1921, pp. 249–51.

4. *EBB Letters*, II, 122, to Miss Mitford, July 15, 1853.

5. Ibid., II, 131, to Chorley, Aug. 10, [1853].

6. In a letter to Milsand. There is no date in Th. Bentzon, "A French Friend," p. 113.

7. *Brownings to George Barrett*, p. 200, Oct. 7, [1853].

8. The friendship between the William Wetmore Storys and the Brownings developed during the summer of 1853, when both families were in Bagni di Lucca. They planned to spend the winter of 1853–4 in Rome. Soon after the Brownings arrived, the six-year-old Joseph Story died and his sister Edith was very ill for a time. This grief and the fear for Pen Browning cast a shadow over the Brownings' first winter in Rome. (*Browning to American Friends*, pp. 3–4.)

9. *EBB Letters*, II, 144, to Sarianna Browning, [Autumn 1853].

10. *Browning to American Friends*, p. 33, June 11, 1854.

11. *New Letters*, p. 77, June 5, 1854.

12. *EBB Letters*, II, 162, to Sarianna Browning, [ca. Mar. 1854].

13. "Letters from Browning," *Century Magazine*, LXXXIV, n.s. LXII, May 1912, 130, to James T. Fields, Aug. 25, 1854.

14. Berg MS, EBB to Arabel, Jan. 10–1, [1855].

15. *EBB Letters*, II, 193, to Mrs. Martin, Apr. 20, 1855; II, 195, to Mrs. Emil Braun, May 13, [1855].

16. Browning gave an account of the experience in a letter to Mrs. William B. Kinney, dated July 25, 1855. This letter was first published by W. L. Phelps in "Robert Browning on Spiritualism" *(Yale Review,* n.s. XXIII, Sept. 1933, 129–38) and more recently by Ronald A. Bosco in "The Brownings and Mrs. Kinney: A Record of Their Friendship" *(Browning Institute Studies,* IV, 1976, 85–9). See also *EBB to Sister,* pp. 219–20, Aug. 17, 1855; and D. D. Home, *Incidents in My Life,* 2d ser. (London: Tinsley Bros., 1892), pp. 105–8.

17. Berg MS, [Sept. 10, 1855].

18. Houghton MS, RB to John Kenyon, Oct. 1, 1855.

19. Ibid. For Elizabeth's comments on the visits, see *EBB to Sister,* p. 230, Oct. 3, 1855; *EBB Letters,* II, 213, to Mrs. Martin, [Oct. 1855].

20. *EBB Letters,* II, 209, to Mrs. Jameson, [July–Aug. 1855].

21. Ibid.

22. Wellesley MS, Mar. 17, 1853.

23. Houghton MS, Oct. 1, 1855.

24. Ibid.

25. William S. Peterson, "The Proofs of Browning's *Men and Women," Browning and His Circle,* III, Fall 1975, 23–39; Allan C. Dooley, "Further Notes on *Men and Women* Proofs," *Browning and His Circle,* V, Spring 1977, 52–4.

26. See *Letters,* Hood, p. 42, Oct. 29, 1855.

27. See *EBB to Sister,* p. 233, Nov. 15, 1855.

28. I have included the *Rambler* in the third group because the perceptive criticism outweighs the objections that originate from the Catholicism of the reviewer. The *New Quarterly Review* (1852–62) was not the *New Quarterly Review* of the forties, which contained reviews discussed in earlier chapters.

29. See, for example, the following: *Letters and Papers of John Addington Symonds,* ed. Horatio F. Brown (New York: Charles Scribner's Sons, 1923), p. 211; Felix Moscheles, *Fragments of an Autobiography* (New York: Harper & Bros., 1899), pp. 341–2; F. Max Müller, *Auld Lang Syne* (New York: Charles Scribner's Sons, 1899), pp. 161–2.

30. H. E. Greene, "Browning's Knowledge of Music," PMLA, LXII, Dec. 1947, 1099.

CHAPTER XVIII: *Limited Recognition*

1. *EBB Letters,* II, 444, W. M. Thackeray to EBB, Apr. 2, 1861.

2. Ibid., II, 245, to Mrs. Jameson, [po. Dec. 26, 1856]; II, 394, to Fanny Haworth, [po. June 16, 1860]. For the reception of *Aurora Leigh,* see Gardner B. Taplin, *The Life of Elizabeth Barrett Browning* (London: John Murray, 1957), pp. 337–47.

3. Houghton MS, RB to John Kenyon, Oct. 1, 1855.

4. *RB and AD,* p. 35, May 22, 1842.

5. *EBB to Sister,* p. 233, Nov. 15, 1855.

6. *New Letters,* p. 85.

7. Ronald A. Bosco, "The Brownings and Mrs. Kinney: A Record of Their Friendship," *Browning Institute Studies,* IV, 1976, 101.

8. *New Letters,* p. 87, Jan. 17, [1856].

9. *RB and EBB,* II, 662, [Apr. 28, 1846].

10. *New Letters,* p. 87, Jan. 17, [1856].

11. "Letters from Browning," *Century Magazine,* LXXXIV, n.s. LXII, May 1912, 130, Aug. 25, 1854.

12. See Ian Jack, "Browning on *Sordello* and *Men and Women:* Unpublished Letters to James T. Fields," *Huntington Library Quarterly,* XLV, Summer 1982, 186–7.

13. See ibid., pp. 186–90, RB to Fields, Sept. 6, Oct. 3, and Oct. 9, 1865.
14. *New Letters,* pp. 86–7, Jan. 17, [1856]; p. 89, Feb. 6, 1856; p. 90, [Apr. 12, 1856].
15. Greer, p. 76.
16. *New Letters,* p. 90.
17. Ibid., p. 92, Apr. 21, 1856.
18. George William Curtis, *From the Easy Chair* (New York: Harper & Bros., 1892), p. 202.
19. For Browning's references to *Sordello* and *Strafford,* see Jack, "Browning on *Sordello* and *Men and Women,"* pp. 187, 189, 190, 191, 196, 197 in letters dated Sept. 6, Oct. 3, Oct. 9, Oct. 26, 1855; and Feb. 4, June 18, 1856.
20. *Letters to William Allingham,* ed. H. Allingham and E. Baumer Williams (London: Longmans, Green & Co., 1911), p. 98.
21. See Jack, "Browning on *Sordello* and *Men and Women,"* p. 197.
22. *New Letters,* p. 97, Dec. 2, 1856. *Aurora Leigh* had a great success with the public though the critics wrote disapprovingly of it. See Taplin, *Elizabeth Barrett Browning,* pp. 310–2, 337–47.
23. K. L. Knickerbocker, "Browning and His Critics," *Sewanee Review,* XLIII, July 1935, 283–91.
24. *Dearest Isa,* p. 17, Sept. 4, 1858.
25. *Allingham: A Diary,* pp. 76–7.
26. *RB and EBB,* II, 906, [July 27, 1846].
27. *EBB Letters,* II, 219, to Ruskin, Nov. 5, [1855].
28. *New Letters,* Appendix B, p. 392.
29. *EBB letters,* II, 368–9, [ca. Mar. 1860].
30. *Dearest Isa,* p. 367, Oct. 1, 1871.
31. *Browning to American Friends,* p. 167, to Edith Story, Jan. 1, 1872.
32. *EBB Letters,* II, 388, to Fanny Haworth, [po. May 18, 1860]. In the same month Elizabeth also wrote Allingham of Browning's work. "Robert is writing, not political poems, but *a poem* in books, a line of which I have not seen — and also certain exquisite lyrics which I have seen." *(Letters to Allingham,* p. 107.)
33. See DeVane, p. 307; Irvine and Honan, p. 373.
34. *EBB Letters,* II, 369–70, [ca. Mar. 1860].
35. See Taplin, *Elizabeth Barrett Browning,* pp. 375–81; Dorothy Hewlett, *Elizabeth Barrett Browning* (New York: Alfred A. Knopf, 1952), pp. 356–7.
36. *EBB Letters,* II, 366, to Isa Blagden, [end of Mar. 1860].
37. Ibid., II, 372, to Isa Blagden, [Apr. 1860].
38. *Browning to American Friends,* pp. 61–2, to the Storys, June 19, 1860.
39. *EBB Letters,* II, 399, to Sarianna Browning, [ca. June 1860].
40. *Dearest Isa,* p. 288, Jan. 19, 1868.
41. *EBB Letters,* II, 434, 435, 436, [end of Mar.] 1861.
42. *Letters of Dante Gabriel Rossetti to William Allingham, 1854–1870,* ed. George Birkbeck Hill (New York: Frederick A. Stokes Co., 1897), p. 238.

CHAPTER XIX: *Nonprofessional Opinion in the Fifties*

1. *Household Words,* IV, Nov. 22, 1851, 213.
2. *English Songs, and Other Small Poems,* new ed. (London: Chapman & Hall, 1851), pp. xxv–xxx.
3. James T. Fields, " 'Barry Cornwall' and Some of His Friends," *Harper's New Monthly Magazine,* LI, Nov. 1875, 782. For Procter's high praise of Browning's originality

in a letter to Thomas Kelsall in the fifties, see *The Browning Box; or, The Life and Works of Thomas Lovell Beddoes,* ed. H. W. Donner (London: Oxford Univ. Press, 1935), p. 50.

4. "Robert Browning," *Pictures of the Living Authors of Britain* (London: Partridge & Oakey, 1851), pp. 61–75.

5. Mary Russell Mitford, *Recollections of a Literary Life* (London: Richard Bentley, 1852), I, 285–91. The comment on Browning's writing journey work is in *Letters of Mary Russell Mitford,* 2d ser., ed. Henry Chorley (London: Richard Bentley & Son, 1872), II, 27.

6. Anna Jameson, *A Commonplace Book of Thoughts, Memories, and Fancies* (London: Longman, Brown, Green, & Longmans, 1854), p. 81.

7. When Dante Gabriel Rossetti was asked to make some of the illustrations for Willmott's collection, he said that if Browning was included he would illustrate his poetry. Two of Browning's poems were included *(Evelyn Hope* and *Two in the Campagna),* but Rossetti did not make the illustrations. He signified his disapproval of the choice of poems *(Letters of Dante Gabriel Rossetti to William Allingham, 1854–1870,* ed. George Birkbeck Hill [New York: Frederick A. Stokes Co., 1897], pp. 173, 190–1). Allingham wrote several times to the Brownings about *Nightingale Valley* and the appearance of their poems in it *(Letters from William Allingham to Mr. and Mrs. Browning* [privately printed, 1914], pp. 7, 8, 9). It included *My Last Duchess, Protus, The Laboratory, Up at a Villa — Down in the City, May and Death* as well as several of Elizabeth's poems. Allingham's name was not on the title page; according to it *Nightingale Valley* was edited by "Giraldus."

8. *Sketches of the Poetical Literature of the Past Half-Century* (Edinburgh: William Blackwood & Sons, 1851), pp. 320–1.

9. *An Essay on the Characteristic Errors of Our Most Distinguished Living Poets* (Dublin: W. B. Kelly, 1853), pp. 25–31.

10. See M. E. Grant Duff, *Notes from a Diary, 1896 to January 23, 1901* (London: John Murray, 1905), I, 299.

11. See Edgar Finley Shannon, Jr., *Tennyson and the Reviewers* (Cambridge: Harvard Univ. Press, 1952), p. 151.

12. *P. R. B. Journal,* p. 96.

13. Texas MS, recorded in a diary of Story's in the W. W. Story Collection.

14. E. F. Bridell-Fox, "Robert Browning," *Argosy,* XLIX, Feb. 1890, 113.

15. Donald Smalley, "Joseph Arnould and Robert Browning: New Letters (1842–50) and a Verse Epistle," PMLA, LXXX, Mar. 1965, 100.

16. Ibid., pp. 92, 95–6.

17. Ibid., p. 100.

18. Macready, II, 464.

19. *Letters from Owen Meredith (Robert, First Earl of Lytton) to Robert and Elizabeth Barrett Browning,* ed. Aurelia Brooks Harlan and J. Lee Harlan, Jr., *Baylor University's Browning Interests,* 10th ser., 1936, p. 31.

20. Aurelia Brooks Harlan, *Owen Meredity: A Critical Biography of Robert, First Earl of Lytton* (New York: Columbia Univ. Press, 1946), pp. 58–9, 75; for continued influence, see pp. 108, 171.

21. *Letters from Owen Meredith,* p. 45.

22. *P. R. B. Journal,* pp. 68, 69, 75.

23. For Lytton's comment on *Men and Women* and his expressed wish to write a review, see *Letters from Owen Meredith,* pp. 114–5, 97–8. The excerpt is from the dedicatory poem *To J. F.* (John Forster) in Lytton's *The Wanderer;* it is quoted in Harlan, *Owen Meredith,* p. 89.

24. *Letters from Owen Meredith,* pp. 114–5.

25. Mrs. Andrew Crosse, *Red-Letter Days of My Life* (London: Richard Bentley & Son, 1892), I, 240.

26. For this paragraph, see Henry S. Salt, *The Life of James Thomson ("B. V.")* (London: Reeves & Turner, 1889), pp. 168, 223–4, 233, 240, 31–2.

27. Crosse, *Red-Letter Days,* I, 274–5.

28. For this paragraph, see *Rossetti to Allingham,* pp. 156–7, 159.

29. *Letters to William Allingham,* ed. H. Allingham and E. Baumer Williams (London: Longmans, Green & Co., 1911), p. 241.

30. Amy Woolner, *Thomas Woolner, R. A., Sculptor and Poet: His Life in Letters* (London: Chapman & Hall, 1917), p. 124; *Ruskin: Rossetti: Preraphaelitism, Papers 1854 to 1862,* ed. William Michael Rossetti (London: George Allen, 1899), p. 134.

31. Woolner's account of this bit of persuasion was given in a letter to Mrs. Tennyson (Amy Woolner, *Woolner,* p. 159); for Woolner's other letter to her, see ibid., p. 115; his letter to Allingham is in *Letters to Allingham,* p. 290.

32. See *Rossetti to Allingham,* p. 178.

33. J. W. Mackail, *The Life of William Morris* (London: Longmans, Green & Co., 1899), I, 46.

34. Ibid., I, 108.

35. Georgiana Burne-Jones, *Memorials of Edward Burne-Jones* (New York: Macmillan Co., 1906), I, 153.

36. Ibid., I, 129.

37. Mackail, *William Morris,* I, 132.

38. Maurice Browning Cramer, "Browning's Literary Reputation at Oxford, 1855–1859," PMLA, LVII, Mar. 1942, 232–40.

39. William Angus Knight, *Memoir of John Nichol* (Glasgow: James MacLehose & Sons, 1896), pp. 145–6.

40. *Dictionary of National Biography,* s.v. "Caird, Edward."

41. Knight, *John Nichol,* p. 157.

42. Ibid., pp. 126–7.

43. See *Oxford and Cambridge Magazine,* no. 12, Dec. 1856, pp. 719, 722, 724 (article reprinted in Nichol's *Fragments of Critcism); Westminster Review,* LXXII, n.s. XVI, Oct. 1, 1859, 512.

44. Knight, *John Nichol,* pp. 169, 181.

45. George Birkbeck Hill, *Writers and Readers* (London: T. Fisher Unwin, 1892), pp. 100–3.

46. Edmund Gosse, *The Life of Algernon Charles Swinburne* (London: Macmillan & Co., 1917), pp. 39–40.

47. *The Swinburne Letters, 1854–1869,* ed. Cecil Y. Lang (New Haven: Yale Univ. Press), I (1959), 16–7.

48. Swinburne wrote, ". . . I believe I am not exaggerating when I say that at nineteen I knew Sordello by heart from end to end — nay, I believe my blood is on your head and his, for I got 'ploughed for smalls' owing to my confining my study for the month previous to *that* in lieu of Euclid — and the hard hearts of examiners would not have accepted a declamation of Salinguerra's soliloquy as compensation for a sum in rule-of-three." *(The Swinburne Letters, 1875–1877,* III [1960], 20.)

49. "Ruskin and the Brownings: Twenty-Five Unpublished Letters," ed. David J. DeLaura, *Bulletin of the John Rylands Library,* LIV, Spring 1972, 314–56.

50. See ibid., p. 322.

51. See *Rossetti to Allingham,* p. 163.

52. "Ruskin and the Brownings," pp. 324, 326.

53. *Rossetti to Allingham,* p. 163.
54. "Ruskin and the Brownings," p. 327.
55. *The Works of John Ruskin,* ed. E. T. Cook and Alexander Wedderburn (London: George Allen), XXXVI (1909), xxxiv–vi.
56. "Ruskin and the Brownings," p. 329.
57. "A Letter from Robert Browning to John Ruskin," *Baylor Browning Interests,* no. 17, 1958, pp. [2–3]; *Works of Ruskin,* V (1904), 336.
58. "Ruskin and the Brownings," p. 335.
59. Ibid., p. 322.
60. Ibid., p. 335.
61. Ibid., p. 336.
62. For the section in Vol. IV of *Modern Painters* that is discussed in this paragraph, see *Works of Ruskin,* VI (1904), 446–9.
63. Ibid., XVI (1905), 458.
64. See ibid., XIV (1904), xxiv and n. 2.
65. "Ruskin and the Brownings," pp. 326–7.
66. *Works of Ruskin,* XXXVI (1909), xxxiv–v.
67. *RB and EBB,* I, 150, [Aug. 10, 1845].
68. "Ruskin and the Brownings," p. 326.
69. *Works of Ruskin,* XXXVI (1909), xxxv.
70. "Ruskin and the Brownings," p. 326.
71. *Works of Ruskin,* XXXVI (1909), xxxv.
72. "Letter from Browning to Ruskin," p. [3].
73. See *Works of Ruskin,* V (1904), 336.
74. For Ruskin's denial that he had Browning in mind in Vol. III, see "Ruskin and the Brownings," p. 330. The quoted passages are in "Letter from Browning to Ruskin," pp. [3–4].
75. *Works of Ruskin,* XXXVI (1909), xxxvi.
76. *The Correspondence of Arthur Hugh Clough,* ed. Frederick L. Mulhauser (Oxford: Clarendon Press, 1957), II, 514.
77. James Grant Wilson, *Thackeray in the United States, 1852–3, 1855–6* (New York: Dodd, Mead & Co., 1904), I, 118; *Allingham: A Diary,* p. 76.
78. *Tennyson and His Friends,* ed. Hallam Tennyson (London: Macmillan & Co., 1912), p. 96.
79. The quotations are from a letter written by Mrs. Jameson to EBB. It is partly quoted by Clara Thomas in her *Love and Work Enough: The Life of Anna Jameson* (Toronto: Univ. of Toronto Press, 1967), p. 211.
80. "Correspondence between Carlyle and Browning," ed. Alexander Carlyle, *Cornhill Magazine,* CXI, n.s. XXXVIII, May 1915, p. 663.
81. Ibid., p. 664, Jan. 23, 1856; also (with slight changes) in *Letters,* Hood, p. 44.
82. Charles Richard Sanders, "Some Lost and Unpublished Carlyle-Browning Correspondence," *Journal of English and Germanic Philology,* LXII, Apr. 1963, 329–30.
83. "Correspondence between Carlyle and Browning," p. 666 (misnumbered 664).
84. "Letter from Browning to Ruskin," p. [4], Feb. 1, 1856.
85. "Correspondence between Carlyle and Browning," p. 666 (misnumbered 664).
86. For Carlyle's comments in this paragraph, see ibid., pp. 666–7.
87. *Letters,* Hood, p. 41, July 25, 1853; and also Ronald A. Bosco, "The Brownings and Mrs. Kinney: A Record of Their Friendship," *Browning Institute Studies,* IV, 1976, 75.
88. "Correspondence between Carlyle and Browning," p. 665 (misnumbered 667), Jan. 23, 1856; also *Letters,* Hood, p. 44.

89. *New Letters,* p. 95, Aug. 20, [1856].
90. Houghton MS, Oct. 1, 1855.
91. Helen Rossetti Angeli, *Dante Gabriel Rossetti: His Friends and Enemies* (London: Hamish Hamilton, 1949), p. 168.
92. Texas MS, Apr. 22, 1856.
93. "Letter from Browning to Ruskin," p. [4].
94. Texas MS.
95. *New Letters,* pp. 92–3, Apr. 21, 1856.
96. See Orr, pp. 346–7. We know that Carlyle manifested his favorable, if sometimes qualified, opinion to Allingham, M. D. Conway, Charles Gavan Duffy, Emerson, Fitzgerald, Forster, Lady Ashburton, and John Tyndall.
97. Texas MS, Apr. 22, 1856.
98. *The Browning Society's Papers* (London: N. Trübner & Co., 1881–91), I, 92; *Rossetti to Allingham,* p. 160.

CHAPTER XX: *Attracting Readers*

1. Forster and Dyce MS, Carlyle to Forster, Aug. 17, 1861.
2. Richard Willard Armour, *Barry Cornwall: A Biography of Bryan Waller Procter* (Boston: Meador Publishing Co., 1935), p. 274.
3. Ibid., p. 276.
4. T. Wemyss Reid, *The Life, Letters, and Friendships of Richard Monckton Milnes,* 2d ed. (London: Cassell & Co., 1890), II, 78–9; Houghton MS, Wednesday, [Feb. 5, 1862]. For the letter from the secretary of the club to Browning telling him of his election, see "Intimate Glimpses from Browning's Letter File," *Baylor University's Browning Interests,* 8th ser., 1934, pp. 29–30.
5. *Dearest Isa,* p. 95; *Browning to American Friends,* p. 99, Feb. 13, 1862.
6. *Dearest Isa,* p. 130, Oct. 18, 1862.
7. *Browning to American Friends,* pp. 100–1, Mar. 19, 1862.
8. Ibid., p. 101, Mar. 19, 1862; pp. 106–7, Apr. 10, 1862.
9. *Dearest Isa,* p. 119, Aug. 18, 1862.
10. William Lyon Phelps, "Robert Browning as Seen by His Son," *Century Magazine,* LXXXV, Jan. 1913, 419.
11. *Browning to American Friends,* p. 101, Mar. 19, 1862. "SCULPTOR & poet" did not appear on the title page of the *Selections.*
12. Ibid., p. 112.
13. *Brownings to George Barrett,* p. 283.
14. John Skelton, *The Table-Talk of Shirley,* 6th ed. (Edinburgh: William Blackwood & Sons, 1896), pp. 128, 129–30.
15. "Intimate Glimpses from Browning's Letter File," p. 30.
16. Skelton, *Table-Talk of Shirley,* p. 288, Mar. 31, 1863. Skelton had written his note on Mar. 16.
17. Ibid., p. 289.
18. *Dearest Isa,* pp. 162–3, May 19, 1863.
19. Ibid., p. 150, Jan. 19, 1863; p. 154, Feb. 19, 1863.
20. *RB and EBB,* I, 39, [Mar. 11, 1845].
21. *Celebrities and I* (London: Hutchinson & Co., 1902), p. 165.
22. See *Allingham: A Diary,* pp. 310–11; Orr, p. 86.
23. Isabella F. Mayo, *Recollections* (London: John Murray, 1910), p. 199; J. Comyns Carr, *Some Eminent Victorians* (London: Duckworth & Co., 1908), p. 203; Robert U. Johnson, *Remembered Yesterdays* (Boston: Little, Brown, & Co., 1923), p. 504. For the effect of

Browning's gloves, see Hall Caine, *Recollections of [D. G.] Rossetti* (London: Cassell & Co., 1928), p. 170.

24. Mrs. Thomas Bailey Aldrich, *Crowding Memories* (Boston: Houghton Mifflin Co., 1920), p. 178–9.

25. *Letters of Dante Gabriel Rossetti to William Allingham, 1854–1870,* ed. George Birkbeck Hill (New York: Frederick A. Stokes Co., 1897), p. 160; *Life and Letters of Sir Charles Hallé,* ed. C. E. Hallé and Marie Hallé (London: Smith, Elder, & Co., 1896), pp. 126–7.

26. Justin McCarthy, *Reminiscences* (London: Chatto & Windus, 1899), I, 46.

27. W[ilfrid] M[eynell], "The 'Detachment' of Browning," *Athenaeum,* Jan. 4, 1890, p. 19.

28. For the impressions given by Mary Gladstone, see *Mary Gladstone (Mrs. Drew): Her Diaries and Letters,* ed. Lucy Masterman (London: Methuen & Co., 1930), pp. 116–7, Mar. 9, 1877, and p. 156, May 29, 1879. For the impression given by Henry James, see his *William Wetmore Story and His Friends* (Boston: Houghton, Mifflin & Co., 1904), II, 88–9 (as well as his short story *The Private Life*).

29. Charles Gavan Duffy, *My Life in Two Hemispheres* (London: T. Fischer Unwin, 1903), II, 259.

30. *Browning's Trumpeter: The Correspondence of Robert Browning and Frederick J. Furnivall, 1872–1889,* ed. William S. Peterson (Washington, D.C.: Decatur House Press, 1979); for a variety of information, see pp. 20, 48, 70–1, 102, 154, 157. Browning's exchange of comments with Julia Wedgwood on *The Ring and the Book* in *RB and JW* will be discussed in Chap. XXVIII.

31. See *Letters,* Hood, to H. Buxton Forman, pp. 174–5, July 27, 1876, and pp. 179–80, July 2, 1877; to Edward Dowden, pp. 91–2, Mar. 5, 1866.

32. "Letters from Robert Browning to the Rev. J. D. Williams, 1874–1889," ed. Thomas J. Collins, asst. Walter J. Pickering, *Browning Institute Studies,* IV, 1976, 34, 38, 40, 46. The reference to Mrs. Orr's "Primer" is on p. 38, in Browning's letter of Sept. 24, 1884.

33. Rudolf Lehmann, *An Artist's Reminiscences* (London: Smith, Elder, & Co., 1894), p. 224.

34. Two were John C. Collins and Lawrence Barrett. See L. C. Collins, *John Churton Collins* (London: John Lane, Bodley Head, 1912), pp. 78–84; and Greer, p. 195.

35. *Memories & Notes of Persons & Places, 1852–1912* (New York: Charles Scribner's Sons, 1921), pp. 83–4.

36. *Browning Institute Studies,* IX, 1981, 59–77.

37. *Learned Lady: Letters from Robert Browning to Mrs. Thomas FitzGerald, 1876–1889,* ed. Edward C. McAleer (Cambridge: Harvard Univ. Press, 1966), p. 151, Aug. 23, 1882.

38. Skelton, *Table-Talk of Shirley,* p. 289.

39. Alice Corkran, "Chapters from the Story of My Girlhood," *Girl's Realm,* Nov. 1904, pp. 279–80. The quotation follows and seems to grow out of Browning's remarks on *The Inn Album.*

40. DeVane, pp. 384–5.

CHAPTER XXI: *A Broad View*

1. *Dearest Isa,* p. 288, Jan. 19, 1868.

2. We learn this from Browning's comment; see ibid., p. 167, July 19, 1863. I have not located the article.

3. *New Letters,* p. 157, Sept. 17, 1863.

4. See ibid., pp. 91–2, Apr. 21, 1856.

5. The dedication to Milsand was quoted in Chap. IV. The one to Forster reads: "I dedicate these volumes to my old friend John Forster, glad and grateful that he who, from the first publication of the various poems they include, has been their promptest and staunchest helper, should seem even nearer to me now than thirty years ago." Following his note in Volume I on the redistribution of his poems, Browning wrote, "Part of these were inscribed to my dear friend John Kenyon: I hope the whole may obtain the honour of an association with his memory." Other dedications that had appeared earlier were reprinted in Volumes II and III with few changes.

6. *Dearest Isa*, p. 176, Sept. 19, 1863.

7. See *RB and EBB*, I, 382, [Jan. 11, 1846]. Browning went so far as to say that a review in the *Athenaeum* would have no great effect on him, yet he was relieved and grateful when one later appeared (ibid.,397–8, [Jan. 17, 1846]).

8. *Browning to American Friends*, p. 135, Nov. 26, 1863.

9. *Dearest Isa*, pp. 180–1, Nov. 19, 1863.

CHAPTER XXII: *Timely Topics and Wider Acceptance*

1. *Dearest Isa*, p. 137, Nov. 19, 1862.

2. *New Letters*, p. 87, Jan. 17, [1856].

3. *Dearest Isa*, p. 134, Nov. 19, 1862.

4. *Browning to American Friends*, p. 118, Mar. 5, 1863.

5. Ibid., p. 130, Sept. 5, 1863.

6. *Dearest Isa*, p. 180, Nov. 19, 1863; *Browning to American Friends*, p. 136, Nov. 26, 1863.

7. *Dearest Isa*, p. 168, July 19, 1863.

8. *Browning to American Friends*, pp. 143–4, May 3, 1864.

9. Early in 1864 Ticknor and Fields had published *Sordello, Strafford,* and *Christmas-Eve and Easter-Day* in an unauthorized volume. Greer defended the publishers. "Had they expected to make money on their *Sordello* volume, these publishers would probably, instead of pirating it, have made some financial arrangement with Browning; for their company was known as one which looked after the material interests of its authors, English as well as Americans, and did not take full advantage of the buccaneering opportunities of that day" (p. 114).

10. In at least two letters Browning reminded Fields that he had not received anything from him for his earlier works, one dated Aug. 25, 1854 ("Letters from Browning," *Century Magazine*, LXXXIV, n.s. LXII, May 1912, 130) and another dated Oct. 16, 1863 (Houghton MS; partly published in James C. Austin, *Fields of the Atlantic Monthly* [San Marino, California: Huntington Library, 1953], p. 401). Some who learned from Browning or from others of his complaints of the practices of Fields were W. W. Story (*Browning to American Friends*, pp. 277–8, Aug. 10, 1853); George Smith (RB to Smith, Dec. 2, 1875, Murray MS); J. R. Lowell (*Browning to American Friends*, pp. 358–9, Sept. 6, 1880).

11. *New Letters*, p. 125, to W. M. Thackeray, Jan. 17, 1860.

12. Houghton MS, RB to James T. Fields, Oct. 16, 1863.

13. Richard Willard Armour, *Barry Cornwall: A Biography of Bryan Waller Procter* (Boston: Meador Publishing Co., 1935), p. 294.

14. Greer, p. 119.

15. Houghton MS, RB to James T. Fields, Oct. 16, 1863.

16. According to a letter Browning later wrote Fields (Houghton MS, po. Aug. 1, 1864), the American firm made nothing — probably lost — by the financial arrangement.

Greer has indicated the generosity of Ticknor and Fields in dealing with the authors whose work they published (pp. 114–5). If payment of £100 for several poems seems unrealistic beside the £60 for the whole of *Dramatis Personae,* we can be reminded of the reports of Browning's declining to contribute a poem to a magazine in one instance in exchange for $1,000 and in another in exchange for any sum he might write on a blank check sent to him (M. E. Grant Duff, *Notes from a Diary, 1886–1888* [London: John Murray, 1900], II, 128; Rudolf Lehmann, *An Artist's Reminiscences* [London: Smith, Elder, & Co., 1894], p. 226, and *Letters,* Hood, p. 244).

17. Moncure Daniel Conway, *Autobiography: Memories and Experiences* (Boston: Houghton, Mifflin & Co., 1904), II, 18.

18. *New Letters,* p. 160, Apr. 26, 1864; p. 161, [May 1864].

19. *Robert Browning: A Bibliography, 1830–1950,* comp. Leslie Nathan Broughton, Clark Sutherland Northup, and Robert Pearsall (Ithaca, New York: Cornell Univ. Press, 1953), p. 14. "New ed.," 1970. (Pearsall says that "updating and some correcting" may be found in the articles on the Brownings.)

20. *Dearest Isa,* p. 180, Nov. 19, 1863. See the chapter "Browning and Higher Criticism" in William O. Raymond's *The Infinite Moment and Other Essays in Robert Browning,* 2d ed. (Toronto: Univ. of Toronto Press, 1965), particularly pp. 29–35.

21. Baden Powell, "On the Study of the Evidences of Christianity," in *Essays and Reviews,* 2d ed. (London: John W. Parker & Son, 1860), p. 117.

22. Quoted in Alexander V. G. Allen, *The Continuity of Christian Thought: A Study of Modern Theology in the Light of Its History* (Boston: Houghton, Mifflin & Co., 1884), p. 286.

23. L. E. Elliott-Binns, *Religion in the Victorian Era,* 2d ed. (London: Lutterworth Press, 1946), p. 285.

24. With introductory remarks (including a statement that there was no connection between him and Browning's portrait of Sludge) and quotations from *Mr. Sludge,* Home reprinted "Mr. Robert Browning on Spiritualism" and "Mr. Home's Account" in his revised *Incidents in My Life.* See the chapter "Sludge, the Medium — Mr. Robert Browning — Fancy Portraits" in D. D. Home, *Incidents in My Life,* 2d ser. (London: Tinsley Bros., 1872), pp. 95–111.

25. For a reference in Browning's letter of Jan. 6, 1871, to Home's account, see *New Letters,* p. 199. The letter is also in Ronald A. Bosco, "The Brownings and Mrs. Kinney: A Record of Their Friendship," *Browning Institute Studies,* IV, 1976, pp. 109–10.

26. *Dearest Isa,* p. 191.

CHAPTER XXIII: *Critics Against Critics*

1. *RB and JW,* pp. 41–2, Aug. 19, 1864. Browning took the story (he lowercased capitals, deleted parenthetical remarks, and made changes in punctuation) from a note on p. 84 of *Travels of Rabbi Benjamin, Son of Jonah of Tudela . . . ,* trans. B. Gerrans, 1783. Browning's grandfather owned a copy of this book (*RB and JW,* p. 42); on p. iv his name appears in a printed list of subscribers. In Sotheby *Travels of Rabbi Benjamin* is listed on p. 73 (Lot 381). The British Library has a copy. A version of the story of the patient teacher Perida (or Pereda) is told in the Talmud, Erubin, 54b. It and the version that Browning used vary in details.

2. *Dearest Isa,* p. 196, Oct. 19, 1864.

3. *RB and JW,* pp. 87–8.

4. Ibid., pp. 93–4.

5. Gwenllian F. Palgrave, *Francis Turner Palgrave: His Journals and Memories of His Life* (New York: Longmans, Green, & Co., 1899), pp. 94–5.

6. *RB and JW,* p. 111.

7. Ibid., p. 101, [Nov. 11, 1864].

8. Bagehot said that in quoting *The Pied Piper* he was illustrating the grotesque "under its best and most satisfactory conditions." But even so, in concentrating on the grotesque he was guilty of giving a disproportionate impression of Browning. Just before the printing of *Dramatic Lyrics* Browning sent *The Pied Piper* to fill in some blank pages (Orr, p. 122). In an incidental mention of the poem after Browning's death his sister indicated that he had never intended to publish it. "Yet is there any of his poems really popular? except, perhaps, the Pied Piper — for which he may thank me and Alfred Domett, as he himself did not think it worth publishing." (Texas MS, Sarianna Browning to Mrs. Miller Morison, Aug. 29, 1899.)

9. *RB and EBB,* I, 221, [Oct. 2, 1845].

10. *RB and JW,* p. 113, [Feb. 1865].

CHAPTER XXIV: *Republications and Inclusive Reviews*

1. *Dearest Isa,* pp. 219–20.

2. See Forster and Dyce MS, Bryan Waller Procter to John Forster, [1865].

3. The revisions were first noticed by Nathaniel I. Hart ("A Browning Letter on 'The Poetical Works' of 1863," *Notes and Queries,* n.s. XXI, June 1974, 213–5). For more detailed discussions, see Allan C. Dooley, "The Textual Significance of Robert Browning's 1865 *Poetical Works,*" *Papers of the Bibliographical Society of America,* LXXI, Second Quarter 1977, 212–8; *Works of Browning,* ed. Jack and Smith, I, Textual Introduction, xix.

4. *Letters of Alexander Macmillan,* ed. George A. Macmillan (Printed for Private Circulation, 1908), p. 186.

5. Baylor MSS, A. Macmillan to RB, July 20, 1865; RB to Frederic Chapman, Saturday morning, [July 22, 1865].

6. *Dearest Isa,* p. 220, Aug. 19, 1865.

7. Wellesley MS, RB to Frederic Chapman, July 5, 1867.

8. Murray MS, RB to George Smith, Nov. 11, 1867.

9. *Rossetti Papers, 1862 to 1870,* p. 299.

10. Betty Miller, without giving her source, wrote that Browning with "extreme repugnance" included *Pauline* to "satisfy" George Smith and she then quoted from his letter to Smith of Dec. 10, 1867. "I will include *Pauline* as you desire" (*Robert Browning: A Portrait* [London: John Murray, 1952], p. 241). According to Michael Meredith, Smith requested Browning's permission to reprint the poem. "Browning stalled, then reluctantly agreed, and sent one of the rare first editions to the printers as copy" ("Browning and the Prince of Publishers," *Browning Institute Studies,* VII, 1979, 9). Meredith did not give the source of this statement. Though he and Miller have suggested that Browning reluctantly included *Pauline* in the 1868 collected edition as the result of Smith's wish, Browning himself, as we have seen, indicated that he did not arrive at his decision to include the poem solely as the result of Smith's wish.

11. Murray MS, RB to George Smith, Jan. 4, 1868.

12. *Rossetti Papers, 1862 to 1870,* pp. 298–9.

13. *Letters,* Hood, pp. 122–3, Oct. 16, 1867; pp. 123–4, Dec. 13, 1867.

14. [V. A. G. R. Lytton], *The Life of Edward Bulwer, First Lord Lytton* (London: Macmillan & Co., 1913), II, 396. The author is not named on the title page, but he is identified as the grandson of Edward Bulwer Lytton.

15. I am indebted to Gerald W. Murray, the librarian at Marlborough College, for answering (in a letter of Sept. 20, 1967) my inquiries concerning this magazine (which was still running a hundred years after the time of these articles on Browning) and giving

me additional related information. He was able to establish the authorship of the first article but not of the second.

16. *Some Eminent Victorians* (London: Duckworth & Co., 1908), p. 199.

17. *Life and Letters of Dean Church,* ed. Mary C. Church (London: Macmillan & Co., 1894), p. 343.

18. For the Browning-Chapman relationship, see *New Letters,* Appendix C (K. L. Knickerbocker, "Why Browning Severed Relations with Chapman and Hall"), pp. 393–400.

19. Baylor MS, RB to Edward Chapman, Feb. 23, 1852.

20. *New Letters,* p. 174, June 26, 1866.

21. *Letters to William Allingham,* ed. H. Allingham and E. Baumer Williams (London: Longmans, Green & Co., 1911), p. 175.

22. Baylor MS, RB to Frederic Chapman, Jan. 8, 1867.

23. NYPL MSS, Frederic Chapman to RB, Nov. 9, 1867, and May 21, 1868.

24. Baylor MS, Christian Bernhard Tauchnitz to RB, Mar. 11, 1867. See Browning's remark to Isa on Jan. 19, 1868, for a follow-up of Tauchnitz's proposal (*Dearest Isa,* p. 289).

25. For their association, see [Leonard Huxley], *The House of Smith Elder* (London: Printed for Private Circulation, 1923), pp. 155–8; Miller, *Robert Browning,* pp. 233, 241–3; L. P. Kelley, "Robert Browning and George Smith: Selections from an Unpublished Correspondence," *Quarterly Review,* CCXCIX, July 1961, 323–35; Meredith, "Browning and the Prince of Publishers," pp. 1–20.

26. On Jan. 19, 1868, Browning indicated in a letter to Isa that she had received £170 from Chapman for one of her novels, which, he said, was £50 more than Chapman had paid him for his three-volume collected edition (*Dearest Isa,* p. 288). On Dec. 31, 1867, he had said that George Smith gave him five times as much for the 1868 edition as Chapman had given him for his earlier collected edition (ibid., p. 286).

27. Murray MS, Dec. 10, 1867.

28. I have based this statement on the large collection of letters from Browning to George Smith, which I examined through the kindness of Mr. John Murray. I am grateful to him for permission to quote from the letters and to Mrs. Virginia Murray for her assistance.

29. *Dearest Isa,* p. 291, Feb. 19, 1868. See the following pages in *Dearest Isa* for the other comments given in this paragraph: pp. 253–4, Feb. 19, 1867; p. 268, June 19, 1867; p. 284, Nov. 19, 1867. The "hint" might have come from George Smith. On Oct. 21, 1867, Browning sent him news of the election: ". . . you get it *first* and can do what you like with it [Murray MS]." Jowett's letters to RB, which are in Baylor University, include two (Jan. 29 and Feb. 14, 1867) on the subject of the professorship.

30. Browning declined this as well as other invitations of the future. See "Intimate Glimpses from Browning's Letter File," *Baylor University's Browning Interests,* 8th ser., 1934, pp. 3–23.

CHAPTER XXV: *The Masterpiece: From Inception to Publication*

1. "Correspondence between Carlyle and Browning," ed. Alexander Carlyle, *Cornhill Magazine,* CXI, n.s. XXXVIII, May 1915, 667.

2. *RB and JW,* p. 154, Jan. 21, 1869.

3. He offered it to Miss Ogle (Orr, p. 251); W. C. Cartwright (Griffin and Minchin, p. 234); A. Trollope (*Allingham: A Diary,* pp. 180); and Tennyson (ibid., 326).

4. *Dearest Isa,* p. 134, Nov. 19, 1862.

5. *Rossetti Papers, 1862 to 1870,* p. 302.

6. *RB and JW*, pp. 43, 79; *Dearest Isa*, p. 193. The letter to Isa was erroneously dated by Orr (p. 250). W. O. Raymond convincingly settled the date as Sept. 19, 1864, in an article published in Nov. 1928 (MLN) and reprinted in his chapter "New Light on the Genesis of 'The Ring and the Book' " in *The Infinite Moment and Other Essays in Robert Browning*, 2d ed. (Toronto: Univ. of Toronto Press, 1965), pp. 75–88.

7. Rudolf Lehmann, *An Artist's Reminiscences* (London: Smith, Elder, & Co., 1894), p. 224.

8. See Paul A. Cundiff, "The Dating of Browning's Conception of the Plan of *The Ring and the Book*," *Studies in Philology*, XXXVIII, July 1941, 543–51. As support of his contention that the Pass was connected in no way with the conception of the poem, Cundiff quoted Browning's own words: ". . . in the spring I print the new poems & a new edition of my things in four vols . . . I am about a long poem to be something remarkable, work at it hard." (The ellipsis dots are Cundiff's; the typographical form makes it seem that he was quoting from one and the same passage, but after the second ellipsis he skipped two or more pages in his source.) Cundiff said that Browning wrote this to Isa on Dec. 19, 1862. Although the first part of the quotation does come from Browning's letter of that date, the last part, which Cundiff emphasized in support of his dating, was not written on Dec. 19, 1862, but on Mar. 18, 1865, and consequently it cannot prove that Browning was working hard on *The Ring and the Book* in 1862. Cundiff had to depend on Browning's letters to Isa as they were printed by A. J. Armstrong (1923). When Edward C. McAleer studied the manuscripts, edited the letters, and published them as *Dearest Isa* (1951), he indicated (p. 145, n. 15) that the last portion of Cundiff's quotation was on a manuscript sheet that belonged to the letter written on Mar. 18, 1865. In this month Browning also wrote to Miss Wedgwood of his hard work on the poem (p. 122). Some scholars (see DeVane, pp. 321, 322–3; and Irvine and Honan, p., 406) who have considered Cundiff's case for an earlier dating of the conception of *The Ring and the Book* have not pointed out that the evidence on which it depends most heavily is invalid. Rossetti's and Lehmann's accounts can be reconciled, as DeVane says. They follow the same general pattern, but Lehmann's does not specify details of time and place.

9. *RB and JW*, p. 79, Oct. 3, 1864; *Dearest Isa*, p. 196, Oct. 19, 1864.

10. *RB and JW*, p. 122, [Mar. 1, 1865]; *Dearest Isa*, p. 239, May 19, 1866; *RB and JW*, p. 126, May 17, 1867; *Dearest Isa*, p. 274, July 19, 1867.

11. *Dearest Isa*, p. 285, Nov. 19, 1867. Browning had also indicated the time of completion to others. On June 12, 1865, he wrote to Edward Twisleton that it would be late autumn (Houghton MS); on Nov. 13, 1865, to Frederick Wedmore that it would be in 1866 (*New Letters*, p. 169); on Oct. 16, 1867, to Edward Dowden that hopefully he would "be rid of it in a few months more" (*Letters*, Hood, p. 123).

12. *Browning to American Friends*, p. 154, July 8, 1865; *Dearest Isa*, p. 239, May 19, 1866.

13. *Dearest Isa*, p. 263, Apr. 23, 1867; *RB and JW*, p. 126, May 17, 1867.

14. *Allingham: A Diary*, p. 195.

15. See *The Ring and the Book*, vol. I, bk. 1, 11. 418–22.

16. Griffin and Minchin, pp. 18–9. See also A. K. Cook, *A Commentary upon Browning's "The Ring and the Book"* (London: Oxford Univ. Press, 1920), pp. 64 (11. 1065–6) and 126 (1. 1078).

17. *Dearest Isa*, p. 124, Sept. 19, 1862.

18. Orr, p. 273, Oct. 17, 1864.

19. Baylor MS, RB to A. Panizzi, Mar. 19, 1866.

20. Houghton MS, A. Panizzi to RB, Mar. 21, 1866.

21. See *Dearest Isa,* p. 238, May 19, 1866; *Letters,* Hood, pp. 105–6, to Seymour Kirkup, Feb. 19, 1867.

22. *Brownings to George Barrett,* p. 288, Jan. 28, 1867. For some further indications of Browning's underground work, see pp. 265–6 (11. 222–4), 295 and n. 3, and 301 of Cook's *Commentary.*

23. See *The Ring and the Book,* vol. IV, bk. 10, 1. 1211.

24. Orr, p. 270; *Allingham: A Diary,* p. 181.

25. *Dearest Isa,* p. 239, May 19, 1866. For other comments on early working hours, see *Rossetti Papers, 1862 to 1870,* p. 298; and Oscar Browning, "Personal Recollections of English Poets," *Empire Review,* XXXVIII, Nov. 1923, 1243.

26. *RB and JW,* p. 162, Feb. 1, 1869.

27. *Dearest Isa,* p. 212, Mar. 18, 1865; p. 220, Aug. 19, 1865.

28. Robert Secor, "Robert Browning and the Hunts of South Kensington," *Browning Institute Studies,* VII, 1979, 118.

29. *Allingham: A Diary,* p. 195.

30. *RB and JW,* p. 162, Feb. 1, 1869.

31. *The Life and Letters of Benjamin Jowett,* ed. Evelyn Abbott and Lewis Campbell, 2d ed. (London: John Murray, 1897), I, 423.

32. *Rossetti Papers, 1862 to 1870,* p. 302.

33. *Letters,* Hood, p. 114, to Fields, Osgood, & Co., July 19, 1867.

34. Murray MS, RB to George Smith, July 8, 1868.

35. Joseph Johnson, *George MacDonald* (New York: Haskell House Publishers, 1973), p. 63.

36. See Berg MS, EBB to Arabel, Jan. 10–1, [1855]. Browning spoke to Thackeray's daughter of this custom. (See Anne Ritchie, *Records of Tennyson, Ruskin, Browning* [New York: Harper & Bros., 1899], p. 162.)

37. *Dearest Isa,* p. 285, Nov. 19, [1867]; *Rossetti Papers, 1862 to 1870,* p. 302.

38. *Dearest Isa,* p. 263, Apr. 23, 1867.

39. Murray MS, RB to George Smith, July 8, 1868.

40. [Leonard Huxley], *The House of Smith Elder* (London: Printed for Private Circulation, 1923), p. 156.

41. Murray MS, RB to George Smith, July 8, 1868.

42. British Library MS, RB to George Smith, Jan. 1, 1869.

43. Richard Willard Armour, *Barry Cornwall: A Biography of Bryan Waller Procter* (Boston: Meador Publishing Co., 1935), p. 324.

44. *Allingham: A Diary,* p. 181.

45. *Letters,* Hood, p. 114, to Fields, Osgood, & Co., July 19, 1867.

46. He might have been thinking of the difficulty his critics had in digesting all the poems in the two volumes of *Men and Women* (1855) when he decided to publish his 1863 collected edition in three volumes at intervals (May, June, Sept.). He was encouraged by the reception of the collected edition.

47. Murray MSS, RB to George Smith, [July 7, 1868], and July 8, 1868.

48. *Browning to American Friends,* p. 130, Sept. 5, 1863.

49. British Library MS, RB to George Smith, July 30, 1868.

50. NYPL MS, Ticknor & Fields to RB, May 14, 1867.

51. Texas MS, Ticknor & Fields to RB, June 18, 1867.

52. *Letters,* Hood, pp. 113–4, to Fields, Osgood, & Co., July 19, 1867.

53. *The Browning Newsletter,* no. 4, Spring 1970, pp. 57–8.

54. *Letters,* Hood, p. 127, to Fields, Osgood, & Co., Sept. 2, 1868.

55. The quotation from Fields' letter (MS is in the Berg Collection in the NYPL) is taken from W. S. Tryon, *Parnassus Corner: A Life of James T. Fields* (Boston: Houghton Mifflin Co., 1963), p. 325. It is also in James C. Austin, *Fields of the Atlantic Monthly* (San Marino, Calif., Huntington Library, 1953), p. 402, and Greer, p. 124. Greer quoted from RB's letter (MS in the Huntington Library in California) and Austin published the whole letter (p. 403).

56. Greer, pp. 124 and 285, n. 41.

57. Baylor MS, James T. Fields to RB, Nov. 12, 1868. See Austin, *Fields,* pp. 403–4, for an unfavorable impression given by Fields and by Mrs. Fields.

CHAPTER XXVI:

No notes.

CHAPTER XXVII:

No notes.

CHAPTER XXVIII: *Nonprofessional Opinion in the Sixties*

1. Frances Power Cobbe, *Italics: Brief Notes on Politics, People, and Places in Italy in 1864* (London: Trübner & Co., 1864), p. 393–4.

2. *From a Victorian Post-Bag: Being Letters Addressed to the Rev. J. Llewelyn Davies by Thomas Carlyle & Others,* ed. C. L. Davies (London: Peter Davies, 1926), p. 75.

3. *Letters of Alexander Macmillan,* ed. George A. Macmillan (Printed for Private Circulation, 1908), p. 178.

4. *Letters of Edward Dowden and His Correspondents,* ed. Elizabeth D. and Hilda M. Dowden (London: J. M. Dent & Sons, 1914), p. 22.

5. *Life of Octavia Hill as Told in Her Letters,* ed. C. Edmund Maurice (London: Macmillan & Co., 1913), pp. 246, 240.

6. "Ruskin and the Brownings: Twenty-Five Unpublished Letters," ed. David J. DeLaura, *Bulletin of the John Rylands Library,* LIV, Spring 1972, 347–8.

7. See ibid., p. 348.

8. [John Skelton], *The Table-Talk of Shirley,* 6th ed. (Edinburgh: William Blackwood & Sons, 1896), p. 130.

9. *Letters to William Allingham,* ed. H. Allingham and E. Baumer Williams (London: Longmans, Green & Co., 1911), p. 175.

10. William Michael Rossetti, *Swinburne's Poems and Ballads: A Criticism* (London: John Camden Hotten, 1866), pp. 48–9.

11. See Swinburne's remarks on Browning in the chapter on Jowett in his *Studies in Prose and Poetry,* 2d ed. (London: Chatto & Windus, 1987), p. 36; and his introductory essay to *The Works of George Chapman* (London: Chatto & Windus, 1875), xiv–xix. For comments in his letters, see *The Swinburne Letters, 1875–1877,* ed. Cecil Y. Lang (New Haven: Yale Univ. Press), III (1960), 40, 87, 166, 212; *1877–1882,* IV (1960), 31, 72; *1890–1909,* VI (1962), 28, 31. Edmund Gosse in his *Portraits and Sketches* (London: William Heinemann, 1913), p. 54, recorded Swinburne's opinion of Browning's works in the seventies.

12. The other occasion was Browning's acceptance of the presidency of the New Shakspere Society in the late seventies at the request of Furnivall, its founder. Swinburne and Furnivall became engaged in a controversy concerning Shakespeare that extended beyond an exchange of views in the literary domain to an exchange of personal abuse with the unfortunate involvement of bystanders. In letters to Browning and others, Swinburne ex-

pressed strong disapproval of Browning's association with Furnivall. See*The Swinburne Letters, 1877–1882,* IV (1960), 100–1, 105–6, 190, 196–7.

13. On pp. 40–60 of *New Writings by Swinburne,* ed. Cecil Y. Lang (Syracuse, New York: Syracuse Univ. Press, 1964). For the account of the details of the situation that led up to the writing of *The Chaotic School,* see K. L. Knickerbocker, "Browning and Swinburne: An Episode," MLN, LXII, Apr. 1947, 240–4. The letter from Browning to Milnes, first published in this article, was later included in *New Letters,* pp. 150–1. See also *New Writings,* pp. 200–3, for other utterances by Swinburne on Browning.

14. *New Writings,* pp. 198–9.

15. *The Swinburne Letters, 1854–1869,* I (1959), 98.

16. Quoted in ibid., p. 100, n. 2.

17. Ibid., p. 100.

18. On Mar. 15, 1865, Swinburne wrote to William Bell Scott, "A year may make some difference to the readers of a Bailey or a Browning — not to mine, whose heel . . . has already bruised the head of the latter Philistine idol. I intend, now the main work is cleared off, that 'that twice-battered God of Palestine,' Dagon-Caliban, shall 'wear my stripes impressed on him, and bear my beating to his grave.' " Ibid., p. 114.

19. Ibid., p. 313.

20. *Rossetti Papers, 1862 to 1870,* pp. 379–80.

21. *The Letters of Algernon Charles Swinburne,* ed. Edmund Gosse and T. J. Wise (New York: John Lane Co., 1919), I, 62–3.

22. *The Swinburne Letters, 1869–1875,* II (1959), 46–7.

23. Rosalie Glynn Grylls, "Rossetti and Browning," *Princeton University Library Chronicle,* XXXIII, Spring 1972, 232–50.

24. Ibid., pp. 243, 245.

25. *Letters of Dante Gabriel Rossetti to William Allingham, 1854–1870,* ed. George Birkbeck Hill (New York: Frederick A. Stokes Co., 1897), pp. 283–4.

26. Rossetti's comments after he read Vols. II, III, and IV are in Grylls, "Rossetti and Browning," pp. 246–8.

27. Berg MSS, Forster to RB.

28. Berg MS, ibid.

29. Theodore Martin, *Helena Faucit* (Edinburgh: William Blackwood & Sons, 1900), pp. 301–2.

30. Hudson Long, "Helena Faucit Martin's Unpublished Letters to Robert Browning," *Baylor University Browning Interests,* 2d ser., 1931, pp. 10–2.

31. *Life and Letters of Dean Church,* ed. Mary C. Church (London: Macmillan & Co., 1894), p. 343.

32. *Letters to a Friend by Connop Thirlwall,* ed. A. P. Stanley (London: Richard Bentley & Son, 1881), p. 184.

33. See *The Browning Box; or, The Life and Works of Thomas Lovell Beddoes,* ed. H. W. Donner (London: Oxford Univ. Press, 1935), pp. lxxi–ii, 165–7.

34. *The Letters of George Meredith,* ed. C. L. Cline (Oxford: Clarendon Press, 1970), I, 413.

35. Baylor MS, Dec. 2, [1868]; see Swinburne, *Studies in Prose and Poetry,* p. 36.

36. A. C. Benson, *Edward Fitzgerald* (New York: Macmillan Co., 1905), p. 148.

37. *Letters and Literary Remains of Edward Fitzgerald,* ed. William Aldis Wright (London: Macmillan & Co., 1903), II, 266, 267–8, 272–3.

38. *Tennyson and His Friends,* ed. Hallam Tennyson (London: Macmillan & Co., 1912), pp. 118–9.

39. Ibid., pp. 51–2.

40. Oscar Browning, "Personal Recollections of English Poets," *Empire Review*, XXXVIII, Nov. 1923, 1243.

41. *Some Reminiscences of William Michael Rossetti* (London: Brown Langham & Co., 1906), I, 233.

42. *Allingham: A Diary*, p. 174. Without giving dates, Allingham jotted down notes on Browning, in which he had some complaints but more praise. See William Allingham, *By the Way: Verses, Fragments, and Notes*, arrgd. Helen Allingham (New York: Longmans, Green & Co., 1912), pp. 107–9.

43. *Allingham: A Diary*, pp. 180–1, 195, 207–8.

44. M. L. Howe, "Robert Browning and William Allingham," *Studies in Philology*, XXXI, Oct. 1934, 571–2, 574.

45. W. Holman Hunt, *Pre-Raphaelitism and the Pre-Raphaelite Brotherhood* (New York: Macmillan Co., 1906), II, 335.

46. See letters written during these years in *Letters from Owen Meredith (Robert, First Earl of Lytton) to Robert and Elizabeth Barrett Browning*, ed. Aurelia Brooks Harlan and J. Lee Harlan, Jr., *Baylor University's Browning Interests*, 10th ser., 1936, pp. 173–217); see also *Personal & Literary Letters of Robert First Earl of Lytton*, ed. Betty Balfour (London: Longmans, Green, & Co., 1906), I, 128, 191.

47. *Personal & Literary Letters of Robert First Earl of Lytton*, I, 255.

48. Ibid.

49. For the revelation of the change in Lytton's feeling and Browning's reaction, see Lytton's letters to Browning dated Mar. 29, 1871, and Apr. 20, 1871 (*Letters from Owen Meredith*, pp. 231–4), and Browning's letter to Isa dated Apr. 25, 1871 (*Dearest Isa*, p. 357).

50. *Letters from Owen Meredith*, pp. 233–4.

51. Richard Willard Armour, *Barry Cornwall: A Biography of Bryan Waller Procter* (Boston: Meador Publishing Co., 1935), p. 315.

52. Ibid., p. 324.

53. Charles Gavan Duffy, *Conversations with Carlyle* (New York: Charles Scribner's Sons, 1892), p. 57.

54. See *Anne Gilchrist: Her Life and Writings*, ed. Herbert Harlakenden Gilchrist (London: T. Fisher Unwin, 1887), pp. 174–5.

55. Sara Norton and M. A. DeWolfe, *Letters of Charles Eliot Norton with Biographical Comment* (Boston: Houghton Mifflin Co., 1913), I, 325.

56. David Alec Wilson and David Wilson MacArthur, *Carlyle in Old Age* (London: Kegan Paul, Trench, Trubner & Co., 1934), pp. 175–6; *Allingham: A Diary*, p. 194; Moncure Daniel Conway, *Autobiography: Memories and Experiences* (Boston: Houghton, Mifflin & Co., 1904), II, 25. For similar remarks, see *Allingham: A Diary*, p. 207; Richard Garnett, *Life of Thomas Carlyle* (London: Walter Scott, 1895), pp. 145–6.

57. Wilson and MacArthur, *Carlyle in Old Age*, p. 175; *Allingham: A Diary*, p. 207.

58. *Allingham: A Diary*, p. 240.

59. See *New Letters*, pp. 262–3, to Bessie Rayner Belloc, Mar. 18, 1881; *Allingham: A Diary*, pp. 310–1, 374; G. W. Smalley, *London Letters and Some Others* (New York: Harper & Bros., 1891), I, 268.

60. Gwenllian F. Palgrave, *Francis Turner Palgrave: His Journals and Memories of His Life* (New York: Longmans, Green, & Co., 1899), p. 103.

61. *Autobiographical Notes of the Life of William Bell Scott*, ed. W. Minto (New York: Harper & Bros., 1892), II, 138.

62. *The Letters of Matthew Arnold to Arthur Hugh Clough*, ed. Howard Foster Lowry (London: Oxford Univ. Press, 1932), pp. 97, 136.

63. *From a Victorian Post-Bag,* pp. 75–6.

64. *Letters of Matthew Arnold, 1848–1888,* ed. George W. E. Russell (London: Macmillan & Co., 1901), II, 10. In giving Arnold's opinion I have depended on his specific statements about Browning. For a stimulating discussion of the contrasting poetic principles of Browning and Arnold, see Philip Drew, *The Poetry of Browning: A Critical Introduction* (London: Methuen & Co., 1970), pp. 354–75.

65. *Letters of Matthew Arnold, 1848–1888,* I, 70.

66. Hallam Tennyson, *Alfred Lord Tennyson: A Memoir* (London: Macmillan & Co., 1905), p. 657.

67. Ibid., p. 610.

68. Ibid., p. 657.

69. *Allingham: A Diary,* p. 128.

70. Hallam Tennyson, *Tennyson: A Memoir,* pp. 465, 466.

71. See Laura Riddling, *Sophia Matilda Palmer, Comtesse de Franqueville, 1852–1915: A Memoir* (London: John Murray, 1919), p. 202.

72. *Letters of Fitzgerald,* II, 266.

73. *Allingham: A Diary,* p. 290.

74. Charles Tennyson, *Alfred Tennyson* (London: Macmillan & Co., 1950), p. 391.

75. *Tennyson and His Friends,* p. 126. This statement goes with another of Tennyson's on Browning made in 1884: ". . . one is constantly aware of the greatness of the man, yet somehow baulked of satisfaction" (*Allingham: A Diary,* p. 326).

76. *RB and JW,* p. 130, Oct. 30, 1868.

77. Ibid., pp. 139, Nov. 15, 1868; 171, Feb. 21, 1869; 137, Nov. 15, 1868.

78. Ibid., pp. 144, Nov. 19, 1868; 176, Feb. 22, 1869; 152, Jan. 21, 1869.

79. Ibid., pp. 178, Mar. 5, 1869; 183, Mar. 8, 1869; 144, Nov. 19, 1868.

80. Ibid., p. 159, Jan. 30, 1869.

81. Ibid., pp. 162–3, Feb. 1, 1869.

82. Ibid., pp. 130, Oct. 30, 1868; 174, Feb. 22, 1869; 177, Feb. 22, 1869.

83. Ibid., p. 153, Jan. 21, 1869.

84. Ibid., p. 165, Feb. 12, 1869.

85. Ibid., pp. 172, Feb. 21, 1869; 150, Dec. 3, 1868.

86. Ibid., p. 176, Feb. 22, 1869.

87. Ibid., p. 143, Nov. 19, 1868.

88. *The Works of John Ruskin,* ed. E. T. Cook and Alexander Wedderburn (London: George Allen), XXXVI (1909), xxxviii.

89. *Dearest Isa,* p. 328, Jan. 19, 1870.

90. *RB and JW,* p. 136, Nov. 15, 1868.

91. Ibid., pp. 162 and 164, Feb. 1, 1869.

92. Ibid., p. 161, Feb. 1, 1869.

93. Ibid., pp. 152, Jan. 21, 1869; 194, June 14, 1870.

94. The letter was dated May 13, 1872. See Th. Bentzon (pseud. for Marie T. de S. Blanc), "A French Friend of Browning — Joseph Milsand," *Scribner's Magazine,* XX, July 1896, 111.

95. *Letters,* Hood, pp. 103–4, Oct. 13, 1866; 124, Dec. 13, 1867.

96. See DeVane, p. 286.

97. See Allan C. Dooley, "The Textual Significance of Robert Browning's 1865 *Poetical Works,*" *Papers of the Bibliographical Society of America,* LXXI, Second Quarter 1977, 212–8; *Works of Browning,* ed. Jack and Smith, I, Textual Introduction, xix-xx.

98. Hallam Tennyson, *Tennyson: A Memoir,* p. 610; see also William Lyon Phelps, "A Conversation with Browning," *A Journal of English Literary History,* XI, June 1944, 156.

99. Mountstuart E. Grant Duff, *Notes from a Diary, 1889–1891* (London: John Murray, 1901), II, 180.

100. Robert Sidney, "Some Browning Memories," *Saturday Review,* CXIII, May 11, 1912, 584.

101. Frederick W. Farrar, *Men I Have Known* (New York: Thomas Y. Crowell & Co., 1897), p. 61.

102. See C. Archer, *William Archer: Life, Work and Friendships* (New Haven: Yale Univ. Press, 1931), p. 297.

103. *Allingham: A Diary,* p. 195.

104. *RB and JW,* p. 165, Feb. 12, 1869.

105. Frederick Pollock, *Personal Remembrances* (London: Macmillan & Co., 1887), II, 202.

106. *RB and JW,* p. 182–3, Mar. 8, 1869. Carlyle gave details of the "interview" (*New Letters of Thomas Carlyle,* ed. Alexander Carlyle [London: John Lane, Bodley Head, 1904], I, 252–5). See also T. Wemyss Reid, *The Life, Letters, and Friendships of Richard Monckton Milnes,* 2d ed. (London: Cassell & Co., 1890), II, 200.

Index

A

Adams, Mrs. William Bridges. *See* Sarah Flower
Ainsworth, William Harrison, 48, 77–8
Aldrich, Mrs. Thomas B., 390
Allingham, William, 144, 267, 341, 356, 357, 361, 467, 470, 471, 524, 528, 533–4, 537; *Nightingale Valley*, 349
Archer, William, 73, 74, 148, 149, 166
Armstrong, Isobel, xxi
Arnold, Matthew, 521, 538–9; *Empedocles on Etna*, 538; Preface to *Poems* (1853), 538
Arnould, Joseph, 76, 89, 132, 133–4, 148, 150, 155, 157, 158, 168, 172, 264; on *Pauline*, 13; on *Paracelsus*, 40; sketch of life, 86; unsound attribution of a review of *Men and Women* to him, 87, 129–30, 351–2; verse epistle to RB, 87, 130; on *Dramatic Lyrics*, 128–30; on *A Blot*, 143–4; on *Christmas-Eve and Easter-Day*, 351–2
Austin, Alfred, 510, 515, 528, 590

B

Bagehot, Walter, 435, 442
Bailey, Philip, 282
Balfour, Lady, 534–5
Bancroft, Squire, 165
Barrett, Arabel, 243, 244–5, 290, 301

Barrett, George, 41, 229, 379, 466–7
Barrett, Lawrence, 148, 161, 163, 164
Beddoes, Thomas L., 67
Benkhausen, Chevalier George de, 24
Bennett, W. C., 230
Blagden, Isa, 342, 377, 406, 409, 411, 412, 438, 444, 445, 446, 458, 464, 465, 469, 470, 535, 544; receives advice from RB, 388–9
Boyle, George, 265
Brimley, George, 311, 317, 373, 514
Browning, Elizabeth Barrett: wants to read *Pauline*, 12–3; on *Paracelsus*, 38; on *Sordello*, 89–90, 92–3; on *Pippa Passes*, 108–10; on *Dramatic Lyrics*, 129; on *A Blot*, 144; hears of Macready's mistreatment of *A Blot*, 155; assists Horne in preparing his *New Spirit of the Age*, 170; refers to RB in her poetry, 187–8; early interest in RB and first letter from him, 188; early exchange of letters with RB, 189; on *Dramatic Romances and Lyrics*, 190, 193–4; on *Luria*, 218–9; on *A Soul's Tragedy*, 221–2; marriage, 239; objects to RB's writing for stage, 271; income from ship *David Lyon*, 288, 289; on RB's concern for finances, 288, 290; on income

from poetry, 297; interest in spiritualism, 301, 423; death, 346;
Lady Geraldine's Courtship, 187;
Greek Christian Poets, 188; *Dead
Pan,* 214; *Aurora Leigh,* 300,
301, 323, 341–2, 345, 379,
411; *Poems before Congress,* 344–5
Browning, Oscar (unrelated), 21,
22, 265, 533
Browning, Reuben (RB's uncle),
289
Browning, Robert (RB's father),
100, 295; schoolmate of Kenyon's, 38–9; teaches RB through
playacting, 45; on *Sordello,* 85;
gets information for *The Ring and
the Book,* 466
Browning, Robert: writes *Incondita,*
1; sees Kean in *Richard III* and
conceives plan of *Pauline,* 2;
paves the way for reviews, 2–3,
12, 27, 210, 397, 414; approaches Fox and receives help,
2–4, 5–6; appreciates criticism,
4, 170, 172, 193, 388, 457–8,
541, 545; Mill's unpublished
criticism of *Pauline,* 7–12, 20–
3; interest in experimentation,
11, 27–8, 218, 273, 300, 469;
requests criticism from friends,
12, 26, 189, 303, 354; compro-
mises with critics, 12, 142–3,
171, 172, 469–70; effect of
R. H. Shepherd's publication of
excerpts from *Pauline,* 14–7; reaction to reception of his early
works, 19–23, 41–4, 73–4,
157, 161; gives impression of
composing with speed and effect
of, 25, 32, 34, 48, 113; search
for publishers, 25–6, 99–100,
243–6, 447–8, 461; reads reviews of his works, 27, 172,
388, 406, 438–9, 441, 446;

heeds criticism, 27, 191, 193–4,
223, 304, 469, 545; publishes
poetry in *Monthly Repository,* 27;
meets Horne and Macready, 37;
goes to Talfourd's *Ion* celebration,
39, 47; tenseness while waiting
for reviews of new work, 43–4,
213–4, 231–2, 546; appeal of
drama and the stage, 45, 46–7,
48, 164; troublesome preparation
for staging *Strafford,* 49–54; production of *Strafford* in eighties,
72–3; extended composition of
Sordello, 75–6; talks freely of
works, 76, 237, 392–3, 460–1,
469–70; slow sale of his works,
90, 269, 287, 345; effort exerted
for clarity, 92–3, 224, 371,
469–70, 546; his high opinion
of *Sordello,* 93, 96–7; agrees to
pamphlet form for *Bells and Pomegranates,* 100; fails to please Macready with the *Druses,* 115–7;
considers how and when to publish, 124, 196–7, 379, 297–8,
447–9; his high opinion of the
Druses, 132; turmoil preceding
performance of *A Blot,* 135–7;
on critics and criticisms, 145,
213, 216, 338, 342, 388–9,
391, 437–42 passim; refers to
acting copy of *A Blot,* 153, 154;
looks ahead in writing, 168,
273, 396; on originality, 171,
192–3; on influence of reviews
on reading public, 212, 231–2;
explains title of *Bells and Pomegranates,* 225; on a writer's learning from experience, 233; confidence in his future, 234; belief in
his destiny and duty to write,
234; importance of socializing,
235, 389–90; marries and goes
to Italy, 239; in Pisa, 243; con-

siders ways to promote sales and enhance reputation, 244, 291, 295–6, 447–8; living in Florence, 268; on difficult task of writing, 268, 339, 379; tries to obtain secretarial post in an embassy, 288–9; financial needs of, 288–91, 301, 342–3, 346; Kenyon's financial assistance, 289; visits England in 1851–2, 289–90, 295; Chapman's negligence and carelessness, 295, 397, 460, 462; return to Florence in 1852, 299; follows regular schedule of writing, 301, 470; reads poetry aloud, 301, 303, 317; takes MS of *Men and Women* to London in 1855, 301; defeated hopes for *Men and Women,* 338–43 passim; defends his artistic method, 365–6, 367, 407–8, 439, 445, 542; returns to England following EBB's death, 375; offered editorship of *Cornhill,* 378–9; publishes poems in *Atlantic Monthly,* 413; payment by his publishers, 461, 471; academic honors, 462; determines plan for *The Ring and the Book* at Pass of Roland, 464–5; presented to the Queen, 547; buried in Westminster Abbey, 547
  WORKS. Each work is repeatedly discussed in the chapter devoted to it. *See* table of contents (v–vi) and also bibliography of reviews (565–80).
Browning, Robert Wiedeman Barrett (RB and EBB's son, Pen), 268, 289, 378, 413, 462
Browning, Sarah Anna Wiedeman (RB's mother), 268
Browning, Sarianna (RB's sister), 17, 45, 164, 343, 344

Browning Society, 17, 72, 147, 148, 161
Buchanan, Robert, 477, 479, 491, 499, 509
Bulwer Lytton, Edward, 47, 54, 67, 113, 131, 152, 155, 458; *Richelieu,* 113, 153
Bulwer, Henry, 54
Burne-Jones, Edward, 357, 358
Busk, Mrs. W., 76, 113
C
Campbell, James Dykes, 17
Carlyle, Jane Welsh (Mrs. Thomas), 85
Carlyle, Thomas, 7, 22, 89, 170, 192, 224, 235, 237, 264, 267, 290, 294, 299, 350, 373–4, 375, 390, 463, 533–4, 547; on *Paracelsus,* 40; on *Pippa Passes* and *Sordello,* 87–8, 110; on RB's writing prose, 110–1, 294, 370; on *Dramatic Lyrics* and *A Soul's Tragedy,* 230; on Essay on Shelley, 294; on *Men and Women,* 368–70; on *The Ring and the Book,* 536–7; *Reminiscences,* 537
Carr, J. Comyns, 459
Cazenova, J. G., 326
Chambers, Robert, *Vestiges of the Natural History of Creation,* 287
Chapman, Edward, 246, 295, 297, 298, 338, 339, 340, 356, 371, 373, 396–7, 411, 447, 460, 461
Chapman, Frederic (nephew of Edward), 345, 447, 460, 461
Chapman, Edward or Frederic, 526
Chapman and Hall, 246, 396, 433, 448, 460–2
Chapman, George, 525
Chapman, John, 517
Charlton, H. B., 595n28
Chignell, T. W., 531–2
Chorley, Henry Fothergill, 109,

632

158, 176–7, 197, 206, 208, 210, 214, 215, 229, 232, 240–1, 245, 246, 264, 344, 351, 390, 518

Church, Richard William, 459, 496, 531

Clarke, Charles Cowden, 25

Clough, Arthur Hugh, 368, 538

Cobbe, Frances Power, 355, 522

Cohen, J. M., 595n28

Coleman, John, 599n32

Colenso, John William, 415, 424; *The Pentateuch and Book of Joshua,* 414

Coleridge, Samuel Taylor, 34, 406–7, 441

Collins, Mortimer, 511

Colvin, Sidney, 393

Conway, Moncure D., 14, 19, 40, 95, 223, 397, 400, 401, 402, 404, 414, 420, 423, 425, 430

Cooper, Robert, 423

Corkran, Alice, 394

Corkran, Henriette, 389

Corkran, Mrs. John F., 394

Cornwall, Barry. *See* Procter, Bryan Waller

Craik, George L., 460

Cramer, Maurice Browning, xxi, 266, 358

Criticism, topics of: along with objections to RB's poetry, recognition of ability, 27, 28, 30, 36, 106, 143; main character delineated by use of subservient characters, 29, 31, 35; periodicity (frequency of publication of periodicals) and RB's reputation, 36, 336–7, 516–7; beginning of objections to RB's obscurity and metrical irregularity, 36; beginning of comments on the dramatic, reflective, philosophical, and human in RB's poetry, 36;

beginning of complaint of lack of the traditional in RB's poetry, 83; beginning of irritability, 83; quips on *Sordello,* 84–6; after *Sordello,* charge that RB did not try to reach readers, 90; lack of understnding accompanied by irritability, 106, 127–8, 208, 278–9, 307–9, 311; suitability of versification to the poem, 199, 200, 201, 277, 281, 318, 319, 450–1, 507–8; diminution of attack on obscurity, 208; critical progress indicated in reception of *Dramatic Romances and Lyrics,* 208–10; sectarian periodicals in relation to criticism, 209, 282–4, 285–7, 323, 337, 518; improvement in tone, 210, 253, 385; desire for prefixed explanation of poem, 242, 251, 470; reader's effort to understand worthwhile, 242, 252, 258, 431; better understanding from merging of critical lines, 248, 249, 314, 320, 432, 498, 509; encouraging signs in late forties, 252–3, 258; interest in *Sordello,* 253–4, 455–7; disappearance of censure of lack of action in plays, 258; relative value of reviews, 259–60, 336; the grotesque, 275, 276, 284, 330–1, 400, 405, 435–6, 451; attraction of timely poetry, 286–7, 332–3, 402, 415–25, 497, 498; RB's individual dramatic quality, 309, 398, 451, 478; obscurity reconsidered, 314–6; achievement of a forward look at RB's verse technique, 316–7, 385, 387, 427–8; objections to nontraditional quality of RB's lyrical poetry, 316, 317, 319, 331–2, 404,

426–7; RB's projection of himself into his characters, 319, 429–30, 480, 490–1; RB's power, originality, and intellect, 320, 478, 501; RB as a religious and moral poet, 322–6, 387–8, 402, 415–25, 453, 492–6, *esp. Christmas-Eve and Easter-Day,* 286, 287, 297, 322, 323, 402; RB's use of the remote in time and place, 322, 383–4, 401, 504–5; questioning of fitness of subject matter for poetry, 207, 322–6, 327–8, 330, 382–3, 384, 430, 502–4; RB's voice in his poetry, 333–4, 452–3, 491–2, 495; RB's place among poets, 334, 384, 385–6, 405, 511–3; critics censuring other critics, 335, 436–7, 442; comparison of RB and Tennyson, 350, 376, 514–5, 524, 532; expenditure of effort for understanding as suitable to changing times, 431, 498–9; objective (dramatic) versus subjective poet, 431, 452, 499; RB's lack of orthodoxy as an advantage, 432; RB seen as a philosophical poet, 453, 493, 496; modernity of study of man as in RB, 497–8; nondidacticism of *The Ring and the Book,* 499–500; comparison of RB with other writers, 514; advantages to RB of character of reviewing in the sixties, 518–20
Crosse, Mrs. Andrew, 264, 355, 356
Cundiff, Paul A., 621n8
Curtis, G. W., 93
D
Dall, Mrs., 96
Darley, C. F., 122; *Plighted Troth,* 133, 150

Darwin, Charles, 421; *Origin of Species,* 287, 414–5
Davies, J. Llewelyn, 522
Davies, James A., 590n6
DeLaura, David, 361, 523
DeVane, William C., xxi, 10, 49, 64, 75–6, 198, 394
de Vere, Aubrey, 67, 350, 523–4
Deverell, Walter, 353
Dickens, Charles, 141, 156–7, 166, 170; opinion of *A Blot,* 134
Domett, Alfred, 76, 79, 84, 94, 110, 115, 124, 126, 129, 130, 134, 136, 143, 145, 148, 150, 151, 154, 155, 157, 163, 168, 169, 172, 173, 174, 175, 187, 192, 195, 216, 234, 235, 236, 264, 297, 338, 390; on *Pauline,* 13; on *Paracelsus,* 40; sketch of life, 86–7; on *Sordello,* 87, 92; poetic attack on critics of RB, 108; *Flotsam and Jetsam,* 108
Dooley, Allan C., 304
Dowden, Edward, 97, 392, 455, 456, 457–8, 517, 519, 522, 545
Dowson, Christopher, 173, 174, 186
Draper, J. W., 417
Drew, Philip, xxi
DuBois, Arthur E., 595n28
Duckworth, F. R. G., xx, 272
Duffy, Charles Gavan, 85, 144, 265
E
Earles, Mr., 85
Edmonds, Cyrus R., 248
Eliot, George, 315, 316, 317, 319, 328, 331, 333, 517; comment on *Gold Hair* influences RB, 545
F
Fane, Julian, 485, 508, 517, 518, 530
Farrar, Frederick W., 20, 22, 546

Faucit, Helen, 38, 67, 74, 146, 148, 179, 183, 186, 246, 295, 531

Fields, James T., 93, 94, 340–1, 348, 412–4, 473

Fitzgerald, Edward, 532–3, 536

Fitzgerald, Mrs. Thomas, 393

Flower, Eliza, 1, 5, 68, 76, 97, 99, 168, 390; on *Sordello,* 85–6; on *Pippa Passes,* 110.

Flower, Sarah, 1, 26, 76

Forman, H. Buxton, 392, 478, 483, 487, 497, 508, 511

Forster, John, 8, 12, 31, 34, 37, 41, 42, 43, 44, 46, 47, 48, 50, 52, 54, 61–2, 63, 64, 66, 69, 70, 76, 77, 84, 90, 104, 113, 114, 117, 119–20, 124–6, 128, 141, 142, 149, 156, 157, 158, 176, 197, 199–200, 225–6, 228, 231–2, 236, 237, 246, 256, 263, 264, 277–8, 287, 298, 300, 303, 305, 306, 314, 315, 318, 319, 333, 351, 354, 376–7, 390, 398, 412, 449, 455, 518, 530–1; description of, 30; author of commentary on *Strafford,* 62–3; as a reviewer of RB, 259; *Sir John Eliot,* 39, 263

Fox, William Johnson, 6–7, 8, 22, 25, 26–7, 37, 76, 77, 85, 89, 110, 211, 235, 237, 303, 304, 305, 351, 518; author of criticisms of RB, 2–4, 5–6, 31–2, 57

Froude, James Anthony, 40, 386, 455, 517, 523, 537

Fry, Charles, 148, 152, 161, 164

Furnivall, F. J., 20, 72, 73, 74, 96, 148, 392, 393

G

Gannon, Nicholas J., 349–50; author of criticism of RB, 350

Gladstone, Mary, 391–2

Goethe, 38

Gosse, Edmund, 20, 43, 73, 74, 132, 147, 148, 546

Greenwood, Frederick, 476

Greer, Louise, 340, 413–4

Griffin, W. H., 85

Grote, George, 547

Grove, George, 44

Gurney, Archer T., 253; author of criticism of RB, 605–6n18; *Love's Legends,* 264

Grylls, Rosalie, 528

H

Hallé, Charles, 391

Hanmer, John, 210–1

Hannay, James, 460

Harness, William J., 213

Hasell, Elizabeth J., 489, 507, 511, 514

Haworth, Euphrasia Fanny, 37, 76, 89, 92, 113, 114, 115, 117, 118, 234, 263, 268, 351, 379, 551, 561; sonnets on RB, 39, 263

Heraud, James A., 204

Hervey, T. K., 82, 85, 104–6, 107, 127–8

Hewlett, Dorothy, x

Hill, Frank, 148–55 passim, 165

Hill, Mrs. Frank, 148, 161, 163, 165

Hill, George Birkbeck, 359, 612n7

Hill, Octavia, 522–3

Home (or Hume), Daniel D., 301, 423

Honan, Park, 107, 118, 587n36, 595n28

Hood, E. P., 450, 451, 452, 456, 457

Hood, Thomas, 190

Horne, Richard H., 37, 67, 68, 85, 90, 130–1, 132, 142, 148, 156, 172, 179, 183, 186, 193, 230, 237, 242, 259, 262, 268,

294, 455, 457, 518, 561; on *Sordello*, 88–9; author of criticisms of RB, 169, 177; RB grateful to, 170; *A New Spirit of the Age*, 122–3, 145, 169, 177
Horner, Francis, 21, 22
Howe, M. L., 534
Hugo, Victor, 532
Hunt, Leigh, 33, 43, 124, 262, 267, 371
Hunt, Margaret, 467
Hunt, William Holman, 266, 534
Hutton, R. H., 282–3, 403, 404, 406–9, 428, 479, 482, 513, 518

I
Innocent XII, Pope, 466, 467
Irving Dramatic Club, 148
Irwin, T. C., 441–2

J
Jack, Ian, xxi
James, Henry, 392
Jameson, Anna, 38, 93, 230, 270–1, 368; *A Commonplace Book of Thoughts, Memories, and Fancies*, 348
Jerrold, Douglas, 85, 90, 200–1, 226–7
Jowett, Benjamin, 359, 462, 467, 470, 532

K
Kean, Charles, 168, 169, 173, 176, 186, 199, 271
Kean, Edmund, 2, 45–6, 173
Keats, John, 195, 443
Keble, John, 452
Kenyon, John, 38–9, 121, 144, 166, 187, 188, 197, 211, 230, 289, 303, 303–4, 341, 371; death and bequest, 346; *A Day at Tivoli*, 263
Khattab, Ezzat A., xxi
King, Roma, 195

Kingsley, Charles, 253, 284–5, 287, 455
Kinney, Mrs. W. B., 339, 371
Kintner, Elvan, 215
Knickerbocker, K. L., xxi, 342, 460
Knowles, James Sheridan, 131

L
Landor, Walter Savage, 40, 47, 89, 213, 230–1, 236, 264, 350; *A Satire on Satirists*, 39–40, 88, 263, 267; poem on RB, 211–2, 267
Lang, Cecil Y., 526
Lee, Sidney, 184–5
Lehmann, Rudolf, 393, 465
Leighton, Frederick, 412
Lewes, George Henry, 81, 142, 243, 279–81, 293
Litzinger, Boyd, xxi, 63, 90, 198
Locker-Lampson, Frederick, 17
Lounsbury, Thomas R., xx, 43, 62, 64, 95, 107, 149, 198, 199
Lushington, Edmund, 368
Luther, Martin, 419
Lyell, Charles, 547; *Principles of Geology*, 287
Lytton, Robert (Owen Meredith), 264, 304, 305, 352–3, 458, 534–5; impossibility of conjectured authorship of review of RB, 354–5

M
McAleer, Edward C., 621n8
McCarthy, Justin, 45, 391
McCormick, James P., xxi
MacDonald, George, 285–6, 470
McElderry, B. R., Jr., xxi
Mackay, Charles, 204, 214, 514
Macmillan, Alexander, 446, 447, 461, 471, 522
McNicoll, Thomas, 514
Macready, William Charles, 10,

39, 46, 47-54 passim, 58, 59,
60, 62, 63, 65, 68, 69, 70, 71,
73, 76, 77, 85, 97, 113, 121-2,
130, 131, 132, 142, 143, 144,
146, 148, 149-57, 161, 163,
164, 165, 166-7, 169, 171,
172, 173, 178, 179, 183, 192,
199, 236, 237, 338, 390, 398;
and RB meet, 37; first performance of *Strafford,* 54; rejects *King
Victor,* 114; rejects the *Druses,*
115-7; and *A Blot,* 133-7; on
Christmas-Eve and Easter-Day,
352
Macrone, John, 77, 78
Marston, John Westland, 92, 134,
169, 276-7; *The Patrician's
Daughter,* 150, 152
Martin, Theodore, 599n32
Martin, Mrs. Theodore. *See* Faucit,
Helen
Martineau, Harriet, 76, 77, 78,
84-5, 90, 237
Massey, Gerald, 386-8, 415, 426,
427-8, 429, 430, 431, 436,
514, 517, 518
Masson, David, 315, 316, 317-8,
320, 328, 331, 332, 335, 339,
436, 437
Meidl, Annaliese, 70
Meredith, George, 265, 532
Metcalf, W. J., 515
Meynell, Wilfred, 391
Mill, J. S., 6-12, 20, 21, 22-3,
27, 78, 79, 290
Millais, John Everett, 266
Milnes, Richard Monckton (Lord
Houghton), 67, 110, 264, 289,
377, 514, 526, 527
Milsand, Joseph, 94, 95, 96, 300,
303, 305, 339, 354, 398, 455,
545
Mitford, Mary Russell, 38, 40,
108-10, 129, 144, 155, 168,

243, 264; *Recollections of a Literary
Life,* 348
Moir, D. M., 349
Monod, Sylvère, 590n6
Morley, John, 482, 484, 498, 499,
502, 519
Morris, William, 316, 317, 335,
357, 358, 372, 452, 514
Moxon, Edward, 25, 26, 79, 123,
124, 137, 191, 195, 196, 197,
212, 213, 216, 243-5, 268,
291, 292, 297, 446, 460; ac-
count of sale of *Sordello,* 90;
agreement to publish *Bells and
Pomegranates,* 99-100; and RB
on publishing collected edition of
1849, 243-5
Mozley, J. R., 480, 490, 496,
497, 500, 503, 511, 517, 518
Munro, Alexander, 356
Murray, Alma (Mrs. Forman), 72,
132, 148, 161, 164-5, 184,
186
Murray, John, 26
N
Nettleship, J. T., 457
New Shakspere Society, 148
Nichol, John, 359, 360
North, Christopher. *See* Wilson,
John
Norton, Charles Eliot, 536
Novello, Mary, 25
Novello, Vincent, 25
O
Old Yellow Book, 463, 502
Oliphant, Mrs. Margaret, 307
Orr, Mrs. Sutherland (Alexandra
Leighton), 78, 146, 156
P
Paine, Mrs., 229
Paley, William, 421-2
Palgrave, Francis Turner, 293,
439-40, 443, 445, 537

Palmer, Frederic, Jr., 194, 195
Partington, Wilfred, 609n34
Patmore, Coventry, 40, 353
Perida, Rabbi, 438, 441
Peterson, William S., 304
Pettigrew, Helen P., xxi
Phelps, Samuel, 136, 146, 151–2, 153, 155, 158, 161, 183, 266
Phelps, W. May, 599n32
Phelps, William Lyon, 14, 15–6, 144
Philips, Ambrose, 514
Pinero, Arthur Wing, 132
Pollock, Frederick, 532, 546
Pollock, Juliet, 37–8, 166
Powell, Baden, 419
Powell, Thomas, 13–4, 156, 204, 205, 295; *The Blind Wife,* 263; *The Living Authors of England* (in America) or *Pictures of the Living Authors of Britain* (in England), 348
Procter, Bryan Waller, 175–6, 235, 236, 347, 376–7, 381, 413, 446, 449, 471, 535–6; *Mirandola,* 175; *A Familiar Epistle to Robert Browning,* 347–8
Procter, Mrs. Bryan Waller, 288, 536

Q
Quarles, Francis, 145–6

R
Reed, Joseph W., Jr., 154
Reeve, Henry, 439
Reeve, Lovell, 460
Renan, Ernest, 424; *La Vie de Jésus,* 414–5, 418
Reviews, reviewers. *See* 563–80
Ripert-Monclar, Amédée de, 24, 41
Robertson, John, 78, 79
Robinson, Henry Crabb, 264
Rogers, Samuel, 264
Rossetti, Dante Gabriel, 13, 73, 265–6, 303, 305, 356, 357, 358, 359, 360, 361, 372, 391, 521, 525, 528–30, 531, 536, 537; sonnet on *Sordello,* 98
Rossetti, William, 72–3, 97, 266, 281–2, 346, 353, 356, 448, 449, 457, 464, 465, 467, 469, 470, 524, 527, 528, 533
Ruskin, John, 334, 361–8, 372–3, 382, 387, 445, 523, 543; on *Men and Women,* 361–2; on *The Bishop Orders His Tomb,* 362–4; *Modern Painters,* Vol. III, 362, 365, 367, 372; *Modern Painters,* Vol. IV, 362–4

S
Sand, George, 192
Saunders and Otley, 26
Scott, William Bell, 54, 65, 357
Shelley, Percy Bysshe, 5, 34, 72; RB and Essay on Shelley, 291–5
Shepherd, Richard Herne, 14–6
Shirley. *See* Skelton, John
Silverthorne, Mrs. Christiana, 2
Simpson, Richard, 317, 319, 324, 327, 330, 482, 494, 496, 508, 513, 514
Skelton, John, 386–8, 393, 456, 482, 483, 496, 499, 508, 513, 515, 517, 518, 519, 523
Smalley, Donald, xxi, 63, 90, 198, 291
Smith, Alexander, 297, 538
Smith, Elder and Co., 245, 448, 461, 462, 471, 474
Smith, George, 245–6, 270, 378, 448, 461, 462, 469, 471, 472
Snyder, Edward, 194, 195
Somervell, D. C., xx
Stephens, Frederic G., 266, 281, 353
Stigand, William, 436, 440–1
Stirling, James H., 450, 518

Story, Emelyn (Mrs. W. W.), 406, 407, 409, 445

Story, William Wetmore, 377, 388, 392, 393, 411–2, 497

Story, Mr. and Mrs. W. W., 300, 379, 444

Strauss, David F., *Das Leben Jesu,* 287, 418

Swinburne, Algernon Charles, 359–60, 521, 524, 525–8, 531, 532

Symonds, J. A., 476, 478, 498, 519

Symons, Arthur, 265

T

Tait, William, 7

Talfourd, Thomas Noon, 54, 100; *Ion,* 39, 41, 43, 47; *Tragedies,* 263; *Sonnet to Robert Browning,* 347

Talmud, 438

Taplin, Gardner B., 611n22

Tauchnitz, Christian Bernhard, 461

Taylor, Harriet, 6

Taylor, Henry, 283, 514; *Philip van Artevelde,* 25, 30, 33–4

Tennyson, Alfred Lord, 25, 109, 124, 170, 171, 195, 264, 283, 297, 307, 317, 332, 334, 357, 359, 368, 521, 532, 539–41, 545, 547; on *Sordello,* 85; and RB read poems, 303; compared with RB, 350, 376, 514–5, 524, 532; on *The Ring and the Book,* 540; *Maud,* 303; *The Holy Grail and Other Poems,* 544

Tennyson, Emily (Lady), 357

Tennyson, Frederick, 533

Thackeray, William Makepeace, 342, 368, 378, 413, 532; *The Rose and the Ring,* 472

Thirlwall, Connop, 531

Thomson, James, 316, 332, 355, 357, 368

Ticknor and Fields, 340, 413–4, 472–3; Ticknor, Reed, and Fields, 341; Fields, Osgood & Co., 473

Toulmin, Camilla (Mrs. Newton Crosland), 203, 210, 215, 228; author of criticism, 226

Twisleton, Edward, 377–8

W

Warburton, Eliot, 201, 250

Watkins, Charlotte Crawford, xxi

Webster, John, 144

Wedgwood, Julia, 392, 437, 438–9, 440, 441, 443, 445, 464, 465, 467, 469, 470, 490, 521–2, 547; criticizes *The Ring and the Book,* 541–5

Wedmore, T. F., 455, 519

Westwood, Thomas, 89, 110

Wilkins, Augustus S., 450, 451, 452

Williams, Rev. J. D., 392–3

Willmott (prompter), 135

Willmott, Robert A., *Poets of the Nineteenth Century,* 348–9

Wilson, Effingham, 26

Wilson, John, 35

Wise, Thomas J., 14, 18, 19, 295

Woolner, Thomas, 266, 357

Wordsworth, William, 34, 38, 39, 40, 47, 170, 264, 332, 392; *Poems, Chiefly of Early and Late Years,* 188

Y

Young, Frederick, 54